This book is dedicated to the memory of Steve Jobs. We continue to be inspired by his spirit and his vision.

—David Mark and Jack Nutting

Dedicated to my mom and dad, who bought my first computer.

—Fredrik Olsson

For my parents and my sister Jackie, who has never had a book dedicated to her before.

—Kim Topley

Beginning iPhone Development

Exploring the iOS SDK

Seventh Edition

David Mark

Jack Nutting

Kim Topley

Fredrik Olsson

Jeff LaMarche

Apress®

Beginning iPhone Development

ISBN-13 (pbk): 978-1-4842-0200-5

ISBN-13 (electronic): 978-1-4842-0199-2

Managing Director: Welmoed Spahr
Lead Editor: Steve Anglin
Development Editor: Matthew Moodie
Technical Reviewer: Felipe Laso Marsetti
Editorial Board: Steve Anglin, Gary Cornell, Louise Corrigan, Jonathan Gennick, Robert Hutchinson, Michelle Lowman, James Markham, Matthew Moodie, Jeff Olson, Jeffrey Pepper, Douglas Pundick, Ben Renow-Clarke, Gwenan Spearing, Matt Wade, Steve Weiss
Coordinating Editor: Anamika Panchoo
Copy Editor: Kimberly Burton
Compositor: SPi Global
Indexer: SPi Global
Artist: SPi Global
Cover Designer: Anna Ishchenko

Distributed to the book trade worldwide by Springer Science+Business Media New York, 233 Spring Street, 6th Floor, New York, NY 10013. Phone 1-800-SPRINGER, fax (201) 348-4505, e-mail orders-ny@springer-sbm.com, or visit www.springeronline.com. Apress Media, LLC is a California LLC and the sole member (owner) is Springer Science + Business Media Finance Inc (SSBM Finance Inc). SSBM Finance Inc is a Delaware corporation.

For information on translations, please e-mail rights@apress.com, or visit www.apress.com.

Apress and friends of ED books may be purchased in bulk for academic, corporate, or promotional use. eBook versions and licenses are also available for most titles. For more information, reference our Special Bulk Sales–eBook Licensing web page at www.apress.com/bulk-sales.

Any source code or other supplementary material referenced by the author in this text is available to readers at www.apress.com/9781484202005. For detailed information about how to locate your book's source code, go to www.apress.com/source-code/.

Contents at a Glance

Contents

About the Authors

Dave Mark is a longtime Mac developer and author who has written a number of books on Mac and iOS development, including *Beginning iOS 6 Development* (Apress, 2013), *More iOS 6 Development* (Apress, 2013), *Learn C on the Mac* (Apress, 2013), *Ultimate Mac Programming* (Wiley, 1995), and the *Macintosh Programming Primer* series (Addison-Wesley, 1992). Dave was one of the founders of MartianCraft, an iOS and Android development house. Dave loves the water and spends as much time as possible on it, in it, or near it. He lives with his wife and three children in Virginia. On Twitter, he's @davemark.

Jack Nutting has been using Cocoa since the olden days, long before it was even called Cocoa. He has used Cocoa and its predecessors to develop software for a wide range of industries and applications, including gaming, graphic design, online digital distribution, telecommunications, finance, publishing, and travel. Jack has written several books on iOS and Mac development, including *Beginning iOS 6 Development* (Apress, 2013), *Learn Cocoa on the Mac* (Apress, 2013), and *Beginning iPad Development for iPhone Developers* (Apress, 2010). Besides writing software and books, he also leads developer training and blogs from time to time at www.nuthole.com. He's @jacknutting on Twitter.

Kim Topley is a software engineer with over 30 years of experience, ranging from mainframe microcode and the UNIX kernel to graphical user interfaces and mobile applications. He is the author of five books on various aspects of Java and JavaFX and has been working with iOS since reading one of the first books published on the subject—the first edition of *Beginning iPhone Development*.

Fredrik Olsson has been using Cocoa since Mac OS X 10.1 and for iPhone since the unofficial toolchain. He has had a long and varied career, ranging from real-time assembly to enterprise Java. He is passionate about Objective-C for its elegance, Cocoa frameworks for its clarity, and both for creating a greater whole than their parts. When away from a keyboard, Fredrik has spoken at conferences and led developer training. You'll find Fredrik on Twitter as @peylow.

Jeff LaMarche is a Mac and an iOS developer with more than 20 years of programming experience. Jeff has written a number of iOS and Mac development books, including *Beginning iOS 6 Development* (Apress, 2013) and *More iOS 6 Development* (Apress, 2013). Jeff is a principal at MartianCraft, an iOS and Android development house. He has written about Cocoa and Objective-C for *MacTech* magazine, as well as articles for Apple's developer web site. Jeff also writes about iOS development for his widely read blog at www.iphonedevelopment.blogspot.com. He can be found on Twitter as @jeff_lamarche.

About the Technical Reviewer

Felipe Laso Marsetti is an iOS programmer working at Lextech Global Services. He loves everything related to Apple, video games, cooking, and playing the violin, piano, or guitar. In his spare time, Felipe loves to read and learn new programming languages or technologies.

Felipe likes to write on his blog at http://iFe.li, create iOS tutorials and articles as a member of www.raywenderlich.com, and work as a technical reviewer for Objective-C and iOS–related books. You can find him on Twitter as @Airjordan12345, on Facebook under his name, or on App.net as @iFeli.

Chapter 1

Welcome to the Jungle

So, you want to write iPhone, iPod touch, and iPad applications? Well, we can't say that we blame you. iOS—the core software of all of these devices—is an exciting platform that has been seeing explosive growth since it first came out in 2007. The rise of the mobile software platform means that people are using software everywhere they go. With the release of iOS 8, Xcode 6, and the latest incarnation of the iOS software development kit (SDK), things have only gotten better and more interesting.

What This Book Is

This book is a guide to help you get started down the path to creating your own iOS applications. Our goal is to get you past the initial difficulties to help you understand the way iOS applications work and how they are built.

As you work your way through this book, you will create a number of small applications, each designed to highlight specific iOS features and to show you how to control or interact with those features. If you combine the foundation you'll gain through this book with your own creativity and determination, and then add in the extensive and well-written documentation provided by Apple, you'll have everything you need to build your own professional iPhone and iPad applications.

> **Tip** Dave, Jack, Jeff, and Fredrik have set up a forum for this book. It's a great place to meet like-minded folks, get your questions answered, and even answer other people's questions. The forum is at `http://forum.learncocoa.org`. Be sure to check it out!

This may seem obvious, but you'll also need an iPhone, iPod touch, or iPad. While much of your code can be tested using the iOS simulator, not all programs can be. And even those that can run on the simulator really need to be thoroughly tested on an actual device before you ever consider releasing your application to the public.

> **Note**   If you are going to sign up for the Standard or Enterprise program, you should do it right now. The approval process can take a while, and you'll need that approval to be able to run your applications on an actual device. Don't worry, though, because while you are waiting, you can run all the projects in the first several chapters and the majority of the applications in this book on the iOS simulator.

What You Need to Know

This book assumes that you already have some programming knowledge. It assumes that you understand the fundamentals of programming in general and object-oriented programming in particular (you know what classes, objects, loops, and variables are, for example). It also assumes that you are familiar with the Objective-C programming language. Cocoa Touch—the part of the SDK that you will be working with through most of this book—uses the latest version of Objective-C, which contains several new features not present in earlier versions. But don't worry if you're not familiar with the more recent additions to the Objective-C language. We highlight any of the new language features that we take advantage of, and explain how they work and why we are using them.

You should also be familiar with iOS itself, as a user. Just as you would with any platform for which you wanted to write an application, get to know the nuances and quirks of the iPhone, iPad, or iPod touch. Take the time to get familiar with the iOS interface and with the way Apple's iPhone and/or iPad applications look and feel.

NEW TO OBJECTIVE-C?

If you have not programmed in Objective-C before, here are a few resources to help you get started:

- *Learn Objective-C on the Mac: For OS X and iOS* (Apress, 2012): This is an excellent and approachable introduction to Objective-C by Mac-programming experts Scott Knaster, Waqar Malik, and Mark Dalrymple. You can find more information at www.apress.com/book/view/9781430241881.

- *Programming with Objective-C: A Primer*: This is Apple's introduction to the language. You can find more information at https://developer.apple.com/library/mac/documentation/cocoa/conceptual/ProgrammingWithObjectiveC.

What's Different About Coding for iOS?

If you have never programmed in Cocoa or its predecessors NeXTSTEP or OpenStep, you may find Cocoa Touch—the application framework you'll be using to write iOS applications—a little alien. It has some fundamental differences from other common application frameworks, such as those used when building .NET or Java applications. Don't worry too much if you feel a little lost at first. Just keep plugging away at the exercises, and it will all start to fall into place after a while.

If you have written programs using Cocoa or NeXTSTEP, a lot in the iOS SDK will be familiar to you. A great many classes are unchanged from the versions that are used to develop for OS X. Even those that are different tend to follow the same basic principles and similar design patterns. However, several differences exist between Cocoa and Cocoa Touch.

Regardless of your background, you need to keep in mind some key differences between iOS development and desktop application development. These differences are discussed in the following sections.

Only One Active Application

On iOS, only one application can be active and displayed on the screen at any given time. Since iOS 4, applications have been able to run in the background after the user presses the **Home** button, but even that is limited to a narrow set of situations, and you must code for it specifically (you'll see exactly how to do that in Chapter 15).

When your application isn't active or running in the background, it doesn't receive any attention whatsoever from the CPU, which will wreak havoc with open network connections and the like. iOS allows background processing, but making your apps play nicely in this situation will require some effort on your part.

Only One Window

Desktop and laptop operating systems allow many running programs to coexist, each with the ability to create and control multiple windows. However, unless you attach an external screen or use AirPlay, and your application is coded to handle more than one screen, iOS gives your application just one "window" to work with. All of your application's interaction with the user takes place inside this one window, and its size is fixed at the size of the screen.

Limited Access

Programs on a desktop or laptop computer pretty much have access to everything the user who launched them does. However, iOS seriously restricts what your application can access.

You can read and write files only from the part of iOS's file system that was created for your application. This area is called your application's **sandbox**. Your sandbox is where your application will store documents, preferences, and every other kind of data it may need to retain.

Your application is also constrained in some other ways. You will not be able to access low-number network ports on iOS, for example, or do anything else that would typically require root or administrative access on a desktop computer.

Limited Response Time

Because of the way it is used, iOS needs to be snappy, and it expects the same of your application. When your program is launched, you need to get your application open, the preferences and data loaded, and the main view shown on the screen as fast as possible—in no more than a few seconds.

At any time when your program is running, it may have the rug pulled out from under it. If the user presses the **Home** button, iOS goes home, and you must quickly save everything before iOS suspends your application in the background. If you take longer than five seconds to save and give up control, your application process will be killed, regardless of whether you finished saving. There is an API that allows your app to ask for additional time to work when it's about to go dark, but you've got to know how to use it.

Limited Screen Size

The iPhone's screen is really nice. When introduced, it was the highest resolution screen available on a handheld consumer device, by far. But even today, the iPhone display isn't all that big, and as a result, you have a lot less room to work with than on modern computers. The screen was just 320 × 480 on the first few iPhone generations, and it was later doubled in both directions to 640 × 960 with the introduction of the iPhone 4's Retina display. Today, the screen of the largest iPhone (the iPhone 6 Plus) measures 1080 × 1920 pixels. That sounds like a decent number of pixels, but keep in mind that these high-density displays (for which Apple uses the term "Retina") are crammed into pretty small form factors, which has a big impact on the kinds of applications and interactivity you can offer on an iPhone and even an iPad. Table 1-1 lists the sizes of the screens of all of the devices that are supported by iOS 8 at the time of writing.

Table 1-1. iOS Device Screen Sizes

Device	Hardware Size	Software Size	Scaling Factor
iPhone 4s	640 × 960	320 × 480	2x
iPhone 5 and 5s	640 × 1136	320 × 568	2x
iPhone 6	750 × 1334	375 × 667	2x
iPhone 6 Plus	1080 × 1920	414 × 736	3x
iPad 2 and iPad mini	768 × 1024	768 × 1024	1x
iPad Air, iPad Retina, and iPad mini Retina	1536 × 2048	768 × 1024	2x

The hardware size is the actual physical size of the screen in pixels. However, when writing software, the size that really matters is the one in the Software Size column. As you can see, in most cases, the software size is only half that of the actual hardware. This situation came about when Apple introduced the first Retina device, which had twice as many pixels in each direction as its predecessor. If Apple had done nothing special, all existing applications would have been drawn at half-scale on the new Retina screen, which would have made them unusable. So Apple chose to internally scale everything that applications draw by a factor of 2, so that they would fill the new screen without any code changes. This internal scaling by a factor of 2 applies to all devices with a Retina display, apart from the iPhone 6 Plus, which has a higher-density screen that requires a scaling factor of 3. For the most part, though, you don't need to worry too much about the fact that your application is being scaled—all you need to do is work within the software screen size and iOS will do the rest.

The only exceptions to this rule are bitmap images. Since bitmap images are, by their nature, fixed in size, for best results you can't really use the same image on a Retina screen as you would on a non-Retina screen. If you try to do that, you'll see that iOS scales your image up for a device that has a Retina screen, which has the effect of introducing blur. You can fix this by including separate copies of each image for the 2x and 3x Retina screens, and iOS will pick the version that matches the screen of the device on which your application is running.

> **Note** If you look back at Table 1-1, you'll see that it appears that the scale factor in the fourth column is the same as the ratio of the hardware size to the software size. For example, on the iPhone 6, the hardware width is 750 and software width is 375, a ratio of 2:1. Look carefully, though, and you'll see that there's something different about the iPhone 6 Plus. The ratio of the hardware width to the software width is 1080/414, which is 2.608:1, and the same applies to the height ratio. So in terms of the hardware, the iPhone 6 Plus does not have a truly 3x Retina display. However, as far as the software is concerned, a 3x scale is used, which means that an application written to use the software screen size of 414 × 736 is first logically mapped to a virtual screen size of 1242 × 2208 and the result is then scaled down a little to match the actual hardware size of 1080 × 1920. Fortunately, this doesn't require you to do anything special because iOS takes care of all the details.

Limited System Resources

Any old-time programmers who are reading this are likely laughing at the idea of a machine with at least 512MB of RAM and 16GB of storage being in any way resource-constrained, but it is true. Developing for iOS is not, perhaps, in exactly the same league as trying to write a complex spreadsheet application on a machine with 48KB of memory. But given the graphical nature of iOS and all it is capable of doing, running out of memory is very easy.

The iOS devices available right now have either 512MB (iPhone 4S, iPad 2, the original iPad mini, the latest iPod touch), or 1024MB of physical RAM (iPhone 5c, iPhone 5s, iPhone 6, iPhone 6 Plus, iPad Air, iPad mini Retina), though this will likely increase over time. Some of that memory is used for the screen buffer and by other system processes. Usually, no more than half of that memory is left for your application to use, and the amount can be considerably less, especially now that other apps can be running in the background.

Although that may sound like it leaves a pretty decent amount of memory for such a small computer, there is another factor to consider when it comes to memory on iOS. Modern computer operating systems like OS X will take chunks of memory that aren't being used and write them out to disk in something called a **swap file**. The swap file allows applications to keep running, even when they have requested more memory than is actually available on the computer. iOS, however, will not write volatile memory, such as application data, out to a swap file. As a result, the amount of memory available to your application is constrained by the amount of unused physical memory in the iOS device.

Cocoa Touch has built-in mechanisms for letting your application know that memory is getting low. When that happens, your application must free up unneeded memory or risk being forced to quit.

No Garbage Collection, But...

We mentioned earlier that Cocoa Touch uses Objective-C, but one of the key Objective-C features of the early 2000s is not available with iOS: Cocoa Touch does not support garbage collection. The need to do manual memory management when programming for iOS has been a bit of a stumbling block for many programmers new to the platform, especially those coming from languages that offer garbage collection.

With the version of Objective-C supported by the latest versions of iOS, however, this particular stumbling block is basically gone. This is thanks to a feature called Automatic Reference Counting (ARC), which gets rid of the need to manually manage memory for Objective-C objects. ARC not only serves as a worthy replacement to garbage collection, it's actually better in most respects. Starting in OS X 10.8, ARC became the default memory management technology for Mac apps, and garbage collection has been deprecated there in favor of ARC. And of course, it's also the default memory management mechanism in iOS as well. We'll talk about ARC in Chapter 3.

Some New Stuff

Since we've mentioned that Cocoa Touch is missing some features that Cocoa has, it seems only fair to mention that the iOS SDK contains some functionality that is not currently present in Cocoa—or, at least, is not available on every Mac:

- The iOS SDK provides a way for your application to determine the iOS device's current geographic coordinates using Core Location.

- Most iOS devices have built-in cameras and photo libraries, and the SDK provides mechanisms that allow your application to access both.

- iOS devices have built-in motion sensors that let you detect how your device is being held and moved.

A Different Approach

Two things iOS devices don't have are a physical keyboard and a mouse, which means you have a fundamentally different way of interacting with the user than you do when programming for a general-purpose computer. Fortunately, most of that interaction is handled for you. For example, if you add a text field to your application, iOS knows to bring up a keyboard when the user touches that field, without you needing to write any extra code.

> **Note**   All iOS devices allow you to connect an external keyboard via Bluetooth, which gives you a nice keyboard experience and saves some screen real estate. Connecting a mouse is not an option.

What's in This Book

Here is a brief overview of the remaining chapters in this book:

- In Chapter 2, you'll learn how to use Xcode's partner in crime, Interface Builder, to create a simple interface, placing some text on the screen.

- In Chapter 3, you'll start interacting with the user, building a simple application that dynamically updates displayed text at runtime based on buttons the user presses.

- Chapter 4 will build on Chapter 3 by introducing you to several more of iOS's standard user-interface controls. We'll also demonstrate how to use alerts and action sheets to prompt users to make a decision or to inform them that something out of the ordinary has occurred.

- In Chapter 5, we'll look at handling rotation and Auto Layout, the mechanisms that allow iOS applications to be used in both portrait and landscape modes.

- In Chapter 6, we'll move into more advanced user interfaces and explore creating applications that support multiple views. We'll show you how to change which view is shown to the user at runtime, which will greatly enhance the potential of your apps.

- Tab bars and pickers are part of the standard iOS user interface. In Chapter 7, we'll look at how to implement these interface elements.

- In Chapter 8, we'll cover table views, the primary way of providing lists of data to the user and the foundation of hierarchical navigation–based applications. You'll also see how to let the user search your application data.

- One of the most common iOS application interfaces is the hierarchical list that lets you drill down to see more data or more details. In Chapter 9, you'll learn what's involved in implementing this standard type of interface.

- From the beginning, all sorts of iOS applications have used table views to display dynamic, vertically scrolling lists of components. More recently, Apple introduced a new class called UICollectionView that takes this concept a few steps further, giving developers lots of new flexibility in laying out visual components. Chapter 10 will get you up and running with collection views.

- In Chapter 11, we'll show you how to build master-detail applications, which present a list of items (such as the e-mails in a mailbox) and let the user view the details of each individual item, one at a time. You'll also see how to use the iOS controls that support this way of working, which were originally developed for the iPad and are now also available on the iPhone.

- In Chapter 12, we'll look at implementing application settings, which is iOS's mechanism for letting users set their application-level preferences.

- Chapter 13 covers data management on iOS. We'll talk about creating objects to hold application data and see how that data can be persisted to iOS's file system. We'll also discuss the basics of using Core Data, which allows you to save and retrieve data easily.

- In iOS 5, Apple introduced iCloud, which allows your document to store data online and sync it between different instances of the application. Chapter 14 shows you how to get started with iCloud.

- iOS developers have access to a powerful library that simplifies multithreaded development called Grand Central Dispatch, or GCD for short. In Chapter 15, we'll introduce you to Grand Central Dispatch and also show you how to use the iOS features that allow you, under certain circumstances, to run your application in the background.

- Everyone loves to draw, so we'll look at doing some custom drawing in Chapter 16, where we'll introduce you to the Core Graphics system.

- In iOS 7, Apple has introduced a new framework called Sprite Kit for creating 2D games. It includes a physics engine and animation systems, and works for making OS X games, too. You'll see how to make a simple game with Sprite Kit in Chapter 17.

- The multitouch screen common to all iOS devices can accept a wide variety of gestural inputs from the user. In Chapter 18, you'll learn all about detecting basic gestures, such as the pinch and swipe. We'll also look at the process of defining new gestures and talk about when new gestures are appropriate.

- iOS is capable of determining its latitude and longitude thanks to Core Location. In Chapter 19, we'll build some code that uses Core Location to figure out where in the world your device is and use that information in our quest for world dominance.

- In Chapter 20, we'll look at interfacing with iOS's accelerometer and gyroscope, which is how your device knows which way it's being held, the speed and direction in which it is moving, and where in the world it's located. We'll also explore some of the fun things your application can do with that information.

- Nearly every iOS device has a camera and a library of pictures, both of which are available to your application, if you ask nicely! In Chapter 21, we'll show you how to ask nicely.

- iOS devices are currently available in more than 90 countries. In Chapter 22, we'll show you how to write your applications in such a way that all parts can be easily translated into other languages. This helps expand the potential audience for your applications.

What's New in This Update?

Since the first edition of this book hit the bookstores, the growth of the iOS development community has been phenomenal. The SDK has continually evolved, with Apple releasing a steady stream of SDK updates. Well, we've been busy, too! Both iOS 8 itself and Xcode 6 contain a lot of new enhancements. We've been hard at work updating the book to cover the new technologies in both iOS 8 and Xcode 6 that you'll need to be aware of to start writing iOS applications. We've rebuilt every project from scratch to ensure not only that the code compiles using the latest version of Xcode and the iOS SDK, but also that each one takes advantage of the latest and greatest features offered by Cocoa Touch. We've also made a ton of subtle changes throughout the book and, of course, we've reshot every screenshot.

Are You Ready?

iOS is an incredible computing platform and an exciting new frontier for your development pleasure. Programming for iOS is going to be a new experience—different from working on any other platform. For everything that looks familiar, there will be something alien—but as you work through the book's code, the concepts should all come together and start to make sense.

Keep in mind that the examples in this book are not simply a checklist that, when completed, magically grant you iOS developer guru status. Make sure you understand what you did and why before moving on to the next project. Don't be afraid to make changes to the code. Observing the results of your experimentation is one of the best ways you can wrap your head around the complexities of coding in an environment like Cocoa Touch.

That said, if you have your iOS SDK installed, turn the page. If not, get to it! Got it? Good. Then let's go!

Chapter 2

Appeasing the Tiki Gods

As you're probably well aware, it has become something of a tradition to call the first project in any book on programming, "Hello, World." We considered breaking with this tradition, but were scared that the Tiki gods would inflict some painful retribution on us for such a gross breach of etiquette. So, let's do it by the book, shall we?

In this chapter, we're going to use Xcode to create a small iOS application that will display the text, "Hello, World!" We'll look at what's involved in creating an iOS application project in Xcode, work through the specifics of using Xcode's Interface Builder to design our application's user interface, and then run our application on the iOS simulator. After that, we'll give our application an icon to make it feel more like a real iOS application.

We have a lot to do here, so let's get going.

Setting Up Your Project in Xcode

By now, you should have Xcode and the iOS SDK installed on your machine. You should also download the book's source code archive from the Apress web site (http://apress.com). While you're at it, take a look at the book forums at http://forum.learncocoa.org/. The book forums are a great place to discuss iOS development, get your questions answered, and meet up with like-minded people.

> **Note** Even though you have the complete set of project files at your disposal in this book's source code archive, you'll get more out of the book if you create each project by hand, rather than simply running the version you downloaded. By doing that, you'll gain familiarity and expertise working with the various application development tools.
>
> There's no substitute for actually creating applications; software development is not a spectator sport.

The project we're going to build in this chapter is contained in the *02 - Hello World* folder of the source code archive.

Before we can start, we need to launch Xcode. Xcode is the tool that we'll use to do most of what we do in this book. After downloading it from the Mac App Store, you'll find it installed in the */Applications* folder, as with most Mac applications. You'll be using Xcode a lot, so you might want to consider dragging it to your dock so you'll have ready access to it.

If this is your first time using Xcode, don't worry; we'll walk you through every step involved in creating a new project. If you're already an old hand but haven't worked with Xcode 6, you will find that quite a bit has changed (mostly for the better, we think).

When you first launch Xcode, you'll be presented with a welcome window like the one shown in Figure 2-1. From here, you can choose to create a new project, connect to a version-control system to check out an existing project, or select from a list of recently opened projects. The welcome window gives you a nice starting point, covering some of the most common tasks you're likely to want to do after launching Xcode. All of these actions can be accessed through the menu as well, so close the window, and we'll proceed. If you would rather not see this window in the future, just uncheck the **Show this window when Xcode launches** check box at the bottom of the window before closing it.

Figure 2-1. The Xcode welcome window

Note   If you have an iPhone, iPad, or iPod touch connected to your machine, you might see a message when you first launch Xcode that asks whether you want to use that device for development. For now, click the **Ignore** button. If you choose to join the paid iOS Developer Program, you will gain access to a program portal that will tell you how to use your iOS device for development and testing. Some of the examples in later chapters require the use of a real device because they use features that are not available on the iOS simulator. You'll need to join the iOS Developer Program to try out those examples.

Create a new project by selecting **New ➤ Project...** from the **File** menu (or by pressing ⇧⌘N). A new project window will open, showing you the project template selection sheet (see Figure 2-2). From this sheet, you'll choose a project template to use as a starting point for building your application. The pane on the left side of the sheet is divided into two main sections: **iOS** and **OS X**. Since we're building an iOS application, select **Application** in the **iOS** section to reveal the iOS application templates.

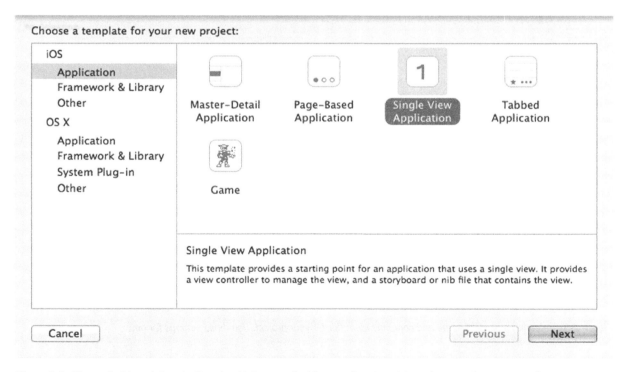

Figure 2-2.   The project template selection sheet lets you select from various templates when creating a new project

Each of the icons shown in the upper-right pane in Figure 2-2 represents a separate project template that can be used as a starting point for your iOS applications. The icon labeled **Single View Application** is the simplest template and the one we'll be using for the first several chapters. The other templates provide additional code and/or resources needed to create common iPhone and iPad application interfaces, as you'll see in later chapters.

Click the **Single View Application** icon (see Figure 2-2), and then click the **Next** button. You'll see the project options sheet, which should look like Figure 2-3. On this sheet, you need to specify the **Product Name** and **Company Identifier** for your project. Xcode will combine these to generate a unique **bundle identifier** for your app. You'll also see a field that lets you enter an **Organization Name**, which Xcode will use to automatically insert a copyright notice into every source code file you create. Name your product *Hello World*, call your organization *Apress*, and then enter *com.apress* in the **Company Identifier** field, as shown in Figure 2-3. Later, after you've signed up for the developer program and learned about provisioning profiles, you'll want to use your own company identifier.

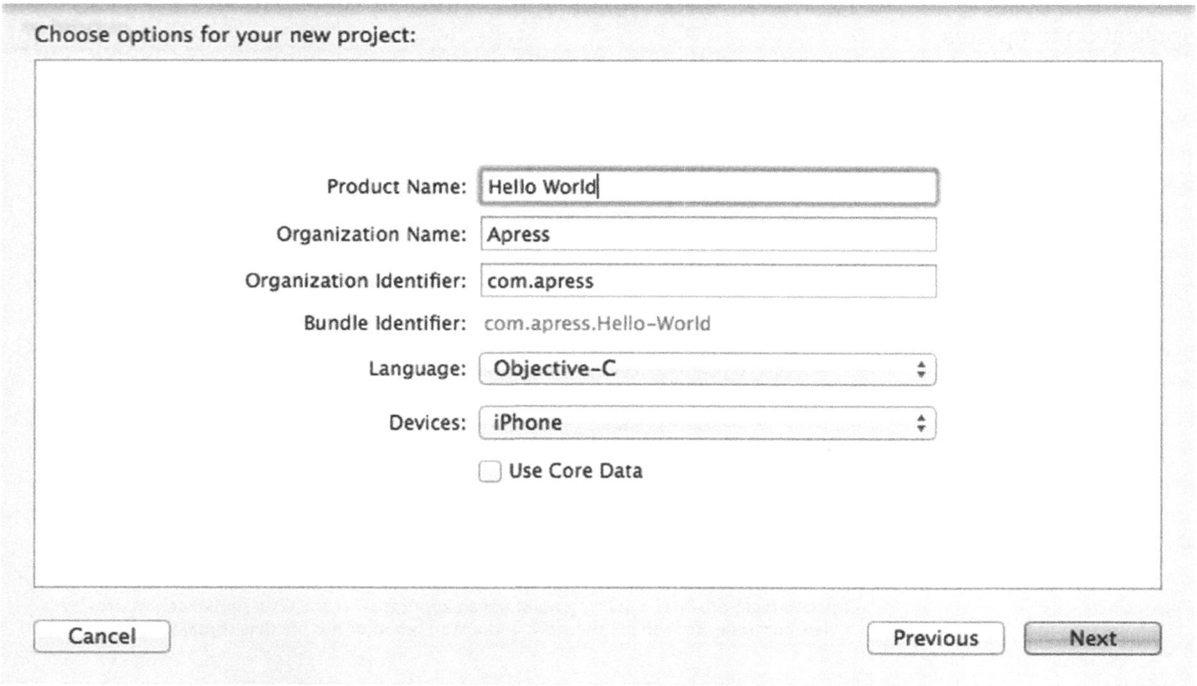

Choose options for your new project:

Product Name:	Hello World|
Organization Name:	Apress
Organization Identifier:	com.apress
Bundle Identifier:	com.apress.Hello–World
Language:	Objective–C ⬍
Devices:	iPhone ⬍
	☐ Use Core Data

Cancel   Previous   Next

Figure 2-3. Selecting a product name and company identifier for your project. Use these settings for now

The **Language** field lets you select the programming language that you want to use. You can choose between Objective-C and Swift. Since you're reading the Objective-C version of this book, the appropriate choice here is, of course, Objective-C.

We also need to specify the **Devices**. In other words, Xcode wants to know if we're building an app for the iPhone and iPod touch, if we're building an app for the iPad, or if we're building a **universal** application that will run on all iOS devices. Select **iPhone** for the **Devices** if it's not already selected. This tells Xcode that we'll be targeting this particular app at the iPhone and iPod touch, which have roughly the same screen size and form factor. For the first few chapters of the book, we'll be using the iPhone device, but don't worry—we'll cover the iPad also.

Leave the **Core Data** check box unchecked—we'll make use of it in Chapter 13. Click **Next** again, and you'll be asked where to save your new project using a standard save sheet (see Figure 2-4). If you haven't already done so, jump over to the Finder, create a new master directory for these book projects, and then return to Xcode and navigate into that directory. Before you click the **Create** button, take note of the **Source Control** check box. We won't be talking about Git in this book, but Xcode includes some support for using Git and other kinds of source control management (SCM) tools. If you are already familiar with Git and want to use it, enable this check box; otherwise, feel free to turn it off.

> **Note**   Source Control Management (SCM) is a technique for keeping track of changes made to an application's source code and resources while it's being built. It also facilitates multiple developers working on the same application at the same time by providing tools to resolve conflicts when they arise. Xcode has built-in support for Git, one of the most popular SCM systems in use today. We won't be dealing with source control issues in this book, so it's up to you to enable it or disable it, whichever works for you.

After choosing whether to create a Git repository, create the new project by clicking the **Create** button.

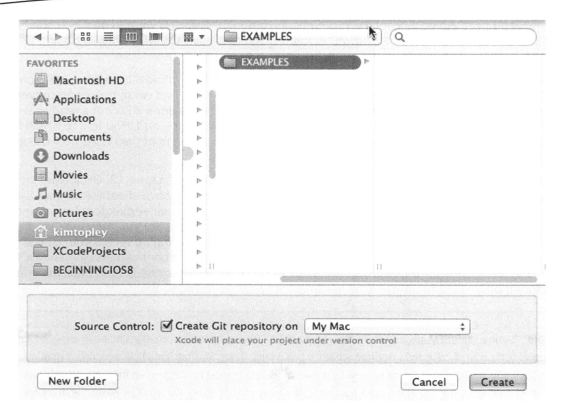

Figure 2-4. Saving your project in a project folder on your hard drive

The Xcode Project Window

After you dismiss the save sheet, Xcode will create and then open your project. You will see a new **project window** (see Figure 2-5). There's a lot of information crammed into this window, and it's where you will be spending a lot of your iOS development time.

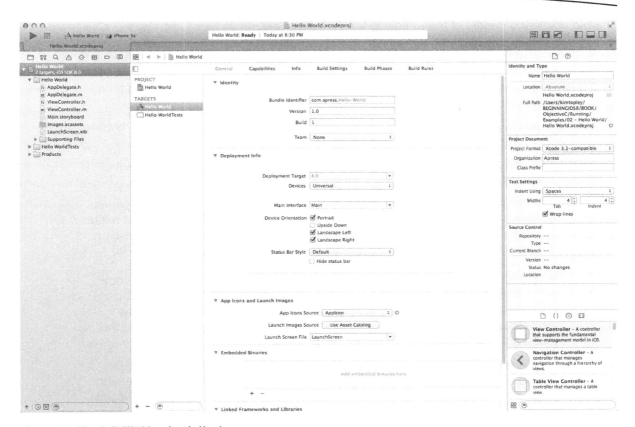

Figure 2-5. The Hello World project in Xcode

Even if you are an old hand with earlier versions of Xcode, you may still benefit from reading through this section, since Apple has a habit of rearranging things and making improvements from release to release. Let's take a quick tour.

The Toolbar

The top of the Xcode project window is called the **toolbar** (see Figure 2-6). On the left side of the toolbar are controls to start and stop running your project, as well as a pop-up menu to select the scheme you want to run. A **scheme** brings together target and build settings, and the toolbar pop-up menus lets you select a specific setup quickly and easily.

Figure 2-6. The Xcode toolbar

The big box in the middle of the toolbar is the **Activity View**. As its name implies, the activity view displays any actions or processes that are currently happening. For example, when you run your project, the activity view gives you a running commentary on the various steps it's taking to build your application. If you encounter any errors or warnings, that information is displayed here, as well. If you click the warning or error, you'll go directly to the **Issue Navigator**, which provides more information about the warning or error, as described in the next section.

On the right side of the toolbar are two sets of buttons. The left set lets you switch between three different editor configurations:

- The **Editor Area** gives you a single pane dedicated to editing a file or project-specific configuration values.

- The incredibly powerful **Assistant Editor** splits the Editor Area into two panes, left and right. The pane on the right is generally used to display a file that relates to the file on the left, or that you might need to refer to while editing the file on the left. You can manually specify what goes into each pane, or you can let Xcode decide what's most appropriate for the task at hand. For example, if you're editing the implementation of an Objective-C class (the .m file), Xcode will automatically show you that class's header file (the .h file) in the right pane. If you're designing your user interface on the left, Xcode will show you the code that the user interface is able to interact with on the right. You'll see the Assistant Editor at work throughout the book.

- The **Version Editor** button converts the editor pane into a time machine–like comparison view that works with version control systems such as Subversion and Git. You can compare the current version of a source file with a previously committed version, or compare any two earlier versions with each other.

To the right of the editor buttons is a set of toggle buttons that show and hide large panes on the left and right sides of the editor view, as well as the debug area at the bottom of the window. Click each of those buttons a few times to see these panes in action. You'll learn more about how these are used soon.

The Navigator

Just below the toolbar, on the left side of the project window, is the **Navigator**. The Navigator offers eight views that show you different aspects of your project. Click each of the icons at the top of the navigator to switch among the following navigators, going from left to right:

- **Project Navigator**: This view contains a list of files in your project (see Figure 2-7). You can store references to everything you expect—from source code files to artwork, data models, property list (or .plist) files (discussed in the "A Closer Look at Our Project" section later in this chapter), and even other project files. By storing multiple projects in a single workspace, those projects can easily share resources. If you click any file in the navigator view, that file will display in the Editor Area. In addition to viewing the file, you can also edit it (if it's a file that Xcode knows how to edit).

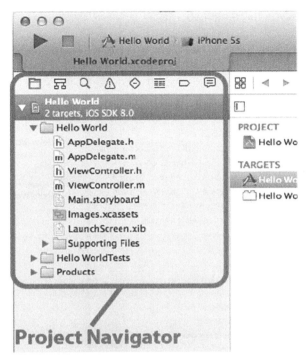

Figure 2-7. *The Xcode Project Navigator. Click one of the eight icons at the top of the view to switch navigators*

■ **Symbol Navigator**: As its name implies, this navigator focuses on the **symbols** defined in the workspace (see Figure 2-8). Symbols are basically the items that the compiler recognizes, such as classes, enumerations, `structs`, and global variables.

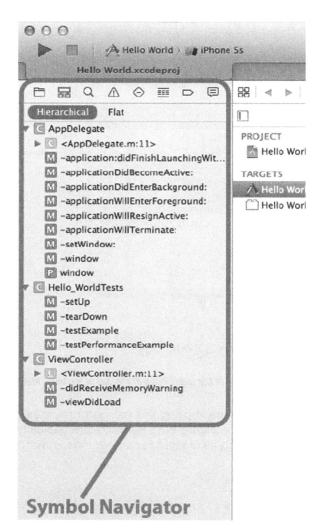

Figure 2-8. The Xcode Symbol Navigator. Open the disclosure triangle to explore the classes, methods, and other symbols defined within each group

■ **Find Navigator**: You'll use this navigator to perform searches on all the files in your workspace (see Figure 2-9). At the top of this pane is a multileveled pop-up control that lets you select **Replace** instead of **Find**, along with other options for applying search criteria to the text you enter. Below the text field, other controls let you choose to search in the entire project or just a portion of it, and specify whether searching should be case-sensitive.

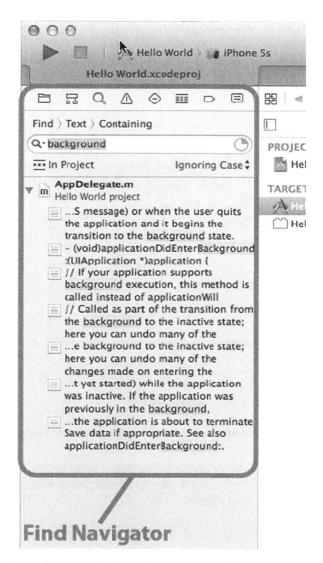

Figure 2-9. *The Xcode Find Navigator. Be sure to check out the pop-up menus hidden under the word Find and under the buttons that are below the search field*

■ **Issue Navigator**: When you build your project, any errors or warnings will appear in this navigator, and a message detailing the number of errors will appear in the activity view at the top of the window (see Figure 2-10). When you click an error in the issue navigator, you'll jump to the appropriate line of code in the editor.

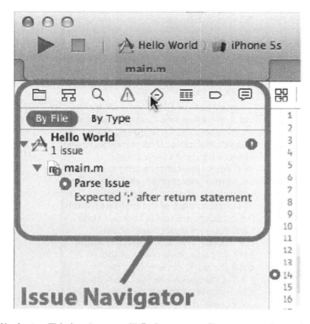

Figure 2-10. The Xcode Issue Navigator. This is where you'll find your compiler errors and warnings

■ **Test Navigator**: If you're using Xcode's integrated unit testing capabilities (a topic that we unfortunately can't fit into this book), this is where you'll see the results of your unit tests (see Figure 2-11).

Figure 2-11. *The Xcode Test Navigator. The output of your unit tests will appear here*

■ **Debug Navigator**: This navigator is your main view into the debugging process (see Figure 2-12). If you are new to debugging, you might check out this part of the *Xcode Overview* (http://developer.apple.com/library/ios/documentation/ ToolsLanguages/Conceptual/Xcode_Overview/DebugYourApp/DebugYourApp.html). The Debug Navigator lists the stack frame for each active thread. A **stack frame** is a list of the functions or methods that have been called previously, in the order they were called. Click a method, and the associated code appears in the editor pane. In the editor, there will be a second pane that lets you control the debugging process, display and modify data values, and access the low-level debugger. A button at the bottom of the debug navigator allows you to control which stack frames are visible, and another lets you choose whether to show all threads or just the threads that have crashed or stopped on a breakpoint.

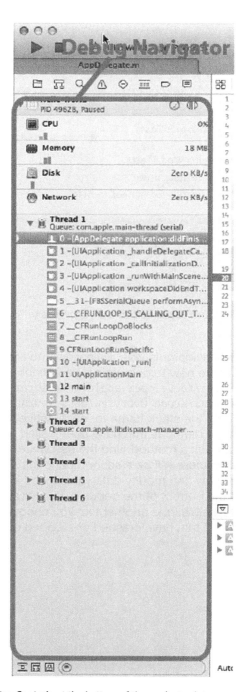

Figure 2-12. The Xcode Debug Navigator. Controls at the bottom of the navigator let you control the level of detail you want to see

■ **Breakpoint Navigator**: The breakpoint navigator lets you see all the breakpoints that you've set (see Figure 2-13). Breakpoints are, as the name suggests, points in your code where the application will stop running (or **break**), so that you can look at the values in variables and do other tasks needed to debug your application. The list of breakpoints in this navigator is organized by file. Click a breakpoint in the list and that line will appear in the editor pane. Be sure to check out the plus sign (+) button at the lower-left corner of the project window when in the breakpoint navigator. This button opens a pop-up that lets you add four different types of breakpoints, including symbolic breakpoints, which are the ones that you will use most often.

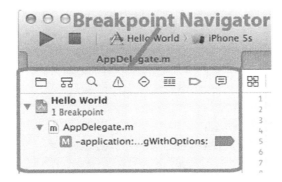

Figure 2-13. The Xcode Breakpoint Navigator. The list of breakpoints is organized by file

■ **Report Navigator**: This navigator keeps a history of your recent build results and run logs (see Figure 2-14). Click a specific log, and the build command and any build issues are displayed in the edit pane.

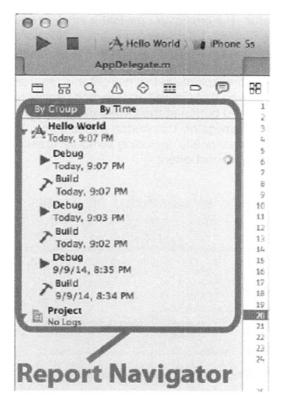

Figure 2-14. The Xcode Report Navigator. The Report Navigator displays a list of builds, with the details associated with a selected view displayed in the editor pane

The Jump Bar

Across the top of the editor, you'll find a special control called the **jump bar**. With a single click, the jump bar allows you to jump to a specific element in the hierarchy you are currently navigating. For example, Figure 2-15 shows a source file being edited in the edit pane. The jump bar is just above the source code. Here's how it breaks down:

- The funky-looking icon at the left end of the jump bar is actually a pop-up menu that displays submenus listing recent files, counterparts, superclasses, and subclasses, siblings, categories, includes, and more! The submenus shown here will take you to just about any other code that touches the code currently open in the editor.

- To the right of the *über* menu are left and right arrows that take you back to the previous file and return you to the next file, respectively.

■ The jump bar includes a segmented pop-up that displays the hierarchical path to reach the selected file in the project. You can click any segment showing the name of a group or a file to see all the other files and groups located at the same point in the hierarchy. The final segment shows a list of items within the selected file. In Figure 2-15, you'll see that the tail end of the jump bar is a pop-up that shows the methods and other symbols contained within the currently selected file. The jump bar shows the file *AppDelegate.m*, with a submenu listing the symbols defined in that file.

Figure 2-15. The Xcode editor pane showing the jump bar, with a source code file selected. The submenu shows the list of methods in the selected file

The jump bar is incredibly powerful. Look for it as you make your way through the various interface elements that make up Xcode.

> **Tip**   Like most of Apple's OS X applications, Xcode includes full support for full-screen mode. Just click the full-screen button in the upper right of the project window to try out distraction-free, full-screen coding!

XCODE KEYBOARD SHORTCUTS

If you prefer navigating with keyboard shortcuts instead of mousing to on-screen controls, you'll like what Xcode has to offer. Most actions that you will do regularly in Xcode have keyboard shortcuts assigned to them, such as ⌘**B** to build your application or ⌘**N** to create a new file.

You can change all of Xcode's keyboard shortcuts, as well as assign shortcuts to commands that don't already have one using Xcode's preferences, under the **Key Bindings** tab.

A really handy keyboard shortcut is ⇧⌘**O**, which is Xcode's Open Quickly feature. After pressing it, start typing the name of a file, setting, or symbol, and Xcode will present you with a list of options. When you narrow down the list to the file you want, hitting the **Return** key will open it in the editing pane, allowing you to switch files in just a few keystrokes.

The Utility Area

As we mentioned earlier, the second-to-last button on the right side of the Xcode toolbar opens and closes the utility area. The upper part of the utility area is a context-sensitive inspector panel, with contents that change depending on what is being displayed in the editor pane. The lower part of the utility area contains a few different kinds of resources that you can drag into your project. You'll see examples throughout the book.

Interface Builder

Earlier versions of Xcode included a separate interface design application called **Interface Builder**, which allowed you to build and customize your project's user interface. One of the major changes introduced in later versions of Xcode is the integration of Interface Builder into the workspace itself. Interface Builder is no longer a separate stand-alone application, which means you don't need to jump back and forth between Xcode and Interface Builder as your code and interface evolve. It's been a few years since this shift occurred, but those of us who remember the days of a separate Interface Builder application are now pretty happy with how the direct integration of Interface Builder in Xcode worked out.

We'll be working extensively with Xcode's interface-building functionality throughout the book, digging into all its nooks and crannies. In fact, we'll do our first bit of interface building a bit later in this chapter.

New Compiler and Debugger

Among the most important changes that were brought in by Xcode 4 lies under the hood: a brand-new compiler and a low-level debugger. Both are significantly faster and smarter than their predecessors and each release since then has added improvements.

For many years, Apple used GCC (the GNU Compiler Collection) as the basis for its compiler technology. But over the course of the past few years, it has shifted over completely to the LLVM (Low Level Virtual Machine) compiler. LLVM generates code that is faster by far than that generated by the traditional GCC. In addition to creating faster code, LLVM also knows more about your code, so it can generate smarter, more precise error messages and warnings.

Xcode is also tightly integrated with LLVM, which gives it some new superpowers. Xcode can offer more precise code completion, and it can make educated guesses as to the actual intent of a piece of code when it produces a warning, offering a pop-up menu of likely fixes. This makes errors like misspelled symbol names, mismatched parentheses, and missing semicolons a breeze to find and fix.

LLVM brings to the table a sophisticated **static analyzer** that can scan your code for a wide variety of potential problems, including problems with Objective-C memory management. In fact, LLVM is so smart about this that it can handle most memory management tasks for you, as long as you abide by a few simple rules when writing your code. We'll begin looking at the wonderful new ARC feature called **Automatic Reference Counting** (ARC) in the next chapter.

A Closer Look at Our Project

Now that we've explored the Xcode project window, let's take a look at the files that make up our new Hello World project. Switch to the Project Navigator by clicking the leftmost of the eight navigator icons on the left side of your workspace (as discussed in the "The Navigator" section earlier in the chapter) or by pressing ⌘**1**.

> **Tip**   The eight navigator configurations can be accessed using the keyboard shortcuts ⌘**1** to ⌘**8**. The numbers correspond to the icons starting on the left, so ⌘**1** is the Project Navigator, ⌘**2** is the Symbol Navigator, and so on up to ⌘**8**, which takes you to the Report Navigator.

The first item in the Project Navigator list bears the same name as your project—in this case, Hello World. This item represents your entire project, and it's also where project-specific configuration can be done. If you single-click it, you'll be able to edit a number of project configuration settings in Xcode's editor. You don't need to worry about those project-specific settings now, however. At the moment, the defaults will work fine.

Flip back to Figure 2-7. Notice that the disclosure triangle to the left of *Hello World* is open, showing a number of subfolders (which are called **groups** in Xcode):

- *Hello World*: The first folder, which is always named after your project, is where you will spend the bulk of your time. This is where most of the code that you write will go, as will the files that make up your application's user interface. You are free to create subfolders under the *Hello World* folder to help organize your code, and you're even allowed to use other groups if you prefer a different organizational approach. While we won't touch most of the files in this folder until the next chapter, there is one file we will explore when we use Interface Builder in the next section:

  - *Main.storyboard* contains the user interface elements specific to your project's main view controller.

- *Supporting Files*: This folder, located inside the *Hello World* folder, contains source code files and resources that aren't Objective-C classes, but that are necessary to your project. Typically, you won't spend a lot of time in the *Supporting Files* folder. When you create a new iOS application project, this folder contains two files:

  - *Info.plist* is a property list that contains information about the application, such as its name, whether it requires any specific features to be present on the devices on which it is run, and so on.

  - *main.m* contains your application's `main()` method. You normally won't need to edit or change this file. In fact, if you don't know what you're doing, it's really a good idea not to touch it.

- ■ *Hello WorldTests*: This folder contains the initial files you'll need if you want to write some unit tests for your application code. We're not going to talk about unit testing in this book, but it's nice that Xcode sets up some of these things for you in each new project you create. Like the *Hello World* folder, this one contains its own *Supporting Files* folder with an *Info.plist* file.

- ■ *Products*: This folder contains the application that this project produces when it is built. If you expand *Products*, you'll see an item called *Hello World.app*, which is the application that this particular project creates. It also contains an item called *Hello WorldTests.xctest*, which represents the testing code. Both of these items are called **build targets**. Because we have never built either of these, they're both red, which is Xcode's way of telling you that a file reference points to something that is not there.

Note   The "folders" in the navigator area do not necessarily correspond to folders in your Mac's file system. These are logical groupings within Xcode to help you keep everything organized and to make it faster and easier to find what you're looking for while working on your application. Often, the items contained in those project folders are stored directly in the project's directory, but you can store them anywhere—even outside your project folder if you want. The hierarchy inside Xcode is completely independent of the file system hierarchy, so moving a file out of the *Supporting Files* folder in Xcode, for example, will not change the file's location on your hard drive.

It is possible to configure a group to use a specific file system directory using the utility pane. However, by default, new groups added to your project are completely independent of the file system, and their contents can be contained anywhere.

Introducing Xcode's Interface Builder

In your project window's Project Navigator, expand the Hello World group, if it's not already open, and then select the file *Main.storyboard*. As soon as you do, the file will open in the editor pane, as shown in Figure 2-16. You should see something resembling an all-white iOS device centered on a plain white background, which makes a nice backdrop for editing interfaces. This is Xcode's Interface Builder (sometimes referred to as IB), which is where you'll design your application's user interface.

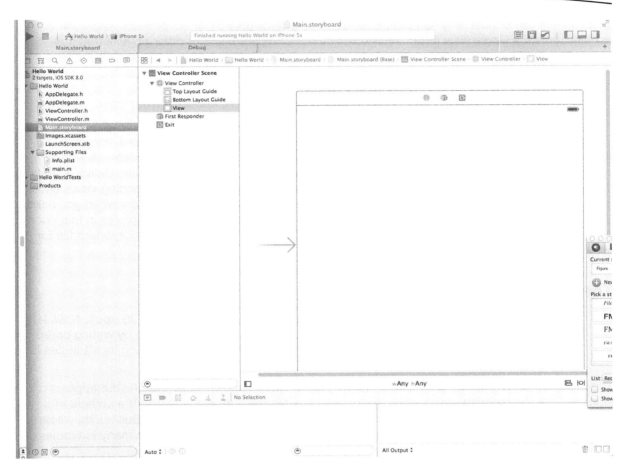

Figure 2-16. We selected Main.storyboard in the Project Navigator. This opened the file in Interface Builder. It looks like this

Interface Builder has a long history. It has been around since 1988 and has been used to develop applications for NeXTSTEP, OpenStep, OS X, and now iOS devices such as the iPhone and the iPad. As we noted earlier, Interface Builder used to be a separate application that was installed along with Xcode and worked in tandem with it. Now, Interface Builder is fully integrated into Xcode.

File Formats

Interface Builder supports a few different file types. The oldest is a binary format that uses the extension *.nib*, whose newer cousin is an XML-based format that uses the extension *.xib*. Both of these formats contain exactly the same sort of document, but the *.xib* version, being a text-based format, has many advantages, especially when you're using any sort of SCM. For the first 20 years of Interface Builder's life, all its files had the extension *.nib*. As a result, most developers took to calling Interface Builder files **nib files**. Interface Builder files are often called nib files, regardless of whether the extension actually used for the file is *.xib* or *.nib*. In fact, Apple still uses the terms **nib** and **nib file** throughout its documentation.

Each nib file can contain any number of objects, but when working on iOS projects, each one will usually contain a single view (often a full-screen view) and controllers or other objects that it is connected to. This lets us compartmentalize our applications, only loading the nib file for a view when it's needed for display. The end result: we save memory when our app is running on a memory-constrained iOS device. A newly-created iOS project contains a nib file called *LaunchScreen.xib* that contains a screen layout that will be shown, by default, when your application launches. We'll talk more about this file at the end of the chapter.

The other file format that IB has supported for the past few years is the **storyboard**. You can think of a storyboard as a "meta-nib file" since it can contain several view controllers, as well as information about how they are connected to each other when the application runs. Unlike a nib file, the contents of which are loaded all at once, a storyboard cannot contain freestanding views and it never loads all its contents at once. Instead, you ask it to load particular controllers when you need them. The iOS project templates in Xcode 6 all use storyboards, so all of the examples in this book will start with a storyboard. Now let's go back to Interface Builder and the *Main.storyboard* file for our Hello World application (Figure 2-16).

The Storyboard

You're now looking at the primary tool you'll use for building user interfaces for iOS apps. Now, let's say that you want to create an instance of a button. You could create that button by writing code, but creating an interface object by dragging a button out of a library and specifying its attributes is so much simpler, and it results in exactly the same thing happening at runtime.

The *Main.storyboard* file we are looking at right now is loaded automatically when your application launches (for the moment, don't worry about how), so it is the right place to add the objects that make up your application's user interface. When you create objects in Interface Builder, they'll be instantiated in your program when that storyboard or nib file is loaded. You'll see many examples of this process throughout this book.

Every storyboard is compartmentalized into one or more pairs of views and controllers. The view is the part you can see graphically and edit in Interface Builder, while the controller is application code you will write to make things happen when a user interacts with your app. The controllers are where the real action of your application happens.

In IB, you often see a view represented by a square, and our current example is no exception. That square represents the screen of an iOS device (actually, it represents a view controller, a concept that you'll be introduced to in the next chapter, but this particular view controller covers the whole screen of the device, so it's pretty much the same thing). Why is the screen square? After all, this is an iPhone project and iPhones just don't look like that! In the early days of iOS, there were just the iPhone and iPod touch. The first versions of Interface Builder that supported iOS development presented an iPhone-shaped design area where you now see a square. When the iPad came along, Interface Builder was enhanced to let you design both iPhone-shaped and iPad-shaped user interfaces. To build an application that worked on both types of device (a universal application), you had to construct one storyboard (or nib file) for the iPhone and another for the iPad. When working with your iPad storyboard, Interface Builder gave you an iPad-shaped outline to design with. In Xcode 6 and iOS 8, things have changed. Now, Apple wants to encourage you to build applications that work as well as possible on screens of any size. Instead of two storyboards, there should be only one.

When your application launches onto a device, it is supposed to adapt itself to the shape of screen that it finds (in fact, Apple refers to applications designed in this way as **adaptive** applications). So now, Interface Builder presents you with a square design area to encourage you not to think in terms of the screen size of any particular device. In the course of the first half of this book, you'll see how to design adaptive applications, but we need to walk before we can run, and our first few examples will be built for iPhone and iPod touch-sized screens.

Returning to our storyboard, click anywhere in the square outline, and you'll see a row of three icons at the top of it, like those in Figure 2-16. Move your mouse over each of them, and you'll see tooltips pop up with their names: View Controller, First Responder, and Exit. Forget about Exit for now, and focus instead on the two that are really important.

- **View Controller** represents a controller object that is loaded from file storage along with its associated view. The task of the view controller is to manage what the user sees on the screen. A typical application has several view controllers, one for each of its screens. It is perfectly possible to write an application with just one screen, and hence one view controller, and many of the examples in this book have only one view controller.

- **First Responder** is, in very basic terms, the object with which the user is currently interacting. If, for example, the user is currently entering data into a text field, that field is the current first responder. The first responder changes as the user interacts with the user interface, and the **First Responder** icon gives you a convenient way to communicate with whatever control or other object is the current first responder, without needing to write code to determine which control or view that might be.

We'll talk more about these objects starting in the next chapter, so don't worry if you're a bit fuzzy right now on when you would use First Responder or how a View Controller gets loaded.

Apart from those icons, the rest of what you see in the editing area is the space where you can place graphical objects. But before we get to that, there's one more thing you should see about IB's editor area: its hierarchy view—or the **Document Outline** to give it its correct name. The Document Outline is shown in Figure 2-17.

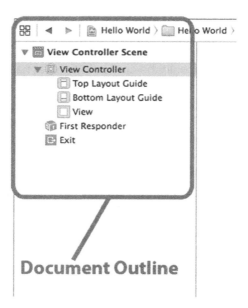

Document Outline

Figure 2-17. The Document Outline contains a useful hierarchical representation of everything in the storyboard

Click the little button in the lower-left corner of the editing area, and you'll see the Document Outline slide in from the left. This shows all the contents of the storyboard, split up into **scenes** containing chunks of related content. In our case, we have just one scene, called the **View Controller Scene**. You'll see that it contains an item called View Controller, which in turn contains an item called the **View** (along with some other things you'll learn about later). This is a pretty handy way of getting an overview of your content. Everything you see in the main editing area is mirrored here.

The **View** icon represents an instance of the UIView class. A UIView object is an area that a user can see and interact with. In this application, we currently have only one view, so this icon represents everything that the user can see in our application. Later, we'll build more complex applications that have several views. For now, just think of this view as an object that the user can see when using your application.

If you click the **View** icon, Xcode will automatically highlight the square screen outline that we were talking about earlier. This is where you can design your user interface graphically.

The Library

The utility view, which makes up the right side of the workspace, is divided into two sections (see Figure 2-18). If you're not currently seeing the utility view, click the rightmost of the three **View** buttons in the toolbar, select **View ➤ Utilities ➤ Show Utilities**, or press ⇧⌘0 (**Option-Command-Zero**).

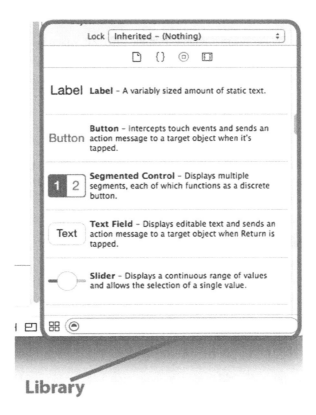

Library

Figure 2-18. The library is where you'll find stock objects from the UIKit that are available for use in Interface Builder. Everything above the library but below the toolbar is known collectively as the Inspector

The bottom half of the utility view is called the **Library Pane**, or just plain **Library**. The library is a collection of reusable items you can use in your own programs. The four icons in the bar at the top of the library pane divide it into four sections:

- **File Template Library**: This section contains a collection of file templates you can use when you need to add a new file to your project. For example, if you want to add a new file to your project, one way to do it is to drag a file of the required type from the file template library.

- **Code Snippet Library**: This section features a collection of code snippets you can drag into your source code files. Can't remember the syntax for Objective-C fast enumeration? That's fine—just drag that particular snippet out of the library, and you don't need to look it up. Have you written something you think you'll want to use again later? Select it in your text editor and drag it to the code snippet library.

- **Object Library**: This section is filled with reusable objects, such as text fields, labels, sliders, buttons, and just about any object you would ever need to design your iOS interface. We'll use the object library extensively in this book to build the interfaces for our sample programs.

- **Media Library**: As its name implies, this section is for all your media, including pictures, sounds, and movies.

> **Note**   The items in the Object Library are primarily from the iOS UIKit, which is a framework of objects used to create an app's user interface. UIKit fulfills the same role in Cocoa Touch as AppKit does in Cocoa. The two frameworks are similar conceptually; however, because of differences in the platforms, there are obviously many differences between them. On the other hand, the Foundation framework classes, such as NSString and NSArray, are shared between Cocoa and Cocoa Touch.

Note the search field at the bottom of the library. Do you want to find a button? Type **button** in the search field, and the current library will show only items with "button" in the name. Don't forget to clear the search field when you are finished searching.

Adding a Label to the View

Let's give Interface Builder a try. Click the **Object Library** icon (it looks like a circle with a square in the center—you can see it in Figure 2-18) at the top of the library to bring up the Object Library. Just for fun, scroll through the library to find a *Table View*. That's it—keep scrolling, and you'll find it. Or wait! There's a better way: just type the words **Table View** in the search field. Isn't that so much easier?

> **Tip**   Here's a nifty shortcut: press ⌃⌥⌘3 to jump to the search field and highlight its contents. Next, you can just type what you want to search for.

Now find a *Label* in the library. Next, drag the label onto the view we saw earlier. (If you don't see the view in your editor pane, click the **View** icon in the Interface Builder Document Outline.) As your cursor appears over the view, it will turn into the standard, "I'm making a copy of something" green plus sign you know from the Finder. Drag the label to the center of the view. A pair of blue guidelines—one vertical and one horizontal—will appear when your label is centered. It's not vital that the label be centered, but it's good to know that those guidelines are there. Figure 2-19 shows what our workspace looked like just before we released our drag.

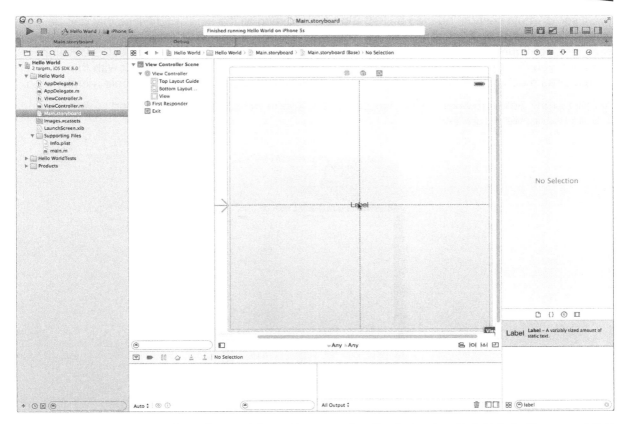

Figure 2-19. *We've found a label in our library and dragged it onto our view. Note that we typed Label into the library search field to limit our object list to those containing the word Label*

User interface items are stored in a hierarchy. Most views can contain **subviews**; however, there are some, like buttons and most other controls, that can't. Interface Builder is smart. If an object does not accept subviews, you will not be able to drag other objects onto it.

By dragging a label directly to the view we're editing, we add it as a subview of that main view (the view named **View**), which will cause it to show up automatically when that view is displayed to the user. Dragging a label from the library to the view called **View** adds an instance of UILabel as a subview of our application's main view.

Let's edit the label so it says something profound. Double-click the label you just created, and type the text, **Hello, World!**. Next, click off the label, and then reselect it and drag the label to recenter it or position it wherever you want it to appear on the screen.

Guess what? Once we save, we're finished. Select **File ➤ Save**, or press ⌘S. Now check out the pop-up menu at the upper left of the Xcode project window. This is actually a multisegment pop-up control. The left side lets you choose a different compilation target and do a few other things, but we're interested in the right side, which lets you pick which device you want to run on. Click the right side and you'll see a list of available devices. At the top, if you have any iOS device plugged in and ready to go, you'll see it listed. Otherwise, you'll just see a generic **iOS Device** entry. Below that, you'll see a whole section, headed by **iOS Simulator**, listing all the kinds of devices that can be used with the iOS simulator. From that lower section, choose **iPhone 5s,** so that our app will run in the simulator, configured as if it were an iPhone 5s. If you are a member of Apple's paid iOS Developer Program, you can try running your app on your own device. In this book, we'll stick with the simulator as much as possible, since running in the simulator doesn't require any paid membership.

Ready to run? Select **Product ➤ Run** or press ⌘R. Xcode will compile your app and launch it in the iOS simulator (see Figure 2-20).

Figure 2-20. Here's the Hello World program in its full iPhone glory! But something is wrong…

Note   If your iOS device is connected to your Mac when you build and run, things might not go quite as planned. In a nutshell, in order to be able to build and run your applications on your iPhone, iPad, or iPod touch, you must sign up and pay for one of Apple's iOS Developer Programs, and then go through the process of configuring Xcode appropriately. When you join the program, Apple will send you the information you'll need to get this done. In the meantime, most of the programs in this book will run just fine using the iPhone or iPad simulator.

Well, that's not quite right. The label was centered in Interface Builder, but on the simulator, it's way off to the right. What went wrong? When you place a view, unless you tell it otherwise, Interface Builder assumes you are positioning it relative to the top-left corner of the view that you dropped it onto. The problem is that the view that we dropped the label onto is wider than the screen of the simulated iPhone that we ran the application on. When we centered the label in Interface Builder, we weren't centering it on the screen we were going to use to test the application. This is a problem that you'll face all the time—the screen of the device that your application ends up running on may not be the same size as the design surface that you used in Interface Builder. As we said earlier, this is deliberate—Apple wants you to design on an abstract square view as much as possible and have your screen layouts adapt to the screens that they meet at runtime.

So how do we fix this? Back in iOS 6, Apple added a technology called **Auto Layout**, which lets you add **constraints** to the views in your design that express how they should change position and/or size to adapt to the space that's actually available on screen. You'll see how to use Interface Builder to configure Auto Layout constraints starting in the next chapter, but for now, let's take a simpler approach—we'll change the square view that we're using as the basis for our design into one that looks more like the iPhone simulator that we're actually running the application on. To this, select *Main.storyboard* in the Project Navigator, and then click the **File Inspector** icon in the Inspector selector pane at the top of the Utility area, as shown in Figure 2-21.

File Inspector Icon

Size Classes Selector

Figure 2-21. Reconfiguring the storyboard for an iPhone

Toward the bottom of the File Inspector pane, you'll see two check boxes labeled **Use Auto Layout** and **Use Size Classes**, both of which are selected. Click the **Use Size Classes** check box to deselect it. When you do this, Xcode prompts you for confirmation and asks whether you want to keep size class data for the iPhone or the iPad. Select to keep the size class data for the iPhone and click **Disable Size Classes**. Immediately, the screen outline in the Editor area resizes itself to look like an iPhone (see Figure 2-22) and you can see clearly why your label did not appear in the correct location.

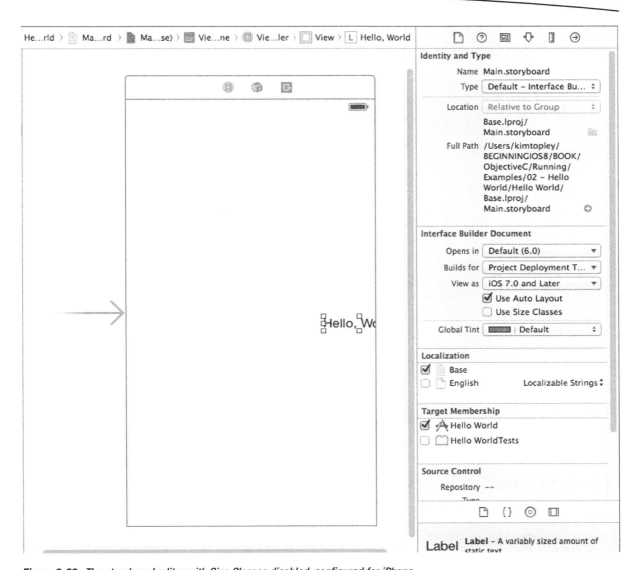

Figure 2-22. *The storyboard editor with Size Classes disabled, configured for iPhone*

Now drag the label back into the center and run the application again—this time, the label should be where you expected it to be (Figure 2-23).

Figure 2-23. The Hello World application working as planned

When you are finished admiring your handiwork, you can head back over to Xcode. Xcode and the simulator are separate applications. Wait a second! That's it? But we didn't write any code. That's right.

Pretty neat, huh?

Well, how about if we wanted to change some of the properties of the label, like the text size or color? We would need to write code to do that, right? Nope. Let's see just how easy it is to make changes.

Changing Attributes

Head back to Xcode and single-click the **Hello World** label to select it. Now turn your attention to the area above the library pane. This part of the utility pane is called the **Inspector**. As you saw in Figure 2-21, the Inspector pane is topped by a series of icons, each of which changes the Inspector to view a specific type of data. To change the attributes of the label, we'll need the fourth icon from the left, which brings up the Attributes Inspector (see Figure 2-24).

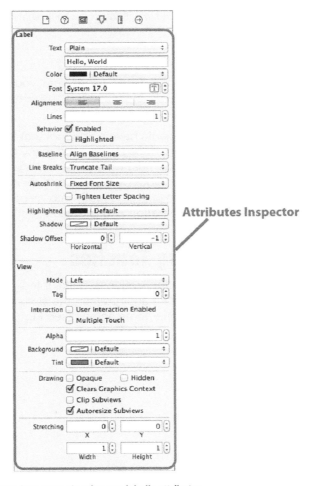

Figure 2-24. The object Attributes Inspector showing our label's attributes

Tip   The Inspector, like the Project Navigator, has keyboard shortcuts corresponding to each of its icons. The Inspector's keyboard shortcuts start with ⌥⌘1 for the leftmost icon, ⌥⌘2 for the next icon, and so on. Unlike the Project Navigator, the number of icons in the Inspector is context-sensitive and changes depending on which object is selected in the navigator and/or editor.

Go ahead and change the label's appearance to your heart's delight. Feel free to play around with the font, size, and color of the text. Note that if you increase the font size, you may need to resize the label itself to make room for larger text. Once you're finished playing, save the file and select **Run** again. The changes you made should show up in your application, once again without writing any code.

Note   Don't worry too much about what all of the fields in the Attributes Inspector mean, or fret if you can't get one of your changes to show up. As you make your way through the book, you'll learn a lot about the Attributes Inspector and what most of the fields do.

By letting you design your interface graphically, Interface Builder frees you to spend time writing the code that is specific to your application, instead of writing tedious code to construct your user interface.

Most modern application development environments have some tool that lets you build your user interface graphically. One distinction between Interface Builder and many of these other tools is that Interface Builder does not generate any code that must be maintained. Instead, Interface Builder creates Objective-C objects, just as you would in your own code, and then serializes those objects into the storyboard or nib file so that they can be loaded directly into memory at runtime. This avoids many of the problems associated with code generation and is, overall, a more powerful approach.

Some iPhone Polish: Finishing Touches

Now let's put a last bit of spit and polish on our application to make it feel a little more like an authentic iPhone application. First, run your project again. When the simulator window appears, press ⇧⌘H. That will bring you back to the iPhone home screen (see Figure 2-25). Notice anything a bit, well, boring?

Figure 2-25. *The Hello World application on the home screen*

Take a look at the **Hello World** icon at the top of the screen. Yeah, that icon will never do, will it? To fix it, you need to create an icon and save it as a portable network graphic (*.png*) file. Actually, for best results you should create five icons, with sizes 180 x 180 pixels, 120 x 120 pixels, 87 x 87 pixels, 80 x 80 pixels and 58 x 58 pixels. Why so many icons? The icons are used on the iPhone home screen, in the Settings app and in the results list for a Spotlight search. That accounts for three of them, but that's not the end of the story—the iPhone 6 Plus, with its larger screen, requires higher resolution icons, adding another three to the list. Fortunately, one of these is the same size as an icon from the other set, so you actually only need to create five versions of your application icon. If you don't supply some of the smaller ones, a larger one will be scaled down appropriately; but for best results, you (or a graphic artist on your team) should probably scale it in advance.

Note   The issue of icon sizes is even more complex than this. Before iOS 7, the side dimension of an icon for all modern iPhones was 114 × 114 pixels. But if you still wanted to support older, non-Retina iPhones, you needed to include an icon at half that resolution too, 57 × 57. Then there's the issue of the iPad, which has still other icons sizes, both Retina and non-Retina, for both iOS 8 and for earlier versions of iOS! For now, we'll avoid diving further down this particular rabbit hole, and just provide icons for iPhones running iOS 8.

Do not try to match the style of the buttons that are already on the phone when you create the icons; your iPhone will automatically round the edges. Just create normal, square images. We have provided a set of icon images in the project archive *02 - Hello World - icons* folder. These images are called *icon-180.png*, *icon-120.png*, *icon-87.png*, *icon-80*, and *icon-58.png*; feel free to use them if you don't want to create your own.

Note   For your application's icon, you must use *.png* images; in fact, you should actually use that format for all images in your iOS projects. Xcode automatically optimizes *.png* images at build time, which makes them the fastest and most efficient image type for use in iOS apps. Even though most common image formats will display correctly, you should use *.png* files unless you have a compelling reason to use another format.

Press ⌘1 to open the Project Navigator, and look inside the Hello World group for an item called *Images.xcassets*. This is something called an **asset catalog**. By default, each new Xcode project is created with an asset catalog, ready to hold your app icon and other images. Select *Images.xcassets* and turn your attention to the editing pane.

On the left side of the editing pane, you'll see a white column with an entry labeled **AppIcon**. Make sure that the **AppIcon** item is selected. To the right of that column, you'll see a white space with the text "AppIcon" in the upper-left corner, as well as dashed-line squares for the five icons we just talked about (see Figure 2-26). This is where we'll drag our app icons.

Figure 2-26. The AppIcon boxes on your project's assets catalog. This is where you can set your application's icon

You'll see that beneath each icon is a bit of text explaining where that version of the icon will be used. It also tells you what size the icon should be. But here's the tricky part: Xcode shows you the size in **points**, not pixels. In this context, a point is a particular size on a screen. It's the size of a single pixel on the earliest iPhones (everything earlier than the iPhone 4), as well as on the iPad 1, iPad 2, and iPad Mini. On most of the later devices with a Retina display, a single point is actually a 2 × 2–pixel square. The exception is the iPhone 6 Plus, where a single point is a 3 × 3–pixel square. The items shown in the asset catalog hint at this with their 2x and 3x labels, but those are really just labels. To figure out what size an item really expects, select one of them and press ⌥⌘**4** to open the Attributes Inspector on the right side of the window. This will show you both the size (again in points) and the scale, which for each of these icons is either 2x or 3x. Multiply the size by the scale, and you'll get the actual pixel size that's required. Select each of the items in the AppIcon box in turn, and the Inspector will give you the details. They should match up with what we described earlier, but you never know what Apple has up its sleeve. Between the time this book goes to print and the time you read this, Apple may have some fantastic new devices that require still more icons!

From the Finder, drag *icon-120.png* to the item labeled "iPhone App 2x" and *icon-180.png* to "iPhone App 3x"—these should be the ones on the right. This will copy those icons into your project and set them as your application's icon. Next, drag *icon-80.png* from the Finder to "iPhone Spotlight 2x" and *icon-120.png* (again) to "iPhone Spotlight 3x", (the group in the middle, not the group on the left), which will set them as your application's **Spotlight** icons. Finally, drag *icon-58.png* to "iPhone Settings 2x" and *icon-87.png* to "iPhone Settings 3x", setting the icons to be used for Settings.

Now compile and run your app. When the simulator has finished launching, press the button with the white square to go home, and check out your snazzy new icon. Ours is shown in Figure 2-27. To see one of the smaller icons in use, swipe down inside the home screen to bring up the spotlight search field, and start typing the word **Hello**—you'll see your new app's icon appear immediately.

Figure 2-27. Your application now has a snazzy icon!

> **Note**   As you work through this book, your simulator's home screen will get cluttered with the icons for the
> example applications that we'll be running. If you want to clear out old applications from the home screen,
> you can choose **iOS Simulator ➤ Reset Content and Settings...** from the iOS simulator's application menu.

The Launch Screen

There's just one more thing we need to talk about before moving on. When you launched your application, you probably noticed the mainly white launch screen that appeared while the application was being loaded. iOS applications have always had a launch screen. Since the process of loading an application into memory takes time (and the larger the application, the longer it takes), the purpose of this screen is to let the user see, as quickly as possible, that something is happening. Prior to iOS 8, you could supply an image (in fact, several images of different sizes) to act as your app's launch screen. iOS would load the correct image and immediately display it before loading the rest of your application. With iOS 8, you still have that option, but Apple now recommends that you use a **launch file** instead of a launch image, or as well as a launch image if your application still needs to support earlier releases.

What's a launch file? It's a nib file or storyboard that contains the user interface for your launch screen. On devices running iOS 8, if a launch file is found, it is used in preference to a launch image. Look in the Project Navigator and you'll see that you already have a launch file in your project—it's called *LaunchScreen.xib*. If you open it in Interface Builder, you'll see that it doesn't contain very much (see Figure 2-28).

Figure 2-28. *Our application's default launch file*

The default launch file consists of two labels, which Xcode creates automatically using the project and organization names that you entered in the project template selection sheet (see Figure 2-3). Apple recommends that you don't try to create a complex or visually impressive launch screen so we're not going to attempt to do that here. Instead, just to show that it works, we're going to change its background color. To do that, select the View icon in the Document Outline and open the Attributes Inspector. Locate the control labeled **Background** and choose any color you like—since this is an Apress book, I chose yellow. Now just run the application again to see the result flash by just before the application itself appears.

Figure 2-29. A yellow launch screen for the Hello, World application

You can read more about the launch file, launch images and application icons in Apple's *Human Interface Guidelines* document, which you'll find online at https://developer.apple.com/library/ios/documentation/UserExperience/Conceptual/MobileHIG/IconMatrix.html.

Bring It on Home

Pat yourself on the back. Although it may not seem like you accomplished all that much in this chapter, we actually covered a lot of ground. You learned about the iOS project templates, created an application, learned a ton about Xcode 6, started using Interface Builder, and learned how to set your application icon.

The Hello World program, however, is a strictly one-way application. We show some information to the users, but we never get any input from them. When you're ready to see how to go about getting input from the user of an iOS device and taking actions based on that input, take a deep breath and turn the page.

3

Handling Basic Interaction

Our Hello World application was a good introduction to iOS development using Cocoa Touch, but it was missing a crucial capability—the ability to interact with the user. Without that, our application is severely limited in terms of what it can accomplish.

In this chapter, we're going to write a slightly more complex application—one that will feature two buttons as well as a label (see Figure 3-1). When the user taps either of the buttons, the label's text will change. This may seem like a rather simplistic example, but it demonstrates the key concepts involved in creating interactive iOS apps. Just for fun, we're also going to introduce you to the NSAttributedString class, which lets you use styled text with many Cocoa Touch GUI elements.

Figure 3-1. The simple two-button application we will build in this chapter

The Model-View-Controller Paradigm

Before diving in, a bit of theory is in order. The designers of Cocoa Touch were guided by a concept called **Model-View-Controller** (MVC), which is a very logical way of dividing the code that makes up a GUI-based application. These days, almost all object-oriented frameworks pay a certain amount of homage to MVC, but few are as true to the MVC model as Cocoa Touch.

The MVC pattern divides all functionality into three distinct categories:

- **Model**: The classes that hold your application's data.

- **View**: Made up of the windows, controls, and other elements that the user can see and interact with.

- **Controller**: The code that binds together the model and view. It contains the application logic that decides how to handle the user's inputs.

The goal in MVC is to make the objects that implement these three types of code as distinct from one another as possible. Any object you create should be readily identifiable as belonging in one of the three categories, with little or no functionality that could be classified as being either of the other two. An object that implements a button, for example, shouldn't contain code to process data when that button is tapped, and an implementation of a bank account shouldn't contain code to draw a table to display its transactions.

MVC helps ensure maximum reusability. A class that implements a generic button can be used in any application. A class that implements a button that does some particular calculation when it is clicked can be used only in the application for which it was originally written.

When you write Cocoa Touch applications, you will primarily create your view components using Interface Builder, although you will also modify, and sometimes even create, your user interfaces from code.

Your model will be created by writing Objective-C classes to hold your application's data or by building a data model using something called Core Data, which you'll learn about in Chapter 13. We won't be creating any model objects in this chapter's application because we do not need to store or preserve data. However, we will introduce model objects as our applications get more complex in future chapters.

Your controller component will typically be composed of classes that you create and that are specific to your application. Controllers can be completely custom classes (NSObject subclasses), but more often they will be subclasses of one of several existing generic controller classes from the UIKit framework, such as UIViewController (as you'll see shortly). By subclassing one of these existing classes, you will get a lot of functionality for free and won't need to spend time recoding the wheel, so to speak.

As we get deeper into Cocoa Touch, you will quickly start to see how the classes of the UIKit framework follow the principles of MVC. If you keep this concept in the back of your mind as you develop, you will end up creating cleaner, more easily maintained code.

Creating Our Project

It's time to create our next Xcode project. We're going to use the same template that we used in the previous chapter: Single View Application. By starting with this simple template again, it will be easier for you to see how the view and controller objects work together in an iOS application. We'll use some of the other templates in later chapters.

Launch Xcode and select **File ➤ New ➤ Project. . .** or press ⌘N. Select the **Single View Application** template, and then click **Next**.

You'll be presented with the same options sheet that you saw in the previous chapter. In the **Product Name** field, type the name of our new application, **Button Fun**. The **Organization Name**, **Company Identifier**, and **Language** fields should still have the values you used in the previous chapter (*Apress*, *com.apress*, and *Objective-C*), so you can leave those alone. In this chapter, we are going to use Auto Layout to create an application that works on all iOS devices, so in the **Devices** field, select **Universal**. Figure 3-2 shows the completed options sheet.

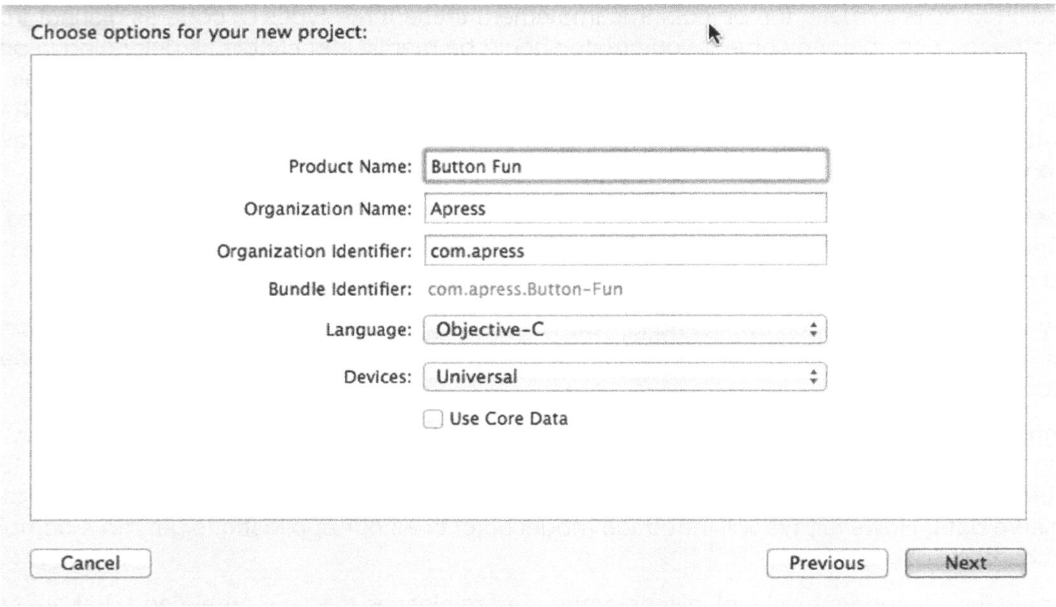

Figure 3-2. Naming your project and selecting options

Hit **Next**, and you'll be prompted for a location for your project. You can leave the **Create Git repository** check box checked or unchecked, whichever you prefer. Press **Create** and save the project with the rest of your book projects.

Looking at the View Controller

A little later in this chapter, we'll design a view (or user interface) for our application using Interface Builder, just as we did in the previous chapter. Before we do that, we're going to look at and make some changes to the source code files that were created for us. Yes, Virginia, we're actually going to write some code in this chapter.

Before we make any changes, let's look at the files that were created for us. In the Project Navigator, the *Button Fun* group should already be expanded; but if it's not, click the disclosure triangle next to it (see Figure 3-3).

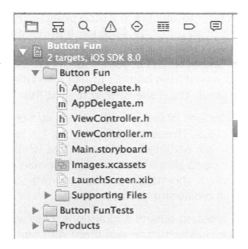

Figure 3-3. *The Project Navigator showing the class files that were created for us by the project template*

The *Button Fun* folder should contain four source code files (the ones that end in *.h* or *.m*) along with a storyboard file, a launch screen file, and an asset catalog for containing any images our app needs. The four source code files implement two classes that our application needs: our application delegate and the view controller for our application's only view.

We'll look at the application delegate a little later in the chapter. First, we'll work with the view controller class that was created for us.

The controller class called `ViewController` is responsible for managing our application's view. The name identifies that this class is, well, a view controller. Click *ViewController.h* in the Project Navigator and take a look at the contents of the class's header file:

```
#import <UIKit/UIKit.h>

@interface ViewController : UIViewController

@end
```

Not much to it, is there? `ViewController` is a subclass of `UIViewController`, which is one of those generic controller classes we mentioned earlier. It is part of the UIKit framework, and by subclassing this class, we get a bunch of functionality for free. Xcode doesn't know what our application-specific functionality is going to be, but it does know that we're going to have some, so it has created this class for us to write that application-specific functionality.

Understanding Outlets and Actions

In Chapter 2, you used Xcode's Interface Builder to design a simple user interface. A moment ago, you saw the shell of a view controller class. There must be some way for the code in this view controller class to interact with the objects in the storyboard, right?

Absolutely! A controller class can refer to objects in a storyboard or nib file by using a special kind of property called an **outlet**. Think of an outlet as a pointer that points to an object within the user interface. For example, suppose you created a text label in Interface Builder (as we did in Chapter 2) and wanted to change the label's text from within your code. By declaring an outlet and connecting that outlet to the label object, you would then be able to use the outlet from within your code to change the text displayed by the label. You'll see how to do just that in this chapter.

Going in the opposite direction, interface objects in our storyboard or nib file can be set up to trigger special methods in our controller class. These special methods are known as **action methods** (or just **actions**). For example, you can tell Interface Builder that when the user taps a button, a specific action method within your code should be called. You could even tell Interface Builder that when the user first touches a button, it should call one action method; and then later, when the finger is lifted off the button, it should call a different action method.

Xcode supports multiple ways of creating outlets and actions. One way is to specify them in our source code before using Interface Builder to connect them with our code. Xcode's Assistant View gives us a much faster and more intuitive approach that lets us create and connect outlets and actions in a single step, a process we're going to look at shortly. But before we start making connections, let's talk about outlets and actions in a little more detail. Outlets and actions are two of the most basic building blocks you'll use to create iOS apps, so it's important that you understand what they are and how they work.

Outlets

Outlets are special Objective-C class properties that are declared using the keyword IBOutlet. Declaring an outlet is done either in your controller's class header file or in a special section (called the **class extension**) of your controller's implementation file. It might look something like this:

```
@property (weak, nonatomic) IBOutlet UIButton *myButton;
```

This example is an outlet called myButton, which can be set to point to any button in the user interface.

The IBOutlet keyword isn't built into the Objective-C language. It's a simple C preprocessor definition in a system header file, where it looks something like this:

```
#ifndef IBOutlet
#define IBOutlet
#endif
```

Confused? IBOutlet does absolutely nothing as far as the compiler is concerned. Its sole purpose is to act as a hint to tell Xcode that this is a property that we're going to want to connect to an object in a storyboard or nib file. Any property that you create and want to connect to an object in a storyboard or nib file must be preceded by the IBOutlet keyword. Fortunately, Xcode will now create outlets for us automatically.

OUTLET CHANGES

Over time, Apple has changed the way that outlets are declared and used. Since you may run across older code at some point, let's look at how outlets have changed.

In the first version of this book, we declared both a property and its underlying instance variable for our outlets. At that time, properties were a new construct in the Objective-C language, and they required you to declare a corresponding instance variable:

```
@interface MyViewController : UIViewController
{
    UIButton *myButton;
}
@property (weak, nonatomic) UIButton *myButton;
@end
```

Back then, we placed the IBOutlet keyword before the instance variable declaration:

```
IBOutlet UIButton *myButton;
```

This was how Apple's sample code was written at the time. It was also how the IBOutlet keyword had traditionally been used in Cocoa and NeXTSTEP.

By the time we wrote the second edition of the book, Apple had moved away from placing the IBOutlet keyword in front of the instance variable, and it became standard to place it within the property declaration:

```
@property (weak, nonatomic) IBOutlet UIButton *myButton;
```

Even though both approaches continued to work (and still do), we followed Apple's lead and changed the book code so that the IBOutlet keyword was in the property declaration rather than in the instance variable declaration.

When Apple switched the default compiler from the GNU C Compiler (GCC) to the Low Level Virtual Machine (LLVM) recently, it stopped being necessary to declare instance variables for properties. If LLVM finds a property without a matching instance variable, it will create one automatically. As a result, in this edition of the book, we've stopped declaring instance variables for our outlets altogether.

All of these approaches do exactly the same thing, which is to tell Interface Builder about the existence of an outlet. Placing the IBOutlet keyword on the property declaration is Apple's current recommendation, so that's what we're going to use. But we wanted to make you aware of the history in case you come across older code that has the IBOutlet keyword on the instance variable.

You can read more about Objective-C properties in the book *Learn Objective-C on the Mac* by Scott Knaster, Waqar Malik, and Mark Dalrymple (Apress, 2012) and in the document called *Introduction to the Objective-C Programming Language*, available from Apple's Developer web site at http://developer.apple.com/library/ios/#documentation/Cocoa/Conceptual/ProgrammingWithObjectiveC.

Actions

In a nutshell, actions are methods that are declared with a special return type, IBAction, which tells Interface Builder that this method can be triggered by a control in a storyboard or nib file. The declaration for an action method will usually look like this:

```
- (IBAction)doSomething:(id)sender;
```

It might also look like this:

```
- (IBAction)doSomething;
```

The actual name of the method can be anything you want, but it must have a return type of IBAction, which is the same as declaring a return type of void. A void return type is how you specify that a method does not return a value. Also, the method must either take no arguments or take a single argument, usually called sender. When the action method is called, sender will contain a pointer to the object that called it. For example, if this action method was triggered when the user tapped a button, sender would point to the button that was tapped. The sender argument exists so that you can respond to multiple controls using a single action method. It gives you a way to identify which control called the action method.

Tip   There's actually a third, less frequently used type of IBAction declaration that looks like this:

```
- (IBAction)doSomething:(id)sender
                forEvent:(UIEvent *)event;
```

We'll begin talking about control events in the next chapter.

It won't hurt anything if you declare an action method with a sender argument and then ignore it. You will likely see a lot of code that does just that. Action methods in Cocoa and NeXTSTEP needed to accept sender whether they used it or not, so a lot of iOS code, especially early iOS code, was written that way.

Now that you understand what actions and outlets are, you'll see how they work as we design our user interface. Before we start doing that, however, we have one quick piece of housekeeping to do to keep everything neat and orderly.

Cleaning Up the View Controller

Single-click *ViewController.m* in the Project Navigator to open the implementation file. As you can see, there's a small amount of boilerplate code in the form of `viewDidLoad` and `didReceiveMemoryWarning` methods that were provided for us by the project template we chose. These methods are commonly used in `UIViewController` subclasses, so Xcode gave us stub implementations of them. If we need to use them, we can just add our code there. However, we don't need either of these stub implementations for this project, so all they're doing is taking up space and making our code harder to read. We're going to do our future selves a favor and clear away methods that we don't need, so go ahead and delete those methods.

At the top of the file, you'll also see an empty class extension ready for us to use. A class extension is a special kind of Objective-C category declaration that lets you declare methods and properties that will only be usable within a class's primary implementation block, within the same file. We'll use the class extension to house our view controller's outlets. This is a typical pattern that you'll see often in iOS applications. We put the outlets in the class extension because they don't need to be visible to code outside the view controller. By contrast, properties and methods that need to be used by other classes would be declared in *ViewController.h* When you're finished, your implementation should look like this:

```objc
#import "ViewController.h"

@interface ViewController ()

@end

@implementation ViewController

@end
```

That's much simpler, huh? Don't worry about those methods you just deleted. You'll find out what they do and how to use them in the rest of the book.

Designing the User Interface

Make sure you save the changes you just made, and then single-click *Main.storyboard* to open your application's view in Xcode's Interface Builder (see Figure 3-4). As you'll remember from the previous chapter, the white window that shows up in the editor represents your application's one and only view. If you look back at Figure 3-1, you can see that we need to add two buttons and a label to this view.

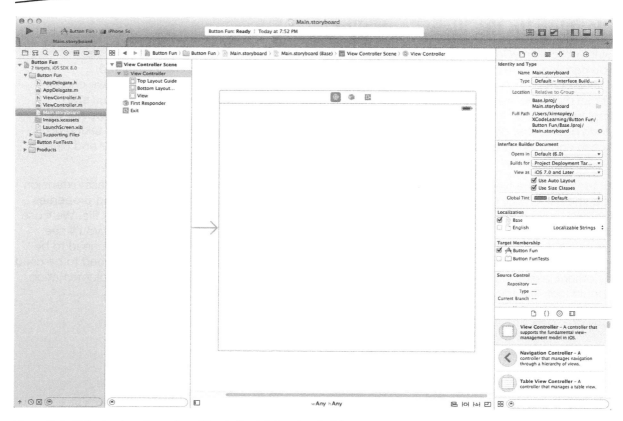

Figure 3-4. Main.storyboard open for editing in Xcode's Interface Builder

Let's take a second to think about our application. We're going to add two buttons and a label to our user interface, and that process is very similar to what we did in the previous chapter. However, we're also going to need outlets and actions to make our application interactive.

The buttons will need to each trigger an action method on our controller. We could choose to make each button call a different action method; but since they're going to do essentially the same task (update the label's text), we will need to call the same action method. We'll differentiate between the two buttons using that sender argument we discussed earlier in the section on actions. In addition to the action method, we'll also need an outlet connected to the label so that we can change the text that the label displays.

Let's add the buttons first and then place the label. We'll create the corresponding actions and outlets as we design our interface. We could also manually declare our actions and outlets, and then connect our user interface items to them, but why do extra work when Xcode will do it for us?

Adding the Buttons and Action Method

Our first order of business is to add two buttons to our user interface. We'll then have Xcode create an empty action method for us, and we will connect both buttons to it. Any code we place in that method will be executed when the user taps the button.

Select **View ➤ Utilities ➤ Show Object Library** or press ^⌥⌘3 to open the object library. Type **UIButton** into the object library's search box (you actually need to type only the first four characters, **uibu**, to narrow down the list—and you can use all lowercase letters to save yourself the trouble of pressing the **Shift** key). Once you're finished typing, only one item should appear in the object library: *Button* (see Figure 3-5).

Figure 3-5. The Button as it appears in the object library

Drag the Button from the library and drop it on the white window inside the editing area. This will add a button to your application's view. Place the button along the left side of the view the appropriate distance from the left edge by using the blue guidelines that appear to place it. For vertical placement, use the blue guidelines to place the button halfway down in the view. You can use Figure 3-1 as a placement guide, if that helps.

> **Note**   The little blue guidelines that appear as you move objects around in Interface Builder are there to help you stick to the *iOS Human Interface Guidelines* (usually referred to as **the HIG**). Apple provides the HIG for people designing iPhone and iPad applications. The HIG tells you how you should—and shouldn't—design your user interface. You really should read it because it contains valuable information that every iOS developer needs to know. You'll find it at `http://developer.apple.com/library/ios/documentation/UserExperience/Conceptual/MobileHIG/`.

Double-click the newly added button. This will allow you to edit the button's title. Give this button a title of *Left*.

Now, it's time for some Xcode magic. Select **View ➤ Assistant Editor ➤ Show Assistant Editor**, or press ⌥⌘↵ to open the Assistant Editor. You can also show and hide the Assistant Editor by clicking the middle editor button in the collection of seven buttons on the upper-right side of the project window (see Figure 3-6).

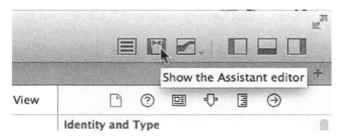

Figure 3-6. *The Show the Assistant Editor toggle button*

The Assistant Editor will appear to the right of the editing pane. The left side will continue to show Interface Builder, but the right will display either *ViewController.h* or *ViewController.m*, which are the header and implementation files for the view controller that "owns" the view you're looking at.

> **Tip**   After opening the Assistant Editor, you may need to resize your window to have enough room to work. If you're on a smaller screen, like the one on a MacBook Air, you might need to close the Utility View and/or Project Navigator to give yourself enough room to use the Assistant Editor effectively. You can do this easily using the three view buttons in the upper right of the project window (see Figure 3-6).

Xcode knows that our view controller class is responsible for displaying the view in the storyboard, and so the Assistant Editor knows to show us the implementation of the view controller class, which is the most likely place we'll want to connect actions and outlets. However, if it is not displaying the file that you want to see, you can use the jump bar at the top of the Assistant Editor to fix that. First, locate the segment of the jump bar that says **Automatic** and click it. In the pop-up menu that appears, select **Manual ➤ Button Fun ➤ Button Fun ➤ ViewController.m**. You should now be looking at the correct file.

As you saw earlier, there's really not much in the ViewController class. It's just an empty UIViewController subclass. But it won't be an empty subclass for long!

We're now going to ask Xcode to automatically create a new action method for us and associate that action with the button we just created. We're going to add these definitions to the view controller's class extension. To do this, begin by clicking the button that you added to the storyboard so that it is selected. Now, hold down the **Control** key on your keyboard, and then click-and-drag from the button over to the source code in the Assistant Editor. You should see a blue line running from the button to your cursor (see Figure 3-7). This blue line is how we connect objects in IB to code or other objects.

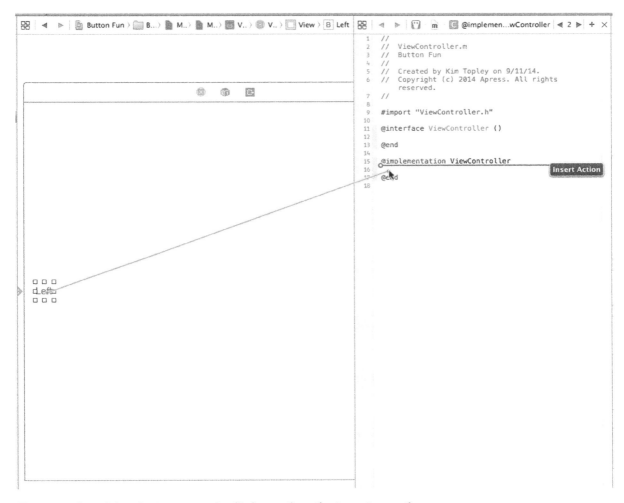

Figure 3-7. Control-dragging to source code will give you the option to create an action

If you move your cursor so it's in the class implementation (between the @implementation and @end keywords—see Figure 3-7), a gray pop-up will appear, letting you know that releasing the mouse button will insert an action for you.

> **Note**   We use actions and outlets in this chapter and we'll use outlet collections later in the book. Outlet collections allow you to connect multiple objects of the same kind to a single NSArray property, rather than creating a separate property for each object.

To finish this connection, release your mouse button, and a floating pop-up will appear, like the one shown in Figure 3-8. This window lets you customize your new action.

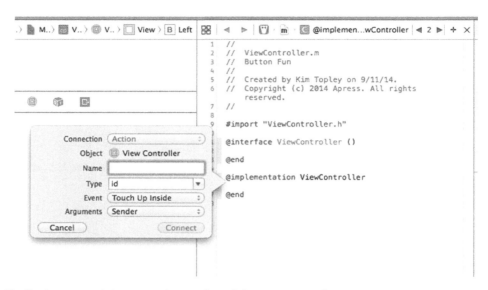

Figure 3-8. The floating pop-up that appears after you Control-drag to source code

In the **Name** field, type **buttonPressed**. When you're finished, do *not* hit the **Return** key. Pressing **Return** would finalize our outlet, and we're not quite ready to do that. Instead, press the **Tab** key to move to the **Type** field and type in **UIButton**, replacing the default value of id.

Note   As you probably remember, an *id* is a generic pointer that can point to any Objective-C object. We could leave this as *id*, and it would work fine; but if we change it to the class we expect to call the method, the compiler can warn us if we try to do this from the wrong type of object. There are times when you'll want the flexibility to be able to call the same action method from different types of controls, and in those cases, you would want to leave this set to *id*. In our case, we're only going to call this method from buttons, so we're letting Xcode and the compiler know that. Now, they can warn us if we unintentionally try to connect something else to it.

There are two fields below **Type**, which we will leave at their default values. The **Event** field lets you specify when the method is called. The default value of **Touch Up Inside** fires when the user lifts a finger off the screen if–and only if–the finger is still on the button. This is the standard event to use for buttons. This gives the user a chance to reconsider. If the user moves a finger off the button before lifting it off the screen, the method won't fire.

The **Arguments** field lets you choose between the three different method signatures that can be used for action methods. We want the sender argument, so that we can tell which button called the method. That's the default, so we just leave it as is. At this point, the pop-up should look like the one in Figure 3-9.

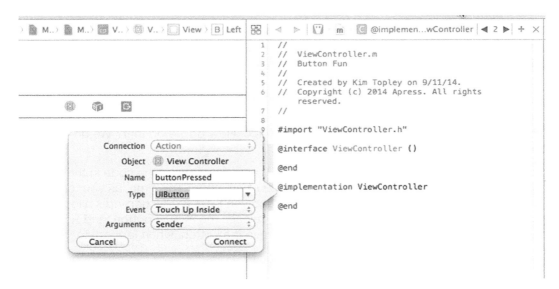

Figure 3-9. *The completed Action pop-up*

Hit the **Return** key or click the **Connect** button, and Xcode will insert the action method for you. The *ViewController.m* file should now look like this:

```
@interface ViewController ()

@end

@implementation ViewController

- (IBAction)buttonPressed:(UIButton *)sender {
}

@end
```

In a few moments, we'll come back here to write the code that needs to run when the user taps either button.

In addition to creating the method stub, Xcode has also connected that button to that method and stored that information in the storyboard. That means we don't need to do anything else to make that button call this method when our application runs.

Go back to *Main.storyboard* and drag out another button, this time placing the button on the right side of the screen. The blue guidelines will appear to help you align it with the right margin, as you saw before, and they will also help you align the button vertically with the other button. After placing the button, double-click it and change its name to *Right*.

> **Tip** Instead of dragging out a new object from the library, you could hold down the ⌥ key (the **Option** key) drag out a copy of the original object (the **Left** button in this example) over. Holding down the ⌥ key tells Interface Builder to make a copy of the object you drag.

This time, we don't want to create a new action method. Instead, we want to connect this button to the existing one that Xcode created for us a moment ago. How do we do that? We do it pretty much the same way as we did for the first button.

After changing the name of the button, Control-click it and drag toward the code in the Assistant Editor. Drag toward the declaration of the buttonPressed: method. This time, as your cursor gets near buttonPressed:, that method should highlight, and you'll get a gray pop-up saying **Connect Action** (see Figure 3-10). When you see that pop-up, release the mouse button, and Xcode will connect the button to the action method. That will cause the button, when tapped, to trigger the same action method as the other button.

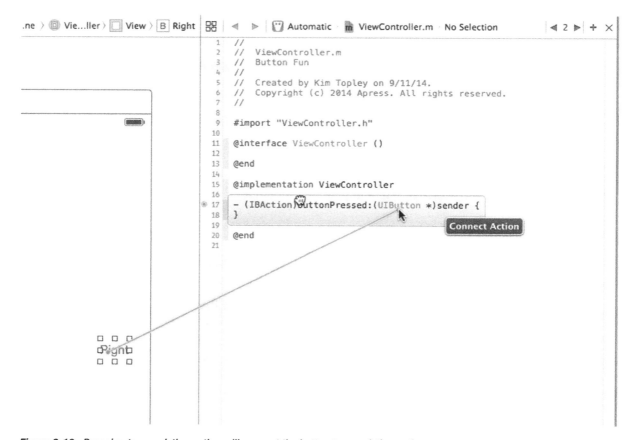

Figure 3-10. Dragging to an existing action will connect the button to an existing action

Adding the Label and Outlet

In the object library, type *Label* into the search field to find the *Label* user interface item (*see* Figure 3-11). Drag the *Label* to your user interface, somewhere above the two buttons you placed earlier. After placing it, use the resize handles to stretch the label from the left margin to the right margin. That should give it plenty of room for the text we'll be displaying to the user.

Figure 3-11. The label as it appears in the object library

The text in a label, by default, is left-aligned, but we want the text in this one to be centered. Select **View ➤ Utilities ➤ Show Attributes Inspector** (or press ⌥⌘4) to bring up the Attributes Inspector (see Figure 3-12). Make sure the label is selected, and then look in the Attributes Inspector for the **Alignment** buttons. Select the middle **Alignment** button to center the label's text.

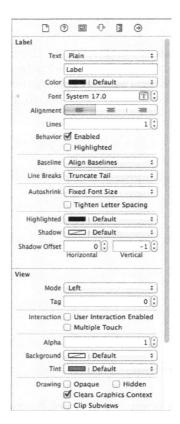

Figure 3-12. The Attributes Inspector for the label

Before the user taps a button, we don't want the label to say anything, so double-click the label (so the text is selected) and press the **Delete** button on your keyboard. That will delete the text currently assigned to the label. Hit **Return** to commit your changes. Even though you won't be able to see the label when it's not selected, don't worry—it's still there.

> **Tip**   If you have invisible user interface elements, like empty labels, and want to be able to see where they are, select **Canvas** from the **Editor** menu. Next, from the submenu that pops up, turn on **Show Bounds Rectangles**.

All that's left is to create an outlet for the label. We do this exactly the way we created and connected actions earlier. Make sure the Assistant Editor is open and displaying *ViewController.m*. If you need to switch files, use the pop-up in the jump bar above the Assistant Editor.

Next, select the label in Interface Builder and Control-drag from the label to the header file. Drag until your cursor is right above the existing action method. When you see something like Figure 3-13, let go of the mouse button, and you'll see a pop-up window that offers to create an Outlet or an Outlet Collection.

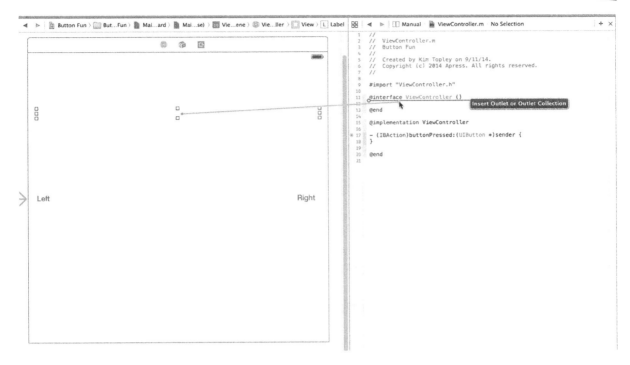

Figure 3-13. Control-dragging to create an outlet

We want to create an outlet, so leave the **Connection** at the default type of **Outlet**. We want to choose a descriptive name for this outlet so we'll remember what it is used for when we're working on our code. Type *statusLabel* into the **Name** field. Leave the **Type** field set to *UILabel*. The final field, labeled **Storage**, can be left at the default value.

Hit **Return** to commit your changes, and Xcode will insert the outlet property into your code. Your class extension should now look like this:

@interface ViewController ()

@property (weak, nonatomic) IBOutlet UILabel *statusLabel;

@end

Now we have an outlet, and Xcode has automagically connected the label to our outlet. This means that if we make any changes to statusLabel in code, those changes will affect the label on our user interface. If we set the text property on statusLabel, for example, it will change what text is displayed to the user.

┌───┐
│   AUTOMATIC REFERENCE COUNTING   │
└───┘

If you're already familiar with Objective-C, or if you've read earlier versions of this book, you might have noticed that we don't have a `dealloc` method. We're not releasing our instance variables!

Warning! Warning! Danger, Will Robinson!

Actually, Will, you can relax. We're quite OK. There's no danger at all—really.

It's no longer necessary to release objects. Well, that's not entirely true. It is necessary, but the LLVM compiler that Apple includes with Xcode these days is so smart that it will release objects for us, using a new feature called **Automatic Reference Counting**, or ARC, to do the heavy lifting. That means less frequent use of `dealloc` methods and no more worrying about calling `release` or `autorelease`. ARC is such a big improvement that we're using it for all examples in this book. ARC has been an option in Xcode for the past couple of years, but now it's enabled by default for each new project you create.

ARC applies only to Objective-C objects, not to Core Foundation objects or to memory allocated with `malloc()` and the like, and there are some caveats and gotchas that can trip you up. But for the most part, worrying about memory management is a thing of the past.

To learn more about ARC, check out the ARC release notes at this URL:

`http://developer.apple.com/library/ios/#releasenotes/ObjectiveC/RN-TransitioningToARC/`

ARC is very cool, but it's not magic. You should still understand the basic rules of memory management in Objective-C to avoid getting in trouble with ARC. To brush up on the Objective-C memory management contract, read Apple's *Memory Management Programming Guide* at this URL:

`http://developer.apple.com/library/ios/#documentation/Cocoa/Conceptual/MemoryMgmt/`

Writing the Action Method

So far, we've designed our user interface and wired up both outlets and actions. All that's left to do is to use those actions and outlets to set the text of the label when a button is pressed. Single-click *ViewController.m* in the Project Navigator to open it in the editor and find the empty `buttonPressed:` method that Xcode created for us earlier.

To differentiate between the two buttons, we're going to use the `sender` parameter. We'll retrieve the title of the button that was pressed using `sender`, and then create a new string based on that title and assign that as the label's text. Add the following bold code to your empty method:

```
- (IBAction)buttonPressed:(UIButton *)sender {
    NSString *title = [sender titleForState:UIControlStateNormal];
    NSString *plainText = [NSString stringWithFormat:@"%@ button pressed.", title];
    _statusLabel.text = plainText;
}
```

This is pretty straightforward. The first line retrieves the tapped button's title using `sender`. Since buttons can have different titles depending on their current state (although not in this example), we use the UIControlStateNormal parameter to specify that we want the title when the button is in its normal, untapped state. This is usually the state you want to specify when asking a control (a button is a type of control) for its title. We'll look at control states in more detail in Chapter 4.

The next line creates a new string by appending this text to the title we retrieved in the previous line: "button pressed." So, if the left button, which has a title of *Left*, is tapped, this line will create a string that says, "Left button pressed." The final line assigns the new string to the label's text property, which is how we change the text that the label is displaying.

MESSAGE NESTING

Objective-C messages are often nested. You may come across code like this in your travels:

```
NSString *plainText = [NSString stringWithFormat:@"%@ button
    pressed.",
    [sender titleForState:UIControlStateNormal]];
```

This one (logical) line of code will function exactly the same as the first two lines of our buttonPressed: method. This is because Objective-C methods can be nested, which essentially substitutes the return value from the nested method call.

For the sake of clarity, we won't generally nest Objective-C messages in the code examples in this book, with the exception of calls to alloc and init, which, by long-standing convention, are almost always nested.

Trying It Out

Guess what? We're almost finished. Are you ready to try out our app? Let's do it!

Select **Product ➤ Run**. If you run into any compile or link errors, go back and compare your code changes to those shown in this chapter. Once your code builds properly, Xcode will launch the iOS simulator and run your application. If you run with an iPhone simulator and tap the **Left** button, you'll see something like Figure 3-14.

Figure 3-14. *Running the application—the layout needs to be fixed*

The left button is in the right place, but the label and the other button are not. In Chapter 2, we fixed a similar problem with the Hello World label by switching off **Size Classes** in the storyboard, which made the design area take on the shape of an iPhone, and then we repositioned the label and tried again. That solution works if you only want to run your application on an iPhone screen of the same size as the one in the storyboard. It doesn't work if you want to support both the iPhone and the iPad—it doesn't even work on all iPhones. Fortunately, there is a better way to approach this problem. Instead of changing the layout to fit the screen size shown in Interface Builder, we'll arrange for it to adapt to the screen that the application is running on, by using Auto Layout. The idea behind Auto Layout is that you use constraints to specify how you want your controls to be placed. In this case, here's what we want to happen:

- The **Left** button should be vertically centered and close to the left margin of the screen.

- The **Right** button should be vertically centered and close to the right margin of the screen.

- The label should be horizontally centered, some way down from the top of the screen.

Each of the preceding statements contains two constraints—one of them a horizontal constraint, the other a vertical constraint. If we apply these constraints to our three views, Auto Layout will take care of positioning them correctly on any screen. So how do we do that?

You can add Auto Layout constraints to views in code by creating instances of the NSLayoutConstraint class. In some cases, that's the only way to create a correct layout, but in this case (and in most cases), you can get the layout that you want by using Interface Builder. Interface Builder lets you add constraints visually by dragging and clicking. Let's see how that works.

We'll start by positioning the label. Select *Main.storyboard* in the Project Navigator and open the Document Outline to show the view hierarchy. Find the icon labeled **View**. This represents the view controller's main view and it's the one relative to which we need to position the other views. Click the disclosure triangle to open the **View** icon if it's not already open, and reveal the two buttons (labeled Left and Right) and the label. Hold down the **Control** key and drag the mouse from the label to its parent view, as shown on the left in Figure 3-15.

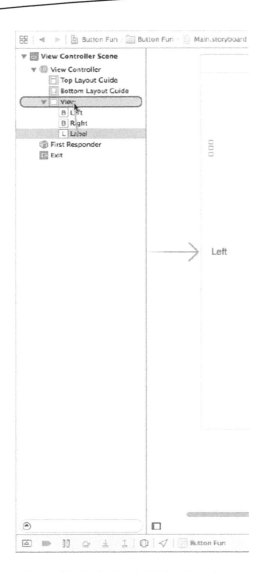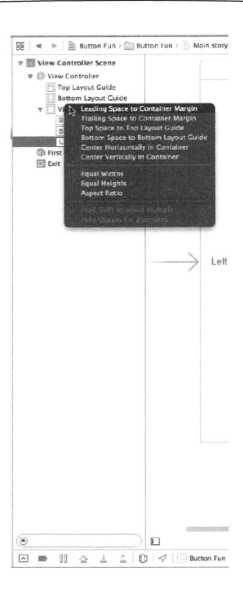

Figure 3-15. Positioning the label with Auto Layout constraints

By dragging from one view to another, you are telling Interface Builder that you want to apply an Auto Layout constraint between them. Release the mouse and a gray pop-up with various choices will appear, as shown on the right in Figure 3-15. Each choice in this pop-up is a single constraint. Clicking any of them will apply that constraint, but we know that we need to apply two constraints to the label and both of them are available in the pop-up. To apply more than one constraint at a time, you need to hold down the **Shift** key while selecting them. So hold down the **Shift** key and click **Center Horizontally in Container** and on **Top Space to Top Layout Guide**. To actually apply the constraints, click the mouse anywhere outside the pop-up. When you do this, the constraints that you have created appear under the heading *Constraints* in the Document Outline and are also represented visually in the storyboard, as shown in Figure 3-16.

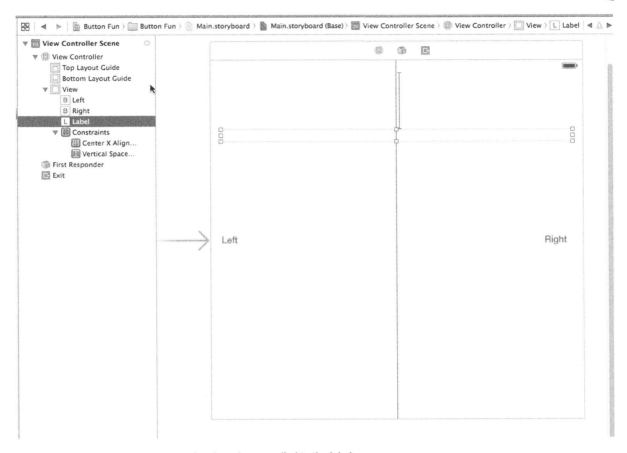

Figure 3-16. Two Auto Layout constraints have been applied to the label

> **Tip**   If you make a mistake when adding a constraint, you can remove it by clicking its representation in the Document Outline, or on the storyboard, and pressing **Delete**.

The two vertical blue lines represent the constraints that you added—the longer one is the constraint that keeps the label horizontally centered, the shorter one shows that it will be placed a fixed distance below the top of the view.

> **Tip**   To see the details for any constraint, select it in the storyboard or the Document Outline and open the Attributes Inspector.

You'll probably also see that the label has an orange outline. Interface Builder uses orange to indicate an Auto Layout problem. There are three typical problems that Interface Builder highlights in this way:

- You don't have enough constraints to fully specify a view's position or size.

- The view has constraints that are ambiguous—that is, they don't uniquely pin down its size or position.

- The constraints are correct, but the position and/or size of the view at runtime will not be the same as it is in Interface Builder.

You can find out more about the problem by clicking the yellow warning triangle in the Activity View to see an explanation in the Issue Navigator. If you do that, you'll see that it says "Frame for 'Label' will be different at run time"—the third of the problems listed. You can clear this warning by having Interface Builder move the label to its correct runtime position and give it its configured size. To do that, look at the bottom-right side of the storyboard editor. You'll see four buttons, as shown in Figure 3-17.

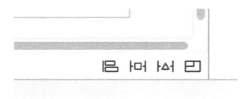

Figure 3-17. *Auto Layout buttons at the bottom right of the storyboard editor*

You can find out what each of these buttons does by hovering your mouse over them. Working from left to right, here's what they are:

- The **Align** button lets you align the selected view relative to another view. If you click this button now, you'll see a pop-up that contains various alignment options. One of them is **Horizontal Center in Container**, a constraint that you have already applied to the label from the Document Outline. There is often more than one way to most Auto Layout-related things in Interface Builder. As you progress through this book, you'll see alternate ways to do the most common Auto Layout tasks.

- The pop-up for the **Pin** button contains controls that let you set the position of a view relative to other views and to apply size constraints. For example, you can set a constraint that constrains the height of one view to be the same as that of another.

- The **Resolve Auto Layout Issues** button lets you correct layout problems. You can use menu items in its pop-up to have Interface Builder remove all constraints for a view (or the entire storyboard), guess at what constraints might be missing and add them, and adjust the frames of one or more views to what they will be at runtime.

- Finally, the **Resizing Behavior** button lets you control the effect of view resizing on existing constraints.

You can fix the label's frame by selecting it in the Document Outline or the storyboard and clicking the **Resolve Auto Layout Issues** button. The pop-up for this button has two identical groups of operations—see Figure 3-18.

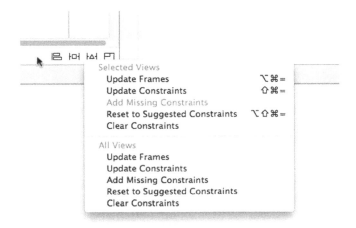

Figure 3-18. The pop-up for the Resolve Auto Layout Issues button

If you select an operation from the top group, it's applied only to the currently selected view, whereas operations from the bottom group are applied to all of the views in the view controller. In this case, we just need to fix the frame for one label, so click **Update Frames** in the top part of the pop-up. When you do this, both the orange outline and the warning triangle in the Activity View disappear, because the label now has the position and size that it will have at runtime. In fact, the label has shrunk to zero width and it's represented in the storyboard by a small, empty square, as shown in Figure 3-19.

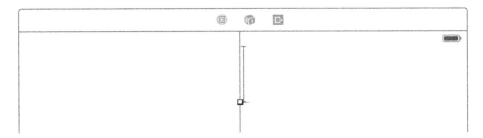

Figure 3-19. After fixing its frame, the label has shrunk to zero size

Can this be correct? Well, it turns out that it *is* correct. Many of the views that UIKit provides, including UILabel, are capable of having Auto Layout set their size based on their actual content. They do this by calculating their **natural** or **intrinsic content size**. At its intrinsic size, the label is just wide enough and tall enough to completely surround the text that it contains. At the moment, this label has no content, so its intrinsic content size really should be zero along both axes. When we run the application and click one of the buttons, the label's text will be set and its intrinsic content size will change. When that happens, Auto Layout will resize the label automatically so that you can see all of the text. Neat, huh?

> **Tip**   You can ensure that Auto Layout gives a view its intrinsic content size by selecting it and then clicking **Editor ➤ Size to Fit Content** in Xcode's menu.

We've taken care of the label, now let's fix the positions of the two buttons. You could use the same technique of Control-dragging from a button to its parent view and applying constraints from the pop-up that appears when you release the mouse, but I am going to take the opportunity to show you another way. Select the **Left** button on the storyboard and click the **Align** button at the bottom right of the storyboard editor (the leftmost button in Figure 3-17). We want the button to be vertically centered, so select **Vertical Center in Container** in the pop-up and then click **Add 1 Constraint** (see Figure 3-20).

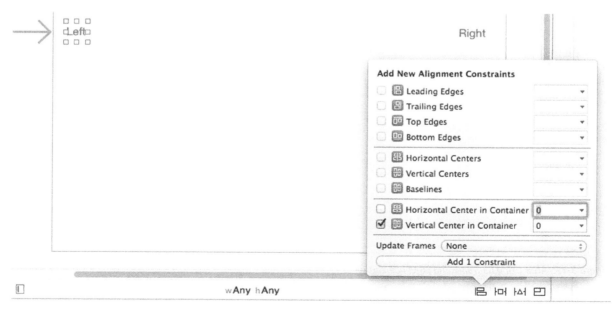

Figure 3-20. Using the Align pop-up to vertically center a view

We need to apply the same constraint to the **Right** button, so select it and repeat the process. While you were doing this, Interface Builder found a couple of new issues, indicated by the orange outlines in the storyboard and the warning triangle in the Activity View. Click the triangle to see the reasons for the warnings in the Issue Navigator, shown in Figure 3-21.

Figure 3-21. Interface Builder warnings for missing constraints

Interface Builder is warning you that the horizontal positions of both buttons are ambiguous. In fact, you haven't yet set any constraint to control the buttons' horizontal positions, so this is not surprising.

> **Note**   While setting Auto Layout constraints, it is normal for warnings like this to appear and you should use them to help you set a complete set of constraints. You should have no warnings once you have completed the layout process. Most of the examples in this book have instructions for setting layout constraints. While you are adding those constraints, you will usually encounter warnings, but don't be concerned unless you still have warnings when you have completed all of the steps. In that case, either you missed a step, you performed a step incorrectly, or there is a bug in the book! In the latter case, please let us know by submitting an erratum on the book's page at http://apress.com.

Let's fix those warnings. We want the **Left** button to be a fixed distance from the left side of its parent view and the **Right** button to be the same distance from the right side of that view. We can set those constraints from the pop-up for the **Pin** button (the one next to the **Align** button in Figure 3-17). Select the **Left** button and click the **Pin** button to open its pop-up. At the top of the pop-up, you'll find four input fields connected to a small square by orange dashed lines, as shown on the left in Figure 3-22.

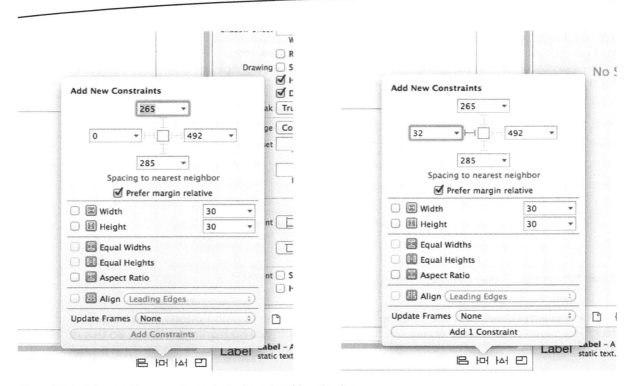

Figure 3-22. Using the Pin pop-up to set the horizontal position of a view

The small square represents the button that we are constraining. The four input fields let you set the distances between the button and its nearest neighbors above it, below it, to its left and to its right. A dashed line indicates that no constraint yet exists. In the case of the **Left** button, we want to set a fixed distance between it and the left side of its parent view, so click the dashed orange line to the left of the square. When you do this, it becomes a solid orange line indicating that there is now a constraint to apply. Next, enter **32** in the left input field to set the distance from the **Left** button to its parent view. The pop-up should now be as shown on the right in Figure 3-22. Press **Add 1 Constraint** to apply the constraint to the button.

To fix the position of the **Right** button, select it, press the **Pin** button, click the orange dashed line to the right of the square (since we are pinning this button to the right side of its parent view), enter **32** in the input field, and press **Add 1 Constraint**.

We have now applied all of the constraints that we need, but there may still be warnings in the Activity View. If you investigate, you'll see that the warnings are because the buttons are not in their correct runtime locations. To fix that, we'll use the **Resolve Auto Layout Issues** button again. Click the button to open its pop-up and then click **Update Frames** from the bottom group of options. We use the option from the bottom group because we need the frames of all of the views in the view controller to be adjusted.

> **Tip**   You may find that none of the options in the pop-up menu is available. If this is the case, select the
> **View Controller** icon in the Document Outline and try again.

The warnings should now go away and our layout is finally complete. Run the application on an iPhone simulator and you'll see a result that's almost like Figure 3-1 at the beginning of this chapter. When you tap the right button, this text should appear: "Right button pressed." If you then tap the left button, the label will change to say, "Left button pressed." So far, so good. But if you look back at Figure 3-1, you'll see that one thing is missing. The screenshot we showed you for our end result displays the name of the chosen button in bold text; however, what we've made just shows a plain string. We'll bring on the boldness using the NSAttributedString class in just a second. First, let's take the opportunity to look at another useful feature of Xcode—layout previews.

Previewing Layout

Return to Xcode and select *Main.storyboard*, and then open the Assistant Editor if it's not already showing (refer back to Figure 3-6 if you need a reminder of how to do this.) At the left of the jump bar at the top of the Assistant Editor, you'll see that the current selection is **Automatic** (unless you changed it to **Manual** to select the file for the Assistant Editor to display). Click to open the pop-up for this segment of the jump bar and you'll see several options, the last of which is **Preview**. When you hover the mouse over **Preview**, a menu containing the name of the application's storyboard will appear. Click it to open the storyboard in the *Preview Editor*.

When the Preview Editor opens, you'll see the application as it appears on an iPhone in portrait mode. This is just a preview, so it won't respond to button clicks, and as a result, you won't see the label. If you move your mouse over the area just below the preview, where it says **iPhone 4-inch**, a control will appear that will let you rotate the phone into landscape mode. You can see the control on the left of Figure 3-23, and the result of clicking it to rotate the phone on the right.

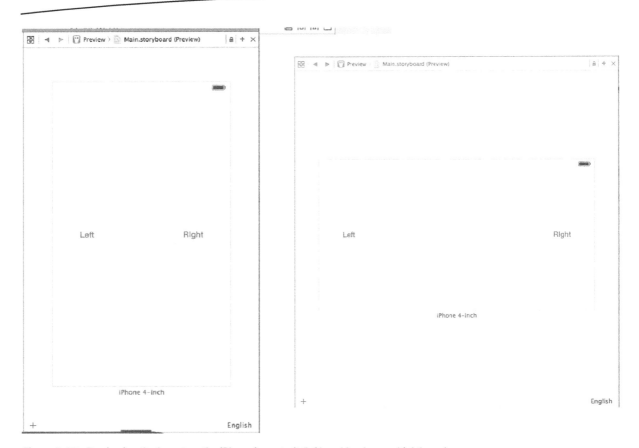

Figure 3-23. *Previewing the layout on the iPhone in portrait (left) and landscape (right) modes*

Thanks to Auto Layout, when the phone rotates, the buttons move so that they remain vertically centered and the same distance away from the sides of the device, as in portrait orientation. If the label were visible, you would see that it is in the correct position too.

We can also use the Preview Assistant to see what happens when we run the application on a different device. At the bottom left of the Preview Assistant (and in Figure 3-23), you'll see a **+** icon. Click this to open a list of devices and then select **iPad** to add an iPad preview to the Preview Assistant. The iPad preview takes up a lot of space, so you may need to close the Document Outline and the Utility View to make enough room to see both the iPhone and iPad. If you still can't see the whole iPad screen, you can zoom the Preview Assistant in a couple of different ways. The easiest is to double-click the Preview Assistant pane—this toggles between a full size view and a much smaller view. If you'd like more control over the zoom level, you can use a pinch gesture on your trackpad (unfortunately, this is not supported on the magic mouse, at least not at the time of writing). Figure 3-24 shows the iPhone and iPad previews, zoomed out to fit in the space available on my screen. Once again, Auto Layout has arranged for the buttons to be in the correct locations. Rotate the iPad preview to see that the layout also works in iPad landscape mode.

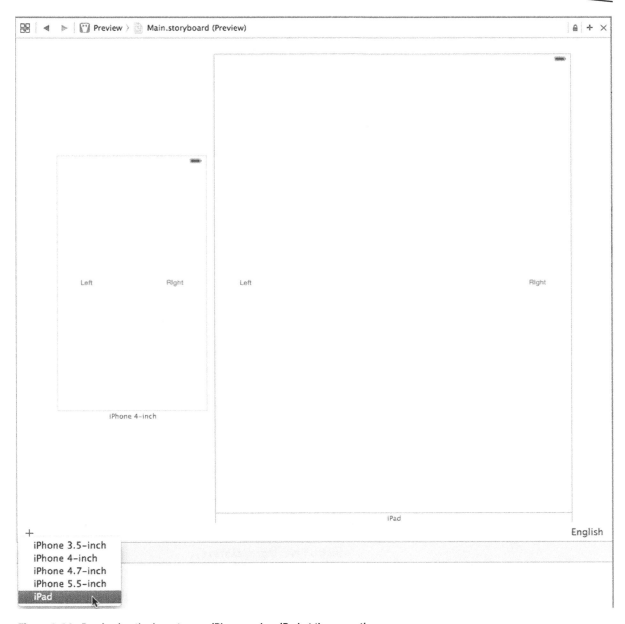

Figure 3-24. Previewing the layout on an iPhone and an iPad at the same time

Using the Preview Assistant can save you a lot of time when building and debugging a layout. You can see how the layout works on more than one device and in both orientations. In fact, you can add another pair of iPhone and iPad previews and rotate them to landscape if you want to see the layout in both orientations on both devices at the same time. The best thing of all is that the preview is live—if you make changes to the layout, the preview updates too!

To see this, go back to the storyboard editor, select one of the buttons and drag it toward the other one, and then release it. Now make sure the button that you dragged is selected in the Document Outline, open the **Resolve Auto Layout Issues** pop-up, and click **Update Constraints**. This tells Interface Builder to change the Auto Layout constraints so that the adjustment you just made to the button becomes permanent. When you do this, you'll see that the button jumps immediately to the new location in both devices in the Preview Assistant. Neat, huh?

Let's move on to adding some boldness to the label's text. Before we do that, though, we need to put that button back where it belongs. You could drag it back into position and adjust its constraints again, but there's a quicker way—just press ⌘Z twice to undo your last change and all should be well.

Adding Some style

The NSAttributedString class lets you attach formatting information, such as fonts and paragraph alignment, to a string. This metadata can be applied to an entire string, or different attributes can be applied to different parts. If you think about the ways that formatting can be applied to pieces of text in a word processor, that's basically the model for how NSAttributedString works.

However, until recently, none of the Apple-provided UIKit classes have been able to do anything with attributed strings. If you wanted to present a label containing both bold text and normal text, you'd have to either use two labels or draw the text directly into a view on your own. Those approaches aren't insurmountable hurdles, but they're tricky enough that most developers would rather not follow those paths too often. iOS 6 brought many improvements for anyone who wants to display styled text, since most of the main UIKit controls now let you use attributed strings. In the case of a UILabel like the one we have here, it's as simple as creating an attributed string, and then passing it to the label via its attributedText property.

So, select *ViewController.m* and update the buttonPressed: method by deleting the crossed-out line and adding the bold lines shown in this snippet:

```
- (IBAction)buttonPressed:(UIButton *)sender {
    NSString *title = [sender titleForState:UIControlStateNormal];
    NSString *plainText = [NSString stringWithFormat:@"%@ button pressed.", title];
    _statusLabel.text = plainText;

    NSMutableAttributedString *styledText = [[NSMutableAttributedString alloc]
                                             initWithString:plainText];
    NSDictionary *attributes =
    @{
      NSFontAttributeName : [UIFont boldSystemFontOfSize:_statusLabel.font.pointSize]
     };

    NSRange nameRange = [plainText rangeOfString:title];

    [styledText setAttributes:attributes range:nameRange];
    _statusLabel.attributedText = styledText;
}
```

The first thing that new code does is create an attributed string—specifically, an `NSMutableAttributedString` instance—based on the string we are going to display. We need a mutable attributed string here because we want to change its attributes.

Next, we create a dictionary to hold the attributes we want to apply to our string. Really, we have just one attribute right now, so this dictionary contains a single key-value pair. The key, `NSFontAttributeName`, lets you specify a font for a portion of an attributed string. The value we pass in is something called the **bold system font**, which is specified to be the same size as the font currently used by the label. Specifying the font this way is more flexible in the long run than specifying a font by name, since we know that the system will always have a reasonable idea of what to use for a bold font.

Tip   If you've been using Objective-C for a while, you may not be familiar with this new dictionary syntax–but it's pretty simple. Instead of requiring an explicit call to a class method on `NSDictionary`, the version of LLVM included with Xcode provides a shorthand form, which is nicer to use. It basically looks like this:

```
@{
  key1 : value1,
  key2 : value2
}
```

Apart from eliminating the need to type the same lengthy class name and method name every time you want to make a dictionary, it also puts the keys and values in the "right order"—at least according to anyone who's ever used a language with built-in dictionaries, such as Ruby, Python, Perl, or JavaScript.

This new dictionary syntax was introduced in 2012, along with similar syntax for arrays and numbers. We'll be using these new pieces of syntax throughout the book.

Next, we ask our `plainText` string to give us the range (consisting of a start index and a length) of the substring where our title is found. We use the range to apply the attributes to the part of the attributed string that corresponds to the title and pass it off to the label.

Now you can hit the **Run** button, and you'll see that the app shows the name of the clicked button in bold text, as shown in Figure 3-1.

Looking at the Application Delegate

Well, cool! Your application works! Before we move on to our next topic, let's take a minute to look through the two source code files we have not yet examined, *AppDelegate.h* and *AppDelegate.m*. These files implement our **application delegate**.

Cocoa Touch makes extensive use of **delegates**, which are objects that take responsibility for doing certain tasks on behalf of another object. The application delegate lets us do things at certain predefined times on behalf of the `UIApplication` class. Every iOS application has exactly one instance of UIApplication, which is responsible for the application's run loop and handles application-level functionality, such as routing input to the appropriate controller class. UIApplication is a standard part of the UIKit, and it does its job mostly behind the scenes, so you generally don't need to worry about it.

At certain well-defined times during an application's execution, UIApplication will call specific methods on its delegate, if the delegate exists and implements the method. For example, if you have code that needs to fire just before your program quits, you would implement the method applicationWillTerminate: in your application delegate and put your termination code there. This type of delegation allows your application to implement common application-wide behavior without needing to subclass UIApplication or, indeed, without needing to know anything about the inner workings of UIApplication. All of the Xcode templates create an application delegate for you and arrange for it to be linked to the UIApplication object when the application launches.

Click *AppDelegate.h* in the Project Navigator to see the application delegate's header file. It should look like this:

```
#import <UIKit/UIKit.h>

@interface AppDelegate : UIResponder <UIApplicationDelegate>

@property (strong, nonatomic) UIWindow *window;

@end
```

One thing worth pointing out is this line of code:

```
@interface AppDelegate : UIResponder <UIApplicationDelegate>
```

Do you see that value between the angle brackets? This indicates that this class conforms to a protocol called UIApplicationDelegate. Hold down the ⌥ key. Your cursor should turn into crosshairs. Move your cursor so that it is over the word UIApplicationDelegate. Your cursor will turn into a question mark, and the word UIApplicationDelegate will be highlighted, as if it were a link in a browser (see Figure 3-25).

```
 9   #import <UIKit/UIKit.h>
10
11   @interface AppDelegate : UIResponder <UIApplicationDelegate>
12
13   @property (strong, nonatomic) UIWindow *window;
14
15
16   @end
```

Figure 3-25. When you hold down the ⌥ key (the Option key) in Xcode and point at a symbol in your code, the symbol is highlighted and your cursor changes into a pointing hand with a question mark

With the ⌥ key still held down, click this link. This will open a small pop-up window showing a brief overview of the UIApplicationDelegate protocol (see Figure 3-26).

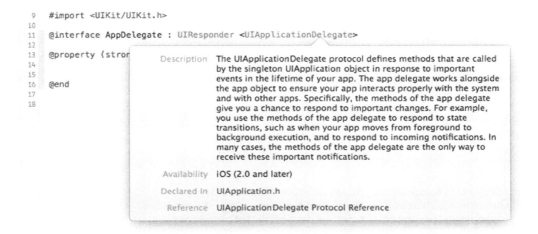

Figure 3-26. *When we Option-clicked <UIApplicationDelegate> from within our source code, Xcode popped up this window, called the Quick Help panel, which describes the protocol*

Notice the two links at the bottom of this new pop-up documentation window (see Figure 3-26). Click the **Reference** link to view the full documentation for this symbol or click the **Declared In** link to view the symbol's definition in a header file. This same trick works with class, protocol, and category names, as well as method names displayed in the editor pane. Just Option-click a word, and Xcode will search for that word in the documentation browser.

Knowing how to look up things quickly in the documentation is definitely worthwhile, but looking at the definition of this protocol is perhaps more important. Here's where you'll find which methods the application delegate can implement and when those methods will be called. It's probably worth your time to read over the descriptions of these methods.

> **Note** If you've worked with Objective-C before but not with Objective-C 2.0, you should be aware that protocols can now specify optional methods. UIApplicationDelegate contains many optional methods. However, you do not need to implement any of the optional methods in your application delegate unless you have a reason to do so.

Back in the Project Navigator, click *AppDelegate.m* to see the implementation of the application delegate. It should look something like this:

```
#import "AppDelegate.h"

@interface AppDelegate ()

@end

@implementation AppDelegate

- (BOOL)application:(UIApplication *)application didFinishLaunchingWithOptions:(NSDictionary *)
launchOptions {
    // Override point for customization after application launch.
    return YES;
}

- (void)applicationWillResignActive:(UIApplication *)application {
    // Sent when the application is about to move from active to inactive
  state. This can occur for certain types of temporary interruptions
  (such as an incoming phone call or SMS message) or when the user quits
  the application and it begins the transition to the background state.
    // Use this method to pause ongoing tasks, disable timers, and throttle down OpenGL ES frame
rates. Games should use this method to pause the game.
}

- (void)applicationDidEnterBackground:(UIApplication *)application {
    // Use this method to release shared resources, save user data,
    invalidate timers, and store enough application state information to
    restore your application to its current state in case it is terminated
    later.
    //
If your application supports background execution, this method is
called instead of applicationWillTerminate: when the user quits.
}

- (void)applicationWillEnterForeground:(UIApplication *)application {
    // Called as part of the transition from the background to the
    inactive state; here you can undo many of the changes made on entering
    the background.
}

- (void)applicationDidBecomeActive:(UIApplication *)application {
    // Restart any tasks that were paused (or not yet started) while
    the application was inactive. If the application was previously
    in the background, optionally refresh the user interface.
}
```

```
- (void)applicationWillTerminate:(UIApplication *)application {
    // Called when the application is about to terminate. Save
    data if appropriate. See also applicationDidEnterBackground:.
}

@end
```

At the top of the file, you can see that our application delegate has implemented one of those protocol methods covered in the documentation, called `application:didFinishLaunchingWithOptions:`. As you can probably guess, this method fires as soon as the application has finished all the setup work and is ready to start interacting with the user. It is often used to create any objects that need to exist for the entire lifetime of the running app.

You'll see more of this later in the book, especially in Chapter 15 where we'll say a lot more about the role that the delegate plays in the application life cycle. We just wanted to give you a bit of background on application delegates and show how this all ties together before closing this chapter.

Bring It on Home

This chapter's simple application introduced you to MVC, creating and connecting outlets and actions, implementing view controllers, and using application delegates. You learned how to trigger action methods when a button is tapped and saw how to change the text of a label at runtime. Although we built a simple application, the basic concepts we used are the same as those that underlie the use of all controls under iOS, not just buttons. In fact, the way we used buttons and labels in this chapter is pretty much the way that we will implement and interact with most of the standard controls under iOS.

It's critical that you understand everything we did in this chapter and why we did it. If you don't, go back and review the parts that you don't fully understand. This is important stuff! If you don't make sure you understand everything now, you will only get more confused as we get into creating more complex interfaces later in this book.

In the next chapter, we'll take a look at some of the other standard iOS controls. You'll also learn how to use alerts to notify the user of important happenings and how to use action sheets to indicate that the user needs to make a choice before proceeding. When you feel you're ready to proceed, give yourself a pat on the back for being such an awesome student and head on over to the next chapter.

Chapter 4

More User Interface Fun

In Chapter 3, we discussed MVC and built an application using it. You learned about outlets and actions, and you used them to tie a button control to a text label. In this chapter, we're going to build an application that will take your knowledge of controls to a whole new level.

We'll implement an image view, a slider, two different text fields, a segmented control, a couple of switches, and an iOS button that looks like buttons did before iOS 7. You'll see how to set and retrieve the values of various controls. You'll learn how to use action sheets to force the user to make a choice, and how to use alerts to give the user important feedback. You'll also learn about control states and the use of stretchable images to make buttons look the way they should.

Because this chapter's application uses so many different user interface items, we're going to work a little differently than we did in the previous two chapters. We'll break our application into pieces, implementing one piece at a time. Bouncing back and forth between Xcode and the iOS simulator, we'll test each piece before we move on to the next. Dividing the process of building a complex interface into smaller chunks makes it much less intimidating, as well as more like the actual process you'll go through when building your own applications. This code-compile-debug cycle makes up a large part of a software developer's typical day.

A Screen Full of Controls

As we mentioned, the application we're going to build in this chapter is a bit more complex than the one we created in Chapter 3. We'll still use only a single view and controller; but as you can see in Figure 4-1, there's a lot more going on in this one view.

Figure 4-1. *The Control Fun application features text fields, labels, a slider, and several other stock iPhone controls*

The logo at the top of the screen is an **image view**. In this application, it does nothing more than display a static image. Below the logo are two **text fields**: one that allows the entry of alphanumeric text and one that allows only numbers. Below the text fields is a **slider**. As the user moves the slider, the value of the label next to it will change so that it always reflects the slider's current value.

Below the slider are a **segmented control** and two **switches**. The segmented control will toggle between two different types of controls in the space below it. When the application first launches, two switches will appear below the segmented control. Changing the value of either switch will cause the other one to change its value to match. Now, this isn't something you would likely do in a real application, but it does demonstrate how to change the value of a control programmatically and how Cocoa Touch animates certain actions without you needing to do any work.

Figure 4-2 shows what happens when the user taps the segmented control. The switches disappear and are replaced by a button. When the **Do Something** button is pressed, an action sheet pops up, asking if the user really meant to tap the button (see Figure 4-3). This is the standard way of responding to input that is potentially dangerous or that could have significant repercussions, and it gives the user a chance to stop potential badness from happening. If **Yes, I'm Sure!** is selected, the application will put up an alert, letting the user know that everything is OK (see Figure 4-4).

Figure 4-2. *Tapping the segmented controller on the left side causes a pair of switches to be displayed. Tapping the right side causes a button to be displayed*

Figure 4-3. *Our application uses an action sheet to solicit a response from the user*

Figure 4-4. Alerts are used to notify the user when important things happen. We use one here to confirm that everything went OK

Active, Static, and Passive Controls

Interface controls are used in three basic modes: active, static (or inactive), and passive. The buttons that we used in the previous chapter are classic examples of active controls. You push them, and something happens—usually, a piece of code that you wrote fires.

Although many of the controls that you will use will directly trigger action methods, not all controls will. The image view that we'll be implementing in this chapter is a good example of a control being used statically. A UIImageView can be configured to trigger action methods, but in our application the image view is passive—the user cannot do anything with it. Labels and image controls are often used in this manner.

Some controls can work in a passive mode, simply holding on to a value that the user has entered until you're ready for it. These controls don't trigger action methods, but the user can interact with them and change their values. A classic example of a passive control is a text field on a web page. Although it's possible to create validation code that fires when the user tabs out of a field, the vast majority of web page text fields are simply containers for data that's submitted to the server when the user clicks the submit button. The text fields themselves usually don't cause any code to fire, but when the submit button is clicked, the text field's data goes along for the ride.

On an iOS device, most of the available controls can be used in all three modes, and nearly all of them can function in more than one mode, depending on your needs. All iOS controls are subclasses of UIControl, which makes them capable of triggering action methods. Many controls can be used passively, and all of them can be made inactive or invisible. For example, using one control might trigger another inactive control to become active. However, some controls, such as buttons, really don't serve much purpose unless they are used in an active manner to trigger code.

There are some behavioral differences between controls on iOS and those on your Mac. Here are a few examples:

■ Because of the multitouch interface, all iOS controls can trigger multiple actions, depending on how they are touched. The user might trigger a different action with a finger swipe across the control than with just a tap.

■ You could have one action fire when the user presses down on a button and a separate action fire when the finger is lifted off the button.

■ You could have a single control call multiple action methods on a single event. For example, you could have two different action methods fire on the Touch Up Inside event when the user's finger is lifted after touching that button.

> **Note**   Although controls can trigger multiple methods on iOS, the vast majority of the time, you're probably better off implementing a single action method that does what you need for a particular use of a control. You won't usually need this capability, but it's good to keep it in mind when working in Interface Builder. Connecting an event to an action in Interface Builder does *not* disconnect a previously connected action from the same control! This can lead to surprising misbehaviors in your app, where a control will trigger multiple action methods. Keep an eye open when retargeting an event in Interface Builder, and make sure you remove old actions before connecting to new ones.

Another major difference between iOS and the Mac stems from the fact that, normally, iOS devices do not have a physical keyboard. The standard iOS software keyboard is actually just a view filled with a series of button controls that are managed for you by the system. Your code will likely never directly interact with the iOS keyboard.

Creating the Application

Let's get started. Fire up Xcode, if it's not already open, and create a new project called *Control Fun*. We're going to use the Single View Application template again, so create your project just as you did in the previous two chapters.

Now that you've created your project, let's get the image we'll use in our image view. The image must be imported into Xcode before it will be available for use inside Interface Builder, so we'll import it now. You'll find three files in the *04 - Logos* folder in the example source code archive folder, named *apress_logo.png*, *apress_logo@2x.png*, and *apress_logo@3x.png*, which are a standard version and two Retina versions of the same image. We're going to add all three of these to the new project's image resource catalog and let the app decide which of them to use at runtime. If you'd rather use an image-pair of your own choosing, make sure that they are *.png* images sized correctly for the space available. The small version should be less than 100 pixels tall and a maximum of 300 pixels wide, so that it can fit comfortably at the top of the view on the narrowest iPhone screen without being resized. The larger ones should be respectively twice and three times the size of the small version.

In Xcode, select *Images.xcassets* in the Project Navigator and click the plus (**+**) button in the lower-left corner of the editor area. This brings up a small menu of choices, from which you should select **New Image Set**. This creates a new spot for adding your actual image files. Right now it's just called *Image*, but we want to give it a unique name so that we can refer to it elsewhere in the project. Select the **Image** item, bring up the Attributes Inspector (⌥⌘4 or **Opt-Cmd-4**), and use it to change the image's name to *apress_logo*.

Now add the images themselves to the *apress_logo* image item by dragging each image from the Finder to the image detail box. Drag *apress_logo.png* to the spot labeled *1x*, *apress_logo@2x.png* to the *2x* slot, and *apress_logo@2x.png* to the *3x* slot.

Implementing the Image View and Text Fields

With the image added to your project, your next step is to implement the five interface elements at the top of the application's screen: the image view, the two text fields, and the two labels (see Figure 4-5).

Figure 4-5. The image view, labels, and text fields we will implement first

Adding the Image View

In the Project Navigator, click *Main.storyboard* to open the file in Interface Builder. You'll see the familiar white background and a single square view where you can lay out your application's interface.

If the Object Library is not open, select **View ➤ Utilities ➤ Show Object Library** to open it. Scroll about one-fourth of the way through the list until you find *Image View* (see Figure 4-6) or just type **image** in the search field. Remember that the Object Library is the third icon on top of the library pane. You won't find Image View under any of the other icons.

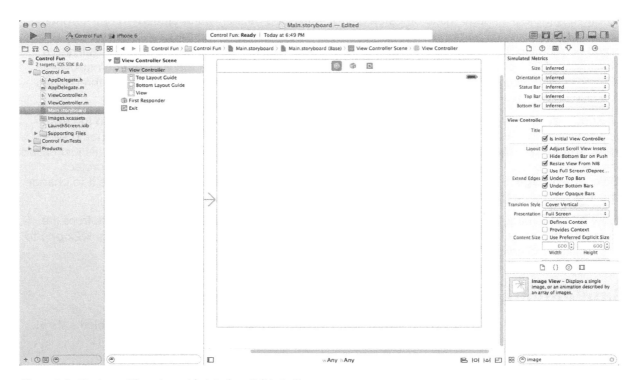

Figure 4-6. The Image View element in Interface Builder's library

Drag an image view onto the view in the storyboard editor. Notice that, as you drag your image view out of the library, it changes size twice. As the drag makes its way out of the library pane, it takes the shape of a horizontal rectangle. Then, when your drag enters the frame of the view, the image view resizes to be the size of the view, including the status bar at the top. This behavior is normal. Indeed, in many cases it is exactly what you want because the first image you place in a view is often a background image. Release the drag inside the view, taking care that the new UIImageView snaps to the sides and bottom of the surrounding view. In this particular case, we actually don't want our image view to take the entire space, so we use the drag handles to resize the image view to the approximate size of the image previously imported into Xcode. Don't worry about getting it exactly right yet; we'll take care of that in the next section. Figure 4-7 shows our resized UIImageView.

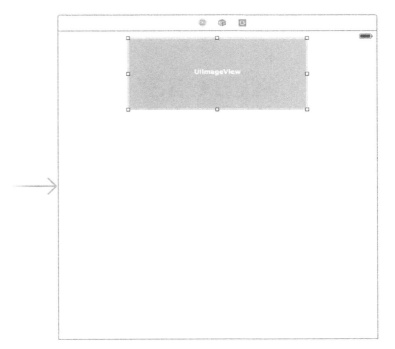

Figure 4-7. *Our resized UIImageView, sized to approximate the dimensions of the image we will place here*

Remember that, if you ever encounter difficulty selecting an item in the editing area, you can open the Document Outline by clicking the small rectangular icon in the lower-left corner. Now, click the item you want selected in the Document Outline and, sure enough, that item will be selected in the editor.

To get at an object that is nested inside another object, click the disclosure triangle to the left of the enclosing object to reveal the nested object. In this case, to select the image view, first click the disclosure triangle to the left of the view. Then, when the image view appears in the Document Outline, click it, and it will be selected in the editing area.

With the image view selected, bring up the object Attributes Inspector by pressing ⌥⌘**4**, and you should see the editable options of the UIImageView class (see Figure 4-8).

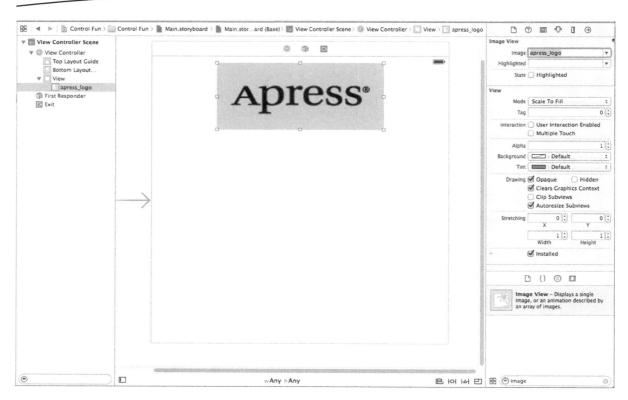

Figure 4-8. *The image view Attributes Inspector. We selected our image from the Image pop-up at the top of the inspector, and this populated the image view with our image*

The most important setting for our image view is the topmost item in the inspector, labeled **Image**. Click the little arrow to the right of the field to see a pop-up menu that lists the available images. This list includes any images you added to your project's image assets catalog. Select the *apress_logo* image you added earlier and it should appear in your image view.

Resizing the Image View

As it turns out, the image we used is a fair amount smaller than the image view in which it was placed. If you take another look at Figure 4-8, you'll notice that the image we used was scaled to completely fill the image view. A big clue that this is so is the Mode setting in the Attributes Inspector, which is set to *Scale To Fill*.

Though we could keep our app this way, it's generally a good idea to do any image scaling before runtime, as image scaling takes time and processor cycles. Let's resize our image view to the exact size of our image.

Make sure the image view is selected and that you can see the resize handles. Now select the image view one more time. You should see the outline of the image view replaced by a thick gray border. Finally, press ⌘= or select **Editor ➤ Size to Fit Content**. This will resize the image view to match the size of its contents. If pressing ⌘= does not work, or **Size to Fit Content** is grayed out, reselect the image view, drag it a little way to the side, and try again.

Now that the image view is resized, let's move it back to its final position by selecting it and choosing **Editor ➤ Align ➤ Horizontal Center in Container**. This creates a constraint that makes the image view always want to remain centered within the view that contains it, even if that view changes size. In Chapter 3, you did the same thing by using the **Horizontal Center in Container** check box in the **Align** pop-up at the bottom of the editing area. You may have noticed the way Interface Builder shows some solid lines running from an edge of one view to an edge of its superview (not to be confused with the dashed blue lines that are shown while you're dragging things around.) These solid lines represent the constraints that express the layout rules that are built directly in Interface Builder. When you select the constraint that you just added by clicking it, you'll see that it becomes a solid orange line, running the entire height of the main view (see Figure 4-9). This specifies that the center of the image view will remain horizontally centered within its parent view, even if the parent view's geometry changes (as it may, for example, when the device is rotated). We'll talk more about constraints throughout the book.

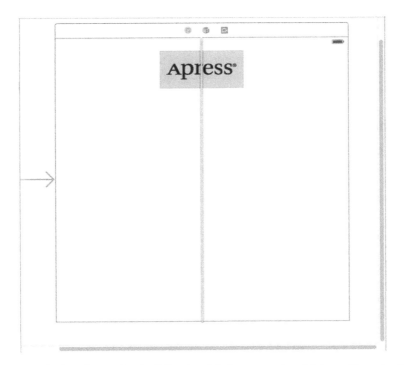

Figure 4-9. Once we have resized our image view to fit the size of its image, we drag it into position using the view's blue guidelines, and create a constraint to keep it centered

Note   You may have noticed that there is an orange warning indicator in the Activity View. If you click it, you'll see that it's telling you that the vertical position of the Image View is ambiguous. What Xcode is telling us is that we need to set a vertical constraint for that view. You can either do so now, using the techniques you saw in Chapter 3, or wait until we fix all the constraints for our layout later in the chapter.

> **Tip** Dragging and resizing views in Interface Builder can be tricky. Don't forget about the Document Outline, which you can open by clicking the small rectangular icon at the bottom left of the editing area. When it comes to resizing, hold down the ⌥ key, and Interface Builder will draw some helpful red lines on the screen that make it much easier to get a sense of the image view's size. This trick won't work with dragging, since the ⌥ key will prompt Interface Builder to make a copy of the dragged object. However, if you select **Editor ➤ Canvas ➤ Show Bounds Rectangles**, Interface Builder will draw a line around all of your interface items, making them easier to see. You can turn off those lines by selecting **Show Bounds Rectangles** a second time.

Setting View Attributes

Select your image view and then switch your attention back over to the Attributes Inspector. Below the Image View section of the inspector is the View section. As you may have deduced, the pattern here is that the attributes that are specific to the selected object are shown at the top, followed by more general attributes that apply to the selected object's parent class. In this case, the parent class of UIImageView is UIView, so the next section is simply labeled **View**, and it contains attributes that any view class will have.

The Mode Attribute

The first option in the view inspector is a pop-up menu labeled **Mode**. The **Mode** menu defines how the view will display its content. This determines how the image will be aligned inside the view and whether it will be scaled to fit. Feel free to play with the various options, but the default value of *Scale To Fill* will work fine for now, because we made the image view exactly the right size for its image.

Keep in mind that choosing any option that causes the image to scale will potentially add processing overhead at runtime, so it's best to avoid those and size your images correctly before you import them. If you want to display the same image at multiple sizes, generally it's better to have multiple copies of the image at different sizes in your project, rather than force the iOS device to do scaling at runtime. Of course, there are times when scaling at runtime is appropriate and even unavoidable; this is a guideline, not a rule.

Tag

The next item, **Tag**, is worth mentioning, though we won't be using it in this chapter. All subclasses of UIView, including all views and controls, have a property called tag, which is just a numeric value that you can set here or in code. The tag is designed for your use—the system will never set or change its value. If you assign a tag value to a control or view, you can be sure that the tag will always have that value unless you change it.

Tags provide an easy, language-independent way of identifying objects in your interface. Let's say you have five different buttons, each with a different label, and you want to use a single action method to handle all five buttons. In that case, you probably need some way to differentiate among the buttons when your action method is called. Sure, you could look at the button's title, but code that does that probably won't work when your application is translated into Swahili or Sanskrit. Unlike labels, tags will never change, so if you set a tag value here in Interface Builder, you can then use that as a fast and reliable way to check which control was passed into an action method in the `sender` argument.

Interaction Check Boxes

The two check boxes in the Interaction section have to do with user interaction. The first check box, **User Interaction Enabled**, specifies whether the user can do anything at all with this object. For most controls, this box will be checked because, if it's not, the control will never be able to trigger action methods. However, image views default to unchecked because they are often used just for the display of static information. Since all we're doing here is displaying a picture on the screen, there is no need to turn this on.

The second check box is **Multiple Touch**, and it determines whether this control is capable of receiving multitouch events. Multitouch events allow complex gestures like the pinch gesture used to zoom in in many iOS applications. We'll talk more about gestures and multitouch events in Chapter 18. Since this image view doesn't accept user interaction at all, there's no reason to turn on multitouch events, so leave this check box unchecked.

The Alpha Value

The next item in the inspector is **Alpha**. Be careful with this one. **Alpha** defines how transparent your image is—how much of what's beneath it shows through. It's defined as a floating-point number between 0.0 and 1.0, where 0.0 is fully transparent and 1.0 is completely opaque. If you use any value less than 1.0, your iOS device will draw this view with some amount of transparency so that any objects behind it show through. With a value of less than 1.0, even if there's nothing interesting behind your image, you will cause your application to spend processor cycles compositing your partially transparent view over the emptiness behind it. Therefore, don't set **Alpha** to anything other than 1.0 unless you have a very good reason for doing so.

Background

The next item down, **Background**, determines the color of the background for the view. For image views, this matters only when an image doesn't fill its view and is letterboxed, or when parts of the image are transparent. Since we've sized our view to perfectly match our image, this setting will have no visible effect, so we can leave it alone.

Tint

The next control lets you specify a tint color for the selected view. This is a color that some views use when drawing themselves. The segmented control that we'll use later in this chapter colors itself using its tint color, but the `UIImageView` not.

Drawing Check Boxes

Below **Tint** is a series of **Drawing** check boxes. The first one is labeled **Opaque**. That should be checked by default; if not, click to check that check box. This tells iOS that nothing behind your view needs to be drawn and allows iOS's drawing methods to do some optimizations that speed up drawing.

You might be wondering why we need to select the **Opaque** check box when we've already set the value of **Alpha** to 1.0 to indicate no transparency. The alpha value applies to the parts of the image to be drawn; but if an image doesn't completely fill the image view, or there are holes in the image thanks to an alpha channel, the objects below will still show through, regardless of the value set in Alpha. By selecting **Opaque**, we are telling iOS that nothing behind this view ever needs to be drawn, no matter what, so it does not need to waste processing time with anything behind our object. We can safely select the **Opaque** check box because we selected **Size To Fit** earlier, which caused the image view to match the size of the image it contains.

The **Hidden** check box does exactly what you think it does. If it's checked, the user can't see this object. Hiding an object can be useful at times, as you'll see later in this chapter when we hide our switches and button; however, the vast majority of the time—including now—you want this to remain unchecked.

The next check box, **Clears Graphics Context**, will rarely need to be checked. When it is checked, iOS will draw the entire area covered by the object in transparent black before it actually draws the object. Again, it should be turned off for the sake of performance and because it's rarely needed. Make sure this check box is unchecked (it is likely checked by default).

Clip Subviews is an interesting option. If your view contains subviews, and those subviews are not completely contained within the bounds of its parent view, this check box determines how the subviews will be drawn. If **Clip Subviews** is checked, only the portions of subviews that lie within the bounds of the parent will be drawn. If **Clip Subviews** is unchecked, subviews will be drawn completely, even if they lie outside the bounds of the parent.

Clip Subviews is unchecked by default. It might seem that the default behavior should be the opposite of what it actually is, so that child views won't be able to draw all over the place. However, calculating the clipping area and displaying only part of the subviews is a somewhat costly operation, mathematically speaking; most of the time, a subview won't lie outside the bounds of its superview. You can turn on **Clip Subviews** if you really need it for some reason, but it is off by default for the sake of performance.

The last check box in this section, **Autoresize Subviews**, tells iOS to resize any subviews if this view is resized. Leave this checked (since we don't allow our view to be resized, it really does not matter whether it's checked).

Stretching

Next up is a section simply labeled **Stretching**. You can leave your yoga mat in the closet, though, because the only stretching going on here is in the form of rectangular views being redrawn as they're resized on the screen. The idea is that, rather than the entire content of a view being stretched uniformly, you can keep the outer edges of a view, such as the beveled edge of a button, looking the same even as the center portion stretches.

The four floating-point values set here let you declare which portion of the rectangle is stretchable by specifying a point at the upper-left corner of the view and the size of the stretchable area, all in the form of a number between 0.0 and 1.0 that represents a portion of the overall view size. For example, if you wanted to keep 10% of each edge not stretchable, you would specify 0.1 for both X and Y, and 0.8 for both Width and Height. In this case, we're going to leave the default values of 0.0 for X and Y, and 1.0 for Width and Height. Most of the time, you will not change these values.

Adding the Text Fields

With your image view finished, it's time to bring on the text fields. Grab a text field from the Object Library and drag it into the View, underneath the image view. Use the blue guidelines to align it with the right margin and make it snug, just under your image view (see Figure 4-10).

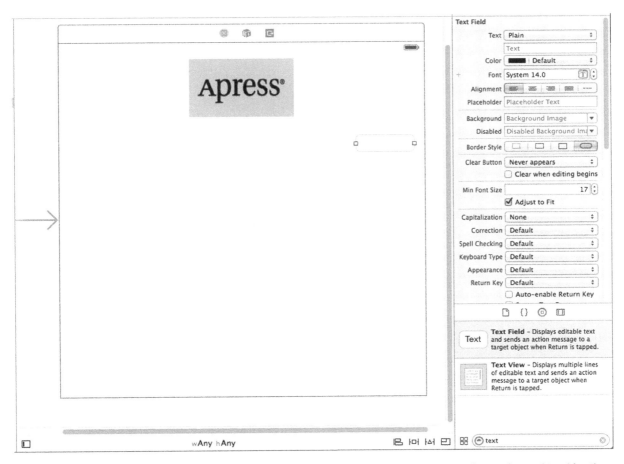

Figure 4-10. We dragged a text field out of the library and dropped it onto the view, just below our image view and touching the right-hand side's blue guideline

A horizontal blue guideline will appear just above the text field when you move it very close to the bottom of your image view. That guideline tells you when the object you are dragging is the minimum reasonable distance from an adjacent object. You can leave your text field there for now, but to give it a balanced appearance, consider moving it a little farther down before moving it to toward the guideline at the right edge. Remember that you can always use Interface Builder to edit your GUI again in order to change the position and size of interface elements—without needing to change code or reestablish connections.

After you drop the text field, grab a label from the library, and then drag that over so it is aligned with the left margin of the view and vertically with the text field you placed earlier. Notice that multiple blue guidelines will pop up as you move the label around, making it easy to align the label to the text field using the top, bottom, or middle of the label. We're going to align the label and the text field using the baseline, which shows up as you're dragging around the middle of those guidelines (see Figure 4-11).

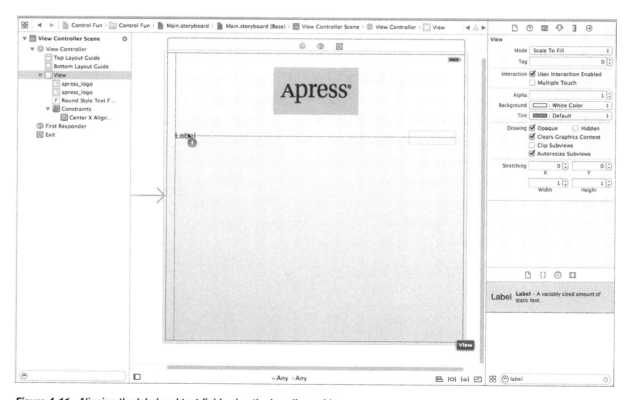

Figure 4-11. Aligning the label and text field using the baseline guide

Double-click the label you just dropped, change it to read *Name:* instead of *Label* (note the colon character at the end of the label), and press the **Enter** key to commit your changes.

Next, drag another text field from the library to the view and use the guidelines to place it below the first text field (see Figure 4-12).

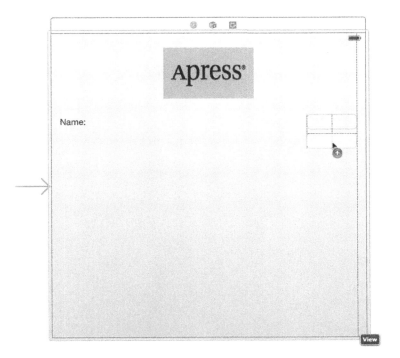

Figure 4-12. Adding the second text field

Once you've added the second text field, grab another label from the library and place it on the left side, below the existing label. Again, use the middle blue guideline to align your new label with the second text field. Double-click the new label and change it to read *Number*: (again, don't forget the colon).

Now, let's expand the size of the bottom text field to the left, so it is snug up against the right side of the label. Why start with the bottom text field? We want the two text fields to be the same size, and the bottom label is longer.

Single-click the bottom text field and drag the left resize dot to the left until a blue guideline appears to tell you that you are as close as you should ever be to the label (see Figure 4-13). This particular guideline is somewhat subtle—it's only as tall as the text field itself, so keep your eyes peeled.

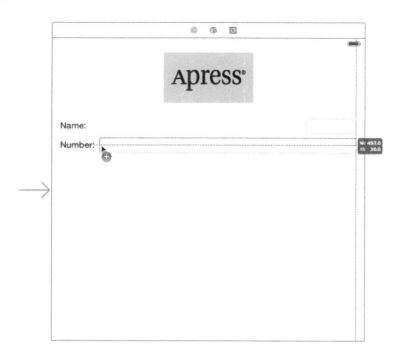

Figure 4-13. Expanding the size of the bottom text field

Now, expand the top text field in the same way, so that it matches the bottom one in size. Once again, a blue guideline provides some help, and this one extends all the way down to the other text field, making it easier to spot.

We're basically finished with the text fields, except for one small detail. Look back at Figure 4-5. Do you see how the **Name:** and **Number:** are right-aligned? Right now, ours are both against the left margin. To align the right sides of the two labels, click the **Name:** label, hold down the ⇧**(Shift)** key, and click the **Number**: label, so both labels are selected. Next, press ⌥⌘**4** to bring up the Attributes Inspector and make sure the **Label** section is expanded, so you can see the label-specific attributes. If it's not expanded, click the **Show** button on the right of the header to open it. Now use the **Alignment** control in the inspector to make the content of these labels right-justified, and then make a constraint to make sure these two fields are always the same width by selecting **Editor ➤ Pin ➤ Widths Equally**.

When you are finished, the interface should look very much like the one shown in Figure 4-5. The only difference is the light-gray text in each text field. We'll add that now.

Select the top text field (the one next to the **Name:** label) and press ⌥⌘**4** to bring up the Attributes Inspector (see Figure 4-14). The text field is one of the most complex iOS controls, as well as one of the most commonly used. Let's take a walk through the settings, beginning from the top of the inspector.

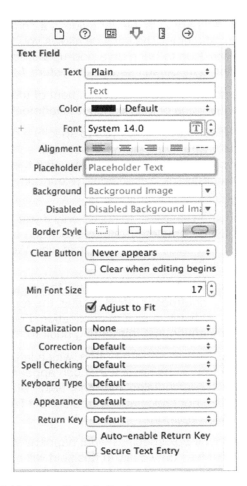

Figure 4-14. The inspector for a text field showing the default values

Text Field Inspector Settings

In the first section, the **Text** label points out two controls that give you some control over the text that will appear in the text field. The upper one is a pop-up button that lets you choose between plain text and attributed text, which can contain a variety of fonts and other attributes. We used attributed text to add bold to part of the text in our example in Chapter 3. Let's leave that pop-up button set to *Plain* for now. Immediately below that, you can set a default value for the text field. Whatever you type here will show up in the text field when your application launches, instead of just a blank space.

After that comes a series of controls that let you set the font and font color. We'll leave the **Color** at the default value of black. Note that the **Color** pop-up is divided into two parts. The right side allows you to select from a set of preselected colors, and the left side gives you access to a color well to more precisely specify your color.

The **Font** setting is divided into three parts. On the right side is a control that lets you increment or decrement the text size, one point at a time. The left side allows you to manually edit the font name and size. Finally, click the T-in-a-box icon to bring up a pop-up window that lets you set the various font attributes. We'll leave the **Font** at its default setting of *System 14.0*.

Below these fields are five buttons for controlling the alignment of the text displayed in the field. We'll leave this setting at the default value of left-aligned (the leftmost button).

Rounding out this first section, **Placeholder** allows you to specify a bit of text that will be displayed in gray inside the text field, but only when the field does not have a value. You can use a placeholder instead of a label if space is tight, or you can use it to clarify what the user should type into this text field. Type in the text **Type in a name** as the placeholder for our currently selected text field, and then hit **Enter** to commit the change.

The next two fields, **Background** and **Disabled**, are used only if you need to customize the appearance of your text field, which is completely unnecessary and actually ill-advised the vast majority of the time. Users expect text fields to look a certain way. We're going to skip over these fields, leaving them set to their defaults.

Next are four buttons labeled **Border Style**. These allow you to change the way the text field's edge will be drawn. The default value (the rightmost button) creates the text field style that users are most accustomed to seeing for normal text fields in an iOS application. Feel free to try all four different styles. When you're finished experimenting, set this setting back to the rightmost button.

Below the border setting is a **Clear Button** pop-up button, which lets you choose when the *clear button* should appear. The clear button is the small X that can appear at the right end of a text field. Clear buttons are typically used with search fields and other fields where you would be likely to change the value frequently. They are not typically included on text fields used to persist data, so leave this at the default value of *Never appears*.

The **Clear when editing begins** check box specifies what happens when the user touches this field. If this box is checked, any value that was previously in this field will be deleted, and the user will start with an empty field. If this box is unchecked, the previous value will remain in the field, and the user will be able to edit it. Leave this check box unchecked.

The next section starts with a control that lets you set the minimum font size that the text field will use for displaying its text. Leave that at its default value for now.

The **Adjust to Fit** check box specifies whether the size of the text should shrink if the text field is reduced in size. Adjusting to fit will keep the entire text visible in the view, even if the text would normally be too big to fit in the allotted space. This check box works in conjunction with the minimum font size setting. No matter the size of the field, the text will not be resized below that minimum size. Specifying a minimum size allows you to make sure that the text doesn't get too small to be readable.

The next section defines how the keyboard will look and behave when this text field is being used. Since we're expecting a name, let's change the **Capitalization** pop-up to *Words*. This causes the first letter of every word to be automatically capitalized, which is what you typically want with names.

The next four pop-ups—**Correction**, **Spell Checking**, **Keyboard**, and **Appearance**—can be left at their default values. Take a minute to look at each to get a sense of what these settings do.

Next is the **Return Key** pop-up. The **Return** key is the key on the lower right of the virtual keyboard, and its label changes based on what you're doing. If you are entering text into Safari's search field, for example, then it says *Search*. In an application like ours, where the text fields share the screen with other controls, *Done* is the right choice. Make that change here.

If the **Auto-enable Return Key** check box is checked, the **Return** key is disabled until at least one character is typed into the text field. Leave this unchecked because we want to allow the text field to remain empty if the user prefers not to enter anything.

The **Secure** check box specifies whether the characters being typed are displayed in the text field. You would check this check box if the text field was being used as a password field. Leave it unchecked for our app.

The next section (which you will probably have to scroll down to see) allows you to set control attributes inherited from `UIControl`; however, these generally don't apply to text fields and, with the exception of the **Enabled** check box, won't affect the field's appearance. We want to leave these text fields enabled, so that the user can interact with them. Leave the default settings in this section.

The last section on the inspector, **View**, should look familiar. It's identical to the section of the same name on the image view inspector we looked at earlier. These are attributes inherited from the `UIView` class; since all controls are subclasses of `UIView`, they all share this section of attributes. As you did earlier for the image view, check the **Opaque** check box and uncheck **Clears Graphics Context** and **Clip Subviews**—for the reasons we discussed earlier.

Setting the Attributes for the Second Text Field

Next, single-click the lower text field (the one next to the **Number:** label) in the View window and return to the inspector. In the **Placeholder** field, type **Type in a number**, and make sure **Clear When Editing Begins** is unchecked. A little farther down, click the **Keyboard** pop-up menu. Since we want the user to enter only numbers, not letters, select **Number Pad**. On the iPhone, this ensures that the users will be presented with a keyboard containing only numbers, meaning they won't be able to enter alphabetical characters, symbols, or anything other than numbers. We don't need to set the Return Key value for the numeric keypad because that style of keyboard doesn't have a **Return** key; therefore, all of the other inspector settings can stay at the default values. As you did earlier, check the **Opaque** check box and uncheck **Clears Graphics Context** and **Clip Subviews**. On the iPad, selecting **Number Pad** has the effect of bringing up a full virtual keyboard in numeric mode when the user activates the text field, but the user can switch back to alphabetic input. This means that in a real application, you would have to verify that the user actually entered a valid number when processing the content of the Number field.

> **Tip**   If you really want to stop the user typing anything other than numbers into a text field, you can do so by creating a class that implements the `textView:shouldChangeTextInRange:replacementText:` method of the `UITextViewDelegate` protocol and making it the text view's delegate. The details are not too complex, but beyond the scope of this book.

Adding Constraints

Before we go on, we need to adjust some constraints for this layout. When you drag a view into another view in Interface Builder (as we just did), Xcode doesn't create any constraints for it automatically. The layout system requires a complete set of constraints, so when it's time to compile your app, Xcode will make a set of default constraints describing the layout. The constraints that are created depend on each object's position within its superview. Depending on whether it's nearer the left or right edge, it will be pinned to the left of the right. Similarly, depending on whether it's nearer the top or the bottom edge, it will be pinned to the top or the bottom. If it's centered in either direction, it will typically get a constraint pinning it to the center.

To complicate matters further, Xcode may also apply automatic constraints pinning each new object to one or more of its "sibling" objects within the same superview. This automatic behavior may or may not be what you want, so normally you're better off creating a complete set of constraints within Interface Builder before your app is compiled and in the last two chapters, you have seen some examples of that.

Let's start poking around what we have so far. To see all the constraints that are in play for any particular view, try selecting it and opening the Size Inspector. If you select any of the labels, text fields, or the slider, you'll see that the Size Inspector shows a message claiming that there are no constraints for the selected view. In fact, this GUI we've been building has only the one constraint that we applied earlier, binding the horizontal centers of the image view and the container view. Click either the container view or the image view to see this constraint in the inspector.

What we really want is a full set of constraints to tell the layout system precisely how to handle all our views and controls, just as it would get at compile time. Fortunately, this is pretty simple to accomplish. Select all the views and controls by click-dragging a box around them, from inside the upper-left corner of our container view down toward the lower right. If you start dragging and find that the view starts moving instead, just release the mouse, move it a little bit further inside the view and try again. When all items are selected, use the menu to execute the **Editor ➤ Resolve Auto Layout Issues ➤ Add Missing Constraints** command. After doing that, you'll see that all our views and controls now have some little blue sticks connecting them to one another and to the container view. Each of those sticks represents a constraint. The big advantage to creating these now instead of letting Xcode create them at compile time is that we now have a chance to modify each constraint if we need to. We'll explore more of what we can do with constraints throughout the book.

Tip   Another way to apply constraints to all the views owned a view controller is to select the view controller in the Document Outline and then use **Editor ➤ Resolve Auto Layout Issues ➤ Add Missing Constraints**.

Normally, the layout we've created here wouldn't require any particular modification of these constraints to make sure it works fine on all devices, but this is not always the case. For example, if you were to add more text fields below the two that we already have until you reach the bottom of the view, and then have Xcode add constraints, you would find that it would tie the whole column of text fields to the bottom of the view, not to the top, so when you run the application on a taller screen than the one in Interface Builder (for example, on an iPhone 6 Plus), the text fields would all move down relative to the image view and not be where you want them to be.

For our current GUI, this isn't a problem, however, which we can verify by using the Preview Assistant again. Open the Assistant Editor by selecting the middle toolbar button labeled **Editor** or by clicking **View ➤ Assistant Editor ➤ Show Assistant Editor**, and then select **Preview** and *Main.storyboard* in the jump bar. When the preview for the 4-inch iPhone appears, add an extra one for the 5.5-inch iPhone and you'll see that the layout remains exactly as it is on the smaller phone, although the text fields are now a little wider because of the larger width of this screen. Later in the book, we'll deal with some GUIs that need a bit of adjustment in this area and in most of the examples that follow, we'll create explicit constraints instead of allowing Xcode to do the work for us, so that you have plenty of opportunity to get used to adding constraints manually.

> **Caution**   For this relatively simple example, Xcode is perfectly capable of creating constraints that will preserve that layout that we need, but that's not always the case. Any time you use the **Editor ➤ Resolve Auto Layout Issues ➤ Add Missing Constraints** command, you should check carefully the constraints that Xcode added. If they don't work as you expected, then delete them and add constraints manually using the techniques that you saw in Chapter 2 and Chapter 3.

Creating and Connecting Outlets

We are almost ready to take our app for its first test drive. For this first part of the interface, all that's left is creating and connecting our outlets. The image view and labels on our interface do not need outlets because we don't need to change them at runtime. The two text fields, however, will hold data we'll need to use in our code, so we need outlets pointing to each of them.

As you probably remember from the previous chapter, Xcode allows us to create and connect outlets at the same time using the Assistant Editor, which should already be open (but if it's not, open it as described earlier).

Make sure your storyboard file is selected in the Project Navigator. If you don't have a large amount of screen real estate, you might also want to select **View ➤ Utilities ➤ Hide Utilities** to hide the utility pane during this step. In the Assistant Editor's jump bar, select **Automatic** and you should see either *ViewController.h* or *ViewController.m* (see Figure 4-15).

Figure 4-15. *The storyboard editing area with the Assistant Editor turned on. You can see the Assistant Editor on the right, showing the code from ViewController.m*

Now comes the fun part. Make sure *ViewController.m* is showing in the Assistant Editor (use the jump bar to return there if necessary). Next, Control-drag from the top text field in the view over to the *ViewController.m* file, right below the @interface line. You should see a gray pop-up that reads **Insert Outlet, Action, or Outlet Collection** (see Figure 4-16). Release the mouse button, and you'll get the same pop-up you saw in the previous chapter. We want to create an outlet called nameField, so type **nameField** into the **Name** field (say that five times fast!), and then hit **Return** or click the **Connect** button.

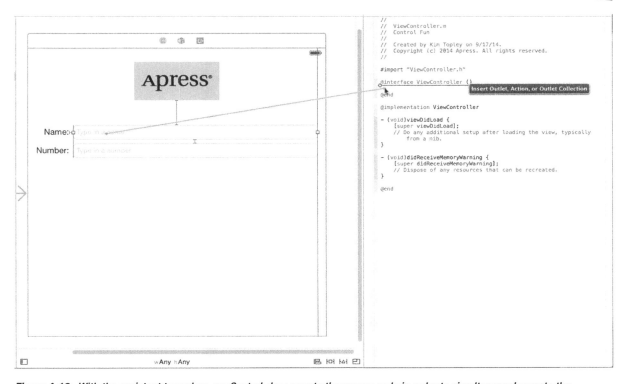

Figure 4-16. *With the assistant turned on, we Control-drag over to the source code in order to simultaneously create the nameField outlet and connect it to the appropriate text field*

You now have a property called `nameField` in `ViewController`, and it has been connected to the top text field. Do the same for the second text field, creating and connecting it to a property called *numberField*.

Closing the Keyboard

Let's see how our app works, shall we? Select **Product ➤ Run**. Your application should come up in the iOS simulator. Click the **Name** text field, and the traditional keyboard should appear. Type in a name and then tap the **Number** field. The numeric keypad should appear (see Figure 4-17). Cocoa Touch gives us all this functionality for free just by adding text fields to our interface.

Figure 4-17. *The keyboard comes up automatically when you touch either the text field or the number field*

Woo-hoo! But there's a little problem. How do you get the keyboard to go away? Go ahead and try. We'll wait right here while you do.

Tip   If the keyboard doesn't show up on the simulator, try selecting **Hardware ➤ Keyboard ➤ Toggle Software Keyboard**.

Closing the Keyboard When Done Is Tapped

Because the keyboard is software-based rather than a physical keyboard, we need to take a few extra steps to make sure the keyboard goes away when the user is finished with it. When the user taps the **Done** button on the text keyboard, a Did End On Exit event will be generated; at that time, we need to tell the text field to give up control so that the keyboard will go away. In order to do that, we need to add an action method to our controller class.

Select *ViewController.m* in the Project Navigator and add the following action method at the bottom of the file, just before the @end:

```
- (IBAction)textFieldDoneEditing:(id)sender {
    [sender resignFirstResponder];
}
```

As you learned in Chapter 2, the first responder is the control with which the user is currently interacting. In our new method, we tell our control to resign as a first responder, giving up that role to the previous control the user worked with. When a text field yields first responder status, the keyboard associated with it goes away.

Save the file you just edited. Let's hop back to the storyboard and trigger this action from both of our text fields.

Select *Main.storyboard* in the Project Navigator, single-click the **Name** text field, and press ⌥⌘6 to bring up the connections inspector. This time, we don't want the Touch Up Inside event that we used in the previous chapter. Instead, we want Did End On Exit since that event will fire when the user taps the **Done** button on the text keyboard.

Drag from the circle next to **Did End On Exit** to the yellow **View Controller** icon in the storyboard, in the bar that's just above the view you've been configuring, and let go. A small pop-up menu will appear containing the name of a single action, the one we just added. Click the `textFieldDoneEditing:` action to select it. You can also do this by dragging to the `textFieldDoneEditing:` method in the assistant view. Repeat this procedure with the other text field, save your changes, and then press ⌘R to run the app again.

When the simulator appears, click the **Name** field, type in something, and then tap the **Done** button. Sure enough, the keyboard drops away, just as you expected. All right! What about the **Number** field, though? Um, where's the **Done** button on that one (see Figure 4-17)?

Well, crud! Not all keyboard layouts feature a **Done** button. We could force the user to tap the **Name** field and then tap **Done**, but that's not very user-friendly, is it? And we most definitely want our application to be user-friendly. Let's see how to handle this situation.

Touching the Background to Close the Keyboard

Can you recall what Apple's iPhone applications do in this situation? Well, in most places where there are text fields, tapping anywhere in the view where there's no active control will cause the keyboard to go away. How do we implement that?

The answer is probably going to surprise you because of its simplicity. Our view controller has a property called `view` that it inherited from `UIViewController`. This `view` property corresponds to the View in the storyboard. The `view` property points to an instance of `UIView` that acts as a container for all the items in our user interface. It is sometimes referred to as a **container view** because its main purpose is to simply hold other views and controls. For all intents and purposes, the container view is the background of our user interface.

Using Interface Builder, we can change the class of the object that `view` points to so that its underlying class is `UIControl` instead of `UIView`. Because `UIControl` is a subclass of `UIView`, it is perfectly appropriate for us to connect our `view` property to an instance of `UIControl`. Remember that when a class subclasses another object, it is just a more specialized version of that class, so a `UIControl` *is* a `UIView`. If we simply change the instance that is created from `UIView` to `UIControl`, we gain the ability to trigger action methods. Before we do that, though, we need to create an action method that will be called when the background is tapped.

We need to add one more action to our controller class. Add the following method to your *ViewController.m* file, just before @end:

```
- (IBAction)backgroundTap:(id)sender {
    [self.nameField resignFirstResponder];
    [self.numberField resignFirstResponder];
}
```

This method simply tells both text fields to yield first responder status if they have it. It is perfectly safe to call `resignFirstResponder` on a control that is not the first responder, so we can call it on both text fields without needing to check whether either is the first responder.

Save this file. Now, select the storyboard again. Make sure your Document Outline is expanded (click the triangle icon at the bottom left of the editing area to toggle this), and then single-click **View** so it is selected. Do *not* select one of your view's subitems; we want the container view itself.

Next, press ⌥⌘3 to bring up the **Identity Inspector** (see Figure 4-18). This is where you can change the underlying class of any object instance in your storyboard.

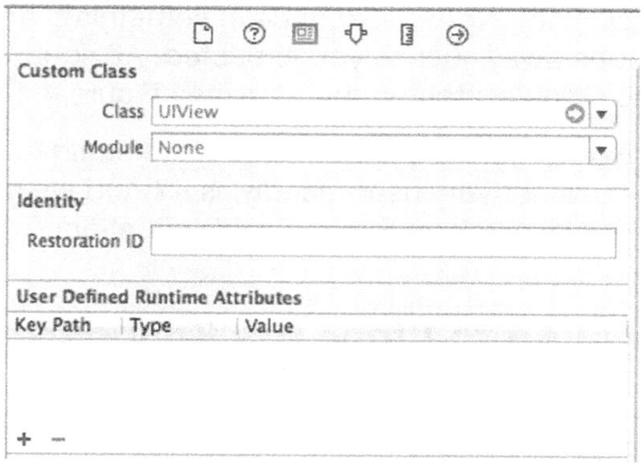

Figure 4-18. We switched Interface Builder to list view and selected our view. We then switched to the Identity Inspector, which allows us to change the underlying class of any object instance in our storyboard

The field labeled **Class** should currently say *UIView*. If not, you likely don't have the container view selected. Now, change that setting to *UIControl* and press **Return** to commit the change. All controls that are capable of triggering action methods are subclasses of UIControl; by changing the underlying class, we have just given this view the ability to trigger action methods. You can verify this by pressing ⌥⌘6 to bring up the connections inspector. You should now see all the events that you saw when you were connecting buttons to actions in the previous chapter.

Drag from the Touch Down event to the **View Controller** icon (see Figure 4-19), and choose the backgroundTap: action. Now, touches anywhere in the view without an active control will trigger our new action method, which will cause the keyboard to retract. Connecting to View Controller like this is exactly the same as connecting to the method in the code. Inside the storyboard, the View Controller is simply an instance of the view controller class, so that was just a slightly different way of achieving the exact same result.

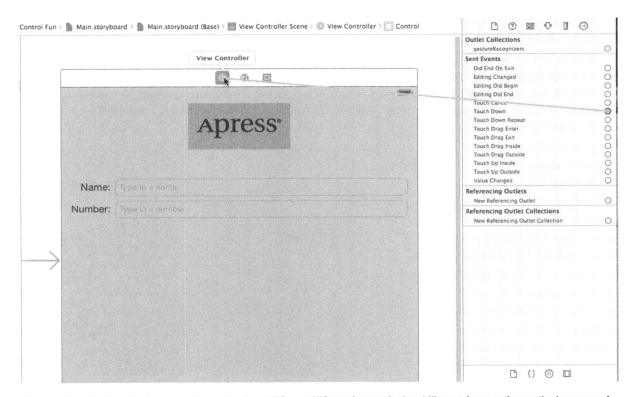

Figure 4-19. *By changing the class of our view from UIView to UIControl, we gain the ability to trigger action methods on any of the standard events. We'll connect the view's Touch Down event to the backgroundTap: action*

Note   You might be wondering why we selected **Touch Down** instead of **Touch Up Inside**, as we did in the previous chapter. The answer is that the background isn't a button. It's not a control in the eyes of the user, so it wouldn't occur to most users to try to drag their finger somewhere to cancel the action.

Save the storyboard, and then compile and run your application again. This time, the keyboard should disappear not only when the **Done** button is tapped, but also when you tap anywhere that's not an active control, which is the behavior that your users will expect.

Excellent! Now that we have this section all squared away, are you ready to move on to the next group of controls?

Adding the Slider and Label

Now it's time to add the slider and accompanying label. Remember that the value in the label will change as the slider is used. Select *Main.storyboard* in the Project Navigator, so we can add more items to our application's user interface.

Before we place the slider, let's add a bit of breathing room to our design. The blue guidelines we used to determine the spacing between the top text field and the image above it are really suggestions for minimum proximity. In other words, the blue guidelines tell you, "Don't get any closer than this." Drag the two text fields and their labels down a bit, using Figure 4-1 as a guide. Now let's add the slider.

From the Object Library, bring over a slider and arrange it below the **Number** text field, using the right-hand side's blue guideline as a stopping point and leaving a little breathing room below the bottom text field. Our slider ended up about halfway down the view. Single-click the newly added slider to select it, and then press ⌥⌘4 to go back to the Attributes Inspector if it's not already visible (see Figure 4-20).

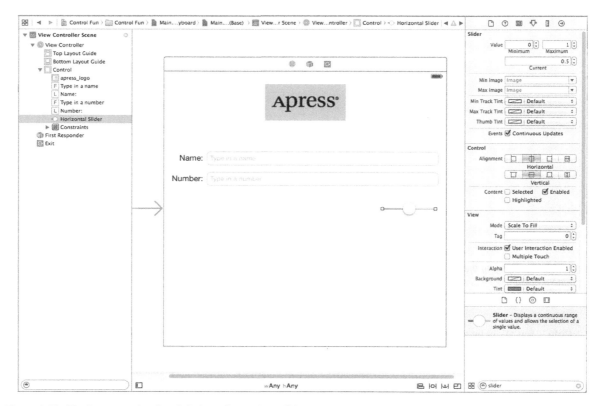

Figure 4-20. The inspector showing default attributes for a slider

A slider lets you choose a number in a given range. Use the inspector to set the **Minimum** value to *1*, the **Maximum** value to *100*, and the **Current** value to *50*. Leave the **Events Continuous Update** check box checked. This ensures a continuous flow of events as the slider's value changes. That's all we need to worry about for now.

Bring over a label and place it next to the slider, using the blue guidelines to align it vertically with the slider and to align its left edge with the left margin of the view (see Figure 4-21).

Figure 4-21. Placing the slider's label

Double-click the newly placed label, and change its text from *Label* to *100*. This is the largest value that the slider can hold, and we can use that to determine the correct width of the slider. Since "100" is shorter than "Label," Interface Builder automatically makes the label smaller for you, as if you had dragged the right-middle resize dot to the edge. Despite this automatic behavior, you're still free to resize the label however you want, of course. If you later decide you want the tool to pick the optimum size for you again, just press ⌘= or select **Editor ➤ Size to Fit Content**.

Next, resize the slider by single-clicking the slider to select it and dragging the left resize dot to the left until the blue guidelines indicate that you're getting close to the label's right-side edge.

Adding More Constraints

Now that we've added two more controls, we need to add the matching Auto Layout constraints. We'll do it the easy way again this time, so just select the **View Controller** icon in the Document Outline and then click **Editor ➤ Resolve Auto Layout Issues ➤ Add Missing Constraints**. That's not all, though. Since we moved the text fields and labels down a little to space out our design, we need to update their constraints to match their new positions. If you don't do this, you'll see warnings in the Activity View telling you that they will appear at different positions at runtime. To fix that, select the **View Controller** icon in the Document Outline again and select **Editor ➤ Resolve Auto Layout Issues ➤ Update Constraints**. Xcode adjusts the constraints so that they match the positions of all of the controls on screen and the warnings in the Activity View should go away.

Creating and Connecting the Actions and Outlets

All that's left to do with these two controls is to connect the outlet and action. We will need an outlet that points to the label, so that we can update the label's value when the slider is used. We're also going to need an action method for the slider to call as it's changed.

Make sure you're using the Assistant Editor and editing *ViewController.m*, and then Control-drag from the slider to just above the @end declaration in the Assistant Editor. When the pop-up window appears, the **Connection** field will be preset to *Action*. Type **sliderChanged** in the **Name** field and set the Type to UISlider, and then hit **Return** to create and connect the action.

Next, Control-drag from the newly added label (the one showing "100") over to the Assistant Editor. This time, drag to just below the last property declaration, in between the @interface and @end at the top of the file. When the pop-up comes up, type **sliderLabel** into the **Name** text field, and then hit **Return** to create and connect the outlet.

Implementing the Action Method

Though Xcode has created and connected our action method, it's still up to us to actually write the code that makes up the action method so it does what it's supposed to do. Add the following code to the sliderChanged: method:

```
- (IBAction)sliderChanged:(UISlider *)sender {
    int progress = (int)lroundf(sender.value);
    self.sliderLabel.text = [NSString stringWithFormat:@"%d", progress];
}
```

The first line in the method retrieves the current value of the slider, rounds it to the nearest integer, and assigns it to an integer variable. The second line of code creates a string containing that number and assigns it to the label.

That takes care of our controller's response to the movements of the slider; but in order to be really consistent, we need to make sure that the label shows the correct slider value before the user even touches it. Add this line to the viewDidLoad method:

```
- (void)viewDidLoad {
    [super viewDidLoad];
    // Do any additional setup after loading the view, typically from a nib.
    self.sliderLabel.text = @"50";
}
```

The preceding method will be executed immediately after the running app loads the view from the storyboard file, but before it's displayed on the screen. The line we added makes sure that the user sees the correct starting value right away.

Save the file. Next, press ⌘R to build and launch your app in the iOS simulator, and try out the slider. As you move it, you should see the label's text change in real time. Another piece falls into place.

But if you drag the slider toward the left (bringing the value below 10) or all the way to the right (setting the value to 100), you'll see an odd thing happen. The label to the left will shrink horizontally when it drops down to showing a single digit, and will grow horizontally when showing three. Now, apart from the text it contains, you don't actually see the label itself, so you can't see its size changing, but what you will see is that the slider actually changes its size along with the label, getting smaller or larger. It's maintaining a size relationship with the label, making sure the gap between the two is always the same.

This isn't anything we've asked for, is it? Not really. It's simply a side effect of the way Interface Builder works, helping you create GUIs that are responsive and fluid. We created some default constraints previously, and here you're seeing one in action. One of the constraints created by Interface Builder keeps the horizontal distance between these elements constant.

Fortunately, you can override this behavior by making your own constraint. Back in Xcode, select the label in your storyboard and select **Editor ➤ Pin ➤ Width** from the menu. This makes a new high-priority constraint that tells the layout system, "Don't mess with the width of this label." If you now press ⌘R to build and run again, you'll see that the label no longer expands and contracts as you drag back and forth across the slider.

We'll see more examples of constraints and their uses throughout the book. But for now, let's look at implementing the switches.

Implementing the Switches, Button, and Segmented Control

Back to Xcode we go once again. Getting dizzy, yet? This back and forth may seem a bit strange, but it's fairly common to bounce around between source code, storyboards, and nib files in Xcode, testing your app in the iOS simulator while you're developing.

Our application will have two switches, which are small controls that can have only two states: on and off. We'll also add a segmented control to hide and show the switches. Along with that control, we'll add a button that is revealed when the segmented control's right side is tapped. Let's implement those next.

Back in the storyboard, drag a segmented control from the Object Library (see Figure 4-22) and place it on the View window, a little below the slider and horizontally centered.

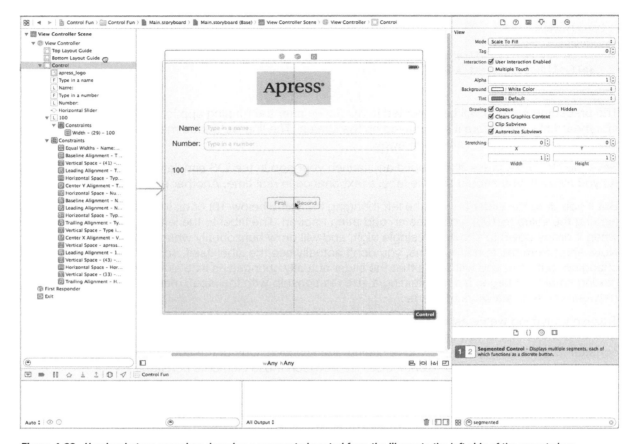

Figure 4-22. Here's what we see when dragging a segmented control from the library to the left side of the parent view

> **Tip**   To give you a sense of the spacing we're going for, take a look at the image view with the Apress logo. We tried to leave about the same amount of space above and below the image view. We did the same thing with the slider: we tried to leave about the same amount of space above and below the slider.

Double-click the word *First* on the segmented control and change the title from *First* to *Switches*. After doing that, repeat the process with the Second segment, renaming it *Button* (see Figure 4-23) and drag the control back into its centered position.

Figure 4-23. Renaming the segments in the segmented control

Adding Two Labeled Switches

Next, grab a switch from the library and place it on the view, below the segmented control and against the left margin. Now drag a second switch and place it against the right margin, aligned vertically with the first switch (see Figure 4-24).

Figure 4-24. Adding the switches to the view

> **Tip**   Holding down the ⌥ key and dragging an object in Interface Builder will create a copy of that item.
> When you have many instances of the same object to create, it can be faster to drag only one object from the
> library, and then Option-drag as many copies as you need.

The three new controls we've added need layout constraints. This time, we'll add the constraints manually. Start by selecting the segmented control and pinning it to the center of the view using **Editor ➤ Align ➤ Horizontal Center in Container** from the menu. Next, select the segmented control with the mouse and then Control-drag upward a little until the background of the main view turns blue. Release the mouse and select **Top Space to Top Layout Guide** in the pop-up menu to fix the distance from the segmented control to the top of the view.

Now let's deal with the switches. Control-drag from the left switch diagonally left and upward, toward the 10 o'clock position relative to the switch, and release the mouse. Hold down the **Shift** key and select **Leading Space to Container Margin** and **Top Space to Top Layout Guide** from the pop-up, and press the **Return** key or click anywhere outside the pop-up to apply the constraints. Do a similar thing with the other switch, but this time Control-drag to the top right (the 2 o'clock position) and select **Trailing Space to Container Margin** and **Top Space to Top Layout Guide**. When you apply constraints by dragging, Xcode offers you different options depending on the direction in which you drag. If you drag horizontally, you'll have options that let you attach the control to the left or right margins of its parent view, whereas if you drag vertically, Xcode assumes you want to set the position of the control relative to the top or bottom of its parent. Here, we needed one horizontal and one vertical constraint for each switch, so we dragged diagonally to indicate that to Xcode, and we got both horizontal and vertical options.

Connecting and Creating Outlets and Actions

Before we add the button, we'll create outlets for the two switches and connect them. The button that we'll be adding next will actually sit on top of the switches, making it harder to Control-drag to and from them, so we want to take care of the switch connections before we add the button. Since the button and the switches will never be visible at the same time, having them in the same physical location won't be a problem.

Using the Assistant Editor, Control-drag from the switch on the left to just below the last outlet in *ViewController.m*. When the pop-up appears, name the outlet *leftSwitch* and hit **Return**. Repeat this process with the other switch, naming its outlet *rightSwitch*.

Now, select the left switch again by single-clicking it. Control-drag once more to the Assistant Editor. This time, drag to right above the @end declaration before letting go. When the pop-up appears, name the new action method switchChanged:, and set the Type of its sender argument to UISwitch. Next, hit **Return** to create the new action. Now repeat this process with the right switch, with one change: instead of creating a new action, drag to the switchChanged: action that was just created and connect to it, instead. Just as we did in the previous chapter, we're going to use a single method to handle both switches.

Finally, Control-drag from the segmented control to the Assistant Editor, right above the @end declaration. Insert a new action method called toggleControls:, just as you've done before. This time, set the Type of its sender parameter to UISegmentedControl.

Implementing the Switch Actions

Save the storyboard and let's add some more code to *ViewController.m*, which is already open in the assistant view. Look for the switchChanged: method that was added for you automatically and add this code to it:

```
- (IBAction)switchChanged:(UISwitch *)sender {
    BOOL setting = sender.isOn;
    [self.leftSwitch setOn:setting animated:YES];
    [self.rightSwitch setOn:setting animated:YES];
}
```

The switchChanged: method is called whenever one of the two switches is tapped. In this method, we simply grab the isOn value of sender (which represents the switch that was pressed) and use that value to set both switches. The idea here is that setting the value of one switch will change the other switch at the other time, keeping them in sync at all times.

Now, sender is always going to be either leftSwitch or rightSwitch, so you might be wondering why we're setting them both. The reason is one of practicality. It's less work to set the value of both switches every time than to determine which switch made the call and set only the other one. Whichever switch called this method will already be set to the correct value, and setting it again to that same value won't have any effect.

Adding the Button

Next, go back to Interface Builder and drag a Button from the library to your view. Add this button directly on top of the leftmost switch, aligning it with the left margin and vertically aligning its top edge with the top edge of the two switches (see Figure 4-25).

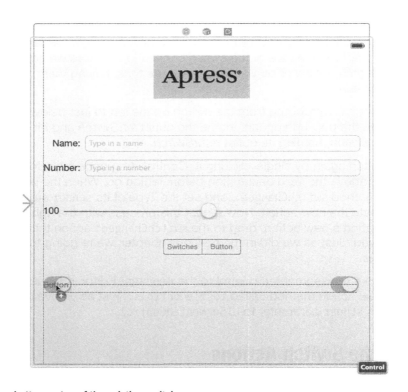

Figure 4-25. Adding a button on top of the existing switches

Now, grab the right-center resize handle and drag all the way to the right until you reach the blue guideline that indicates the right-side margin. The button should completely overlay the space occupied by the two switches, but because the default button is transparent, you will still see the switches (see Figure 4-26).

Figure 4-26. *The round rect button, once placed and resized, will fill the space occupied by the two switches*

Double-click the newly added button and give it a title of *Do Something*.

The button needs Auto Layout constraints. We're going to pin it to the top and to both sides of the main view. Control-drag upward from the button until the view background turns blue, and then release the mouse and select **Top Space to Top Layout Guide**. Then Control-drag horizontally until the main view background turns blue again and select **Leading Space to Container Margin**. You'll only get this option if you drag far enough to the left, so if you don't see it, try again and drag left until the mouse is outside the bounds of the button. Finally, Control-drag to the right until the main view background turns blue, and then select **Trailing Space to Container Margin**. Now run the application to see what we've just done.

Spiffing Up the Button

If you compare your running application to Figure 4-2, you might notice an interesting difference. Your **Do Something** button doesn't look like the one in the figure. That's because, starting with iOS 7, the default button has a very simple appearance: it's just a piece of plain text with no outline, border, background color, or other decorative features. That conforms nicely to Apple's design guidelines for iOS 7 and later, but there are still cases where you'll want to use custom buttons, so we're going to show you how it's done.

Many of the buttons you see on your iOS device are drawn using images. We've provided images that you can use for this example in the *04 – Button Images* folder of the source code archive for this book. In the Project Navigator in Xcode, select *Images.xcassets* (the same assets catalog that we used earlier when we added images for the Apress logo), and then just drag both images from the *04 – Button Images* folder in the Finder straight into the editing area in your Xcode window. The images are added to your project and will be immediately available to your app.

Stretchable Images

Now, if you look at the two button images we just added, you'll probably be struck by the size of them. They're very small and seem much too narrow to fill out the button you added to the storyboard. That's because these graphics are meant to be stretchable. It so happens that UIKit can stretch graphics to nicely fill just about any size you want. Stretchable images are an interesting concept. A stretchable image is a resizable image that knows how to resize itself intelligently, so that it maintains the correct appearance. For these button templates, we don't want the edges to stretch evenly with the rest of the image. **Edge insets** are the parts of an image (measured in pixels) that should not be resized. We want the bevel around the edges to stay the same, no matter what size we make the button, so we need to specify how much nonstretchable space makes up each edge.

In the past, this could only be accomplished in code. You'd have to use a graphics program to measure pixel boundaries of your images, and then use those numbers to set edge insets in your code. Xcode 6 eliminates the need for this by letting you visually "slice" any image you have in an assets catalog! That's what we're going to do next.

Select the *Images.xcassets* asset catalog in Xcode, and inside that select **whiteButton**. At the bottom of the editing area, you'll see a button labeled **Show Slicing**. Click that to initiate the slicing process, which begins by simply putting a **Start Slicing** button right on top of your image. That's where the magic begins, so click it! You'll see three new buttons that let you choose whether you want the image to be sliced (and therefore stretchable) vertically, horizontally, or both. Choose the button in the middle to slice both ways. Xcode does a quick analysis of your image, and then finds the sections that seem to have unique pixels around the edges, and vertical and horizontal slices in the middle that should be repeatable. You'll see these boundaries represented by dashed lines, as shown in Figure 4-27. If you have a tricky image, you may need to adjust these (it's easy to do, just drag them with the mouse); but for this image, the automatic edge insets will work fine.

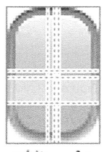

whit...- 1x

Figure 4-27. *This is what the default slicing for the white button looks like*

Next, select **blueButton** and do the same automatic slicing for it. All done! Now it's time to put these graphics to use.

Go back to the storyboard you've been working on and single-click the **Do Something** button. With the button selected, press ⌥⌘4 to open the Attributes Inspector. In the inspector, use the first pop-up menu to change the type from *System* to *Custom*. You'll see in the inspector that you can specify an Image and a Background for your button. We're going to use the Background to show our resizable graphic, so click in the **Background** pop-up and select **whiteButton**. You'll see that the button now shows the white graphic, perfectly stretched to cover the entire button frame. Nice!

Now we want to use the blue button to define the look of this button's highlighted state, which is what you see while the button is pressed. We'll talk more about control states in the next section of this chapter; but for now, just take a look at the second pop-up from the top, labeled **State Config**. A UIButton can have multiple states, each with its own text and images. Right now we've been configuring the default state, so switch this pop-up to *Highlighted*, so that we can configure that state. You'll see that the **Background** pop-up has been cleared; click it to select **blueButton**, and you're done!

There's just one problem with this new button appearance: the default UIButton size isn't tall enough to properly show the gradient buttons we imported. In fact, there's a warning in the Activity View indicating that the button will have a different frame at runtime. You can fix this by selecting the button, and then clicking **Editor ➤ Resolve Auto Layout Issues ➤ Update Frames** in the menu.

Configuring this button introduces two new concepts: **stretchable images** and **control states**. We already talked about the former, so now let's tackle the latter.

Control States

Every iOS control has four possible control states and is always in one, and only one, of these states at any given moment:

- **Normal**: The most common state is the normal control state, which is the default state. It's the state that controls are in when not in any of the other states.

- **Highlighted**: The highlighted state is the state a control is in when it's currently being used. For a button, this would be while the user has a finger on the button.

- **Disabled**: Controls are in the disabled state when they have been turned off, which can be done by unchecking the **Enabled** check box in Interface Builder or setting the control's enabled property to NO.

- **Selected**: Only some controls support the selected state. It is usually used to indicate that the control is turned on or selected. Selected is similar to highlighted, but a control can continue to be selected when the user is no longer directly using that control.

Certain iOS controls have attributes that can take on different values depending on their state. For example, by specifying one image for UIControlStateNormal and a different image for UIControlStateHighlighted, we are telling iOS to use one image when the user has a finger on the button and a different image the rest of the time. That's essentially what we did when we configured two different background states for the button in the storyboard.

Connecting and Creating the Button Outlets and Actions

Control-drag from the new button to the Assistant Editor, just below the last outlet already in the section at the top of the file. When the pop-up appears, create a new outlet called *doSomethingButton*. After you've done that, Control-drag from the button a second time to just above the @end declaration at the bottom of the file. There, create an action called buttonPressed: and set the Type to UIButton.

If you save your work and take the application for a test drive, you'll see that the segmented control will be live, but it won't do anything particularly useful yet. We need to add some logic to make the button and switches hide and unhide.

We also need to mark our button as hidden from the start. We didn't want to do that before because it would have made it harder to connect the outlets and actions. Now that we've done that, however, let's hide the button. We'll show the button when the user taps the right side of the segmented control; but when the application starts, we want the button hidden. In the storyboard, select the button and press ⌥⌘4 to bring up the Attributes Inspector. Scroll down to the **View** section and click the **Hidden** check box. The button will still be visible in Interface Builder, but will look faded out and transparent, to indicate its hidden status.

Implementing the Segmented Control Action

Save the storyboard and focus once again on *ViewController.m*. Look for the toggleControls: method that Xcode created for us and add the code in bold to it:

```
- (IBAction)toggleControls:(UISegmentedControl *)sender {
    // 0 == switches index
    if (sender.selectedSegmentIndex == 0) {
        self.leftSwitch.hidden = NO;
        self.rightSwitch.hidden = NO;
        self.doSomethingButton.hidden = YES;
    } else {
        self.leftSwitch.hidden = YES;
        self.rightSwitch.hidden = YES;
        self.doSomethingButton.hidden = NO;
    }
}
```

This code looks at the selectedSegmentIndex property of sender, which tells us which of the sections is currently selected. The first section, called switches, has an index of 0. We've noted this fact in a comment, so that when we revisit the code later, we will know what's going on. Depending on which segment is selected, we hide or show the appropriate controls.

Before we run the application, let's apply a small tweak to make it look a little better. With iOS 7, Apple has introduced some new GUI paradigms. One of these is that the status bar at the top of the screen is transparent in iOS 7 apps, so that your content shines right through it. Right now, that yellow Apress icon really sticks out like a sore thumb against our app's white background, so let's extend that yellow color to cover our entire view. In *Main.storyboard*, select the main content view, and press ⌥⌘4 to bring up the Attributes Inspector. Click the color swatch labeled **Background** to open the standard OS X color picker. One feature of this color picker is that it lets you choose any color you see on the screen. With the color picker open, click the Apress image view in the storyboard to select it. Now click the icon showing a magnifying glass at the upper left of the color picker and click the Apress image view again. You should now see the background color of the Apress image at the top of the color picker, next to the magnifying glass. To set it as the background color for the main content view, select the main view in the Document Outline (it's called **Control** because we changed its class to UIControl a while ago) and then click the color in the color picker. When you're done, close the color picker.

On your screen, you may find that the background and the Apress image seem to have slightly different colors, but when run in the simulator or on a device, they will be the same. These colors appear to be different in Interface Builder because OS X automatically adapts colors depending on the display you're using. On an iOS device and in the simulator, that doesn't happen.

Now run your app, and you'll see that the yellow color fills the entire screen, with no visible distinction between the status bar and your app's content. If you don't have full-screen scrolling content, or other content that requires the use of a navigation bar or other controls at the top of the screen, this can be a nice way to show full-screen content that isn't interrupted by the status bar quite as much.

If you've typed everything correctly, you should also be able to switch between the button and the pair of switches using the segmented control. And if you tap either switch, the other one will change its value as well. The button, however, still doesn't do anything. Before we implement it, we need to talk about action sheets and alerts.

Implementing the Action Sheet and Alert

Action sheets and **alerts** are both used to provide the user with feedback:

- Action sheets are used to force the user to make a choice between two or more items. On iPhones, the action sheet comes up from the bottom of the screen and displays a series of buttons (see Figure 4-3). On the iPad, you specify the position of the action sheet relative to another view, typically a button. Users are unable to continue using the application until they have tapped one of the buttons. Action sheets are often used to confirm a potentially dangerous or irreversible action, such as deleting an object.

- Alerts appear as a rounded rectangle in the middle of the screen (see Figure 4-4). Like action sheets, alerts force users to respond before they are allowed to continue using the application. Alerts are usually used to inform the user that something important or out of the ordinary has occurred. Like action sheets, alerts may be presented with only a single button, although you have the option of presenting multiple buttons if more than one response is appropriate.

Note   A view that forces users to make a choice before they are allowed to continue using their application is known as a modal view.

Showing an Action Sheet

Let's switch over to *ViewController.m* and implement the button's action method. Begin by looking for the empty buttonPressed: method that Xcode created for you, and then add the code in bold to that method to create and show the action sheet:

```
- (IBAction)buttonPressed:(UIButton *)sender {
    UIAlertController *controller =
        [UIAlertController alertControllerWithTitle:@"Are You Sure?"
            message:nil preferredStyle:UIAlertControllerStyleActionSheet];
    UIAlertAction *yesAction =
        [UIAlertAction actionWithTitle:@"Yes, I'm sure!"
                style:UIAlertActionStyleDestructive
                handler:^(UIAlertAction *action){
        NSString *msg;
        if ([self.nameField.text length] > 0) {
            msg = [NSString stringWithFormat:
                    @"You can breathe easy, %@, everything went OK.",
                    self.nameField.text];
        } else {
            msg = @"You can breathe easy, everything went OK.";
        }
        UIAlertController *controller2 =
                [UIAlertController
                    alertControllerWithTitle:@"Something Was Done"
                    message:msg
                    preferredStyle:UIAlertControllerStyleAlert];
        UIAlertAction *cancelAction =
                [UIAlertAction actionWithTitle:@"Phew!"
                    style: UIAlertActionStyleCancel handler:nil];
        [controller2 addAction:cancelAction];
        [self presentViewController:controller2 animated:YES completion:nil];
    }];
    UIAlertAction *noAction = [UIAlertAction actionWithTitle:@"No way!"
                    style:UIAlertActionStyleCancel handler:nil];
    [controller addAction:yesAction];
    [controller addAction:noAction];

    UIPopoverPresentationController *ppc =
            controller.popoverPresentationController;
    if (ppc != nil) {
        ppc.sourceView = sender;
        ppc.sourceRect = sender.bounds;
    }
    [self presentViewController:controller animated:YES completion:nil];
}
```

What exactly did we do there? Well, first, in the doSomething: action method, we allocated and initialized a UIAlertController, which is a view controller subclass that can display either an action sheet or an alert:

```
UIAlertController *controller =
    [UIAlertController alertControllerWithTitle:@"Are You Sure?"
        message:nil preferredStyle:UIAlertControllerStyleActionSheet];
```

The initializer method takes a number of parameters. Let's look at each of them in turn.

The first parameter is the title to be displayed. Refer back to Figure 4-3 to see how the title we're supplying will be displayed at the top of the action sheet. The second parameter is a message that will be displayed immediately below the title, in a smaller font. For this example, we're not using the message so we supply the value nil for this parameter. The final parameter specifies whether we want the controller to display an alert (value UIAlertControllerStyleAlert) or an action sheet (**UIAlertControllerStyleActionSheet**). Since we need an action sheet, we supply the value **UIAlertControllerStyleActionSheet** here.

The alert controller does not supply any buttons by default—you have to create a UIAlertAction object for each button that you want and add it to the controller. Here's part of the code that creates the two buttons for our action sheet:

```
UIAlertAction *yesAction =
    [UIAlertAction actionWithTitle:@"Yes, I'm sure!"
        style:UIAlertActionStyleDestructive
        handler:^(UIAlertAction *action){
  // Code omitted - see below.
}];
UIAlertAction *noAction = [UIAlertAction actionWithTitle:@"No way!"
            style:UIAlertActionStyleCancel handler:nil];
```

For each button, you specify the title, the style, and a handler to be called when the button is pressed. There are three possible styles to choose from:

- UIAlertActionStyleDestructive should be used when the button triggers a destructive, dangerous, or irreversible action, such as deleting or overwriting a file. The title for a button with this style is drawn in red in a bold font.

- Use UIAlertActionStyleDefault for a normal button, such as an **OK** button, when the action that will be triggered is not destructive. The title is drawn in a regular blue font.

- UIAlertStyleCancel is used for the **Cancel** button. The title is drawn in a bold blue font.

Finally, you add the buttons to the controller:

```
[controller addAction:yesAction];
[controller addAction:noAction];
```

To make the alert or action sheet visible, you need to ask the current view controller to *present* the alert controller. Here's how you present an action sheet:

```
UIPopoverPresentationController *ppc =
            controller.popoverPresentationController;
if (ppc != nil) {
    ppc.sourceView = sender;
    ppc.sourceRect = sender.bounds;
}
[self presentViewController:controller animated:YES completion:nil];
```

The first five lines configure where the action sheet will appear by getting the alert controller's popover presentation controller and setting its sourceView and sourceRect properties. We'll say more about these properties shortly. Finally, we make the action sheet visible by calling our view controller's presentViewController:animated:completion: method, passing it the alert controller as the controller to be presented. When a view controller is presented, its view temporarily replaces that of the view controller that's presenting it. In the case of the alert view controller, the action sheet or alert partially covers the presenting view controller's view; the rest of the view is covered by a dark, translucent background that lets you see the underlying view but makes it clear that you can't interact with it until you dismiss the presented view controller.

Now let's revisit the popover presentation controller configuration. On the iPhone, the action sheet always pops up from the bottom of the screen, as shown in Figure 4-3, but on the iPad, it's displayed in a **popover**—a small, rounded rectangle with an arrow that points toward another view, usually the one that caused it to appear. Figure 4-28 shows how our action sheet looks on the iPad simulator.

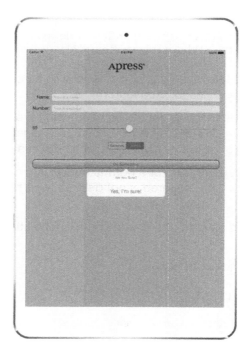

Figure 4-28. An action sheet on iPad

As you can see, the popover's arrow points to the **Do Something** button. That's because we set the `sourceView` property of the alert controller's popover presentation controller to point to that button and its `sourceRect` property to the button's bounds:

```
if (ppc != nil) {
        ppc.sourceView = sender;
        ppc.sourceRect = sender.bounds;
    }
```

Notice the `ppc != nil` check—we make this check because on the iPhone, the alert controller does not present the action sheet in a popover, so its `popoverPresentationController` property is `nil`. Strictly speaking, this check is not required because sending a message to a `nil` object reference is perfectly legal in Objective-C and does nothing. However, having the check in the code makes it clear that there are circumstances under which `ppc` may be `nil` and the popover view controller configuration is not required.

In Figure 4-28, the popover appears below the source button, but you can change this, if you need to, by setting the popover presentation controller's `permittedArrowDirections` property, which is a mask of permitted directions for the popover's arrow. The following code moves the popover above the source button by setting this property to `UIPopoverArrowDirectionDown`:

```
if (ppc != nil) {
    ppc.sourceView = sender;
    ppc.sourceRect = sender.bounds;
    ppc.permittedArrowDirections = UIPopoverArrowDirectionDown;
}
```

If you compare Figure 4-28 and Figure 4-3, you'll see that the **No Way!** button is missing on the iPad. The alert controller does not use buttons with style `UIAlertStyleCancel` on the iPad, because users are accustomed to dismissing a popover without taking any action by tapping anywhere outside of it.

Showing an Alert

When the user presses the **Yes, I'm Sure!** button, we want to pop up an alert with a message. When a button that was added to an alert controller is pressed, the action sheet (or alert) is dismissed and the button's handler block is called with a reference to the `UIAlertAction` from which the button was created. The code that's executed when the **Yes, I'm Sure!** button is pressed is shown in bold:

```
UIAlertAction *yesAction =
    [UIAlertAction actionWithTitle:@"Yes, I'm sure!"
           style:UIAlertActionStyleDestructive
           handler:^(UIAlertAction *action){
    NSString *msg;
    if ([self.nameField.text length] > 0) {
        msg = [NSString stringWithFormat:
                @"You can breathe easy, %@, everything went OK.",
                self.nameField.text];
```

```
    } else {
        msg = @"You can breathe easy, everything went OK.";
    }
    UIAlertController *controller2 =
            [UIAlertController
                alertControllerWithTitle:@"Something Was Done"
                message:msg
                preferredStyle:UIAlertControllerStyleAlert];
    UIAlertAction *cancelAction =
            [UIAlertAction actionWithTitle:@"Phew!"
                style: UIAlertActionStyleCancel handler:nil];
    [controller2 addAction:cancelAction];
    [self presentViewController:controller2 animated:YES completion:nil];
}];
```

The first thing we do in the handler block is create a new string that will be displayed to the user. In a real application, this is where you would do whatever processing the user requested. We're just going to pretend we did something, and notify the user by using an alert. If the user has entered a name in the top text field, we'll grab that, and we'll use it in the message that we'll display in the alert. Otherwise, we'll just craft a generic message to show:

```
NSString *msg = nil;

if ([self.nameField.text length] > 0) {
    msg = [NSString stringWithFormat:
            @"You can breathe easy, %@, everything went OK.",
            self.nameField.text];
}
else {
    msg = @"You can breathe easy, everything went OK.";
}
```

The next few lines of code are going to look kind of familiar. Alert views and action sheets are created and used in a very similar manner. We always start by creating a UIAlertController:

```
UIAlertController *controller2 =
        [UIAlertController
            alertControllerWithTitle:@"Something Was Done"
            message:msg
            preferredStyle:UIAlertControllerStyleAlert];
```

Again, we pass a title to be displayed. This time, we also pass a more detailed message, which is that string we just created. The final parameter is the style, which we set to UIAlertControllerStyleAlert because we want an alert, not an action sheet. Next, we create a UIAlertAction for the alert's cancel button and add it to the controller:

```
UIAlertAction *cancelAction =
        [UIAlertAction actionWithTitle:@"Phew!"
            style: UIAlertActionStyleCancel handler:nil];
[controller2 addAction:cancelAction];
```

Finally, we make the alert appear by present the alert view controller:

```
[self presentViewController:controller2 animated:YES completion:nil];
```

You can see the alert that's created by this code in Figure 4-4. You'll notice that our code does not attempt to get and configure the alert controller's popover presentation controller. That's because alerts appear in a small, rounded view in the center of the screen on both iPhone and iPad, so there is no popover presentation controller to configure.

Save *ViewController.m* and then build, run, and try out the completed application.

Crossing the Finish Line

This was a big chapter. Conceptually, we didn't hit you with too much new stuff, but we took you through the use of a good number of controls and showed you many different implementation details. You got a lot more practice with outlets and actions, saw how to use the hierarchical nature of views to your advantage, and got some more practice adding Auto Layout constraints. You learned about control states and stretchable images, and you also learned how to use both action sheets and alerts.

There's a lot going on in this little application. Feel free to go back and play with it. Change values, experiment by adding and modifying code, and see what different settings in Interface Builder do. There's no way we could take you through every permutation of every control available in iOS, but the application you just put together is a good starting point and covers a lot of the basics.

In the next chapter, we're going to look at what happens when the user rotates an iOS device from portrait to landscape orientation or vice versa. You're probably well aware that many apps change their displays based on the way the user is holding the device, and we're going to show you how to do that in your own applications.

Chapter 5

Rotation and Adaptive Layout

The iPhone and iPad are amazing pieces of engineering. Apple engineers found all kinds of ways to squeeze maximum functionality into a pretty darn-small package. One example of this is how these devices can be used in either portrait (tall and skinny) or landscape (short and wide) mode, and how that orientation can be changed at runtime simply by rotating the device. You can see an example of this behavior, which is called **autorotation**, in iOS's web browser, Mobile Safari (see Figure 5-1). In this chapter, we'll cover rotation in detail. We'll start with an overview of the ins and outs of autorotation, and then move on to different ways of implementing that functionality in your apps.

Figure 5-1. *Like many iOS applications, Mobile Safari changes its display based on how it is held, making the most of the available screen space*

Prior to iOS 8, if you wanted to design an application that would run on both iPhones and iPads, you would have to create one storyboard with a layout for the iPhones and another one with your iPad layout. In iOS 8, that's all changed. Apple has added APIs to UIKit and tools in Xcode that make it possible to build an application that runs on (or, using their terminology, *adapts to*) any device—even the new large-screen iPhone 6 Plus—with a single storyboard. You still have to design carefully for the different form factor of each type of device, but now you can do it all in one place. Even better, using the Preview feature that we introduced in Chapter 3, you can see immediately how your application would look on any device without even having to start up the simulator. We'll take a look at how to build adaptive application layouts in the second part of this chapter.

The Mechanics of Rotation

The ability to run in both portrait and landscape orientations might not be right for every application. Several of Apple's iPhone applications (such as the Weather app) support only a single orientation. However, iPad applications are different. Apple recommends that most applications (with the exception of immersive apps like games that are inherently designed around a particular layout) should support every orientation when running on an iPad.

In fact, most of Apple's own iPad apps work fine in both orientations. Many of them use the orientations to show different views of your data. For example, the Mail and Notes apps use landscape orientation to display a list of items (folders, messages, or notes) on the left and the selected item on the right. In portrait orientation, however, these apps let you focus on the details of just the selected item.

For iPhone apps, the base rule is that, if autorotation enhances the user experience, you should add it to your application. For iPad apps, the rule is you should add autorotation unless you have a compelling reason not to. Fortunately, Apple did a great job of hiding the complexities of handling orientation changes in iOS and in the UIKit, so implementing this behavior in your own iOS applications is actually quite easy.

Permission to rotate the user interface is specified in the view controller. If the user rotates the device, the active view controller will be asked if it's okay to rotate to the new orientation (which you'll see how to do in this chapter). If the view controller responds in the affirmative, the application's window and views will be rotated, and the window and view will be resized to fit the new orientation.

On the iPhone and iPod touch, a view that starts in portrait mode will be taller than it is wide—you can see the actual available space for any given device by referring to the Software Size column of Table 1-1 in Chapter 1. Note, however, that the vertical screen real estate available for your app will be decreased by 20 points vertically if your app is showing the **status bar**, which is the 20-point strip at the top of the screen (see Figure 5-1) that shows information like signal strength, time, and battery charge.

When the device rotates to landscape mode, the vertical and horizontal dimensions switch around, so, for example, an application running on an iPhone 6 would see a screen that's 375 points wide × 667 points high in portrait, but 667 points wide × 375 points high in landscape. Again though, on iPads the vertical space actually available to your app is reduced by 20 points if you're showing the status bar, which most apps do. On iPhones, as of iOS 8, the status bar is hidden in landscape orientation.

Points, Pixels, and the Retina Display

You might be wondering why we're talking about "points" instead of pixels. Earlier versions of this book did, in fact, refer to screen sizes in pixels rather than points. The reason for this change is Apple's introduction of the **Retina display**.

The Retina display is Apple's marketing term for the high-resolution screen on all versions of the iPhone starting with iPhone 4 and later-generation iPod touches, as well as newer variants of the iPad. As you can see by looking back at Table 1-1 again, it doubles the hardware screen resolution for most models and almost triples it for the iPhone 6 Plus.

Fortunately, you don't need to do a thing in most situations to account for this. When we work with on-screen elements, we specify dimensions and distances in *points*, not in pixels. For older iPhones, and the iPad, iPad 2, and iPad Mini 1, points and pixels are equivalent. One point is one pixel. On more recent-model iPhones, iPads, and iPod touches, however, a point equates to a 4-pixel square (2 pixels wide × 2 pixels high) and the iPhone 5s screen (for example) still appears to be 320 points wide, even though it's actually 640 pixels across. On iPhone 6 Plus, the scaling factor is 3, so each point maps to a 9-pixel square. Think of it as a "virtual resolution," with iOS automatically mapping points to the physical pixels of your screen. We'll talk more about this in Chapter 16.

In typical applications, most of the work in actually moving the pixels around the screen is managed by iOS. Your application's main job in all this is making sure everything fits nicely and looks proper in the resized window.

Handling Rotation

To handle device rotation, you need to specify the correct **constraints** for all of the objects that make up your interface. Constraints tell the iOS device how your controls should behave when their enclosing view is resized. How does that relate to device rotation? When the device rotates, the dimensions of the screen are (more or less) interchanged—so the area in which your views are laid out changes size. If you've worked with Cocoa on OS X, you may already be familiar with the basic process because it is the same one used to specify how Cocoa controls behave when the user resizes the window in which they are contained.

The simplest way of using constraints is to configure them in Interface Builder (IB). Interface Builder lets you define constraints that describe how your GUI components will be repositioned and resized as their parent view changes or as other views move around. You did a little bit of this in Chapter 4 and will delve further into this subject in this chapter. You can think of constraints as equations that make statements about view geometry and the iOS view system itself as a "solver" that will rearrange things as necessary to make those statements true. You can also add constraints in code, but we're not going to cover that in this book.

Constraints were added to iOS 6, but have been present on the Mac for a bit longer than that. On both iOS and OS X, constraints can be used in place of the old "springs and struts" system that came before. Constraints can do everything the old technology could do, and a whole lot more.

Let's get started, shall we? Before we get into the different ways you can configure your GUI to shuffle its views around, we'll show you how to specify which orientations your app will allow.

Choosing Your View Orientations

We'll create a simple app to show you how to pick which orientations you want your app to work with. Start a new Single View Application project in Xcode, and call it *Orientations*. Choose *Universal* from the **Devices** pop-up, and save it along with your other projects.

Before we lay out our GUI in the storyboard, we need to tell iOS that our view supports interface rotation. There are actually two ways of doing this. You can create an app-wide setting that will be the default for all view controllers, and you can further tweak things for each individual view controller. We'll do both of these things, starting with the app-wide setting.

Supported Orientations at the App Level

First, we need to specify which orientations our application supports. When your new Xcode project window appeared, it should have opened to your project settings. If not, click the top line in the Project Navigator (the one named after your project), and then make sure you're on the **General** tab. Among the options available in the summary, you should see a section called *Deployment Info* and, within that, a section called *Device Orientation* (*see* Figure 5-2) with a list of check boxes.

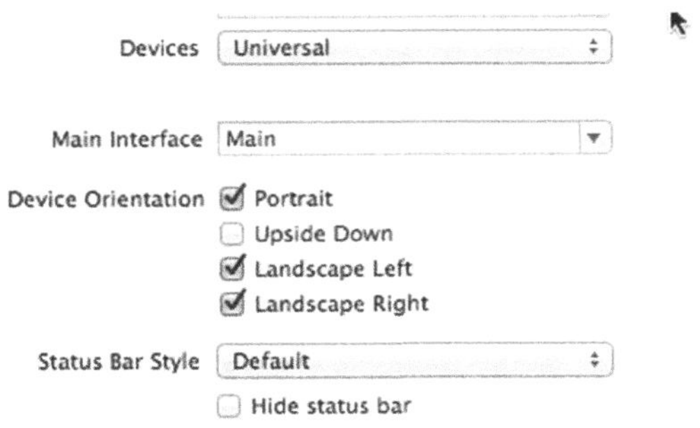

Figure 5-2. The General tab for our project shows, among other things, the supported device orientations

This is how you identify which orientations your application supports. It doesn't necessarily mean that every view in your application will use all of the selected orientations; but if you're going to support an orientation in any of your application's views, that orientation must be selected here.

Have you noticed that the **Upside Down** orientation is off by default? That's because, if the phone rings while it is being held upside down, the phone is likely to remain upside down when you answer it.

Open the **Devices** drop-down that's just above the check boxes and you'll see that you can actually configure separate sets of allowed orientations for the iPhone and the iPad. If you choose **iPad**, you'll see that all four check boxes are selected, because the iPad is meant to be used in any orientation.

Note   The four check boxes shown in Figure 5-2 are actually just a shortcut to adding and deleting entries in your application's *Info.plist* file. If you single-click *Info.plist* in the *Supporting Files* folder in the Project Navigator, you should see two entries called *Supported interface orientations* and *Supported interface orientations (iPad)*, with subentries for the orientations that are currently selected. Selecting and deselecting those check boxes in the project summary simply adds and removes items from these arrays. Using the check boxes is easier and less prone to error, so using the check boxes is definitely recommended. However, you should know what they do.

Now, select *Main.storyboard*. Find a Label in the Object Library and drag it into your view, dropping it so that it's horizontally centered and somewhere near the top, as shown in Figure 5-3. Select the label's text and change it to *This way up*. Changing the text may shift the label's position, so drag it to make it horizontally centered again.

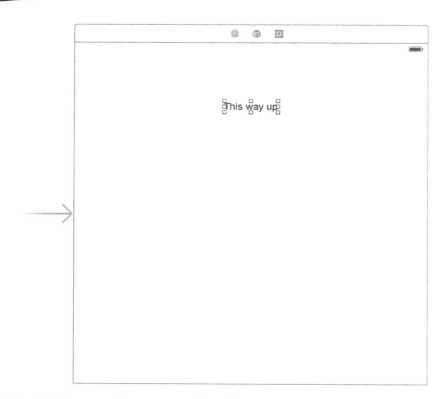

Figure 5-3. A useful reminder in case you lose your sense of gravity

We need to add Auto Layout constraints to pin the label in place before running the application, so Control-drag from the label upward until the background of the containing view turns blue, and then release the mouse. Hold down the **Shift** key and select **Top Space to Top Layout Guide** and **Center Horizontally in Container** in the pop-up, and then press **Return**. Now, press ⌘**R** to build and run this simple app on the iPhone simulator. When it comes up in the simulator, try rotating the device a few times by pressing ⌘**-Left-Arrow** or ⌘**-Right-Arrow**. You'll see that the entire view (including the label you added) rotates to every orientation except upside down, just as we configured it to do. Run it on the iPad simulator to confirm that it rotates to all four possible orientations.

We've identified the orientations our app will support, but that's not all we need to do. We can also specify a set of accepted orientations for each view controller, giving us more fine-grained control over which orientations will work in different parts of our apps.

Per-Controller Rotation Support

Let's configure our view controller to allow a different, smaller set of accepted orientations. The global configuration for the app specifies a sort of absolute upper limit for allowed orientations. If the global configuration doesn't include upside-down orientation, for example, there's no way that any individual view controller can force the system to rotate the display to upside down. All we can do in the view controller is place further limits on what is acceptable.

In the Project Navigator, single-click *ViewController.m*. Here we're going to implement a method, defined in the UIViewController superclass, that lets us specify which orientations we'll accept:

```
- (NSUInteger)supportedInterfaceOrientations {
    return (UIInterfaceOrientationMaskPortrait |
            UIInterfaceOrientationMaskLandscapeLeft);
}
```

This method lets us return a C-style mask of acceptable orientations. This is iOS's way of asking a view controller if it's okay to rotate to a specific orientation. In this case, we're returning a value that indicates that we'll accept two orientations: the default portrait orientation and the orientation you get when you turn your phone 90° clockwise, so that the phone's left edge is at the top. We use the Boolean OR operator (the vertical bar symbol) to combine these two orientation masks and return the combined value.

UIApplication.h defines the following orientation masks, which you can combine in any way you like using the OR operator, as previously discussed:

- ▦ UIInterfaceOrientationMaskPortrait

- ▦ UIInterfaceOrientationMaskLandscapeLeft

- ▦ UIInterfaceOrientationMaskLandscapeRight

- ▦ UIInterfaceOrientationMaskPortraitUpsideDown

In addition, there are some predefined combinations of these for common use cases. These are functionally equivalent to OR'ing them together on your own, but can save you some typing and make your code more readable:

- ▦ UIInterfaceOrientationMaskLandscape

- ▦ UIInterfaceOrientationMaskAll

- ▦ UIInterfaceOrientationMaskAllButUpsideDown

When the iOS device is changed to a new orientation, the supportedInterfaceOrientations method is called on the active view controller. Depending on whether the return value includes the new orientation, the application determines whether it should rotate the view. Because every view controller subclass can implement this differently, it is possible for one application to support rotation with some of its views but not with others, or for one view controller to support certain orientations under certain conditions.

CODE COMPLETION IN ACTION

Have you noticed that the defined system constants on the iPhone are always designed so that values that work together start with the same letters? One reason why `UIInterfaceOrientationMaskPortrait`, `UIInterfaceOrientationMaskPortraitUpsideDown`, `UIInterfaceOrientationMaskLandscapeLeft`, and `UIInterfaceOrientationMaskLandscapeRight` all begin with `UIInterfaceOrientationMask` is to let you take advantage of Xcode's **code completion** feature.

You've probably noticed that as you type, Xcode frequently tries to complete the word you are typing. That's code completion in action.

Developers cannot possibly remember all the various defined constants in the system, but you can remember the common beginning for the groups you use frequently. When you need to specify an orientation, simply type **UIInterfaceOrientationMask** (or even **UIInterf**), and you'll see a list of all matches pop up. (In Xcode's preferences, you can configure the list to pop up only when you press the **Esc** key.) You can use the arrow keys to navigate the list that appears and make a selection by pressing the **Tab** or **Return** key. This is much faster than needing to look up the values in the documentation or header files.

Feel free to play around with this method by returning different orientation mask combinations. You can force the system to constrict your view's display to whichever orientations make sense for your app, but don't forget the global configuration we talked about earlier! Remember that if you haven't enabled upside down there (for example), none of your views will ever appear upside down, no matter what their views say.

> **Note**   iOS actually has two different types of orientations. The one we're discussing here is the **interface orientation**. There's also a separate but related concept of **device orientation**. Device orientation specifies how the device is currently being held. Interface orientation is which way the views on the screen are rotated. If you turn a standard iPhone upside down, the device orientation will be upside down, but the interface orientation will almost always be one of the other three, since iPhone apps typically don't support portrait upside down.

Designing an Interface Using Constraints

In Xcode, make another new project based on the Single View Application template and name it *Layout*. Select *Main.storyboard* to edit the interface file in Interface Builder. One nice thing about using constraints is that they accomplish quite a lot using very little code. We do need to specify which orientations we support in code (unless we plan to support the default set), but the details of the layout are specified right here in Interface Builder.

To see how this works, drag four Labels from the library over to your view, and place them as shown in Figure 5-4. Use the dashed blue guidelines to help you line up each one near its respective corner. In this example, we're using instances of the `UILabel` class to show how to use constraints with your GUI layout, but the same rules apply to all kinds of GUI objects.

Double-click each label and assign a title to each one so that you can tell them apart later. We've used *UL* for the upper-left label, *UR* for the upper-right label, *LL* for the lower-left label, and *LR* for the lower-right label. After setting the text for each label, drag all of them into position so that they are lined up evenly with respect to the container view's corners (see Figure 5-4).

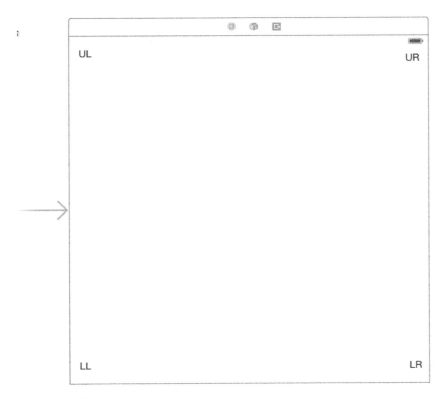

Figure 5-4. Adding four labels to the interface

Let's see what happens now, given that we haven't set any Auto Layout constraints. Build and run the app on the iPhone 5s simulator. Once the simulator starts up, you'll find that you can see the label at the upper left and a small part of the one at lower left—the other two are off-screen to the right. Furthermore, the label that started at the lower left is only just visible. Select **Hardware ➤ Rotate Left**, which will simulate turning the iPhone to landscape mode, and you'll find that you can now see the top-left label and part of the one at the top right, as shown in Figure 5-5.

Figure 5-5. *So far, not so good. What happened?*

As you can see, things aren't looking so good. The top-left label is in the right spot after rotating, but all of the others are in the wrong places and some of them aren't visible at all! What's happened is that every object has maintained its distance relative to the upper-left corner of the view in the storyboard.

What we really want is to have each label sticking tightly to its nearest corner after rotating. The labels on the right should shift horizontally to match the view's new width, and the labels on the bottom should move vertically to match the new height instead of disappearing off the bottom edge. Fortunately, we can easily set up constraints in Interface Builder to make these changes happen for us.

In fact, as you've seen in earlier chapters, Interface Builder is smart enough to examine this set of objects and create a set of default constraints that will do exactly what we want. It uses some rules of thumb to figure out that if we have objects near edges, we probably want to keep them there. To make it apply these rules, first select all four labels. You can do this by clicking one label, and then holding down the **Shift** or ⌘ key while clicking each of the other three. With all of them selected, choose **Editor ➤ Resolve Auto Layout Issues ➤ Add Missing Constraints** from the menu (you'll find there are two menu items with this name—in this case, you can use either of them). Next, just press the **Run** button to launch the app in the simulator, and then verify that it works.

Knowing that this works is one thing, but to use constraints like this most effectively, it's pretty important to understand how it works, too. So, let's dig into this a bit. Back in Xcode, click the upper-left label to select it. You'll notice that you can see some solid blue lines attached to the label. These blue lines are different from the dashed blue guidelines you see when dragging objects around the screen (see Figure 5-6).

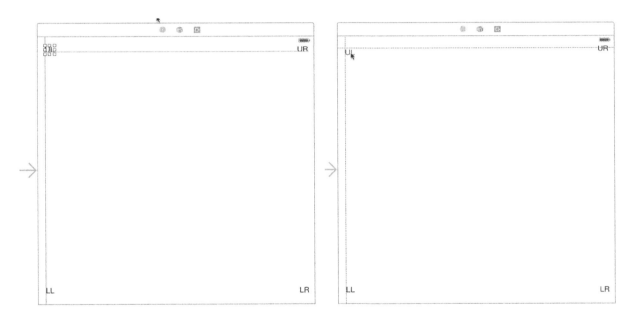

Figure 5-6. *On the right, the dashed blue lines help you line up objects while you're dragging. On the left, the solid blue lines show constraints that are configured for the chosen object*

Each of those solid blue lines represents a constraint. If you now press ⌥⌘5 to open the Size Inspector, you'll see that it contains a list of constraints. Figure 5-7 shows a typical set of constraints, but the constraints that Xcode creates depends on exactly where you placed the labels, so you may see something different.

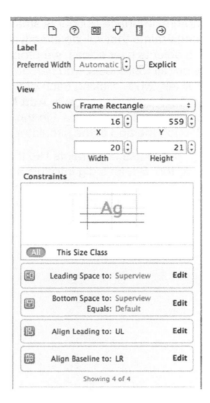

Figure 5-7. *Four constraints generated by Xcode to pin a label in its parent view*

In this case, two of the constraints deal with this label's position relative to its superview, the container view: it specifies the **leading space**, which generally means the space to the left, and the **bottom space** (i.e., the space below the label). These constraints cause the label to maintain the same distance to the bottom and left edges of its superview when the superview's size changes, as it does when the device is rotated. The other two constraints are attached to two of the other labels and work to keep them lined up with this label. Examine each of the other labels to see what constraints they have and make sure that you understand how those constraints work to keep the four labels in the corners of their superview.

Note that in languages where text is written and read from right to left, "leading space" is on the right, so a leading constraint may cause a GUI to be laid out in the opposite direction if the user has picked a language such as Arabic for their device. For now, let's just act as if "leading space" means "left space."

Overriding Default Constraints

Grab another label from the library and drag it over to the layout area. This time, instead of moving toward a corner, drag it toward the left edge of your view, lining up the label's left edge with the left edges of the other labels on the left side, and centering it vertically in the view. Dashed lines will appear to help you out. Figure 5-8 shows you what this looks like.

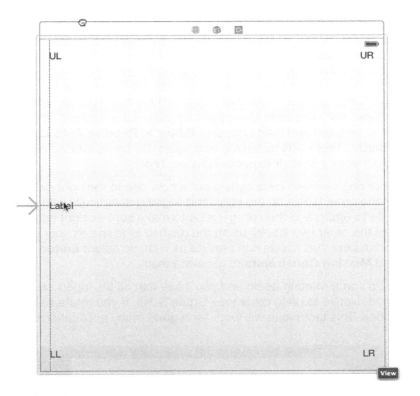

Figure 5-8. Placing the Left label

After placing the left label, give it a title like "Left." Press ⌘R to run your app in the simulator. Rotate it to landscape mode and you'll see that the left label maintains its distance from the top, placing it a long way below the center (see Figure 5-9). Oops!

Figure 5-9. The Left label is not where it should be!

We need to create a new constraint to make this work, so go back to Xcode and select the left label in your storyboard. Adding a constraint to force this label to stay vertically centered is really easy—just select **Editor ➤ Align ➤ Vertical Center in Container**. When you do this, Xcode creates a new constraint and immediately selects the new constraint itself in the editor view. This is slightly confusing, but don't worry! Just click the label again to select it. Make sure the Size Inspector is on display by pressing ⌥⌘5, and you'll see that this label now has a constraint aligning its center Y value to that of its superview. The label also needs a horizontal constraint. You can add this by making sure the label is selected and then choosing **Editor ➤ Resolve Auto Layout Issues ➤ Add Missing Constraints**. Press ⌘R to run the app again. Do some rotating and you'll see that all the labels now move perfectly into their expected places. Nice!

Now, let's complete our ring of labels by dragging out a new one to the right side of the view, lining up its right edge with the other labels on the right, and aligning it vertically with the **Left** label. Change this label's title to *Right*, and then drag it a bit to make sure its right edge is vertically aligned with the right edges of the other two labels, using the dashed blue line as your guide. We want to use the automatic constraints that Xcode can provide us with, so select **Editor ➤ Resolve Auto Layout Issues ➤ Add Missing Constraints** to generate them.

Build and run again. Do some rotating again and you'll see that all the labels stay on the screen and are correctly positioned relative to each other (see Figure 5-10). If you rotate back, they should return to their original positions. This technique will work for a great many applications.

Figure 5-10. The labels in their new positions after rotating

That's all fine, but we can do a lot more with just a few clicks! Let's say that we've been struck by a great visionary idea and decide that we want the two uppermost labels, UL and UR, to form a sort of header, filling the entire width of the screen. With a bit of resizing and some constraints, we'll sort that out in no time.

Full-Width Labels

We're going to create some constraints that make sure that our labels stay the same width as each other, with tight spacing to keep them stretched across the top of the view even when the device rotates. Figure 5-11 shows what we're shooting for.

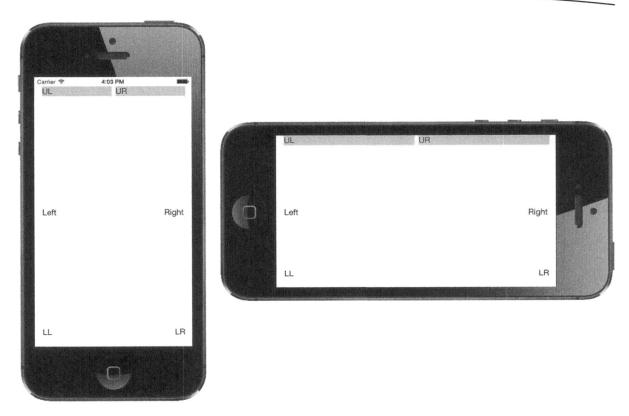

Figure 5-11. *The top labels, spread across the entire width of the display, in both portrait and landscape orientations*

The hardest part about this is being able to visually verify that we've got the result we want, where each label is precisely centered within its half of the screen. In order to make it easier to see whether we've got it right, let's temporarily set a background color for the labels. In the storyboard, select both the **UL** and **UR** labels, open the Attributes Inspector, and scroll down to the View section. Use the **Background** control to select a nice, bright color. You'll see that the entire frame of each label fills with the color you chose.

Now, direct your attention to the UL label and drag the resizing control on its right edge, pulling it almost to the horizontal midpoint of the view. You don't have to be exact here, for reasons that will become clear soon. After doing this, resize the UR label by dragging its left-edge resizing control to the left until you see the dashed blue guideline appear, which tells you that it's the recommended width from the label to its left. Now we'll add a constraint to make these labels fill the whole width of their superview. Select both the **UL** and **UR** labels, and then select **Editor ➤ Pin ➤ Horizontal Spacing** from the menu. That constraint tells the layout system to hold these labels beside one another with the same horizontal space they have right now. Build and run to see what happens. You'll probably see something like Figure 5-12.

Figure 5-12. The labels are stretched across the display, but not evenly

That's pretty close, but not really what we had in mind. So what's missing? We've defined constraints that control each label's position relative to its superview and the allowed distance between the two labels, but we haven't said anything about the size of the labels. This leaves the layout system free to size them in whatever way it wants (which, as we've just seen, can be quite wrong). To remedy this, we need to add one more constraint.

Make sure the **UL** label is selected, and then hold down the **Shift** key (⇧) and click the **UR** label. With both labels selected, you can make a constraint that affects both of them. From the menu, select **Editor ➤ Pin ➤ Widths Equally** to make the new constraint. You'll now see a new constraint appear, and just like before, it's automatically selected, as shown in Figure 5-13. You may also note that if the two labels weren't exactly the same width before you created this constraint, they certainly are now, as the existence of this new constraint snaps them into place. You'll also notice that the constraints are colored orange; this means that the current positions of the labels in the storyboard do not match what you will see at runtime. To fix this, select **Editor ➤ Resolve Auto Layout Issues ➤ Update Frames**. The constraints should change to blue.

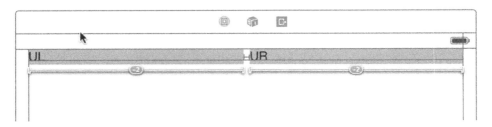

Figure 5-13. *The top labels are now made equal in width by a constraint*

If you run again at this point, you should see the labels spread across the entire screen, in both portrait and landscape orientations (see Figure 5-11).

In this example, all of our labels are visible and correctly laid out in multiple orientations; however, there is a lot of unused space on the screen. Perhaps it would be better if we also set up the other two rows of labels to fill the width of the view or allowed the height of our labels to change so that there will be less empty space on the interface? Feel free to experiment with the constraints of these six labels and perhaps even add some others. Apart from what we've covered so far, you'll find more actions that create constraints in the **Editor ➤ Pin** menu. And if you end up making a constraint that doesn't do what you want, you can delete it by selecting it and pressing the **Delete** key, or try configuring it in the Attributes Inspector. Play around until you feel comfortable with the basics of how constraints work. We'll use them constantly throughout the book; but if you want the full details, just search for "Auto Layout" in Xcode's documentation window.

Creating Adaptive Layouts

The layout for the simple example that we just created works well in portrait and landscape orientations and it also works on iPhones and iPads, despite the difference in screen dimensions between these devices. In fact, as already noted, handling device rotation and creating a user interface that works on devices with different screen sizes are really the same problem—after all, from the point of view of your application, when the device rotates, the screen effectively changes size. In the simplest cases, you handle both by assigning Auto Layout constraints to make sure that all of your views are positioned and sized where you want them to be. However, that's not always possible. Some layouts work well when the device is in portrait mode, but not so well when it's rotated to landscape; and similarly, some designs suit the iPhone but not the iPad. When this happens, you really have no choice but to create separate designs for each case. Prior to iOS 8, this meant either implementing your whole layout in code, having multiple storyboards, or a combination of the two. Fortunately, with iOS 8 and Xcode 6, Apple has made it possible to design *adaptive* applications that work in both orientations and on different devices while still using only a single storyboard. Let's take a look at how this works.

The Restructure Application

To set the scene, we'll design a user interface that works well for an iPhone in portrait mode, but not so well when the phone is rotated or when the application runs on an iPad. Then we'll see how to use the new tools in Xcode 6 to adapt the design so that it works well everywhere.

Start by making a new Single View project like you've done before, naming this one *Restructure*. We're going to construct a GUI that consists of one large content area and a small set of buttons that perform various (fictional) actions. We'll place the buttons at the bottom of the screen and let the content area take up the rest of the space, as shown in Figure 5-14.

Figure 5-14. The initial GUI of the Restructure app, in portrait orientation on the iPhone

Select *Main.storyboard* to start editing the GUI. Since we don't really have an interesting content view we want to display, we'll just use a large colored rectangle. Drag a single UIView from the Object Library into your container view. You'll notice as you do so that it expands to fill your container view completely, which is really not what we want. While it's still selected, resize it so that it fills the top three-quarters or so of the available space, leaving a small margin above it and on both sides, as shown in Figure 5-15. Next, switch over to the Attributes Inspector and use the **Background** pop-up to pick some other background color. You can choose anything you like, as long as it's not white, so that the view stands out from the background. In the storyboard in the example source code archive, this view is green, so from now on we'll call it the green view.

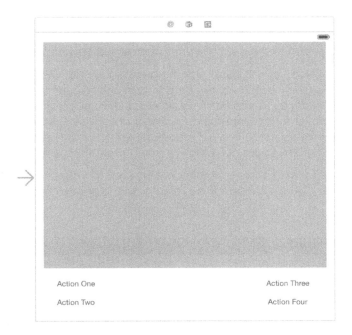

Figure 5-15. *The basic portrait layout for the Restructure view*

Drag a button from the Object Library and place it in the lower left of the empty space below the green view. Double-click to select the text in its label, and change it to *Action One*. Now Option-drag three copies of this button and place them in two columns, like those in Figure 5-15. You don't have to line them up perfectly because we're going to use constraints to finalize their positions, but you should try to place the two button groups approximately equal distances from their respective sides of the containing view. Change their titles to *Action Two*, *Action Three*, and *Action Four*. Finally, drag the lower edge of the green view downward until it's a little way above the top row of buttons. Use the blue guidelines to line everything up, as shown in Figure 5-15.

Now let's set up the Auto Layout constraints. Start by selecting the green view. We're going to start by pinning this to the top and to the left and right sides of the main view. That's still not enough to fully constrain it because its height isn't specified yet; we're going to fix that by anchoring it to the top of the buttons, once we've fixed the buttons themselves. Click the **Pin** button at the bottom right of the storyboard editor. At the top of the pop-up, you'll see the now familiar group of four input fields surrounding a small square. Leave the **Constrain to margins** check box checked. Click the red dashed lines above, to the left, and to the right of the small square to attach the view to the top, left, and right sides of its superview. Click **Add 3 Constraints**.

Next, hold down the **Shift** key and click to select both the **Action One** and **Action Two** buttons. Click the **Align** button, check **Horizontal Centers** in the pop-up, and then click **Add 1 Constraint**. This fixes these two buttons in a column. Repeat this procedure with the **Action Three** and **Action Four** buttons.

Select the **Action Two** button again and open the **Pin** pop-up. With **Constrain to margins** checked, select the red dashed lines to the left of, above, and below the square at the top of the pop-up, and then click **Add 3 Constraints**. These constraints fix this button in the lower-left corner of the main view and sets the vertical distance between it and the **Action One** button. The positions of both of these buttons are now fully specified. Now do something similar with the other column of buttons. Leaving **Constrain to margins** checked, select **Action Four**, and open the **Pin** pop-up. Select the dashed lines below, above, and to the right of the square, and then click **Add 3 Constraints**.

All that's left is to fix the position of the bottom of the green view relative to the buttons. To do that, Control-drag from the green view to the **Action One** button and release the mouse. In the pop-up, select **Vertical Spacing**. That's all the constraints we need. If there are any warnings in the Activity View, select the view controller in the Document Outline and choose **Editor ➤ Resolve Auto Layout Issues ➤ Update Frames** in the menu bar. If this doesn't work, or the layout isn't as it should be, go back over the preceding steps to figure out which of your constraints is wrong or missing.

Build and run the application in an iPhone simulator. If you got all your constraints right, you should see something like Figure 5-14. Now rotate the simulator to the right to see what happens to the layout (see Figure 5-16).

Figure 5-16. Rotating the Restructure application to landscape orientation. Not bad, but it could be better

That doesn't look too bad—the green view resized properly and we can see all of the views. This arrangement might work, but we can do better. There is a lot of white space at the bottom around the buttons. And the long, thin green view might not be so good if it were a UIImageView—either the image would be stretched, or it would be lost in the middle of the view, depending on the mode property of the UIImageView. How about the iPad? Try it out for yourself (see Figure 5-17).

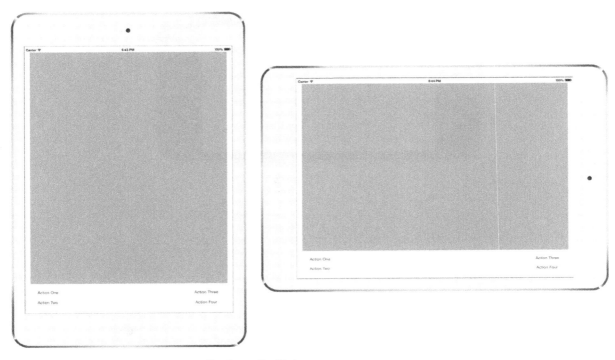

Figure 5-17. *Running the Restructure application on the iPad*

Once again, the layout adapts very well, but we still have the problem of the extra white space between the buttons. This is a perfect example of a layout that needs to be modified for different screen sizes (and therefore different orientations). We're actually going to create two extra variants of this layout—one that we'll use for the iPhone in landscape orientation and the other for the iPad. You can see what we're aiming for in Figure 5-18.

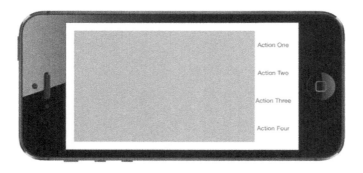

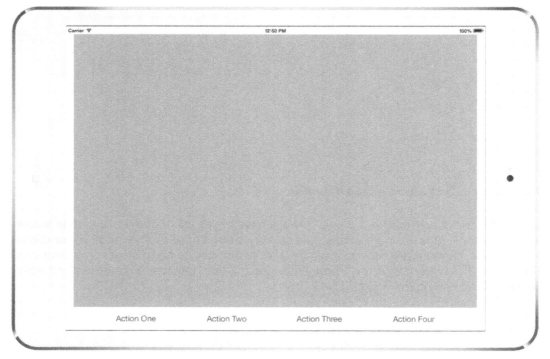

Figure 5-18. Modifying the Restructure application for the iPhone in landscape and for the iPad

To create these two different layouts, we need two more sets of constraints. We can do that while still using only one storyboard, thanks to a new feature in iOS 8 called *Size Classes*.

Size Classes

Take a look at the bottom of the storyboard editor. In the toolbar, you'll see a control that we haven't mentioned so far. It's called the Size Classes control and it looks like a label with the text "w**Any** h**Any**". Click this control and a pop-up containing a grid with nine cells will appear, as shown in Figure 5-19. We'll be using this control to help us create our two extra sets of constraints, but first we need to explain what size classes are all about.

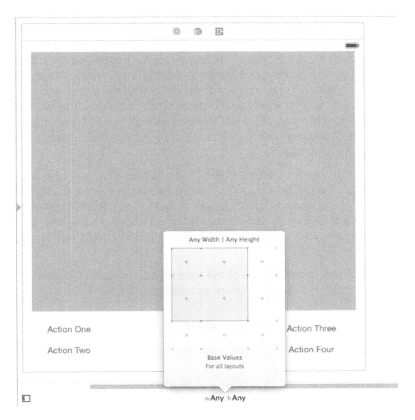

Figure 5-19. *The Size Classes control*

The cells in the grid correspond to different combinations of horizontal (width) and vertical (height) size classes. A **size class** is a loose classification of the width or the height of a device. There are two concrete size classes—*Compact* and *Regular*—that are used to describe real devices, and a third—*Any*—that can be used in the designer (and in code) as a wildcard, matching either Compact or Regular. Table 5-1 shows how the four possible combinations of concrete horizontal and vertical size classes map to devices and their orientations.

Table 5-1. *Mapping of size classes to device and orientation*

Width	Height	Device and Orientation
Compact	Compact	All iPhones (apart from iPhone 6 Plus) in landscape.
Compact	Regular	All iPhones in portrait.
Regular	Compact	iPhone 6 Plus in landscape.
Regular	Regular	All iPads in both landscape and portrait.

In general, Compact implies something smaller than Regular, but there are a couple of interesting points to note:

- In portrait, iPhones have compact width and regular height, which makes sense because the width is less than the height in this orientation. However, when rotated to landscape, the size class of both dimensions is compact, whereas you might have expected regular width and compact height. The exception to this is the larger iPhone 6 Plus, which does indeed have regular width and compact height. This illustrates that you need to consider both size classes when making layout decisions.

- iPads have regular width and height size classes in both landscape and portrait orientations. That means that you can't use size classes alone to determine the orientation of the iPad. In many cases, however, this won't matter; because the screen of the iPad is relatively large and much closer to square than that of an iPhone, you can often use the same layout in both portrait and landscape orientations.

Figure 5-20 shows a pictorial representation of the information in Table 5-1, which you may find useful to refer to while we modify the Restructure application.

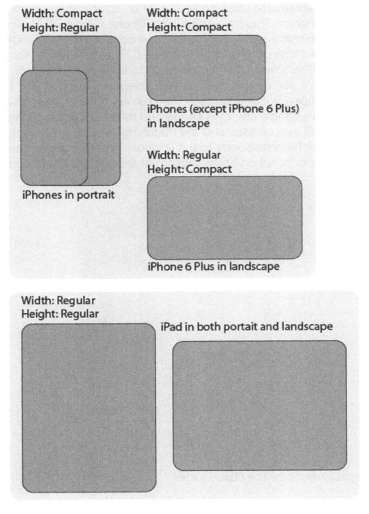

Figure 5-20. *A pictorial representation of size class combinations*

Size Classes and Storyboards

Now that you know what size classes are, let's return to the Restructure application. Look again at the Size Classes control in the storyboard editor. By default, it's set to w**Any** h**Any**. That means that the design in the storyboard editor applies to devices with any width and height size classes. We'll refer to this as the **base design**. You should always start out by creating the base design. Once you've done that, you can derive any other designs you need by modifying the base design. You can modify the design to suit a particular combination of size classes without affecting the base design by selecting that combination in the Size Classes control. We already know that we need two additional designs for the Restructure application—one for iPhones in landscape, the other for iPads. Let's start by creating the landscape iPhone design, which is shown at the top in Figure 5-18.

The first question to ask is: Which size class combination or combinations correspond to the layout that we're about to design? For all iPhones—apart from iPhone 6 Plus—that would be compact width, compact height, which translates to a Size Classes control setting of w**Compact**, h**Compact**. However, we want to use the same design for the iPhone 6 Plus, which maps to w**Regular**, h**Compact** instead. Putting those two together, we need to implement a design that works for any width and compact height. We can do that by using the pseudo size class *Any* for the width. Click the **Size Classes** control to open the pop-up, and then move your mouse over the squares in the grid. As you do so, the blue rectangle changes shape and the description changes to indicate the corresponding combination of size classes and the matching devices and orientations. We need to select w**Any**, h**Compact**, which corresponds to the leftmost two squares on the top row of the grid, as shown in Figure 5-21. The description at the bottom of the pop-up confirms that we have the correct selection.

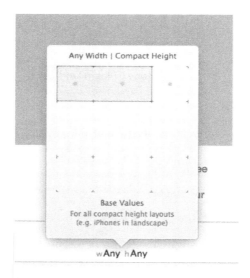

Figure 5-21. Selecting wAny, hCompact in the Size Classes control

To actually make the selection, click the rightmost blue square in the grid. You'll see that the Size Classes control updates and the toolbar changes color to indicate that you are no longer editing the base design. The shape of the view controller area in the storyboard also changes to look more like a landscape iPhone, as shown in Figure 5-22.

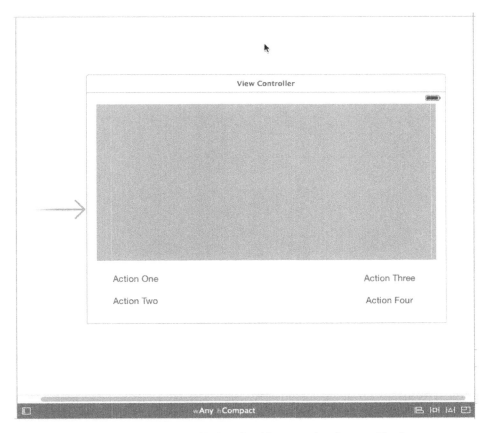

Figure 5-22. *The storyboard editor updated to work with the wAny, hCompact size class combination*

There are three things that you can do to modify the design for any given combination of size classes. The changes that you make apply only to devices and orientations that map to the current size class combination:

- You can add, remove, or modify constraints.

- You can add or remove views.

- You can change the font of some of the UIKit controls (in iOS 8, UILabel, UITextField, UITextView, and UIButton support this).

The design that we're working with is so different from the base design that we'll need to remove all of the existing constraints, since all of the views need to change position. Before we make any changes, with the storyboard selected, open the Assistant Editor and select **Preview** in the jump bar, and then open a preview of the storyboard, showing the iPhone in portrait orientation. We'll use this preview to make sure that the changes that we are about to make don't affect the base design.

Creating the iPhone Landscape Layout

Let's start making changes. In the storyboard, resize the green view so that it's positioned on the left side of the main view, leaving room for the column of four buttons that we're going to build on the right (see Figure 5-23).

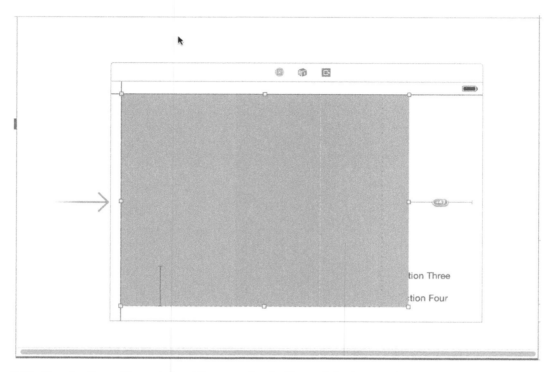

Figure 5-23. *Changing the position and size of the green view for iPhones in landscape orientation*

Next, we need to move the four buttons into place. As things stand now, you might find it difficult to drag the two buttons on the left, because they may be covered by the green view. So let's first get the green view out of the way by temporarily resizing it again. Drag the bottom of the green view upward until you can see all of the buttons, and then drag the **Action One** and **Action Two** buttons over to the empty area on the right, without worrying too much about exact placement for the moment. Once you've done that, select the green view again and drag it back to the location shown in Figure 5-23. Once again, check the Preview Assistant to make sure that the portrait design is unaffected. You should make it a habit to do this every time you make a change, so that you can quickly fix anything that goes wrong.

> **Warning**   If something does go wrong, don't attempt to fix it by making more changes—instead, use ⌘Z to undo as many steps as necessary to get back to an earlier version of the layout that was correct, and then try again.

Currently, the green view and the buttons all have constraints that link them to each other and to the sides of the main view. We need to replace all of these constraints with new ones. You might be tempted to do this by selecting them in the Document Outline and deleting them, but that would be a mistake—deleting constraints removes them from the design for *all* size class combinations. Instead of deleting them, you need to *uninstall* them for the size class combination that you're editing.

Select the **Action One** button in the storyboard and open the Size Inspector, where you'll find the three constraints that currently apply to this button (see the left of Figure 5-24).

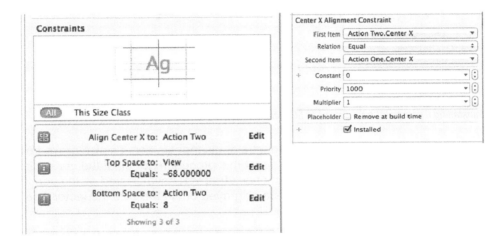

Figure 5-24. Viewing a constraint in the Size Inspector

Double-click the top constraint to show the details (see the right of Figure 5-24). At the bottom, you'll see an Installed check box that's currently checked. We need to uninstall the constraint for this design. To do that, press the **+** button to the left of the check box and select **Any Width | Compact Height** in the pop-up that appears. This adds a new check box that applies to the w**Any** h**Compact** layout only. Clear this check box to uninstall the constraint for this combination of size classes while leaving it installed for the base design, as shown on the left of Figure 5-25.

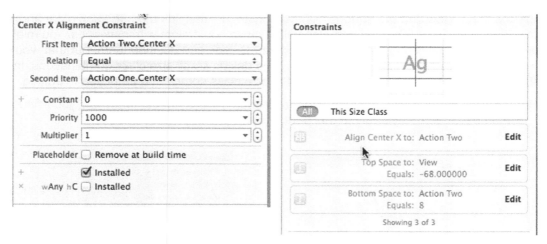

Figure 5-25. *Uninstalling a constraint from the wAny hCompact layout*

Back in the storyboard, you'll notice that the constraint disappears and it's also grayed out in the Document Outline and in the Size Inspector. Repeat this procedure for all of the constraints attached to the four buttons and the green view. You can check that you have cleared all the constraints by selecting each button and checking that they are all grayed out in the Size Inspector (see the right of Figure 5-25).

Now let's add the constraints that we need for the new design, starting with the green view. We need to pin this view to the top, left, right, and bottom edges of the main view. To do that, select the green view in the Document Outline (it's the one that has the same level of nesting as the Action buttons) and click the **Pin** button. In the pop-up menu, uncheck **Constrain to margins**, and then click the dashed red lines above, below, and to the left of the square, but do not click the line to the right. In the input fields above, below, and to the left of the square, enter **20** and then click **Add 3 Constraints** (see Figure 5-26).

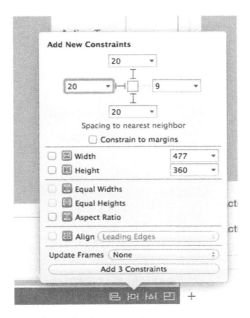

Figure 5-26. *Fixing the position of the green view in landscape mode*

To fix the right side of the green view, Control-drag from its center to the right until the main view's background turns blue. Release the mouse and click **Trailing Space to Container Margin**.

Next, we need to arrange the four buttons in a column, so drag them into roughly the layout that we need (refer back to Figure 5-18 if necessary). At this point, we can't make the buttons line up exactly in the storyboard because we don't have all the constraints that we need, so continue to ignore all of the Auto Layout warnings for now. Your layout should now look like Figure 5-27.

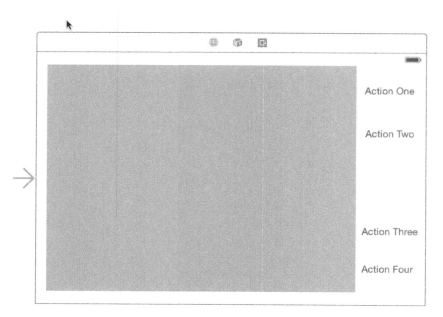

Figure 5-27. The buttons in a column to the right of the green content view

We now need to position the buttons vertically and horizontally. We'd like the buttons to be horizontally centered in their column and to be equally spaced vertically. There's no easy way to do that by applying constraints to the buttons using Interface Builder, since there's no way to say something like "make this vertical gap between these two buttons the same height as the gaps between the other buttons," which is what we really need. However, we *can* constrain views to be of equal height—and that gives us a way to get what we need. We're going to add hidden filler views in the gaps between the buttons, and force those hidden views to take up all of the available space and to be of equal heights. That's the same as making the gaps all the same size. We can use the same hidden views to center the buttons horizontally as well. We'll make the hidden views occupy all the horizontal space in the button column, and then we'll make their centers and the centers of the buttons align along the same vertical line. If you don't have the plan clear in your mind, take a sneak peek at Figure 5-28, where the filler views are shown in gray. Neat, huh?

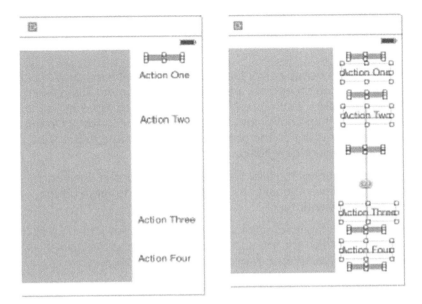

Figure 5-28. Adding filler views to the button column

Let's get started. I suggest you make a copy of your project at this point so that you can revert to it if things don't work out as you follow the instructions in the next few paragraphs. Although what we're doing is quite simple, there are a lot of steps and it's easy to go wrong.

Let's first create the filler views. Grab a UIView from the Object Library and drop it on top of the green view. Resize it so that it's small enough to fit into the gaps between the buttons, both horizontally and vertically. Its height should be no more than 10 pixels. Use the Attributes Inspector to give it a gray background so that we can see it more easily. Now drag and resize this view so that it fits between the top of the Action One button and the bottom of the status bar, as shown on the left of Figure 5-28. Make sure that the top of this view is below the top of the green view and that the bottom is above the top of the Action One button. *There must be no overlap at all*. Select the **Action One** button so that you can see its outline to make sure of this. Another way to check this is to make the bounds rectangles of every view visible by selecting **Editor ➤ Canvas ➤ Show Bounds Rectangles**. This setting is a toggle, so select it again to switch it off when you have finished.

With the filler view selected, hold down the **Option** (⌥) key and drag downward to create another copy. Place it between the Action One and Action Two buttons, again with no overlap. Repeat the process until you have a filler view between every pair of buttons, and between the bottom button and the bottom of the main view, as shown on the right in Figure 5-28. As before, make sure there is no vertical overlap between each filler view and the buttons above and below it, selecting each button in turn (or enabling **Editor ➤ Canvas ➤ Show Bounds Rectangles** again) and inspecting its frame outline to make sure.

Note   The filler views that you just added will appear only on the iPhone in landscape mode because we added them while designing for the w**Any** h**Compact** combination.

Select all of the filler views and click the **Pin** button. In the pop-up, check **Equal Widths** and **Equal Heights,** and then click **Add 8 Constraints**. The fillers will now all be the same height and width at runtime.

Next, let's make the filler views occupy all of the available horizontal space. We only need to make one of them do that, since all the other ones are constrained to be the same width. Select the top filter view and click the **Pin** button. In the pop-up, click the dashed red lines to the left and right of the square. Enter **0** in the left and right input fields, and then click **Add 2 Constraints**. These constraints force the filler view to link to the green view on its left and to the right margin of the main view on its right, thereby spanning the whole column.

We also need to align the centers of the filler views and the buttons in one vertical line. That's easy to do: just select all of the filler views and all of the buttons, press the **Align** button, check **Horizontal Centers**, and click **Add 8 Constraints**.

We are almost done. The final step is to make sure that the filler views take up all the vertical space between the buttons, and between the top and bottom buttons and the main view. We do that by forcing the vertical spacing between each pair of these views to be zero.

Select all of the filler views and click the **Pin** button. In the pop-up, clear the **Constrain to margins** check box. Click the red dashed lines above and below the square. Enter **0** in the input fields above and below the square, and then click **Add 10 Constraints**.

Now we can finally see the results of all this work. In the Document Outline, click the view controller and choose **Editor ➤ Resolve Auto Layout Issues ➤ Update Frames**. You should see the result shown in Figure 5-29. If you don't get the correct result, revert to the saved copy of your project and try again. If you see that the filler views overlap vertically, you probably haven't properly separated them from the buttons.

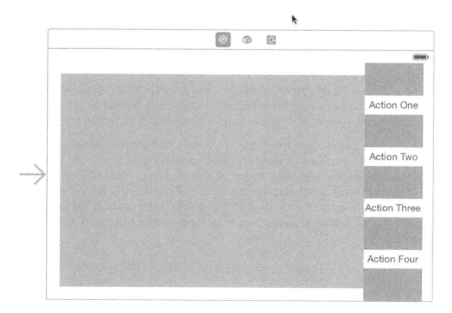

Figure 5-29. *The iPhone landscape layout, including the filler views*

To finish this layout, select each of the filler views in turn and check the **Hidden** property in the Attributes Inspector, and then run the example in the iPhone simulator to verify that the layout is correct in both portrait and landscape modes, and that it also works for the iPhone 6 Plus. You can see what it is supposed to look like in Figure 5-18.

Next, we're going to add the iPad layout, but before we do so, now would be a good time to make another backup copy of your project, in case you need to revert while following the next set of instructions.

Adding the iPad Layout

To add the iPad layout to the storyboard, we need to switch the editor to the correct combination of size classes. Click the **Size Classes** control and click in the bottom-right corner of the grid to select **Regular Width | Regular Height**. The view controller in the editing area should switch to a square outline. Before we make any changes, in the Assistant Editor, use the jump bar to open a preview of the storyboard (if it's not already open) and add another iPhone four-inch preview, this time in landscape mode. We'll use this and the existing portrait preview to make sure that our changes for iPad do not affect the iPhone layouts.

The constraints for our new layout are inherited from the base design. As was the case when we constructed the iPhone landscape layout, we need to delete all of the inherited constraints. It's not always necessary to do this—sometimes you can keep some or even all of the constraints from the base design. In this case, though, it's easier to see what we're doing if we remove them. To do this, proceed as you did before: open the Size Inspector and then select each of the enable constraints in the Document Outline in turn. For each constraint, add a new entry in the Size Inspector for **Regular Width | Regular Height** (wR hR), marking it as not installed. You don't need to make any changes to the constraints that are grayed out because those belong to the iPhone landscape design, and therefore do not apply to this layout.

Next, we'll pin the top, left, and right sides of the green view in their correct positions. We won't fix the bottom of the view yet because we're going to move it downward shortly. Select the green view and click the **Pin** button. At the top of the pop-up, click the dashed red lines above, to the left, and to the right of the square, and then click **Add 3 Constraints**.

For the iPad, we're going to arrange the four buttons in a single row underneath the green view, and because there's more space available, we'll make the button text larger. Let's do that now before we start moving things around.

Select the **Action One** button, open the Attributes Inspector, and locate the **Font** property. Any changes you make to the font will apply to all size classes, which is not what we want. To make a change for the current design only, click the **+** button to the left of the **Font** field and select **Regular Width | Regular Height** from the pop-up to add a new Font field labeled w**R** h**R** (see Figure 5-30). Click the **T** in the **Font** field and change the font size from *15* to *20*.

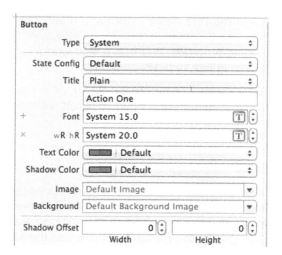

Figure 5-30. *Changing the font of a button for iPad only*

Apply the same change to the other three buttons. Since we are making this font change while designing for the size class combination w**R** h**R**, it applies only to iPads. Check the iPhone previews to see that this is the case.

Next, drag the four buttons to make a single row at the bottom of the main view, aligning the bottom edges of the buttons with the bottom blue layout guide, and resize each button so that you can see all of its text. Make sure that there is plenty of empty space to the left and right of each button. You don't need to be too exact with this because Auto Layout will ensure that the buttons are properly sized at runtime. When you've done that, drag down the bottom of the green view so that it's close to the tops of the buttons, as shown in Figure 5-31.

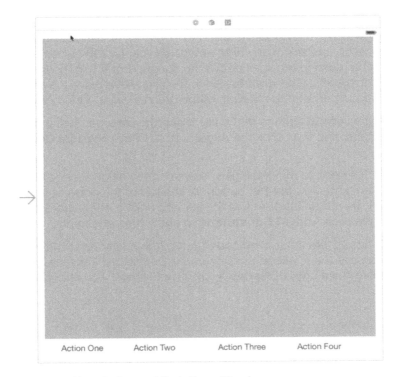

Figure 5-31. *The buttons arranged in a single row at the bottom of the view*

Now we can add a constraint to fix the bottom of the green view. Control-drag from the green view downward until the background of the main view turns blue, and then release the mouse and select **Bottom Space to Bottom Layout Guide**. The green view is now in its final position.

The next step is to add the constraints that will position the buttons. This is really the same problem as the one we solved when creating the iPhone landscape layout—we want the buttons to be equally spaced along the row. The only difference is the orientation. We're going to use the same solution again: create filler views and add constraints that give them equal sizes. Start by dragging a UIView onto the green view. Use the Attributes Inspector to give it a gray background and resize it so that it's small enough to fit into any of the gaps between the buttons, and then drag it so that it's between the left side of the view and the Action One button, with no overlap. With the filler view selected, hold down the **Option** (⌥) key and drag to create another four filler views, placing one between each pair of buttons and one between the rightmost button and the right side of the main view, as shown in Figure 5-32. As before, select each button in turn to make sure there is overlap between the button frames (which are larger than the area occupied by the text) and the filler views.

Figure 5-32. *The filler views for the iPad layout. The buttons are selected to ensure that there is no overlap between the filler views and the buttons*

To make all of the filler views the same size, select all of them and click the **Pin** button. And then in the pop-up, click **Equal Widths** and **Equal Heights**, followed by **Add 8 Constraints**. To make them all fill the available vertical space, select any filler view and click the **Pin** button again. At the top of the content menu, click the dashed red lines above the square. Enter **0** in the input fields at the top and bottom, and then click **Add 2 Constraints**. Since the filler views have the same height, they will now all fill the vertical space between the bottom of the green view and the bottom of the main view.

Next, we need to align the vertical centers of the fillers and the buttons. Select all of the filler views and all of the buttons, and then click the **Align** button. Check **Vertical Centers** and **Add 8 Constraints**.

To complete the layout, we need to make the filler views occupy all of the free horizontal space. This time, select all of the fillers and click the **Pin** button. At the top of the pop-up, uncheck **Constrain to margins**, and then click the red dashed lines to the left and right of the square. Enter **0** in the left and right input fields, and then click **Add 10 Constraints** to apply the constraints.

With all the constraints added, we can have Xcode update the positions of the all of the views in the layout so that we can see the result. In the Document Outline, click the view controller, and then choose **Editor ➤ Resolve Auto Layout Issues ➤ Update Frames**. You should see the result shown in Figure 5-33.

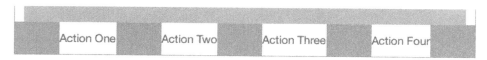

Figure 5-33. The four buttons equally spaced below the green view in the iPad layout

To finish up, select all of the filler views again, open the Attributes Inspector, and make sure that the **Hidden** property is checked. Run the application on the iPad simulator and verify that you get the correct result in both portrait and landscape orientations (see Figure 5-18). Rerun the application on the iPhone simulator to check that those layouts still work too.

Rotating Out of Here

In this chapter, you learned how to support rotation in your applications. You discovered how to use constraints to define view layout and you also saw how to restructure your views by creating multiple layouts in the storyboard to handle different screen sizes and device rotation.

In the next chapter, we're going to start looking at true multiview applications. Every application we've written so far has used a single view controller and a single content view. A lot of complex iOS applications, such as Mail and Contacts, are made possible only by the use of multiple views and view controllers, and we're going to look at exactly how that works in Chapter 6.

Multiview Applications

Up until this point, we've written applications with a single view controller. While there certainly is a lot you can do with a single view, the real power of the iOS platform emerges when you can switch out views based on user input. Multiview applications come in several different flavors, but the underlying mechanism is the same, regardless of how the app may appear on the screen.

In this chapter, we're going to focus on the structure of multiview applications and the basics of swapping content views by building our own multiview application from scratch. We will write our own custom controller class that switches between two different content views, establishing a strong foundation for taking advantage of the various multiview controllers that Apple provides.

But before we start building our application, let's see how multiple-view applications can be useful.

Common Types of Multiview Apps

Strictly speaking, we have worked with multiple views in our previous applications, since buttons, labels, and other controls are all subclasses of UIView and they can all go into the view hierarchy. But when Apple uses the term **view** in documentation, it is generally referring to a UIView or one of its subclasses that has a corresponding view controller. These types of views are also sometimes referred to as **content views** because they are the primary container for the content of your application.

The simplest example of a multiview application is a **utility application**. A utility application focuses primarily on a single view, but offers a second view that can be used to configure the application or to provide more detail than the primary view. The Stocks application that ships with iPhone is a good example (see Figure 6-1). If you click the button in the lower-right corner, the view transitions to a configuration view that lets you configure the list of stocks tracked by the application.

Figure 6-1. *The Stocks application that ships with iPhone has two views: one to display the data and another to configure the stock list*

There are also several **tab bar applications** that ship with the iPhone, including the Phone application (see Figure 6-2) and the Clock application. A tab bar application is a multiview application that displays a row of buttons, called the **tab bar**, at the bottom of the screen. Tapping one of the buttons causes a new view controller to become active and a new view to be shown. In the Phone application, for example, tapping **Contacts** shows a different view than the one shown when you tap **Keypad**.

Figure 6-2. *The Phone application is an example of a multiview application using a tab bar*

Another common kind of multiview iPhone application is the **navigation-based application**, which features a navigation controller that uses a **navigation bar** to control a hierarchical series of views. The Settings application is a good example. In Settings, the first view you get is a series of rows, each row corresponding to a cluster of settings or a specific app. Touching one of those rows takes you to a new view where you can customize one particular set of settings. Some views present a list that allows you to dive even deeper. The navigation controller keeps track of how deep you go and gives you a control to let you make your way back to the previous view.

For example, if you select the **Sounds** preference, you'll be presented a view with a list of sound-related options. At the top of that view is a navigation bar with a left arrow labeled **Settings** that takes you back to the previous view if you tap it. Within the sound options is a row labeled **Ringtone**. Tap **Ringtone**, and you're taken to a new view featuring a list of ringtones and a navigation bar that takes you back to the main Sounds preference view (see Figure 6-3). A navigation-based application is useful when you want to present a hierarchy of views.

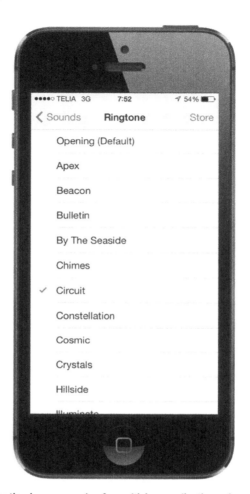

Figure 6-3. The iPhone Settings application is an example of a multiview application using a navigation bar

On the iPad, most navigation-based applications, such as Mail, are implemented using a **split view**, where the navigation elements appear on the left side of the screen, and the item you select to view or edit appears on the right. You'll learn more about split views in Chapter 11.

Because views are themselves hierarchical in nature, it's even possible to combine different mechanisms for swapping views within a single application. For example, the iPhone's Music application uses a tab bar to switch between different methods of organizing your music, and a navigation controller and its associated navigation bar to allow you to browse your music based on that selection. In Figure 6-4, the tab bar is at the bottom of the screen and the navigation bar is at the top of the screen.

Figure 6-4. *The Music application uses both a navigation bar and a tab bar*

Some applications use a **toolbar**, which is often confused with a tab bar. A tab bar is used for selecting one and only one option from among two or more options. A toolbar can hold buttons and certain other controls, but those items are not mutually exclusive. A perfect example of a toolbar is at the bottom of the main Safari view (see Figure 6-5). If you compare the toolbar at the bottom of the Safari view with the tab bar at the bottom of the Phone or Music application, you'll find the two pretty easy to tell apart. The tab bar has multiple segments, exactly one of which (the selected one) is highlighted with a tint color; but on a toolbar, normally every enabled button is highlighted.

Figure 6-5. Mobile Safari features a toolbar at the bottom. The toolbar is like a free-form bar that allows you to include a variety of controls

Each of these multiview application types uses a specific controller class from the UIKit. Tab bar interfaces are implemented using the class `UITabBarController` and navigation interfaces are implemented using `UINavigationController`. We'll describe their use in detail in the next few chapters.

The Architecture of a Multiview Application

The application we're going to build in this chapter, View Switcher, is fairly simple in appearance; however, in terms of the code we're going to write, it's by far the most complex application we've yet tackled. View Switcher will consist of three different controllers, a storyboard, and an application delegate.

When first launched, View Switcher will look like Figure 6-6, with a toolbar at the bottom containing a single button. The rest of the view will contain a blue background and a button yearning to be pressed.

Figure 6-6. *When you first launch the View Switcher application, you'll see a blue view with a button and a toolbar with its own button*

When the **Switch Views** button is pressed, the background will turn yellow and the button's title will change (see Figure 6-7).

Figure 6-7. *When you press the Switch Views button, the blue view flips over to reveal the yellow view*

If either the **Press Me** or **Press Me, Too** button is pressed, an alert will pop up indicating which view's button was pressed (see Figure 6-8).

Figure 6-8. When the Press Me or Press Me, Too button is pressed, an alert is displayed

Although we could achieve this same functionality by writing a single-view application, we're taking this more complex approach to demonstrate the mechanics of a multiview application. There are actually three view controllers interacting in this simple application: one that controls the blue view, one that controls the yellow view, and a third special controller that swaps the other two in and out when the **Switch Views** button is pressed.

Before we start building our application, let's talk about the way iPhone multiview applications are put together. Most multiview applications use the same basic pattern.

The Root Controller

The storyboard is a key player here since it will contain all the views and view controllers for our application. We're going to create a storyboard with an instance of a controller class that is responsible for managing which other view is currently being shown to the user. We call this controller the **root controller** (as in "the root of the tree" or "the root of all evil") because it is the first controller the user sees and the controller that is loaded when the application loads. This root controller is often an instance of UINavigationController or UITabBarController, although it can also be a custom subclass of UIViewController.

In a multiview application, the job of the root controller is to take two or more other views and present them to the user as appropriate, based on the user's input. A tab bar controller, for example, will swap in different views and view controllers based on which tab bar item was last tapped. A navigation controller will do the same thing as the user drills down and backs up through hierarchical data.

> **Note**   The root controller is the primary view controller for the application; and, as such, it is the view that specifies whether it is OK to automatically rotate to a new orientation. However, the root controller can pass responsibility for tasks like that to the currently active controller.

In multiview applications, most of the screen will be taken up by a content view, and each content view will have its own view controller with its own outlets and actions. In a tab bar application, for example, taps on the tab bar will go to the tab bar controller, but taps anywhere else on the screen will go to the controller that corresponds to the content view currently being displayed.

Anatomy of a Content View

In a multiview application, each view controller controls a content view, and these content views are where the bulk of your application's user interface is built. Taken together, each of these pairings is called a **scene** within a storyboard. Each scene consists of a view controller and a content view, which may be an instance of UIView or one of its subclasses. Unless you are doing something really unusual, your content view will always have an associated view controller and will sometimes subclass UIView. Although you can create your interface in code rather than using Interface Builder, few people choose that route because it is more time-consuming and the code is difficult to maintain.

In this project, we'll be creating a new controller class for each content view. Our root controller controls a content view that consists of a toolbar that occupies the bottom of the screen. The root controller then loads a blue view controller, placing the blue content view as a subview to the root controller view. When the root controller's **Switch Views** button (the button is in the toolbar) is pressed, the root controller swaps out the blue view controller and swaps in a yellow view controller, instantiating that controller if it needs to do so. Confused? If so, don't worry because this will become clearer as we walk through the code.

Building View Switcher

Enough theory! Let's go ahead and build our project. Select **File ➤ New ➤ Project...** or press ⇧⌘N. When the template selection sheet opens, select **Single View Application** and then click **Next**. On the next page of the assistant, enter **View Switcher** as the **Product Name**, set the **Language** to *Objective-C* and the **Devices** pop-up button to *Universal*. Also make sure the check box labeled **Use Core Data** is unchecked. When everything is set up correctly, click **Next** to continue. On the next screen, navigate to wherever you're saving your projects on disk and click the **Create** button to create a new project directory.

Renaming the View Controller

As you've already seen, the Single View Application template supplies an application delegate, a view controller, and a storyboard. The view controller class is called `ViewController`. In this application, we are going to be dealing with three view controllers, but most of the logic will be in the main view controller. Its task will be to switch the display so that the view from one of the other view controllers is showing at all times. To make the role of the main view controller clear, we'd like to give it a better name, such as `SwitchingViewController`. There are several places in the project where the view controller's class name is referenced. To change its name, we need to update all of those places. Fortunately, Xcode has a nifty feature that will do that for us. In the Project Navigator, select *ViewController.h*, and then double-click the class name after `@interface` in the editor area to select it and right-click it. In the menu that appears, select **Refactor** and then **Rename...** (see Figure 6-9).

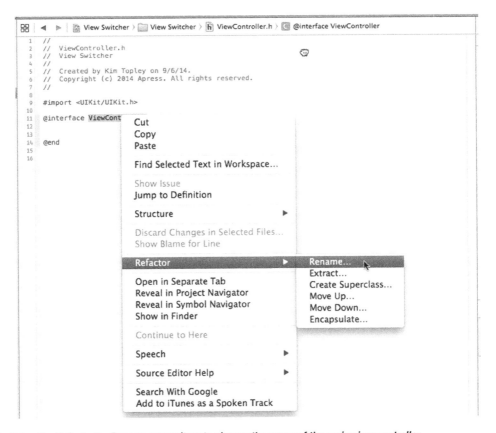

Figure 6-9. Using the Refactor ➤ Rename menu item to change the name of the main view controller

In the dialog that appears, make sure that **Rename related files** is checked and change the view controller name to SwitchingViewController, as shown in Figure 6-10.

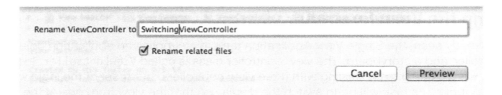

Figure 6-10. *Renaming the view controller*

Press **Preview** and Xcode opens a new window showing all of the places where it needs to change the view controller's name (see Figure 6-11).

Figure 6-11. *Previewing the changes that Xcode will make to change the name of the view controller*

Press **Save** to continue with the rename operation. Xcode will prompt you to enable automatic snapshots. Doing so is a good idea, because if you decide later that you don't want to go through with the change, you can easily revert it. Press **Enable** and Xcode will complete the rename. When it's done, you should see that the name of the view controller has changed in the Project Navigator and the content of the file in the editor area has also changed, as shown in Figure 6-12.

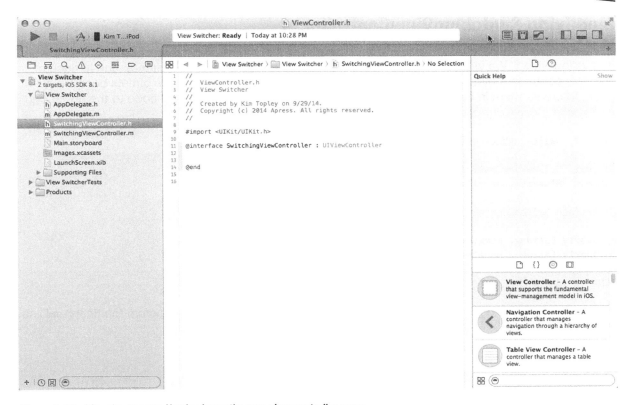

Figure 6-12. After the rename, Xcode shows the new view controller name

> **Tip**   You can create a snapshot at any time by selecting Create Snapshot… from Xcode's File menu. Once you have a snapshot, you can revert your workspace by using **File ➤ Restore Snapshot…**. Xcode will show a list of the snapshots from which you can choose the one to be used for the restore.

Adding the Content View Controllers

We'll need two additional view controllers to display the content views. In the Project Navigator, right-click the **View Switcher** group and select **New File…**. In the template dialog, choose **Cocoa Touch Class** from the **iOS Source** section and press **Next**. Name the new class *BlueViewController*, make it a subclass of UIViewController, and make sure that the **Also create XIB file** check box is not checked, since we are going to add this controller to the storyboard a little later. Press **Next** and then press **Create** to save the files for the new view controller. Repeat this process to create the second content view controller, giving it the name YellowViewController.

Modifying SwitchingViewController.m

The SwitchingViewController class will need an action method that will toggle between the blue and yellow views. We won't create any outlets, but we will need two other pointers: one to each of the view controllers that we'll be swapping in and out. These don't need to be outlets because we're going to create them in code rather than in the storyboard. Add the following code to the upper part of *SwitchingViewController.m*:

```
#import "SwitchingViewController.h"

#import "YellowViewController.h"
#import "BlueViewController.h"

@interface SwitchingViewController ()

@property (strong, nonatomic) YellowViewController *yellowViewController;
@property (strong, nonatomic) BlueViewController *blueViewController;

@end
```

Next, add the following empty action method toward the end of the file, just before the final @end line:

```
- (IBAction)switchViews:(id)sender {

}

@end
```

In the past, we've added action methods directly within Interface Builder, but here you'll see that we can work the other way around just as well, since IB can see what outlets and actions are already defined in our source code. Now that we've declared the action we need, we can set up the minimal user interface for this controller in our storyboard.

Building a View with a Toolbar

We now need to set up the view for SwitchingViewController. As a reminder, this view controller will be our root view controller—the controller that is in play when our application is launched. SwitchingViewController's content view will consist of a toolbar that occupies the bottom of the screen. Its job is to switch between the blue view and the yellow view, so it will need a way for the user to change the views. For that, we're going to use a toolbar with a button. Let's build the toolbar view now.

In the Project Navigator, select *Main.storyboard*. In the IB editor view, you'll see our switching view controller. As you can see in Figure 6-13, it's currently empty and quite dull. This is where we'll start building our GUI.

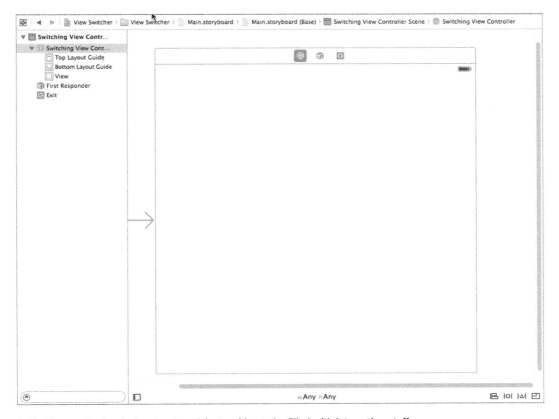

Figure 6-13. The empty view in the storyboard, just waiting to be filled with interesting stuff

Now, let's add a toolbar to the bottom of the view. Grab a **Toolbar** from the library, drag it onto your view, and place it at the bottom so that it looks like Figure 6-14.

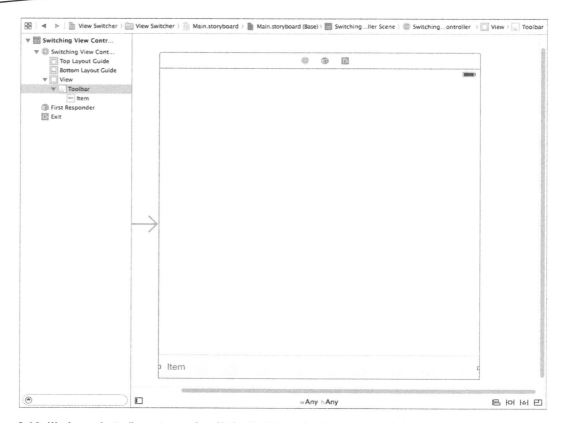

Figure 6-14. We dragged a toolbar onto our view. Notice that the toolbar features a single button, labeled Item

We want to keep this toolbar stretched across the bottom of the content view no matter what size the view has. To do that, we need to add three layout constraints—one that pins the toolbar to the bottom of the view and another two that pin it to the view's left and right sides. To do this, select the toolbar in the Document Outline, click the **Pin** button on the toolbar beneath the storyboard, and change the values in the pop-up, as shown in Figure 6-15.

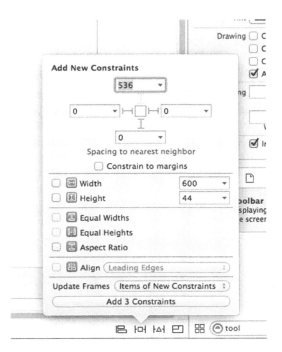

Figure 6-15. *Pinning the toolbar to the bottom of the content view*

Start by unchecking the **Constrain to margins** check box, because we want to position the toolbar relative to the edges of the content view, not the blue guidelines that appear near its edges. Next, set the distances to the nearest left, right, and bottom neighbors to zero (if you have correctly positioned the toolbar, they should already be zero). In this case, the nearest neighbor of the toolbar is the content view. You can see this by clicking the small arrow in one of the distance boxes: it opens a pop-up that shows the nearest neighbor and any other neighbors relative to which you could place the toolbar—in this case, there are none. To indicate that these distance constraints should be active, click the three dashed red lines that link the distance boxes to the small square in the center, so that they become solid lines. Finally, change **Update Frames** to *Items of New Constraints* (so that the toolbar's representation in the storyboard moves to its new constrained location) and click **Add 3 Constraints**.

Now, to make sure you're on the right track, click the **Run** button to make this app launch in the iOS simulator. You should see a plain white app start up, with a pale gray toolbar at the bottom containing a lone button. If not, go back and retrace your steps to see what you missed. Rotate the simulator and verify that the toolbar stays fixed at the bottom of the view and stretched right across the screen. If this doesn't happen, you need to fix the constraints that you just applied to the toolbar.

Linking the Toolbar Button to the View Controller

The toolbar has a single button. We'll use that button to let the user switch between the different content views. Double-click the button in the storyboard and change its title to *Switch Views*. Press the **Return** key to commit your change.

Now we can link the toolbar button to our action method in SwitchingViewController. Before doing that, though, you should be aware that toolbar buttons aren't like other iOS controls. They support only a single target action, and they trigger that action only at one well-defined moment—the equivalent of a touch up inside event on other iOS controls.

Selecting a toolbar button in Interface Builder can be tricky. The easiest way to do it is to expand the **Switching View Controller** icon in the Document Outline until you can see the button, which is now labeled **Switch Views**, and then click it. Once you have the **Switch Views** button selected, Control-drag from it over to the yellow **Switching View Controller** icon at the top of the scene, as shown in Figure 6-16. Release the mouse and select the **switchViews:** action from the pop-up. If the *switchViews:* action doesn't appear, and instead you see an outlet called *delegate*, you've most likely Control-dragged from the toolbar rather than the button. To fix it, just make sure you have the button rather than the toolbar selected, and then redo your Control-drag.

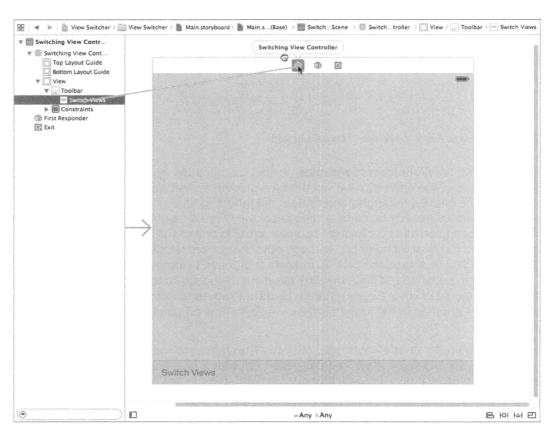

Figure 6-16. Linking the toolbar button to the switchViews: method in the view controller class

We have one more thing to point out in this scene, which is SwitchingViewController's view outlet. This outlet is already connected to the view in the scene. The view outlet is inherited from the parent class, UIViewController, and gives the controller access to the view it controls. When we created the project, Xcode created both the controller and its view, and hooked them up for us. Nice.

That's all we need to do here, so save your work. Next, let's get started implementing SwitchingViewController.

Writing the Root View Controller

It's time to write our root view controller. Its job is to switch between the blue view and the yellow view whenever the user clicks the **Switch Views** button. In the Project Navigator, select *SwitchingViewController.m* and modify the viewDidLoad method to set some things up by adding the lines shown here in bold:

```
- (void)viewDidLoad {
    [super viewDidLoad];
    // Do any additional setup after loading the view, typically from a nib.

    self.blueViewController = [self.storyboard
                                 instantiateViewControllerWithIdentifier:
                                 @"Blue"];

    self.blueViewController.view.frame = self.view.frame;
    [self switchViewFromViewController:nil
            toViewController:self.blueViewController];

}
```

Our implementation of viewDidLoad overrides a UIViewController method that is called when the storyboard is loaded. How could we tell? Hold down the ⌥ key (the **Option** key) and single-click the method named viewDidLoad. A documentation pop-up window will appear (see Figure 6-17). Alternatively, you can select **View ➤ Utilities ➤ Show Quick Help Inspector** to view similar information in the Quick Help panel. viewDidLoad is defined in our superclass, UIViewController, and is intended to be overridden by classes that need to be notified when the view has finished loading.

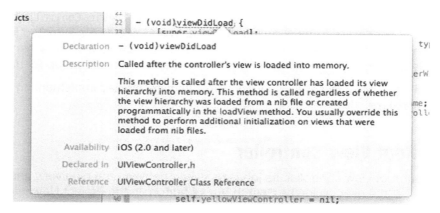

Figure 6-17. This documentation window appears when you option-click the viewDidLoad method name

This version of viewDidLoad creates an instance of BlueViewController. We use the instantiateViewControllerWithIdentifier: method to load the BlueViewController instance from the same storyboard that contains our root view controller. To access a particular view controller from a storyboard, we use a string as an identifier—in this case "Blue" —which we'll set up when we configure our storyboard a little more. Once the BlueViewController is created, we assign this new instance to our blueViewController property:

```
self.blueViewController = [self.storyboard
        instantiateViewControllerWithIdentifier:
        @"Blue"];
```

Next, we set the frame of the blue view controller's view to be the same as that of the switch view controller's content view, and switch to the blue view controller so that its view appears on the screen:

```
self.blueViewController.view.frame = self.view.frame;
[self switchViewFromViewController:nil
        toViewController:self.blueViewController];
```

Since we need to perform a view controller switch in several places, the code to do this is in the helper method switchFromViewController:toViewController: that we'll see shortly.

Now, why didn't we load the yellow view controller here also? We're going to need to load it at some point, so why not do it now? Good question. The answer is that the user may never tap the **Switch Views** button. The user might just use the view that's visible when the application launches, and then quit. In that case, why use resources to load the yellow view and its controller?

Instead, we'll load the yellow view the first time we actually need it. This is called **lazy loading**, and it's a standard way of keeping memory overhead down. The actual loading of the yellow view happens in the switchViews: method. Fill in the stub of this method that you created earlier by adding the cold shown in bold:

```
- (IBAction)switchViews:(id)sender {
    // Create the new view controller, if required.
    if (!self.yellowViewController.view.superview) {
        if (!self.yellowViewController) {
            self.yellowViewController = [self.storyboard
                instantiateViewControllerWithIdentifier:@"Yellow"];
        }
    } else {
        if (!self.blueViewController) {
            self.blueViewController = [self.storyboard
                instantiateViewControllerWithIdentifier:@"Blue"];
        }
    }

    // Switch view controllers.
    if (!self.yellowViewController.view.superview) {
        self.yellowViewController.view.frame = self.view.frame;
        [self switchViewFromViewController:self.blueViewController
                toViewController:self.yellowViewController];
    } else {
        self.blueViewController.view.frame = self.view.frame;
        [self switchViewFromViewController:self.yellowViewController
                toViewController:self.blueViewController];
    }
}
```

switchViews: first checks which view is being swapped in by seeing whether yellowViewController's view's superview is nil. This will be true if one of two things is true:

■ If yellowViewController exists but its view is not being shown to the user, that view will not have a superview because it's not presently in the view hierarchy, and the expression will evaluate to true.

■ If yellowViewController doesn't exist because it hasn't been created yet or was flushed from memory, it will also return true.

We then check to see whether yellowViewController exists:

```
if (!self.yellowViewController.view.superview) {
```

If it's a nil pointer, that means there is no instance of yellowViewController, and we need to create one. This could happen because it's the first time the button has been pressed or because the system ran low on memory and it was flushed. In this case, we need to create an instance of YellowViewController as we did for the BlueViewController in the viewDidLoad method:

```
if (!self.yellowViewController) {
    self.yellowViewController = [self.storyboard
        instantiateViewControllerWithIdentifier:@"Yellow"];
}
```

If we're switching in the blue controller, we need to perform the same check to see whether it still exists (since it could have been flushed from memory) and create it if it does not. This is just the same code again, referencing the blue controller instead:

```
} else {
    if (!self.blueViewController) {
        self.blueViewController = [self.storyboard
            instantiateViewControllerWithIdentifier:@"Blue"];
    }
}
```

At this point, we know that we have a view controller instance because either we already had one or we just created it. We then set the view controller's frame to match that of the switch view controller's content view and then we use our switchFromViewController:toViewController: method to actually perform the switch:

```
// Switch view controllers.
if (!self.yellowViewController.view.superview) {
    self.yellowViewController.view.frame = self.view.frame;
    [self switchViewFromViewController:self.blueViewController
            toViewController:self.yellowViewController];
} else {
    self.blueViewController.view.frame = self.view.frame;
    [self switchViewFromViewController:self.yellowViewController
            toViewController:self.blueViewController];
}
```

The first branch of the if statement is taken if we are switching from the blue view controller to the yellow and vice versa for the else branch.

In addition to not using resources for the yellow view and controller if the **Switch Views** button is never tapped, lazy loading also gives us the ability to release whichever view is not being shown to free up its memory. iOS will call the UIViewController method didReceiveMemoryWarning, which is inherited by every view controller, when memory drops below a system-determined level.

Since we know that either view will be reloaded the next time it is shown to the user, we can safely release either controller, provided it is not currently on display. We can do this by adding a few lines to the existing didReceiveMemoryWarning method:

```
- (void)didReceiveMemoryWarning {
    [super didReceiveMemoryWarning];

    if (!self.blueViewController.view.superview) {
        self.blueViewController = nil;
    } else {
        self.yellowViewController = nil;
    }
}
```

This newly added code checks to see which view is currently being shown to the user and releases the controller for the other view by assigning nil to its property. This will cause the controller, along with the view it controls, to be deallocated, freeing up its memory.

> **Tip**   Lazy loading is a key component of resource management on iOS, and you should implement it anywhere you can. In a complex, multiview application, being responsible and flushing unused objects from memory can be the difference between an application that works well and one that crashes periodically because it runs out of memory.

The final piece of the puzzle is the switchFromViewController:toViewController: method, which is responsible for the view controller switch. Switching view controllers is a two-step process. First, we need to remove the view for the controller that's currently displayed, and then we need to add the view for the new view controller. But that's not quite all—we need to take care of some housekeeping as well. Add the implementation of this method as shown:

```
- (void)switchViewFromViewController:(UIViewController *)fromVC
              toViewController:(UIViewController *)toVC {
    if (fromVC != nil) {
        [fromVC willMoveToParentViewController:nil];
        [fromVC.view removeFromSuperview];
        [fromVC removeFromParentViewController];
    }

    if (toVC != nil) {
        [self addChildViewController:toVC];
        [self.view insertSubview:toVC.view atIndex:0];
        [toVC didMoveToParentViewController:self];
    }
}
```

The first block of code removes the outgoing view controller, but let's look at the second block first, where we add the incoming view controller. Here's the first line of code in that block:

```
[self addChildViewController:toVC];
```

This code makes the incoming view controller a child of the switching view controller. View controllers like SwitchingViewController that manage other view controllers are referred to as **container view controllers**. The standard classes UITabBarController and UINavigationController are both container view controllers and they have code that does something similar to what the s witchFromViewController:toViewController: method is doing. Making the new view controller a child of the SwitchingViewController ensures that certain events that are delivered to the root view controller are correctly passed to the child controller when required—for example, it makes sure that rotation is handled properly.

Next, the child view controller's view is added to that of the SwitchingViewController:

```
[self.view insertSubview:toVC.view atIndex:0];
```

Note that the view is inserted in the subviews list of SwitchingViewController at index zero, which tells iOS to put this view *behind* everything else. Sending the view to the back ensures that the toolbar we created in Interface Builder a moment ago will always be visible on the screen, since we're inserting the content views behind it. Finally, we notify the incoming view controller that it has been added as the child of another controller:

```
[toVC didMoveToParentViewController:self];
```

This is necessary in case the child view controller overrides this method to take some action when it's become the child of another controller.

Now that you've seen how a view controller is added, the code that removes a view controller from its parent is much easier to understand—all we do is reverse each of the steps that we performed when adding it:

```
if (fromVC != nil) {
    [fromVC willMoveToParentViewController:nil];
    [fromVC.view removeFromSuperview];
    [fromVC removeFromParentViewController];
}
```

Implementing the Content Views

At this point, the code is complete, but we can't run the application yet because we don't have the blue and yellow content controllers in the storyboard. These two controllers are extremely simple. They each have one action method that is triggered by a button, and neither one needs any outlets. The two views are also nearly identical. In fact, they are so similar that they could have been represented by the same class. We chose to make them two separate classes because that's how most multiview applications are constructed.

The two action methods we're going to implement do nothing more than show an alert (as we did in Chapter 4's Control Fun application), so go ahead and add this code to *BlueViewController.m:*

```
#import "BlueViewController.h"

@implementation BlueViewController

- (IBAction)blueButtonPressed {
    UIAlertController *alert = [UIAlertController
        alertControllerWithTitle:@"Blue View Button Pressed"
        message:@"You pressed the button on the blue view"
        preferredStyle:UIAlertControllerStyleAlert];
    UIAlertAction *action =
        [UIAlertAction actionWithTitle:@"Yep, I did"
            style:UIAlertActionStyleDefault handler:nil];
    [alert addAction:action];
    [self presentViewController:alert animated:YES completion:nil];
}
```

Save the file. Next, switch over to *YellowViewController.m* and add this very similar code to that file:

```
#import "YellowViewController.h"

@implementation YellowViewController

- (IBAction)yellowButtonPressed {
    UIAlertController *alert = [UIAlertController
        alertControllerWithTitle:@"Yellow View Button Pressed"
        message:@"You pressed the button on the yellow view"
        preferredStyle:UIAlertControllerStyleAlert];
    UIAlertAction *action =
        [UIAlertAction actionWithTitle:@"Yep, I did"
            style:UIAlertActionStyleDefault handler:nil];
    [alert addAction:action];
    [self presentViewController:alert animated:YES completion:nil];
}
```

Save this file as well.

Next, select *Main.storyboard* to open it in Interface Builder so that we can make a few changes. First, we need to add a new scene for BlueViewController. Up until now, each storyboard we've dealt with contained just a single controller-view pairing, but the storyboard has more tricks up its sleeve, and holding multiple scenes is one of them. From the object library, drag out another View Controller and drop it in the editing area next to the existing one. Now your storyboard has two scenes, each of which can be loaded dynamically and independently while your application is running. In the row of icons at the top of the new scene, single-click the yellow **View Controller** icon and press ⌥⌘3 to bring up the Identity Inspector. In the **Custom Class** section, **Class** defaults to UIViewController; change it to BlueViewController.

We also need to create an identifier for this new view controller so that our code can find it inside the storyboard. Just below the **Custom Class** section in the Identity Inspector, you'll see a **Storyboard ID** field. Click there and type **Blue** to match what we used in our code.

So now you have two scenes. We showed you earlier how to configure your app to load this storyboard at launch time, but we didn't mention anything about scenes there. How will the app know which of these two views to show? The answer lies in the big arrow pointing at the first scene, as shown in Figure 6-18. That arrow points out the storyboard's default scene, which is what the app shows when it starts up. If you want to choose a different default scene, all you have to do is drag the arrow to point at the scene you want.

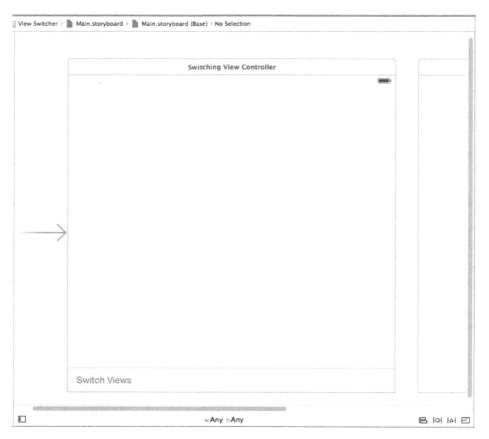

Figure 6-18. We just added a second scene to our storyboard. The big arrow points at the default scene

Single-click the big square view in the new scene you just added, and then press ⌥⌘4 to bring up the Attributes Inspector. In the inspector's **View** section, click the color well that's labeled **Background**, and use the pop-up color picker to change the background color of this view to a nice shade of blue. Once you are happy with your blue, close the color picker.

Drag a Button from the library over to the view, using the guidelines to center the button in the view, both vertically and horizontally. We want to make sure that the button stays centered no matter what, so make two constraints to that effect. First select **Editor ➤ Align ➤ Horizontal Center in Container** from the menu. Then click the new button again and select **Editor ➤ Align ➤ Vertical Center in Container** from the menu.

Double-click the button and change its title to *Press Me*. Next, with the button still selected, switch to the Connections Inspector (by pressing ⌥⌘6), drag from the Touch Up Inside event to the yellow **View Controller** icon at the top of the scene, and connect to the blueButtonPressed action method. You'll notice that the text of the button is a blue color by default. Since our background is also blue, there's a pretty big risk that this button's text will be hard to see! Switch to the Attributes Inspector with ⌥⌘4, and then use the combined color-picker/pop-up button to change the **Text Color** value to something else. Depending on how dark your background color is, you might want to choose either white or black.

Now it's time to do pretty much the same set of things for YellowViewController. Grab yet another View Controller from the object library and drag it into the editor area. Don't worry if things are getting crowded; you can stack those scenes on top of each other, and no one will mind! Click the **View Controller** icon for the new scene in the Document Outline and use the Identity Inspector to change its class to YellowViewController and its **Storyboard ID** to *Yellow*.

Next, select the YellowViewController's view and switch to the Attributes Inspector. There, click the **Background** color well, select a bright yellow, and then close the color picker.

Next, drag out a Button from the library and use the guidelines to center it in the view. Use the menu actions to create constraints aligning its horizontal and vertical center, just like for the last button. Now change its title to *Press Me, Too*. With the button still selected, use the Connections Inspector to drag from the Touch Up Inside event to the **View Controller** icon, and connect to the yellowButtonPressed action method.

When you're finished, save the storyboard and get ready to take the app for a spin. Hit the **Run** button in Xcode, and your app should start up and present you with a full screen of blue.

When our application launches, it shows the blue view we built. When you tap the **Switch Views** button, it will change to show the yellow view that we built. Tap it again, and it goes back to the blue view. If you tap the button centered on the blue or yellow view, you'll get an alert view with a message indicating which button was pressed. This alert shows that the correct controller class is being called for the view that is being shown.

The transition between the two views is kind of abrupt, though. Gosh, if only there were some way to make the transition look nicer.

Of course, there is a way to make the transition look nicer! We can animate the transition to give the user visual feedback of the change.

Animating the Transition

UIView has several class methods we can call to indicate that the transition between views should be animated, to indicate the type of transition that should be used, and to specify how long the transition should take.

Go back to *SwitchingViewController.m* and enhance your switchViews: method by adding the lines shown here in bold:

```
- (IBAction)switchViews:(id)sender {
    // Create the new view controller, if required.
    if (!self.yellowViewController.view.superview) {
        if (!self.yellowViewController) {
            self.yellowViewController = [self.storyboard
                instantiateViewControllerWithIdentifier:@"Yellow"];
        }
    } else {
        if (!self.blueViewController) {
            self.blueViewController = [self.storyboard
                instantiateViewControllerWithIdentifier:@"Blue"];
        }
    }

    // Switch view controllers.
    [UIView beginAnimations:@"View Flip" context:NULL];
    [UIView setAnimationDuration:0.4];
    [UIView setAnimationCurve:UIViewAnimationCurveEaseInOut];
    if (!self.yellowViewController.view.superview) {
        [UIView setAnimationTransition:
                    UIViewAnimationTransitionFlipFromRight
                forView:self.view cache:YES];
        self.yellowViewController.view.frame = self.view.frame;
        [self switchViewFromViewController:self.blueViewController
                toViewController:self.yellowViewController];
    } else {
        [UIView setAnimationTransition:
                    UIViewAnimationTransitionFlipFromLeft
                forView:self.view cache:YES];
        self.blueViewController.view.frame = self.view.frame;
        [self switchViewFromViewController:self.yellowViewController
                toViewController:self.blueViewController];
    }
    [UIView commitAnimations];
}
```

Compile this new version and run your application. When you tap the **Switch Views** button, instead of the new view just snapping into place, the old view will flip over to reveal the new view, as shown in Figure 6-19.

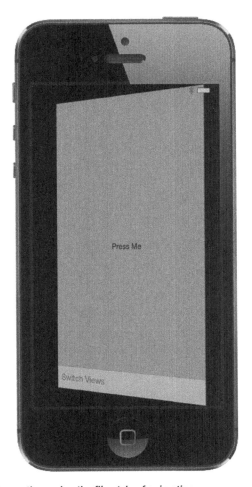

Figure 6-19. One view transitioning to another, using the flip style of animation

To tell iOS that we want a change animated, we need to declare an **animation block** and specify how long the animation should take. Animation blocks are declared by using the UIView class method beginAnimations:context:, like so:

```
[UIView beginAnimations:@"View Flip" context:NULL];
[UIView setAnimationDuration:0.4];
```

beginAnimations:context: takes two parameters. The first is an animation block title. This title comes into play only if you take more direct advantage of Core Animation, the framework behind this animation. For our purposes, we could have used nil. The second parameter is a (void *) that allows you to specify an object (or any other C data type) whose pointer you would like associated with this animation block. We used NULL here, since we don't need to do that. We also set the duration of the animation, which tells UIView how long (in seconds) the animation should last.

After that, we set the **animation curve**, which determines the timing of the animation. The default, which is a linear curve, causes the animation to happen at a constant speed. The option we set here, `UIViewAnimationCurveEaseInOut`, specifies that the animation should start slow but speed up in the middle, and then slow down again at the end. This gives the animation a more natural, less mechanical appearance:

```
[UIView setAnimationCurve:UIViewAnimationCurveEaseInOut];
```

Next, we need to specify the transition to use. At the time of this writing, five iOS view transitions are available:

- `UIViewAnimationTransitionFlipFromLeft`

- `UIViewAnimationTransitionFlipFromRight`

- `UIViewAnimationTransitionCurlUp`

- `UIViewAnimationTransitionCurlDown`

- `UIViewAnimationTransitionNone`

We chose to use two different effects, depending on which view was being swapped in. Using a left flip for one transition and a right flip for the other makes the view seem to flip back and forth. The value `UIViewAnimationTransitionNone` causes an abrupt transition from one view controller to another. Of course, if you wanted that effect, you wouldn't bother creating an animation block at all.

The cache option speeds up drawing by taking a snapshot of the view when the animation begins, and uses that image rather than redrawing the view at each step of the animation. You should always cache the animation unless the appearance of the view may need to change during the animation:

```
[UIView setAnimationTransition:UIViewAnimationTransitionFlipFromRight
               forView:self.view cache:YES];
```

When we're finished specifying the changes to be animated, we call `commitAnimations` on `UIView`. Everything between the start of the animation block and the call to `commitAnimations` will be animated together.

Thanks to Cocoa Touch's use of Core Animation under the hood, we're able to do fairly sophisticated animation with only a handful of code.

Switching Off

Whoo-boy! Creating our own multiview controller was a lot of work, wasn't it? You should have a very good grasp of how multiview applications are put together, now that you've built one from scratch.

Although Xcode contains project templates for the most common types of multiview applications, you need to understand the overall structure of these types of applications so that you can build them yourself from the ground up. The standard container controllers (`UITabBarController`, `UINavigationController`, and `UIPageViewController`) are incredible time-savers and you should use them when you can, but, at times, they simply won't meet your needs.

In the next few chapters, we're going to continue building multiview applications to reinforce the concepts from this chapter and to give you a feel for how more complex applications are put together. In Chapter 7, we'll construct a tab bar application. Let's get going!

Tab Bars and Pickers

In the previous chapter, you built your first multiview application. In this chapter, you're going to build a full tab bar application with five different tabs and five different content views. Building this application will reinforce a lot of what you learned in Chapter 6. Now, you're too smart to spend a whole chapter doing stuff you already sort of know how to do, so we're going to use those five content views to demonstrate a type of iOS control that we have not yet covered. The control is called a **picker view**, or just a **picker**.

You may not be familiar with the name, but you've almost certainly used a picker if you've owned an iPhone or iPod touch for more than, say, 10 minutes. Pickers are the controls with dials that spin. You use them to input dates in the Calendar application or to set a timer in the Clock application (see Figure 7-1). On the iPad, the picker view isn't quite as common since the larger display lets you present other ways of choosing among multiple items; but even there, it's used in the Calendar application.

Figure 7-1. A picker in the Clock application

Pickers are a bit more complex than the iOS controls you've seen so far; and as such, they deserve a little more attention. Pickers can be configured to display one dial or many. By default, pickers display lists of text, but they can also be made to display images.

The Pickers Application

This chapter's application, Pickers, will feature a tab bar. As you build Pickers, you'll change the default tab bar so that it has five tabs, add an icon to each of the tab bar items, and then create a series of content views and connect each view to a tab.

The application's content views will feature five different pickers:

- **Date picker:** The first content view we'll build will have a date picker, which is the easiest type of picker to implement (see Figure 7-2). The view will also have a button that, when tapped, will display an alert that shows the date that was picked.

Figure 7-2. The first tab will show a date picker

■ **Single-component picker:** The second tab will feature a picker with a single list of values (see Figure 7-3). This picker is a little more work to implement than a date picker. You'll learn how to specify the values to be displayed in the picker by using a delegate and a data source.

Figure 7-3. A picker displaying a single list of values

■ **Multicomponent picker:** In the third tab, we're going to create a picker with two separate wheels. The technical term for each of these wheels is a **picker component**, so here we are creating a picker with two components. You'll see how to use the data source and delegate to provide two independent lists of data to the picker (see Figure 7-4). Each of this picker's components can be changed without impacting the other one.

Figure 7-4. A two-component picker, showing an alert that reflects our selection

■ **Picker with dependent components:** In the fourth content view, we'll build another picker with two components. But this time, the values displayed in the component on the right will change based on the value selected in the component on the left. In our example, we're going to display a list of states in the left component and a list of that state's ZIP codes in the right component (see Figure 7-5).

Figure 7-5. In this picker, one component is dependent on the other. As you select a state in the left component, the right component changes to a list of ZIP codes in that state

■ **Custom picker with images:** Last, but most certainly not least, we're going to have some fun with the fifth content view. We'll demonstrate how to add image data to a picker, and we're going to do it by writing a little game that uses a picker with five components. In several places in Apple's documentation, the picker's appearance is described as looking a bit like a slot machine. Well then, what could be more fitting than writing a little slot machine game (see Figure 7-6)? For this picker, the user won't be able to manually change the values of the components, but will be able to select the **Spin** button to make the five wheels spin to a new, randomly selected value. If three copies of the same image appear in a row, the user wins.

Figure 7-6. *Our fifth component picker. Note that we do not condone using your iPhone as a tiny casino*

Delegates and Data Sources

Before we dive in and start building our application, let's look at what makes pickers more complex than the other controls you've used so far. With the exception of the date picker, you can't use a picker by just grabbing one in the object library, dropping it on your content view, and configuring it. You also need to provide each picker with both a picker **delegate** and a picker **data source**.

By this point, you should be comfortable using delegates. We've already used application delegates and the basic idea is the same here. The picker defers several jobs to its delegate. The most important of these is the task of determining what to actually draw for each of the rows in each of its components. The picker asks the delegate for either a string or a view that will be drawn at a given spot on a given component. The picker gets its data from the delegate.

In addition to the delegate, pickers need to have a data source. The data source tells the picker how many components it will be working with and how many rows make up each component. The data source works like the delegate in that its methods are called at certain, prespecified times. Without a data source and a delegate, pickers cannot do their job; in fact, they won't even be drawn.

It's very common for the data source and the delegate to be the same object. And it's just as common for that object to be the view controller for the picker's enclosing view, which is the approach we'll be using in this application. The view controllers for each of our application's content panes will be the data source and the delegate for their picker.

> **Note**   Here's a pop quiz: Is the picker data source part of the model, view, or controller portion of the application? It's a trick question. A data source sounds like it must be part of the model, but it's actually part of the controller. The data source isn't usually an object designed to hold data. In simple applications, the data source might hold data, but its true job is to retrieve data from the model and pass it along to the picker.

Let's fire up Xcode and get to it.

Creating the Pickers Application

Although Xcode provides a template for tab bar applications, we're going to build ours from scratch. It's not much extra work and it's good practice.

Create a new project, select the **Single View Application** template again, and choose **Next** to go to the next screen. In the **Product Name** field, type **Pickers**. Make sure the check box that says **Use Core Data** is unchecked, and set the **Language** to *Objective-C* and the **Devices** pop-up to *Universal*. Then choose **Next** again. Xcode will let you select the folder where you want to save your project.

We're going to walk you through the process of building the whole application; but at any step of the way, if you feel like challenging yourself by moving ahead, by all means do so. If you get stumped, you can always come back. If you don't feel like skipping ahead, that's just fine. We love the company.

Creating the View Controllers

In the previous chapter, we created a root view controller ("root controller" for short) to manage the process of swapping our application's other views. We'll be doing that again this time, but we won't need to create our own root view controller class. Apple provides a very good class for managing tab bar views, so we're just going to use an instance of UITabBarController as our root controller.

First, we need to create five new classes in Xcode: the five view controllers that the root controller will swap in and out.

Expand the *Pickers* folder in the Project Navigator. There, you'll see the source code files that Xcode created to start off the project. Single-click the *Pickers* folder, and press ⌘**N** or select **File ➤ New ➤ File. . ..**

Select **iOS** and then **Source** in the left pane of the new file assistant, and then select the icon for **Cocoa Touch Class** and click **Next** to continue. The next screen lets you give your new class a name. Enter **DatePickerViewController** in the **Class** field. Ensure that the **Subclass of** field contains *UIViewController*. Make sure that the **Also create XIB file** check box is unchecked, set the **Language** to *Objective-C*, and then click **Next**.

You'll be shown a folder selection window, which lets you choose where the class should be saved. Choose the *Pickers* directory, which already contains the `AppDelegate` class and a few other files. Make sure also that the **Group** pop-up has the *Pickers* folder selected and that the target check box for **Pickers** is checked.

After you click the **Create** button, two new files will appear in your *Pickers* folder: *DatePickerViewController.h* and *DatePickerViewController.m.*

Repeat those steps four more times, using the names *SingleComponentPickerViewController, DoubleComponentPickerViewController, DependentComponentPickerViewController*, and *CustomPickerViewController*. At the end of all this, the *Pickers* folder should contain all the fresh files, nicely bunched together (see Figure 7-7).

Figure 7-7. The Project Navigator should contain all these files after creating the five view controller classes

Creating the Tab Bar Controller

Now, let's create our tab bar controller. The project template already contains a view controller called `ViewController`, which is a subclass of `UIViewController`. To convert it to a tab bar controller, all we need to do is change its base class. Open *ViewController.h* and make the following change shown in bold:

```
#import <UIKit/UIKit.h>

@interface ViewController : UITabBarController
```

Next, we need to set the tab bar controller up in the storyboard, so open *Main.storyboard*. The template added an initial view controller, which we're going to replace, so select it in the Document Outline or the editor area and delete it by pressing the **Delete** key. In the Object Library, locate a Tab Bar Controller and drag it over to the editing area (see Figure 7-8).

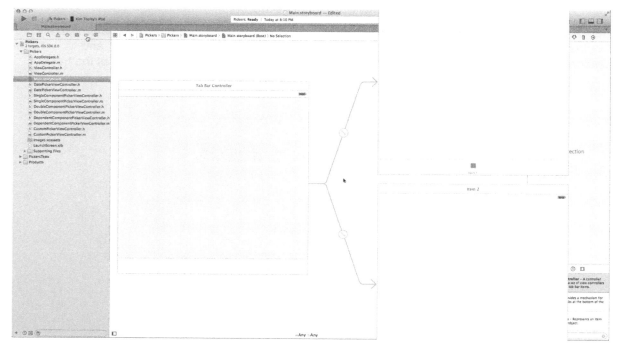

Figure 7-8. Dragging a tab bar controller from the library into the editor area. That's one heck of a big thing you're dragging around there

While you're dragging, you'll see that, unlike the other controllers we've been asking you to drag out from the object library, this one actually pulls out three complete view-controller pairs at once, all of which are connected to each other with curved lines. This is actually more than just a tab bar controller; it's also two child controllers, already connected and ready to use.

Once you drop the tab bar controller onto the editing area, three new scenes are added to the storyboard. If you expand the document view on the left, you will see a nice overview of all the scenes contained in the storyboard (see Figure 7-9). You'll also see the curvy lines still in place connected the tab bar controller with each of its children. Those lines will always adjust themselves to stay connected if you move the scenes around, which you are always free to do. The on-screen position of each scene within a storyboard has no impact on your app's appearance when it runs.

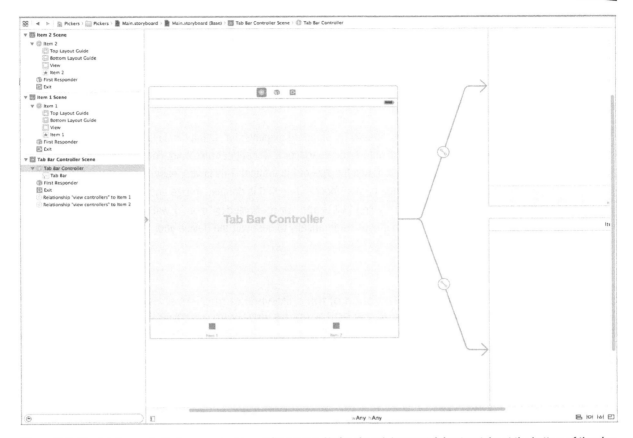

Figure 7-9. The tab bar controller's scene, and two child scenes. Notice the tab bar containing two tabs at the bottom of the view and the curved lines connected to each of the child view controllers

This tab bar controller will be our root controller. As a reminder, the root controller controls the very first view that the user will see when your program runs. It is responsible for switching the other views in and out. Since we'll connect each of our views to one of the tabs in the tab bar, the tab bar controller makes a logical choice as a root controller. We need to tell iOS that the tab bar controller is the one that it should load from *Main.storyboard* when the application starts. To do this, select the **Tab Bar Controller** icon in the Document Outline and open the Attributes Inspector; and then in the **View Controller** section, check the **Is Initial View Controller** check box. With the view controller still selected, switch to the Identity Inspector and change the **Class** to ViewController.

Tab bars can use icons to represent each of the tabs, so we should also add the icons we're going to use before editing the storyboard. You can find some suitable icons in the *07 - ImageSets* folder of the source code archive for this book. Each subfolder of *07 - ImageSets* contains three images (one for devices with a standard display, two for Retina devices). In the Xcode Project Navigator, select *Images.xcassets*, which already contains default graphics for an icon and a launch image. Next, drag each subfolder from the *07 - ImageSets* folder and drop it into the left column of the editing area, underneath AppIcon, to copy them all into the project.

If you want to make your own icons instead, there are some guidelines for how they should be created. The icons you use should be 24 × 24 pixels and saved in *.png* format. The icon file should have a transparent background. Don't worry about trying to color the icons so that they match the appearance of the tab bar. Just as it does with the application icon, iOS will take your image and make it look just right.

Tip   An image size of 24 × 24 pixels is actually for standard displays; for Retina displays on iPhone 4 and later, and for the new iPad, you need a double-sized image, or it will appear pixelated. For the iPhone 6 Plus, you need to provide an image that's three times the size of the original. This is very easy: for any image *foo.png*, you should also provide an image named *foo@2x.png* that is doubled in size and another called *foo@3x.png* that is three times the size. Calling [UIImage imageNamed:@"foo"] will return the normal-sized image or the double-sized image automatically to best suit the device your app is currently running on.

Back in the storyboard, you can see that each of the child view controllers shows a name like "Item 1" at the top and has a single bar item at the bottom of its view, with a simple label matching what is present in the tab bar. We might as well set these two up so that they have the right names from the start, so select the **Item 1** view controller, and then click the tab bar item at the bottom or in the Document Outline. Open the Attributes Inspector, and you'll see a text field for setting the **Title** of the **Bar Item**, which currently contains the text *Item 1*. Replace the text with *Date* and press the **Enter** key. This immediately changes the text of the bar item at the bottom of this view controller, as well as the corresponding tab bar item in the tab bar controller. While you're still in the inspector, click the **Image** pop-up and select **clockicon** to set the icon, too. Couldn't be simpler!

Now repeat the same steps for the second child view controller, but name this one *Single* and use the **singleicon** image for its bar item.

Our next step is to complete our tab bar controller so it reflects the five tabs shown in Figure 7-2. Each of those five tabs represents one of our five pickers. The way we're going to do this is by simply adding three more view controllers to the storyboard (in addition to the two that were added along with the tab bar controller), and then connecting each of them so that the tab bar controller can activate them. Get started by dragging out a normal View Controller from the object library. Next, Control-drag from the tab bar controller to your new view controller, release the mouse button, and select **view controllers** from the **Relationship Segue** section of the small pop-up window that appears. This tells the tab bar controller that it has a new child to maintain, so the tab bar immediately acquires a new item, and your new view controller gets a bar item in the bottom of its view, just like the others already had. Now do the same steps outlined previously to give this latest view controller's bar item *Double* as a title and **doubleicon** for its image.

Now we are really getting somewhere. Drag out two more view controllers and connect each of them to the tab bar controller as described previously. One at a time, select each of their bar items, naming one of them *Dependent* with **dependenticon** as its image, and the other *Custom* with **toolicon** as its image.

Now that all our view controllers are in place, it's time to set up each of them with the correct controller class. This will let us have different functionality in each of these views. In the Document Outline, select the view controller labeled **Item 1** and bring up the Identity Inspector. In the **Custom Class** section of the inspector, change the class to *DatePickerViewController*, and press **Return** or **Tab** to set it. You'll see that the name of the selected control in the Document Outline changes to *Date,* mirroring the change you made.

Now repeat this same process for the next four view controllers, in the order in which they appear at the bottom of the tab bar controller. In the Identity Inspector for each, use the class names *SingleComponentPickerViewController*, *DoubleComponentPickerViewController*, *DependentComponentPickerViewController*, and *CustomPickerViewController*, respectively.

Before moving on to the next bit of GUI editing, save your storyboard file.

The Initial Test Run

At this point, the tab bar and the content views should all be hooked up and working. Compile and run, and your application should launch with a tab bar that functions (see Figure 7-10). Click each of the tabs in turn. Each tab should be selectable.

Figure 7-10. The application with five empty but selectable tabs

There's nothing in the content views now, so the changes won't be very dramatic. In fact, you won't see any difference at all, except for the highlighting tab bar items. But if everything went OK, the basic framework for your multiview application is now set up and working, and we can start designing the individual content views.

> **Tip**   If your simulator bursts into flames when you click one of the tabs, don't panic! Most likely, you've either missed a step or made a typo. Go back and make sure the connections are right and the class names are all set correctly.

If you want to make doubly sure everything is working, you can add a different label or some other object to each of the content views, and then relaunch the application. At this point, you should see the content of the different views change as you select different tabs.

Implementing the Date Picker

To implement the date picker, we'll need a single outlet and a single action. The outlet will be used to grab the value from the date picker. The action will be triggered by a button and will put up an alert to show the date value pulled from the picker. We'll add both of these from inside Interface Builder while editing the *Main.storyboard* file, so select it in the Project Navigator if it's not already front-and-center.

The first thing we need to do is find a Date Picker in the Object Library and drag it over to the Date Scene in the editing area. Click the **Date** icon in the Document Outline to bring the correct view controller to the front, and then drag the date picker from the Object Library and place it at the top of the view, right up against the top of the display. It's OK if it overlaps the status bar because this control has so much built-in vertical padding at the top that no one will notice.

Now we need to apply Auto Layout constraints so that the date picker is correctly placed when the application runs on any kind of device. We want the picker to be horizontally centered and anchored to the top of the view, so we need two constraints. Click the **Align** button below the storyboard, check the **Horizontal Center in Container** box, and then click **Add 1 Constraint**. Click the **Pin** button (which is next to the **Align** button). Using the four distance boxes at the top of the pop-up, set the distance between the picker and the top of edge of the view above it to zero by entering zero in the top box, and then click the dashed red line below it so that it becomes a solid line. At the bottom of the pop-up, set **Update Frames** to *Items of New Constraints*, and then click **Add 1 Constraint**. The date picker will resize and move to its correct position, as shown in Figure 7-11.

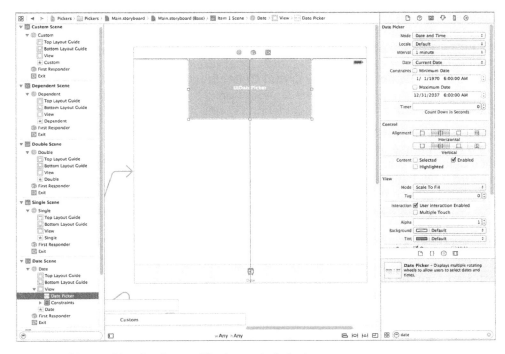

Figure 7-11. The date picker, positioned at the top of its view controller's view

Single-click the date picker if it's not already selected and go back to the Attributes Inspector. As you can see in Figure 7-12, a number of attributes can be configured for a date picker. We're going to leave most of the values at their defaults (but feel free to play with the options when we're finished, to see what they do). The one thing we will do is limit the range of the picker to reasonable dates. Look for the heading that says **Constraints** and check the box that reads **Minimum Date**. Leave the value at the default of *1/1/1970*. Also check the box that reads **Maximum Date** and set that value *to 12/31/2200*.

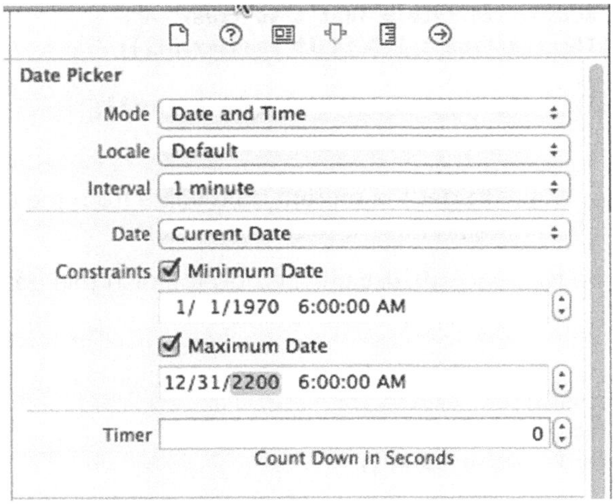

Figure 7-12. The Attributes Inspector for a date picker. Set the maximum date, but leave the rest of the settings at their default values

Now let's connect this picker to its controller. Press ⌥⌘**Enter** to open the Assistant Editor and make sure the jump bar at the top of the Assistant Editor is set to **Automatic**. That should make *DatePickerViewController.m* show up there. Next, Control-drag from the picker to the class extension part of *DatePickerViewController.m*, between the @interface and @end lines, releasing the mouse button when the **Insert Outlet, Action, or Outlet Collection** tooltip appears. In the pop-up window that appears after you let go, make sure the **Connection** is set to *Outlet*, enter **datePicker** as the **Name**, and then press **Enter** to create the outlet and connect it to the picker.

Next, grab a Button from the library and place it a small distance below the date picker. Double-click the button and give it a title of *Select*. We want this button to be horizontally centered and to stay a fixed distance below the date picker. With the button selected, click the **Align** button at the bottom of the storyboard, check the **Horizontal Center in Container** box, and click **Add 1 Constraint**. To fix the distance between them, Control-drag from the button to the date picker and release the mouse. In the pop-up that appears, select **Vertical Spacing**. Finally, click the **Resolve Auto Layout Issues** button at the bottom of the storyboard and then click **Update Frames** in the top section of the pop-up. The button should move to its correct location and there should no longer be any Auto Layout warnings.

Now Control-drag from the button to the source code in the assistant view, this time dragging it down near the bottom, just above the final @end line, until you see the **Insert Action** tooltip appear. Name the new action *buttonPressed* and press **Enter** to connect it. Doing so creates an empty method called buttonPressed:, which you should now complete with the following bold code:

```
- (IBAction)buttonPressed:(id)sender {
    NSDate *date = self.datePicker.date;
    NSString *message = [[NSString alloc] initWithFormat:
                        @"The date and time you selected is %@", date];
    UIAlertController *alert =
            [UIAlertController alertControllerWithTitle:
                    @"Date and Time Selected"
                    message:message
                    preferredStyle:UIAlertControllerStyleAlert];
    UIAlertAction *action =
            [UIAlertAction actionWithTitle:@"That's so true!"
                    style:UIAlertActionStyleDefault handler:nil];
    [alert addAction:action];
    [self presentViewController:alert animated:YES completion:nil];
}
```

Here, we use our datePicker outlet to get the current date value from the date picker, and then we construct a string based on that date and use it to show an alert.

Next, add a bit of setup code to the viewDidLoad: method to finish this controller class:

```
- (void)viewDidLoad {
    [super viewDidLoad];
    // Do any additional setup after loading the view.
    NSDate *now = [NSDate date];
    [self.datePicker setDate:now animated:NO];
}
```

In `viewDidLoad`, we create a new `NSDate` object. An `NSDate` object created this way will hold the current date and time. We then set `datePicker` to that date, which ensures that every time this view is loaded from the storyboard, the picker will reset to the current date and time.

Go ahead and build and run to make sure your date picker checks out. If everything went OK, your application should look like Figure 7-2 when it runs. If you choose the **Select** button, an alert will pop up, telling you the date and time currently selected in the date picker.

Note   The date picker does not allow you to specify seconds or a time zone. The alert displays the time with seconds and in Greenwich Mean Time (GMT). We could have added some code to simplify the string displayed in the alert, but isn't this chapter long enough already? If you're interested in customizing the formatting of the date, take a look at the `NSDateFormatter` class.

Implementing the Single-Component Picker

Our next picker lets the user select from a list of values. In this example, we're going to use an `NSArray` to hold the values we want to display in the picker.

Pickers don't hold any data themselves. Instead, they call methods on their data source and delegate to get the data they need to display. The picker doesn't really care where the underlying data lives. It asks for the data when it needs it, and the data source and delegate (which are often, in practice, the same object) work together to supply that data. As a result, the data could be coming from a static list, as we'll do in this section. It also could be loaded from a file or a URL, or even made up or calculated on the fly.

For the picker class to ask its controller for data, we must ensure that the controller implements the right methods. One part of doing that is declaring in the controller's interface that it will implement a couple of protocols. In the Project Navigator, single-click *SingleComponentPickerViewController.h*. This controller class will act as both the data source and the delegate for its picker, so we need to make sure it conforms to the protocols for those two roles. Add the following code:

```
#import <UIKit/UIKit.h>

@interface SingleComponentPickerViewController : UIViewController
    <UIPickerViewDelegate, UIPickerViewDataSource>

@end
```

Building the View

Now select *Main.storyboard* again, since it's time to edit the content view for the second tab in our tab bar. In the Document Outline, click the **Single** icon to bring the view controller into the foreground in the editor area. Next, bring over a Picker View from the library (see Figure 7-13) and add it to your view, placing it snugly into the top of the view, as you did with the date picker view.

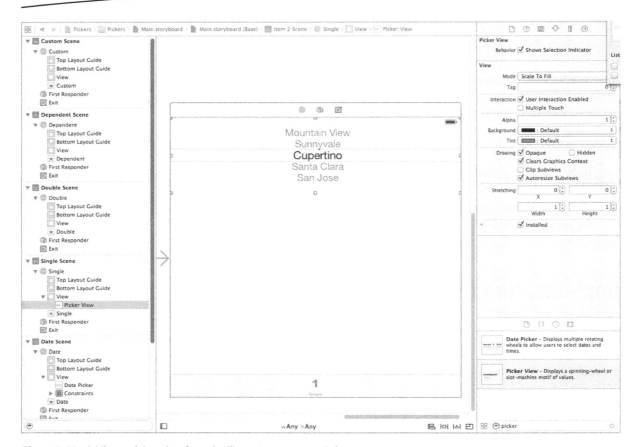

Figure 7-13. Adding a picker view from the library to your second view

The picker needs to be horizontally centered and pinned to the top of the scene. You can do this by adding the same Auto Layout constraints to the picker that you added to the Date Picker in the previous example. If you can't remember how to do that, refer back to the instructions in the "Implementing the Date Picker" section. We're going to be using these constraints again and again in this chapter, so it's worth remembering how to create them, or writing them down.

Now let's connect this picker to its controller. The procedure here is just like for the previous picker view: open the Assistant Editor, set the jump bar to show the *.m* file, Control-drag from the picker to the @interface section at the top of *SingleComponentPickerViewController.m*, and create an outlet named singlePicker.

Next, with the picker selected, press ⌥⌘6 to bring up the Connections Inspector. If you look at the connections available for the picker view, you'll see that the first two items are **dataSource** and **delegate**. If you don't see those outlets, make sure you have the picker selected, rather than the UIView that contains it! Drag from the circle next to **dataSource** to the **View Controller** icon at the top of the scene in the storyboard or in the Document Outline, and then drag from the circle next to **delegate** to the **View Controller** icon. Now this picker knows that the instance of the SingleComponentPickerViewController class in the storyboard is its data source and delegate, and the picker will ask it to supply the data to be displayed. In other words, when the picker needs information about the data it is going to display, it asks the `SingleComponentPickerViewController` instance that controls this view for that information.

Drag a Button to the view, place it just below the picker. Double-click the button and give it the title *Select.* Press **Return** to commit the change. In the Connections Inspector, drag from the circle next to Touch Up Inside to code in the assistant view, releasing it just above the @end at the bottom to make a new action method. Name this action `buttonPressed` and you'll see that Xcode fills in an empty method.

As always when we add a view to a storyboard, we need to set its Auto Layout constraints. In the case of the button, these constraints need to center it horizontally and make sure its distance below the picker remains fixed. You saw how to do this when we added a similar button to the Data Picker scene, so just use the same constraints here. Now you've finished building the GUI for the second tab. Save the storyboard and let's get back to some coding.

Implementing the Controller As a Data Source and Delegate

To make our controller work properly as the picker's data source and delegate, we'll start with some code you should feel comfortable with, and then add a few methods that you've never seen before.

Single-click *SingleComponentPickerViewController.m* in the Project Navigator and add the following property to the @interface section at the top. This will let us keep a pointer to an array with the names of several well-known movie characters:

```
@interface SingleComponentPickerViewController ()

@property (weak, nonatomic) IBOutlet UIPickerView *singlePicker;
@property (strong, nonatomic) NSArray *characterNames;

@end
```

Next, add this initialization code to the `viewDidLoad` method to set up the contents of the character name array:

```
- (void)viewDidLoad {
    [super viewDidLoad];
    // Do any additional setup after loading the view.
    self.characterNames = @[@"Luke", @"Leia", @"Han", @"Chewbacca",
                            @"Artoo", @"Threepio", @"Lando"];
}
```

And then, add the following code to the `buttonPressed:` method:

```
- (IBAction)buttonPressed:(id)sender {
    NSInteger row = [self.singlePicker selectedRowInComponent:0];
    NSString *selected = self.characterNames[row];
    NSString *title = [[NSString alloc] initWithFormat:
                       @"You selected %@!", selected];
```

```
    UIAlertController *alert =
        [UIAlertController alertControllerWithTitle:title
            message:@"Thank you for choosing."
            preferredStyle:UIAlertControllerStyleAlert];
    UIAlertAction *action =
        [UIAlertAction actionWithTitle:@"You're welcome"
            style:UIAlertActionStyleDefault handler:nil];
    [alert addAction:action];
    [self presentViewController:alert animated:YES completion:nil];
}
```

These two methods should be familiar to you by now. The buttonPressed: method is nearly identical to the one we used with the date picker, but unlike the date picker, a regular picker can't tell us what data it holds because it doesn't maintain the data. It hands off that job to the delegate and data source. Instead, the buttonPressed: method needs to ask the picker which row is selected, and then grabs the corresponding data from your pickerData array. Here is how we ask it for the selected row:

```
NSInteger row = [self.singlePicker selectedRowInComponent:0];
```

Notice that we needed to specify which component we want to know about. We have only one component in this picker, so we simply pass in 0, which is the index of the first component.

> **Note**   Did you notice that there is no asterisk between NSInteger and row in our request for the selected row? Throughout most of the iOS SDK, the prefix NS often indicates an Objective-C class from the Foundation framework, but this is one of the exceptions to that general rule. NSInteger is always defined as an integer datatype, either an int or a long. We use NSInteger rather than int or long because, with NSInteger, the compiler automatically chooses whichever size is best for the platform for which we are compiling. It will create a 32-bit int when compiling for a 32-bit processor and a longer 64-bit long when compiling for a 64-bit architecture. Now that Apple has begun releasing 64-bit iOS devices, using these types makes a lot of sense. You might also write classes for your iOS applications that you'll later want to recycle and use in Cocoa applications for OS X, which has been running on both 32- and 64-bit machines for several years.

In viewDidLoad, we assign an array with several objects to the characterNames property so that we have data to feed the picker. Usually, your data will come from other sources, like a property list in your project's *Resources* folder or a web service query. By embedding a list of items in our code the way we've done here, we are making it much harder on ourselves if we need to update this list or if we want to have our application translated into other languages. But this approach is the quickest and easiest way to get data into an array for demonstration purposes. Even though you won't usually create your arrays like this, you will almost always configure some form of access to your application's model objects here in the viewDidLoad method, so that you're not constantly going to disk or to the network every time the picker asks you for data.

> **Tip** If you're not supposed to create arrays from lists of objects in your code, as we just did in `viewDidLoad`, how should you do it? Embed the lists in property list files and add those files to the *Resources* folder of your project. Property list files can be changed without recompiling your source code, which means there is little risk of introducing new bugs when you do so. You can also provide different versions of the list for different languages, as you'll see in Chapter 22. Property lists can be created directly in Xcode, which offers a template for creating one in the Resource section of the new file assistant and supports the editing of property lists in the editor pane. Both `NSArray` and `NSDictionary` offer a method called `initWithContentsOfFile:` to allow you to initialize instances from a property list file, as we'll do later in this chapter when we implement the Dependent tab. Property lists are discussed in more detail in Chapter 13.

Finally, insert the following new code at the end of the file:

```
#pragma mark -
#pragma mark Picker Data Source Methods
- (NSInteger)numberOfComponentsInPickerView:(UIPickerView *)pickerView {
    return 1;
}

- (NSInteger)pickerView:(UIPickerView *)pickerView
numberOfRowsInComponent:(NSInteger)component {
    return [self.characterNames count];
}

#pragma mark Picker Delegate Methods
- (NSString *)pickerView:(UIPickerView *)pickerView
            titleForRow:(NSInteger)row
          forComponent:(NSInteger)component {
    return self.characterNames[row];
}

@end
```

These three methods are required to implement the picker. The first two methods are from the `UIPickerViewDataSource` protocol, and they are both required for all pickers (except date pickers). Here's the first one:

```
- (NSInteger)numberOfComponentsInPickerView:(UIPickerView *)pickerView {
    return 1;
}
```

Pickers can have more than one spinning wheel, or component, and this is how the picker asks how many components it should display. We want to display only one list this time, so we return a value of 1. Notice that a `UIPickerView` is passed in as a parameter. This parameter points to the picker view that is asking us the question, which makes it possible to have multiple pickers being controlled by the same data source. In our case, we know that we have only one picker, so we can safely ignore this argument because we already know which picker is calling us.

The second data source method is used by the picker to ask how many rows of data there are for a given component:

```
- (NSInteger)pickerView:(UIPickerView *)pickerView
        numberOfRowsInComponent:(NSInteger)component{
    return [self.characterNames count];
}
```

Once again, we are told which picker view is asking and which component that picker is asking about. Since we know that we have only one picker and one component, we don't bother with either of the arguments and simply return the count of objects from our sole data array.

#PRAGMA WHAT?

Did you notice the following lines of code from *SingleComponentPickerViewController.m*?

```
#pragma mark -
#pragma mark Picker Data Source Methods
```

Any line of code that begins with #pragma is technically a compiler directive. More specifically, a #pragma marks a **pragmatic**, or compiler-specific, directive that won't necessarily work with other compilers or in other environments. If the compiler doesn't recognize the directive, it ignores it, though it may generate a warning. In this case, the #pragma directives are actually directives to the IDE, not the compiler, and they tell Xcode's editor to put a break in the pop-up menu of methods and functions at the top of the editor pane. The first one puts the break in the menu. The second creates a text entry containing whatever the rest of the line holds, which you can use as a sort of descriptive header for groups of methods in your source code.

Some of your classes, especially some of your controller classes, are likely to get rather long, and the methods and functions pop-up menu makes navigating around your code much easier. Putting in #pragma directives and logically organizing your code will make that pop-up more efficient to use.

After the two data source methods, we implement one delegate method. Unlike the data source methods, all of the delegate methods are optional. The term *optional* is a bit deceiving because you do need to implement at least one delegate method. You will usually implement the method that we are implementing here. However, if you want to display something other than text in the picker, you must implement a different method instead, as you'll see when we get to the custom picker later in this chapter:

```
#pragma mark Picker Delegate Methods
- (NSString *)pickerView:(UIPickerView *)pickerView
            titleForRow:(NSInteger)row
            forComponent:(NSInteger)component {
    return self.characterNames[row];
}
```

In this method, the picker is asking us to provide the data for a specific row in a specific component. We are provided with a pointer to the picker that is asking, along with the component and row that it is asking about. Since our view has one picker with one component, we simply ignore everything except the row argument and use that to return the appropriate item from our data array.

Go ahead and compile and run again. When the simulator comes up, switch to the second tab—the one labeled **Single**—and check out your new custom picker, which should look like Figure 7-3.

When you're done reliving all those *Star Wars* memories, come on back to Xcode and we'll show you how to implement a picker with two components. If you feel up to a challenge, this next content view is actually a good one for you to attempt on your own. You've already seen all the methods you'll need for this picker, so go ahead and take a crack at it. We'll wait here. You might want to start with a good look at Figure 7-4, just to refresh your memory. When you're finished, read on and you'll see how we tackled this problem.

Implementing a Multicomponent Picker

The next tab will have a picker with two components, or wheels, each independent of the other. The left wheel will have a list of sandwich fillings and the right wheel will have a selection of bread types. We'll write the same data source and delegate methods that we did for the single-component picker. We'll just need to write a little additional code in some of those methods to make sure we're returning the correct value and row count for each component.

Declaring Outlets and Actions

Single-click *DoubleComponentPickerViewController.h* and add the following code:

```
#import <UIKit/UIKit.h>

@interface DoubleComponentPickerViewController : UIViewController
<UIPickerViewDelegate, UIPickerViewDataSource>

@end
```

Here, we simply conform our controller class to both the delegate and data source. Save this and click *Main.storyboard* to work on the GUI.

Building the View

Select the **Double Scene** in the Document Outline and click its **View Controller** icon to bring the view controller to the front in the editor area. Now add a picker view and a button to the view, change the button label to **Select**, and then make the necessary connections. We're not going to walk you through it this time, but you can refer to the previous section if you need a step-by-step guide, since the two view controllers are identical in terms of connections in the storyboard. Here's a summary of what you need to do:

1. Create an outlet called doublePicker in the class extension of the DoubleComponentPickerViewController class to connect the view controller to the picker.

2. Connect the **dataSource** and **delegate** connections on the picker view to the view controller (use the Connections Inspector).

3. Connect the Touch Up Inside event of the button to a new action called buttonPressed on the view controller (use the Connections Inspector).

4. Add Auto Layout constraints to the picker and the button to pin them in place.

Make sure you save your storyboard before you dive back into the code. Oh, and dog-ear this page (or use a bookmark, if you prefer). You'll be referring to it in a bit.

Implementing the Controller

Select *DoubleComponentPickerViewController.m* and add the following code at the top of the file:

```
#import "DoubleComponentPickerViewController.h"

#define kFillingComponent 0
#define kBreadComponent   1

@interface DoubleComponentPickerViewController ()

@property (weak, nonatomic) IBOutlet UIPickerView *doublePicker;
@property (strong, nonatomic) NSArray *fillingTypes;
@property (strong, nonatomic) NSArray *breadTypes;

@end
```

As you can see, we start out by defining two constants that will represent the two components, which is just to make our code easier to read. Picker components are referred to by number, with the leftmost component being assigned zero and increasing by one each move to the right. Next, we declare properties for two arrays to hold the data for our two picker components.

Now implement the buttonPressed: method, as shown here:

```
- (IBAction)buttonPressed:(id)sender {
    NSInteger fillingRow = [self.doublePicker selectedRowInComponent:
                               kFillingComponent];
    NSInteger breadRow = [self.doublePicker selectedRowInComponent:
                               kBreadComponent];


    NSString *filling = self.fillingTypes[fillingRow];
    NSString *bread = self.breadTypes[breadRow];

    NSString *message = [[NSString alloc] initWithFormat:
            @"Your %@ on %@ bread will be right up.", filling, bread];


    UIAlertController *alert =
    [UIAlertController
            alertControllerWithTitle:@"Thank you for your order"
            message:message
            preferredStyle:UIAlertControllerStyleAlert];
    UIAlertAction *action = [UIAlertAction actionWithTitle:@"Great!"
                style:UIAlertActionStyleDefault handler:nil];
    [alert addAction:action];
    [self presentViewController:alert animated:YES completion:nil];
}
```

Next, add the following lines of code to the viewDidload method:

```
- (void)viewDidLoad {
    [super viewDidLoad];
    // Do any additional setup after loading the view.
    self.fillingTypes = @[@"Ham", @"Turkey", @"Peanut Butter",
                            @"Tuna Salad", @"Chicken Salad",
                            @"Roast Beef", @"Vegemite"];
    self.breadTypes = @[@"White", @"Whole Wheat", @"Rye",
                          @"Sourdough", @"Seven Grain"];
}
```

Also, add the delegate and data source methods at the bottom, before the final @end line:

```
#pragma mark -
#pragma mark Picker Data Source Methods
- (NSInteger)numberOfComponentsInPickerView:(UIPickerView *)pickerView {
    return 2;
}
```

```
- (NSInteger)pickerView:(UIPickerView *)pickerView
      numberOfRowsInComponent:(NSInteger)component {
    if (component == kBreadComponent) {
        return [self.breadTypes count];
    } else {
        return [self.fillingTypes count];
    }
}

#pragma mark Picker Delegate Methods
- (NSString *)pickerView:(UIPickerView *)pickerView
              titleForRow:(NSInteger)row
            forComponent:(NSInteger)component {
    if (component == kBreadComponent) {
        return self.breadTypes[row];
    } else {
        return self.fillingTypes[row];
    }
}

@end
```

The buttonPressed: method is a bit more involved this time, but there's very little there that's new to you. We just need to specify which component we are talking about when we request the selected row using those constants we defined earlier, kBreadComponent and kFillingComponent:

```
NSInteger fillingRow = [self.doublePicker selectedRowInComponent:
                            kFillingComponent];
NSInteger breadRow   = [self.doublePicker selectedRowInComponent:
                            kBreadComponent];
```

You can see here that using the two constants instead of 0 and 1 makes our code considerably more readable. From this point on, the buttonPressed: method is fundamentally the same as the last one we wrote.

viewDidLoad is also very similar to the version we wrote for the previous picker. The only difference is that we are loading two arrays with data rather than just one array. Again, we're just creating arrays from a hard-coded list of strings—something you generally won't do in your own applications.

When we get down to the data source methods, that's where things start to change a bit. In the first method, we specify that our picker should have two components rather than just one:

```
- (NSInteger)numberOfComponentsInPickerView:(UIPickerView *)pickerView {
    return 2;
}
```

This time, when we are asked for the number of rows, we need to check which component the picker is asking about and return the correct row count for the corresponding array:

```
- (NSInteger)pickerView:(UIPickerView *)pickerView
          numberOfRowsInComponent:(NSInteger)component {
    if (component == kBreadComponent) {
        return [self.breadTypes count];
    } else {
        return [self.fillingTypes count];
    }
}
```

Next, in our delegate method, we do the same thing. We check the component and use the correct array for the requested component to fetch and return the correct value:

```
- (NSString *)pickerView:(UIPickerView *)pickerView
            titleForRow:(NSInteger)row
            forComponent:(NSInteger)component {
    if (component == kBreadComponent) {
        return self.breadTypes[row];
    } else {
        return self.fillingTypes[row];
    }
}
```

That wasn't so hard, was it? Compile and run your application, and make sure the **Double** content pane looks like Figure 7-4.

Notice that the wheels are completely independent of each other. Turning one has no effect on the other. That's appropriate in this case, but there will be times when one component is dependent on another. A good example of this is in the date picker. When you change the month, the dial that shows the number of days in the month may need to change, because not all months have the same number of days. Implementing this isn't really hard once you know how, but it's not the easiest thing to figure out on your own, so let's do that next.

Implementing Dependent Components

We're picking up steam now. For this next section, we're not going to hold your hand quite as much when it comes to material we've already covered. Instead, we'll focus on the new stuff. Our new picker will display a list of US states in the left component and a list of corresponding ZIP codes in the right component.

We'll need a separate list of ZIP code values for each item in the left-hand component. We'll declare two arrays, one for each component, as we did last time. We'll also need an NSDictionary. In the dictionary, we're going to store an NSArray for each state (see Figure 7-14). Later, we'll implement a delegate method that will notify us when the picker's selection changes. If the value on the left changes, we will grab the correct array out of the dictionary and assign it to the array being used for the right-hand component. Don't worry if you didn't catch all that; we'll talk about it more as we get into the code.

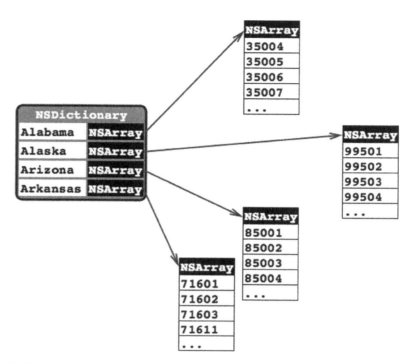

Figure 7-14. Our application's data. For each state, there will be one entry in a dictionary with the name of the state as the key. Stored under that key will be an NSArray instance containing all the ZIP codes from that state

Add the following code to your *DependentComponentPickerViewController.h* file:

```
#import <UIKit/UIKit.h>

@interface DependentComponentPickerViewController : UIViewController
<UIPickerViewDelegate, UIPickerViewDataSource>

@end
```

Next, add the following to *DependentComponentPickerViewController.m*:

```
#import "DependentComponentPickerViewController.h"

#define kStateComponent 0
#define kZipComponent   1
```

```
@interface DependentComponentPickerViewController ()

@property (strong, nonatomic) NSDictionary *stateZips;
@property (strong, nonatomic) NSArray *states;
@property (strong, nonatomic) NSArray *zips;

@end
```

Now it's time to build the content view. That process will be almost identical to the previous two component views we built. If you get lost, flip back to the "Building the View" section for the single-component picker and follow those step-by-step instructions. Here's a hint: start off by opening *Main.storyboard*, find the view controller for the DependentComponentPickerViewController class, and then repeat the same basic steps you've done for all the other content views in this chapter. You should end up with an outlet property called dependentPicker connected to a picker, an empty buttonPressed: method connected to a button, and both the delegate and dataSource properties of the picker connected to the view controller. Don't forget to add the Auto Layout constraints to both views! When you're finished, save the storyboard.

OK, take a deep breath. Let's implement this controller class. This implementation may seem a little gnarly at first. By making one component dependent on the other, we have added a whole new level of complexity to our controller class. Although the picker displays only two lists at a time, our controller class must know about and manage 51 lists. The technique we're going to use here actually simplifies that process. The data source methods look almost identical to the one we implemented for the DoublePickerViewController. All of the additional complexity is handled elsewhere, between viewDidLoad and a new delegate method called pickerView:didSelectRow: inComponent:.

Before we write the code, we need some data to display. Up till now, we've created arrays in code by specifying a list of strings. Because we didn't want you to need to type in several thousand values, and because we figured we should show you the correct way to do this, we're going to load the data from a property list. As mentioned, both NSArray and NSDictionary objects can be created from property lists. We've included a property list called *statedictionary.plist* in the project archive, under the *07 – Picker Data* folder.

Drag that file into the *Pickers* folder in your Xcode project. If you single-click the *.plist* file in the Project Navigator, you can see and even edit the data that it contains (see Figure 7-15).

Key	Type	Value
▼ Root	Dictionary	(50 items)
▶ Alabama	Array	(657 items)
▶ Alaska	Array	(251 items)
▶ Arizona	Array	(376 items)
▶ Arkansas	Array	(618 items)
▶ California	Array	(1757 items)
▶ Colorado	Array	(501 items)
▶ Connecticut	Array	(276 items)
▶ Delaware	Array	(68 items)
▶ Florida	Array	(972 items)
▶ Georgia	Array	(736 items)
▶ Hawaii	Array	(92 items)
▶ Idaho	Array	(292 items)
▶ Illinois	Array	(1375 items)
▶ Indiana	Array	(780 items)
▶ Iowa	Array	(972 items)
▶ Kansas	Array	(721 items)
▶ Kentucky	Array	(799 items)
▶ Louisiana	Array	(542 items)
▶ Maine	Array	(415 items)
▶ Maryland	Array	(466 items)
▶ Massachusetts	Array	(519 items)
▶ Michigan	Array	(987 items)
▶ Minnesota	Array	(892 items)
▶ Mississippi	Array	(447 items)
▶ Missouri	Array	(1040 items)
▶ Montana	Array	(364 items)
▶ Nebraska	Array	(590 items)
▶ Nevada	Array	(158 items)
▶ New Hampshire	Array	(238 items)
▶ New Jersey	Array	(604 items)
▶ New Mexico	Array	(366 items)
▶ New York	Array	(1677 items)
▶ North Carolina	Array	(809 items)
▶ North Dakota	Array	(392 items)
▼ Ohio	Array	(1189 items)
Item 0	String	43001
Item 1	String	43002
Item 2	String	43003
Item 3	String	43004
Item 4	String	43005
Item 5	String	43006

Figure 7-15. The statedictionary.plist file, showing our list of states. Within Ohio, you can see the start of a list of ZIP codes

Now, let's write some code. In *DependentComponentPickerViewController.m,* we're going to first show you some whole methods to implement, and then we'll break it down into more digestible chunks. Start with the implementation of buttonPressed::

```objc
- (IBAction)buttonPressed:(id)sender {
    NSInteger stateRow = [self.dependentPicker
                          selectedRowInComponent:kStateComponent];
    NSInteger zipRow = [self.dependentPicker
                        selectedRowInComponent:kZipComponent];

    NSString *state = self.states[stateRow];
    NSString *zip = self.zips[zipRow];

    NSString *title = [[NSString alloc] initWithFormat:
                       @"You selected zip code %@.", zip];
    NSString *message = [[NSString alloc] initWithFormat:
                         @"%@ is in %@", zip, state];

    UIAlertController *alert =
    [UIAlertController alertControllerWithTitle:title
                  message:message
                  preferredStyle:UIAlertControllerStyleAlert];
    UIAlertAction *action = [UIAlertAction actionWithTitle:@"OK"
                        style:UIAlertActionStyleDefault handler:nil];
    [alert addAction:action];
    [self presentViewController:alert animated:YES completion:nil];
}
```

Next, add the following code to the existing viewDidLoad method:

```objc
- (void)viewDidLoad {
    [super viewDidLoad];
    // Do any additional setup after loading the view from its nib.
    NSBundle *bundle = [NSBundle mainBundle];
    NSURL *plistURL = [bundle URLForResource:@"statedictionary"
                               withExtension:@"plist"];

    self.stateZips = [NSDictionary
                      dictionaryWithContentsOfURL:plistURL];

    NSArray *allStates = [self.stateZips allKeys];
    NSArray *sortedStates = [allStates sortedArrayUsingSelector:
                       @selector(compare:)];
    self.states = sortedStates;

    NSString *selectedState = self.states[0];
    self.zips = self.stateZips[selectedState];
}
```

And, finally, add the delegate and data source methods at the bottom of the file:

```
#pragma mark -
#pragma mark Picker Data Source Methods
- (NSInteger)numberOfComponentsInPickerView:(UIPickerView *)pickerView {
    return 2;
}

- (NSInteger)pickerView:(UIPickerView *)pickerView
           numberOfRowsInComponent:(NSInteger)component {
    if (component == kStateComponent) {
        return [self.states count];
    } else {
        return [self.zips count];
    }
}

#pragma mark Picker Delegate Methods
- (NSString *)pickerView:(UIPickerView *)pickerView
             titleForRow:(NSInteger)row
            forComponent:(NSInteger)component {
    if (component == kStateComponent) {
        return self.states[row];
    } else {
        return self.zips[row];
    }
}

- (void)pickerView:(UIPickerView *)pickerView
      didSelectRow:(NSInteger)row
       inComponent:(NSInteger)component {
    if (component == kStateComponent) {
        NSString *selectedState = self.states[row];
        self.zips = self.stateZips[selectedState];
        [self.dependentPicker reloadComponent:kZipComponent];
        [self.dependentPicker selectRow:0
                            inComponent:kZipComponent
                               animated:YES];
    }
}

@end
```

There's no need to talk about the buttonPressed: method since it's fundamentally the same as the previous one. We should talk about the viewDidLoad method, though. There's some stuff going on there that you need to understand, so pull up a chair and let's chat.

The first thing we do in this new viewDidLoad method is grab a reference to our application's main bundle:

```
NSBundle *bundle = [NSBundle mainBundle];
```

What is a bundle, you ask? Well, a **bundle** is just a special type of folder, the contents of which follow a specific structure. Applications and frameworks are both bundles, and this call returns a bundle object that represents our application.

One of the primary uses of NSBundle is to get to resources that you added to the *Resources* folder of your project. Those files will be copied into your application's bundle when you build your application. We've added resources like images to our projects; but up to now, we've used those only in Interface Builder. If we want to get to those resources in our code, we usually need to use NSBundle. We use the main bundle to retrieve the URL of the resource in which we're interested:

```
NSURL *plistURL = [bundle URLForResource:@"statedictionary"
                         withExtension:@"plist"];
```

This will return a URL containing the location of the *statedictionary.plist* file. We can then use that URL to create an NSDictionary object. Once we do that, the entire contents of that property list will be loaded into the newly created NSDictionary object; that is, it is assigned to stateZips:

```
self.stateZips = [NSDictionary
                 dictionaryWithContentsOfURL:plistURL];
```

The dictionary we just loaded uses the names of the states as the keys and contains an NSArray with all the ZIP codes for that state as the values. To populate the array for the left-hand component, we get the list of all keys from our dictionary and assign those to the states array. Before we assign it, though, we sort it alphabetically:

```
NSArray *allStates = [self.stateZips allKeys];
NSArray *sortedStates = [allStates sortedArrayUsingSelector:
                        @selector(compare:)];
self.states = sortedStates;
```

Unless we specifically set the selection to another value, pickers start with the first row (row 0) selected. To get the zips array that corresponds to the first row in the states array, we grab the object from the states array that's at index 0. That will return the name of the state that will be selected at launch time. We then use that state name to grab the array of ZIP codes for that state, which we assign to the zips array that will be used to feed data to the right-hand component:

```
NSString *selectedState = self.states[0];
self.zips = self.stateZips[selectedState];
```

The two data source methods are practically identical to the previous version. We return the number of rows in the appropriate array. The same is true for the first delegate method we implemented. The second delegate method is the new one, and it's where the magic happens:

```
- (void)pickerView:(UIPickerView *)pickerView
      didSelectRow:(NSInteger)row
       inComponent:(NSInteger)component {
```

```
    if (component == kStateComponent) {
        NSString *selectedState = self.states[row];
        self.zips = self.stateZips[selectedState];
        [self.dependentPicker reloadComponent:kZipComponent];
        [self.dependentPicker selectRow:0
                            inComponent:kZipComponent
                                animated:YES];
    }
}
```

In this method, which is called any time the picker's selection changes, we look at the component and see whether the left-hand component changed. If it did, we grab the array that corresponds to the new selection and assign it to the zips array. Next, we set the right-hand component back to the first row and tell it to reload itself. By swapping the zips array whenever the state changes, the rest of the code remains pretty much the same as it was in the DoublePicker example.

We're not quite finished yet. Compile and run your application, and then check out the **Dependent** tab (see Figure 7-16). Do you see anything there you don't like?

Figure 7-16. Do we really want the two components to be of equal size? Notice the clipping of a long state name

The two components are equal in size. Even though the ZIP code will never be more than five characters long, it has been given equal billing with the state. Since state names like Mississippi and Massachusetts won't fit in half of the picker on the screens of the iPhone 4s, iPhone 5, and iPhone 5s, this seems less than ideal. Fortunately, there's another delegate method we can implement to indicate how wide each component should be. Add the following method to the delegate section of *DependentComponentPickerViewController.m*:

```
- (CGFloat)pickerView:(UIPickerView *)pickerView
            widthForComponent:(NSInteger)component {
    CGFloat pickerWidth = pickerView.bounds.size.width;
    if (component == kZipComponent) {
        return pickerWidth/3;
    } else {
        return 2 * pickerWidth/3;
    }
}
```

In this method, we return a number that represents how many pixels wide each component should be, and the picker will do its best to accommodate this. We've chosen to give the state component two-thirds of the available width and the rest goes to the ZIP component. Feel free to experiment with other values to see how the distribution of space between the components changes as you modify them. Save, compile, and run, and the picker on the **Dependent** tab will look more like the one shown in Figure 7-5.

By this point, you should be pretty darn comfortable with both pickers and tab bar applications. We have one more thing to show you about pickers, and we plan to have a little fun while doing it. Let's create a simple slot machine game.

Creating a Simple Game with a Custom Picker

Next up, we're going to create an actual working slot machine. Well, OK, it won't dispense silver dollars, but it does look pretty cool. Take a look back at Figure 7-6 before proceeding, so you know what we're building.

Writing the Controller Header File

Begin by adding the following code to *CustomPickerViewController.h*:

```
#import <UIKit/UIKit.h>

@interface CustomPickerViewController : UIViewController
<UIPickerViewDataSource, UIPickerViewDelegate>

@end
```

Next, switch to *CustomerPickerViewController.m* and add the following property to the class extension near the top of the file:

```
#import "CustomPickerViewController.h"

@interface CustomPickerViewController ()

@property (strong, nonatomic) NSArray *images;

@end
```

At this point, all we've added to the class is a property for an NSArray object that will hold the images to use for the symbols on the spinners of the slot machine. The rest will come a little later.

Building the View

Even though the picker in Figure 7-6 looks quite a bit fancier than the other ones we've built, there's actually very little difference in the way we'll design our nib. All the extra work is done in the delegate methods of our controller.

Make sure you've saved your new source code, and then select *Main.storyboard* in the Project Navigator and select the **Custom Scene** to edit the GUI. Add a picker view, a label below that, and a button below that. Give the button the title *Spin*.

With the label selected, bring up the Attributes Inspector. Set the **Alignment** to centered. Then click **Text Color** and set the color to something bright. Next, let's make the text a little bigger. Look for the **Font** setting in the inspector, and click the icon inside it (it looks like the letter T inside a little box) to pop up the font selector. This control lets you switch from the device's standard system font to another if you like, or simply change the size. For now, just change the size to *48* and delete the word *Label*, since we don't want any text displayed until the first time the user wins.

Now add Auto Layout constraints to center the label and button horizontally and to fix the vertical gaps between them and between the label and the picker. You'll probably find it easiest to drag from the label in the Document Outline when adding its Auto Layout constraints, because the label on the storyboard is empty and so very difficult to find!

After that, make all the connections to outlets and actions. Create a new outlet called picker to connect the view controller to the picker view, another called winLabel to connect the view controller to the label. Again, you'll find it easiest to use the label in the Document Outline than the one on the storyboard. Next, connect the button's Touch Up Inside event to a new action method called spin:. After that, just make sure to connect the **delegate** and **data source** for the picker.

Oh, and there's one additional thing that you need to do. Select the picker and bring up the Attributes Inspector. You need to uncheck the check box labeled **User Interaction Enabled** within the **View** settings, so that the user can't manually change the dial and cheat. Once you've done all that, save the changes you've made to the storyboard.

FONTS SUPPORTED BY IOS DEVICES

Be careful when using the fonts palette in Interface Builder for designing iOS interfaces. The Attribute Inspector's font selector will let you assign from a wide range of fonts, but not all iOS devices have the same set of fonts available. At the time of writing, for instance, there are several fonts that are available on the iPad, but not on the iPhone or iPod touch. You should limit your font selections to one of the font families found on the iOS device you are targeting. This post on Jeff LaMarche's excellent iOS blog shows you how to grab this list programmatically: http://iphonedevelopment. blogspot.com/2010/08/fonts-and-font-families.html.

In a nutshell, create a view-based application and add this code to the method application: didFinishLaunchingWithOptions: in the application delegate:

```
for (NSString *family in [UIFont familyNames]) {
    NSLog(@"%@", family);
    for (NSString *font in [UIFont fontNamesForFamilyName:family]) {
        NSLog(@"\t%@", font);
    }
}
```

Run the project in the appropriate simulator, and your fonts will be displayed in the project's console log.

Implementing the Controller

We have a bunch of new stuff to cover in the implementation of this controller. Select *CustomPickerViewController.m* and get started by filling in the contents of the spin: method:

```
- (IBAction)spin:(id)sender {
    BOOL win = NO;
    int numInRow = 1;
    int lastVal = -1;
    for (int i = 0; i < 5; i++) {
        int newValue = arc4random_uniform((uint)[self.images count]);

        if (newValue == lastVal) {
            numInRow++;
        } else {
            numInRow = 1;
        }
        lastVal = newValue;

        [self.picker selectRow:newValue inComponent:i animated:YES];
        [self.picker reloadComponent:i];
        if (numInRow >=3) {
            win = YES;
        }
    }
```

```
    if (win) {
        self.winLabel.text = @"WINNER!";
    } else {
        self.winLabel.text = @" "; // Note ths space between the quotes
    }
}
```

Next, insert the following code into the viewDidLoad method:

```
- (void)viewDidLoad {
    [super viewDidLoad];
    // Do any additional setup after loading the view.
    self.images = @[[UIImage imageNamed:@"seven"],
                    [UIImage imageNamed:@"bar"],
                    [UIImage imageNamed:@"crown"],
                    [UIImage imageNamed:@"cherry"],
                    [UIImage imageNamed:@"lemon"],
                    [UIImage imageNamed:@"apple"]];
    self.winLabel.text = @" "; // Note ths space between the quotes
}
```

Finally, add the following code to the end of the file, before the final @end line:

```
#pragma mark -
#pragma mark Picker Data Source Methods
- (NSInteger)numberOfComponentsInPickerView:(UIPickerView *)pickerView {
    return 5;
}

- (NSInteger)pickerView:(UIPickerView *)pickerView
        numberOfRowsInComponent:(NSInteger)component {
    return [self.images count];
}

#pragma mark Picker Delegate Methods
- (UIView *)pickerView:(UIPickerView *)pickerView
        viewForRow:(NSInteger)row
      forComponent:(NSInteger)component reusingView:(UIView *)view {
    UIImage *image = self.images[row];
    UIImageView *imageView = [[UIImageView alloc] initWithImage:image];
    return imageView;
}

- (CGFloat)pickerView:(UIPickerView *)pickerView
    rowHeightForComponent:(NSInteger)component {
    return 64;
}

@end
```

There's a lot going on here, huh? Let's take the new stuff, method by method.

The spin Method

The spin method fires when the user touches the **Spin** button. In it, we first declare a few variables that will help us keep track of whether the user has won. We'll use win to keep track of whether we've found three in a row by setting it to YES if we have. We'll use numInRow to keep track of how many of the same value we have in a row so far, and we will keep track of the previous component's value in lastVal, so that we have a way to compare the current value to the previous value. We initialize lastVal to -1 because we know that value won't match any of the real values:

```
BOOL win = NO;
int numInRow = 1;
int lastVal = -1;
```

Next, we loop through all five components and set each one to a new, randomly generated row selection. We get the count from the images array to do that, which is a shortcut we can use because we know that all five columns use the same number of images:

```
for (int i = 0; i < 5; i++) {
    int newValue = arc4random_uniform((uint)[self.images count])
```

We compare the new value to the previous value and increment numInRow if it matches. If the value didn't match, we reset numInRow back to 1. We then assign the new value to lastVal, so we'll have it to compare the next time through the loop:

```
if (newValue == lastVal) {
    numInRow++;
} else {
    numInRow = 1;
}
lastVal = newValue;
```

After that, we set the corresponding component to the new value, telling it to animate the change, and we tell the picker to reload that component:

```
[self.picker selectRow:newValue inComponent:i animated:YES];
[self.picker reloadComponent:i];
```

The last thing we do each time through the loop is check whether we have three in a row, and then set win to YES if we do:

```
if (numInRow >=3) {
    win = YES;
}
```

Once we're finished with the loop, we set the label to say whether the spin was a win:

```
if (win) {
    self.winLabel.text = @"WINNER!";
} else {
    self.winLabel.text = @" "; // Note ths space between the quotes
}
```

The viewDidLoad Method

Looking back at what we added here, the first thing was to load six different images, which we added to *Images.xcassets* right back at the beginning of the chapter. We did this using the imageNamed: convenience method of the UIImage class:

```
self.images = @[[UIImage imageNamed:@"seven"],
[UIImage imageNamed:@"bar"], [UIImage imageNamed:@"crown"],
[UIImage imageNamed:@"cherry"], [UIImage imageNamed:@"lemon"],
[UIImage imageNamed:@"apple"]];
```

The last thing we did in this method was to make sure the label contains exactly one space. We want the label to be empty, but if we really make it empty, it collapses to zero height. By including a space, we make sure the label is shown at its correct height:

```
self.winLabel.text = @" "; // Note ths space between the quotes
```

That was really simple, wasn't it? But, um, what do we do with those six images? If you scroll down through the code you just typed, you'll see that two data source methods look pretty much the same as before; however, if you look further into the delegate methods, you'll see that we're using a completely different delegate method to provide data to the picker. The one that we've used up to now returned an NSString *, but this one returns a UIView *.

Using this method instead, we can supply the picker with anything that can be drawn into a UIView. Of course, there are limitations on what will work here and look good at the same time, given the small size of the picker. But this method gives us a lot more freedom in what we display, although it is a bit more work:

```
- (UIView *)pickerView:(UIPickerView *)pickerView
      viewForRow:(NSInteger)row
    forComponent:(NSInteger)component reusingView:(UIView *)view {
  UIImage *image = self.images[row];
  UIImageView *imageView = [[UIImageView alloc] initWithImage:image];
  return imageView;
}
```

This method returns one UIImageView object initialized with one of the images for the symbols. To do that, we first get the image for the symbol for the row. Next, create and return an image view with that symbol. For views more complex than a single image, it can be beneficial to create all needed views first (e.g., in viewDidLoad), and then return these pre-created views to the picker view when requested. But for our simple case, creating the needed views on the fly works well.

Wow, take a deep breath. You got through all of it in one piece, and now you get to take it for a spin. So, build and run the application and have fun!

Final Details

Our game is rather fun, especially when you think about how little effort it took to build it. Now let's improve it with a couple more tweaks. There are two things about this game right now that really bug us:

- It's so darn quiet. Slot machines aren't quiet!

- It tells us that we've won before the dials have finished spinning, which is a minor thing, but it does tend to eliminate the anticipation. To see this in action, run your application again. It is subtle, but the label really does appear before the wheels finish spinning.

The *07 - Picker Sounds* folder in the project archive that accompanies the book contains two sound files: *crunch.wav* and *win.wav*. Drag both of these files to your project's *Pickers* folder. These are the sounds we'll play when the users tap the **Spin** button and when they win, respectively.

To work with sounds, we'll need access to the iOS Audio Toolbox classes. Insert the following line shown in bold above the existing #import line at the top of *CustomPickerViewController.m*:

```
#import <AudioToolbox/AudioToolbox.h>
#import "CustomPickerViewController.h"
```

Next, we need to add an outlet that will point to the button. While the wheels are spinning, we're going to hide the button. We don't want users tapping the button again until the current spin is all done. Add the following bold line of code to *CustomPickerViewController.m*:

```
@interface CustomPickerViewController ()

@property (strong, nonatomic) NSArray *images;
@property (weak, nonatomic) IBOutlet UIPickerView *picker;
@property (weak, nonatomic) IBOutlet UILabel *winLabel;
@property (weak, nonatomic) IBOutlet UIButton *button;

@end
```

After you type that and save the file, click *Main.storyboard* to edit the GUI. Once it's open, Control-drag from the **Custom** icon below the **Custom Scene** in the Document Outline to the **Spin** button and connect it to the new button outlet we just created. Save the storyboard.

Now, we need to do a few things in the implementation of our controller class. First, we need some instance variables to hold references to the loaded sounds. Open *CustomPickerViewController.m* and add the following new properties:

```
@interface CustomPickerViewController ()

@property (strong, nonatomic) NSArray *images;
@property (weak, nonatomic) IBOutlet UIPickerView *picker;
@property (weak, nonatomic) IBOutlet UILabel *winLabel;
@property (weak, nonatomic) IBOutlet UIButton *button;
```

```
@property (assign, nonatomic) SystemSoundID winSoundID;
@property (assign, nonatomic) SystemSoundID crunchSoundID;

@end
```

We also need a couple of methods added to our controller class. Add the following two methods to *CustomPickerViewController.m*:

```
- (void)showButton {
    self.button.hidden = NO;
}

- (void)playWinSound {
    if (_winSoundID == 0) {
        NSURL *soundURL = [[NSBundle mainBundle] URLForResource:@"win"
                                                  withExtension:@"wav"];
        AudioServicesCreateSystemSoundID((__bridge CFURLRef)soundURL,
                                         &_winSoundID);
    }
    AudioServicesPlaySystemSound(_winSoundID);
    self.winLabel.text = @"WINNER!";
    [self performSelector:@selector(showButton)
               withObject:nil
               afterDelay:1.5];
}
```

The first method is used to show the button. As noted previously, we're going to hide the button when the user taps it because, if the wheels are already spinning, there's no point in letting them spin again until they've stopped.

The second method will be called when the user wins. First, we check if we have already loaded the winning sound. Properties are initialized as zero and valid identifiers for loaded sounds are not zero, so we can check whether the sound is loaded yet by comparing the identifier to zero. To load a sound, we first ask the main bundle for the path to the sound called *win.wav*, just as we did when we loaded the property list for the Dependent picker view. Once we have the path to that resource, the next three lines of code load the sound file in and play it. Next, we set the label to *WINNER!* and call the showButton method; however, we call the showButton method in a special way using a method called performSelector:withObject:afterDelay:. This is a very handy method available to all objects. It lets you call the method sometime in the future—in this case, one and a half seconds in the future, which will give the dials time to spin to their final locations before telling the user the result.

> **Note**   You may have noticed something a bit odd about the way we called the
> `AudioServicesCreateSystemSoundID` function. That function takes a URL as its first parameter, but
> it doesn't want an instance of `NSURL`. Instead, it wants a `CFURLRef` structure. Apple provides C interfaces
> to many common components—such as URLs, arrays, strings, and much more—via the Core Foundation
> framework. This allows even applications written entirely in C some access to the functionality that we
> normally use from Objective-C. The interesting thing is that these C components are "bridged" to their
> Objective-C counterparts, so that a `CFURLRef` is functionally equivalent to an `NSURL` pointer, for example.
> That means that certain kinds of objects created in Objective-C can be pushed over the bridge to use C APIs,
> and vice versa. This is accomplished by using a C language cast, putting the type you want your variable to
> be interpreted as inside parentheses before the variable name. Starting in iOS 5, with the use of ARC, the type
> name itself must be preceded by the keyword __bridge, which gives ARC a hint about how it should handle
> this Objective-C object as it passes into a C API call.

We also need to make some changes to the `spin:` method. We will write code to play a sound
and to call the `playWinSound` method if the player won. Make the following changes to the `spin:`
method now:

```objc
- (IBAction)spin:(id)sender {
    BOOL win = NO;
    int numInRow = 1;
    int lastVal = -1;
    for (int i = 0; i < 5; i++) {
        int newValue = random() % [self.images count];

        if (newValue == lastVal) {
            numInRow++;
        } else {
            numInRow = 1;
        }
        lastVal = newValue;

        [self.picker selectRow:newValue inComponent:i animated:YES];
        [self.picker reloadComponent:i];
        if (numInRow >=3) {
            win = YES;
        }
    }
    if (_crunchSoundID == 0) {
        NSString *path = [[NSBundle mainBundle] pathForResource:@"crunch"
                                                        ofType:@"wav"];
        NSURL *soundURL = [NSURL fileURLWithPath:path];
        AudioServicesCreateSystemSoundID((__bridge CFURLRef)soundURL,
                                        &_crunchSoundID);

    }
    AudioServicesPlaySystemSound(_crunchSoundID);
```

```
    if (win) {
        [self performSelector:@selector(playWinSound)
                    withObject:nil
                    afterDelay:.5];
    } else {
        [self performSelector:@selector(showButton)
                    withObject:nil
                    afterDelay:.5];
    }
    self.button.hidden = YES;
    self.winLabel.text = @" ";   // Note the space between the quotes

        if (win) {
            self.winLabel.text = @"WINNER!";
        } else {
            self.winLabel.text = @"";
        }
}
```

First, we load the crunch sound if needed, just as we did with the win sound before. Now play the crunch sound to let the player know the wheels have been spun. Next, instead of setting the label to *WINNER!* as soon as we know the user has won, we do something tricky. We call one of the two methods we just created, but we do it after a delay using performSelector:afterDelay:. If the user won, we call our playWinSound method half a second into the future, which will give time for the dials to spin into place; otherwise, we just wait a half a second and reenable the **Spin** button. While waiting for the result, we hide the button and clear the label's text.

Now you're done! Hit the Xcode **Run** button and click the final tab to see and hear this slot machine in action. Tapping the **Spin** button should play a little cranking sound, and a win should produce a winning sound. Hooray!

Final Spin

By now, you should be comfortable with tab bar applications and pickers. In this chapter, we built a full-fledged tab bar application containing five different content views from scratch. You learned how to use pickers in a number of different configurations, how to create pickers with multiple components, and even how to make the values in one component dependent on the value selected in another component. You also saw how to make the picker display images rather than just text.

Along the way, you learned about picker delegates and data sources, and saw how to load images, play sounds, and create dictionaries from property lists. It was a long chapter, so congratulations on making it through! When you're ready to tackle table views, turn the page and we'll keep going.

Chapter 8

Introduction to Table Views

Over the course of the next few chapters, we're going to build some hierarchical navigation-based applications similar to the Mail application that ships on iOS devices. Applications of this type, usually called **master-detail applications**, allow the user to drill down into nested lists of data and edit that data. But before we can build applications like that, you need to master the concept of table views. And that's the goal of this chapter.

Table views are the most common mechanism used to display lists of data to the user. They are highly configurable objects that can be made to look practically any way you want them to look. Mail uses table views to show lists of accounts, folders, and messages; however, table views are not limited to just the display of textual data. Table views are also used in the Settings, Music, and Clock applications, even though those applications have very different appearances (see Figure 8-1).

Figure 8-1. *Though they all look different, the Settings, Music, and Clock applications use table views to display their data*

Table View Basics

Tables display lists of data. Each item in a table's list is a row. iOS tables can have an unlimited number of rows, constrained only by the amount of available memory. iOS tables can be only one column wide.

Table Views and Table View Cells

A table view is the view object that displays a table's data and is an instance of the class UITableView. Each visible row in a table is implemented by an instance of the class UITableViewCell (see Figure 8-2).

Figure 8-2. *Each table view is an instance of UITableView, and each visible row is an instance of UITableViewCell*

Table views are not responsible for storing your table's data. They store only enough data to draw the rows that are currently visible. Table views get their configuration data from an object that conforms to the UITableViewDelegate protocol and their row data from an object that conforms to the UITableViewDataSource protocol. You'll see how all this works when we get into our sample programs later in the chapter.

As mentioned, all tables are implemented as a single column. The Clock application, shown on the right side of Figure 8-1, does give the appearance of having two columns, but in reality, that's not the case—each row in the table is represented by a single UITableViewCell. By default, a UITableViewCell object can be configured with an image, some text, and an optional accessory icon, which is a small icon on the right side (we'll cover accessory icons in detail in the next chapter).

You can put even more data in a cell if you need to by adding subviews to UITableViewCell. You do this using one of two basic techniques: by adding subviews programmatically when creating the cell or by loading them from a storyboard or nib file. You can lay out the table view cell in any way you like and include any subviews you desire. So, the single-column limitation is far less limiting than it probably sounds at first. If this is confusing, don't worry—we'll show you how to use both of these techniques in this chapter.

Grouped and Plain Tables

Table views come in two basic styles:

- **Grouped**: A grouped table view contains one or more sections of rows. Within each section, all rows sit tightly together in a nice little group; but between sections, there are clearly visible gaps, as shown in the leftmost picture in Figure 8-3. Note that a grouped table can consist of a single group.

- **Plain**: Plain is the default style. In this style, the sections are slightly closer together, and each section's header can optionally be styled in a custom manner. When an index is used, this style is also referred to as **indexed** (see Figure 8-3, right).

Figure 8-3. *The same table view displayed as a grouped table (left); a plain table without an index (middle); and a plain table with an index, which is also called an indexed table (right)*

If your data source provides the necessary information, the table view will let the user navigate your list using an index that is displayed down the right side.

Each division of your table is known to your data source as a **section**. In a grouped table, each section is represented visually as a group. In an indexed table, each indexed grouping of data is a section. For example, in the indexed table shown in Figure 8-3, all the names beginning with *A* would be one section, those beginning with *B* would be another, and so on.

Caution   Even though it is technically possible to create a grouped table with an index, you should not do so. The *iPhone Human Interface Guidelines* specifically state that grouped tables should not provide indexes.

Implementing a Simple Table

Let's look at the simplest possible example of a table view to get a feel for how it works. In this example, we're just going to display a list of text values.

Create a new project in Xcode. For this chapter, we're going back to the Single View Application template, so select that one. Call your project *Simple Table*, set Objective-C as the **Language**, set the **Devices** field to *Universal* and make sure that **Use Core Data** is unchecked.

Designing the View

In the Project Navigator, expand the top-level *Simple Table* project and the *Simple Table* folder. This is such a simple application that we're not going to need any outlets or actions. Go ahead and select *Main.storyboard* to edit the storyboard. If the View window isn't visible in the layout area, single-click its icon in the Document Outline to open it. Next, look in the object library for a Table View (see Figure 8-4) and drag that over to the View window.

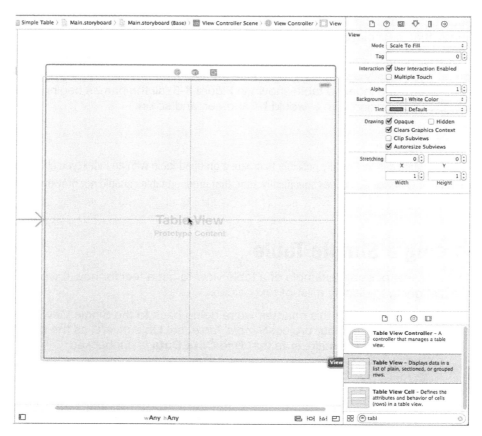

Figure 8-4. *Dragging a table view from the library onto our main view. Notice that the table view automatically resizes to the full size of the view*

The table view should automatically size itself to the height and width of the view. This is exactly what we want. Table views are designed to fill the entire width of the screen and most of the height as well—whatever isn't taken up by your application's navigation bars, toolbars, and tab bars. Drop the table view onto the View window and line it up to be centered in its parent view. Now let's add Auto Layout constraints to make sure that the table view is positioned and sized correctly no matter what size the screen is. Select the table in the Document Outline, and then click the **Pin** icon at the bottom right of the storyboard editor (see Figure 8-5).

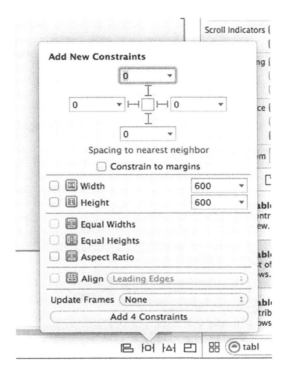

Figure 8-5. *Pinning the table view so that it fits the screen*

At the top of the pop-up, clear the **Constrain to margins** check box, click all four dashed lines, and set the distances in the four input fields to zero. This will have the effect of pinning all four edges of the table view to those of its parent view. To apply the constraints, change **Update Frames** to *Items of New Constraints*, and click the **Add 4 Constraints** button.

Select the table view again in the Document Inspector and press ⌥⌘6 to bring up the Connections Inspector. You'll notice that the first two available connections for the table view are the same as the first two for the picker views that we used in the last chapter: *dataSource* and *delegate*. Drag from the circle next to each of those connections over to the **View Controller** icon in the Document Outline or above the view controller in the storyboard editor. This makes our controller class both the data source and delegate for this table.

After setting the connections, save your storyboard and get ready to dig into some `UITableView` code.

Writing the Controller

The next stop is our controller class's header file. Single-click *ViewController.m* and add the following code at the top of the file:

```
#import "ViewController.h"

@interface ViewController () <UITableViewDataSource, UITableViewDelegate>

@property (copy, nonatomic) NSArray *dwarves;

@end

@implementation ViewController

- (void)viewDidLoad
{
    [super viewDidLoad];
    // Do any additional setup after loading the view, typically from a nib.
    self.dwarves = @[@"Sleepy", @"Sneezy", @"Bashful", @"Happy",
                     @"Doc", @"Grumpy", @"Dopey",
                     @"Thorin", @"Dorin", @"Nori", @"Ori",
                     @"Balin", @"Dwalin", @"Fili", @"Kili",
                     @"Oin", @"Gloin", @"Bifur", @"Bofur",
                     @"Bombur"];
}
```

Next, add the following code at the end of the file:

```
- (NSInteger)tableView:(UITableView *)tableView
          numberOfRowsInSection:(NSInteger)section {
    return [self.dwarves count];
}

- (UITableViewCell *)tableView:(UITableView *)tableView
        cellForRowAtIndexPath:(NSIndexPath *)indexPath {
    static NSString *SimpleTableIdentifier = @"SimpleTableIdentifier";

    UITableViewCell *cell = [tableView dequeueReusableCellWithIdentifier:
                                        SimpleTableIdentifier];
    if (cell == nil) {
        cell = [[UITableViewCell alloc]
                initWithStyle:UITableViewCellStyleDefault
                reuseIdentifier:SimpleTableIdentifier];
    }

    cell.textLabel.text = self.dwarves[indexPath.row];
    return cell;
}

@end
```

First, we conformed our class to the two protocols that are needed for it to act as the delegate and data source for the table view. Then we declared an array that will hold the data to be displayed. And finally, we added three methods to the controller. You should be comfortable with the first one, viewDidLoad, since we've done similar things in the past. We're simply creating an array of data to display in the table. In a real application, this array would come from another source, such as a text file, a property list, or a web service.

Next, we added two data source methods. The first one, tableView:numberOfRowsInSection:, is used by the table to ask how many rows are in a particular section. As you might expect, the default number of sections is one, and this method will be called to get the number of rows in the one section that makes up the list. We just return the number of items in our array.

The next method probably requires a little explanation, so let's look at it more closely:

```
- (UITableViewCell *)tableView:(UITableView *)tableView
        cellForRowAtIndexPath:(NSIndexPath *)indexPath
```

This method is called by the table view when it needs to draw one of its rows. Notice that the second argument to this method is an NSIndexPath instance. NSIndexPath is a structure that table views use to wrap the section and row indexes into a single object. To get the row index or the section index out of an NSIndexPath, you just access its row property or its section property, both of which return an integer value.

The first parameter, tableView, is a reference to the table that's being constructed. This allows us to create classes that act as a data source for multiple tables.

Next, we declare a static string instance:

```
static NSString *SimpleTableIdentifier = @"SimpleTableIdentifier";
```

This string will be used as a key to represent the type of our table cell. In this example, the table uses only a single type of cell, but in a more complex table, you might need to format different types of cells according to their content or position, in which case you would use a separate table cell identifier for each distinct cell type.

A table view can display only a few rows at a time, but the table itself can conceivably hold considerably more. Remember that each row in the table is represented by an instance of UITableViewCell, a subclass of UIView, which means each row can contain subviews. With a large table, this could represent a huge amount of overhead if the table were to try to keep one table view cell instance for every row in the table, regardless of whether that row was currently being displayed. Fortunately, tables don't work that way.

Instead, as table view cells scroll off the screen, they are placed into a queue of cells available to be reused. If the system runs low on memory, the table view will get rid of the cells in the queue. But as long as the system has some memory available for those cells, it will hold on to them in case you want to use them again.

Every time a table view cell rolls off the screen, there's a pretty good chance that another one just rolled onto the screen on the other side. If that new row can just reuse one of the cells that has already rolled off the screen, the system can avoid the overhead associated with constantly creating and releasing those views. To take advantage of this mechanism, we'll ask the table view to give us a previously used cell of the specified type using the NSString identifier we declared earlier. In effect, we're asking for a reusable cell of type SimpleTableIdentifier:

```
UITableViewCell *cell = [tableView dequeueReusableCellWithIdentifier:
                                 SimpleTableIdentifier];
```

Now, it's completely possible that the table view won't have any spare cells (e.g., when it's being initially populated), so we check the cell after the call to see whether it's nil. If it is, we manually create a new table view cell using that identifier string. At some point, we'll inevitably reuse one of the cells we create here, so we need to make sure that we create it using SimpleTableIdentifier:

```
if (cell == nil) {
    cell = [[UITableViewCell alloc]
            initWithStyle:UITableViewCellStyleDefault
            reuseIdentifier:SimpleTableIdentifier];
}
```

Curious about UITableViewCellStyleDefault? Hold that thought. We'll get to it when we look at the table view cell styles.

We now have a table view cell that we can return for the table view to use. So, all we need to do is place whatever information we want displayed in this cell. Displaying text in a row of a table is a very common task, so the table view cell provides a UILabel property called textLabel that we can set to display strings. That just requires getting the correct string from our dwarves array and using it to set the cell's textLabel.

To get the correct value, however, we need to know which row the table view is asking for. We get that information from the indexPath's row property. We use the row number of the table to get the corresponding string from the array, assign it to the cell's textLabel.text property, and then return the cell:

```
cell.textLabel.text = self.dwarves[indexPath.row];
return cell;
```

That wasn't so bad, was it?

Compile and run your application, and you should see the array values displayed in a table view, as shown on the left of Figure 8-6.

Figure 8-6. *The Simple Table application, in all its dwarven glory*

That looks good, but there is a small problem—scroll the table up a little way and you'll see that its content appears behind the status bar, as shown on the right in Figure 8-6. The problem arises because we made the table view fill the whole screen. Sometimes that's exactly what you want, but in this case the text in the table cells conflicts with the text in the status bar, which looks ugly, so let's fix it. All we need to do is change the constraint that pins the table view to the top of the screen so that it's pinned to the bottom of the status bar instead. To do that, select *Main.storyboard* in the Project Navigator and make sure that the table view is selected in the Document outline. Grab the top of the table view and drag it down until you see a blue guideline appear below the status bar, like the one shown in Figure 8-7, and then release it.

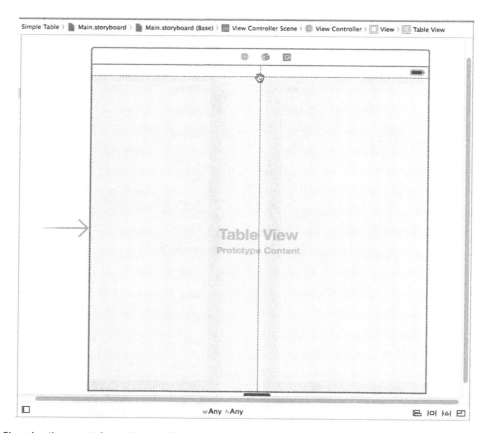

Figure 8-7. Changing the constraint on the top of the table view so that it doesn't extend behind the status bar

With the table view still selected, click the **Resolve Auto Layout Issues** button at the bottom right of the storyboard editor and then click **Update Constraints** to change the top constraint to match the new position of the top of the table view. Now run the application again and you'll see that the table view's content no longer scrolls underneath the status bar.

Adding an Image

It would be nice if we could add an image to each row. Guess we would need to create a subclass of UITableViewCell or add subviews to do that, huh? Actually, no, not if you can live with the image being on the left side of each row. The default table view cell can handle that situation just fine. Let's check it out.

Drag the files *star.png* and *star2.png* from the *08 – Star Image* folder in the example source code archive to your project's *Images.xcassets*. We're going to arrange for these icons to appear on every row of the table view. All we need to do is create a UIImage for each of them and assign it to the

UITableViewCell when the table view asks its data source for the cell for each row. To do this, in the file *ViewController.m*, add the following code in bold to the tableView:cellForRowAtIndexPath: method:

```
- (UITableViewCell *)tableView:(UITableView *)tableView
         cellForRowAtIndexPath:(NSIndexPath *)indexPath {
    static NSString *SimpleTableIdentifier = @"SimpleTableIdentifier";

    UITableViewCell *cell = [tableView dequeueReusableCellWithIdentifier:
                                       SimpleTableIdentifier];
    if (cell == nil) {
        cell = [[UITableViewCell alloc]
                initWithStyle:UITableViewCellStyleDefault
                reuseIdentifier:SimpleTableIdentifier];
    }

    UIImage *image = [UIImage imageNamed:@"star"];
    cell.imageView.image = image;
    UIImage *highlightedImage = [UIImage imageNamed:@"star2"];
    cell.imageView.highlightedImage = highlightedImage;

    cell.textLabel.text = self.dwarves[indexPath.row];
    return cell;
}
```

Yep, that's it. Each cell has an imageView property of type UIImage, which in turn has properties called image and highlightedImage. The image given by the image property appears to the left of the cell's text and is replaced by the highlightedImage, if one is provided, when the cell is selected. You just set the cell's imageView.image and imageView.highlightedImage properties to whatever images you want to display.

If you compile and run your application now, you should get a list with a bunch of nice little blue star icons to the left of each row (see Figure 8-8). If you select any row, you'll see that its icon switches from blue to green, which is the color of the image in the *star2.png* file. Of course, we could have included a different image for each row in the table, or, with very little effort, we could have used one icon for all of Mr. Disney's dwarves and a different one for Mr. Tolkien's.

Figure 8-8. We used the cell's imageView property to add an image to each of the table view's cells

Note   UIImage uses a caching mechanism based on the file name, so it won't load a new image property each time imageNamed: is called. Instead, it will use the already cached version.

Using Table View Cell Styles

The work you've done with the table view so far has used the default cell style shown in Figure 8-8, represented by the constant UITableViewCellStyleDefault. But the UITableViewCell class includes several other predefined cell styles that let you easily add a bit more variety to your table views. These cell styles use three different cell elements:

- **Image**: If an image is part of the specified style, the image is displayed to the left of the cell's text.

- **Text label**: This is the cell's primary text. In the case of the UITableViewCellStyleDefault style that we have been using so far, the text label is the only text shown in the cell.

- **Detail text label**: This is the cell's secondary text, usually used as an explanatory note or label.

To see what these new style additions look like, add the following code to tableView:cellForRowAtIndexPath: in *ViewController.m*:

```
- (UITableViewCell *)tableView:(UITableView *)tableView
        cellForRowAtIndexPath:(NSIndexPath *)indexPath
{
    static NSString *SimpleTableIdentifier = @"SimpleTableIdentifier";

    UITableViewCell *cell = [tableView dequeueReusableCellWithIdentifier:
                                    SimpleTableIdentifier];
    if (cell == nil) {
        cell = [[UITableViewCell alloc]
                initWithStyle:UITableViewCellStyleDefault
                reuseIdentifier:SimpleTableIdentifier];
    }

    UIImage *image = [UIImage imageNamed:@"star"];
    cell.imageView.image = image;
    UIImage *highlightedImage = [UIImage imageNamed:@"star2"];
    cell.imageView.highlightedImage = highlightedImage;

    cell.textLabel.text = self.dwarves[indexPath.row];

    if (indexPath.row < 7) {
        cell.detailTextLabel.text = @"Mr. Disney";
    } else {
        cell.detailTextLabel.text = @"Mr. Tolkien";
    }
    return cell;
}
```

All we've done here is set the cell's detail text. We use the string @"Mr. Disney" for the first seven rows and the string @"Mr. Tolkien" for the rest. When you run this code, each cell will look just as it did before (see Figure 8-9). That's because we are using the style UITableViewCellStyleDefault, which does not use the detail text.

Figure 8-9. *The default cell style shows the image and text label in a straight line*

Now change UITableViewCellStyleDefault to UITableViewCellStyleSubtitle like this:

```
if (cell == nil) {
    cell = [[UITableViewCell alloc]
            initWithStyle:UITableViewCellStyleSubtitle
            reuseIdentifier:SimpleTableIdentifier];
}
```

Now run the app again. With the subtitle style, both text elements are shown, one below the other (see Figure 8-10).

Figure 8-10. *The subtitle style shows the detail text in smaller gray letters below the text label*

Next, change UITableViewCellStyleSubtitle to UITableViewCellStyleValue1, and then build and run again. This style places the text label and detail text label on the same line, but on opposite sides of the cell (see Figure 8-11).

Figure 8-11. *The style value 1 will place the text label on the left side in black letters and the detail text right-justified on the right side in blue letters*

Finally, change UITableViewCellStyleValue1 to UITableViewCellStyleValue2. This format is often used to display information along with a descriptive label. It doesn't show the cell's icon, but places the detail text label to the left of the text label (see Figure 8-12). In this layout, the detail text label acts as a label describing the type of data held in the text label.

Sneezy Mr. Disney

Figure 8-12. *The style value 2 does not display the image and places the detail text label in blue letters to the left of the text label*

Now that you've seen the cell styles that are available, go ahead and change back to the `UITableViewCellStyleDefault` style before continuing. Later in this chapter, you'll see how to create custom table view cells. But before you do that, make sure you consider the available cell styles to see whether one of them will suit your needs.

You may have noticed that we made our controller both the data source and delegate for this table view; but up until now, we haven't actually implemented any of the methods from the `UITableViewDelegate` protocol. Unlike picker views, simpler table views don't require the use of a delegate to do their thing. The data source provides all the data needed to draw the table. The purpose of the delegate is to configure the appearance of the table view and to handle certain user interactions. Let's take a look at a few of the configuration options now. We'll discuss a few more in the next chapter.

Setting the Indent Level

The delegate can be used to specify that some rows should be indented. In the file *ViewController.m*, add the following method to your code, just above the @end declaration:

```
- (NSInteger)tableView:(UITableView *)tableView
indentationLevelForRowAtIndexPath:(NSIndexPath *)indexPath {
    return indexPath.row % 4;
}
```

This method sets the **indent level** for each row based on its row number; so row 0 will have an indent level of 0, row 1 will have an indent level of 1, and so on. Because of the % operator, row 4 will revert back to an indent level of 0 and the cycle begins again. An indent level is simply an integer that tells the table view to move that row a little to the right. The higher the number, the further to the right the row will be indented. You might use this technique, for example, to indicate that one row is subordinate to another row, as Mail does when representing subfolders.

When you run the application again, you'll see that the rows indent in blocks of four, as shown in Figure 8-13.

Figure 8-13. *Indented table rows*

Handling Row Selection

The table's delegate has two methods that allow you to handle row selection. One method is called before the row is selected, and it can be used to prevent the row from being selected or even to change which row gets selected. Let's implement that method and specify that the first row is not selectable. Add the following method to the end of *ViewController.m*, just before the @end declaration:

```
- (NSIndexPath *)tableView:(UITableView *)tableView
         willSelectRowAtIndexPath:(NSIndexPath *)indexPath {
    if (indexPath.row == 0) {
        return nil;
    } else {
        return indexPath;
    }
}
```

This method is passed an `indexPath` that represents the item that's about to be selected. Our code looks at which row is about to be selected, and if it's the first row, which is always index zero, then it returns `nil`, which indicates that no row should actually be selected. Otherwise, it returns the unmodified `indexPath`, which is how we indicate that it's OK for the selection to proceed.

Before you compile and run, let's also implement the delegate method that is called after a row has been selected, which is typically where you'll actually handle the selection. In the next chapter, we'll use this method to handle drill-downs in a master-detail application, but in this chapter, we'll just put up an alert to show that the row was selected. Add the following method to the bottom of *ViewController.m*, just before the @end declaration again:

```
- (void)tableView:(UITableView *)tableView
        didSelectRowAtIndexPath:(NSIndexPath *)indexPath {
    NSString *rowValue = self.dwarves[indexPath.row];
    NSString *message = [[NSString alloc] initWithFormat:
                            @"You selected %@", rowValue];

    UIAlertController *controller =
        [UIAlertController alertControllerWithTitle:@"Row Selected!"
                            message:message
                            preferredStyle: UIAlertControllerStyleAlert];
    UIAlertAction *cancelAction =
            [UIAlertAction actionWithTitle:@"Yes I Did"
                            style: UIAlertActionStyleDefault
                            handler: nil];
    [controller addAction:cancelAction];
    [self presentViewController:controller animated:YES completion:nil];

    [tableView deselectRowAtIndexPath:indexPath animated:YES];
}
```

Once you've added this method, compile and run the app, and then take it for a spin. For example, see whether you can select the first row (you shouldn't be able to), and then select one of the other rows. The selected row should be highlighted and your alert should pop up, telling you which row you selected while the selected row fades in the background (see Figure 8-14).

Figure 8-14. In this example, the first row is not selectable, and an alert is displayed when any other row is selected

Note that you can also modify the index path before you pass it back, which would cause a different row and/or section to be selected. You won't do that very often, as you should have a very good reason for changing the user's selection. In the vast majority of cases where you use the `tableView:willSelectRowAtIndexPath:` method, you will either return `indexPath` unmodified to allow the selection or return `nil` to disallow it. If you really want to change the selected row and/or section, use the `NSIndexPath indexPathForRow:inSection:` method to create a new `NSIndexPath` object and return it. For example, the following code would ensure that if you tried to select an even-numbered row, you would actually select the row that follows it:

```
- (NSIndexPath *)tableView:(UITableView *)tableView
        willSelectRowAtIndexPath:(NSIndexPath *)indexPath {
    if (indexPath.row == 0) {
        return nil;
```

```
    } else if (indexPath.row % 2 == 0) {
        return [NSIndexPath indexPathForRow:indexPath.row + 1
            inSection:indexPath.section];
    } else {
        return indexPath;
    }
}
```

Changing the Font Size and Row Height

Let's say that we want to change the size of the font being used in the table view. In most situations, you shouldn't override the default font; it's what users expect to see. But sometimes there are valid reasons to change the font. Add the following line of code to your tableView:cellForRowAtIndexPath: method:

```
- (UITableViewCell *)tableView:(UITableView *)tableView
         cellForRowAtIndexPath:(NSIndexPath *)indexPath {
    static NSString *SimpleTableIdentifier = @"SimpleTableIdentifier";

    UITableViewCell *cell = [tableView dequeueReusableCellWithIdentifier:
                                        SimpleTableIdentifier];
    if (cell == nil) {
        cell = [[UITableViewCell alloc]
                initWithStyle:UITableViewCellStyleDefault
                reuseIdentifier:SimpleTableIdentifier];
    }

    UIImage *image = [UIImage imageNamed:@"star"];
    cell.imageView.image = image;
    UIImage *highlightedImage = [UIImage imageNamed:@"star2"];
    cell.imageView.highlightedImage = highlightedImage;

    cell.textLabel.text = self.dwarves[indexPath.row];
    cell.textLabel.font = [UIFont boldSystemFontOfSize:50];

    if (indexPath.row < 7) {
        cell.detailTextLabel.text = @"Mr. Disney";
    } else {
        cell.detailTextLabel.text = @"Mr. Tolkien";
    }
    return cell;
}
```

When you run the application now, the values in your list are drawn in a really large font size, but they don't exactly fit in the row (see Figure 8-15). In iOS 8, the table view automatically adjusts the height of each row based on its content, unless you tell it otherwise, but as you can see, in this case the new row height is larger than it really should be.

Figure 8-15. Changing the font used to draw table view cells

There are a couple of ways to fix this. First, we can tell the table that all of its rows should have a given, fixed height. To do that, we set its rowHeight property, like this:

```
tableView.rowHeight = 70;
```

If you need different rows to have different heights, you can implement the UITableViewDelegate's tableView:heightForRowAtIndexPath: method. Go ahead and add this method to your controller class, just before @end:

```
- (CGFloat)tableView:(UITableView *)tableView
          heightForRowAtIndexPath:(NSIndexPath *)indexPath {
    return indexPath.row == 0 ? 120 : 70;
}
```

We've just told the table view to set the row height for all rows to 70 points, except for the first row, which will be a little larger. Compile and run, and your table's rows should be a better fit for their content now (see Figure 8-16).

Figure 8-16. *Changing the row size using the delegate. Notice that the first row is much taller than the rest*

There are more tasks that the delegate handles, but most of the remaining ones come into play when you start working with hierarchical data, which we'll do in the next chapter. To learn more, use the documentation browser to explore the UITableViewDelegate protocol and see what other methods are available.

Customizing Table View Cells

You can do a lot with table views right out of the box; but often, you will want to format the data for each row in ways that simply aren't supported by UITableViewCell directly. In those cases, there are three basic approaches: one that involves adding subviews to UITableViewCell programmatically when creating the cell, a second that involves loading a cell from a nib file, and a third that is similar, but loads the cell from a storyboard. We'll take a look at the first two techniques in this chapter and you'll see an example that creates a cell from a storyboard in Chapter 9.

Adding Subviews to the Table View Cell

To show how to use custom cells, we're going to create a new application with another table view. In each row, we'll display two lines of information along with two labels (see Figure 8-17). Our application will display the name and color of a series of potentially familiar computer models, and we'll show both of those pieces of information in the same table cell by adding subviews to the table view cell.

Figure 8-17. Adding subviews to the table view cell can give you multiline rows

Create a new Xcode project using the Single View Application template. Name the project *Table Cells* and use the same settings as your last project. Click *Main.storyboard* to edit the GUI in Interface Builder.

Add a Table View to the main view and resize it so that it fills the whole view, except that the top of the table should be aligned with the bottom of the status bar, not the top of the view. Use the Connections Inspector to set its data source to the view controller, as we did for the Simple Table application. Then, use the **Pin** button at the bottom of the window to create constraints between the table view's edges and those of its parent view and the status bar. You can actually use the same settings as in Figure 8-5, since the values that you specify in the input boxes at the top of the pop-up are, by default, the distances between the table view and its nearest neighbor in all four directions. Last time, the nearest neighbor above the table view was the main view itself, but now it's the status bar, so Xcode will create constraints that ensure that the top of the table view is right below the bottom of the status bar. Finally, save the storyboard.

Creating a UITableViewCell Subclass

Until this point, the standard table view cells we've been using have taken care of all the details of cell layout for us. Our controller code has been kept clear of the messy details about where to place labels and images, and it has been able to just pass off the display values to the cell. This keeps presentation logic out of the controller, and that's a really good design to stick to. For this project, we're going to make a new cell UITableViewCell subclass of our own that takes care of the details of the new layout, which will keep our controller as simple as possible.

Adding New Cells

Select the *Table Cells* folder in the Project Navigator, and press ⌘**N** to create a new file. In the assistant that pops up, select **Cocoa Touch Class** from the **iOS** section and press **Next**. On the following screen, enter **NameAndColorCell** as the name of the new class, select *UITableViewCell* in the **Subclass of** pop-up list, click **Next** again, and on the next screen, click **Create**.

Now select *NameAndColorCell.h* in the Project Navigator and add the following code:

```
#import <UIKit/UIKit.h>

@interface NameAndColorCell : UITableViewCell

@property (copy, nonatomic) NSString *name;
@property (copy, nonatomic) NSString *color;

@end
```

Here, we've added two properties to our cell's interface that our controller will use to pass values to each cell. Note that instead of declaring the NSString properties with strong semantics, we're using copy. Doing so with NSString values is always a good idea because there's a risk that the string value passed into a property setter may actually be an NSMutableString, which the sender can modify later on, leading to problems. Copying each string that's passed in to a property gives us a stable, unchangeable snapshot of what the string contains at the moment the setter is called.

Now switch over to *NameAndColorCell.m* and add the following code:

```
#import "NameAndColorCell.h"

@interface NameAndColorCell ()

@property (strong, nonatomic) UILabel *nameLabel;
@property (strong, nonatomic) UILabel *colorLabel;

@end
```

Here, we've added a class extension defining two properties that we'll use to access some of the subviews we'll be adding to our cell. Our cell will contain four subviews, two of which are labels that have fixed content and another two for which the content will be changed for every row and therefore require outlets.

Those are all the properties we need to add, so let's move on to the @implementation section. We're going to add some code to the initWithStyle:reuseIdentifier: method to create the views that we'll need to display:

```
- (id)initWithStyle:(UITableViewCellStyle)style
            reuseIdentifier:(NSString *)reuseIdentifier {
    self = [super initWithStyle:style reuseIdentifier:reuseIdentifier];
    if (self) {
        // Initialization code
        CGRect nameLabelRect = CGRectMake(0, 5, 70, 15);
        UILabel *nameMarker = [[UILabel alloc] initWithFrame:nameLabelRect];
        nameMarker.textAlignment = NSTextAlignmentRight;
        nameMarker.text = @"Name:";
        nameMarker.font = [UIFont boldSystemFontOfSize:12];
        [self.contentView addSubview:nameMarker];

        CGRect colorLabelRect = CGRectMake(0, 26, 70, 15);
        UILabel *colorMarker = [[UILabel alloc] initWithFrame:colorLabelRect];
        colorMarker.textAlignment = NSTextAlignmentRight;
        colorMarker.text = @"Color:";
        colorMarker.font = [UIFont boldSystemFontOfSize:12];
        [self.contentView addSubview:colorMarker];

        CGRect nameValueRect = CGRectMake(80, 5, 200, 15);
        self.nameLabel = [[UILabel alloc] initWithFrame:
                            nameValueRect];
        [self.contentView addSubview:_nameLabel];

        CGRect colorValueRect = CGRectMake(80, 25, 200, 15);
        self.colorLabel = [[UILabel alloc] initWithFrame:
                            colorValueRect];
        [self.contentView addSubview:_colorLabel];
    }
    return self;
}
```

That should be pretty straightforward. We create four `UILabels` and add them to the table view cell. The table view cell already has a `UIView` subview called `contentView`, which it uses to group all of its subviews. As a result, we don't add the labels as subviews directly to the table view cell, but rather to its `contentView`.

Two of these labels contain static text. The label `nameMarker` contains the text *Name*:, and the label `colorMarker` contains the text *Color*:. Those are just labels that we won't change. Both of these labels have right-aligned text using `NSTextAlignmentRight`.

We'll use the other two labels to display our row-specific data. Remember that we need some way of retrieving these fields later, so we keep references to both of them in the properties that we declared earlier.

Now let's put the finishing touches on the `NameAndColorCell` class by adding these two setter methods just before the `@end`:

```
- (void)setName:(NSString *)n {
    if (![n isEqualToString:_name]) {
        _name = [n copy];
        self.nameLabel.text = _name;
    }
}

- (void)setColor:(NSString *)c {
    if (![c isEqualToString:_color]) {
        _color = [c copy];
        self.colorLabel.text = _color;
    }
}
```

You already know that using `@property`, as we did in the header file, implicitly creates getter and setter methods for each property. Yet, here we're defining our own setters for both `name` and `color`! As it turns out, this is just fine. Any time a class defines its own getters or setters, those will be used instead of the default methods. In this class, we're using the default synthesized getters, but defining our own setters. Whenever we are passed new values for the `name` or `color` properties, we update the labels we created earlier.

Implementing the Controller's Code

Now, let's set up the simple controller to display values in our nice new cells. Start off by selecting *ViewController.h*, where you need to add the following code:

```
#import <UIKit/UIKit.h>

@interface ViewController : UIViewController
    <UITableViewDataSource>

@end
```

In our controller, we need to set up some data to use, and then implement the table data source methods to feed that data to the table. Switch to *ViewController.m* and add the following code at the beginning of the file:

```
#import "ViewController.h"
#import "NameAndColorCell.h"

static NSString *CellTableIdentifier = @"CellTableIdentifier";

@interface ViewController ()

@property (copy, nonatomic) NSArray *computers;
@property (weak, nonatomic) IBOutlet UITableView *tableView;

@end

@implementation ViewController

- (void)viewDidLoad
{
    [super viewDidLoad];
    // Do any additional setup after loading the view, typically from a nib.

    self.computers = @[@{@"Name" : @"MacBook Air", @"Color" : @"Silver"},
                       @{@"Name" : @"MacBook Pro", @"Color" : @"Silver"},
                       @{@"Name" : @"iMac", @"Color" : @"Silver"},
                       @{@"Name" : @"Mac Mini", @"Color" : @"Silver"},
                       @{@"Name" : @"Mac Pro", @"Color" : @"Black"}];

    [self.tableView registerClass:[NameAndColorCell class]
             forCellReuseIdentifier:CellTableIdentifier];
}
```

This version of viewDidLoad assigns an array of dictionaries to the computers property. Each dictionary contains the name and color information for one row in the table. The name for that row is held in the dictionary under the key Name, and the color is held under the key Color.

> **Note** Remember when Macs came in different colors, like beige, platinum, black, and white? And that's not to mention the original iMac and iBook series, with their beautiful assortment of rainbow hues. Now, except for the newest Mac Pro, there's just one color: silver. Harrumph. Well, at least we can now comfort ourselves with colorful iPhones.

We also added an outlet for the table view, so we need to connect it in the storyboard. Select the *Main.storyboard* file. In the Document Outline, Control-drag from the **View Controller** icon to the **Table View** icon. Release the mouse and select tableView in the pop-up to link the table view to the outlet.

Now add this code at the end of *ViewController.m*, above the @end declaration:

```
- (NSInteger)tableView:(UITableView *)tableView
 numberOfRowsInSection:(NSInteger)section {
    return [self.computers count];
}

- (UITableViewCell *)tableView:(UITableView *)tableView
         cellForRowAtIndexPath:(NSIndexPath *)indexPath {
    NameAndColorCell *cell =
        [tableView dequeueReusableCellWithIdentifier:
                                    CellTableIdentifier
                    forIndexPath:indexPath];

    NSDictionary *rowData = self.computers[indexPath.row];
    cell.name = rowData[@"Name"];
    cell.color = rowData[@"Color"];

    return cell;
}
```

@end

You have already seen these methods in our previous example—they belong to the UITableViewDataSource protocol. Let's focus on tableView:cellForRowWithIndexPath: since that's where we're really getting into some new stuff. Here we're using an interesting feature: a table view can use a sort of registry to create a new cell when needed. That means that as long as we've registered all the reuse identifiers that we're going to use for a table view, we can always get access to an available cell. In our previous example, we used the dequeueReusableCellWithIdentifier: method. That method also uses the registry, but it returns nil if the identifier that we give it isn't registered. The nil return value is used as a signal that we need to create and populate a new UITableViewCell object. The dequeueReusableCellWithIdentifier:forIndexPath: method that we're using here never returns nil, so how does it get a table cell object? It uses the identifier that we pass to it as the key to its registry and we added an entry to the registry that's mapped to our table cell identifier in the viewDidLoad method:

```
[tableView registerClass:[NameAndColorCell class]
   forCellReuseIdentifier:CellTableIdentifier];
```

What happens if we pass an identifier that's not registered? In that case, the dequeueReusableCellW ithIdentifier:forIndexPath: method crashes. Crashing sounds bad, but in this case, it would be the result of a bug that you would discover right away during development. Therefore, we don't need to include code that checks for a nil return value since that will never happen.

Once we've got our new cell, we use the `indexPath` argument that was passed in to determine which row the table is requesting a cell for, and then use that row value to grab the correct dictionary for the requested row. Remember that the dictionary has two key/value pairs—one with `name` and another with `color`:

```
NSDictionary *rowData = self.computers[indexPath.row];
```

Now, all that's left to do is populate the cell with data from the chosen row, using the properties we defined in our subclass:

```
cell.name = rowData[@"Name"];
cell.color = rowData[@"Color"];
```

As you saw earlier, setting these properties causes the value to be copied to the name and color labels in the table view cell.

Compile and run your application. You should see a table of rows, each with two lines of data, as shown in Figure 8-17.

Being able to add views to a table view cell provides a lot more flexibility than using the standard table view cell alone, but it can get a little tedious creating, positioning, and adding all the subviews programmatically. Gosh, it sure would be nice if we could design the table view cell graphically by using Xcode's GUI editing tools. Well, we're in luck. As we mentioned earlier, you can use Interface Builder to design your table view cells, and then simply load the views from a storyboard or a nib file when you create a new cell.

Loading a UITableViewCell from a Nib

We're going to re-create that same two-line interface we just built in code using the visual layout capabilities that Xcode provides in Interface Builder. To do this, we'll create a new nib file that will contain the table view cell and lay out its views using Interface Builder. Then, when we need a table view cell to represent a row, instead of creating a standard table view cell, we'll just load the nib file and use the properties we already defined in our cell class to set the name and color. In addition to using Interface Builder's visual layout, we'll also simplify our code in a few other places. Before proceeding, you might want to take a copy of the Table Cells project in which you can make the changes that follow. Alternatively, you'll find a copy of the Table Cells project in its current state that you can use as a starting point in the *Table Cells 2* folder in the example source code archive.

First, we'll make a few changes to the `NameAndColorCell` class, inside *NameAndColorCell.m*. The first step is to mark up our properties as outlets, so we can use them in Interface Builder. Make these changes in the class extension near the top:

```
@interface NameAndColorCell ()

@property (strong, nonatomic) IBOutlet UILabel *nameLabel;
@property (strong, nonatomic) IBOutlet UILabel *colorLabel;

@end
```

Now, remember that setup we did in `initWithStyle:reuseIdentifier:`, where we created our labels? All that can go. In fact, you should just delete the entire method since all that setup will now be done in Interface Builder!

After all that, you're left with a cell class that's even smaller and cleaner than before. Its only real function now is to shuffle data to the labels. Now we need to re-create the cell and its labels in Interface Builder.

Right-click the *Table Cells* folder in Xcode and select **New File...** from the contextual menu. In the left pane of the new file assistant, click **User Interface** (making sure to pick it in the **iOS** section, rather than the **OS X** section). From the upper-right pane, select **Empty**, and then click **Next**. On the following screen, use the file name *NameAndColorCell.xib.* Make sure that the main project directory is selected in the file browser and that the **Table Cells** group is selected in the **Group** pop-up. Press **Create** to create a new nib file.

Designing the Table View Cell in Interface Builder

Next, select *NameAndColorCell.xib* in the Project Navigator to open the file for editing. Until now, we've been doing all of our GUI editing inside of storyboards, but now we're using a nib file instead. Most things are similar and will look very familiar to you, but there are a few differences. One of the main differences is that, while a storyboard file is centered around scenes that pair up a view controller and a view, inside a nib file there's no such forced pairing. In fact, a nib file often doesn't contain a real controller object at all, just a proxy that is called *File's Owner*. If you open the Document Outline, you'll see it there, right above First Responder.

Look in the library for a Table View Cell (see Figure 8-18) and drag one of those over to the GUI layout area.

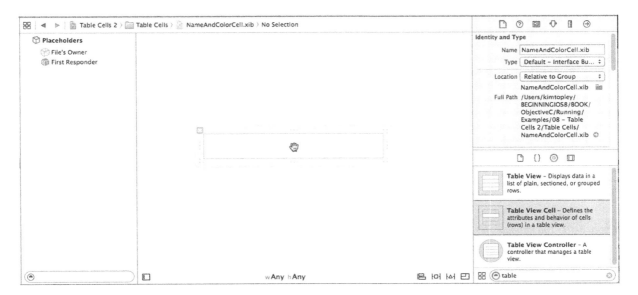

Figure 8-18. We dragged a table view cell from the library into the nib editor

Next, press ⌥⌘4 to go to the Attributes Inspector (see Figure 8-19). One of the first fields you'll see there is **Identifier**. That's the reuse identifier that we've been using in our code. If this does not ring a bell, scan back through the chapter and look for CellTableIdentifier. Set the **Identifier** value to *CellTableIdentifier*.

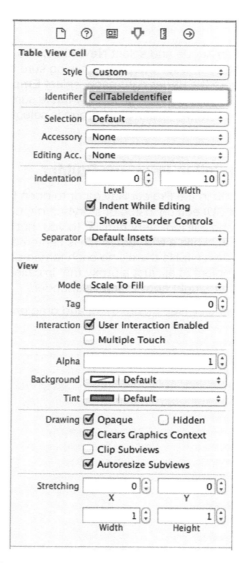

Figure 8-19. The Attributes Inspector for a table view cell

The idea here is that, when we retrieve a cell for reuse, perhaps because of scrolling a new cell into view, we want to make sure we get the correct cell type. When this particular cell is instantiated from the nib file, its reuse identifier instance variable will be prepopulated with the name you entered in the **Identifier** field of the Attributes Inspector—*CellTableIdentifier*, in this case.

Imagine a scenario where you created a table with a header and then a series of "middle" cells. If you scroll a middle cell into view, it's important that you retrieve a middle cell to reuse and not a header cell. The **Identifier** field lets you tag the cells appropriately.

Our next step is to edit our table cell's content view. First, select the table cell in the editing area and drag down its lower edge to make the cell a little taller. Keep dragging until the height is *65*. Go to the library, drag out four Label controls, and place them in the content view, using Figure 8-20 as a guide. The labels will be too close to the top and bottom for those guidelines to be of much help, but the left guideline and the alignment guidelines should serve their purpose. Note that you can drag out one label, and then Option-drag to create copies, if that approach makes things easier for you.

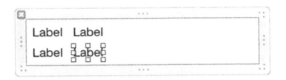

Figure 8-20. The table view cell's content view, with four labels dragged in

Next, double-click the upper-left label and change it to *Name:*, and then change the lower-left label to *Color:*.

Now, select both the **Name:** and **Color:** labels and press the small **T** button in the Attribute Inspector's **Font** field. This will open a small panel containing a **Font** pop-up button. Click that and choose **System Bold** as the typeface. If needed, select the two unchanged label fields on the right and drag them a little more to the right to give the design a bit of breathing room, and then resize the other two labels so that you can see the text that you just set. Next, resize the two right-side labels so that they stretch all the way to the right guideline. Figure 8-21 should give you a sense of our final cell content view.

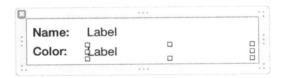

Figure 8-21. The table view cell's content view with the left label names changed and set to bold, and with the right labels slightly moved and resized

As always when we create a new layout, we need to add Auto Layout constraints. The general idea is to pin the left side labels to the left side of the cell and the right side labels to its right. We'll also make sure that the vertical separation between the labels and the top and bottom of the cell and between the labels is preserved. We'll link each left side label to the one on its right. Here are the steps:

1. Click the **Name:** label, hold down **Shift**, and then click the **Color:** label. Choose **Editor ➤ Pin ➤ Widths Equally** from the menu. You'll see some Auto Layout warnings appear when you do this—don't worry about them, because we'll fix them as we add more constraints.

2. With the two labels still selected, open the Size Inspector and find the section headed **Content Hugging Priority**. If you don't see it, try deselecting and reselecting both labels. The values in these fields determine how resistant the labels are to expanding into extra space. We don't want these labels to expand at all in the horizontal, so change the value in the **Horizontal** field from *251* to *500*. Any value greater than 251 will do—we just need it to be greater than the **Content Hugging Priority** of the two labels on the right, so that any extra horizontal space is allocated to them.

3. Control-drag from the **Color:** label up to the **Name:** label, select **Vertical Spacing** from the pop-up, and press **Return**.

4. Control-drag diagonally up and left from the **Name:** label toward the top-left corner of the cell until the cell's background turns completely blue. In the pop-up, hold down **Shift** and select **Leading Space to Container Margin** and **Top Space to Container Margin**, and then press **Return**.

5. Control-drag diagonally down and left from the **Color:** label toward the bottom-left corner of the cell, until its background is blue. In the pop-up, hold down **Shift** and select **Leading Space to Container Margin** and **Bottom Space to Container Margin**, and then press **Return**.

6. Control-drag from the **Name:** label to the label to its right. In the pop-up, hold down **Shift**, select **Horizontal Spacing** and **Baseline**, and press **Return**. Control-drag from the top label on the right toward the right edge of the cell, until the cell's background turns blue. In the pop-up, select **Trailing Space to Container Margin**.

7. Similarly, Control-drag from the **Color:** label to the label to its right. In the pop-up, hold down **Shift**, select **Horizontal Spacing** and **Baseline**, and press **Return**. Control-drag from the bottom label on the right toward the right edge of the cell, until the cell's background turns blue. In the pop-up, select **Trailing Space to Container Margin**.

8. Finally, select the **Content View** icon in the Document Outline and then choose **Editor ➤ Resolve Auto Layout Issues ➤ Update Frames** from the menu, if it's enabled. The four labels should move to their final locations, as shown in Figure 8-21. If you see something different, delete all of the constraints in the Document Outline and try again.

Now, we need to let Interface Builder know that this table view cell isn't just a normal cell, but an instance of our special subclass. Otherwise, we wouldn't be able to connect our outlets to the relevant labels. Select the table view cell by clicking **CellTableIdentifier** in the Document Outline, bring up the Identity Inspector by pressing ⌥⌘3, and choose **NameAndColorCell** from the **Class** control.

Next, switch to the Connections Inspector (⌥⌘6), where you'll see the *colorLabel* and *nameLabel* outlets. Drag from the *nameLabel* outlet to the top label on the right in the table cell and from the *colorLabel* outlet to the bottom label on the right.

Using the New Table View Cell

To use the cell we designed, we just need to make a few pretty simple changes to the viewDidLoad: method in *ViewController.m*:

```
- (void)viewDidLoad
{
    [super viewDidLoad];
    // Do any additional setup after loading the view, typically from a nib.

    self.computers = @[@{@"Name" : @"MacBook Air", @"Color" : @"Silver"},
                       @{@"Name" : @"MacBook Pro", @"Color" : @"Silver"},
                       @{@"Name" : @"iMac", @"Color" : @"Silver"},
                       @{@"Name" : @"Mac Mini", @"Color" : @"Silver"},
                       @{@"Name" : @"Mac Pro", @"Color" : @"Black"}];

    [self.tableView registerClass:[NameAndColorCell class]
                  forCellReuseIdentifier:CellTableIdentifier];
    UINib *nib = [UINib nibWithNibName:@"NameAndColorCell" bundle:nil];
    [self.tableView registerNib:nib
              forCellReuseIdentifier:CellTableIdentifier];
}
```

Just as it can associate a class with a reuse identifier (as you saw in the previous example), a table view can keep track of which nib files are meant to be associated with particular reuse identifiers. This allows you to register cells for each row type you have using classes or nib files once, and dequeueReusableCellWithIdentifier:forIndexPath: will always provide a cell ready for use.

That's it. Build and run. Now your two-line table cells are based on your Interface Builder design skills.

You may have noticed that we didn't explicitly set the table's row height or implement the tableView:heightForRowAtIndexPath: methods of its UITableViewDelegate. Despite that, the rows are all of the correct height. Here's how the table figures out the height of a row:

- If the tableView:heightForRowAtIndexPath: method is implemented, the table view gets the height for each row by calling it.

- If not, then the table view uses its rowHeight property. If this property has the special value UITableViewAutomaticDimension *and* the table cell comes from a nib or a storyboard, *and* its content is laid out using Auto Layout constraints, it gets the row height for that cell from the cell itself, based on its Auto Layout constraints. If the rowHeight property has any other value, it's used as the height for every row in the table.

In this example, we placed all of the cell's content using Auto Layout, so the table is able to work out how tall the cell needs to be, saving us the trouble of having to calculate it ourselves. This even works if different rows have content that would lead to different row heights. Since the default value of the `rowHeight` property is `UITableViewAutomaticDimension`, you get this behavior for free as long as you use Auto Layout constraints when constructing your custom cell.

So, now that you've seen a couple of approaches to building a custom cell, what do you think? Many people who delve into iOS development are somewhat confused at first by the focus on Interface Builder, but as you've seen, it has a lot going for it. Besides having the obvious appeal of letting you visually design your GUI, this approach promotes the proper use of nib files, which helps you stick to the MVC architecture pattern. Also, you can make your application code simpler, more modular, and just plain easier to write. As our good buddy Mark Dalrymple says, "No code is the best code!" In Chapter 9, you'll see that you can also design table cells directly in the storyboard, which means that you don't need to create an extra nib file. That approach works only if you don't want to share cell designs between different tables.

Grouped and Indexed Sections

Our next project will explore another fundamental aspect of tables. We're still going to use a single table view—no hierarchies yet—but we'll divide data into sections. Create a new Xcode project using the Single View Application template again, this time calling it *Sections*. As usual, set the **Language** to *Objective-C* and the **Devices** to *Universal*.

Building the View

Open the *Sections* folder and click *Main.storyboard* to edit the file. Drop a table view onto the View window, as we did before. Arrange the top of the table view to be below the status bar and add the same Auto Layout constraints that we used in the Table Cell example. Then press ⌥⌘6 and connect the **dataSource** connection to the **View Controller** icon.

Next, make sure the table view is selected and press ⌥⌘4 to bring up the Attributes Inspector. Change the table view's **Style** from *Plain* to *Grouped* (see Figure 8-22). Save the storyboard and move along. (We discussed the difference between indexed and grouped styles at the beginning of the chapter.)

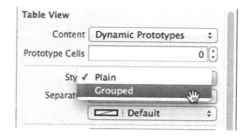

Figure 8-22. The Attributes Inspector for the table view, showing the Style pop-up with Grouped selected

Importing the Data

This project needs a fair amount of data to do its thing. To save you a few hours of typing, we've provided another property list for your tabling pleasure. Grab the file named *sortednames.plist* from the *08 Sections Data* subfolder in this book's example source code archive and drag it into your project's *Sections* folder in Xcode.

Once *sortednames.plist* is added to your project, single-click it just to get a sense of what it looks like (see Figure 8-23). It's a property list that contains a dictionary, with one entry for each letter of the alphabet. Underneath each letter is a list of names that start with that letter.

Key	Type	Value
▼ Root	Dictionary	(26 items)
▶ A	Array	(245 items)
▶ B	Array	(93 items)
▶ C	Array	(141 items)
▶ D	Array	(117 items)
▶ E	Array	(92 items)
▶ F	Array	(27 items)
▶ G	Array	(64 items)
▶ H	Array	(51 items)
▶ I	Array	(35 items)
▼ J	Array	(206 items)
Item 0	String	Jabari
Item 1	String	Jace
Item 2	String	Jacey
Item 3	String	Jack
Item 4	String	Jackson
Item 5	String	Jaclyn
Item 6	String	Jacob
Item 7	String	Jacoby
Item 8	String	Jacqueline
Item 9	String	Jacquelyn

Figure 8-23. The sortednames.plist property list file. The letter J is open to give you a sense of one of the dictionaries

We'll use the data from this property list to feed the table view, creating a section for each letter.

Implementing the Controller

Single-click the *ViewController.h* file and make the class conform to the UITableViewDataSource protocol by adding the following code shown in bold:

```
#import <UIKit/UIKit.h>

@interface ViewController : UIViewController
    <UITableViewDataSource>

@end
```

Now, switch over to *ViewController.m* and add the following code to the beginning of that file:

```
#import "ViewController.h"

static NSString *SectionsTableIdentifier = @"SectionsTableIdentifier";

@interface ViewController ()

@property (copy, nonatomic) NSDictionary *names;
@property (copy, nonatomic) NSArray *keys;

@end
```

Next, open the Assistant Editor and use the jump bar to select *ViewController.m*. In the Document Outline, select *Main.storyboard* and Control-drag from the table view to the class extension in the Assistant Editor to create an outlet for the table just below the definition of the keys property:

```
@interface ViewController ()

@property (copy, nonatomic) NSDictionary *names;
@property (copy, nonatomic) NSArray *keys;
@property (weak, nonatomic) IBOutlet UITableView *tableView;

@end
```

Back in *ViewController.m*, add the following code in bold to the viewDidLoad method:

```
@implementation ViewController

- (void)viewDidLoad
{
    [super viewDidLoad];
    // Do any additional setup after loading the view, typically from a nib.

    [self.tableView registerClass:[UITableViewCell class]
            forCellReuseIdentifier:SectionsTableIdentifier];
```

```
    NSString *path = [[NSBundle mainBundle] pathForResource:@"sortednames"
                                        ofType:@"plist"];
    self.names = [NSDictionary dictionaryWithContentsOfFile:path];
    self.keys = [[self.names allKeys] sortedArrayUsingSelector:
                @selector(compare:)];
}
```

Most of this isn't too different from what you've seen before. In the class extension at the top, we added property declarations for both an NSDictionary and an NSArray. The dictionary will hold all of our data, while the array will hold the sections sorted in alphabetical order. In the viewDidLoad method, we registered the default table view cell class that should be displayed for each row, using our declared identifier. After that, we created an NSDictionary instance from the property list we added to our project and assigned it to the names property. Next, we grabbed all the keys from that dictionary and sorted them to give us an ordered NSArray with all the key values in the dictionary in alphabetical order. Remember that the NSDictionary uses the letters of the alphabet as its keys, so this array will have 26 letters sorted from A to Z, and we'll use the array to help us keep track of the sections.

Next, add the following code at the end of the file, just above the @end declaration:

```
#pragma mark -
#pragma mark Table View Data Source Methods
- (NSInteger)numberOfSectionsInTableView:(UITableView *)tableView {
    return [self.keys count];
}

- (NSInteger)tableView:(UITableView *)tableView
 numberOfRowsInSection:(NSInteger)section {
    NSString *key = self.keys[section];
    NSArray *nameSection = self.names[key];
    return [nameSection count];
}

- (NSString *)tableView:(UITableView *)tableView
titleForHeaderInSection:(NSInteger)section {
    return self.keys[section];
}

- (UITableViewCell *)tableView:(UITableView *)tableView
        cellForRowAtIndexPath:(NSIndexPath *)indexPath {
    UITableViewCell *cell =
    [tableView dequeueReusableCellWithIdentifier:SectionsTableIdentifier
                                    forIndexPath:indexPath];

    NSString *key = self.keys[indexPath.section];
    NSArray *nameSection = self.names[key];

    cell.textLabel.text = nameSection[indexPath.row];
    return cell;
}

@end
```

These are all table data source methods. The first one we added to our class specifies the number of sections. We didn't implement this method in the earlier examples because we were happy with the default setting of 1. This time, we're telling the table view that we have one section for each key in our dictionary:

```
- (NSInteger)numberOfSectionsInTableView:(UITableView *)tableView {
    return [self.keys count];
}
```

The next method calculates the number of rows in a specific section. In the previous example, we had only one section, so we just returned the number of rows in our array. This time, we need to break it down by section. We can do this by retrieving the array that corresponds to the section in question and returning the count from that array:

```
- (NSInteger)tableView:(UITableView *)tableView
      numberOfRowsInSection:(NSInteger)section {
    NSString *key = self.keys[section];
    NSArray *nameSection = self.names[key];
    return [nameSection count];
}
```

The method `tableView:titleForHeaderInSection:` allows you to specify an optional header value for each section, and we simply return the letter for this group, which is the group's key:

```
- (NSString *)tableView:(UITableView *)tableView
    titleForHeaderInSection:(NSInteger)section {
    return self.keys[section];
}
```

In our `tableView:cellForRowAtIndexPath:` method, we need to extract both the section key and the names array using the section and row properties from the index path, and then use those to determine which value to use. The section will tell us which array to pull out of the names dictionary, and then we can use the row to figure out which value from that array to use. Everything else in that method is basically the same as the version in the Table Cells application we built earlier in the chapter.

Compile and run the project, and revel in its grooviness. Remember that we changed the table's **Style** to *Grouped*, so we ended up with a grouped table with 26 sections, which should look like Figure 8-24.

Figure 8-24. A grouped table with multiple sections

As a contrast, let's change our table view back to the plain style and see what a plain table view with multiple sections looks like. Select *Main.storyboard* to edit the file in Interface Builder again. Select the table view and use the Attributes Inspector to switch the view to *Plain*. Save the project, and then build and run it—same data, different grooviness (see Figure 8-25).

Figure 8-25. *A plain table with sections and no index*

Adding an Index

One problem with our current table is the sheer number of rows. There are 2,000 names in this list. Your finger will get awfully tired looking for Zachariah or Zayne, not to mention Zoie.

One solution to this problem is to add an index down the right side of the table view. Now that we've set our table view style back to *Plain*, that's relatively easy to do. Add the following method to the bottom of *ViewController.m*, just above the @end:

```
- (NSArray *)sectionIndexTitlesForTableView:(UITableView *)tableView {
    return self.keys;
}
```

Yep, that's it. In this method, the table is asking for an array of the values to display in the index. You must have more than one section in your table view to use the index, and the entries in this array must correspond to those sections. The returned array must have the same number of entries as you have sections, and the values must correspond to the appropriate section. In other words, the first item in this array will take the user to the first section, which is section 0. Compile and run the app again, and you'll have yourself a nice index (see Figure 8-26).

Figure 8-26. *The table view with an index*

Implementing a Search Bar

The index is helpful, but even so, we still have a whole lot of names here. If we want to see whether the name Arabella is in the list, for example, we'll need to scroll for a while even after using the index. It would be nice if we could let the user pare down the list by specifying a search term, wouldn't it? That would be darn user-friendly. Well, it's a bit of extra work, but it's not too bad. We're going to implement a standard iOS search bar using a search controller, like the one shown on the left in Figure 8-27.

Figure 8-27. The application with a search bar added to the table

As the user types into the search bar, the list of names reduces to only those that contain the entered text as a substring. As a bonus, the search bar also allows you to define scope buttons that you can use to qualify the search in some way. We'll add three scope buttons to our search bar—the **Short** button will limit the search to names that are less than six characters long, the **Long** button will consider only those names that have at least six characters, and the **All** button includes all names in the search. The scope buttons appear only when the user is typing into the search bar; you can see them in action on the right of Figure 8-27.

In iOS 8, adding search functionality is quite easy. You need only three things:

- Some data to be searched. In our case, that's the list of names.

- A view controller to display the search results. This view controller temporarily replaces the one that's providing the data. It can choose to display the results in any way, but usually the source data is presented in a table and the results view controller will use another table that looks very similar to it, thus creating the impression that the search is simply filtering the original table. As you'll see, though, that's not actually what's happening.

- A `UISearchController` that provides the search bar and manages the display of the search results in the results view controller.

Let's start by creating the skeleton of the results view controller. We are going to display our search results in a table, so our results view controller needs to contain a table. We could drag a view controller onto the storyboard and add a table view to it as we have done in the earlier examples in the chapter, but let's do something different this time. We're going to use a `UITableViewController`, which is a view controller with an embedded `UITableView` that is preconfigured as both the data source and the delegate for its table view. In the Project Navigator, right-click the **Sections** group and select **New File…** from the pop-up menu. In the file template chooser, select **Cocoa Touch Class** from the **iOS Source** group and press **Next**. Name your new class *SearchResultsController* and make it a subclass of `UITableViewController`. Press **Next**, choose the location for the new files, and let Xcode create them.

Select *SearchResultsController.h* in the Project Navigator and make the following changes to it:

```
#import <UIKit/UIKit.h>

@interface SearchResultsController : UITableViewController
                <UISearchResultsUpdating>

- (instancetype)initWithNames:(NSDictionary *)names keys:(NSArray *)keys;

@end
```

We're going to implement the search logic in this view controller, so we conformed it to the `UISearchResultsUpdating` protocol, which allows us to assign it as a delegate of the `UISearchController` class. As you'll see later, the single method defined by this protocol is called to update the search results as the user types into the search bar.

Since it's going to implement the search operation for us, `SearchResultsController` needs access to the list of names that the main view controller is displaying, so we also added an initializer so that we can pass to it the names dictionary and the list of keys that we're using for display in the main view controller. Let's add this initializer to *SearchResultsController.m*. If you open this file in the editor, you'll see that it already contains some incomplete code that provides a partial implementation of the `UITableViewDataSource` protocol and some commented-out code blocks for other methods that `UITableViewController` subclasses frequently need to implement. We're not going to use most of them in this example, so feel free to delete all of the commented-out code, and then make the following changes at the top of the file:

```
#import "SearchResultsController.h"

static NSString *SectionsTableIdentifier = @"SectionsTableIdentifier";

@interface SearchResultsController ()

@property (strong, nonatomic) NSDictionary *names;
@property (strong, nonatomic) NSArray *keys;
@property (strong, nonatomic) NSMutableArray *filteredNames;

@end
```

We added the SectionsTableIdentifier variable to hold the identifier for the table cells in this view controller. We're using the same identifier as we did in the main view controller, although we could have used any name at all. We also added three properties—two that will hold the names dictionary and the list of keys that we'll use when searching, and another that will keep a reference to an array that will hold the search results. Next, add the implementation of the initializer:

```
@implementation SearchResultsController

- (instancetype)initWithNames:(NSDictionary *)names keys:(NSArray *)keys {
    if (self = [super initWithStyle:UITableViewStylePlain]) {
        self.names = names;
        self.keys = keys;
        self.filteredNames = [[NSMutableArray alloc] init];
    }
    return self;
}
```

This code is very straightforward. We start by calling one of the initializers of the UITableViewController class, setting the style of its embedded table view to plain. We then set the values of the names and keys properties and allocate the array for the search results. It's important to note that the names and keys properties were both declared as (strong, nonatomic), which means that they will just hold references to the data from the main view controller. This is more efficient than making a copy of the source data.

Finally, add a line of code to the viewDidLoad method to register out the table cell identifier with the results controller's embedded table view:

```
- (void)viewDidLoad {
    [super viewDidLoad];

    [self.tableView registerClass:[UITableViewCell class]
            forCellReuseIdentifier:SectionsTableIdentifier];
}
```

That's all we need to do in the results view controller for now, so let's switch back to our main view controller for a while and add the search bar to it. Select *ViewController.m* in the Project Navigator and make the changes shown in bold to the code at the top of the file:

```
#import "ViewController.h"
#import "SearchResultsController.h"

static NSString *SectionsTableIdentifier = @"SectionsTableIdentifier";

@interface ViewController ()

@property (copy, nonatomic) NSDictionary *names;
@property (copy, nonatomic) NSArray *keys;
@property (weak, nonatomic) IBOutlet UITableView *tableView;
@property (strong, nonatomic) UISearchController *searchController;

@end
```

We first imported the header file for our search results controller, which we'll need shortly, and then we added a property to hold a reference to the UISearchController instance that will do most of the hard work for us in this example.

Next, add the code that creates the search controller to the viewDidLoad method:

```
- (void)viewDidLoad {
    [super viewDidLoad];
    // Do any additional setup after loading the view, typically from a nib.

    [self.tableView registerClass:[UITableViewCell class]
            forCellReuseIdentifier:SectionsTableIdentifier];

    NSString *path = [[NSBundle mainBundle] pathForResource:@"sortednames"
                                                     ofType:@"plist"];
    self.names = [NSDictionary dictionaryWithContentsOfFile:path];
    self.keys = [[self.names allKeys] sortedArrayUsingSelector:
                    @selector(compare:)];

    SearchResultsController *resultsController =
            [[SearchResultsController alloc] initWithNames:self.names
                    keys:self.keys];
    self.searchController = [[UISearchController alloc]
            initWithSearchResultsController:resultsController];

    UISearchBar *searchBar = self.searchController.searchBar;
    searchBar.scopeButtonTitles = @[@"All", @"Short", @"Long"];
    searchBar.placeholder = @"Enter a search term";
    [searchBar sizeToFit];
    self.tableView.tableHeaderView = searchBar;
    self.searchController.searchResultsUpdater = resultsController;
}
```

We start by creating the results controller using the initializer that we just implemented in the *SearchResultsController.m* file. Then, we create the UISearchController, passing it a reference to our results controller—UISearchController presents this view controller when it has search results to display:

```
self.searchController = [[UISearchController alloc]
     initWithSearchResultsController:resultsController];
```

The next three lines of code get and configure the UISearchBar, which is created by the UISearchController and which we can get from its searchBar property:

```
UISearchBar *searchBar = self.searchController.searchBar;
searchBar.scopeButtonTitles = @[@"All", @"Short", @"Long"];
searchBar.placeholder = @"Enter a search term";
```

The search bar's scopeButtonTitles property contains the names to be assigned to its scope buttons. By default there are no scope buttons, but here we install the names of the three buttons that we discussed earlier in this section. We also set some placeholder text to let the user know what the search bar is for. You can see the placeholder text on the left in Figure 8-27.

So far, we have created the `UISearchController` but we haven't connected it to our user interface. To do that, we get the search bar and install it as the header view of the table in our main view controller:

```
[searchBar sizeToFit];
self.tableView.tableHeaderView = searchBar;
```

The table's header view is managed automatically by the table view. It always appears before the first row of the first table section. Notice that we use the `sizeToFit` method to give the search bar the size that's appropriate for its content. We do this so that it is given the correct height—the width that's set by this method is not important, because the table view will make sure that it stretches the whole width of the table and will resize it automatically if the table changes size (typically because the device has been rotated.)

The final change to `viewDidLoad` assigns a value to the `UISearchController`'s `searchResultsUpdater` property, which is of type `id<UISearchResultsUpdating>`:

```
self.searchController.searchResultsUpdater = resultsController;
```

Each time the user types something into the search bar, `UISearchController` uses the object stored in its `searchResultsUpdater` property to update the search results. As mentioned, we are going to handle the search in the `SearchResultsController` class, which is why we needed to make it conform to the `UISearchResultsUpdating` protocol.

Believe it or not, that's all we need to do to in our main view controller to add the search bar and have the search results displayed. Next, we need to return to *SearchResultsController.m*, where we have two tasks to complete—add the code that implements the search and the `UITableDataSource` methods for the embedded table view.

Let's start with the code for the search. As the user types into the search bar, the `UISearchController` calls the `updateSearchResultsForSearchController:` method of its search results updater, which is our `SearchResultsController`. In this method, we need to get the search text from the search bar and use it to construct a filtered list of names in the `filteredNames` array. We'll also use the scope buttons to limit the names that we include in the search. Add the following code to *SearchResultsController.m*:

```
#pragma mark - UISearchResultsUpdating Conformance

static const NSUInteger longNameSize = 6;
static const NSInteger shortNamesButtonIndex = 1;
static const NSInteger longNamesButtonIndex = 2;

- (void)updateSearchResultsForSearchController:
                (UISearchController *)controller {
    NSString *searchString = controller.searchBar.text;
    NSInteger buttonIndex =
                controller.searchBar.selectedScopeButtonIndex;
    [self.filteredNames removeAllObjects];
```

```
    if (searchString.length > 0) {
        NSPredicate *predicate =
          [NSPredicate
            predicateWithBlock:^BOOL(NSString *name, NSDictionary *b) {
                // Filter out long or short names depending on which
                // scope button is selected.
                NSUInteger nameLength = name.length;
                if ((buttonIndex == shortNamesButtonIndex &
                            & nameLength >= longNameSize)
                    || (buttonIndex == longNamesButtonIndex
                            && nameLength < longNameSize)) {
                    return NO;
                }
                NSRange range = [name rangeOfString:searchString
                                        options:NSCaseInsensitiveSearch];
                return range.location != NSNotFound;
          }];
        for (NSString *key in self.keys) {
            NSArray *matches = [self.names[key]
                                filteredArrayUsingPredicate: predicate];
            [self.filteredNames addObjectsFromArray:matches];
        }
    }
    [self.tableView reloadData];
}
```

Let's walk through this code to see what it's doing. First, we get the search string from the search bar and the index of the scope button that's selected, and then we clear the list of filtered names:

```
NSString *searchString = controller.searchBar.text;
NSInteger buttonIndex =
            controller.searchBar.selectedScopeButtonIndex;
[self.filteredNames removeAllObjects];
```

Next, we check that the search string is not empty—we do not display any matching results for an empty search string:

```
if (searchString.length > 0) {
```

Now we define a predicate for matching names against the search string. A predicate is an object that tests an input value, returning YES if the value matches and NO if there's no match. The predicate will be called for each name in the names dictionary. We first check that the length of the name is consistent with the selected scope button and return NO if it isn't:

```
    NSPredicate *predicate =
      [NSPredicate
        predicateWithBlock:^BOOL(NSString *name, NSDictionary *b) {
            // Filter out long or short names depending on which
            // scope button is selected.
            NSUInteger nameLength = name.length;
```

```
            if ((buttonIndex == shortNamesButtonIndex &
                        & nameLength >= longNameSize)
                || (buttonIndex == longNamesButtonIndex
                        && nameLength < longNameSize)) {
                return NO;
            }
```

If the name passes this test, we look for the search string as a substring of the name. If we find it, then we have a match:

```
            NSRange range = [name rangeOfString:searchString
                                    options:NSCaseInsensitiveSearch];
            return range.location != NSNotFound;
        }];
```

Next, we iterate over all the keys in the names dictionary, each of which corresponds to an array of names (key A maps to the names that start with the letter A, and so on). For each key, we get its array of names and apply our predicate to it by using the filteredArrayUsingPredicate: method of NSArray. This gets us a (possibly empty) filtered array of the names that match, which we add to the filteredNames array:

```
    for (NSString *key in self.keys) {
        NSArray *matches = [self.names[key]
                            filteredArrayUsingPredicate: predicate];
        [self.filteredNames addObjectsFromArray:matches];
    }
```

Once all the name arrays have been processed, we have the complete set of matching names in the filteredNames array. Now all we need to do is arrange for them to be displayed in the table in our SearchResultsController. We start by telling the table that it needs to redisplay its content:

```
}
[self.tableView reloadData];
```

We need the table view to display one name from the filteredNames array in each row. To do that, we implement the methods of the UITableViewDataSource protocol in our SearchResultsController class. Recall that SearchResultsController is a subclass of UITableViewController, so it automatically acts as its table's data source. Add the following code to *SearchResultsController.m*:

```
- (NSInteger)tableView:(UITableView *)tableView
            numberOfRowsInSection:(NSInteger)section {
    return [self.filteredNames count];
}

- (UITableViewCell *)tableView:(UITableView *)tableView
        cellForRowAtIndexPath:(NSIndexPath *)indexPath {
    UITableViewCell *cell =
    [tableView dequeueReusableCellWithIdentifier:SectionsTableIdentifier
                                    forIndexPath:indexPath];
    cell.textLabel.text = self.filteredNames[indexPath.row];
    return cell;
}
```

You can now run the app and try filtering the list of names, as shown in Figure 8-28.

Figure 8-28. *The application with a search bar added to the table. Note that before tapping the search bar, it appears truncated on the right side of the screen*

We're almost done—there's just one more thing to fix. If you look back on the left of Figure 8-27, you'll see that there is a visual "glitch": the search bar seems to be mysteriously chopped off near the right edge. In fact, what you're seeing is the upper end of the vertical section index bar on the right. Our search bar is a part of the table view (since we set it up to be the header view). When a table view shows a section index, it automatically squashes all its other views in from the right. Since the default section index background color is white, it pretty much blends in with the rows of the table view, which makes its appearance next to the search bar stick out like a sore thumb!

To remedy this, let's set some colors on the section index in our original table. We'll use a contrasting color to make it stick out like a sore thumb the whole way up and down the table, so that users can see what's going on more clearly. Just add these lines to the end of the `viewDidLoad` method in *ViewController.m*:

```
self.tableView.sectionIndexBackgroundColor =
            [UIColor blackColor];
self.tableView.sectionIndexTrackingBackgroundColor =
            [UIColor darkGrayColor];
self.tableView.sectionIndexColor = [UIColor whiteColor];
```

First, we set the main background color for the section index, which is what users see when they're not touching it. Then we set the tracking background color to let the entire column light up a bit when the user touches it and drags up and down the edge. Finally, we set the text color for the index items themselves. Figure 8-29 shows the final result.

Figure 8-29. With a more visually pronounced section index , it's clearer to the user that this is actually a control surface

How Many Tables?: View Debugging

The `UISearchController` class does a good job of switching between the two tables in our last example—so good that you might find it hard to believe that there is a switch going on at all! Apart from the fact that you've seen all the code, there are also a couple of visual clues—the search table is a plain table, so you don't see the names grouped like they are in the main table, and it has no section index. If you want even more proof, you can get it by using a neat new feature of Xcode 6 called View Debugging, which lets you take snapshots of the view hierarchy of a running application and examine them in Xcode's editor area. This feature works on both the simulator and real devices, and you'll probably find it invaluable at some point or another when you're trying to find out why one of your views appears to be missing or is not where you expect it to be.

Let's start by looking at what View Debugging makes of our application when it's showing the full name list. Run the application again and in Xcode's menu bar, select **Debug ➤ View Debugging ➤ Capture View Hierarchy**. Xcode grabs the view hierarchy from the simulator or device, and displays it as shown in Figure 8-30.

Figure 8-30. The view hierarchy of the Sections application

That probably doesn't look very useful—we can't really see anything more than we could in the simulator. To reveal the view hierarchy, you need to rotate the image of the application so that you can look at it "from the side." To do so, click the mouse in the editor area, somewhere just to the left of the captured image, and drag it to the right. As you do so, the layering of views in the application will reveal itself. If you rotate through about 45 degrees, you'll see something like Figure 8-31.

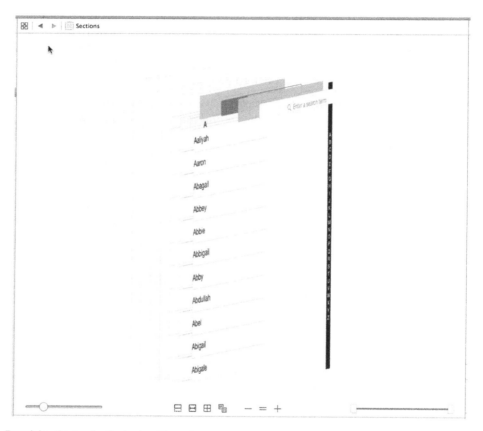

Figure 8-31. Examining the application's view hierarchy

If you click the various views in the stack, you'll see that the jump bar at the top changes to show you the class name of the view that you've clicked and those of all of its ancestor views. Click each of the views from the back to the front to get familiar with how the table is constructed. You should be able to find the view controller's main view, the table view itself, some table view cells, the search bar, the search bar index, and various other views that are part of the table's implementation.

Now let's see what the view hierarchy looks like while we are searching. Xcode pauses your application to let you examine the view snapshot, so first resume execution by clicking **Debug ➤ Continue**. Now start typing into the application's search bar and capture the view hierarchy again using **Debug ➤ View Debugging ➤ Capture View Hierarchy**. When the view hierarchy appears, rotate it a little and you'll see something like Figure 8-32.

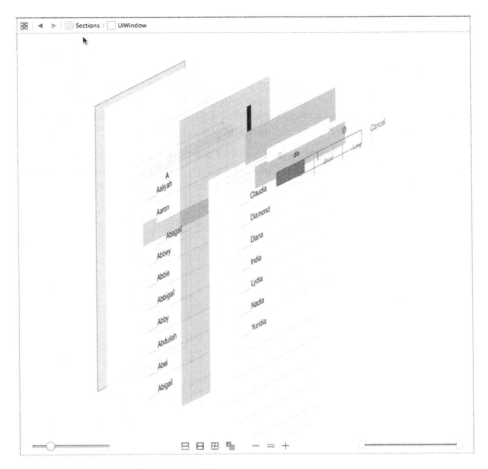

Figure 8-32. *The view hierarchy while using the search bar*

Now it's pretty clear that there are indeed two tables in use. You can see the original table about half way through the view stack and above (i.e., to the right of) it, you can see the table view that belongs to the search results view controller. Just behind that, there's a translucent gray view that covers the original table—that's the view that dims the original table when you first start typing in the search bar.

Experiment a little with the buttons at the bottom of the editor area—you can use them to turn on and off the display of Auto Layout constraints, reset the view to the top-down view shown in Figure 8-30, and zoom in and zoom out. You can also use the slider on the left to change the spacing between views, and use the one on the right to remove layers at the top or bottom of the hierarchy so that you can see what's behind them. View Debugging is a very powerful tool!

Putting It All on the Table

Well, how are you doing? This was a pretty hefty chapter and you've learned a ton! You should have a very solid understanding of the way that flat tables work. You should know how to customize tables and table view cells, as well as how to configure table views. You also saw how to implement a search bar, which is a vital tool in any iOS application that presents large volumes of data. Finally, you met View Debugging, a new and extremely useful feature in iOS 8. Make sure you understand everything we did in this chapter because we're going to build on it.

We're going to continue working with table views in the next chapter. For example, you'll learn how to use them to present hierarchical data. And you'll see how to create content views that allow the user to edit data selected in a table view, as well as how to present checklists in tables, embed controls in table rows, and delete rows.

Chapter 9

Navigation Controllers and Table Views

In the previous chapter, you mastered the basics of working with table views. In this chapter, you'll get a whole lot more practice because we're going to explore **navigation controllers**.

Table views and navigation controllers work hand in hand. Strictly speaking, a navigation controller doesn't need a table view to do its thing. As a practical matter, however, when you implement a navigation controller, you almost always implement at least one table (and usually several) because the strength of the navigation controller lies in the ease with which it handles complex hierarchical data. On the iPhone's small screen, hierarchical data is best presented using a succession of table views.

In this chapter, we're going to build an application progressively, just as we did with the Pickers application back in Chapter 7. We'll get the navigation controller and the root view controller working, and then we'll start adding more controllers and layers to the hierarchy. Each view controller we create will reinforce some aspect of table use or configuration:

- How to drill down from table views into child table views
- How to drill down from table views into content views, where detailed data can be viewed and even edited
- How to use multiple sections within a table view
- How to use edit mode to allow rows to be deleted from a table view
- How to use edit mode to let the user reorder rows within a table view

That's a lot, isn't it? Well, let's get started with an introduction to navigation controllers.

Navigation Controller Basics

The main tool you'll use to build hierarchical applications is UINavigationController. UINavigationController is similar to UITabBarController in that it manages, and swaps in and out, multiple content views. The main difference between the two is that UINavigationController is implemented as a stack, which makes it well suited to working with hierarchies.

Do you already know everything there is to know about stacks? If so, scan through the following subsection (or skip it altogether), and we'll meet you at the beginning of the next subsection, "A Stack of Controllers." If you're new to stacks, continue reading. Fortunately, stacks are a pretty easy concept to grasp.

Stacky Goodness

A **stack** is a commonly used data structure that works on the principle of "last in, first out." Believe it or not, a Pez dispenser is a great example of a stack. Ever try to load one? According to the little instruction sheet that comes with each and every Pez dispenser, there are a few easy steps. First, unwrap the pack of Pez candy. Second, open the dispenser by tipping its head straight back. Third, grab the stack (notice the clever way we inserted the word "stack" in there!) of candy, holding it firmly between your pointer finger and thumb, and insert the column into the open dispenser. Fourth, pick up all the little pieces of candy that flew all over the place because these instructions just never work.

OK, so far this example has not been particularly useful. But what happens next is. As you pick up the pieces and jam them, one at a time, into the dispenser, you are working with a stack. Remember that we said a stack was last in, first out? That also means first in, last out. The first piece of Pez you push into the dispenser will be the last piece that pops out. The last piece of Pez you push in will be the first piece you pop out. A computer stack follows the same rules:

- When you add an object to a stack, it's called a push. You push an object onto the stack.

- The first object you push onto the stack is called the base of the stack.

- The last object you pushed onto the stack is called the top of the stack (at least until it is replaced by the next object you push onto the stack).

- When you remove an object from the stack, it's called a pop. When you pop an object off the stack, it's always the last one you pushed onto the stack. Conversely, the first object you push onto the stack will always be the last one you pop off the stack.

A Stack of Controllers

A navigation controller maintains a stack of view controllers. When you design your navigation controller, you'll need to specify the very first view the user sees. As we've discussed in previous chapters, that view's controller is called the **root view controller**, or just **root controller**, and is the base of the navigation controller's stack of view controllers. As the user selects the next view to display, a new view controller is pushed onto the stack, and the view it controls appears. We refer to these new view controllers as **subcontrollers.** As you'll see, this chapter's application, Fonts, is made up of a navigation controller and several subcontrollers.

Take a look at Figure 9-1. Notice the **title** centered in the navigation bar and the **back button** on the left side of the navigation bar. The title of the navigation bar is populated with the title property of the top view controller in the navigation controller's stack, and the title of the back button is populated with the title of the previous view controller. The back button acts similar to a web browser's back button. When the user taps that button, the current view controller is popped off the stack, and the previous view becomes the current view.

Figure 9-1. The Settings application uses a navigation controller. The back button at the upper left pops the current view controller off the stack, returning you to the previous level of the hierarchy. The title of the current content view controller is also displayed

We love this design pattern. It allows us to build complex hierarchical applications iteratively. We don't need to know the entire hierarchy to get things up and running. Each controller only needs to know about its child controllers, so it can push the appropriate new controller object onto the stack when the user makes a selection. You can build up a large application from many small pieces this way, which is exactly what we're going to do in this chapter.

The navigation controller is really the heart and soul of many iPhone apps; however, when it comes to iPad apps, the navigation controller plays a more marginal role. A typical example of this is the Mail app, which features a hierarchical navigation controller to let users navigate among all their mail servers, folders, and messages. In the iPad version of Mail, the navigation controller never fills the screen, but appears either as a sidebar or a temporary view covering part of the main view. We'll dig into that usage a little later, in Chapter 11.

Fonts: A Simple Font Browser

The application we're about to build will show you how to do most of the common tasks associated with displaying a hierarchy of data. When the application launches, you'll be presented with a list of all the **font families** that are included with iOS, as shown in Figure 9-2. A font family is a group of closely related fonts, or fonts that are stylistic variations on one another. For example, Helvetica, Helvetica-Bold, Helvetic-Oblique, and other variations are all included in the Helvetica font family.

Figure 9-2. This chapter application's root view controller. Note the accessory icons on the right side of the view. This particular type of accessory icon is called a disclosure indicator. It tells the user that touching that row drills down to another table view

Selecting any row in this top-level view will push a view controller onto the navigation controller's stack. The icons on the right side of each row are called **accessory icons**. This particular accessory icon (the gray arrow) is called a **disclosure indicator**, and its presence lets the user know that touching that row drills down to another table view.

Meet the Subcontrollers

Before we start building the Fonts application, let's take a quick look at each of the views displayed by our subcontrollers.

The Font List Controller

Touching any row of the table shown in Figure 9-2 will bring up the child view shown in Figure 9-3.

Figure 9-3. The first of the Fonts application's subcontrollers implements a table in which each row contains a detail disclosure button

The accessory icon to the right of each row in Figure 9-3 is a bit different. This accessory is known as a **detail disclosure button**. Unlike the disclosure indicator, the detail disclosure button is not just an icon—it's a control that the user can tap. This means that you can have two different options available for a given row: one action is triggered when the user selects the row, and another action is triggered when the user taps the button. Tapping the small info button within this accessory should allow the user to view, and perhaps edit, more detailed information about the current row. Meanwhile, the presence of the right-pointing arrow should indicate to the user that there is some deeper navigation to be found by tapping elsewhere in the row.

The Font Sizes View Controller

Touching any row of the table shown in Figure 9-3 will bring up the child view shown in Figure 9-4.

Figure 9-4. Located one layer deeper than the Font List View Controller, the Font Sizes View Controller shows multiple sizes of the chosen font, one per row

Here's a recap of when to use disclosure indicators and detail disclosure buttons:

- If you want to offer a single choice for a row tap, don't use an accessory icon if a row tap will *only* lead to a more detailed view of that row.

- Mark the row with a disclosure indicator (right-pointing arrow) if a row tap will lead to a new view listing more items (*not* a detail view).

- If you want to offer two choices for a row, mark the row with either a detail disclosure indicator or a detail button. This allows the user to tap the row for a new view or the disclosure button for more details.

The Font Info View Controller

Our final application subcontroller—the only one that is not a table view—is shown in Figure 9-5. This is the view that appears when you tap on the info icon for any row in the Font List View Controller shown in Figure 9-2.

Figure 9-5. *The final view controller in the Fonts application allows you to view the chosen font at any size you want*

This view lets the user drag a slider to adjust the size of the displayed font. It also includes a switch that lets the user specify whether this font should be listed among the user's favorites. If any fonts are set as favorites, they'll appear within a separate group in the root view controller.

The Fonts Application's Skeleton

Xcode offers a perfectly good template for creating navigation-based applications, and you will likely use it much of the time when you need to create hierarchical applications. However, we're not going to use that template today. Instead, we'll construct our navigation-based application from the ground up, so we get a feel for how everything fits together. We'll also walk through it one piece at a time, so it should be easy to keep up.

In Xcode, press ⌘⇧N to create a new project. Select **Single View Application** from the iOS template list, and then click **Next** to continue. Set *Fonts* as the **Product Name**, *Objective-C* as the **Language**, and select *Universal* for **Devices**. Make sure that **Use Core Data** is not checked, click **Next**, and choose the location to save your project.

Setting Up the Navigation Controller

We now need to create the basic navigation structure for our application. At the core of this will be a UINavigationController, which manages the stack of view controllers that a user can navigate between, and a UITableViewController that shows the top-level list of rows we're going to display. As it turns out, Interface Builder makes this remarkably easy to do.

Select *Main.storyboard*. The template has created a basic view controller for us, but we need to use a UINavigationController instead, so select the view controller in either the editor area or the Document Outline and delete it to leave the storyboard empty. Now use the Object Library to search for UINavigationController and drag an instance into the editing area. You'll see that you actually get two scenes instead of one, similar to what you saw when creating a tab view controller in Chapter 7. On the left is the UINavigationController itself. Select this controller, open the Attributes Inspector, and check **Is Initial View Controller** in the **View Controller** section to make this the controller that appears when the application is launched.

The UINavigationController has a connection wired to the second scene, which contains a UITableViewController. You'll see that the table has the title *Root View Controller*. Click that title, open the Attributes Inspector, and then set the title to *Fonts*.

It's worth taking a moment to think about this. What exactly do we get by configuring our application to load the initial scene from this storyboard? First, we get the view created by the navigation controller, a composite view that contains a combination of two things: the navigation bar at the top of the screen (which usually contains some sort of title and often a back button of some kind on the left) and the content of whatever the navigation controller's current view controller wants to display. In our case, the lower part of the display will be filled with the table view that was created alongside the navigation controller.

You'll learn more about how to control what the navigation controller shows in the navigation bar as we go forward. You'll also gain an understanding of how the navigation controller shifts focus from one subordinate view controller to another. For now, you've laid enough groundwork that you can start defining what your custom view controllers are going to do.

At this point, the application skeleton is essentially complete. You'll see a warning about setting a reuse identifier for a prototype table cell, but we can ignore that for now. Save all your files, and then build and run the app. If all is well, the application should launch, and a navigation bar with the title *Fonts* should appear. You haven't given the table view any information about what to show yet, so no rows will display at this point (see Figure 9-6).

Figure 9-6. *The application skeleton in action*

Keeping Track of Favorites

At several points in this application, we're going to let the user maintain a list of favorite fonts by letting them add chosen fonts, view a whole list of already-chosen favorites, and remove fonts from the list. In order to manage this list in a consistent way, we're going to make a new class that will hang onto an array of favorites and store them in the user's preferences settings for this application. You'll learn a lot more about user preferences in Chapter 12, but here we'll just touch on some basics.

Start by creating a new class. Select the *Fonts* folder in the Project Navigator and press ⌘**N** to bring up the new file assistant. Select **Cocoa Touch Class** from the **iOS Source** section and then click **Next**. On the following screen, name the new class *FavoritesList* and choose NSObject in the **Subclass of** field. After creating the files for this class, select *FavoritesList.h* and add the following code shown in bold:

```
#import <Foundation/Foundation.h>

@interface FavoritesList : NSObject

+ (instancetype)sharedFavoritesList;
```

```
- (NSArray *)favorites;

- (void)addFavorite:(id)item;
- (void)removeFavorite:(id)item;
```

@end

In the preceding snippet, we declared the API for our new class. For starters, we declared a factory method called sharedFavoritesList that returns an instance of this class. No matter how many times this method is called, the same instance will always be returned. The idea is that FavoritesList should work as a singleton; instead of using multiple instances, we'll just use one instance throughout the application.

> **Note**   The declaration for sharedFavoritesList has a return type that you may not recognize: instancetype. This is a fairly recent addition to Objective-C. It's now recommended that all factory methods and init methods that would have otherwise used id as their return type should now use instancetype instead. The problem with using id is the lack of type safety. In the past, you could easily write wrong-headed code like "NSString *s = [NSArray array];" and the compiler wouldn't complain (though your program would crash later, when you tried to send one of NSString's methods to the NSArray you created). Using instancetype lets you keep a level of genericness, while still telling the compiler that the return value should really be limited to the type of the message recipient (or one of its subclasses). In iOS 8, pretty much all of Apple's public APIs use instancetype instead of id.

Next, we defined methods for accessing the array, as well as adding and deleting items.

Now we want to switch over to *FavoritesList.m*, so we can start implementing it. For starters, create a class extension at the top of the file and add a property to it:

```
#import "FavoritesList.h"

@interface FavoritesList ()

@property (strong, nonatomic) NSMutableArray *favorites;

@end
```

Note that we're declaring a property named favorites of type NSMutableArray. In our header file, we just declared a method called favorites that returns an NSArray. Since declaring a property also typically declares the existence of a getter and a setter, won't this lead to a conflict? Fortunately, no. Since our property's type is a subclass of what we are using in the header, it will work just fine. This means that internally, within our class, we can use a mutable array; however, what we expose through our API seems to be an immutable NSArray. The API that this class provides, as defined in *FavoritesList.h*, should be considered by any users of this code to be a contract. If another piece of code digs deep, discovers that this class is actually returning an NSMutableArray, and uses it directly as such, then that code is effectively breaking the contract, and that is Not Our Problem.

Moving on, add the implementation of the sharedFavoritesList factory method to *FavoritesList.m*:

```
@implementation FavoritesList

+ (instancetype)sharedFavoritesList {
    static FavoritesList *shared = nil;
    static dispatch_once_t onceToken;
    dispatch_once(&onceToken, ^{
        shared = [[self alloc] init];
    });
    return shared;
}

@end
```

This may look complicated, but it really just does one thing: it creates a new instance of the class and returns it. The creation part is tucked inside a block of code which is passed off to the dispatch_once() function, which makes sure that the code in question runs exactly one time. Every time this method is called after the first time, the instance has already been created, so it is simply returned.

Now, it's time for the init method. Add this code right before the @end line:

```
- (instancetype)init {
    self = [super init];
    if (self) {
        NSUserDefaults *defaults = [NSUserDefaults standardUserDefaults];
        NSArray *storedFavorites = [defaults objectForKey:@"favorites"];
        if (storedFavorites) {
            self.favorites = [storedFavorites mutableCopy];
        } else {
            self.favorites = [NSMutableArray array];
        }
    }
    return self;
}
```

This method uses the NSUserDefaults class (more about that in Chapter 12) to see if there are any favorites stored in preferences. If so, it puts a mutable copy of the favorites into the favorites property; otherwise, it puts a new, empty mutable array in there instead.

Let's finish up by implementing the two methods for adding and removing favorites, as well as a method they will both call to immediately save their changes. Add both of these methods before the @end line:

```
- (void)addFavorite:(id)item {
    [_favorites insertObject:item atIndex:0];
    [self saveFavorites];
}

- (void)removeFavorite:(id)item {
    [_favorites removeObject:item];
    [self saveFavorites];
}
```

```
- (void)saveFavorites {
    NSUserDefaults *defaults = [NSUserDefaults standardUserDefaults];
    [defaults setObject:self.favorites forKey:@"favorites"];
    [defaults synchronize];
}
```

Both addFavorite: and removeFavorite: are very straightforward. The only thing worth noting here is the fact that, instead of accessing the array through self.favorites (the preferred style through most of this book), we're accessing the underlying instance variable _favorites instead. The reason for this is subtle: even though we've defined the property in the class extension as an NSMutableArray, the compiler will find what we declared in the @interface in the header file when trying to resolve self.favorites, and that's an immutable NSArray! This workaround diverges from our normal style, but it will work just fine.

Both of those methods call the saveFavorites method, which uses the NSUserDefaults class to save the array in the user's preferences. You'll learn more about how this works in Chapter 12; but for now, it's enough to know that the NSUserDefaults object that we use here acts like a sort of persistent dictionary, and anything that we put in there will be available the next time we ask for it, even if the application has been stopped and restarted.

Creating the Root View Controller

Now we're ready to start working on our first view controller. In the previous chapter, we used simple arrays of strings to populate our table rows. We're going to do something similar here, but this time we'll use the UIFont class to get a list of font families, and then use the names of those font families to populate each row. We'll also use the fonts themselves to display the font names, so that each row will contain a small preview of what the font family contains.

It's time to create the first controller class for this application. The template created a view controller for us, but its name—ViewController—isn't very useful, because there are going to be several view controllers in this application. So first select both *ViewController.h* and *ViewController.m* in the Project Navigator and press **Delete** to delete them and move them to the trash. Next, select the *Fonts* folder in the Project Navigator and press ⌘**N** to bring up the new file assistant. Select **Cocoa Touch Class** from the **iOS Source** section and then click **Next**. On the following screen, name the new class *RootViewController* and enter **UITableViewController** for **Subclass of**. Click **Next** and then click **Create** to create the new class. In the Project Navigator, select *RootViewController.m* and add the bold lines in the snippet that follows to import the header for our favorites list and add a few properties:

```
#import "RootViewController.h"
#import "FavoritesList.h"

@interface RootViewController ()

@property (copy, nonatomic) NSArray *familyNames;
@property (assign, nonatomic) CGFloat cellPointSize;
@property (strong, nonatomic) FavoritesList *favoritesList;

@end
```

We'll assign values to each of those properties from the outset, and then use them at various times while this class is in use. The familyNames array will contain a list of all the font families we're going to display; the cellPointSize property will contain the font size that we want to use in all of our table view cells; and favoritesList will contain a pointer to the FavoritesList singleton.

> **Note**   You may notice that the familyNames property is declared using the copy keyword instead of strong. What's up with that? Why should we be copying arrays willy-nilly? The reason is the potential existence of mutable arrays.
>
> Imagine if we had declared the property using strong, and an outside piece of code passed in an instance of NSMutableArray to set the value of the familyNames property. If that original caller later decides to change the contents of that array, the RootViewController instance will end up in an inconsistent state, where the contents of familyNames is no longer in sync with what's on the screen! Using copy eliminates that risk, since calling copy on any NSArray (including any mutable subclasses) always gives us an immutable copy. Also, we don't need to worry about the performance impact too much. As it turns out, sending copy to any immutable object doesn't actually copy the object. Instead, it returns the same object after increasing its reference count. In effect, calling copy on an immutable object is the same as calling retain, which is what ARC might do behind the scenes anytime you set a strong property. So, it works out just fine for everyone, since the object can never change.
>
> This situation applies to all **value classes** where the base class is immutable, but mutable subclasses exist. These value classes include NSArray, NSDictionary, NSSet, NSString, NSData, and a few more. Any time you want to hang onto an instance of one of these in a property, you should probably declare the property's storage with copy instead of strong to avoid any problems.

Set up all of this class's properties by adding the bold code shown here to the viewDidLoad method:

```
- (void)viewDidLoad {
    [super viewDidLoad];

    self.familyNames = [[UIFont familyNames]
                        sortedArrayUsingSelector:@selector(compare:)];
    UIFont *preferredTableViewFont = [UIFont preferredFontForTextStyle:
                                      UIFontTextStyleHeadline];
    self.cellPointSize = preferredTableViewFont.pointSize;
    self.favoritesList = [FavoritesList sharedFavoritesList];
}
```

In the preceding snippet, we populated familyNames by asking the UIFont class for all known family names, and then sorting the resulting array. We then used UIFont once again to ask for the preferred font for use in a headline. We did this using a piece of functionality added in iOS 7, which builds on the font size setting that can be specified in the Settings app. This dynamic font sizing lets the user set an overall font scaling for system-wide use. Here, we used that font's `pointSize` property to establish a baseline font size that we'll use elsewhere in this view controller. Finally, we grabbed the singleton favorites list object.

Before we go on, let's delete the `didReceiveMemoryWarning` method, as well as any commented-out table view delegate or data source methods—we're not going to use any of them in this class.

The idea behind this view controller is to show two sections. The first section is a list of all available font families, each of which leads to a list of all the fonts in the family. The second selection is for favorites, and it contains just a single entry that will lead the user to a list of their favorite fonts. However, if the user has no favorites (for example, when the app is launched for the first time), we'd rather not show that second section at all, since it would just lead the user to an empty list. So, we'll have to do a few things throughout the rest of this class to compensate for this eventuality. The first of these is to implement this method, which is called just before the root view controller's view appears on the screen:

```
- (void)viewWillAppear:(BOOL)animated {
    [super viewWillAppear:animated];
    [self.tableView reloadData];
}
```

The reason for this is that there may be times when the set of things we're going to display might change from one viewing to the next. For example, the user may start with no favorites, but then drill down, view a font, set it as a favorite, and then come back out to the root view. At that time, we need to reload the table view, so that the second section will appear.

Next, we're going to implement a sort of utility method for use within this class. At a couple of points, while configuring the table view via its data source methods, we'll need to be able to figure out which font we want to display in a cell. We put that functionality into a method of its own:

```
- (UIFont *)fontForDisplayAtIndexPath:(NSIndexPath *)indexPath {
    if (indexPath.section == 0) {
        NSString *familyName = self.familyNames[indexPath.row];
        NSString *fontName = [[UIFont fontNamesForFamilyName:familyName]
                                                firstObject];
        return [UIFont fontWithName:fontName size:self.cellPointSize];
    } else {
        return nil;
    }
}
```

The preceding method uses the `UIFont` class, first to find all the font names for the given family name, and then later to grab the first font name within that family. We don't necessarily know that the first named font in a family is the best one to represent the whole family, but it's as good a guess as any.

Now, let's move on to the meat of this view controller: the table view data source methods. First up, let's look at the number of sections:

```
- (NSInteger)numberOfSectionsInTableView:(UITableView *)tableView {
#warning Potentially incomplete method implementation.
    // Return the number of sections.
    if ([self.favoritesList.favorites count] > 0) {
        return 2;
    } else {
        return 1;
    }
    return 0;
}
```

We use the favorites list to determine whether we want to show the second section. Next, we tackle the number of sections in each row:

```
- (NSInteger)tableView:(UITableView *)tableView
            numberOfRowsInSection:(NSInteger)section {
#warning Incomplete method implementation.
    // Return the number of rows in the section.
    if (section == 0) {
        return [self.familyNames count];
    } else {
        return 1;
    }
    return 0;
}
```

That one's also pretty simple. We just use the section number to determine whether the section is showing all family names, or a single cell linking to the list of favorites. Now let's define one other method, an optional method in the UITableViewDataSource protocol that lets us specify the title for each of our sections:

```
- (NSString *)tableView:(UITableView *)tableView
            titleForHeaderInSection:(NSInteger)section {
    if (section == 0) {
        return @"All Font Families";
    } else {
        return @"My Favorite Fonts";
    }
}
```

This is another straightforward method. It uses the section number to determine which header title to use. The final core method that every table view data source must implement is the one for configuring each cell, and ours looks like this:

```
- (UITableViewCell *)tableView:(UITableView *)tableView
        cellForRowAtIndexPath:(NSIndexPath *)indexPath {
    static NSString *FamilyNameCell = @"FamilyName";
    static NSString *FavoritesCell = @"Favorites";
    UITableViewCell *cell = nil;
```

```
// Configure the cell...
if (indexPath.section == 0) {
    cell = [tableView dequeueReusableCellWithIdentifier:FamilyNameCell
                                          forIndexPath:indexPath];
    cell.textLabel.font = [self fontForDisplayAtIndexPath:indexPath];
    cell.textLabel.text = self.familyNames[indexPath.row];
    cell.detailTextLabel.text = self.familyNames[indexPath.row];
} else {
    cell = [tableView dequeueReusableCellWithIdentifier:FavoritesCell
                                          forIndexPath:indexPath];
}

return cell;
}
```

We define two different cell identifiers that we will use to load two different cell prototypes from the storyboard (much like we loaded a table cell from a nib file in Chapter 8). We haven't configured those cell prototypes yet, but we will soon! Next, we use the section number to determine which of those cells we want to show for the current indexPath. If the cell is meant to contain a font family name, then we put the family name into both its label and its detailLabel. We also use a font from the family (the one we get from the fontForDisplayAtIndexPath: method) within the text label, so that we'll see the font family name shown in the font itself, as well as a smaller version in the standard system font.

Initial Storyboard Setup

Now that we have a view controller that we think should show something, let's configure the storyboard to make things happen. Select *Main.storyboard* in the Project Navigator. You'll see the navigation controller and the table view controller that we added earlier. The first thing we need to configure is the table view controller. By default, the controller's class is set to UITableViewController. We need to change that to our root view controller class. In the Document Outline, select the yellow icon labeled **Root View Controller**, and then use the Identity Inspector to change the view controller's **Class** to *RootViewController*.

The other configuration we'll need to do right now is to set up a pair of prototype cells to match the cell identifiers we used in our code. From the start, the table view has a single prototype cell. Select it and press ⌘D to duplicate it, and you'll see that you now have two cells. Select the first one, and then use the Attributes Inspector to set its **Style** to *Subtitle*, its **Identifier** to *FamilyName*, and its **Accessory** to *Disclosure Indicator*. Next, select the second prototype cell, and then set its **Style** to *Basic*, its **Identifier** to *Favorites*, and its **Accessory** to *Disclosure Indicator*. Also, double-click the title shown in the cell itself and change the text from *Title* to *Favorites*.

> **Tip** The prototype cells that we are using in this example both have standard table view cell styles. If you set the **Style** to *Custom*, you can design the layout of the cell right in the cell prototype, just as you created a cell in a nib file in Chapter 8.

Now build and run this app on your device or the simulator, and you should see a nice list of fonts. Scroll around a bit and you'll see that not all of the fonts produce text of the same height. Scroll right to the end, for example, and you'll see that the sample text for the Zapfino font is much larger than all the others, as shown in Figure 9-7. Despite this, all of the cells are tall enough to contain their content, even though we didn't do anything special to make this happen.

Figure 9-7. *The root view controller displays the installed font families*

As you saw in Chapter 8, this is because of a new feature in iOS 8 that calculates the correct cell height for cells that obey certain rules. Here, we are using standard table view cell styles, which follow the rules out of the box. In earlier versions of iOS, you would have had to implement the UITableViewDelegate protocol method tableView:heightForRowAtIndexPath: to achieve the same result.

First Subcontroller: The Font List View

Our app currently just shows a list of font families, and nothing more. We want to add the ability for a user to touch a font family and see all the fonts it contains, so let's make a new view controller that can manage a list of fonts. Use Xcode's new file assistant to create a new Objective-C class called *FontListViewController* as a subclass of UITableViewController. After creating the class, select its header file and add the following properties:

```
#import <UIKit/UIKit.h>

@interface FontListViewController : UITableViewController

@property (copy, nonatomic) NSArray *fontNames;
@property (assign, nonatomic) BOOL showsFavorites;

@end
```

The fontNames property is what we'll use to tell this view controller what to display. We also created a showsFavorites property that we'll use to let this view controller know if it's showing the list of favorites instead of just a list of fonts in a family, since this will be useful later on.

Now switch over to *FontListController.m* and import a header and declare a property at the top of the file:

```
#import "FontListViewController.h"
#import "FavoritesList.h"

@interface FontListViewController ()

@property (assign, nonatomic) CGFloat cellPointSize;

@end
```

We'll use the cellPointSize property to hold the preferred display size for displaying each font, once again using UIFont to find the preferred size. We do this by implementing viewDidLoad as follows:

```
- (void)viewDidLoad {
    [super viewDidLoad];

    // Uncomment the following line to preserve selection between presentations.
    // self.clearsSelectionOnViewWillAppear = NO;

    // Uncomment the following line to display an Edit button in the navigation
    // bar for this view controller.
    // self.navigationItem.rightBarButtonItem = self.editButtonItem;

    UIFont *preferredTableViewFont = [UIFont preferredFontForTextStyle:
                                                    UIFontTextStyleHeadline];
    self.cellPointSize = preferredTableViewFont.pointSize;
}
```

The next thing we want to do is create a little utility method for choosing the font to be shown in each row, similar to what we have in RootViewController. Here it's a bit different, though. Instead of holding onto a list of font families, in this view controller we're holding onto a list of font names, and we'll use the UIFont class to get each named font, like this:

```
- (UIFont *)fontForDisplayAtIndexPath:(NSIndexPath *)indexPath {
    NSString *fontName = self.fontNames[indexPath.row];
    return [UIFont fontWithName:fontName size:self.cellPointSize];
}
```

Now it's time for a small addition in the form of a viewWillAppear: implementation. Remember how in RootViewController we implemented this method in case the list of favorites might change, requiring a refresh? Well, the same applies here. This view controller might be showing the list of favorites, and the user might switch to another view controller, change a favorite (we'll get there later), and then come back here. We need to reload the table view then, and this method takes care of that:

```
- (void)viewWillAppear:(BOOL)animated {
    [super viewWillAppear:animated];
    if (self.showsFavorites) {
        self.fontNames = [FavoritesList sharedFavoritesList].favorites;
        [self.tableView reloadData];
    }
}
```

The basic idea is that this view controller, in normal operation, is passed a list of font names before it displays, and that the list stays the same the whole time this view controller is around. In one particular case (which you'll see later), this view controller needs to reload its font list.

Moving on, we delete the numberOfSectionsInTableView: method entirely. We'll only have one section here, and just skipping that method is the equivalent of implementing it and returning 1. Next, we implement the two other main data source methods, like this:

```
- (NSInteger)tableView:(UITableView *)tableView
        numberOfRowsInSection:(NSInteger)section {
#warning Incomplete method implementation.
    // Return the number of rows in the section.
    return [self.fontNames count];
    return 0;
}


- (UITableViewCell *)tableView:(UITableView *)tableView
            cellForRowAtIndexPath:(NSIndexPath *)indexPath {
    static NSString *CellIdentifier = @"FontName";
    UITableViewCell *cell = [tableView
                        dequeueReusableCellWithIdentifier:CellIdentifier
                        forIndexPath:indexPath];
```

```
    // Configure the cell...
    cell.textLabel.font = [self fontForDisplayAtIndexPath:indexPath];
    cell.textLabel.text = self.fontNames[indexPath.row];
    cell.detailTextLabel.text = self.fontNames[indexPath.row];

    return cell;
}
```

Neither of these methods really needs any explanation, because they are similar to what we used in RootViewController, but even simpler.

We'll add some more to this class later, but first we want to see it in action. To make this happen, we'll need to configure the storyboard some more, and then make some modifications to RootViewController. Switch over to *Main.storyboard* to get started.

Storyboarding the Font List

The storyboard currently contains a table view controller that displays the list of font families, embedded inside a navigation controller. We need to add one new layer of depth to incorporate the view controller that will display the fonts for a given family. Find a Table View Controller in the Object Library and drag one out into the editing area, to the right of the existing table view controller. Select the new table view controller and use the Identity Inspector to set its class to *FontListViewController*. Select the prototype cell in the table view and open the Attributes Inspector to make some adjustments. Change its **Style** to *Subtitle*, its **Identifier** to *FontName*, and its **Accessory** to *Detail Disclosure*. Using the detail disclosure accessory will let rows of this type respond to two kinds of taps so that users can trigger two different actions, depending on whether they tap the accessory or any other part of the row.

One way to make a user action in one view controller cause the instantiation and display of another view controller is to create a **segue** connecting the two of them. This is probably an unfamiliar word for many people, so let's get this out of the way: segue essentially means "transition," and it is sometimes used by writers and filmmakers to describe making a smooth movement from one paragraph or scene to the next. Apple could have been a little straightforward and just called it a transition; but since that word appears elsewhere in the UIKit APIs, maybe Apple decided to use a distinct term to avoid confusion. We should also mention here that the word "segue" is pronounced exactly the same as the name of the Segway personal transportation product (and now you know why the Segway is called that).

Often, segues are created entirely within Interface Builder. The idea is that an action in one scene can trigger a segue to load and display another scene. If you're using a navigation controller, the segue can push the next controller onto the navigation stack automatically. We'll be using this functionality in our app, starting right now!

In order for the cells in the root view controller to make the Font List View Controller appear, you need to create a couple of segues connecting the two scenes. This is done simply by Control-dragging from the first of the two prototype cells in the Fonts scene over to the new scene; you'll see the entire scene highlight when you drag over it, indicating it's ready to connect, as shown in Figure 9-8.

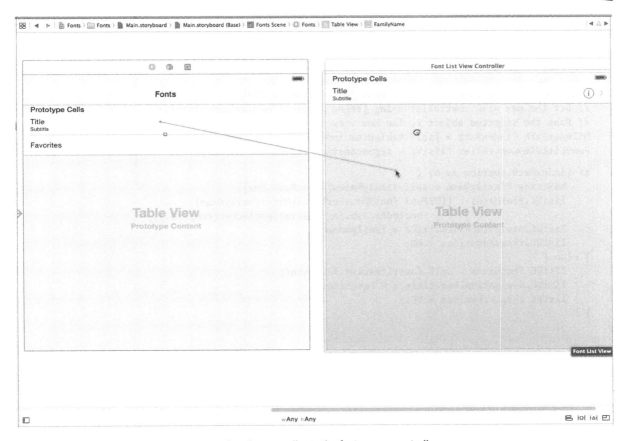

Figure 9-8. Creating a show segue from the font list controller to the font names controller

Release the mouse button and select **show** from the **Selection Segue** section of the pop-up menu that appears. Now do the same for the other prototype cell. Creating these segues means that as soon as the user taps any of these cells, the view controller at the other end of the connection will be allocated and made ready.

Making the Root View Controller Prepare for Segues

Save your changes and switch back to *RootViewController.m*. Note that we're not talking about our latest class, FontListViewController, but instead its "parent" controller. This is the place where you'll need to respond to the user's touches in the root table view by preparing the new FontListViewController (specified by one of the segues you just created) for display and by passing it the values it needs to display. Start by importing the header for the new class:

```
#import "RootViewController.h"
#import "FavoritesList.h"
#import "FontListViewController.h"
```

The actual preparation of the new view controller is done using the `prepareForSegue:sender:` method. Add an implementation of this method as shown here:

```
#pragma mark - Navigation

- (void)prepareForSegue:(UIStoryboardSegue *)segue sender:(id)sender {
    // Get the new view controller using [segue destinationViewController].
    // Pass the selected object to the new view controller.
    NSIndexPath *indexPath = [self.tableView indexPathForCell:sender];
    FontListViewController *listVC = segue.destinationViewController;

    if (indexPath.section == 0) {
        NSString *familyName = self.familyNames[indexPath.row];
        listVC.fontNames = [[UIFont fontNamesForFamilyName:familyName]
                               sortedArrayUsingSelector:@selector(compare:)];
        listVC.navigationItem.title = familyName;
        listVC.showsFavorites = NO;
    } else {
        listVC.fontNames = self.favoritesList.favorites;
        listVC.navigationItem.title = @"Favorites";
        listVC.showsFavorites = YES;
    }
}
```

This method uses the `sender` (the `UITableViewCell` that was tapped) to determine which row was tapped and asks the segue for its `destinationViewController`, which is the `FontListViewController` instance that is about to be displayed. We then pass some values along to the new view controller, depending on whether the user tapped a font family (section 0) or the favorites cell (section 1). As well as setting the custom properties for the target view controller, we also access the controller's `navigationItem` property in order to set a `title`. The `navigationItem` property is an instance of `UINavigationItem`, which is a UIKit class that contains information about what should be displayed in the navigation bar for any given view controller.

Now run the app. You'll see that touching the name of any font family shows you a list of all the individual fonts it contains, as seen in Figure 9-3. Furthermore, you can tap the **Fonts** label in the header of the fonts list navigation controller to go back to its parent controller to select another font.

Creating the Font Sizes View Controller

What you'll notice, however, is that the app currently doesn't let you go any further. Figures 9-4 and 9-5 show additional screens that let you view a chosen font in various ways, and we're not there yet. But soon, we will be! Let's create the view shown in Figure 9-4, which shows multiple font sizes at once. Using the same steps as you used to create `FontListViewController`, add a new view controller that subclasses `UITableViewController`, and name it *FontSizesViewController*.

The only parameter this class will need from its parent controller is a font, which you should add to *FontSizesViewController.h*, like this:

```
#import <UIKit/UIKit.h>

@interface FontSizesViewController : UITableViewController

@property (strong, nonatomic) UIFont *font;

@end
```

Now switch over to *FontSizesViewController.m*. This is going to be a pretty simple table view controller that just implements some standard table view data source methods, plus a few private internal methods. For starters, go ahead and delete the viewDidLoad, didReceiveMemoryWarning, and numberOfSectionsInTableView: methods, along with all of the commented-out methods at the bottom. Again, you're not going to need any of those.

What you will need instead are a couple of internal private methods. One will return a list of the point sizes that the chosen font will be displayed in. The other will return a font corresponding to an index path, similar to those used for each of our other view controllers:

```
- (NSArray *)pointSizes {
    static NSArray *pointSizes = nil;
    static dispatch_once_t onceToken;
    dispatch_once(&onceToken, ^{
        pointSizes = @[@9,
                       @10,
                       @11,
                       @12,
                       @13,
                       @14,
                       @18,
                       @24,
                       @36,
                       @48,
                       @64,
                       @72,
                       @96,
                       @144];
    });
    return pointSizes;
}

- (UIFont *)fontForDisplayAtIndexPath:(NSIndexPath *)indexPath {
    NSNumber *pointSize = self.pointSizes[indexPath.row];
    return [self.font fontWithSize:pointSize.floatValue];
}
```

Note that the pointSizes method uses the same dispatch_once() function we used earlier to ensure that a piece of code is run exactly once. In this case, it initializes a list of numbers that will be used to specify fonts for each row in the table.

For this view controller, we're going to skip the method that lets us specify the number of sections to display, since we're going to just use the default number (1). However, we must implement the methods for specifying the number of rows and the content of each cell. Here are those two methods:

```
- (NSInteger)tableView:(UITableView *)tableView
             numberOfRowsInSection:(NSInteger)section {
#warning Incomplete method implementation.
    // Return the number of rows in the section.
    return [self.pointSizes count];
    return 0;
}

- (UITableViewCell *)tableView:(UITableView *)tableView
        cellForRowAtIndexPath:(NSIndexPath *)indexPath {
    static NSString *CellIdentifier = @"FontNameAndSize";
    UITableViewCell *cell = [tableView
                      dequeueReusableCellWithIdentifier:CellIdentifier
                      forIndexPath:indexPath];

    // Configure the cell...
    cell.textLabel.font = [self fontForDisplayAtIndexPath:indexPath];
    cell.textLabel.text = self.font.fontName;
    cell.detailTextLabel.text = [NSString stringWithFormat:@"%@ point",
                            self.pointSizes[indexPath.row]];

    return cell;
}
```

There's really nothing in any of these methods we haven't seen before, so let's move on to setting up the GUI for this.

Storyboarding the Font Sizes View Controller

Go back to *Main.storyboard* and drag another Table View Controller into the editing area. Use the Identity Inspector to set its class to *FontSizesViewController*. You'll need to make a segue connection from its parent, the FontListViewController. So find that controller and Control-drag from its prototype cell to the newest view controller, and then select **show** from the **Selection Segue** section of the pop-up menu that appears. Next, select the prototype cell in the new scene you just added, and then use the Attributes Inspector to set its **Style** to *Subtitle* and its **Identifier** to *FontNameAndSize*.

Making the Font List View Controller Prepare for Segues

Now, just like the last time we extended our storyboard's navigation hierarchy, we need to jump up to the parent controller so that it can configure its child. That means we need to go to *FontListViewController.m* and import the header for the new child controller:

```
#import "FontListViewController.h"
#import "FavoritesList.h"
#import "FontSizesViewController.h"
```

Next, down at the bottom of the @implementation section, implement the prepareForSegue:sender: method like this:

```
#pragma mark - Navigation

- (void)prepareForSegue:(UIStoryboardSegue *)segue sender:(id)sender {
    // Get the new view controller using [segue destinationViewController].
    // Pass the selected object to the new view controller.
    NSIndexPath *indexPath = [self.tableView indexPathForCell:sender];
    UIFont *font = [self fontForDisplayAtIndexPath:indexPath];
    [segue.destinationViewController navigationItem].title = font.fontName;

    FontSizesViewController *sizesVC = segue.destinationViewController;
    sizesVC.font = font;
}
```

That probably all looks pretty familiar by now, so we won't dwell on it further.

Run the app, select a font family, select a font (by tapping a row anywhere except the accessory on the right), and you'll now see the multisize listing shown in Figure 9-4.

Creating the Font Info View Controller

The final view controller we're going to create is the one shown in Figure 9-5. This one isn't based on a table view. Instead, it features a large text label, a slider for setting text size, and a switch for toggling whether this font should be included in the list of favorites. Create a new Cocoa Touch class in your project using UIViewController as the superclass, and then name it *FontInfoViewController*. Like most of the other controllers in this app, this one needs to have a couple of parameters passed in by its parent controller. Enable this by defining these properties in *FontInfoViewController.h*:

```
#import <UIKit/UIKit.h>

@interface FontInfoViewController : UIViewController

@property (strong, nonatomic) UIFont *font;
@property (assign, nonatomic) BOOL favorite;

@end
```

Now switch over to *FontInfoViewController.m* and add a single import and a handful of IBOutlet properties at the top:

```
#import "FontInfoViewController.h"
#import "FavoritesList.h"

@interface FontInfoViewController ()

@property (weak, nonatomic) IBOutlet UILabel *fontSampleLabel;
@property (weak, nonatomic) IBOutlet UISlider *fontSizeSlider;
@property (weak, nonatomic) IBOutlet UILabel *fontSizeLabel;
@property (weak, nonatomic) IBOutlet UISwitch *favoriteSwitch;

@end
```

Next, implement `viewDidLoad` and a pair of action methods that will be triggered by the slider and switch, respectively:

```
- (void)viewDidLoad
{
    [super viewDidLoad];
    // Do any additional setup after loading the view.

    self.fontSampleLabel.font = self.font;
    self.fontSampleLabel.text = @"AaBbCcDdEeFfGgHhIiJjKkLlMmNnOoPpQqRrSsTtUuVv"
                                 "WwXxYyZz 0123456789";
    self.fontSizeSlider.value = self.font.pointSize;
    self.fontSizeLabel.text = [NSString stringWithFormat:@"%.0f",
                                self.font.pointSize];
    self.favoriteSwitch.on = self.favorite;
}

- (IBAction)slideFontSize:(UISlider *)slider {
    float newSize = roundf(slider.value);
    self.fontSampleLabel.font = [self.font fontWithSize:newSize];
    self.fontSizeLabel.text = [NSString stringWithFormat:@"%.0f", newSize];
}

- (IBAction)toggleFavorite:(UISwitch *)sender {
    FavoritesList *favoritesList = [FavoritesList sharedFavoritesList];
    if (sender.on) {
        [favoritesList addFavorite:self.font.fontName];
    } else {
        [favoritesList removeFavorite:self.font.fontName];
    }
}
```

These methods are all pretty straightforward. The `viewDidLoad` method sets up the display based on the chosen font; `slideFontSize:` changes the size of the font in the `fontSampleLabel` label based on the value of the slider; and `toggleFavorite:` either adds the current font to the favorites list or removes it from the favorites list, depending on the value of the switch.

Storyboarding the Font Info View Controller

Now head back over to *Main.storyboard* to build the GUI for this app's final view controller. Use the Object Library to find a plain View Controller. Drag it into the editing area and use the Identity Inspector to set its class to *FontInfoViewController*. Next, use the Object Library to find some more objects and drag them into your new scene. You need three labels, a switch, and a slider. Lay them out roughly, as shown in Figure 9-9.

Figure 9-9. Each of the labels here has been given a light-gray background color, just for purposes of this illustration. Yours should have white backgrounds

Notice that we left some space above the upper label, since we're going to end up having a navigation bar up there. Also, we want the upper label to be able to display long pieces of text across multiple lines, but by default the label is set to show only one line. To change that, select the label, open the Attributes Inspector, and set the number in the **Lines** field to *0*.

Figure 9-8 also shows changed text in the lower two labels. Go ahead and make the same changes yourself. What you can't see here is that the Attributes Inspector was used to right-align both of them. You should do the same, since they both have layouts that essentially tie them to their right edges. Also, select the slider at the bottom, and then use the Attributes Inspector to set its **Minimum** to *1* and its **Maximum** to *200*.

Now it's time to wire up all the connections for this GUI. Start by selecting the view controller and opening the Connections Inspector. When we have so many connections to make, the overview shown by that inspector is pretty nice. Make connections for each of the outlets by dragging from the small circles next to *favoriteSwitch*, *fontSampleLabel*, *fontSizeLabel*, and *fontSizeSlider* to the appropriate objects in the scene. In case it's not obvious, *fontSampleLabel* should be connected to the label at the top, *fontSizeLabel* to the label at the bottom right, and the *favoriteSwitch* and *fontSizeSlider* outlets to the only places they can go. To connect the actions to the controls, you can continue to use the Connections Inspector. In the **Received Actions** section of the Connections Inspector for the view controller, drag from the little circle next to **slideFontSize:** over to the slider, release the mouse button, and select **Value Changed** from the context menu that appears. Next, drag from the little circle next to **toggleFavorite:** over to the switch and again select **Value Changed**.

One more thing we need to do here is create a segue so that this view can be shown. Remember that this view is going to be displayed whenever a user taps the detail accessory (the little blue "i" in a circle) when the Font List View Controller is displayed. So, find that controller, Control-drag from its prototype cell to the new font info view controller you've been working on, and select **show** from the **Accessory Action** section of the context menu that appears. Note that we just said **Accessory Action**, not **Selection Segue**. The accessory action is the segue that is triggered when the user taps the detail accessory, whereas the selection segue is the segue that is triggered by a tap anywhere else in the row. We already set this cell's selection segue to open a FontSizesViewController.

Now we have two different segues that can be triggered by touches in different parts of a row. Since these will present different view controllers, with different properties, we need to have a way to differentiate them. Fortunately, the UIStoryboardSegue class, which represents a segue, has a way to accomplish this: we can use an identifier, just as we do with table view cells!

All you have to do is select a segue in the editing area and use the Attributes Inspector to set its Identifier. You may need to shift your scenes around a bit, so that you can see both of the segues that are snaking their way out of the right-hand side of the Font List View Controller. Select the one that's pointing at the Font Sizes View Controller and set its **Identifier** to *ShowFontSizes*, as shown in Figure 9-10. Next, select the one that's pointing at the Font Info View Controller and set its **Identifier** to *ShowFontInfo*.

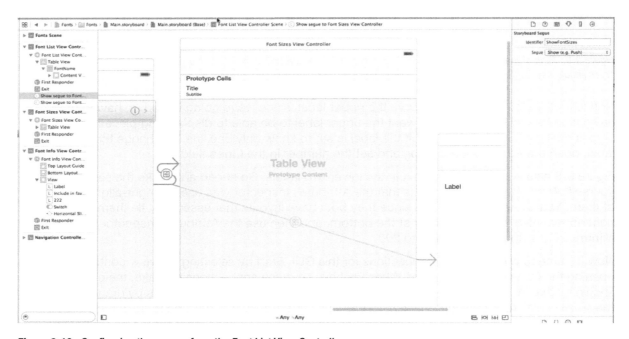

Figure 9-10. Configuring the segues from the Font List View Controller

Setting Up Constraints

Setting up that segue lets Interface Builder know that our new scene will be used within the context of the navigation controller like everything else, so that scene automatically receives a blank navigation bar at the top. Now that the real confines of our view are in place, it's a good time to set up the constraints. This is a fairly complex view with several subviews, especially near the bottom, so we can't quite rely on the system's automatic constraints to do the right thing for us. We'll use the **Pin** button at the bottom of the editing area and the pop-up window it triggers to build most of the constraints we'll need.

Start with the uppermost label. Click **Pin**, and then in the pop-up window, select the little red bars above, to the left, and to the right of the little square—but not the one below it. Now click the **Add 3 Constraints** button at the bottom.

Next, select the slider at the bottom and click the **Pin** button. This time, select the red bars below, to the left, and to the right of the little square—but not the one above it. Again, click **Add 3 Constraints** to put them in place.

For each of the two remaining labels and for the switch, follow this procedure: select the object, click **Pin**, select the red bars below and to the right of the little square, turn on the check boxes for **Width** and **Height**, and finally, click **Add 4 Constraints**. Setting those constraints for all three of those objects will bind them to the lower-right corner.

There's just one more constraint to make. We want the top label to grow to contain its text, but to never grow so large that it overlaps the views at the bottom. We can accomplish this with a single constraint! Control-drag from the upper label to the **Include in favorites** label, release the mouse button, and select **Vertical Spacing** from the context menu that appears. Next, click the new constraint to select it (it's a blue vertical bar connecting the two labels) and open the Attributes Inspector, where you'll see some configurable attributes for the constraint. Change the **Relation** pop-up to *Greater Than or Equal*, and then set the **Constant** value to *10*. That ensures that the expanding upper label won't push past the other views at the bottom.

Adapting the Font List View Controller for Multiple Segues

Now head back over to good old *FontListViewController.m*. Since this class will now be able to trigger segues to two different child view controllers, it now needs to import the header for the latest view controller:

```
#import "FontListViewController.h"
#import "FavoritesList.h"
#import "FontSizesViewController.h"
#import "FontInfoViewController.h"
```

You also need to adapt the prepareForSegue:sender: method, as shown here:

```
- (void)prepareForSegue:(UIStoryboardSegue *)segue sender:(id)sender {
    // Get the new view controller using [segue destinationViewController].
    // Pass the selected object to the new view controller.
    NSIndexPath *indexPath = [self.tableView indexPathForCell:sender];
    UIFont *font = [self fontForDisplayAtIndexPath:indexPath];
    [segue.destinationViewController navigationItem].title = font.fontName;

    if ([segue.identifier isEqualToString:@"ShowFontSizes"]) {
        FontSizesViewController *sizesVC = segue.destinationViewController;
        sizesVC.font = font;
    } else if ([segue.identifier isEqualToString:@"ShowFontInfo"]) {
        FontInfoViewController *infoVC = segue.destinationViewController;
        infoVC.font = font;
        infoVC.favorite = [[FavoritesList sharedFavoritesList].favorites
                            containsObject:font.fontName];
    }
}
```

Now run the app and let's see where we are! Select a font family that contains many fonts (for example, Gill Sans), and then tap the middle of the row for any font. You'll be taken to the same list you saw earlier, which shows the font in multiple sizes. Press the navigation button at the upper left (It's labeled **Gill Sans**) to go back, and then tap another row; however, this time tap on the right-hand side where the detail accessory is shown. This should bring up the final view controller, which shows a sample of the font with a slider at the bottom that lets you pick whatever size you want.

Also, you can now use the **Include in favorites** switch to mark this font as a favorite. Do that, and then hit the navigation button at the top-left corner a couple of times to get back to the root controller view.

My Favorite Fonts

Scroll down to the bottom of the root view controller, and you'll see something new: the second section is now there, as you can see in Figure 9-11.

Figure 9-11. Now that we've picked at least one favorite font, we can see a list of them by tapping the new row that appears at the bottom of the root view controller

Tap the **Favorites** row, and you'll see a listing of any fonts you've chosen as favorites. From there, you can do the same things you could do with the other font listing: you can tap a row to see a list of multiple font sizes, or you can tap a detail accessory to see the slider-adjustable font view and the favorites switch. You can even try turning off that switch and hitting the back button, and you'll see that the font you were just looking at is no longer listed.

Table View Niceties

Now the basic functionality of our app is complete. But before we can really call it a day, there are a couple more features we should implement. If you've been using iOS for a while, you're probably aware that you can often delete a row from a table view by swiping from right to left. For example, in Mail you can use this technique to delete a message in a list of messages. Performing this gesture brings up a small GUI, right inside the table view row. This GUI asks you to confirm the deletion, and then the row disappears and the remaining rows slide up to fill the gap. That whole interaction—including handling the swipe, showing the confirmation GUI, and animating any affected rows—is taken care of by the table view itself. All you need to do is implement two methods in your controller to make it happen.

Also, the table view provides easy functionality for letting the user reorder rows within a table view by dragging them up and down. As with swipe-to-delete, the table view takes care of the entire user interaction for us. All we have to do is one line of setup (to create a button that activates the reordering GUI), and then implement a single method that is called when the user has finished dragging. The table view gives us so much for free, it would be criminal not to use it!

Implementing Swipe-to-Delete

In this app, the FontListViewController class is a typical example of where this feature should be used. Whenever the app is showing the list of favorites, we should let the user delete a favorite with a swipe, saving them the step of tapping the detail accessory and then turning off the switch. Select *FontListViewController.m* in Xcode to get started. Both of the methods we need to implement are already included in each view controller source file by default, but they are commented out. We're going to uncomment each of them and provide them with real implementations.

Start by adding an implementation of the tableView:canEditRowAtIndexPath: method:

```
- (BOOL)tableView:(UITableView *)tableView
       canEditRowAtIndexPath:(NSIndexPath *)indexPath {
    // Return NO if you do not want the specified item to be editable.
    return self.showsFavorites;
}
```

That method will return YES if it's showing the list of favorites, and NO otherwise. This means that the editing functionality that lets you delete rows is only enabled while displaying favorites. If you were to try to run the app and delete rows with just this change, you wouldn't see any difference. The table view won't bother to deal with the swipe gesture because it sees that we haven't implemented the other method that is required to complete a deletion. So, let's put that in place, too. Add an implementation for the `tableView:commitEditingStyle:forRowAtIndexPath:` method as follows:

```
- (void)tableView:(UITableView *)tableView
      commitEditingStyle:(UITableViewCellEditingStyle)editingStyle
      forRowAtIndexPath:(NSIndexPath *)indexPath {
    if (!self.showsFavorites) return;

    if (editingStyle == UITableViewCellEditingStyleDelete) {
        // Delete the row from the data source
        NSString *favorite = self.fontNames[indexPath.row];
        [[FavoritesList sharedFavoritesList] removeFavorite:favorite];
        self.fontNames = [FavoritesList sharedFavoritesList].favorites;

        [tableView deleteRowsAtIndexPaths:@[indexPath]
                        withRowAnimation:UITableViewRowAnimationFade];
    }
}
```

This method is pretty straightforward, but there are some subtle things going on. The first thing we do is check to make sure we're showing the favorites list; and if not, we just bail. Normally, this should never happen, since we specified with the previous method that only the favorites list should be editable. Nevertheless, we're doing a bit of defensive programming here. After that, we check the editing style to make sure that the particular edit operation we're going to conclude really was a deletion. It's possible to do insertion edits in a table view, but not without additional setup that we're not doing here, so we don't need to worry about other cases. Next, we determine which font should be deleted, remove it from the `FavoritesList` singleton, and update our local copy of the favorites list.

Finally, we tell the table view to delete the row and make it disappear with a visual fade animation. It's important to understand what happens when you tell the table view to delete a row. Intuitively, you might think that calling that method would delete some data, but that's not what happened. In fact, we've already deleted the data! That final method call is really our way of telling the table view, "Hey, I've made a change, and I want you to animate away this row. Ask me if you need anything more." When that happens, the table view will start animating any rows that are below the deleted row by moving them up, which means that it's possible that one or more rows that were previously off-screen will now come on-screen, at which time it will indeed ask the controller for cell data via the usual methods. For that reason, it's important that our implementation of the `tableView:commitE ditingStyle:forRowAtIndexPath:` method makes necessary changes to the data model (in this case, the `FavoritesList` singleton) before telling the table view to delete a row.

Now run the app again, make sure you have some favorite fonts set up, and then go into the Favorites list and delete a row by swiping from right to left. The row slides partly off-screen, and a **Delete** button appears on the right (see Figure 9-12). Tap the **Delete** button, and the row goes away.

Figure 9-12. *A favorite font row with the Delete button showing*

Implementing Drag-to-Reorder

The final feature we're going to add to the font list will let users rearrange their favorites just by dragging them up and down. In order to accomplish this, we're going to add one method to the FavoritesList class, which will let us reorder its items however we want. Open *FavoritesList.h* and add the following declaration to the @interface section:

```
- (void)moveItemAtIndex:(NSInteger)from toIndex:(NSInteger)to;
```

Next, switch over to *FavoritesList.m* and add this method to the @implementation section:

```
- (void)moveItemAtIndex:(NSInteger)from toIndex:(NSInteger)to {
    id item = _favorites[from];
    [_favorites removeObjectAtIndex:from];
    [_favorites insertObject:item atIndex:to];
    [self saveFavorites];
}
```

This new method provides the underpinnings for what we're going to do. Now select *FontListViewController.m* and add the following lines at the end of the `viewDidLoad` method:

```
if (self.showsFavorites) {
    self.navigationItem.rightBarButtonItem = self.editButtonItem;
}
```

We've mentioned the navigation item previously. It's an object that holds the information about what should appear in the navigation bar for a view controller. It has a property called `rightBarButtonItem` that can hold an instance of `UIBarButtonItem`, a special sort of button meant only for navigation bars and tool bars. Here, we're pointing that at `editButtonItem`, a property of `UIViewController` that gives us a special button item that's preconfigured to activate the table view's editing/reordering GUI.

With that in place, try running the app again and go into the Favorites list. You'll see that there's now an **Edit** button in the upper-right corner. Pressing that button toggles the table view's editing GUI, which right now means that each row acquires a delete button on the left, while its content slides a bit to the right to make room. This enables yet another way that users can delete rows, using the same methods we already implemented.

But our main interest here is in adding reordering functionality. For that, all we need to do is the following method in *FontListViewController.m*:

```
- (void)tableView:(UITableView *)tableView
             moveRowAtIndexPath:(NSIndexPath *)fromIndexPath
             toIndexPath:(NSIndexPath *)toIndexPath {
    [[FavoritesList sharedFavoritesList] moveItemAtIndex:fromIndexPath.row
                                                 toIndex:toIndexPath.row];
    self.fontNames = [FavoritesList sharedFavoritesList].favorites;
}
```

This method is called as soon as the user finishes dragging a row. All we do here is tell the `FavoritesList` singleton to do the reordering, and then refresh our list of font names, just as we did after deleting an item. To see this in action, run the app, go into the Favorites list, and tap the **Edit** button. You'll see that the edit mode now includes little "dragger" icons on the right side of each row (see Figure 9-13), and you can use the draggers to rearrange items.

Figure 9-13. The favorite font list with reordering controls enabled

With that, our app is complete! At least, it's complete as far as this book is concerned. If you can think of more useful things to do with these fonts, have at it!

Breaking the Tape

This chapter was a marathon. And if you're still standing, you should feel pretty darn good about yourself. Dwelling on these mystical table view and navigation controller objects is important because they are the backbone of a great many iOS applications, and their complexity can definitely get you into trouble if you don't truly understand them.

As you start building your own tables, refer back to this chapter and the previous one, and don't be afraid of Apple's documentation, either. Table views are extraordinarily complex, and it would be impossible to cover every conceivable permutation; however, you should now have a very good set of table view building blocks that you can use as you design and build your own applications. As always, feel free to reuse this code in your own applications. It's a gift from the authors to you. Enjoy!

Chapter 10

Collection View

In this chapter, we're going to look at a fairly recent addition to UIKit: the UICollectionView class. You'll see how it relates to the familiar UITableView, how it differs, and how it can be extended to do things that UITableView can't even dream about.

For years, iOS developers have used the UITableView component to create a huge variety of interfaces. With its ability to let you define multiple cell types, create them on the fly as needed, and handily scroll them vertically, UITableView has become a key component of thousands of apps. And Apple has truly given its table view class lots of API love over the years, adding new and better ways to supply it with content in each major new iOS release.

However, it's still not the ultimate solution for all large sets of data. If you want to present data in multiple columns, for example, you need to combine all the columns for each row of data into a single cell. There's also no way to make a UITableView scroll its content horizontally. In general, much of the power of UITableView has come with a particular trade-off: developers have no control of the overall layout of a table view. You can define the look of each individual cell all you want; but at the end of the day, the cells are just going to be stacked on top of each other in one big scrolling list!

Well, apparently Apple realized this, too. In iOS 6, it introduced a new class called UICollectionView that addresses these shortcomings. Like a table view, this class lets you display a bunch of "cells" of data and handles things like queuing up unused cells for later use. But unlike a table view, UICollectionView doesn't lay these cells out in a vertical stack for you. In fact, UICollectionView doesn't lay them out at all! Instead, it uses a helper class to do layout, as you'll see soon.

Creating the DialogViewer Project

To show some of the capabilities of UICollectionView, we're going to use it to lay out some paragraphs of text. Each word will be placed in a cell of its own, and all the cells for each paragraph will be clustered together in a section. Each section will also have its own header. This may not seem too exciting, considering that UIKit already contains other perfectly good ways of laying out text. However, this process will be instructive anyway, since you'll get a feel for just how flexible this thing is. You certainly wouldn't get very far doing something like Figure 10-1 with a table view!

Figure 10-1. *Each word is a separate cell, with the exception of the headers, which are, well, headers. All of this is laid out using a single UICollectionView, and no explicit geometry calculations of our own*

In order to make this work, we'll define a couple of custom cell classes, we'll use UICollectionViewFlowLayout (the one and only layout helper class included in UIKit at this time), and, as usual, we'll use our view controller class to glue it all together. Let's get started!

Use Xcode to create a new Single View Application, as you've done many times by now. Name your project *DialogViewer* and use the standard settings we've used throughout the book (set **Language** to *Objective-C* and choose *Universal* for **Devices**).

Fixing the View Controller's Class

There's nothing in particular we need to do with the app delegate in this app, so let's jump straight into *ViewController.h* and make just one simple change, switching the super class to UICollectionView:

```
@interface ViewController : UIViewController
@interface ViewController : UICollectionViewController
```

Next, open *Main.storyboard*. We need to set up the view controller to match what we just specified in the header. Select the one and only **View Controller** in the Document Outline and delete it, leaving an empty storyboard. Now use the Object Library to locate a *Collection View Controller* and drag it into the editing area. Select the icon for the **View Controller** you just dragged out and use the Identity Inspector to change its class to ViewController. In the Attributes Inspector, ensure that the **Is Initial View Controller** check box is checked. Next, select the **Collection View** in the Document Outline and use the Attributes Inspector to change its background to white. Finally, you'll see that the **Collection View** object in the Document Outline has a child called **Collection View Cell**. This a prototype cell that you can use to design the layout for your actual cells in Interface Builder. We're not going to do that in this chapter, so select that cell and delete it.

Defining Custom Cells

Now let's define some cell classes. As you saw in Figure 10-1, we're displaying two basic kinds of cells: a "normal" one containing a word and another that is used as a sort of header. Any cell you're going to create for use in a UICollectionView needs to be a subclass of the system-supplied UICollectionViewCell, which provides basic functionality similar to UITableViewCell. This functionality includes a backgroundView, a contentView, and so on. Because our two cells will have some shared functionality, we'll actually make one a subclass of the other and use the subclass to override some functionality.

Start by creating a new Cocoa Touch class in Xcode. Name the new class *ContentCell* and make it a subclass of UICollectionViewCell. Select the new class's header file and add declarations for three properties and one class method:

```
#import <UIKit/UIKit.h>

@interface ContentCell : UICollectionViewCell

@property (strong, nonatomic) UILabel *label;
@property (copy, nonatomic) NSString *text;
@property (assign, nonatomic) CGFloat maxWidth;

+ (CGSize)sizeForContentString:(NSString *)s forMaxWidth:(CGFloat)maxWidth;

@end
```

The `label` property will point at a `UILabel` used for display. We'll use the `text` property to tell this cell what to display, the `maxWidth` property to control the cell's maximum width, and we'll use the `sizeFo rContentString:forMaxWidth:` method to ask how big the cell needs to be to display a given string. This will come in handy when creating and configuring instances of our cell classes.

Now switch over to *ContentCell.m*, where several pieces of work await us. Let's start by adding an `initWithFrame:` method, as shown here:

```
- (id)initWithFrame:(CGRect)frame {
    self = [super initWithFrame:frame];
    if (self) {
        // Initialization code
        self.label = [[UILabel alloc] initWithFrame:self.contentView.bounds];
        self.label.opaque = NO;
        self.label.backgroundColor = [UIColor colorWithRed:0.8
                                                     green:0.9
                                                      blue:1.0
                                                     alpha:1.0];
        self.label.textColor = [UIColor blackColor];

        self.label.textAlignment = NSTextAlignmentCenter;
        self.label.font = [[self class] defaultFont];
        [self.contentView addSubview:self.label];
    }
    return self;
}
```

That code is pretty simple. It just creates a label, sets its display properties, and adds the label to the cell's `contentView`. The only mysterious thing here is that it uses the `defaultFont` method to get a font, which is used to set the label's font. The idea is that this class should define which font will be used for displaying content, while also allowing any subclasses to declare their own display font by overriding the `defaultFont` method. But we haven't created this method yet, so let's do so:

```
+ (UIFont *)defaultFont {
    return [UIFont preferredFontForTextStyle:UIFontTextStyleBody];
}
```

Pretty straightforward. This uses the `preferredFontForTextStyle:` method of the `UIFont` class to get the user's preferred font for body text. The user can use the Settings app to change the size of this font. By using this method instead of hard-coding a font size, we make our apps a bit more user-friendly.

To finish off this class, let's add the method we mentioned in the header, the one that computes an appropriate size for the cell:

```
+ (CGSize)sizeForContentString:(NSString *)string forMaxWidth:(CGFloat)maxWidth {

    CGSize maxSize = CGSizeMake(maxWidth, 1000);

    NSStringDrawingOptions opts = NSStringDrawingUsesLineFragmentOrigin |
    NSStringDrawingUsesFontLeading;
```

```
NSMutableParagraphStyle *style = [[NSMutableParagraphStyle alloc] init];
[style setLineBreakMode:NSLineBreakByCharWrapping];

NSDictionary *attributes = @{ NSFontAttributeName : [self defaultFont],
                              NSParagraphStyleAttributeName : style };

CGRect rect = [string boundingRectWithSize:maxSize
                                   options:opts
                                attributes:attributes
                                   context:nil];


    return rect.size;
}
```

That method does a lot of things, so it's worth walking through it. First, we declare a maximum size so that no word will be allowed to be wider than the value of the maxWidth argument, which will be set from the width of the UICollectionView. Next, we define some options that will help the system calculate the right dimensions for the string we're dealing with. We also create a paragraph style that allows for character wrapping, so in case our string is too big to fit in our given maximum width, it will wrap around to a subsequent line. We also create an attributes dictionary that contains the default font we defined for this class and the paragraph style we just created. Finally, we use some NSString functionality provided in UIKit that lets us calculate sizes for a string. We pass in an absolute maximum size and the other options and attributes we set up, and we get back a size.

All that's left for this class is some special handling of the text property. Instead of letting this use an implicit instance variable as we normally do, we're going to define methods that get and set the value based on the UILabel we created earlier, basically using the UILabel as storage for the displayed value. By doing so, we can also use the setter to recalculate the cell's geometry when the text changes. Here's what this looks like:

```
- (NSString *)text {
    return self.label.text;
}

- (void)setText:(NSString *)text {
    self.label.text = text;
    CGRect newLabelFrame = self.label.frame;
    CGRect newContentFrame = self.contentView.frame;
    CGSize textSize = [[self class] sizeForContentString:text forMaxWidth:_maxWidth];
    newLabelFrame.size = textSize;
    newContentFrame.size = textSize;
    self.label.frame = newLabelFrame;
    self.contentView.frame = newContentFrame;
}
```

The getter is nothing special; but the setter is doing some extra work. Basically, it's modifying the frame for both the label and the content view, based on the size needed for displaying the current string.

That's all we need for our base cell class. Now let's make a cell class to use for a header. Use Xcode to make another new Cocoa Touch class, naming this one *HeaderCell* and making it a subclass of ContentCell. We don't need to touch the header file at all, so jump straight to *HeaderCell.m* to make some changes. All we're going to do in this class is override a couple of methods from the ContentCell class to change the cell's appearance, making it look different from the normal content cell:

```
- (id)initWithFrame:(CGRect)frame {
    self = [super initWithFrame:frame];
    if (self) {
        // Initialization code
        self.label.backgroundColor = [UIColor colorWithRed:0.9
                                                      green:0.9
                                                       blue:0.8
                                                      alpha:1.0];
        self.label.textColor = [UIColor blackColor];

    }
    return self;
}

+ (UIFont *)defaultFont {
    return [UIFont preferredFontForTextStyle:UIFontTextStyleHeadline];
}
```

That's all we need to do to give the header cell a distinct look, with its own colors and font.

Configuring the View Controller

Now let's focus our attention on our view controller. Select *ViewController.m* and start by importing the headers for our custom cells and declaring an array to contain the content we want to display:

```
#import "ViewController.h"
#import "ContentCell.h"
#import "HeaderCell.h"

@interface ViewController ()
@property (copy, nonatomic) NSArray *sections;
@end
```

Next, we'll use `viewDidLoad` to create that data. The `sections` array will contain a list of dictionaries, each of which will have two keys: *header* and *content*. We'll use the values associated with those keys to define our display content. The actual content we're using is adapted from a well-known play:

```
- (void)viewDidLoad
{
    [super viewDidLoad];
    // Do any additional setup after loading the view, typically from a nib.
    self.sections =
    @[
      @{ @"header" : @"First Witch",
         @"content" : @"Hey, when will the three of us meet up later?" },
      @{ @"header" : @"Second Witch",
         @"content" : @"When everything's straightened out." },
      @{ @"header" : @"Third Witch",
         @"content" : @"That'll be just before sunset." },
      @{ @"header" : @"First Witch",
         @"content" : @"Where?" },
      @{ @"header" : @"Second Witch",
         @"content" : @"The dirt patch." },
      @{ @"header" : @"Third Witch",
         @"content" : @"I guess we'll see Mac there." },
    ];

}
```

Much like `UITableView`, `UICollectionView` lets us register the class of a reusable cell based on an identifier. Doing this lets us call a dequeuing method later on, when we're going to provide a cell. If no cell is available, the collection view will create one for us—just like `UITableView`! Add this line to the end of `viewDidLoad` to make this happen:

```
[self.collectionView registerClass:[ContentCell class]
        forCellWithReuseIdentifier:@"CONTENT"];
```

We'll make just one more change to `viewDidLoad`. Since this application has no navigation bar, the main view will interfere with the status bar. To prevent that, add the following lines to the end of `viewDidLoad`:

```
UIEdgeInsets contentInset = self.collectionView.contentInset;
contentInset.top = 20;
[self.collectionView setContentInset:contentInset];
```

That's enough configuration in viewDidLoad, at least for now. Before we get to the code that will populate the collection view, we need to write one little helper method. All of our content is contained in lengthy strings, but we're going to need to deal with them one word at a time to be able to put each word into a cell. So let's create an internal method of our own to split those strings apart. This method takes a section number, pulls the relevant content string from our section data, and splits it into words:

```
- (NSArray *)wordsInSection:(NSInteger)section {
    NSString *content = self.sections[section][@"content"];
    NSCharacterSet *space = [NSCharacterSet whitespaceAndNewlineCharacterSet];
    NSArray *words = [content componentsSeparatedByCharactersInSet:space];
    return words;
}
```

Providing Content Cells

Now it's time for the group of methods that will actually populate the collection view. These next three methods are remarkably similar to their UITableView correspondents. First, we need a method to let the collection view know how many sections to display:

```
- (NSInteger)numberOfSectionsInCollectionView:(UICollectionView *)collectionView {
    return [self.sections count];
}
```

Next, we have a method to tell the collection how many items each section should contain. This uses the wordsInSection: method we defined earlier:

```
- (NSInteger)collectionView:(UICollectionView *)collectionView
    numberOfItemsInSection:(NSInteger)section {
    NSArray *words = [self wordsInSection:section];
    return [words count];
}
```

And here's the method that actually returns a single cell, configured to contain a single word. This method uses our wordsInSection: method. As you can see, it uses a dequeuing method on UICollectionView, similar to UITableView. Since we've registered a cell class for the identifier we're using here, we know that the dequeuing method always returns an instance:

```
- (UICollectionViewCell *)collectionView:(UICollectionView *)collectionView
                cellForItemAtIndexPath:(NSIndexPath *)indexPath {
    NSArray *words = [self wordsInSection:indexPath.section];

    ContentCell *cell = [self.collectionView
                        dequeueReusableCellWithReuseIdentifier:@"CONTENT"
                        forIndexPath:indexPath];
    cell.maxWidth = collectionView.bounds.size.width;
    cell.text = words[indexPath.row];
    return cell;
}
```

Judging by the way that UITableView works, you might think that at this point we'd have something that works, in at least a minimal way. Build and run your app, and you'll see that we're not really at a useful point yet (see Figure 10-2).

Figure 10-2. This isn't very useful

We can see some of the words, but there's no "flow" going on here. Each cell is the same size, and everything is all jammed together. The reason for this is that we have more delegate responsibilities we have to take care of to make things work.

Making the Layout Flow

Until now, we've been dealing with the UICollectionView, but as we mentioned earlier, this class has a sidekick that takes care of the actual layout. UICollectionViewFlowLayout, which is the default layout helper for UICollectionView, has some delegate methods of its own that it will use to try to pull more information out of us. We're going to implement one of these right now. The layout object calls this method for each cell to find out how large it should be. Here we're once again using our wordsInSection: method to get access to the word in question, and then using a method we defined in the ContentCell class to see how large it needs to be. Add this method to *ViewController.m*. This works because the UICollectionViewController class makes itself the default delegate of its UICollectionViewFlowLayout:

```
- (CGSize)collectionView:(UICollectionView *)collectionView
                layout:(UICollectionViewLayout*)collectionViewLayout
  sizeForItemAtIndexPath:(NSIndexPath *)indexPath {
    NSArray *words = [self wordsInSection:indexPath.section];
    CGSize size = [ContentCell sizeForContentString:words[indexPath.row]
                                      forMaxWidth:collectionView.bounds.size.width];

    return size;
}
```

Now build and run the app again, and you'll see that we've taken a pretty large step forward (see Figure 10-3).

Figure 10-3. Paragraph flow is starting to take shape

You can see that the cells are now flowing and wrapping around so that the text is readable, and that the beginning of each section drops down a bit. But each section is jammed really tightly against the ones before and after it. They're also pressing all the way out to the sides, which doesn't look too nice. Let's fix that by adding a bit more configuration. Add these lines to the end of the viewDidLoad method:

```
UICollectionViewLayout *layout = self.collectionView.collectionViewLayout;
UICollectionViewFlowLayout *flow = (UICollectionViewFlowLayout *)layout;
flow.sectionInset = UIEdgeInsetsMake(10, 20, 30, 20);
```

Here we're grabbing the layout object from our collection view. We assign this first to a temporary UICollectionViewLayout pointer, primarily to highlight a point: UICollectionView only knows about this generic layout class, but it's really using an instance of UICollectionFlowLayout, which is a subclass of UICollectionViewLayout. Knowing the true type of the layout object, we can use a typecast to assign it to another variable, enabling us to access methods that only that subclass has—in this case, we need the setter method for the sectionInset property.

Build and run again, and you'll see that our text cells have gained some much-needed breathing room (see Figure 10-4).

Figure 10-4. Now much less cramped

Providing Header Views

The only thing missing now is the display of our header objects, so it's time to fix that. You will recall that UITableView has a system of header and footer views, and it asks for those specifically for each section. UICollectionView has made this concept a bit more generic, allowing for more flexibility in the layout. The way this works is that, along with the system of accessing normal cells from the delegate, there is a parallel system for accessing additional views that can be used as headers, footers, or anything else. Add this bit of code to the end of viewDidLoad to let the collection view know about our header cell class:

```
[self.collectionView registerClass:[HeaderCell class]
        forSupplementaryViewOfKind:UICollectionElementKindSectionHeader
               withReuseIdentifier:@"HEADER"];
```

As you can see, in this case we're not only specifying a cell class and an identifier, but we're also specifying a "kind." The idea is that different layouts may define different kinds of supplementary views and may ask the delegate to supply views for them. UICollectionFlowLayout is going to ask for one section header for each section in the collection view, and we'll apply them like this:

```
- (UICollectionReusableView *)collectionView:(UICollectionView *)collectionView
         viewForSupplementaryElementOfKind:(NSString *)kind
                               atIndexPath:(NSIndexPath *)indexPath {
    if ([kind isEqual:UICollectionElementKindSectionHeader]) {
        HeaderCell *cell = [self.collectionView
                               dequeueReusableSupplementaryViewOfKind:kind
                               withReuseIdentifier:@"HEADER"
                               forIndexPath:indexPath];

        cell.maxWidth = collectionView.bounds.size.width;
        cell.text = self.sections[indexPath.section][@"header"];
        return cell;
    }
    return nil;
}
```

Build and run, and you'll see... wait! Where are those headers? As it turns out, UICollectionFlowLayout won't give the headers any space in the layout unless we tell it exactly how large they should be. So go back to viewDidLoad and add the following line at the end:

```
flow.headerReferenceSize = CGSizeMake(100, 25);
```

Build and run once more, and now you'll see the headers in place, as Figure 10-1 showed earlier and Figure 10-5 shows again.

Figure 10-5. The completed DialogViewer app

In this chapter, we've really just dipped our toes into UICollectionView and what can be accomplished with the default UICollectionFlowLayout class. You can get even fancier with it by defining your own layout classes, but that is a topic for another book.

Now that you've gotten familiar with all the major big-picture components, it's time to look at how to create master-detail apps like the iOS Mail application; so turn the page and let's get started with that in Chapter 11.

Using Split Views and Popovers

In Chapter 9, you spent a lot of time dealing with app navigation based on selections in table views, where each selection causes the top-level view, which fills the entire screen, to slide to the left and bring in the next view in the hierarchy (or perhaps yet another table view). Plenty of iPhone and iPod touch apps work this way, including some of Apple's own apps. One typical example is Mail, which lets you drill down through mail accounts and folders until you finally make your way to a message. Technically, this approach can work on the iPad as well, but it leads to a user interaction problem.

On a screen the size of the iPhone or iPod touch, having a screen-sized view slide away to reveal another screen-sized view works well. On a screen the size of the iPad, however, that same interaction feels a little wrong, a little exaggerated, and even a little overwhelming. In addition, consuming such a large display with a single table view is inefficient in most cases. As a result, you'll see that the built-in iPad apps do not actually behave that way. Instead, any drill-down navigation functionality, like that used in Mail, is relegated to a narrow column whose contents slide left or right as the user drills down or backs out. With the iPad in landscape mode, the navigation column is in a fixed position on the left, with the content of the selected item displayed on the right. This is what's called a **split view** (see Figure 11-1) and applications built this way are called **master-detail applications**.

Figure 11-1. *This iPad, in landscape mode, is showing a split view. The navigation column is on the left. Tap an item in the navigation column—in this case, a specific mail account—and that item's content is displayed in the area on the right*

The split view is perfect for developing master-detail applications like the Mail app. Prior to iOS 8, the split view class (UISplitViewController) was only available on the iPad, which meant that if you wanted to build a universal master-detail application, you had to do it one way on the iPad and another way on the iPhone. Now, UISplitViewController is also available everywhere, which means that you no longer need to write special code to handle the iPhone.

When used on the iPad, the left side of the split view is 320 points wide by default, which is the same width as an iPhone in its vertical position. The split view itself, with navigation and content side by side, typically appears only in landscape mode. If you turn the device to portrait orientation, the split view is still in play, but it's no longer visible in the same way. The navigation view loses its permanent location and can be activated only by swiping in from the left side of the view or pressing a toolbar button, which causes it to slide in from the left, in a view that floats in front of everything else on the screen (see Figure 11-2).

Figure 11-2. This iPad, in portrait mode, does not show the same split view as seen in landscape mode. Instead, the information that made up the left side of the split view in landscape mode appears only when the user swipes in from the left side of the split view or taps a toolbar button

Some applications don't follow this rule strictly, though. The iPad Settings app, for instance, uses a split view that is visible all the time, and the left side neither disappears nor covers the content view on the right. In this chapter, however, we'll stick to the standard usage pattern.

In this chapter's example project, you'll see how to create a master-detail application that uses a split view controller. Initially, we'll test the application on the iPad simulator, but when it's finished, you'll see that the same code also works on the iPhone, although it doesn't quite look the same. You'll also learn how to customize the split view's appearance and behavior, and how to create and display a popover that's like the one that you saw in Chapter 4 when we discussed alert views and action sheets. Unlike the popover in Figure 4-28, which wrapped an action sheet, this one will contain content that is specific to the example application—specifically, a list of languages (see Figure 11-3).

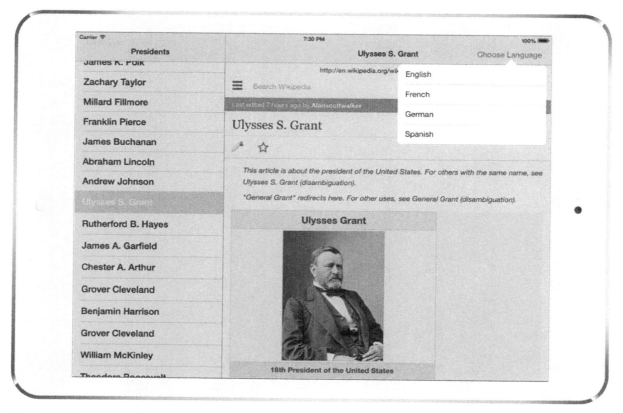

Figure 11-3. A popover, which visually seems to sprout from the button that triggered its appearance

Building Master-Detail Applications with UISplitViewController

We're going to start off with an easy task: taking advantage of one of Xcode's predefined templates to create a split view project. We'll build an app that lists all the US presidents and shows the Wikipedia entry for whichever one you select.

Go to Xcode and select **File ➤ New ➤ Project. . ..** From the **iOS Application** section, select **Master-Detail Application** and click **Next**. On the next screen, name the new project *Presidents*, set the **Language** to *Objective-C* and **Devices** to *Universal*. Make sure that the **Use Core Data** check box is unchecked. Click **Next**, choose the location for your project, and then click **Create**. Xcode will do its usual thing, creating a handful of classes and a storyboard file for you, and then showing the project. If it's not already open, expand the *Presidents* folder and take a look at what it contains.

From the start, the project contains an app delegate (as usual), a class called MasterViewController, and a class called DetailViewController. Those two view controllers represent, respectively, the views that will appear on the left and right sides of the split view in landscape orientation. MasterViewController defines the top level of a navigation structure and DetailViewController defines what's displayed in the larger area when a navigation element is selected. When the app launches, both of these are contained inside a split view, which, as you may recall, does a bit of shape-shifting as the device is rotated.

To see what this particular application template gives you in terms of functionality, build the app and run it in the iPad simulator (the application works on the iPhone too, but its behavior is slightly different, so we'll defer discussing that aspect of the split view controller until later in the chapter.) If the application launches into portrait mode, you'll see just the detail view controller, as shown on the left in Figure 11-4. Tap the **Master** button on the toolbar or swipe from the left edge of the view to the right to slide in the master view controller over the top of the detail view, as shown on the right in Figure 11-4.

Figure 11-4. The default master-detail application in portrait mode. The layout on the right is similar to Figure 11-2

Rotate the simulator (or device) left or right, into landscape mode. In this mode, the split view works by showing the navigation view on the left and the detail view on the right (see Figure 11-5).

Figure 11-5. *The default master-detail application in landscape mode. Note the similar layouts shown in this figure and Figure 11-1*

We're going to build on this to make the president-presenting app, but first let's dig into what's already there.

The Storyboard Defines the Structure

Right off the bat, you have a pretty complex set of view controllers in play:

- A split view controller that contains all the elements
- A navigation controller to handle what's happening on the left side of the split
- A master view controller (displaying a master list of items) inside the navigation controller

- A detail view controller on the right

- Another navigation controller as a container for the detail view controller on the right

In the default master-detail application template that we used, these view controllers are set up and interconnected primarily in the main storyboard file, rather than in code. Apart from doing GUI layout, Interface Builder really shines as a way of letting you connect different components without writing a bunch of code just to establish relationships. Let's dig into the project's storyboard to see how things are set up.

Select *Main.storyboard* to open it in Interface Builder. This storyboard really has a lot of stuff going on. You'll definitely want to open the Document Outline for the best results (see Figure 11-6). Zooming out (by right-clicking the storyboard editor and choosing a magnification level from the pop-up) can also help you see the big picture.

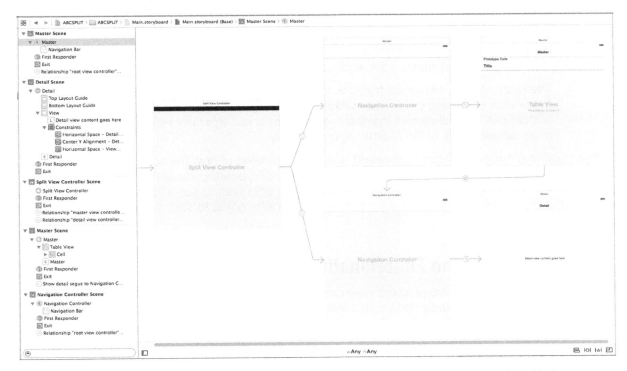

Figure 11-6. MainStoryboard.storyboard open in Interface Builder. This complex object hierarchy is best viewed in the Document Outline

To get a better sense of how these controllers relate to one another, open the Connections Inspector, and then spend some time clicking each of the view controllers in turn. Here's a quick summary of what you'll find:

- The UISplitViewController has relationship segues called **master view controller** and **detail view controller** to two UINavigationControllers. These are used to tell the UISplitViewController what it should use for the narrow strip it displays on the left (the master view controller), as well as what it should use for the larger display area (the detail view controller).

- The UINavigationController linked via the **master view controller** segue has a **root view controller relationship** to its own root view controller, which is the MasterViewController class generated by the template. The master view controller is a subclass of UITableViewController, which you should be familiar with from Chapter 9.

- Similarly, the other UINavigationController has a **root view controller relationship** to the detail view controller, which is the template's DetailVIewController class. The detail view controller generated by the template is a plain UIViewController subclass, but you are at liberty to use any view controller that meets your application's requirements.

- There is a storyboard segue from the cells in the master view controller to the detail view controller, of type **showDetail**. This segue causes the item in the clicked cell to be shown in the detail view. More about this later when we take a more detailed look at the master view controller.

At this point, the content of *Main.storyboard* is really a definition of how the app's various controllers are interconnected. As in most cases where you're using storyboards, this eliminates a lot of code, which is usually a good thing. If you're the kind of person who likes to see all such configuration done in code, you're free to do so; but for this example, we're going to stick with what Xcode has provided.

The Code Defines the Functionality

One of the main reasons for keeping the view controller interconnections in a storyboard is that they don't clutter up your source code with configuration information that doesn't need to be there. What's left is just the code that defines the actual functionality.

Let's look at what we have as a starting point. Xcode defined several classes for us when the project was created, and we're going to peek into each of them before we start making any changes.

The App Delegate

First up is *AppDelegate.h*, which looks something like this:

```
#import <UIKit/UIKit.h>

@interface AppDelegate : UIResponder <UIApplicationDelegate>

@property (strong, nonatomic) UIWindow *window;

@end
```

This is pretty similar to several other application delegates you've seen in this book so far. Now switch over to the implementation in *AppDelegate.m*. The code at the start of this file looks something like the following (most comments and empty methods have been deleted here for the sake of brevity):

```
#import "AppDelegate.h"
#import "DetailViewController.h"

@interface AppDelegate () <UISplitViewControllerDelegate>

@end

@implementation AppDelegate

- (BOOL)application:(UIApplication *)application
                    didFinishLaunchingWithOptions:(NSDictionary *)launchOptions {
    UISplitViewController *splitViewController =
                    (UISplitViewController *)self.window.rootViewController;
    UINavigationController *navigationController =
                    [splitViewController.viewControllers lastObject];
    navigationController.topViewController.navigationItem.leftBarButtonItem =
                    splitViewController.displayModeButtonItem;
    splitViewController.delegate = self;
    return YES;
}
```

Let's look at the last part of this code first:

```
splitViewController.delegate = self;
```

This line sets the UISplitViewController's delegate property, pointing it at the application delegate itself. Later in this chapter, when we look at how split views behave on the iPhone, we'll see why this delegate connection is required. But why make this connection here in code, instead of having it hooked up directly in the storyboard? After all, just a few paragraphs ago, you were told that elimination of boring code—"connect this thing to that thing"—is one of the main benefits of both nibs and storyboards. And we've hooked up delegates in Interface Builder plenty of times, so why can't we do that here?

To understand why using a storyboard to make the connections can't really work here, you need to consider how a storyboard differs from a nib file. A nib file is really a frozen object graph. When you load a nib into a running application, the objects it contains all "thaw out" and spring into existence, including all the interconnections specified in the file. The system creates a fresh instance of every single object in the file, one after another, and connects all the outlets and connections between objects.

A storyboard, however, is something more than that. You could say that each scene in a storyboard corresponds roughly to a nib file. When you add in the metadata describing how the scenes are connected via segues, you end up with a storyboard. However, unlike a single nib, a complex storyboard is not normally loaded all at once. Instead, any activity that causes a new scene to be activated will end up loading that particular scene's frozen object graph from the storyboard. This means that the objects you see when looking at a storyboard won't necessarily all exist at the same time.

Since Interface Builder has no way of knowing which scenes will coexist, it actually forbids you from making any outlet or target/action connections from an object in one scene to an object in another scene. In fact, the only connections it allows you to make from one scene to another are segues.

But don't take our word for it, try it out yourself! First, select the **Split View Controller** in the storyboard (you'll find it within the dock in the Split View Controller Scene). Now bring up the Connections Inspector and try to drag a connection from the *delegate* outlet to another view controller or object. You can drag all over the layout view and the list view, and you won't find any spot that highlights (which would indicate it was ready to accept a drag). The only way to make this connection is in code. All in all, this extra bit of code is a small price to pay, considering how much other code is eliminated by our use of storyboards.

Now let's rewind and look at what happens at the start of the `application:didFinishLaunchingWithOptions:` method:

```
UISplitViewController *splitViewController =
    (UISplitViewController *)self.window.rootViewController;
```

This grabs the window's `rootViewController`, which is the one indicated in the storyboard by the free-floating arrow. If you look back at Figure 11-6, you'll see that the arrow points at our `UISplitViewController` instance. This code comes next:

```
UINavigationController *navigationController =
    [splitViewController.viewControllers lastObject];
```

On this line, we dig into the `UISplitViewController`'s `viewControllers` array. When the split view is loaded from the storyboard, this array has references to the navigation controllers wrapping the master and detail view controllers. We grab the last item in this array, which points to the `UINavigationController` for our detail view. Finally, we see this:

```
navigationController.topViewController.navigationItem.leftBarButtonItem =
        splitViewController.displayModeButtonItem;
```

This assigns the `displayModeButtonItem` of the split view controller to the navigation bar of the detail view controller. The `displayModeButtonItem` is a bar button item that is created and managed by the split view itself. This code is actually adding the **Master** button that you can see on the navigation bar on the left in Figure 11-4. On the iPad, the split view shows this button when the device is in portrait mode and the master view controller is not visible. When the device rotates to landscape orientation or the user presses the button to make the master view controller visible, the button is hidden. You'll see later that this button is also used on the iPhone to allow the user to manually show and hide the master view controller.

The Master View Controller

Now, let's take a look at `MasterViewController`, which controls the setup of the table view containing the app's navigation. *MasterViewController.h* looks like this:

```
#import <UIKit/UIKit.h>

@class DetailViewController;

@interface MasterViewController : UITableViewController

@property (strong, nonatomic) DetailViewController *detailViewController;

@end
```

Its corresponding *MasterViewController.m* file starts off like this (we're just looking at the first few methods now and will deal with the rest later):

```
#import "MasterViewController.h"
#import "DetailViewController.h"

@interface MasterViewController ()

@property NSMutableArray *objects;
@end

@implementation MasterViewController

- (void)awakeFromNib {
    [super awakeFromNib];
    if ([[UIDevice currentDevice] userInterfaceIdiom] == UIUserInterfaceIdiomPad) {
        self.clearsSelectionOnViewWillAppear = NO;
        self.preferredContentSize = CGSizeMake(320.0, 600.0);
    }
}

- (void)viewDidLoad {
    [super viewDidLoad];
    // Do any additional setup after loading the view, typically from a nib.
    self.navigationItem.leftBarButtonItem = self.editButtonItem;
```

```
    UIBarButtonItem *addButton = [[UIBarButtonItem alloc]
            initWithBarButtonSystemItem:UIBarButtonSystemItemAdd target:self
            action:@selector(insertNewObject:)];
    self.navigationItem.rightBarButtonItem = addButton;
    self.detailViewController = (DetailViewController *)
            [[self.splitViewController.viewControllers lastObject] topViewController];
}
.
@end
```

A fair amount of configuration is happening here. Fortunately, Xcode provides all of this code as part of the split view template. First, the awakeFromNib method starts like this:

```
- (void)awakeFromNib {
    [super awakeFromNib];
    if ([[UIDevice currentDevice] userInterfaceIdiom] == UIUserInterfaceIdiomPad) {
        self.clearsSelectionOnViewWillAppear = NO;
```

The if statement gets the user interface idiom from the UIDevice object that represents the device on which the application is running and tests whether it's an iPad. If it is, it sets the view controller's clearsSelectionOnViewWillAppear property to NO. This property is defined by the UITableViewController class (which is the superclass of MasterViewController) and lets us tweak the controller's behavior a bit. By default, UITableViewController is set up to deselect all rows each time it's displayed. That may be OK in an iPhone app, where each table view is usually displayed on its own; however, in an iPad app featuring a split view, you probably don't want that selection to disappear. To revisit an earlier example, consider the Mail app. The user selects a message on the left side and expects that selection to remain there, even if the message list disappears (due to rotating the iPad or closing the popover containing the list). This line fixes that.

Next, the awakeFromNib method sets the view's preferredContentSize property. That property sets the size of the view if this view controller should happen to be used to provide the display for some other view controller that allows a variable size. In this case, it's intended to be used when the master view controller is displayed in portrait mode. Although this property is set here, in iOS 8 it does not appear to have any effect—you'll see the correct way to control the width of the master view controller in portrait mode in "Customizing the Split View" later in this chapter.

The final point of interest here is the viewDidLoad method. In previous chapters, when you implemented a table view controller that responds to a user row selection, you typically responded to the user selecting a row by creating a new view controller and pushing it onto the navigation controller's stack. In this app, however, the view controller we want to show is already in place, and it will be reused each time the user makes a selection on the left. It's the instance of DetailViewController contained in the storyboard file. Here, we're grabbing that DetailViewController instance and hanging saving it in a property, anticipating that we'll want to use it later. However, this property is not used in the rest of the template code.

The viewDidLoad method also adds a button to the toolbar. This is the + button that you can see on the right of master view controller's navigation bar in Figure 11-4 and Figure 11-5. The template application uses this button to create and add a new entry to the master view controller's table view. Since we don't need this button in our Presidents application, we'll be removing this code shortly.

There are several more methods included in the template for this class, but don't worry about those right now. We're going to delete some of those and rewrite the others, but only after taking a detour through the detail view controller.

The Detail View Controller

The final class created for us by Xcode is DetailViewController, which takes care of the actual display of the item the user chooses from the table in the master view controller. Here's what *DetailViewController.h* looks like:

```
#import <UIKit/UIKit.h>

@interface DetailViewController : UIViewController

@property (strong, nonatomic) id detailItem;
@property (weak, nonatomic) IBOutlet UILabel *detailDescriptionLabel;

@end
```

This is very straightforward—the detailItem property is where the view controller stores its reference to the object that the user selected in the master view controller, and detailDescriptionLabel is an outlet that connects to a label in the storyboard. In the template application, the label simply displays a description of the object in the detailItem property.

Switch over to *DetailViewController.m*, where you'll find the following:

```
#import "DetailViewController.h"

@interface DetailViewController ()

@end

@implementation DetailViewController

#pragma mark - Managing the detail item

- (void)setDetailItem:(id)newDetailItem {
    if (_detailItem != newDetailItem) {
        _detailItem = newDetailItem;

        // Update the view.
        [self configureView];
    }
}

- (void)configureView {
    // Update the user interface for the detail item.
    if (self.detailItem) {
        self.detailDescriptionLabel.text = [self.detailItem description];
    }
}
```

```objc
- (void)viewDidLoad {
    [super viewDidLoad];
    // Do any additional setup after loading the view, typically from a nib.
    [self configureView];
}

- (void)didReceiveMemoryWarning {
    [super didReceiveMemoryWarning];
    // Dispose of any resources that can be recreated.
}

@end
```

The most important thing in this class is this method:

```objc
- (void)setDetailItem:(id)newDetailItem {
    if (_detailItem != newDetailItem) {
        _detailItem = newDetailItem;

        // Update the view.
        [self configureView];
    }
}
```

The setDetailItem: method may seem surprising to you. We did, after all, define detailItem as a property, and the compiler would automatically create the getter and setter for us, so why create a setter ourselves? In this case, we need to be able to react whenever the setter is called (we'll see exactly how this happens in the "How the Master-Detail Template Application Works" section later in this chapter), so that we can update the display. Implementing the setter ourselves is the easiest way to do that.

The first part of the method just stores the new property value in the instance variable that the compiler creates for us. Then, the configureView method is called. This is another method that's generated for us. All it does is call the description method of the detail object and then uses the result to set the text property of the label in the storyboard:

```objc
- (void)configureView {
    // Update the user interface for the detail item.
    if (self.detailItem) {
        self.detailDescriptionLabel.text = [self.detailItem description];
    }
}
```

The description method is implemented by every subclass of NSObject. If your class doesn't override it, it returns a default value that's probably not very useful. However, in this example, the detail objects are all instances of the NSDate class and NSDate's implementation of the description method returns the date and time, formatted in a generic way.

How the Master-Detail Template Application Works

Now you've seen all of the pieces of the template application, but you're probably still not very clear on how it works, so let's run it and take a look at what it actually does.

Run the application on an iPad simulator and rotate the device to landscape mode so that the master view controller appears. You can see that the label in the detail view controller currently has the default text that's assigned to it in the storyboard. What we're going to see in this section is how the act of selecting an item in the master view controller causes that text to change. There currently aren't any items in the master view controller. To fix that, press the + button at the top right of its navigation bar a few times. Every time you do that, a new item is added to the controller's table view, as shown in Figure 11-7.

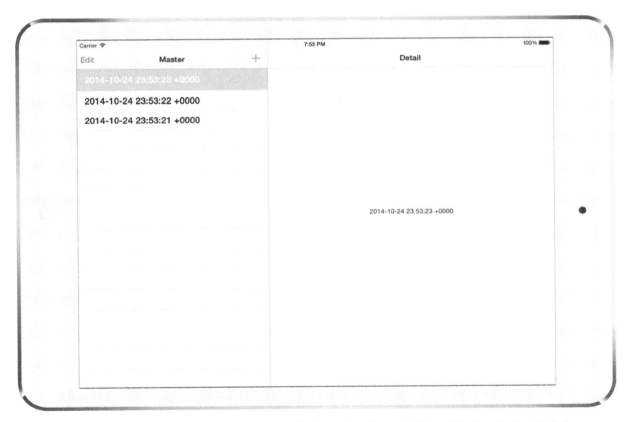

Figure 11-7. The template application with an item selected in the master view controller and displayed in the detail view controller

All of the items in the master view controller table are dates. Select one of them, and the label in the detail view updates to show the same date. You've already seen the code that does this—it's the configureView method in *DetailViewController.m*, which is called when a new value is stored in the detail view controller's detailItem property. What is it that causes a new property value to be set?

Take a look back at the storyboard in Figure 11-6. There's a segue that links the prototype table cell in the master view controller's table cell to the detail view controller. If you click this segue and open the Attributes Inspector, you'll see that this is a **Show Detail** segue with the identifier showDetail (see Figure 11-8).

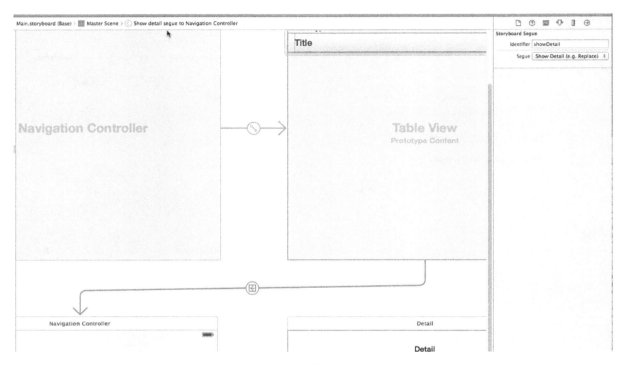

Figure 11-8. The Show Detail segue linking the master and detail view controllers

As you saw in Chapter 9, a segue that's linked to a table view cell is triggered when that cell is selected, so when you select a row in the master view controller's table view, iOS performs the Show Detail segue, with the navigation controller wrapping the detail view controller as the segue destination. This causes two things to happen:

- A new instance of the detail view controller is created and its view is added to the view hierarchy.

- The prepareForSegue:sender: method in the master view controller is called.

The first step takes care of making sure the detail view controller is visible. In the second step, your master view controller needs to display the object selected in the master view controller in some way. Here's how the template code in *MasterViewController.m* handles this:

```
- (void)prepareForSegue:(UIStoryboardSegue *)segue sender:(id)sender {
    if ([[segue identifier] isEqualToString:@"showDetail"]) {
        NSIndexPath *indexPath = [self.tableView indexPathForSelectedRow];
        NSDate *object = self.objects[indexPath.row];
        DetailViewController *controller =
                (DetailViewController *)[[segue destinationViewController] topViewController];
        [controller setDetailItem:object];
        controller.navigationItem.leftBarButtonItem = self.splitViewController.
        displayModeButtonItem;
        controller.navigationItem.leftItemsSupplementBackButton = YES;
    }
}
```

First, the segue identifier is checked to make sure that it's the one that is expected and that the NSDate object from the selected object in the view controller's table is obtained. Next, the master view controller finds the DetailViewController instance from the topViewController property of the destination view controller in the segue that caused this method to be called. Now that we have both the selected object and the detail view controller, all we have to do is set the detail view controller's detailItem property to cause the detail view to be updated. The final two lines of the prepareForSegue:sender: method add the display mode button to the detail view controller's navigation bar. When the device is in landscape mode, this doesn't do anything because the display mode button isn't visible, but if you rotate to portrait orientation, you'll see that the button (it's the **Master** button) appears.

So now you know how the selected item in the master view controller gets displayed in the detail view controller. Although it doesn't look like much is going on here, in fact there is a great deal happening under the hood to make this work correctly on both the iPad and the iPhone, in portrait and landscape orientations. The beauty of the split view controller is that it takes care of all the details and leaves you free to worry about how to implement your custom master and detail view controllers.

That concludes the overview of what Xcode's Master-Detail Application template gives you. It might be a lot to absorb at a glance, but, ideally, presenting it a piece at a time has helped you understand how all the pieces fit together.

Here Come the Presidents

Now that you've seen the basic layout of our project, it's time to fill in the blanks and turn the template app into something all your own. Start by looking in the book's source code archive, where the folder *11 – Presidents Data* contains a file called *PresidentList.plist*. Drag that file into your project's *Presidents* folder in Xcode to add it to the project, making sure that the check box telling Xcode to copy the file itself is checked. This *.plist* file contains information about all the US presidents so far, consisting of just the name and the Wikipedia entry URL for each of them.

Now, let's look at the master view controller and see how we need to modify it to handle the presidential data properly. It's going to be a simple matter of loading the list of presidents, presenting them in the table view, and passing a URL to the detail view for display. In *MasterViewController.m*, start off by adding the bold line shown here to the class extension and removing the crossed-out line:

```
@interface MasterViewController ()

@property NSMutableArray *objects;
@property (copy, nonatomic) NSArray *presidents;

@end
```

Instead of holding our list of presidents in the mutable array that was created by Xcode, we create our own immutable array with a more meaningful name.

Now divert your attention to the viewDidLoad method, where the changes are a little more involved (but still not too bad). You're going to add a few lines to load the list of presidents, and then remove a few other lines that set up edit and insertion buttons in the toolbar:

```
- (void)viewDidLoad {
    [super viewDidLoad];
    // Do any additional setup after loading the view, typically from a nib.
    self.navigationItem.leftBarButtonItem = self.editButtonItem;

    NSString *path = [[NSBundle mainBundle] pathForResource:@"PresidentList"
                                                     ofType:@"plist"];
    NSDictionary *presidentInfo = [NSDictionary
                                   dictionaryWithContentsOfFile:path];
    self.presidents = [presidentInfo objectForKey:@"presidents"];

    UIBarButtonItem *addButton = [[UIBarButtonItem alloc]
                   initWithBarButtonSystemItem:UIBarButtonSystemItemAdd target:self
                   action:@selector(insertNewObject:)];
    self.navigationItem.rightBarButtonItem = addButton;
    self.detailViewController = (DetailViewController *)
            [[self.splitViewController.viewControllers lastObject] topViewController];
}
```

This template-generated class also includes a method called insertNewObject: for adding items to the objects array. We don't even have that array anymore, so we delete the entire method:

```
- (void)insertNewObject:(id)sender {
    if (!_objects) {
        _objects = [[NSMutableArray alloc] init];
    }
    [_objects insertObject:[NSDate date] atIndex:0];
    NSIndexPath *indexPath = [NSIndexPath indexPathForRow:0 inSection:0];
    [self.tableView insertRowsAtIndexPaths:@[indexPath]
                          withRowAnimation:UITableViewRowAnimationAutomatic];
}
```

Also, we have a couple of data source methods that deal with letting users edit rows in the table view. We're not going to allow any editing of rows in this app, so let's just remove this code before adding our own:

```
- (BOOL)tableView:(UITableView *)tableView
                        canEditRowAtIndexPath:(NSIndexPath *)indexPath {
    // Return NO if you do not want the specified item to be editable.
    return YES;
}

- (void)tableView:(UITableView *)tableView
                    commitEditingStyle:(UITableViewCellEditingStyle)editingStyle
                    forRowAtIndexPath:(NSIndexPath *)indexPath {
    if (editingStyle == UITableViewCellEditingStyleDelete) {
        [self.objects removeObjectAtIndex:indexPath.row];
        [tableView deleteRowsAtIndexPaths:@[indexPath]
                        withRowAnimation:UITableViewRowAnimationFade];
    } else if (editingStyle == UITableViewCellEditingStyleInsert) {
        // Create a new instance of the appropriate class, insert it into the array,
        //          and add a new row to the table view.
    }
}
```

Now it's time to get to the main table view data source methods, adapting them for our purposes. Let's start by editing the method that tells the table view how many rows to display:

```
- (NSInteger)tableView:(UITableView *)tableView
                        numberOfRowsInSection:(NSInteger)section {
    return self.objects.count;
    return [self.presidents count];
}
```

After that, edit the tableView:cellForRowAtIndexPath: method to make each cell display a president's name:

```
- (UITableViewCell *)tableView:(UITableView *)tableView
                            cellForRowAtIndexPath:(NSIndexPath *)indexPath {
    UITableViewCell *cell =
            [tableView dequeueReusableCellWithIdentifier:@"Cell" forIndexPath:indexPath];

    NSDate *object = self.objects[indexPath.row];
    cell.textLabel.text = [object description];

    NSDictionary *president = self.presidents[indexPath.row];
    cell.textLabel.text = president[@"name"];

    return cell;
}
```

Finally, edit the prepareForSegue:sender: method to pass the data for the selected president (which is an NSDictionary) to the detail view controller, as follows:

```
- (void)prepareForSegue:(UIStoryboardSegue *)segue sender:(id)sender {
    if ([[segue identifier] isEqualToString:@"showDetail"]) {
        NSIndexPath *indexPath = [self.tableView indexPathForSelectedRow];
        NSDate *object = self.objects[indexPath.row];
        DetailViewController *controller =
                (DetailViewController *)[[segue destinationViewController] topViewController];
        [controller setDetailItem:object];
        NSDictionary *president = self.presidents[indexPath.row];
        controller .detailItem = president;

        controller.navigationItem.leftBarButtonItem =
                        self.splitViewController.displayModeButtonItem;
        controller.navigationItem.leftItemsSupplementBackButton = YES;
    }
}
```

That's all we need to do in the master view controller.

Next, select *Main.storyboard* and click the **Master** icon in the **Master Scene** in the Document Outline to select the master view controller, and then double-click its title bar and replace *Master* with *Presidents* and save the storyboard.

At this point, you can build and run the app. Switch to landscape mode, or tap the **Master** button in the upper-left corner to bring up the master view controller, showing a list of presidents (see Figure 11-9). Tap a president's name to display a not-very-useful string in the detail view.

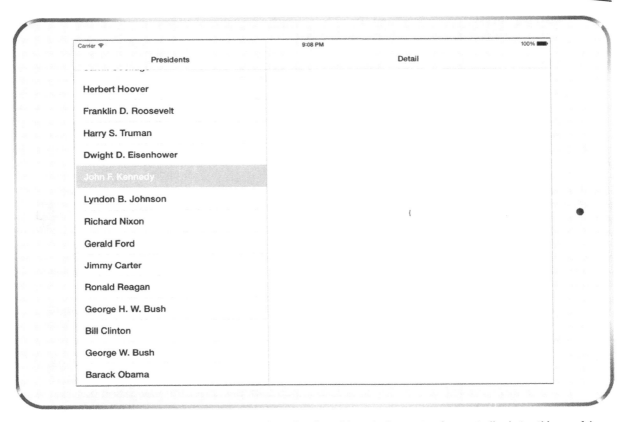

Figure 11-9. Our first run of the Presidents app, showing a list of presidents in the master view controller, but nothing useful in the detail view

Let's finish this example by making the detail view do something a little more useful with the data that it's given. Start with *DetailViewContoller.h*, where we'll add an outlet for a web view to display the Wikipedia page for the selected president. Add the bold line shown here:

```
@interface DetailViewController : UIViewController

@property (strong, nonatomic) id detailItem;
@property (weak, nonatomic) IBOutlet UILabel *detailDescriptionLabel;
@property (weak, nonatomic) IBOutlet UIWebView *webView;

@end
```

Next, switch to *DetailViewController.m*, where we have a bit more to do (though really, not too much). Scroll down to the configureView method and replace it with the following code:

```
- (void)configureView {
    // Update the user interface for the detail item.
    if (self.detailItem) {
        NSDictionary *dict = (NSDictionary *)self.detailItem;
```

```
        NSString *urlString = dict[@"url"];
        self.detailDescriptionLabel.text = urlString;

        NSURL *url = [NSURL URLWithString:urlString];
        NSURLRequest *request = [NSURLRequest requestWithURL:url];
        [self.webView loadRequest:request];

        NSString *name = dict[@"name"];
        self.title = name;
    }
}
```

The detailItem that was set by the master view controller is an NSDictionary containing two key-value pairs: one with a key name that stores the president's name and another with a key url that gives the URL of the president's Wikipedia page. We use the URL to set the text of the detail description label and to construct an NSURLRequest that the UIWebView will use to load the page. We use the name to set the detail view controller's title. When a view controller is a container in a UINavigationController, the value in its title property is displayed in the navigation controller's navigation bar. That's all we need to get our web view to load the requested page.

The final changes we need to make are in *Main.storyboard*. Open it for editing and find the detail view at the lower right. Let's first take care of the label in the GUI (the text of which reads, "Detail view content goes here").

Start by selecting the label. You might find it easiest to select the label in the Document Outline, in the section labeled *Detail Scene*. Once the label is selected, drag it to the top of the window. The label should run from the left-to-right blue guideline and fit snugly under the navigation bar (resize it to make sure that is the case). This label is being repurposed to show the current URL. But when the application launches, before the user has chosen a president, we want this field to give the user a hint about what to do.

Double-click the label and change it to *Select a President*. You should also use the Size Inspector to make sure that the label's position is constrained to both the left and right sides of its superview, as well as the top edge (see Figure 11-10). If you need to adjust these constraints, use the methods described earlier to set them up. You can probably get almost exactly what you want by selecting the label and then choosing **Editor ➤ Resolve Auto Layout Issues ➤ Reset to Suggested Constraints** from the menu.

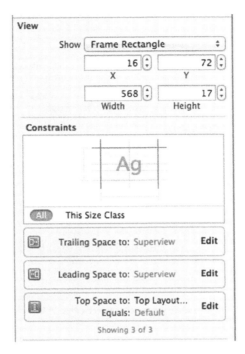

Figure 11-10. *The Size Inspector, showing the constraints settings for the "Select a President" label at the bottom*

Next, use the library to find a UIWebView and drag it into the space below the label you just moved. After dropping the web view there, use the resize handles to make it fill the rest of the view below the label. Make it go from the left edge to the right edge, and from the blue guideline just below the bottom of the label all the way to the very bottom of the window. Now use the Size Inspector to constrain the web view to the left, bottom, and right edges of the superview, as well as to the label for the top edge (see Figure 11-11). Once again, you can probably get exactly what you need by selecting **Editor ➤ Resolve Auto Layout Issues ➤ Reset to Suggested Constraints** from the menu.

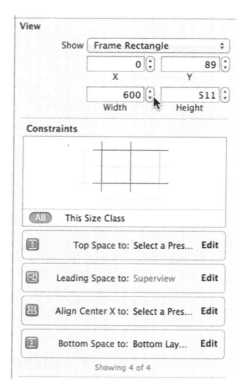

Figure 11-11. The Size Inspector, showing the constraints settings for the web view

Now select the **Master** view controller in the Document Outline and open the Attributes Editor. In the **View Controller** section, change the **Title** from *Master* to *Presidents*. This changes the title of the navigation button at the top of the detail view controller to something more useful.

We have one last step to complete. To hook up the outlet for the web view that you created, Control-drag from the **Detail** icon (in the Detail Scene section in the Document Outline) to our new Web View (same section, just below the label in the Document Outline, or in the storyboard), and connect the webView outlet. Save your changes, and you're finished!

Now you can build and run the app, and it will let you see the Wikipedia entries for each of the presidents (see Figure 11-12). Rotate the display between the two orientations, and you'll see how the split view controller takes care of everything for you, with a little help from the detail view controller.

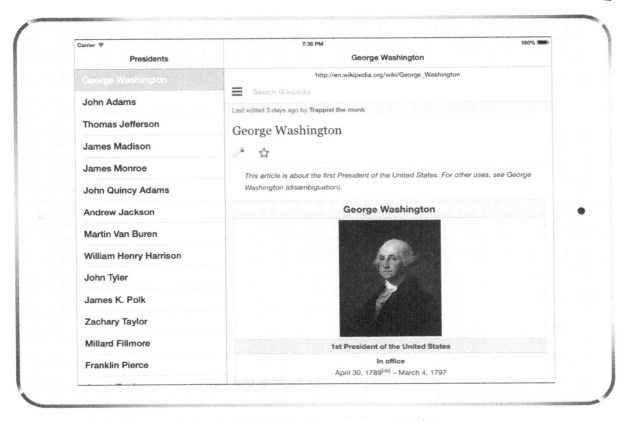

Figure 11-12. *The Presidents application, showing the Wikipedia page for George Washington*

Creating Your Own Popover

Back in Chapter 4, you saw that you can display an action sheet in what looks like a cartoon speech bubble (see Figure 4-28). That speech bubble is the visual representation of a **popover controller**, or *popover* for short. The popover that you get with an action sheet is created for you when the action sheet is presented by a UIPopoverPresentationController, which you have very little control over. However, you can create your own popover by using the UIPopoverController class, which can come in handy when you want to present your own view controllers.

To see how this works, we're going to add a popover to be activated by a permanent toolbar item (unlike the one in the UISplitView, which is meant to come and go). This popover will display a table view containing a list of languages. If the user picks a language from the list, the web view will load (in the new language) whatever Wikipedia entry that was already showing. This will be simple enough to do, since switching from one language to another in Wikipedia is just a matter of changing a small piece of the URL that contains an embedded country code. Figure 11-3 shows what we are aiming for. It's important to note, however, that UIPopoverController is available only on the iPad, so when this application is run on the iPhone, the language selector will be missing.

> **Note**   The use of a popover in this example is in the service of showing a UITableView, but don't let that mislead you—UIPopoverController can be used to handle the display of any view controller content you like! We're sticking with table views for this example because it's a common use case, it's easy to show in a relatively small amount of code, and it's something with which you should already be quite familiar.

Start by right-clicking the *Presidents* folder in Xcode and selecting **New File. . .** from the pop-up menu. When the assistant appears, select **Cocoa Touch Class** from the **iOS Source** section, and then click **Next**. On the next screen, name the new class *LanguageListController* and select UITableViewController from the **Subclass of** field. Click **Next**, double-check the location where you're saving the file, and click **Create**.

The LanguageListController is going to be a pretty standard table view controller class. It will display a list of items and let the detail view controller know when a choice is made, by using a pointer back to the detail view controller. Edit *LanguageListController.h*, adding the bold lines shown here:

```
#import <UIKit/UIKit.h>

@class DetailViewController;

@interface LanguageListController : UITableViewController

@property (weak, nonatomic) DetailViewController *detailViewController;
@property (copy, nonatomic) NSArray *languageNames;
@property (copy, nonatomic) NSArray *languageCodes;

@end
```

These additions define a pointer back to the detail view controller (which we'll set from code in the detail view controller itself when we're about to display the language list), as well as a pair of arrays for containing the values that will be displayed (English, French, etc.) and the underlying values that will be used to build an URL from the chosen language (en, fr, and so on). Note that we've declared these arrays to have copy storage semantics instead of strong. This means that whenever some piece of code calls one of these setters, the parameter is sent a copy message instead of just being held as a strong pointer. This is done to prevent a situation where another class might send in an NSMutableArray instead of an NSArray, and then make changes to the array without our knowledge. Sending copy to an NSMutableArray instance always returns an immutable NSArray, so we know that the array we're using can't be changed by someone else. At the same time, sending copy to an NSArray, which is already immutable, doesn't actually make a new copy, it just returns a strong pointer to self, so sending it a copy message isn't wasteful in any way.

If you copied and pasted this code from the book's source archive (or e-book) into your own project or typed it yourself a little sloppily, you may not have noticed an important difference in how the detailViewController property was declared earlier. Unlike most properties that reference an object pointer, we declared this one using weak instead of strong. This is something that we must do to avoid a **retain** cycle.

What's a retain cycle? It's a situation where a set of two or more objects have references to each other, in a circular fashion. Each object is keeping the memory of the other object from being freed. Most potential retain cycles can be avoided by carefully considering the creation of your objects, often by trying to figure out which object "owns" which. In this sense, an instance of DetailViewController owns an instance of LanguageListController because it's the DetailViewController that actually creates the LanguageListController to get a piece of work done. Whenever you have a pair of objects that need to refer to one another, you'll usually want the owner object to retain the other object, while the other object should specifically not retain its owner. Since we're using the ARC feature that Apple introduced in Xcode 4.2, the compiler does most of the work for us. Instead of paying attention to the details about releasing and retaining objects, all we need to do is declare a property that refers to an object that we do not own with the weak keyword instead of strong. ARC will do the rest!

Now, switch over to *LanguageListController.m* to implement the following changes. At the top of the file, start by importing the header for DetailViewController:

```
#import "LanguageListController.h"
#import "DetailViewController.h"
.
.
.
```

Next, scroll down a bit to the viewDidLoad method and add a bit of setup code:

```
- (void)viewDidLoad {
    [super viewDidLoad];

    self.languageNames = @[@"English", @"French", @"German", @"Spanish"];
    self.languageCodes = @[@"en", @"fr", @"de", @"es"];
    self.clearsSelectionOnViewWillAppear = NO;
    self.preferredContentSize = CGSizeMake(320.0,
                                      [self.languageCodes count] * 44.0);

    [self.tableView registerClass:[UITableViewCell class]
            forCellReuseIdentifier:@"Cell"];

}
```

This sets up the language arrays and also defines the size that the view controller's view will use if shown in a popover (which, as we know, it will be). Without defining the size, we would end up with a popover stretching vertically to fill nearly the whole screen, even if it can be displayed in full with a much smaller view. And finally, we register a default table view cell class to use, as explained in Chapter 8.

Further down, we have a few methods generated by Xcode's template that don't contain particularly useful code—just a warning and some placeholder text. Let's replace those with something real:

```
- (NSInteger)numberOfSectionsInTableView:(UITableView *)tableView {
#warning Potentially incomplete method implementation.
    return 0;
    return 1;
}
```

```
- (NSInteger)tableView:(UITableView *)tableView
    numberOfRowsInSection:(NSInteger)section {
#warning Incomplete method implementation.
    // Return the number of rows in the section.
    return 0;
    return [self.languageCodes count];
}
```

Now add the `tableView:cellForRowAtIndexPath:` method to get a cell object and put a language name into a cell:

```
- (UITableViewCell *)tableView:(UITableView *)tableView
                        cellForRowAtIndexPath:(NSIndexPath *)indexPath {
    UITableViewCell *cell =
        [tableView dequeueReusableCellWithIdentifier:@"Cell" forIndexPath:indexPath];

    // Configure the cell...
    cell.textLabel.text = self.languageNames[indexPath.row];

    return cell;
}
```

Next, implement `tableView:didSelectRowAtIndexPath:` so that you can respond to a user's touch by passing the language selection back to the detail view controller:

```
- (void)tableView:(UITableView *)tableView
             didSelectRowAtIndexPath:(NSIndexPath *)indexPath {
    self.detailViewController.languageString =
                self.languageCodes[indexPath.row];
}
```

> **Note** DetailViewController doesn't actually have a `languageString` property yet, so you will see a compiler error. We'll take care of that in just a bit.

Now it's time to make the changes required for `DetailViewController` to handle the popover, as well as to generate the correct URL whenever the user either changes the display language or picks a different president. Start by making the following changes in *DetailViewController.h*:

```
#import <UIKit/UIKit.h>

@interface DetailViewController : UIViewController

@property (strong, nonatomic) id detailItem;
@property (weak, nonatomic) IBOutlet UILabel *detailDescriptionLabel;
@property (weak, nonatomic) IBOutlet UIWebView *webView;
@property (strong, nonatomic) UIBarButtonItem *languageButton;
@property (strong, nonatomic) UIPopoverController *languagePopoverController;
@property (copy, nonatomic) NSString *languageString;

@end
```

Here, we added some properties to keep track of the GUI components required for the popover and the user's selected language. All we need to do now is fix *DetailViewController.m* so that it can handle the language popover and the URL construction. Start by adding this import somewhere at the top and conforming the class to the `UIPopoverControllerDelegate` protocol so that it can respond to messages from the `UIPopoverController`:

```
#import "DetailViewController.h"
#import "LanguageListController.h"

@interface DetailViewController () <UIPopoverControllerDelegate>

@end
```

The next thing we're going to add is a function that takes as arguments a URL pointing to a Wikipedia page and a two-letter language code, and then returns a URL that combines the two. We'll use this at appropriate spots in our controller code later. You can place this function just about anywhere, including within the class's implementation. The compiler is smart enough to always treat a function as just a function. Place it just after the `setDetailItem:` method:

```
static NSString * modifyUrlForLanguage(NSString *url, NSString *lang) {
    if (!lang) {
        return url;
    }

    // We're relying on a particular Wikipedia URL format here. This
    // is a bit fragile!
    // URL is like http://en.wikipedia...
    NSRange codeRange = NSMakeRange(7, 2);
    if ([[url substringWithRange:codeRange] isEqualToString:lang]) {
        return url;
    } else {
        NSString *newUrl = [url stringByReplacingCharactersInRange:codeRange
                                                        withString:lang];
        return newUrl;
    }
}
```

Why make this a function instead of a method? There are a couple of reasons. First, instance methods in a class are typically meant to do something involving one or more instance variables, or accessing an object's internal state either through getters and setters or through direct instance variable access. This function does not use any instance variables. It simply performs an operation on two strings and returns another. We could have made it a class method, but even that feels a bit wrong, since what the method does isn't really related specifically to the controller class. Sometimes, a function is just what you need.

Our next move is to update the configureView: method. This method will use the function we just defined to combine the URL that's passed in with the chosen languageString to generate the correct URL:

```objc
- (void)configureView {
    // Update the user interface for the detail item.
    if (self.detailItem) {
        NSDictionary *dict = (NSDictionary *)self.detailItem;

        NSString *urlString = modifyUrlForLanguage(dict[@"url"], self.languageString);
        self.detailDescriptionLabel.text = urlString;

        NSURL *url = [NSURL URLWithString:urlString];
        NSURLRequest *request = [NSURLRequest requestWithURL:url];
        [self.webView loadRequest:request];

        NSString *name = dict[@"name"];
        self.title = name;
    }
}
```

Now let's update the viewDidLoad method. Here, we're going to create a UIBarButtonItem and put it into the UINavigationItem at the top of the screen, but only if we are running on an iPad:

```objc
- (void)viewDidLoad {
    [super viewDidLoad];

    if (UI_USER_INTERFACE_IDIOM() == UIUserInterfaceIdiomPad) {
        self.languageButton =
        [[UIBarButtonItem alloc] initWithTitle:@"Choose Language"
                                         style:UIBarButtonItemStylePlain
                                        target:self
                                        action:@selector(toggleLanguagePopover)];
        self.navigationItem.rightBarButtonItem = self.languageButton;
    }
    [self configureView];
}
```

You'll get a compiler warning here because the code you just added refers to a method called toggleLanguagePopover that doesn't exist. We'll fix that soon. Here, we use UI_USER_INTERFACE_ IDIOM() to determine whether we're running on an iPad or an iPhone. We only want to add the button on an iPad, because iPhones do not support UIPopoverController.

Next, we implement setLanguageString:, which is called when the value of the languageString property is changed. This property setter method calls configureView so that the URL can be regenerated (and the new page loaded) immediately, and dismisses the language selection popover if it's visible. Add this method to the bottom of the file, just above the @end:

```
- (void)setLanguageString:(NSString *)newString {
    if (![newString isEqualToString:self.languageString]) {
        _languageString = [newString copy];
        [self configureView];
    }
    if (self.languagePopoverController != nil) {
        [self.languagePopoverController dismissPopoverAnimated:YES];
        self.languagePopoverController = nil;
    }
}
```

Now, let's define what will happen when the user taps the **Choose Language** button. Simply put, we create a LanguageListController, wrap it in a UIPopoverController, and display it. Place this method after the viewDidLoad method:

```
- (void)toggleLanguagePopover {
    if (self.languagePopoverController == nil) {
        LanguageListController *languageListController =
            [[LanguageListController alloc] init];
        languageListController.detailViewController = self;
        UIPopoverController *poc =
            [[UIPopoverController alloc]
                initWithContentViewController:languageListController];
        [poc presentPopoverFromBarButtonItem:self.languageButton
                    permittedArrowDirections:UIPopoverArrowDirectionAny
                                    animated:YES];
        self.languagePopoverController = poc;
    } else {
        [self.languagePopoverController dismissPopoverAnimated:YES];
        self.languagePopoverController = nil;
    }
}
```

Finally, we need to implement one more method to handle the situation where the user taps to open our Languages popover, and then taps somewhere outside the popover to make it go away. In that case, our toggleLanguagePopover method isn't called. However, we can implement a method declared in the UIPopoverControllerDelegate protocol to be notified when that happens, and then remove the language Popovers:

```
- (void)popoverControllerDidDismissPopovers:
    (UIPopoverController *)popoverController  {
    if (popoverController == self.languagePopoverController) {
        self.languagePopoverController = nil;
    }
}
```

And that's all! You should now be able to run the app in all its glory, switching willy-nilly between presidents and languages. Switching from one language to another should always leave the chosen president intact. Likewise, switching from one president to another should leave the language intact—but actually, it doesn't. Try this: choose a president, change the language to (say) Spanish, and then choose another president. Unfortunately, the language is no longer Spanish.

Why did this happen? If you go back to "How the Master-Detail Template Application Works" section, you'll discover the problem—the Show Detail segue creates a new instance of the detail view controller every time it's performed. That means that the language setting, which is stored as a property of the detail view controller, is going to be lost each time a new president is selected. To fix it, we need to add a few lines of code in the master view controller. Open *MasterViewController.m* and make the following changes to the prepareForSegue:sender: method:

```
- (void)prepareForSegue:(UIStoryboardSegue *)segue sender:(id)sender {
    if ([[segue identifier] isEqualToString:@"showDetail"]) {
        NSIndexPath *indexPath = [self.tableView indexPathForSelectedRow];

        DetailViewController *controller =
                (DetailViewController *)[[segue destinationViewController] topViewController];
        controller.languageString = self.detailViewController.languageString;
        self.detailViewController = controller;

        NSDictionary *president = self.presidents[indexPath.row];
        controller.detailItem = president;

        controller.navigationItem.leftBarButtonItem = self.splitViewController.
        displayModeButtonItem;
        controller.navigationItem.leftItemsSupplementBackButton = YES;
    }
}
```

Recall that we saved a reference to the detail view controller in the detailViewController property in the master view controller's viewDidLoad method. Here, when we are about to perform the segue, we use that reference to get the value of the languageString property from the old instance of the detail view controller and copy it to the new instance, which has already replaced the old one in the split view controller's view hierarchy. Then, we update the detailViewController property of the new instance. That's all we need to do. Now run the application again. You'll find that you can switch between presidents without losing your chosen language.

Split Views on the iPhone

As of iOS 8, the split view controller is available on the iPhone as well as the iPad. However, the smaller screen size of the iPhone means that the split view controller works slightly differently than it does on the iPad. Select the iPhone 5s simulator and run the Presidents app in portrait mode. You'll see the difference immediately (see Figure 11-13): the list of presidents in the master view controller is visible, but the detail view controller's view is missing. Rotate the device to landscape, and you'll see that you can still see only the master view controller.

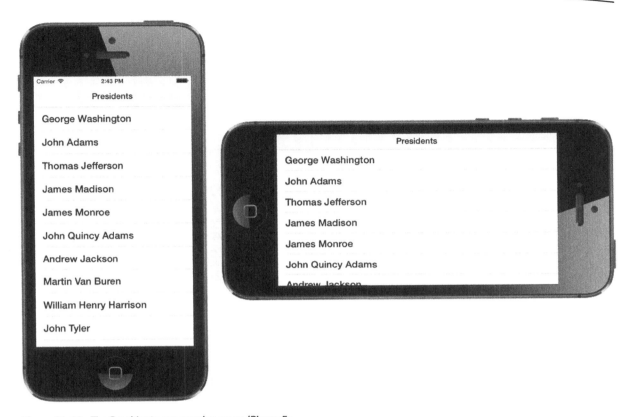

Figure 11-13. *The Presidents app running on an iPhone 5s*

To activate the detail view controller, just select a president. The detail view controller's view slides in from the right and the **Presidents** button appears at the top of the navigation bar, as shown in Figure 11-14. Notice also that the **Choose Language** button is missing, because we don't create one when running on an iPhone. If you press the **Back** button, the detail view controller's view slides out to the right and the list of presidents reappears.

Figure 11-14. The Presidents app's detail view controller on iPhone

It's important to note that we haven't had to change any code to make the application work on the iPhone. The split view controller sets itself up differently in the constrained screen space of the iPhone, initially showing only the master view controller. In this mode, the split view controller is said to be **collapsed**. In collapsed mode, the Set Detail segue that we used to link the master view controller to the detail view controller behaves differently—instead of displaying the detail view controller in its own dedicated space on the screen, the split view pushes it onto the view controller stack of the master view controller's UINavigationController. When you press the **Presidents** button to redisplay the presidents list, the detail view controller is popped off the stack, exposing the table view controller that was underneath it.

Split Views on the iPhone 6 Plus

The behavior you have just seen applies to all iPhones, with the exception of the iPhone 6 Plus. In landscape mode, the iPhone 6 Plus has a large enough screen to permit the split view to show both view controllers side by side, as it does on the iPad, but only when in landscape mode. Run the application on the iPhone 6 Plus simulator. You'll initially see just the master view controller, as usual. Now rotate to landscape mode, and you'll see both view controllers (Figure 11-15).

Figure 11-15. The President's app in landscape mode on the iPhone 6 Plus

This is similar to, but not exactly the same as, on the iPad. If you compare Figure 11-15 with Figure 11-3, you'll see that the iPhone version has an extra, double-headed button at the top left of the detail view controller's navigation bar. This is actually the **Presidents** button (the one obtained from the `displayModeButtonItem` property of the `UISplitViewController` in the application delegate), drawn differently to reflect its modified function. If you press this button, the master view controller is removed, leaving the detail view controller with the whole screen, and the button reverts to its normal appearance. Press the button again to bring the master view controller back into view.

The difference in behavior of the iPhone 6 Plus is another feature that you get for free from `UISplitViewController`. There are various ways to customize the behavior of the split view, usually by implementing various methods of the `UISplitViewDelegate` protocol. We're not going to say anything more about that here, except to point out one detail that you'll observe if you restart the application and turn the simulator to portrait mode. At this point, as always, you'll see the master view controller. If you switch between portrait and landscape modes, you'll continue to see the same controller. Now rotate to landscape mode and select a president, and then rotate back to portrait mode. This time, the detail view controller remains visible—the split view controller did not switch back to the master view controller. This behavior is the result of a `UISplitViewDelegate` method that's implemented in *AppDelegate.m* and is the reason why the application delegate is registered as the split view's delegate when the application launches. Here's how that method is implemented:

```
- (BOOL)splitViewController:(UISplitViewController *)splitViewController
            collapseSecondaryViewController:(UIViewController *)secondaryViewController
            ontoPrimaryViewController:(UIViewController *)primaryViewController {
    if ([secondaryViewController isKindOfClass:[UINavigationController class]]
            && [[(UINavigationController *)secondaryViewController topViewController]
                            isKindOfClass:[DetailViewController class]]
            && ([(DetailViewController *)
                        [(UINavigationController *)secondaryViewController topViewController]
                            detailItem] == nil)) {
        // Return YES to indicate that we have handled the collapse by doing nothing;
            the secondary controller will be discarded.
        return YES;
    } else {
        return NO;
    }
}
```

This method is called when the split view controller is switching between expanded mode (when both view controllers are active) and collapsed mode (when there is only one). If it returns YES, the detail view controller will be removed; but if it returns NO, the detail view controller will stay in view. The code that the Xcode template produces ensures that the detail view controller is not removed if its detailItem property is not nil—that is, if it is currently displaying something. Interestingly, if you stub out this method so that it always returns NO, you'll find that the split view controller opens with the detail view controller visible instead of the master view controller.

Getting the iPhone 6 Plus Behavior on All iPhones

It's possible to get the split view to behave as it does on the iPhone 6 Plus on all iPhones. To see how this is possible, you have to understand why the split view shows both view controllers in landscape mode on the iPhone 6 Plus but not on any other iPhone models. They key to this is a concept that was introduced back in Chapter 5—size classes. If you look at Figure 5-20, you'll see that the horizontal size class for all iPhones in all orientations is Compact, apart from the iPhone 6 Plus, which has Regular size class in landscape mode. The split view controller operates in collapsed mode in a horizontally compact environment and in expanded mode otherwise. That's why you can see both view controllers on the iPhone 6 Plus when it's in landscape orientation. As it turns out, you can use this fact to get the same behavior on all iPhones. All you have to do is convince the split view controller that its horizontal size class is Regular.

Size class information is propagated to a view controller from its parent view controller, if it has one, or from its window if it's the top-level view controller. The size class information is delivered as part of a **trait collection**, represented by the UITraitCollection class, when the view controller's view is displayed and when the device is rotated, if that would cause either its horizontal or vertical size class to change. All view controllers conform to the `UITraitEnvironment` protocol, which means that they have a `traitCollection` property that holds the current set of traits and they implement the following method, which is called after the value of the `traitCollection` property has been changed:

```
- (void)traitCollectionDidChange:(UITraitCollection *)previousTraitCollection
```

To make the split view controller believe that it has a Regular horizontal size class, we need to change the trait collection that's passed to it by its parent view controller. That brings up a problem: in the storyboard that's created by the Master-Detail application template (see Figure 11-6), the split view controller is the root view controller of its window, so it doesn't have a parent view controller. To change its trait collection, we'll first have to give it a parent view controller, so let's do that.

Select *Main.storyboard*, open the Object Library, and drag a `UINavigationController` onto the storyboard. We're going to make this controller the parent of the split view controller. It already has a `UITableViewController` child, which we don't need, so select it (it's the one labeled **Root View Controller** in the Document Outline) and delete it. Next, Control-drag from the navigation controller to the split view controller, and then release the mouse. In the pop-up, select **Root View Controller** from the **Relationship Segue** section to make the navigation controller the parent of the `UISplitViewController`. There are two final steps to complete. Select the navigation controller and open the Attributes Inspector. In the **Navigation Controller** section, uncheck **Shows Navigation Bar** (since we don't need to be able to navigate) and in the **View Controller** section, check **Is Initial View Controller** to make the navigation controller the root view controller of the application window.

> **Note**   If you are wondering why we used a `UINavigationController` as the root view controller instead of a plain `UIViewController`, the reason is that Interface Builder won't let you drag to create a controller connection from an ordinary `UIViewController`, because there is no `rootViewController` property. You could create the connection in code (as we did in Chapter 6), but it's easier to just use a `UINavigationController` and switch off the navigation bar.

At this point, your storyboard should look something like Figure 11-16.

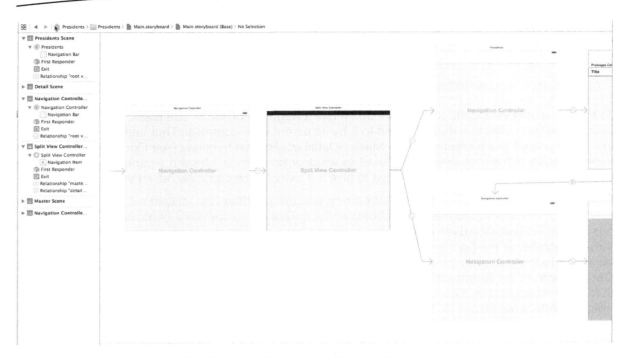

Figure 11-16. The storyboard of the Presidents app with a new root view controller

Now that we've given the split view a parent view controller, we need to override its traitCollectionDidChange: method. To do that, we need to substitute our own UINavigationController subclass for the one in the storyboard. Right-click the *Presidents* folder in the Project Navigator and select **New File. . .**, and then choose **Cocoa Touch Class** from the **iOS Source** section of the new file chooser and click **Next**. Give the new class the name RootViewController, make it a subclass of UINavigationController, and create it. Select the navigation controller in *Main.storyboard*, open the Identity Inspector, and set its **Class** to RootViewController.

So now our navigation controller subclass is the window's root view controller and we are almost ready to override its traitCollectionDidChange: method, but we have one more thing to fix before we do that. The template-generated code in application:didFinishLaunchingWithOptions: in *AppDelegate.m* assumes that the split view controller is the root view controller. Since that's no longer the case, we have to make a small change. Open *AppDelegate.m* and make the following changes shown in bold:

```
- (BOOL)application:(UIApplication *)application
                        didFinishLaunchingWithOptions:(NSDictionary *)launchOptions {
    // Override point for customization after application launch.
    UISplitViewController *splitViewController =
                            (UISplitViewController *)self.window.rootViewController;
    UINavigationController *rootViewController =
                            (UINavigationController *)self.window.rootViewController;
```

```
UISplitViewController *splitViewController =
                    (UISplitViewController *)rootViewController.viewControllers[0];
UINavigationController *navigationController = [splitViewController.viewControllers lastObject];
navigationController.topViewController.navigationItem.leftBarButtonItem =
                    splitViewController.displayModeButtonItem;
splitViewController.delegate = self;
return YES;
}
```

Now let's do what we set out to do. Open *RootViewController.m* in the editor and add the following code to it:

```
- (void)traitCollectionDidChange:(UITraitCollection *)previousTraitCollection {
    UIViewController *spltVC = self.viewControllers[0];
    UITraitCollection *newTraits = self.traitCollection;
    if (newTraits.horizontalSizeClass == UIUserInterfaceSizeClassCompact
            && newTraits.verticalSizeClass == UIUserInterfaceSizeClassCompact) {
        UITraitCollection *childTraits = [UITraitCollection
                    traitCollectionWithHorizontalSizeClass:UIUserInterfaceSizeClassRegular];
        [self setOverrideTraitCollection:childTraits forChildViewController:spltVC];
    } else {
        [self setOverrideTraitCollection:nil forChildViewController:spltVC];
    }
    [super traitCollectionDidChange:previousTraitCollection];
}
```

The first thing we do is get the newly installed set of traits from the root view controller's `traitCollection` property. If both the horizontal and vertical size classes are Compact, then we must be running on an iPhone that's been rotated to landscape. This is the case in which we need to change the horizontal size class that the split view will see from Compact to Regular. We do that by creating a trait for the regular size class using a class method of `UITraitCollection`:

```
UITraitCollection *childTraits = [UITraitCollection
        traitCollectionWithHorizontalSizeClass:UIUserInterfaceSizeClassRegular];
```

Next, we tell the root view controller to override the traits of its split view controller child with this new trait:

```
[self setOverrideTraitCollection:childTraits forChildViewController:spltVC];
```

On the other hand, if we have any other combination of size classes, we don't need to change them, so we install a `nil` override:

```
[self setOverrideTraitCollection:nil forChildViewController:spltVC];
```

Now build and run the application, and then run it on any iPhone simulator. Rotate to landscape, and you'll see both view controllers, just like you would on the iPhone 6 Plus.

Incidentally, you can even force the split view controller to show both view controllers in portrait mode by modifying the `traitCollectionDidChange:` method so that it always installs an override trait. It's worth trying that just to see that it works, but the screen is too narrow for this to be useful in most cases.

Customizing the Split View

There are a couple of split view controller customizations available that are worth experimenting with. These work on any device. First, you can control the width of the area allocated to the master view controller when both view controllers are visible. To do this, you need to set the split view controller's `preferredPrimaryColumnWidthFraction` and `maximumPrimaryColumnWidth` properties. The former sets the width of the master view controller as a fraction of the total space available and requires a value between 0 and 1. The latter acts as an upper bound on its width, so you need to set this property if you need the master view controller to be wider than the default value calculated by the split view controller.

To see how this works, make the following changes to `application:didFinishLaunchingWithOptions:` in *AppDelegate.m*:

```objc
- (BOOL)application:(UIApplication *)application
              didFinishLaunchingWithOptions:(NSDictionary *)launchOptions {
    // Override point for customization after application launch.
    UINavigationController *rootViewController =
                  (UINavigationController *)self.window.rootViewController;
    UISplitViewController *splitViewController =
                  (UISplitViewController *)rootViewController.viewControllers[0];
    UINavigationController *navigationController =
                  [splitViewController.viewControllers lastObject];
    navigationController.topViewController.navigationItem.leftBarButtonItem =
                  splitViewController.displayModeButtonItem;
    splitViewController.delegate = self;

    splitViewController.preferredPrimaryColumnWidthFraction = 0.5;
    splitViewController.maximumPrimaryColumnWidth = 600;

    return YES;
}
```

Run the application again on any simulator and rotate to landscape mode. You'll see that the master view controller now occupies half of the screen (see Figure 11-17), because we set `preferredPrimaryColumnWidthFraction` to 0.5 and increased `maximumPrimaryColumnWidth` to a value that's large enough that it doesn't limit the master view controller's width on any current device.

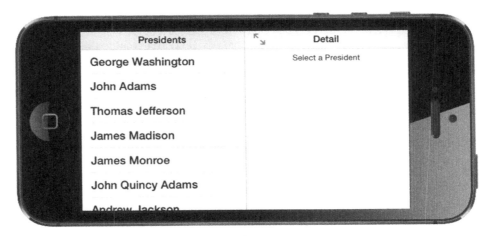

Figure 11-17. Increasing the width of the master view controller in a split view

The second customization controls the way in which the master view controller is managed. By default, the split view controller determines when this controller is visible and how it appears and disappears. For example, on the iPad in portrait mode, the master view controller is initially invisible and slides in from the left of the screen; whereas in landscape mode, it's initially visible and cannot be hidden. This behavior is controlled by the split view controller's preferredDisplayMode property. By default, this is set to UISplitViewControllerDisplayModeAutomatic, but there are three other choices available:

- UISplitViewControllerDisplayModePrimaryOverlay: Places the master view controller on the left, overlaying the detail view controller. When the master view controller is dismissed, it slides away to the left.

- UISplitViewControllerDisplayModePrimaryHidden: The same as UISplitViewControllerDisplayModePrimaryOverlay, except that the master view controller is initially hidden.

- UISplitViewControllerDisplayModeAllVisible: Makes both view controllers initially visible on the screen.

The actual behavior depends on the type of device. For example, in horizontal Compact mode, this property has no effect, since both view controllers are never on the screen at the same time.

You can try out each of these modes by setting the preferredDisplayMode property in the application:didFinishLaunchingWithOptions: method. For example:

```
- (BOOL)application:(UIApplication *)application
            didFinishLaunchingWithOptions:(NSDictionary *)launchOptions {
    // Override point for customization after application launch.
    UINavigationController *rootViewController =
                (UINavigationController *)self.window.rootViewController;
    UISplitViewController *splitViewController =
                (UISplitViewController *)rootViewController.viewControllers[0];
```

```
UINavigationController *navigationController =
                [splitViewController.viewControllers lastObject];
navigationController.topViewController.navigationItem.leftBarButtonItem =
                splitViewController.displayModeButtonItem;
splitViewController.delegate = self;

splitViewController.preferredPrimaryColumnWidthFraction = 0.5;
splitViewController.maximumPrimaryColumnWidth = 600;

splitViewController.preferredDisplayMode = UISplitViewControllerDisplayModePrimaryOverlay;

return YES;
}
```

Time to Wrap Up and Split

In this chapter, you learned about the split view controller and its role in the creation of Master-Detail applications. You also saw that a complex application with several interconnected view controllers can be configured entirely within Interface Builder. Although split views are now available on all devices, they are probably still most useful in the larger screen space of the iPhone 6 Plus and the iPad. If you want to dig even further into the particulars of iPad development, you may want to take a look at *Beginning iPad Development for iPhone Developers* by David Mark, Jack Nutting, and Dave Wooldridge (Apress, 2010).

Next up, it's time to visit application settings and user defaults.

Chapter 12

Application Settings and User Defaults

All but the simplest computer programs today have a preferences window where the user can set application-specific options. On Mac OS X, the **Preferences…** menu item is usually found in the application menu. Selecting it brings up a window where the user can enter and change various options. The iPhone and other iOS devices have a dedicated application called Settings, which you no doubt have played with any number of times. In this chapter, we'll show you how to add settings for your application to the Settings application and how to access those settings from within your application.

Getting to Know Your Settings Bundle

The Settings application lets the user enter and change preferences for any application that has a settings bundle. A **settings bundle** is a group of files built in to an application that tells the Settings application which preferences the application wishes to collect from the user.

Pick up your iOS device and locate your Settings icon. Touch the icon to launch the Settings app. Ours is shown in Figure 12-1.

Figure 12-1. *The Settings application*

The Settings application acts as a common user interface for the iOS User Defaults mechanism. User Defaults is the part of the system that stores and retrieves preferences.

In an iOS application, User Defaults is implemented by the NSUserDefaults class. If you've done Cocoa programming on the Mac, you're probably already familiar with NSUserDefaults because it is the same class that is used to store and read preferences on the Mac. You will have your applications use NSUserDefaults to read and store preference data using pairs of keys and values, just as you would access keyed data from an NSDictionary. The difference is that NSUserDefaults data is persisted to the file system rather than stored in an object instance in memory.

In this chapter, we're going to create an application, add and configure a settings bundle, and then access and edit those preferences from the Settings application and from within our own application.

One nice thing about the Settings application is that it provides a solution, so you don't need to design your own user interface for your preferences. You create a property list describing your application's available settings, and the Settings application creates the interface for you.

Immersive applications, such as games, generally should provide their own preferences view so that the user doesn't need to quit to make a change. Even utility and productivity applications might, at times, have preferences that a user should be able to change without leaving the application. We'll also show you to how to collect preferences from the user directly in your application and store those in iOS's User Defaults.

One additional complication is that the user can actually switch to the Settings application, change a preference, and then switch back to your still-running application. We'll show you how to handle that situation at the end of this chapter.

The Bridge Control Application

In this chapter, we're going to build a simple application that keeps track of some aspects of managing the bridge of a starship, which I'm sure you'll agree is a useful enterprise. Our first step will be to create a settings bundle so that, when the user launches the Settings application, there will be an entry for our application, Bridge Control (see Figure 12-2).

Figure 12-2. The Settings application, which shows an entry for our Bridge Control application in the simulator

If the user selects our application, Settings will drill down into a view that shows the preferences relevant to our application. As you can see in Figure 12-3, the Settings application uses text fields, secure text fields, switches, and sliders to coax values out of our intrepid user.

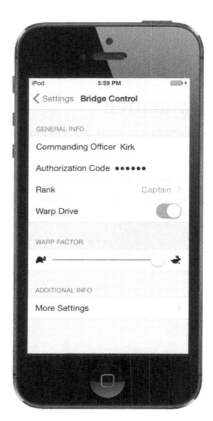

Figure 12-3. *Our application's primary settings view*

Also notice the two items in the view that have disclosure indicators. The first one, *Rank*, takes the user to another table view that displays the options available for that item. From that table view, the user can select a single value (see Figure 12-4).

Figure 12-4. *Selecting a single preference item from a list*

The More Settings disclosure indicator allows the user to drill down to another set of preferences (see Figure 12-5). This child view can have the same kinds of controls as the main settings view and can even have its own child views. You may have noticed that the Settings application uses a navigation controller, which it needs because it supports the construction of hierarchical preference views.

Figure 12-5. A child settings view for our application

When users launch our application, they will be presented with a list of the preferences gathered in the Settings application (see Figure 12-6).

Figure 12-6. Our application's main view

To show how to update preferences from within our application, we also provide a second view where they can change additional preferences directly in the application (see Figure 12-7).

Figure 12-7. Setting some preferences directly in our application

Let's get started building Bridge Control, shall we?

Creating the Project

In Xcode, press ⇧⌘N or select **File ➤ New ➤ Project…**. When the new project assistant comes up, select **Application** from under the iOS heading in the left pane, click the **Tabbed Application** icon, and then click **Next**. On the next screen, name your project *Bridge Control*. Set Devices to *Universal*, and then click the **Next** button. Finally, choose a location for your project and click **Create**.

The Bridge Control application is based on the UITabBarController class that we used in Chapter 7. The template creates two tabs, which is all we'll need. Each tab requires an icon. You'll find these in the *12 – Images* folder in the example source code archive. In Xcode, select *Images.xcassets*, and then drag the *singleicon.imageset* and *doubleicon.imageset* folders from *12 – Images* into the editing area.

Next, we'll assign the icons to their tab bar items. Select *Main.storyboard* and you'll see the tab bar controller and the two child controllers for its tabs, one labeled *First View*, the other *Second View*. Select the first child controller, and then click its tab bar item, which currently shows a round circle and the title *First*. In the Bar Item section of the Attributes Inspector, change the Title to *Main* and the Image to *singleicon*, as shown in Figure 12-8. Now select the tab bar item for the second child controller and change the title from *Second* to *Settings* and the image from *second* to *doubleicon*. Finally, select *Images.xcassets* again and delete the `first` and `second` image sets that the template created—we don't need them anymore. That's enough work on the application itself for now—before doing anything more, let's create its settings bundle.

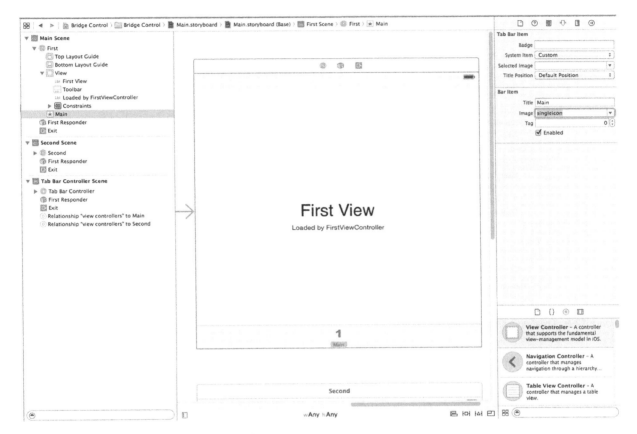

Figure 12-8. Setting the icon for the first tab bar item

Working with the Settings Bundle

The Settings application uses the contents of each application's settings bundle to construct a settings view for that application. If an application has no settings bundle, then the Settings app doesn't show anything for it. Each settings bundle must contain a property list called *Root.plist* that defines the root-level preferences view. This property list must follow a very precise format, which we'll talk about when we set up the property list for our app's settings bundle.

When the Settings application starts up, it checks each application for a settings bundle and adds a settings group for each application that includes a settings bundle. If we want our preferences to include any subviews, we need to add property lists to the bundle and add an entry to *Root.plist* for each child view. You'll see exactly how to do that in this chapter.

Adding a Settings Bundle to Our Project

In the Project Navigator, click the *Bridge Control* folder, and then select **File ➤ New ➤ File…** or press ⌘N. In the left pane, select **Resource** under the iOS heading, and then select the **Settings Bundle** icon (see Figure 12-9). Click the **Next** button, leave the default name of *Settings.bundle*, and click **Create**.

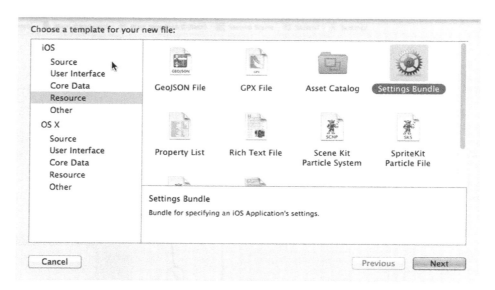

Figure 12-9. Creating a settings bundle in Xcode

You should now see a new item in the project window called *Settings.bundle*. Expand the *Settings. bundle* item, and you should see two subitems: a folder named *en.lproj* that contains a file named *Root.strings*, and another named *Root.plist*. We'll discuss *en.lproj* in Chapter 22 when we talk about localizing your application into other languages. Here, we'll concentrate on *Root.plist*.

Setting Up the Property List

Select *Root.plist* and take a look at the editor pane. You're looking at Xcode's property list editor (see Figure 12-10).

Key	Type	Value
▼ iPhone Settings Schema	Dictionary	(2 items)
▶ Preference Items	Array	(4 items)
Strings Filename	String	Root

Figure 12-10. Root.plist in the property list editor pane. If your editing pane looks slightly different, don't panic. Simply Control-click in the editing pane and select Show Raw Keys/Values from the contextual menu that appears

Notice the organization of the items in the property list. Property lists are essentially dictionaries, storing item types and values and using a key to retrieve them, just as an NSDictionary does.

Several different types of nodes can be put into a property list. The *Boolean*, *Data*, *Date*, *Number*, and *String* node types are meant to hold individual pieces of data, but you also have a couple of ways to deal with whole collections of nodes, as well. In addition to *Dictionary* node types, which allow you to store other dictionaries, there are *Array* nodes, which store an ordered list of other nodes similar to an NSArray. The Dictionary and Array types are the only property list node types that can contain other nodes.

> **Note**   Although you can use most kinds of objects as keys in an NSDictionary, keys in property list dictionary nodes must be strings. However, you are free to use any node type for the values.

When creating a settings property list, you need to follow a very specific format. Fortunately, *Root.plist*, the property list that came with the settings bundle you just added to your project, follows this format exactly. Let's take a look.

In the *Root.plist* editor pane, names of keys can either be displayed in their true, "raw" form or in a slightly more human-readable form. We're big fans of seeing things as they truly are whenever possible, so right-click anywhere in the editor and make sure the **Show Raw Keys/Values** option in the contextual menu is checked (see Figure 12-11). The rest of our discussion here uses the real names for all the keys we're going to talk about, so this step is important.

Figure 12-11. Control-click anywhere in the property list editing pane and make sure the Show Raw Keys/Values item is checked. This will ensure that real names are used in the property list editor, which makes your editing experience more precise

> **Caution**   At the time of writing, leaving the property list, either by editing a different file or by quitting Xcode, resets the **Show Raw Keys/Values** item to be unchecked. If your text suddenly looks a little different, take another look at that menu item and make sure it is checked.

One of the items in the dictionary is *StringsTable*. A strings table is used in translating your application into another language. We'll discuss the translation of strings in Chapter 22 when we get into localization. We won't be using it in this chapter, but feel free to leave it in your project since it won't do any harm.

In addition to *StringsTable*, the property list contains a node named *PreferenceSpecifiers*, which is an array. This array node is designed to hold a set of dictionary nodes, where each node represents either a single preference item that the user can modify or a single child view that the user can drill down into.

Click the disclosure triangle to the left of *PreferenceSpecifiers* to expand that node. You'll notice that Xcode's template kindly gave us four child nodes (see Figure 12-12). Those nodes aren't likely to reflect our actual preferences, so delete *Item 1*, *Item 2*, and *Item 3* (select each one and press the **Delete** key, one after another), leaving just *Item 0* in place.

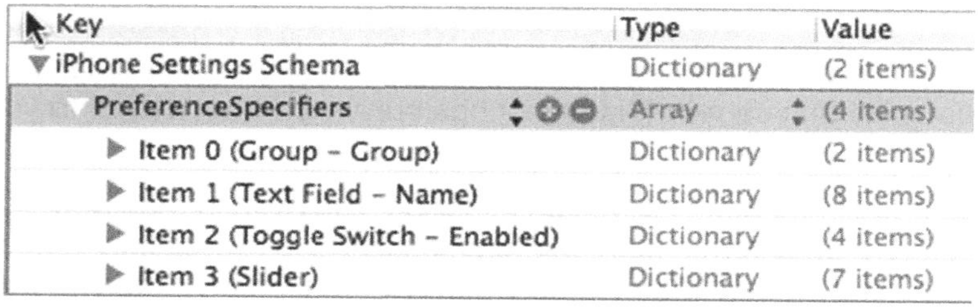

Key	Type	Value
▼ iPhone Settings Schema	Dictionary	(2 items)
▼ PreferenceSpecifiers	Array	(4 items)
▶ Item 0 (Group – Group)	Dictionary	(2 items)
▶ Item 1 (Text Field – Name)	Dictionary	(8 items)
▶ Item 2 (Toggle Switch – Enabled)	Dictionary	(4 items)
▶ Item 3 (Slider)	Dictionary	(7 items)

Figure 12-12. Root.plist in the editor pane, this time with PreferenceSpecifiers expanded

Note   To select an item in the property list, it is best to click one side or the other of the Key column to avoid bringing up the Key column's drop-down menu.

Single-click **Item 0** but don't expand it. Xcode's property list editor lets you add rows simply by pressing the **Return** key. The current selection state—including which row is selected and whether it's expanded—determines where the new row will be inserted. When an unexpanded array or dictionary is selected, pressing **Return** adds a sibling node after the selected row. In other words, it will add another node at the same level as the current selection. If you were to press **Return** (but don't do that now), you would get a new row called *Item 1* immediately after Item 0. Figure 12-13 shows an example of hitting **Return** to create a new row. Notice the drop-down menu that allows you to specify the kind of preference specifier this item represents—more on this in a bit.

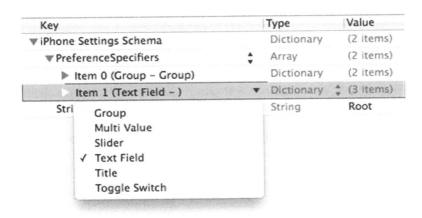

Figure 12-13. We selected Item 0 and hit Return to create a new sibling row. Note the drop-down menu that appears, allowing us to specify the kind of preference specifier this item represents

Now expand Item 0 and see what it contains (see Figure 12-14). The editor is now ready to add child nodes to the selected item. If you were to press **Return** at this point (again, don't actually press it now), you would get a new first child row inside Item 0.

Key		Type	Value
▼ iPhone Settings Schema		Dictionary	(2 items)
▼ PreferenceSpecifiers	↕	Array	(1 item)
▽ Item 0 (Group – Group)	▼	Dictionary ↕	(2 items)
Title	↕	String	Group
Type	↕	String	PSGroupSpecifier

Figure 12-14. When you expand Item 0, you'll find a row with a key of Type and a second row with a key of Title. This represents a group with a title of Group

One of the items inside Item 0 has a key of *Type*. Every property list node in the *PreferenceSpecifiers* array must have an entry with this key. The *Type* key is typically the second entry, but order doesn't matter in a dictionary, so the *Type* key doesn't need to be second. The *Type* key tells the Settings application what type of data is associated with this item.

In Item 0, the *Type* item has a value of *PSGroupSpecifier*. This indicates that the item represents the start of a new group. Each item that follows will be part of this group—until the next item with a Type of *PSGroupSpecifier*.

If you look back at Figure 12-3, you'll see that the Settings application presents the application settings in a grouped table. Item 0 in the *PreferenceSpecifiers* array in a settings bundle property list should always be a *PSGroupSpecifier*, so that the settings start in a new group. This is important because you need at least one group in every Settings table.

The only other entry in Item 0 has a key of *Title*, and this is used to set an optional header just above the group that is being started.

Now take a closer look at the Item 0 row itself, and you'll see that it's actually shown as *Item 0 (Group – Group)*. The values in parentheses represent the value of the *Type* item (the first *Group*) and the *Title* item (the second *Group*). This is a nice shortcut that Xcode gives you so that you can visually scan the contents of a settings bundle.

As shown back in Figure 12-3, we called our first group *General Info*. Double-click the value next to Title, and change it from *Group* to *General Info* (see Figure 12-15). When you enter the new title, you may notice a slight change to Item 0. It's now shown as *Item 0 (Group – General Info)* to reflect the new title. In the Settings application, the title is shown in uppercase, so the user will actually see GENERAL INFO instead. You can see this in Figure 12-3.

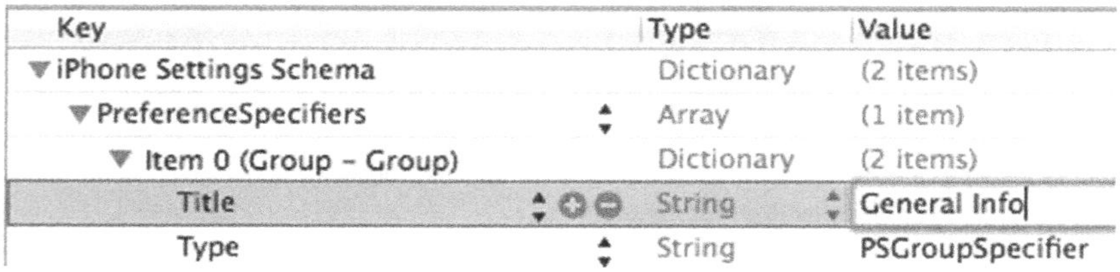

Key		Type	Value
▼ iPhone Settings Schema		Dictionary	(2 items)
▼ PreferenceSpecifiers	⬍	Array	(1 item)
▼ Item 0 (Group – Group)		Dictionary	(2 items)
Title	⬍ ⊕ ⊖	String ⬍	General Info|
Type	⬍	String	PSGroupSpecifier

Figure 12-15. We changed the title of the Item 0 group from Group to General Info

Adding a Text Field Setting

We now need to add a second item in this array, which will represent the first actual preference field. We're going to start with a simple text field.

If you single-click the **PreferenceSpecifiers** row in the editor pane (don't do this, just keep reading) and press **Return** to add a child, the new row will be inserted at the beginning of the list, which is not what we want. We want to add a row at the end of the array.

To add the row, click the disclosure triangle to the left of Item 0 to close it, and then select **Item 0** and press **Return**. This gives you a new sibling row after the current row (see Figure 12-16). As usual, when the item is added, a drop-down menu appears, showing the default value of *Text Field*.

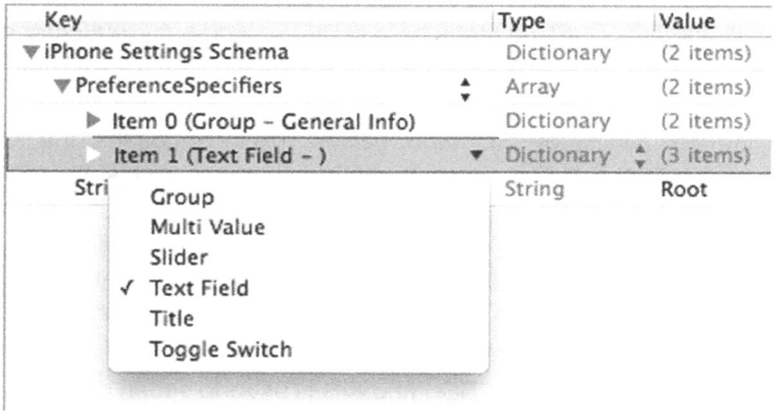

Key		Type	Value
▼ iPhone Settings Schema		Dictionary	(2 items)
▼ PreferenceSpecifiers	⬍	Array	(2 items)
▶ Item 0 (Group – General Info)		Dictionary	(2 items)
▶ Item 1 (Text Field –)	▼	Dictionary ⬍	(3 items)
Stri Group		String	Root
Multi Value			
Slider			
✓ Text Field			
Title			
Toggle Switch			

Figure 12-16. Adding a new sibling row to Item 0

Click somewhere outside the drop-down menu to make it go away, and then click the disclosure triangle next to Item 1 to expand it. You'll see that it contains a Type row set to *PSTextFieldSpecifier*. This is the *Type* value used to tell the Settings application that we want the user to edit this setting in a text field. It also contains two empty rows for Title and Key (see Figure 12-17).

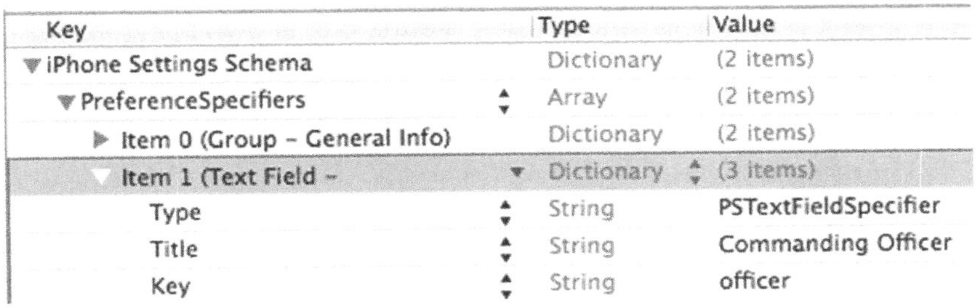

Key		Type		Value
▼ iPhone Settings Schema		Dictionary		(2 items)
▼ PreferenceSpecifiers	↕	Array		(2 items)
▶ Item 0 (Group – General Info)		Dictionary		(2 items)
Item 1 (Text Field –	▼	Dictionary	↕	(3 items)
Type	↕	String		PSTextFieldSpecifier
Title	↕	String		Commanding Officer
Key	↕	String		officer

Figure 12-17. Our text field item, expanded to show the type, title, and key

Select the **Title** row, and then double-click in the whitespace of the Value column. Type in **Commanding Officer** to set the Title value. This is the text that will appear in the Settings app.

Now do the same for the Key row (no, that's not a misprint, you're really looking at a key called *Key*). For a value, type in **officer** (note the lowercase first letter). Remember that user defaults work like an NSDictionary. This entry tells the Settings application which key to use when it stores the value entered in this text field.

Recall what we said about NSUserDefaults? It lets you store values using a key, similar to an NSDictionary. Well, the Settings application will do the same thing for each of the preferences it saves on your behalf. If you give it a key value of *foo*, then, later in your application, you can request the value for *foo*, and it will give you the value the user entered for that preference. We will use this same key value later to retrieve this setting from the user defaults in our application.

> **Note** Our Title has a value of *Commanding Officer* and our Key has a value of *officer*. This uppercase/lowercase difference will happen frequently, and here we're even compounding the difference by using two words for the displayed title, and a single word for the key. The *Title* is what appears on the screen; so the capital C and O, and putting a space between the words, all makes sense. The *Key* is a text string we'll use to retrieve preferences from the user defaults, so all lowercase makes sense there. Could we use all lowercase for *Title*? You bet. Could we use all capitals for *Key*? Sure! As long as you capitalize it the same way when you save and when you retrieve, it doesn't matter which convention you use for your preference keys.

Now select the last of the three Item 1 rows (the one with a Key of *Key*) and press **Return** to add another entry to the Item 1 dictionary, giving this one a key of *AutocapitalizationType*. Note that, as soon as you start typing **AutocapitalizationType**, Xcode presents you with a list of matching choices, so you can simply pick one from the list instead of typing the whole name. After you've entered *AutocapitalizationType*, press the **Tab** key or click the small up/down arrow icon on the right of the Value column to open a list where you can select from the available options. Choose **Words**. This specifies that the text field should automatically capitalize each word that the user types in this field.

Create one last new row and give it a key of *AutocorrectionType* and a value of *No*. This will tell the Settings application not to autocorrect values entered into this text field. In any situation where you do want the text field to use autocorrection, you would set the value in this row to *Yes*. Again, Xcode presents you with a list of matching choices as you begin entering **AutocorrectionType**, and it shows you a list of valid options in a pop-up.

When you're finished, your property list should look like the one shown in Figure 12-18.

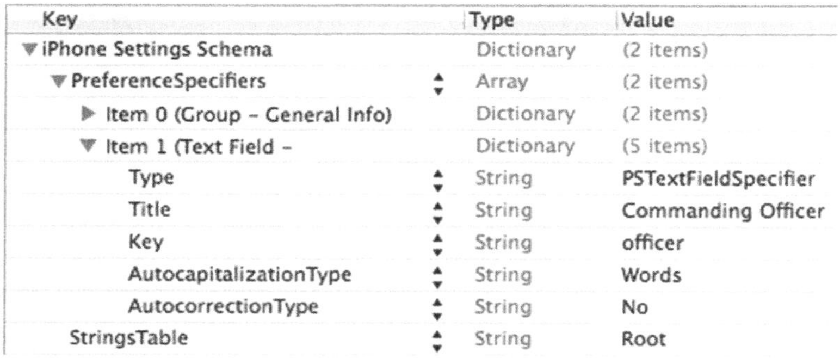

Key		Type	Value
▼ iPhone Settings Schema		Dictionary	(2 items)
▼ PreferenceSpecifiers	‡	Array	(2 items)
▶ Item 0 (Group – General Info)		Dictionary	(2 items)
▼ Item 1 (Text Field –		Dictionary	(5 items)
Type	‡	String	PSTextFieldSpecifier
Title	‡	String	Commanding Officer
Key	‡	String	officer
AutocapitalizationType	‡	String	Words
AutocorrectionType	‡	String	No
StringsTable	‡	String	Root

Figure 12-18. The finished text field specified in Root.plist

Adding an Application Icon

Before we try our new setting, let's add an application icon to the project. You've done this before.

Save *Root.plist*, the property file you just edited. Next, use the Project Navigator to select the *Images.xcassets* item, and then select the *AppIcon* item it contains. There, you'll find a set of drop targets where icons can be placed.

In the Finder, navigate first to the source code archive, and then into the *12 – Images* folder. Drag the file *SettingsIcon.png* into the iPad Settings 1x slot of the *Images.xcassets* editor in Xcode, and drag *SettingsIcon@2x.png* into the iPhone Settings 2x and iPad Settings 2x slots. While you're here, let's add icons for the application itself. Drag *AppIcon-iPhone@2x.png* onto the iPhone App slot, *AppIcon-iPad.png* onto the iPad App 1x slot, and *AppIcon-iPad@2x.png* onto the iPad App 2x slot. When you're done, the editor should look like Figure 12-19.

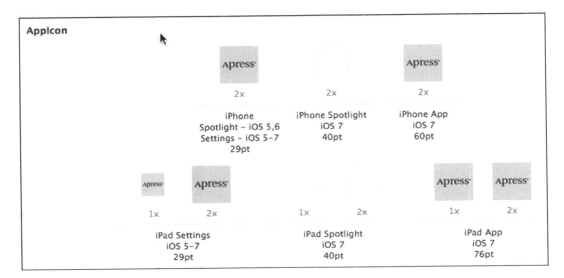

Figure 12-19. Adding the settings and app icons for our application

That's it. Now compile and run the application by selecting **Product ➤ Run**. You haven't built any sort of GUI for the app yet, so you'll just see the first tab of the tab bar controller. Press the **Home** button, and then tap the icon for the Settings application. You will find an entry for our application, which uses the icon added earlier (see Figure 12-2). Click the **Bridge Control** row, and you will be presented with a simple settings view with a single text field, as shown in Figure 12-20.

Figure 12-20. Our root view in the Settings application after adding a group and a text field

Quit the simulator and go back to Xcode. We're not finished yet, but you should now have a sense of how easy it is to add preferences to your application. Let's add the rest of the fields for our root settings view. The first one we'll add is a secure text field for the user's authorization code.

Adding a Secure Text Field Setting

Click *Root.plist* to return to your setting specifiers (don't forget to turn on **Show Raw Keys/Values**, assuming Xcode's editing area has reset this). Collapse Item 0 and Item 1, and then select **Item 1**. Press ⌘C to copy it to the clipboard, and then press ⌘V to paste it back. This will create a new Item 2 that is identical to Item 1. Expand the new item and change the Title to *Authorization Code* and the Key to *authorizationCode*. Remember that the *Title* is what's shown in an on-screen label, and the *Key* is what's used for saving the value.

Next, add one more child to the new item. Remember that the order of items does not matter, so feel free to place it directly below the *Key* item you just edited. To do this, select the **Key/authorizationCode** row, and then hit **Return**.

Give the new item a Key of *IsSecure* (note the leading uppercase I) and press **Tab**, and you'll see that Xcode automatically changes the Type to *Boolean*. Now change its Value from *NO* to *YES*, which tells the Settings application that this field needs to hide the user's input like a password field, rather than behaving like an ordinary text field. Finally, change AutocapitalizationType to *None*. Our finished Item 2 is shown in Figure 12-21.

Key	Type	Value
▼ iPhone Settings Schema	Dictionary	(2 items)
▼ PreferenceSpecifiers	Array	(3 items)
▶ Item 0 (Group – General Info)	Dictionary	(2 items)
▶ Item 1 (Text Field – Commanding Officer)	Dictionary	(5 items)
▼ Item 2 (Text Field – Authorization Code)	Dictionary	(6 items)
Type	String	PSTextFieldSpecifier
Title	String	Authorization Code
Key	String	authorizationCode
IsSecure	Boolean	YES
AutocapitalizationType	String	None
AutocorrectionType	String	No

Figure 12-21. Our finished Item 2, a text field designed to accept an authorizationCode

Adding a Multivalue Field

The next item we're going to add is a **multivalue field**. This type of field will automatically generate a row with a disclosure indicator. Clicking it will let users drill down to another table, where they can select one of several rows.

Collapse Item 2, select the row, and then press **Return** to add Item 3. Use the pop-up attached to the Key field to select **Multi Value**, and then expand Item 3 by clicking the disclosure triangle.

The expanded Item 3 already contains a few rows. One of them, the Type row, is set to *PSMultiValueSpecifier*. Look for the Title row and set its value to *Rank*. Then find the Key row and give it a value of *rank*. The next part is a little tricky, so let's talk about it before we do it.

We're going to add two more children to Item 3, but they will be *Array* type nodes, not *String* type nodes, as follows:

- One array, called *Titles*, will hold a list of the values from which the user can select.

- The other array, called *Values*, will hold a list of the values that are stored in the user defaults.

So, if the user selects the first item in the list, which corresponds to the first item in the *Titles* array, the Settings application will actually store the first value from the *Values* array. This pairing of *Titles* and *Values* lets you present user-friendly text to the user, but actually stores something else, like a number, a date, or a different string.

Both of these arrays are required. If you want them to be the same, you can create one array, copy it, paste it back in, and then change the key so that you have two arrays with the same content, but stored under different keys. We'll actually do just that.

Select **Item 3** (leave it open) and press **Return** to add a new child. You'll see that, once again, Xcode is aware of the type of file we're editing and even seems to anticipate what we want to do: the new child row already has its Key set to *Titles* and is configured to be an *Array*, which is just what we wanted! Press **Return** to stop editing the Key field, and then expand the Titles row and hit **Return** to add a child node. Repeat this five more times, so you have a total of six child nodes. All six nodes should be *String* type and should be given the following values: *Ensign*, *Lieutenant*, *Lieutenant Commander*, *Commander*, *Captain*, and *Commodore*.

Once you've created all six nodes and entered their values, collapse **Titles** and select it. Next, press ⌘**C** to copy it and press ⌘**V** to paste it back. This will create a new item with a key of *Titles - 2*. Double-click the key *Titles - 2* and change it to *Values*.

We're almost finished with our multivalue field. There's just one more required value in the dictionary, which is the default value. Multivalue fields must have one—and only one—row selected. So, we need to specify the default value to be used if none has yet been selected, and it needs to correspond to one of the items in the *Values* array (not the *Titles* array, if they are different). Xcode already added a DefaultValue row when we created this item, so all we need to do now is give it a value of *Ensign*. Go ahead and do that now. Figure 12-22 shows our finalized version of Item 3.

Key	Type	Value
▼ iPhone Settings Schema	Dictionary	(2 items)
▼ PreferenceSpecifiers	Array	(4 items)
▶ Item 0 (Group – General Info)	Dictionary	(2 items)
▶ Item 1 (Text Field – Commanding Officer)	Dictionary	(5 items)
▶ Item 2 (Text Field – Authorization Code)	Dictionary	(6 items)
▽ Item 3 (Multi Value – Rank)	Dictionary	(6 items)
▼ Titles	Array	(6 items)
Item 0	String	Ensign
Item 1	String	Lieutenant
Item 2	String	Lieutenant Commander
Item 3	String	Commander
Item 4	String	Captain
Item 5	String	Commodore
▼ Values	Array	(6 items)
Item 0	String	Ensign
Item 1	String	Lieutenant
Item 2	String	Lieutenant Commander
Item 3	String	Commander
Item 4	String	Captain
Item 5	String	Commodore
Type	String	PSMultiValueSpecifier
Title	String	Rank
Key	String	rank
DefaultValue	String	Ensign

Figure 12-22. Our finished Item 3, a multivalue field designed to let the user select from one of five possible values

Let's check our work. Save the property list, and build and run the application again. When your application starts, press the **Home** button and launch the Settings application. When you select **Bridge Control**, you should see three fields on your root-level view (see Figure 12-23). Go ahead and play with your creation, and then let's move on.

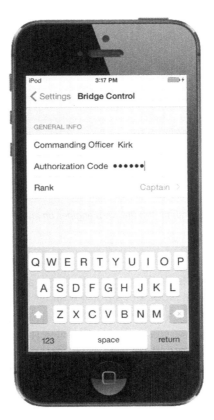

Figure 12-23. Three fields down. Not too shabby!

Adding a Toggle Switch Setting

The next item we need to get from the user is a Boolean value that indicates whether our warp engines are turned on. To capture a Boolean value in our preferences, we are going to tell the Settings application to use a UISwitch by adding another item to our *PreferenceSpecifiers* array with a type of *PSToggleSwitchSpecifier*.

Collapse Item 3 if it's currently expanded, and then single-click it to select it. Press **Return** to create Item 4. Use the drop-down menu to select **Toggle Switch**, and then click the disclosure triangle to expand Item 4. You'll see there's already a child row with a Key of *Type* and a Value of *PSToggleSwitchSpecifier*. Give the empty Title row a value of *Warp Drive* and set the value of the Key row to *warp*.

We have one more required item in this dictionary, which is the default value. Just as with the Multi Value setup, here Xcode has already created a DefaultValue row for us. Let's turn on our warp engines by default by giving the DefaultValue row a value of *YES*. Figure 12-24 shows our completed Item 4.

Key		Type	Value
▼ iPhone Settings Schema		Dictionary	(2 items)
▼ PreferenceSpecifiers	‡	Array	(5 items)
▶ Item 0 (Group – General Info)		Dictionary	(2 items)
▶ Item 1 (Text Field –		Dictionary	(5 items)
▶ Item 2 (Text Field –		Dictionary	(6 items)
▶ Item 3 (Multi Value – Rank)		Dictionary	(6 items)
▼ Item 4 (Toggle Switch – Warp	▼	Dictionary ‡	(4 items)
Type	‡	String	PSToggleSwitchSpecifier
Title	‡	String	Warp Drive
Key	‡	String	warp
DefaultValue	‡	Boolean	YES

Figure 12-24. Our finished Item 4, a toggle switch to turn the warp engines on and off. Engage!

Adding the Slider Setting

The next item we need to implement is a slider. In the Settings application, a slider can have a small image at each end, but it can't have a label. Let's put the slider in its own group with a header, so that the user will know what the slider does.

Start by collapsing Item 4. Now single-click **Item 4** and press **Return** to create a new row. Use the pop-up to turn the new item into a *Group*, and then click the item's disclosure triangle to expand it. You'll see that Type is already set to *PSGroupSpecifier*. This will tell the Settings application to start a new group at this location. Double-click the value in the row labeled *Title* and change the value to *Warp Factor*.

Collapse **Item 5** and select it, and then press **Return** to add a new sibling row. Use the pop-up to change the new item into a *Slider*, which indicates to the Settings application that it should use a UISlider to get this information from the user. Expand Item 6 and set the value of the Key row to *warpFactor*, so that the Settings application knows which key to use when storing this value.

We're going to allow the user to enter a value from 1 to 10, and we'll set the default to *warp 5*. Sliders need to have a minimum value, a maximum value, and a starting (or default) value; and all of these need to be stored as numbers, not strings, in your property list. Fortunately, Xcode has already created rows for all these values. Give the DefaultValue row a value of *5*, the MinimumValue row a value of *1*, and the MaximumValue row a value of *10*.

If you want to test the slider, go ahead, but hurry back. We're going to do just a bit more customization.

As noted, you can place an image at each end of the slider. Let's provide little icons to indicate that moving the slider to the left slows us down and moving it to the right speeds us up.

Adding Icons to the Settings Bundle

In the *12 – Images* folder in the project archive that accompanies this book, you'll find two icons called *rabbit.png* and *turtle.png*. We need to add both of these to our settings bundle. Because these images need to be used by the Settings application, we can't just put them in our *Bridge Control* folder; we need to put them in the settings bundle, so the Settings application can access them.

To do that, find the *Settings.bundle* in the Project Navigator. We'll need to open this bundle in the Finder. Control-click the *Settings.bundle* icon in the Project Navigator. When the contextual menu appears, select **Show in Finder** (see Figure 12-25) to show the bundle in the Finder.

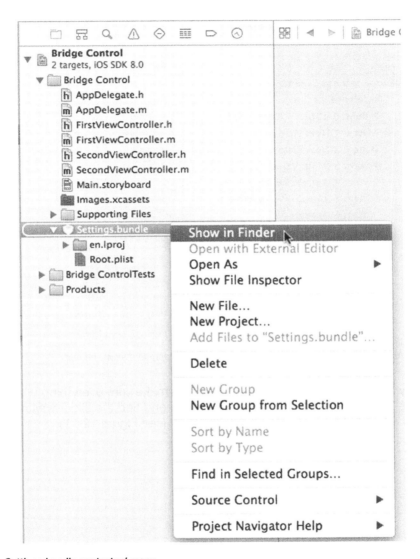

Figure 12-25. The Settings.bundle contextual menu

Remember that bundles look like files in the Finder, but they are really folders. When the Finder window opens to show the *Settings.bundle* file, Control-click the file and select **Show Package Contents** from the contextual menu that appears. This will open the settings bundle in a new Finder window, and you should see the same two items that you see in *Settings.bundle* in Xcode. Copy the two icon files, *rabbit.png* and *turtle.png*, from the *12 – Images* folder into the *Settings.bundle* package contents in the Finder window, next to *en.proj* and *Root.plist*.

You can leave this window open in the Finder, as we'll need to copy another file here soon. Now we'll return to Xcode and tell the slider to use these two images.

Back in Xcode, return to *Root.plist* and add two more child rows under Item 6. Give one a key of *MinimumValueImage* and a value of *turtle*. Give the other a key of *MaximumValueImage* and a value of *rabbit*. Figure 12-26 shows our finished Item 6.

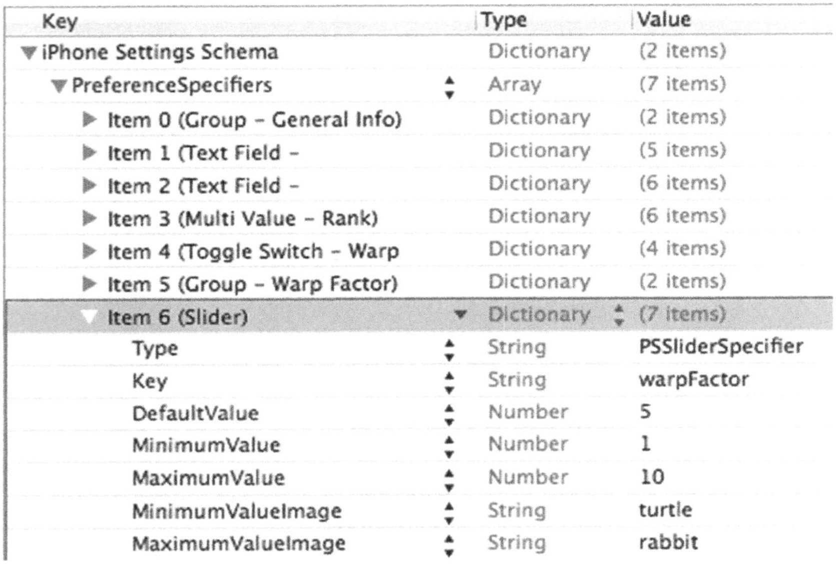

Key		Type	Value
▼ iPhone Settings Schema		Dictionary	(2 items)
▼ PreferenceSpecifiers	↕	Array	(7 items)
▶ Item 0 (Group – General Info)		Dictionary	(2 items)
▶ Item 1 (Text Field –		Dictionary	(5 items)
▶ Item 2 (Text Field –		Dictionary	(6 items)
▶ Item 3 (Multi Value – Rank)		Dictionary	(6 items)
▶ Item 4 (Toggle Switch – Warp		Dictionary	(4 items)
▶ Item 5 (Group – Warp Factor)		Dictionary	(2 items)
▼ Item 6 (Slider)	▼	Dictionary ↕	(7 items)
Type	↕	String	PSSliderSpecifier
Key	↕	String	warpFactor
DefaultValue	↕	Number	5
MinimumValue	↕	Number	1
MaximumValue	↕	Number	10
MinimumValueImage	↕	String	turtle
MaximumValueImage	↕	String	rabbit

Figure 12-26. *Our finished Item 6: a slider with turtle and rabbit icons to represent slow and fast*

Save your property list, and then build and run the app to make sure everything is still hunky-dory. You should be able to navigate to the Settings application and find the slider waiting for you, with the sleepy turtle and the happy rabbit at their respective ends (see Figure 12-27).

Figure 12-27. We have text fields, multivalue fields, a toggle switch, and a slider. We're almost finished

Adding a Child Settings View

We're going to add another preference specifier to tell the Settings application that we want it to display a child settings view. This specifier will present a row with a disclosure indicator that, when tapped, will take the user down to a whole new view full of preferences. Let's get to it.

Since we don't want this new preference to be grouped with the slider, first we'll copy the group specifier in Item 0 and paste it at the end of the *PreferenceSpecifiers* array to create a new group for our child settings view.

In *Root.plist*, collapse all open items, and then single-click **Item 0** to select it and press ⌘C to copy it to the clipboard. Next, select **Item 6**, and then press ⌘V to paste in a new Item 7. Expand Item 7 and double-click the Value column next to the key *Title*, changing it from *General Info* to *Additional Info*.

Now collapse **Item 7** again. Select it and press **Return** to add Item 8, which will be our actual child view. Expand it by clicking the disclosure triangle. Find the Type row, give it a value of *PSChildPaneSpecifier*, and then set the value of the Title row to *More Settings*.

We need to add one final row to Item 8, which will tell the Settings application which property list to load for the More Settings view. Add another child row, and give it a key of *File* (you can do this by changing the key of the last row in the group from *Key* to *File*) and a value of *More* (see Figure 12-28). The file extension *.plist* is assumed and must not be included (if it is, the Settings application won't find the *.plist* file).

Key		Type	Value
▼ iPhone Settings Schema		Dictionary	(2 items)
▼ PreferenceSpecifiers	▲▼	Array	(9 items)
▶ Item 0 (Group – General Info)		Dictionary	(2 items)
▶ Item 1 (Text Field –		Dictionary	(5 items)
▶ Item 2 (Text Field –		Dictionary	(6 items)
▶ Item 3 (Multi Value – Rank)		Dictionary	(6 items)
▶ Item 4 (Toggle Switch – Warp		Dictionary	(4 items)
▶ Item 5 (Group – Warp Factor)		Dictionary	(2 items)
▶ Item 6 (Slider)		Dictionary	(7 items)
▼ Item 7 (Group – Additional Info)		Dictionary	(2 items)
Title	▲▼	String	Additional Info
Type	▲▼	String	PSGroupSpecifier
▼ Item 8 (Child Pane – More	▼	Dictionary ▲▼	(3 items)
Type	▲▼	String	PSChildPaneSpecifier
Title	▲▼	String	More Settings
File	▲▼	String	More

Figure 12-28. Our finished Items 7 and 8, setting up the new Additional Info settings group and providing the child pane link to the file, More.plist

We are adding a child view to our main preference view. The settings in that child view are specified in the *More.plist* file. We need to copy *More.plist* into the settings bundle. We can't add new files to the bundle in Xcode, and the Property List Editor's Save dialog will not let us save into a bundle. So, we need to create a new property list, save it somewhere else, and then drag it into the *Settings.bundle* window using the Finder.

You've now seen all the different types of preference fields that you can use in a settings bundle *.plist* file. To save yourself some typing, you can grab *More.plist* out of the *12 – Images* folder in the project archive that accompanies this book, and then drag it into that *Settings.bundle* window we left open earlier, alongside *Root.plist*.

> **Tip**   When you create your own child settings views, the easiest approach is to make a copy of *Root.plist* and give it a new name. Next, delete all of the existing preference specifiers except the first one and add whatever preference specifiers you need for that new file.

We're finished with our settings bundle. Feel free to compile, run, and test the Settings application. You should be able to reach the child view and set values for all the other fields. Go ahead and play with it, and make changes to the property list if you want.

> **Tip**   We've covered almost every configuration option available (at least at the time of this writing). You can find the full documentation of the settings property list format in the document called *Settings Application Schema Reference* in the iOS Dev Center. You can get that document, along with a ton of other useful reference documents, from this page: `http://developer.apple.com/library/ios/navigation/`.

Before continuing, select the *Images.xcassets* item in Xcode's Project Navigator, and then copy the *rabbit.png* and *turtle.png* icons from the *12 – Images* folder in the project archive into the left side of the editor area. This will add these icons to the project as new images resources, ready for use. We'll use them in our application to show the value of the current settings.

You might have noticed that the two icons you just added are exactly the same ones you added to your settings bundle earlier, and you might be wondering why. Remember that iOS applications can't read files out of other applications' sandboxes. The settings bundle doesn't become part of our application's sandbox—it becomes part of the Settings application's sandbox. Since we also want to use those icons in our application, we need to add them separately to our *Bridge Control* folder, so they are copied into our application's sandbox, as well.

Reading Settings in Our Application

We've now solved half of our problem. The user can use the Setting app to declare their preferences, but how do we get to them from within our application? As it turns out, that's the easy part.

Retrieving User Settings

We'll use a class called `NSUserDefaults` to access the user's settings. `NSUserDefaults` is implemented as a singleton, which means there is only one instance of `NSUserDefaults` running in our application. To get access to that one instance, we call the class method `standardUserDefaults`, like so:

```
NSUserDefaults *defaults = [NSUserDefaults standardUserDefaults];
```

Once we have a pointer to the standard user defaults, we use it much like an `NSDictionary`. To get a value from it, we can call `objectForKey:`, which will return an Objective-C object, such as an `NSString`, `NSDate`, or `NSNumber`. If we want to retrieve the value as a scalar—like an `int`, `float`, or `BOOL`—we can use another method, such as `intForKey:`, `floatForKey:`, or `boolForKey:`.

When you were creating the property list for this application, you added an array of *PreferenceSpecifiers* inside a *.plist* file. Within the Settings application, some of those specifiers were used to create groups, while others were used to create interface objects for user interaction. Those are the specifiers we are really interested in because they hold the keys the real settings data. Every specifier that was tied to a user setting has a Key named *Key*. Take a minute to go back and check. For example, the *Key* for our slider has a value of *warpFactor*. The *Key* for our Authorization Code field is *authorizationCode*. We'll use those keys to retrieve the user settings.

Instead of using strings for each key directly in our methods, we'll use some precompiler #define statements for the values. That way we can use these makeshift constants in our code instead of inline strings, where we would run the risk of mistyping something. We'll set these up in a header file, since we're going to use some of them in more than just this class later on. So, in Xcode, press ⌘N and, from the iOS section of the file creation window, choose **Source** and then **Header File**. Press **Next**, call the header file *Constants.h*, and press **Create**. Open the newly created header file and add these bold lines:

```
#ifndef Bridge_Control_Constants_h
#define Bridge_Control_Constants_h

#define kOfficerKey              @"officer"
#define kAuthorizationCodeKey    @"authorizationCode"
#define kRankKey                 @"rank"
#define kWarpDriveKey            @"warp"
#define kWarpFactorKey           @"warpFactor"
#define kFavoriteTeaKey          @"favoriteTea"
#define kFavoriteCaptainKey      @"favoriteCaptain"
#define kFavoriteGadgetKey       @"favoriteGadget"
#define kFavoriteAlienKey        @"favoriteAlien"

#endif
```

These constants are the keys that we used in our *.plist* file for the different preference fields. Now that we have a place to display the settings, let's quickly set up our main view with a bunch of labels. Before going over to Interface Builder, let's create outlets for all the labels we'll need. Single-click *FirstViewController.m*, and make the following changes:

```
#import "FirstViewController.h"
#import "Constants.h"

@interface FirstViewController ()

@property (weak, nonatomic) IBOutlet UILabel *officerLabel;
@property (weak, nonatomic) IBOutlet UILabel *authorizationCodeLabel;
@property (weak, nonatomic) IBOutlet UILabel *rankLabel;
@property (weak, nonatomic) IBOutlet UILabel *warpDriveLabel;
@property (weak, nonatomic) IBOutlet UILabel *warpFactorLabel;
@property (weak, nonatomic) IBOutlet UILabel *favoriteTeaLabel;
@property (weak, nonatomic) IBOutlet UILabel *favoriteCaptainLabel;
@property (weak, nonatomic) IBOutlet UILabel *favoriteGadgetLabel;
@property (weak, nonatomic) IBOutlet UILabel *favoriteAlienLabel;

@end
```

There's nothing new here. We import *Constants.h* so that we can use the settings keys and we declare nine properties, all of them labels with the IBOutlet keyword to make them connectable in Interface Builder.

Save your changes. Now that we have our outlets declared, let's head over to the storyboard file to create the GUI.

Creating the Main View

Select *Main.storyboard* to edit it in Interface Builder. When it comes up, you'll see the tab bar view controller on the left and the view controllers for the two tabs on the right, one above the other. The upper one is for the first tab, corresponding to the FirstViewController class, and the lower one is for the second tab, which will be implemented in the SecondViewController class.

We're going to start by adding a bunch of labels to the *View* of FirstViewController, so it looks like the one shown in Figure 12-29. We'll need a grand total of 18 labels. Half of them, on the left side of the screen, will be right-aligned and bold; the other half, on the right side of the screen, will be used to display the actual values retrieved from the user defaults and will have outlets pointing to them. All of the changes that we make here will be to the view controller for the first tab, which is the upper one on the right of the storyboard.

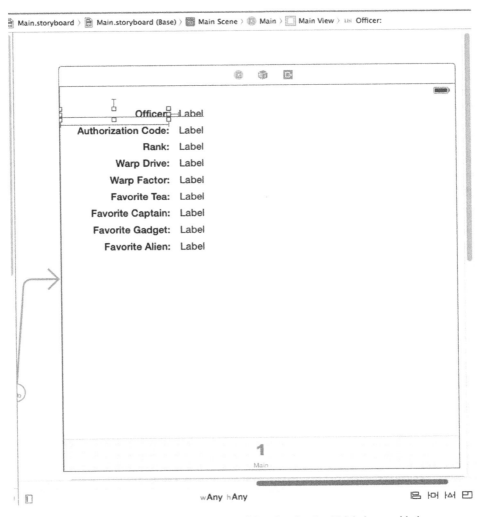

Figure 12-29. The view controller for the first tab in Interface Builder, showing the 18 labels we added

Start by expanding the node for Main Scene in the Document Outline, and then expand the *View* item. You'll find three child views already in place—delete them all. Next, rename the *View* item to *Main View*. Now drag a **Label** from the Object Library and drop it near the top left of the view. Drag it all the way to the left of the window (or at least to the left blue guideline), and then widen it by dragging its right edge toward the center of the view, like the Officer label in Figure 12-29. In the Attributes Inspector, make the text right aligned and change the font to *System Bold 15*. Now Option-drag the label downward to create eight more copies, lining them up neatly to form the left column. Change the label texts so that they match the ones in Figure 12-29.

Building the right-hand column is slightly easier. Drag another label onto the View and place it to the right of the Officer label, leaving a small gap between them. In the Attributes Inspector, set the font to *System 15*. Option-drag this label downward to create eight more copies, each of them lined up with the corresponding label in the left column.

Now we need to set the auto layout constraints. Let's start by linking the top two labels together. Control-drag from the **Officer** label to the label to its right. Release the mouse and hold down **Shift**. In the pop-up menu, select **Horizontal Spacing** and **Baseline**, and then click outside the pop-up. Do the same for the other eight rows, to link each pair of labels together.

Next, we'll fix the positions of the labels in the left column relative to the left and top of the view. In the Document Outline, Control-drag from the **Officer** label to **Main View**. Release the mouse, hold down the **Shift** key, and select **Leading Space to Container Margin** and **Top Space to Top Layout Guide**, and then click outside the pop-up to apply the constraints. Do the same with the other eight labels in the left column.

Finally, we need to fix the widths of the labels in the left column. Select the **Officer** label and click the **Pin** button below the storyboard editor. In the pop-up, check the **Width** check box followed by **Add 1 Constraint**. Repeat this process for all of the labels in the left column.

All of the labels should now be properly constrained, so select the view controller **First** in the Document Outline, and then click the **Resolve Auto Layout Issues** button underneath the storyboard editor, and select **Update Frames** (if this option is not enabled, all of the labels are already in their correct positions in the storyboard). If all is well, the labels will move to their final positions.

The next thing we need to do is link the labels in the right column to their outlets. Open *FirstViewController.m* in the Assistant Editor and Control-drag from the top label in the right column to the officerLabel outlet to connect them. Control-drag from the second label in the right column to authorizationLabel, and repeat until all nine labels in the right column are connected to their outlets. Save the *Main.storyboard* file.

Updating the First View Controller

In Xcode, select *FirstViewController.m* and add the following code to the class's @implementation section:

```
@implementation FirstViewController

- (void)refreshFields {
    NSUserDefaults *defaults = [NSUserDefaults standardUserDefaults];
    self.officerLabel.text = [defaults objectForKey:kOfficerKey];
    self.authorizationCodeLabel.text = [defaults
                            objectForKey:kAuthorizationCodeKey];
```

```
    self.rankLabel.text = [defaults objectForKey:kRankKey];
    self.warpDriveLabel.text = [defaults boolForKey:kWarpDriveKey]
                                ? @"Engaged" : @"Disabled";
    self.warpFactorLabel.text = [[defaults objectForKey:kWarpFactorKey]
                                  stringValue];
    self.favoriteTeaLabel.text = [defaults objectForKey:kFavoriteTeaKey];
    self.favoriteCaptainLabel.text = [defaults
                                        objectForKey:kFavoriteCaptainKey];
    self.favoriteGadgetLabel.text = [defaults objectForKey:kFavoriteGadgetKey];
    self.favoriteAlienLabel.text = [defaults objectForKey:kFavoriteAlienKey];
}

- (void)viewWillAppear:(BOOL)animated {
    [super viewWillAppear:animated];
    [self refreshFields];
}.
```

There's not really much here that should throw you. The refreshFields method does two things. First, it grabs the standard user defaults. Second, it sets the text property of all the labels to the appropriate object from the user defaults using the same key values that we put in our *.plist* file. Notice that for warpFactorLabel, we're calling stringValue on the object returned. Most of our other preferences are strings, which come back from the user defaults as NSString objects. The preference stored by the slider, however, comes back as an NSNumber, but we need a string for display purposes, so we call stringValue on it to get a string representation of the value it holds.

After that, we overrode our superclass's viewWillAppear: method, and there we called our refreshFields method. This causes the values that the user sees to be updated whenever the view appears—which includes when the application starts and when the user switches from the second tab to the first tab.

If you run the application at this point, you should see the user interface that you built for the first tab, but some or all of the fields will be empty. Don't worry, this is not a bug. It is correct behavior, believe it or not. You'll see why, and how to fix it, in the upcoming "Registering Default Values" section.

Changing Defaults from Our Application

Now that we have the main view up and running, let's build the second tab. As you can see in Figure 12-30, the second tab features our warp drive switch, as well as the warp factor slider. We'll use the same controls that the Settings application uses for these two items: a switch and a slider. In addition to declaring our outlets, we'll also declare a method called refreshFields, just as we did in FirstViewController, and two action methods that will be triggered by the user touching the controls.

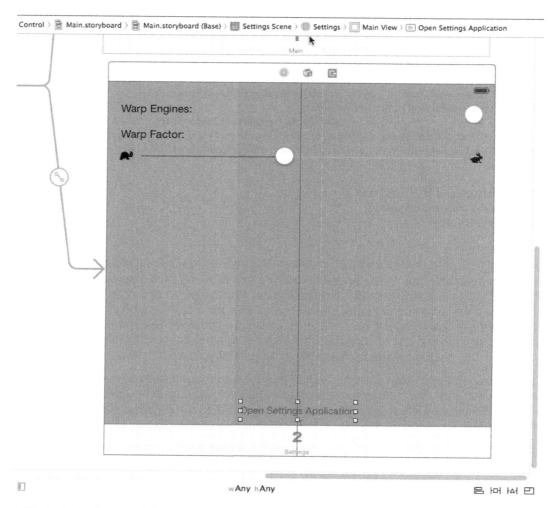

Figure 12-30. Designing the second view controller in Interface Builder

Select *SecondViewController.m* and make the following changes:

```
@interface SecondViewController()

@property (weak, nonatomic) IBOutlet UISwitch *engineSwitch;
@property (weak, nonatomic) IBOutlet UISlider *warpFactorSlider;

@end
```

Now, save your changes and select *Main.storyboard* to edit the GUI in Interface Builder, this time focusing on the Settings Scene in the Document Outline. Hold down the **Option** key and click the disclosure triangle to expand Settings Scene and everything below it. Change the name of the *View* item to *Main View* and delete all of its child nodes.

Next, select **Main View** in the Settings Scene in the Document Outline and then bring up the Attributes Inspector. Change the background color by using the Background pop-up to select **Light Gray Color**.

Next, drag two labels from the library and place them on Main View in the storyboard. Make sure you drag them onto the Settings Scene controller, which is the one at the bottom right of the storyboard. Double-click one of them, and change it to read *Warp Engines:*. Double-click the other, and call it *Warp Factor:*. Place both labels against the left guideline, one above the other. You can use Figure 12-30 as a placement guide.

Next, drag over a **Switch** from the library and place it against the right side of the view, across from the label that reads *Warp Engines*. Control-drag from the **View Controller** icon at the top of the Settings Scene to the new switch, and connect it to the **engineSwitch** outlet. Next, open SecondViewController in the Assistant Editor and Control-drag from the switch to a point just above the @end line at the bottom of the file. Release the mouse and create an *Action* called *engineSwitchTapped*, leaving all the other selections in the pop-up at their default values.

Drag over a **Slider** from the library and place it below the label that reads *Warp Factor:*. Resize the slider so that it stretches from the blue guideline on the left margin to the one on the right. Now Control-drag from the **View Controller** icon at the top of the Settings Scene to the slider, and then connect it to the **warpFactorSlider** outlet. Next, Control-drag from the slider to the end of the SecondViewController class and create an *Action* called *warpSliderTouched*, leaving all the other selections in the pop-up at their default values.

Single-click the slider if it's not still selected and bring up the Attributes Inspector. Set Minimum to *1.00*, Maximum to *10.00*, and Current to *5.00*. Next, select **turtle** for Min Image and **rabbit** for Max Image. If those don't show up in the pop-up buttons, make sure you dragged the images into the *Images.xcassets* assets catalog.

To complete the user interface, drag a button from the Object Library, drop it at the bottom of the view, and change its name to *Open Settings Application*. Control-drag from the button to just below the warpSliderTouched method in SecondViewController and create an *Action* called *settingsButtonClicked*. We'll use this button at the end of the chapter.

It's time to add the auto layout constraints. Start by selecting *Main.storyboard*. In the Document Outline, Control-drag from the **Warp Engines** label to **Main View** and release the mouse. Hold down **Shift** and select **Leading Space to Container Margin** and **Top Space to Top Layout Guide**, and click outside the pop-up to apply the constraints. Repeat this for the Warp Factor label.

Next, Control-drag from the switch to **Main View** and release the mouse. Hold down **Shift** and select **Trailing Space to Container Margin** and **Top Space to Top Layout Guide,** and click outside the pop-up. Control-drag from the slider to **Main View** and release the mouse. Hold down **Shift** and this time select **Leading Space to Container Margin**, **Trailing Space to Container Margin**, and **Top Space to Top Layout Guide**, and then click outside the pop-up to apply the constraints.

Finally, we need to fix the position of the button at the bottom of the view. Control-drag from the button to **Main View**, release the mouse and select **Bottom Space to Bottom Layout Guide** and **Center Horizontally in Container** while holding down the **Shift** key, and then click anywhere outside the pop-up. That completes the auto layout constraints.

Now, let's finish the settings view controller. Select *SecondViewController.m* and add the following import at the top of the file:

```
#import "Constants.h"
```

Next, make the following changes within the class's implementation:

```
- (void)viewWillAppear:(BOOL)animated {
    [super viewWillAppear:animated];
    [self refreshFields];
}

- (void)refreshFields {
    NSUserDefaults *defaults = [NSUserDefaults standardUserDefaults];
    self.engineSwitch.on = [defaults boolForKey:kWarpDriveKey];
    self.warpFactorSlider.value = [defaults floatForKey:kWarpFactorKey];
}

- (IBAction)engineSwitchTapped:(id)sender {
    NSUserDefaults *defaults = [NSUserDefaults standardUserDefaults];
    [defaults setBool:self.engineSwitch.on forKey:kWarpDriveKey];
}

- (IBAction)warpSliderTouched:(id)sender {
    NSUserDefaults *defaults = [NSUserDefaults standardUserDefaults];
    [defaults setFloat:self.warpFactorSlider.value forKey:kWarpFactorKey];
}
```

When the view controller's view appears (e.g., when the tab is selected), we call our refreshFields method. This method's three lines of code get a reference to the standard user defaults, and then use the outlets for the switch and slider to make them display the values stored in the user defaults. We also implemented the engineSwitchTapped and warpSliderTouched action methods, so that we could stuff the values from our controls back into the user defaults when the user changes them.

Now you should be able to run the app, switch to the second tab, edit the values presented there, and see them reflected in the first tab when you switch back.

Registering Default Values

We've created a settings bundle, including some default settings for a few values, to give the Settings app access to our app's preferences. We've also set up our own app to access the same information, with a GUI to let the user see and edit it. However, one piece is missing: our app is completely unaware of the default values specified in the settings bundle. You can see this for yourself by deleting the Bridge Control app from the iOS simulator or the device you're running on (thereby deleting the preferences stored for the app), and then running it from Xcode again. At the start of a fresh launch, the app will show you blank values for all the settings. Even the default values for the warp drive settings, which we defined in the settings bundle, are nowhere to be seen. If you then switch over to the Settings app, you'll see the default values; however, unless you actually change the values there, you'll never see them back in the Bridge Control app!

The reason our default settings disappeared is that our app knows nothing about the settings bundle it contains. So, when it tries to read the value from NSUserDefaults for *warpFactor*, and finds nothing saved under that key, it has nothing to show us. Fortunately, NSUserDefaults includes a method called registerDefaults: that lets us specify the default values that we should find if we try to look up a key/value that hasn't been set. To make this work throughout the app, it's best if this is called early during app start-up. Select *AppDelegate.m* and include this header file somewhere at the top of the file, so we can access the key names we defined earlier:

```
#import "Constants.h"
```

Next, modify the application:didFinishLaunchingWithOptions: method:

```
- (BOOL)application:(UIApplication *)application
    didFinishLaunchingWithOptions:(NSDictionary *)launchOptions
{
    // Override point for customization after application launch.

    NSDictionary *defaults = @{kWarpDriveKey : @YES,
                               kWarpFactorKey : @5,
                               kFavoriteAlienKey : @"Vulcan"};
    [[NSUserDefaults standardUserDefaults] registerDefaults:defaults];
    return YES;
}
```

The first thing we do here is create a dictionary that contains three key/value pairs, one for each of the keys available in Settings that requires a default value. We're using the same key names we defined earlier to reduce the risk of mistyping a key name. Note that in addition to the @{} shortcut syntax for initializing a dictionary, we're also using the @*<numeric value>* syntax for creating NSNumber instances wrapping the Boolean value YES and the integer 5.

We pass that entire dictionary to the standard NSUserDefaults instance's registerDefaults: method. From that point on, NSUserDefaults will give us the values we specify here, as long as we haven't set different values either in our app or in the Settings app.

This class is complete. You should be able to compile and run your application. It will look something like Figure 12-6, except yours will be showing whatever values you entered in your Settings application, of course. Couldn't be much easier, could it?

Keeping It Real

Now you should be able to run your app, view the settings, and then press the **Home** button and open the Settings app to tweak some values. Hit the **Home** button again, launch your app again, and you may be in for a surprise. When you go back to your app, you won't see the settings change! They'll remain as they are, showing the old values.

Here's the deal: in iOS, hitting the **Home** button while an app is running doesn't actually quit the app. Instead, the operating system suspends the app in the background, leaving it ready to be quickly fired up again. This is great for switching back and forth between applications, since the amount of time it takes to reawaken a suspended app is much shorter than what it takes to launch it from scratch. However, in our case, we need to do a little more work, so that when our app wakes up, it effectively gets a slap in the face, reloads the user preferences, and redisplays the values they contain.

You'll learn more about background applications in Chapter 15, but we'll give you a sneak peek at the basics of how to make your app notice that it has been brought back to life. To do this, we're going to sign up each of our controller classes to receive a notification that is sent by the application when it wakes up from its state of suspended execution.

A **notification** is a lightweight mechanism that objects can use to communicate with each other. Any object can define one or more notifications that it will publish to the application's **notification center**, which is a singleton object that exists only to pass these notifications between objects. Notifications are usually indications that some event occurred, and objects that publish notifications include a list of notifications in their documentation. The UIApplication class publishes a number of notifications (you can find them in the Xcode documentation viewer, toward the bottom of the *UIApplication* page). The purpose of most notifications is usually pretty obvious from their names, but the documentation contains further information if you're unclear about a given notification's purpose.

Our application needs to refresh its display when the application is about to come to the foreground, so we are interested in the notification called UIApplicationWillEnterForegroundNotification. We'll modify the viewWillAppear: method of our view controllers to subscribe to that notification and tell the notification center to call another method when that notification happens. Add the following code to both *FirstViewController.m* and *SecondViewController.m*:

```
- (void)applicationWillEnterForeground:(NSNotification *)notification {
    NSUserDefaults *defaults = [NSUserDefaults standardUserDefaults];
    [defaults synchronize];
    [self refreshFields];
}
```

The method itself is quite simple. First, it gets a reference to the standard user defaults object and calls its synchronize method, which forces the User Defaults system to save any unsaved changes and also reload any unmodified preferences from storage. In effect, we're forcing it to reread the stored preferences so that we can pick up the changes that were made in the Settings app. Next, the applicationWillEnterForeground: method calls the refreshFields method, which each class uses to update its display.

Now we need to make each of our controllers subscribe to the notification. Add the following code in bold to the viewWillAppear: method in both *FirstViewController.m* and *SecondViewController.m*:

```
- (void)viewWillAppear:(BOOL)animated {
    [super viewWillAppear:animated];
    [self refreshFields];

    UIApplication *app = [UIApplication sharedApplication];
    [[NSNotificationCenter defaultCenter] addObserver:self
            selector:@selector(applicationWillEnterForeground:)
            name:UIApplicationWillEnterForegroundNotification
            object:app];
}
```

We start by getting a reference to our application instance, and then use that to subscribe to the UIApplicationWillEnterForegroundNotification, using the default NSNotificationCenter instance and a method called addObserver:selector:name:object:. We then pass the following to this method:

- For the observer, we pass self, which means that our controller class (each of them individually, since this code is going into both of them) is the object that needs to be notified.

- For selector, we pass a selector to the applicationWillEnterForeground: method we just wrote, telling the notification center to call that method when the notification is posted.

- The third parameter, UIApplicationWillEnterForegroundNotification, is the name of the notification that we're interested in receiving.

- The final parameter, app, is the object from which we're interested in getting the notification. We use a reference to our own application for this. If we passed nil for the final parameter instead, we would get notified any time any application posted the UIApplicationWillEnterForegroundNotification.

That takes care of updating the display, but we also need to consider what happens to the values that are put into the user defaults when the user manipulates the controls in our app. We need to make sure that they are saved to storage before control passes to another app. The easiest way to do that is to call synchronize as soon as the settings are changed, by adding one line to each of our new action methods in *SecondViewController.m*:

```
- (IBAction)engineSwitchTapped {
    NSUserDefaults *defaults = [NSUserDefaults standardUserDefaults];
    [defaults setBool:self.engineSwitch.on forKey:kWarpDriveKey];
    [defaults synchronize];
}

- (IBAction)warpSliderTouched {
    NSUserDefaults *defaults = [NSUserDefaults standardUserDefaults];
    [defaults setFloat:self.warpFactorSlider.value forKey:kWarpFactorKey];
    [defaults synchronize];
}
```

> **Note** Calling the synchronize method is a potentially expensive operation because the entire contents of the user defaults in memory must be compared with what's in storage. When you're dealing with a whole lot of user defaults at once and want to make sure everything is in sync, it's best to try to minimize calls to synchronize, so that this whole comparison isn't performed over and over again. However, calling it once in response to each user action, as we're doing here, won't cause any noticeable performance problems.

There's one more thing to take care of to make this work as cleanly as possible. You already know that you must clean up your memory by setting properties to nil when they're no longer in use, as well as performing other clean-up tasks. The notification system is another place where you need to clean up after yourself by telling the default NSNotificationCenter that you don't want to listen to any more notifications. In our case, where we've registered each view controller to observe this notification in its viewWillAppear: method, we should unregister in the matching viewDidDisappear: method. So, in both *FirstViewController.m* and *SecondViewController.m*, add the following method:

```
- (void)viewDidDisappear:(BOOL)animated {
    [super viewDidDisappear:(BOOL)animated];
    [[NSNotificationCenter defaultCenter] removeObserver:self];
}
```

Note that it's possible to unregister for specific notifications using the removeObserver:name:object: method by passing in the same values that were used to register your observer in the first place. In any case, the preceding line is a handy way to make sure that the notification center forgets about our observer completely, no matter how many notifications it was registered for.

With that in place, it's time to build and run the app and see what happens when you switch between your app and the Settings app. Changes you make in the Settings app should now be immediately reflected in your app when you switch back to it.

Switching to the Settings Application

To switch from the Bridge Control application to its settings, you need to go to the Home screen, launch the Settings application, find the Bridge Control entry, and select it. That's a lot of steps. It's so tiresome that many applications have opted to include their own settings screen rather than make the user go through all of that. Wouldn't it be much nicer if you could just take the user directly to screen for your settings in the Settings application? Well, as of iOS 8, you can do just that. Remember the **Open Settings Application** button we added to SecondViewController in Figure 12-30? We wired it up to the settingButtonClicked: method in the view controller, but we didn't put any code in that method. Let's fix that now. Add the following code shown in bold:

```
- (IBAction)settingsButtonClicked:(id)sender {
    [[UIApplication sharedApplication]
        openURL:[NSURL URLWithString:UIApplicationOpenSettingsURLString]];
}
```

This code uses a system-defined URL stored in the external constant UIApplicationOpenSettingsURLString (it's value is actually app-settings:) to launch the Settings application right from our view controller. Run the application, switch to the second tab, and click the **Open Settings Application** button—you'll be taken directly to our settings screen, the one shown in Figure 12-3. That's a great improvement. Unfortunately, though, there's no quick way back—to return to our application, you have to go via the Home screen again. Maybe that's something that will get fixed in a later iOS release.

Beam Me Up, Scotty

At this point, you should have a very solid grasp on both the Settings application and the User Defaults mechanism. You know how to add a settings bundle to your application and how to build a hierarchy of views for your application's preferences. You also learned how to read and write preferences using NSUserDefaults, as well as how to let the user change preferences from within your application. You even got a chance to use a new project template in Xcode. There really shouldn't be much in the way of application preferences that you are not equipped to handle now.

In the next chapter, we're going to show you how to keep your application's data around after your application quits. Ready? Let's go!

Chapter 13

Basic Data Persistence

So far, we've focused on the controller and view aspects of the MVC paradigm. Although several of our applications have read data out of the application bundle, none of them has saved data to any form of persistent storage—nonvolatile storage that survives a restart of the computer or device. So far, with the exception of Application Settings (in Chapter 12), every sample application either did not store data or used volatile (i.e., nonpersistent) storage. Every time one of the sample applications launched, it appeared with exactly the same data it had the first time you launched it.

This approach has worked for us up to this point. But in the real world, your applications will need to persist data. When users make changes, they usually like to find those changes when they launch the program again.

A number of different mechanisms are available for persisting data on an iOS device. If you've programmed in Cocoa for OS X, you've likely used some or all of these techniques.

In this chapter, we're going to look at four different mechanisms for persisting data to the iOS file system:

- Property lists
- Object archives (or archiving)
- SQLite3 (iOS's embedded relational database)
- Core Data (Apple's provided persistence tool)

We will write example applications that use all four approaches.

> **Note**   Property lists, object archives, SQLite3, and Core Data are not the only ways you can persist data on iOS; they are just the most common and easiest. You always have the option of using traditional C I/O calls like fopen( ) to read and write data. You can also use Cocoa's low-level file-management tools. In almost every case, doing so will result in a lot more coding effort and is rarely necessary, but those tools are there if you want them.

Your Application's Sandbox

All four of this chapter's data-persistence mechanisms share an important common element: your application's */Documents* folder. Every application gets its own */Documents* folder, and applications are allowed to read and write from their own */Documents* directory.

To give you some context, let's take a look at how applications are organized in iOS by examining the folder layout used by the iPhone simulator. To see this, you'll need to look inside the *Library* directory contained in your home directory. On OS X 10.6 and earlier, this was no problem; however, starting with OS X 10.7, Apple decided to make the *Library* folder hidden by default, so there's a small extra hoop to jump through. Open a Finder window and navigate to your home directory. If you can see your *Library* folder, that's great. If not, hold down the **Alt** key and select **Go ➤ Library**. The **Library** option is hidden unless you hold down the **Alt** key.

Within the *Library* folder, drill down into *Developer/CoreSimulator/Devices/.* Within that directory, you'll see one subdirectory for each simulator in your current Xcode installation. The subdirectory names are globally unique identifiers (GUIDs) that are generated automatically by Xcode, so it's impossible to know just by looking at them which directory corresponds to which simulator. To find out, look for a file called *device.plist* in any of the simulator directories and open it. You'll find a key that maps to the simulated device's name. Figure 13-1 shows the *device.plist* file for the iPad 2 simulator.

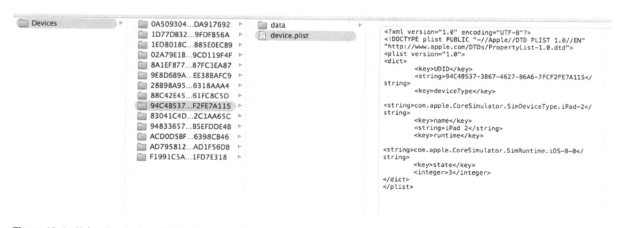

Figure 13-1. Using the device.plist file to map a directory to a simulator

Choose a device and drill down into its *data* directory until you reach the subdirectory *data/Containers/ Data/Application*. Here again you'll see subdirectories with names that are GUIDs. In this case, each one of them represents either a preinstalled application or an application that you have run on that simulator. Select one of the directories and open it. You'll see something like Figure 13-2.

Containers	Bundle	Application	0A9BC3BD...1D30E16D	Documents
Documents	Data	PluginKitPlugin	4DEBC486...79987245	Library
Library	Shared	VPNPlugin	5BCB7F90...45DDC060	tmp
Media			7D2D4DD...C0B6B18E0	
Root			28EC063D...370E626F	
tmp			66D8615A...1C370B08	
var			78C830D5...C5EA5D57	
			84E377C1...45C4FDED	
			91E0FE93...CC8731436	
			422CF6D7...4FFD75A5	
			530FA91D...6D791402	
			252237A7...76220022	
			9926847E...F8D9BBA39	
			BB479DCD...E760FA6C	
			C8EC72E9...F014F7C1	
			DE8BA961...46754D19	
			E916DA8D...87CFF00B	
			F71D9901...CB9B2F563	
			F987DF43...B0C5FA155	
			FD66BBEC...BB1446F67	

Figure 13-2. The sandbox for an application on the simulator

Although this listing represents the simulator, the file structure is similar to what's on the actual device. To see the sandbox for an application on a device, plug it onto your Mac and open the Xcode Devices window (**Window ➤ Devices**). You should see your device in the window sidebar. Select it and then choose an application from the Installed Apps table. Below the table, there's an icon that looks like a gear. Click it and select **Show Container** from the pop-up to see the contents of the application's sandbox. You can also download everything in the sandbox to your Mac. Figure 13-3 shows the application sandbox for the Bridge Control application that we created in Chapter 12.

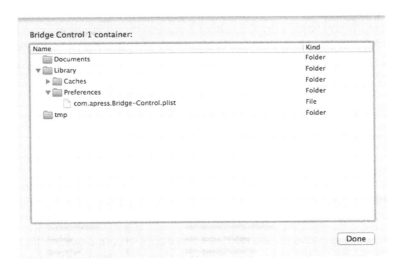

Figure 13-3. The sandbox for an application on a real device

Every application sandbox contains these three directories:

▪ *Documents*: Your application can store data in *Documents*. If you enable iTunes file sharing for your application, the user can see the contents of this directory (and any subdirectories that your application creates) in iTunes and can also upload files to it.

Tip   To enable file sharing for your application, open its *Info.plist* file and add the key **Application supports iTunes file sharing** with the value *YES*.

▪ *Library*: This is another place that your application can use to store its data. Use it for files that you do not want to share with the user. You can create your own subdirectories if required. As you can see in Figure 13-3, the system creates subdirectories called *Cache* and *Preferences*. The latter contains the *.plist* file that stores the application's preferences, set using the `NSUserDefaults` class, which we discussed in Chapter 12.

▪ *tmp*: The *tmp* directory offers a place where your application can store temporary files. Files written into *tmp* will not be backed up by iTunes when your iOS device syncs; but to avoid filling up the file system, your application does need to take responsibility for deleting the files in *tmp* once they are no longer needed.

Getting the Documents and Library Directories

Since our application is in a folder with a seemingly random name, how do we retrieve the full path to the *Documents* directory so that we can read and write our files? It's actually quite easy. The C function `NSSearchPathForDirectoriesInDomain()` will locate various directories for you. This is a Foundation function, so it is shared with Cocoa for OS X. Many of its available options are designed for OS X and won't return any values on iOS, either because those locations don't exist on iOS (such as the *Downloads* folder) or because your application doesn't have rights to access the location due to iOS's sandboxing mechanism.

Here's some code to retrieve the path to the *Documents* directory:

```
NSArray *paths = NSSearchPathForDirectoriesInDomains(NSDocumentDirectory,
    NSUserDomainMask, YES);
NSString *documentsDirectory = paths[0];
```

The constant `NSDocumentDirectory` says we are looking for the path to the *Documents* directory. The second constant, `NSUserDomainMask`, indicates that we want to restrict our search to our application's sandbox. In OS X, this same constant is used to indicate that we want the function to look in the user's home directory, which explains its somewhat odd name.

Though an array of matching paths is returned, we can count on our *Documents* directory residing at index zero in the array. Why? We know that only one directory meets the criteria we've specified, since each application has only one *Documents* directory.

We can create a file name by appending another string onto the end of the path we just retrieved. We'll use an NSString method called stringByAppendingPathComponent: that was designed for just that purpose:

```
NSString *filename = [documentsDirectory
    stringByAppendingPathComponent:@"theFile.txt"];
```

After this call, filename would contain the full path to a file called *theFile.txt* in our application's *Documents* directory, and we can use filename to create, read, and write from that file.

You can use the same C function with first argument NSLibraryDirectory to locate the *Library* directory:

```
NSArray *paths = NSSearchPathForDirectoriesInDomains(NSLibraryDirectory,
    NSUserDomainMask, YES);
NSString *libraryDirectory = paths[0];
```

Getting the tmp Directory

Getting a reference to your application's temporary directory is even easier than getting a reference to the *Documents* directory. The Foundation function called NSTemporaryDirectory() will return a string containing the full path to your application's temporary directory. To create a file name for a file that will be stored in the temporary directory, first find the temporary directory:

```
NSString *tempPath = NSTemporaryDirectory();
```

Next, create a path to a file in that directory by appending a file name to that path, like this:

```
NSString *tempFile = [tempPath
    stringByAppendingPathComponent:@"tempFile.txt"];
```

File-Saving Strategies

All four approaches we're going to look at in this chapter use the iOS file system. In the case of SQLite3, you'll create a single SQLite3 database file and let SQLite3 worry about storing and retrieving your data. In its simplest form, Core Data takes care of all the file system management for you. With the other two persistence mechanisms—property lists and archiving—you need to put some thought into whether you are going to store your data in a single file or in multiple files.

Single-File Persistence

Using a single file for data storage is the easiest approach; and with many applications, it is a perfectly acceptable one. You start by creating a root object, usually an NSArray or NSDictionary (your root object can also be based on a custom class when using archiving). Next, you populate your root object with all the program data that needs to be persisted. Whenever you need to save, your code rewrites the entire contents of that root object to a single file. When your application launches, it reads the entire contents of that file into memory. When it quits, it writes out the entire contents. This is the approach we'll use in this chapter.

The downside of using a single file is that you need to load all of your application's data into memory, and you must write all of it to the file system for even the smallest changes. But if your application isn't likely to manage more than a few megabytes of data, this approach is probably fine, and its simplicity will certainly make your life easier.

Multiple-File Persistence

Using multiple files for persistence is an alternative approach. For example, an e-mail application might store each e-mail message in its own file.

There are obvious advantages to this method. It allows the application to load only data that the user has requested (another form of lazy loading); and when the user makes a change, only the files that changed need to be saved. This method also gives you the opportunity to free up memory when you receive a low-memory notification. Any memory that is being used to store data that the user is not currently viewing can be flushed and then simply reloaded from the file system the next time it's needed.

The downside of multiple-file persistence is that it adds a fair amount of complexity to your application. For now, we'll stick with single-file persistence.

Next, we'll get into the specifics of each of our persistence methods: property lists, object archives, SQLite3, and Core Data. We'll explore each of these in turn and build an application that uses each mechanism to save some data to the device's file system. We'll start with property lists.

Using Property Lists

Several of our sample applications have used property lists, most recently when we used a property list to specify our application settings and preferences in Chapter 12. Property lists are convenient. They can be edited manually using Xcode or the Property List Editor application. Also, both NSDictionary and NSArray instances can be written to and created from property lists, as long as the dictionary or array contains only specific serializable objects.

Property List Serialization

A **serialized object** is one that has been converted into a stream of bytes so that it can be stored in a file or transferred over a network. Although any object can be made serializable, only certain objects can be placed into a collection class, such as an NSDictionary or NSArray, and then stored to a property list using the collection class's writeToFile:atomically: or writeToURL:atomically: methods. The following Foundation classes can be serialized this way:

- NSArray
- NSMutableArray
- NSDictionary
- NSMutableDictionary
- NSData

- NSMutableData
- NSString
- NSMutableString
- NSNumber
- NSDate

If you can build your data model from just these objects, you can use property lists to save and load your data.

If you're going to use property lists to persist your application data, you'll use either an NSArray or an NSDictionary to hold the data that needs to be persisted. Assuming that all the objects that you put into the NSArray or NSDictionary are serializable objects from the preceding list, you can write out a property list by calling the writeToFile:atomically: method on the dictionary or array instance, like so:

```
[myArray writeToFile:@"/some/file/location/output.plist" atomically:YES];
```

> **Note** In case you were wondering, the atomically parameter tells the method to write the data to an auxiliary file, not to the specified location. Once it has successfully written the file, it will then copy that auxiliary file to the location specified by the first parameter. This is a safer way to write a file, because if the application crashes during the save, the existing file (if there was one) will not be corrupted. It adds a bit of overhead; but in most situations, it's worth the cost.

One problem with the property list approach is that custom objects cannot be serialized into property lists. You also can't use other classes from Cocoa Touch that aren't specified in the list of serializable object types, which means that classes like NSURL, UIImage, and UIColor cannot be used directly.

Apart from the serialization issue, keeping all your model data in the form of property lists means that you can't easily create derived or calculated properties (such as a property that is the sum of two other properties), and some of your code that really should be contained in model classes must be moved to your controller classes. Again, these restrictions are OK for simple data models and simple applications. Most of the time, however, your application will be much easier to maintain if you create dedicated model classes.

Simple property lists can still be useful in complex applications. They are a great way to include static data in your application. For example, when your application has a picker, often the best way to include the list of items for it is to create a .plist file and place that file in your project's Resources folder, which will cause it to be compiled into your application.

Let's a build a simple application that uses property lists to store its data.

The First Version of the Persistence Application

We're going to build a program that lets you enter data into four text fields, saves those fields to a *.plist* file when the application quits, and then reloads the data back from that *.plist* file the next time the application launches (see Figure 13-4).

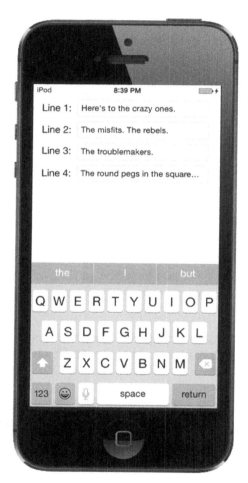

Figure 13-4. The Persistence application

> **Note**   In this chapter's applications, we won't be taking the time to set up all the user interface niceties that we have added in previous examples. Tapping the **Return** key, for example, will neither dismiss the keyboard nor take you to the next field. If you want to add such polish to the application, doing so would be good practice, so we encourage you to do that on your own.

Creating the Persistence Project

In Xcode, create a new project using the Single View Application template and name it *Persistence*. This project contains all the files that we'll need to build our application, so we can dive right in.

Before we build the view with the four text fields, let's create the outlets we need. In the Project Navigator, single-click the *ViewController.m* file and make the following changes:

```
#import "ViewController.h"

@interface ViewController ()

@property (strong, nonatomic) IBOutletCollection(UITextField) NSArray *lineFields;

@end
```

Now select *Main.storyboard* to edit the GUI.

Designing the Persistence Application View

Once Xcode switches over to Interface Builder mode, you'll see the View Controller scene in the editing pane. Expand the **View Controller** icon and change the name of the View item to *Main View*. Drag a **Text Field** from the library and place it against the top and right blue guidelines. Bring up the Attributes Inspector. Make sure the box labeled **Clear when editing begins** is unchecked.

Now drag a **Label** to the window and place it to the left of the text field using the left blue guideline, and then use the horizontal blue guideline to line up the label's vertical center with that of the text field. Double-click the label and change it to say *Line 1:*. Finally, resize the text field using the left resize handle to bring it close to the label. Use Figure 13-5 as a guide.

Figure 13-5. Designing the Persistence application's view

Next, select the label and text field, hold down the **Option** key, and drag down to make a copy below the first set. Use the blue guidelines to guide your placement. Now select both labels and both text fields, hold down the **Option** key, and drag down again. You should have four labels next to four text fields. Double-click each of the remaining labels and change their names to *Line 2:*, *Line 3:*, and *Line 4:*. Again, compare your results with Figure 13-5.

Once you have all four text fields and labels placed, Control-drag from the **View Controller** icon to each of the four text fields. Connect them all to the lineFields outlet collection, making sure to connect them in order from top to bottom. Save the changes you made to *Main.storyboard*.

Now let's add the Auto Layout constraints to make sure that the design works the same way on all devices. Starting by Control-dragging from the Line 1 label to the text field to its right, and then release the mouse. Hold down the **Shift** key and select **Horizontal Spacing** and **Baseline**, and then click outside the pop-up. Do the same for the other three labels and text fields.

Next, we'll fix the positions of the text fields. In the Document Outline, Control-drag from the top text field to Main View, release the mouse, hold down the **Shift** key and select **Trailing Space to Container Margin** and **Top Space to Top Layout Guide**, and then click outside the pop-up. Do the same for the other three text fields.

We need to fix the widths of the labels so that they don't resize if the user types more text than will fit in any of the text fields. Select the top label and click the **Pin** button below the storyboard editor. In the pop-up, select the **Width** check box and press **Add 1 Constraint**. Do the same for all of the labels.

Finally, back in the Document Outline, Control-drag from the Line 1 label to Main View, release the mouse, and select **Leading Space to Container Margin**. Do the same for all of the labels and that's it—all the required Auto Layout constraints have been set. Build and run the application and compare the result with Figure 13-5.

Editing the Persistence Classes

In the Project Navigator, select *ViewController.m* and add the following code to the class's @implementation section:

```
@implementation ViewController

- (NSString *)dataFilePath
{
    NSArray *paths = NSSearchPathForDirectoriesInDomains(
                         NSDocumentDirectory, NSUserDomainMask, YES);
    NSString *documentsDirectory = [paths objectAtIndex:0];
    return [documentsDirectory stringByAppendingPathComponent:@"data.plist"];
}
```

The dataFilePath method returns the full pathname of our data file by finding the *Documents* directory and appending our file name to it. This method will be called from any code that needs to load or save data.

Find the viewDidLoad method and add the following code to it, as well as a new method for receiving notifications named applicationWillResignActive: just below it, like this:

```
- (void)viewDidLoad
{
    [super viewDidLoad];
    // Do any additional setup after loading the view, typically from a nib.
    NSString *filePath = [self dataFilePath];
    if ([[NSFileManager defaultManager] fileExistsAtPath:filePath]) {
        NSArray *array = [[NSArray alloc] initWithContentsOfFile:filePath];
        for (int i = 0; i < 4; i++) {
            UITextField *theField = self.lineFields[i];
            theField.text = array[i];
        }
    }
}
```

```
    UIApplication *app = [UIApplication sharedApplication];
    [[NSNotificationCenter defaultCenter]
     addObserver:self
        selector:@selector(applicationWillResignActive:)
            name:UIApplicationWillResignActiveNotification
          object:app];
}

- (void)applicationWillResignActive:(NSNotification *)notification {
    NSString *filePath = [self dataFilePath];
    NSArray *array = [self.lineFields valueForKey:@"text"];
    [array writeToFile:filePath atomically:YES];
}
```

In the viewDidLoad method, we do a few more things. First, we use the NSFileManager class to check whether a data file already exists. If there isn't one, we don't want to bother trying to load it. If the file does exist, we instantiate an array with the contents of that file, and then copy the objects from that array to our four text fields. Because arrays are ordered lists, we copy them in the same order as we save them (the code for which you haven't yet seen), so that we are always sure to get the correct values in the correct fields:

```
NSString *filePath = [self dataFilePath];
if ([[NSFileManager defaultManager] fileExistsAtPath:filePath]) {
    NSArray *array = [[NSArray alloc] initWithContentsOfFile:filePath];
    for (int i = 0; i < 4; i++) {
        UITextField *theField = self.lineFields[i];
        theField.text = array[i];
    }
}
```

After we load the data from the property list, we get a reference to our application instance and use that to subscribe to UIApplicationWillResignActiveNotification, using the default NSNotificationCenter instance and a method called addObserver:selector:name:object:. We pass self as the first parameter, specifying that our ViewController instance is the observer that should be notified. For the second parameter, we pass a selector to the applicationWillResignActive: method, telling the notification center to call that method when the notification is posted. The third parameter, UIApplicationWillResignActiveNotification, is the name of the notification that we're interested in receiving. This is a string constant defined by the UIApplication class. The final parameter, app, is the object we're interested in getting the notification from:

```
UIApplication *app = [UIApplication sharedApplication];
[[NSNotificationCenter defaultCenter]
addObserver:self
    selector:@selector(applicationWillResignActive:)
        name:UIApplicationWillResignActiveNotification
      object:app];
```

The final new method is called applicationWillResignActive:. Notice that it takes a pointer to an NSNotification as an argument. You probably recognize this pattern from Chapter 12. applicationWillResignActive: is a notification method, and all notifications take a single NSNotification instance as their argument.

Our application needs to save its data before it is terminated or sent to the background, so we are interested in the notification called UIApplicationWillResignActiveNotification. This notification is posted whenever an app is no longer the one with which the user is interacting. This happens when the user taps the **Home** button, as well as when the application is pushed to the background by some other event, such as an incoming phone call. Earlier, in the viewDidLoad method, we used the notification center to subscribe to that particular notification. This method is called when that notification happens:

```
- (void)applicationWillResignActive:(NSNotification *)notification {
    NSString *filePath = [self dataFilePath];
    NSArray *array = [self.lineFields valueForKey:@"text"];
    [array writeToFile:filePath atomically:YES];
}
```

This method is pretty short, but really does a lot with just a few method calls. We construct an array of strings by calling the text method on each of the text fields in our lineFields array. To accomplish this, we use a clever shortcut: instead of explicitly iterating through our array of text fields, asking each for its text value, and adding that value to a new array, we simply call valueForKey: on our array, passing @"text" as a parameter. The NSArray implementation of valueForKey: does the iteration for us, asks each UITextField instance it contains for its text value, and returns a new array containing all the values. After that, we write the contents of that array out to our *.plist* file. That's all there is to saving our data using property lists.

That wasn't too bad, was it? When our main view is finished loading, we look for a *.plist* file. If it exists, we copy data from it into our text fields. Next, we register to be notified when the application becomes inactive (either by being quit or pushed to the background). When that happens, we gather the values from our four text fields, stick them in a mutable array, and write that mutable array to a property list.

Why don't you compile and run the application? It should build and then launch in the simulator. Once it comes up, you should be able to type into any of the four text fields. When you've typed something in them, press the **Home** button (the circular button with the rounded square in it at the bottom of the simulator window). It's very important that you press the **Home** button. If you just exit the simulator, that's the equivalent of forcibly quitting your application. In that case, the view controller will never receive the notification that the application is going inactive, and your data will not be saved. After pressing the **Home** button, you may quit the simulator, or stop the app from Xcode and run it again. Your text will be restored the next time the app starts.

> **Note**   It's important to understand that pressing the **Home** button doesn't typically quit the app—at least not at first. The app is put into a background state, ready to be instantly reactivated in case the user switches back to it. We'll dig into the details of these states and their implications for running and quitting apps in Chapter 15. In the meantime, if you want to verify that the data really was saved, you can quit the iOS simulator entirely and then restart your app from Xcode. Quitting the simulator is basically the equivalent of rebooting an iPhone. The next time your app starts, it will give the user a fresh relaunch experience.

Property list serialization is pretty cool and easy to use. However, it's a little limiting, since only a small selection of objects can be stored in property lists. Let's look at a somewhat more robust approach.

Archiving Model Objects

In the Cocoa world, the term **archiving** refers to another form of serialization, but it's a more generic type that any object can implement. Any model object specifically written to hold data should support archiving. The technique of archiving model objects lets you easily write complex objects to a file and then read them back in.

As long as every property you implement in your class is either a scalar (e.g., int or float) or an instance of a class that conforms to the NSCoding protocol, you can archive your objects completely. Since most Foundation and Cocoa Touch classes capable of storing data do conform to NSCoding (though there are a few noteworthy exceptions, such as UIImage), archiving is relatively easy to implement for most classes.

Although not strictly required to make archiving work, another protocol should be implemented along with NSCoding: the NSCopying protocol, which allows your object to be copied. Being able to copy an object gives you a lot more flexibility when using data model objects.

Conforming to NSCoding

The NSCoding protocol declares two methods, which are both required. One encodes your object into an archive; the other one creates a new object by decoding an archive. Both methods are passed an instance of NSCoder, which you work with in very much the same way as NSUserDefaults, introduced in the previous chapter. You can encode and decode both objects and native datatypes like int and float values using key-value coding.

A method to encode an object might look like this:

```
- (void)encodeWithCoder:(NSCoder *)encoder {
    [encoder encodeObject:foo forKey:kFooKey];
    [encoder encodeObject:bar forKey:kBarKey];
    [encoder encodeInt:someInt forKey:kSomeIntKey];
    [encoder encodeFloat:someFloat forKey:kSomeFloatKey]
}
```

To support archiving in our object, we need to encode each of our instance variables into encoder using the appropriate encoding method. If you are subclassing a class that also conforms to NSCoding, you need to make sure you call encodeWithCoder: on your superclass to ensure that the superclass encodes its data. Therefore, your method would look like this instead:

```
- (void)encodeWithCoder:(NSCoder *)encoder {
    [super encodeWithCoder:encoder];  // Let superclass encode its state
    [encoder encodeObject:foo forKey:kFooKey];
    [encoder encodeObject:bar forKey:kBarKey];
    [encoder encodeInt:someInt forKey:kSomeIntKey];
    [encoder encodeFloat:someFloat forKey:kSomeFloatKey]
}
```

We also need to implement a method that initializes an object from an NSCoder, allowing us to restore an object that was previously archived. Implementing the initWithCoder: method is slightly more complex than implementing encodeWithCoder:. If you are subclassing NSObject directly or subclassing some other class that doesn't conform to NSCoding, your method would look something like the following:

```
- (id)initWithCoder:(NSCoder *)decoder {
    if (self = [super init]) {
        foo = [decoder decodeObjectForKey:kFooKey];
        bar = [decoder decodeObjectForKey:kBarKey];
        someInt = [decoder decodeIntForKey:kSomeIntKey];
        someFloat = [decoder decodeFloatForKey:kAgeKey];
    }
    return self;
}
```

The method initializes an object instance using [super init]. If that's successful, it sets its properties by decoding values from the passed-in instance of NSCoder. When implementing NSCoding for a class with a superclass that also conforms to NSCoding, the initWithCoder: method needs to look slightly different. Instead of calling init on super, it needs to call initWithCoder:, like so:

```
- (id)initWithCoder:(NSCoder *)decoder {
    if (self = [super initWithCoder:decoder]) {
        foo = [decoder decodeObjectForKey:kFooKey];
        bar = [decoder decodeObjectForKey:kBarKey];
        someInt = [decoder decodeIntForKey:kSomeIntKey];
        someFloat = [decoder decodeFloatForKey:kAgeKey];
    }
    return self;
}
```

And that's basically it. As long as you implement these two methods to encode and decode all your object's properties, your object is archivable and can be written to and read from archives.

Implementing NSCopying

As mentioned earlier, conforming to NSCopying is a very good idea for any data model objects. NSCopying has one method, called copyWithZone:, which allows objects to be copied. Implementing NSCopying is similar to implementing initWithCoder:. You just need to create a new instance of the same class, and then set all of that new instance's properties to the same values as this object's properties. Here's what a copyWithZone: method might look like:

```
- (id)copyWithZone:(NSZone *)zone {
    MyClass *copy = [[[self class] allocWithZone:zone] init];
    copy.foo = [self.foo copyWithZone:zone];
    copy.bar = [self.bar copyWithZone:zone];
    copy.someInt = self.someInt;
    copy.someFloat = self.someFloat;
    return copy;
}
```

> **Note** Don't worry too much about the NSZone parameter. This pointer is to a struct that is used by the system to manage memory. Only in rare circumstances did developers ever need to worry about zones or create their own, and nowadays, it's almost unheard of to have multiple zones. Calling copy on an object is the same as calling copyWithZone: using the default zone, which is always what you want. In fact, on the modern iOS, zones are completely ignored. The fact that NSCopying uses zones at all is a historical oddity for the sake of backward compatibility.

Archiving and Unarchiving Data Objects

Creating an archive from an object (or objects) that conforms to NSCoding is relatively easy. First, we create an instance of NSMutableData to hold the encoded data, and then we create an NSKeyedArchiver instance to archive objects into that NSMutableData instance:

```
NSMutableData *data = [[NSMutableData alloc] init];
NSKeyedArchiver *archiver = [[NSKeyedArchiver alloc]
    initForWritingWithMutableData:data];
```

After creating both of those, we then use key-value coding to archive any objects we wish to include in the archive, like this:

```
[archiver encodeObject:myObject forKey:@"keyValueString"];
```

Once we've encoded all the objects we want to include, we just tell the archiver we're finished, and then we write the NSMutableData instance to the file system:

```
[archiver finishEncoding];
BOOL success = [data writeToFile:@"/path/to/archive" atomically:YES];
```

If anything went wrong while writing the file, success will be set to NO. If success is YES, the data was successfully written to the specified file. Any objects created from this archive will be exact copies of the objects that were last written into the file.

There is a quicker way to achieve the same thing, using the NSKeyedArchiver archiveDataWithRootObject: method, which allocates an NSData object and encodes the object into it in a single step, then returns the NSData object:

```
NSData *data = [NSKeyedArchiver archivedDataWithRootObject:object];
BOOL success = [data writeToFile:@"/path/to/archive" atomically:YES];
```

You can also go straight from the object to the file using the archiveRootObject:toFile: method:

```
BOOL success = [NSKeyedArchiver archiveRootObject:object
                    toFile:@"/path/to/archive"];
```

To reconstitute objects from the archive, we go through a similar process. We create an NSData instance from the archive file and create an NSKeyedUnarchiver to decode the data:

```
NSData *data = [[NSData alloc] initWithContentsOfFile:@"/path/to/archive"];
NSKeyedUnarchiver *unarchiver = [[NSKeyedUnarchiver alloc]
    initForReadingWithData:data];
```

After that, we read our objects from the unarchiver using the same key that we used to archive the object:

```
self.object = [unarchiver decodeObjectForKey:@"keyValueString"];
```

Finally, we tell the archiver we are finished:

```
[unarchiver finishDecoding];
```

As with the archiving step, there are convenience methods that let you unarchive directly from an NSData object or from a file without allocating an NSKeyedUnarchiver instance.

If you're feeling a little overwhelmed by archiving, don't worry. It's actually fairly straightforward. We're going to retrofit our Persistence application to use archiving, so you'll get to see it in action. Once you've done it a few times, archiving will become second nature, as all you're really doing is storing and retrieving your object's properties using key-value coding.

The Archiving Application

Let's redo the Persistence application, so it uses archiving instead of property lists. We're going to be making some fairly significant changes to the Persistence source code, so you should make a copy of your entire project folder before continuing.

Implementing the FourLines Class

Once you're ready to proceed and have a copy of your Persistence project open in Xcode, press ⌘N or select **File ➤ New ➤ File...**. When the new file assistant comes up, from the iOS section, select **Cocoa Touch Class** and click **Next**. On the next screen, name the class *FourLines* and select **NSObject** in the **Subclass of** control. Click **Next** again. Now choose the *Persistence* folder to save the files, and then click **Create**. This class is going to be our data model. It will hold the data that we're currently storing in a dictionary in the property list application.

Single-click *FourLines.h* and make the following changes:

```
#import <Foundation/Foundation.h>

@interface FourLines : NSObject <NSCoding, NSCopying>

@property (copy, nonatomic) NSArray *lines;

@end
```

This is a very straightforward data model class with an array property of four strings. Notice that we've conformed the class to the NSCoding and NSCopying protocols. Now switch over to *FourLines.m* and add the following code:

```
#import "FourLines.h"

static NSString * const kLinesKey = @"kLinesKey";

@implementation FourLines

#pragma mark - Coding

- (id)initWithCoder:(NSCoder *)aDecoder {
    self = [super init];
    if (self) {
        self.lines = [aDecoder decodeObjectForKey:kLinesKey];
    }
    return self;
}

- (void)encodeWithCoder:(NSCoder *)aCoder; {
    [aCoder encodeObject:self.lines forKey:kLinesKey];
}

#pragma mark - Copying

- (id)copyWithZone:(NSZone *)zone; {
    FourLines *copy = [[[self class] allocWithZone:zone] init];
    NSMutableArray *linesCopy = [NSMutableArray array];
    for (id line in self.lines) {
        [linesCopy addObject:[line copyWithZone:zone]];
    }
    copy.lines = linesCopy;
    return copy;
}

@end
```

We just implemented all the methods necessary to conform to NSCoding and NSCopying. We encoded the lines property in encodeWithCoder: and decoded it using the same key value in initWithCoder:. In copyWithZone:, we created a new FourLines object and copied the array of strings to it. See? It's not hard at all; just make sure you did not forget to change anything if you did a lot of copying and pasting.

Implementing the ViewController Class

Now that we have an archivable data object, let's use it to persist our application data. Select *ViewController.m* and make the following changes:

```
#import "ViewController.h"
#import "FourLines.h"

static NSString * const kRootKey = @"kRootKey";

@interface ViewController ()

@property (strong, nonatomic) IBOutletCollection(UITextField) NSArray *lineFields;

@end

@implementation ViewController

- (void)viewDidLoad
{
    [super viewDidLoad];
    // Do any additional setup after loading the view, typically from a nib.
    NSString *filePath = [self dataFilePath];
    if ([[NSFileManager defaultManager] fileExistsAtPath:filePath]) {
        NSArray *array = [[NSArray alloc] initWithContentsOfFile:filePath];
        for (int i = 0; i < 4; i++) {
            UITextField *theField = self.lineFields[i];
            theField.text = array[i];
        }
        NSData *data = [[NSMutableData alloc]
                          initWithContentsOfFile:filePath];
        NSKeyedUnarchiver *unarchiver = [[NSKeyedUnarchiver alloc]
                                           initForReadingWithData:data];
        FourLines *fourLines = [unarchiver decodeObjectForKey:kRootKey];
        [unarchiver finishDecoding];

        for (int i = 0; i < 4; i++) {
            UITextField *theField = self.lineFields[i];
            theField.text = fourLines.lines[i];
        }
    }

    UIApplication *app = [UIApplication sharedApplication];
    [[NSNotificationCenter defaultCenter]
      addObserver:self
        selector:@selector(applicationWillResignActive:)
            name:UIApplicationWillResignActiveNotification
          object:app];
}
```

```
- (void)applicationWillResignActive:(NSNotification *)notification
{
    NSString *filePath = [self dataFilePath];
    NSArray *array = [self.lineFields valueForKey:@"text"];
    [array writeToFile:filePath atomically:YES];

    FourLines *fourLines = [[FourLines alloc] init];
    fourLines.lines = [self.lineFields valueForKey:@"text"];
    NSMutableData *data = [[NSMutableData alloc] init];
    NSKeyedArchiver *archiver = [[NSKeyedArchiver alloc]
                                 initForWritingWithMutableData:data];
    [archiver encodeObject:fourLines forKey:kRootKey];
    [archiver finishEncoding];
    [data writeToFile:filePath atomically:YES];
}

- (NSString *)dataFilePath
{
    NSArray *paths = NSSearchPathForDirectoriesInDomains(
                        NSDocumentDirectory, NSUserDomainMask, YES);
    NSString *documentsDirectory = [paths objectAtIndex:0];
    return [documentsDirectory stringByAppendingPathComponent:@"data.plist"];
    return [documentsDirectory stringByAppendingPathComponent:@"data.archive"];
}

@end
```

Save your changes and take this version of Persistence for a spin.

Not very much has changed, really. We started off by specifying a new file name so that our program doesn't try to load the old property list as an archive. We also defined a new constant that will be the key value we use to encode and decode our object. Next, we redefined the loading and saving by using FourLines to hold the data and using its NSCoding methods to do the actual loading and saving. The GUI is identical to the previous version.

This new version takes several more lines of code to implement than property list serialization, so you might be wondering if there really is an advantage to using archiving over just serializing property lists. For this application, the answer is simple: no, there really isn't any advantage. But imagine we had an array of archivable objects, such as the FourLines class that we just built, we could archive the entire array by archiving the array instance itself. Collection classes like NSArray, when archived, archive all of the objects they contain. As long as every object you put into an array or dictionary conforms to NSCoding, you can archive the array or dictionary and restore it so that all the objects that were in it when you archived it will be in the restored array or dictionary. The same is not true of property link persistence, which only works for a small set of Foundation object types—you cannot use it to persist custom classes without writing additional code to convert instances of those classes to and from an NSDictionary, with one key for each object property.

In other words, the NSCoding approach scales beautifully (in terms of code size, at least). No matter how many objects you add, the work to write those objects to disk (assuming you're using single-file persistence) is exactly the same. With property lists, the amount of work increases with every object you add.

Using iOS's Embedded SQLite3

The third persistence option we're going to discuss is using iOS's embedded SQL database, called SQLite3. SQLite3 is very efficient at storing and retrieving large amounts of data. It's also capable of doing complex aggregations on your data, with much faster results than you would get doing the same thing using objects.

Consider a couple scenarios. What if your application needs to calculate the sum of a particular field across all the objects in your application? Or, what if you need the sum from just the objects that meet certain criteria? SQLite3 allows you to get this information without loading every object into memory. Getting aggregations from SQLite3 is several orders of magnitude faster than loading all the objects into memory and summing their values. Being a full-fledged embedded database, SQLite3 contains tools to make it even faster by, for example, creating table indexes that can speed up your queries.

> **Note**   There are several schools of thought about the pronunciation of "SQL" and "SQLite." Most official documentation says to pronounce "SQL" as "Ess-Queue-Ell" and "SQLite" as "Ess-Queue-Ell-Light." Many people pronounce them, respectively, as "Sequel" and "Sequel Light." A small cadre of hardened rebels prefer "Squeal" and "Squeal Light." Pick whatever works best for you (and be prepared to be mocked and shunned by the infidels if you choose to join the "Squeal" movement).

SQLite3 uses the Structured Query Language (SQL), the standard language used to interact with relational databases. Whole books have been written on the syntax of SQL (hundreds of them, in fact), as well as on SQLite itself. So if you don't already know SQL and you want to use SQLite3 in your application, you have a little work ahead of you. We'll show you how to set up and interact with the SQLite database from your iOS applications, and we'll also show you some of the basics of the syntax in this chapter. But to really make the most of SQLite3, you'll need to do some additional research and exploration. A couple of good starting points are "An Introduction to the SQLite3 C/C++ Interface" (www.sqlite.org/cintro.html) and "SQL As Understood by SQLite" (www.sqlite.org/lang.html).

Relational databases (including SQLite3) and object-oriented programming languages use fundamentally different approaches to storing and organizing data. The approaches are different enough that numerous techniques and many libraries and tools for converting between the two have been developed. These different techniques are collectively called **object-relational mapping** (ORM). There are currently several ORM tools available for Cocoa Touch. In fact, we'll look at one ORM solution provided by Apple, called Core Data, later in the chapter.

But before we do that, we're going to focus on the SQLite3 basics, including setting it up, creating a table to hold your data, and using the database in an application. Obviously, in the real world, an application as simple as the one we're working on wouldn't warrant the investment in SQLite3. But this application's simplicity is exactly what makes it a good learning example.

Creating or Opening the Database

Before you can use SQLite3, you must open the database. The function that's used to do that, sqlite3_open(), will open an existing database; or, if none exists at the specified location, the function will create a new one. Here's what the code to open a database might look like:

```
sqlite3 *database;
int result = sqlite3_open("/path/to/database/file", &database);
```

If result is equal to the constant SQLITE_OK, then the database was successfully opened. Note that the path to the database file must be passed in as a C string, not as an NSString. SQLite3 was written in portable C, not Objective-C, and it has no idea what an NSString is. Fortunately, there is an NSString method that generates a C string from an NSString instance:

```
const char *stringPath = [pathString UTF8String];
```

When you're finished with an SQLite3 database, close it:

```
sqlite3_close(database);
```

Databases store all their data in tables. You can create a new table by crafting an SQL CREATE statement and passing it in to an open database using the function sqlite3_exec, like so:

```
char *errorMsg;
const char *createSQL = "CREATE TABLE IF NOT EXISTS PEOPLE"
    "(ID INTEGER PRIMARY KEY AUTOINCREMENT, FIELD_DATA TEXT)";
int result = sqlite3_exec(database, createSQL, NULL, NULL, &errorMsg);
```

> **Tip** If two inline strings are separated by nothing but white space, including line breaks, they are concatenated into a single string.

As before, you need to verify that result is equal to SQLITE_OK to make sure your command ran successfully. If it didn't, errorMsg will contain a description of the problem that occurred.

The function sqlite3_exec is used to run any command against SQLite3 that doesn't return data, including updates, inserts, and deletes. Retrieving data from the database is a little more involved. You first need to prepare the statement by feeding it your SQL SELECT command:

```
NSString *query = @"SELECT ID, FIELD_DATA FROM FIELDS ORDER BY ROW";
sqlite3_stmt *statement;
int result = sqlite3_prepare_v2(database, [query UTF8String],
    -1, &statement, nil);
```

> **Note** All of the SQLite3 functions that take strings require an old-fashioned C string. In the example, we created and passed a C string. Specifically, we created an NSString and derived a C string by using one of NSString's methods called UTF8String. Either method is acceptable. If you need to do manipulation on the string, using NSString or NSMutableString will be easier; however, converting from NSString to a C string incurs a bit of extra overhead.

If result equals SQLITE_OK, your statement was successfully prepared, and you can start stepping through the result set. Here is an example of stepping through a result set and retrieving an int and an NSString from the database:

```
while (sqlite3_step(statement) == SQLITE_ROW) {
    int rowNum = sqlite3_column_int(statement, 0);
    char *rowData = (char *)sqlite3_column_text(statement, 1);
    NSString *fieldValue = [[NSString alloc] initWithUTF8String:rowData];
    // Do something with the data here
}
sqlite3_finalize(statement);
```

Using Bind Variables

Although it's possible to construct SQL strings to insert values, it is common practice to use something called **bind variables** for this purpose. Handling strings correctly—making sure they don't have invalid characters and that quotes are inserted properly—can be quite a chore. With bind variables, those issues are taken care of for us.

To insert a value using a bind variable, you create your SQL statement as normal, but put a question mark (?) into the SQL string. Each question mark represents one variable that must be bound before the statement can be executed. Next, you prepare the SQL statement, bind a value to each of the variables, and execute the command.

Here's an example that prepares an SQL statement with two bind variables, binds an int to the first variable and a string to the second variable, and then executes and finalizes the statement:

```
char *sql = "insert into foo values (?, ?);";
sqlite3_stmt *stmt;
if (sqlite3_prepare_v2(database, sql, -1, &stmt, nil) == SQLITE_OK) {
    sqlite3_bind_int(stmt, 1, 235);
    sqlite3_bind_text(stmt, 2, "Bar", -1, NULL);
}
if (sqlite3_step(stmt) != SQLITE_DONE)
    NSLog(@"This should be real error checking!");
sqlite3_finalize(stmt);
```

There are multiple bind statements available, depending on the datatype you wish to use. Most bind functions take only three parameters:

- The first parameter to any bind function, regardless of the datatype, is a pointer to the `sqlite3_stmt` used previously in the `sqlite3_prepare_v2()` call.

- The second parameter is the index of the variable to which you're binding. This is a one-indexed value, meaning that the first question mark in the SQL statement has index 1, and each one after it is one higher than the one to its left.

- The third parameter is always the value that should be substituted for the question mark.

A few bind functions, such as those for binding text and binary data, have two additional parameters:

- The first additional parameter is the length of the data being passed in the third parameter. In the case of C strings, you can pass -1 instead of the string's length, and the function will use the entire string. In all other cases, you need to tell it the length of the data being passed in.

- The final parameter is an optional function callback in case you need to do any memory cleanup after the statement is executed. Typically, such a function would be used to free memory allocated using `malloc()`.

The syntax that follows the bind statements may seem a little odd since we're doing an insert. When using bind variables, the same syntax is used for both queries and updates. If the SQL string had an SQL query, rather than an update, we would need to call `sqlite3_step()` multiple times until it returned `SQLITE_DONE`. Since this is an update, we call it only once.

The SQLite3 Application

In Xcode, create a new project using the Single View Application template and name it *SQLite Persistence*. This project will start off identical to the previous project, so begin by opening the *ViewController.m* file, and then make the following changes:

```
#import "ViewController.h"

@interface ViewController ()

@property (strong, nonatomic) IBOutletCollection(UITextField) NSArray *lineFields;

@end
```

Next, select *Main.storyboard*. Design the view and connect the outlet collection by following the instructions in the "Designing the Persistence Application View" section earlier in this chapter. Once your design is complete, save the storyboard file.

We've covered the basics, so let's see how this would work in practice. We're going to retrofit our Persistence application again, this time storing its data using SQLite3. We'll use a single table and store the field values in four different rows of that table. We'll also give each row a row number that corresponds to its field. For example, the value from the first line will get stored in the table with a row number of 0, the next line will be row number 1, and so on. Let's get started.

Linking to the SQLite3 Library

SQLite 3 is accessed through a procedural API that provides interfaces to a number of C function calls. To use this API, we'll need to link our application to a dynamic library called *libsqlite3.dylib*. The process of linking a dynamic library into your project is exactly the same as that of linking in a framework.

Select the **SQLite Persistence** item at the very top of the Project Navigator list (leftmost pane), and then select **SQLite Persistence** from the **TARGETS** section in the main area (see the middle pane of Figure 13-6). (Be careful that you have selected SQLite Persistence from the **TARGETS** section, not from the **PROJECT** section.)

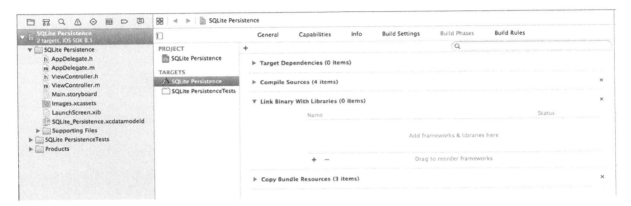

Figure 13-6. *Selecting the SQLite Persistence project in the Project Navigator; selecting the SQLite Persistence target; and finally, selecting the Build Phases tab*

With the SQLite Persistence target selected, click the **Build Phases** tab in the rightmost pane. You'll see a list of items, initially all collapsed, which represent the various steps Xcode goes through to build the application. Expand the item labeled **Link Binary With Libraries**. This section contains the libraries and frameworks that Xcode links with your application. By default, it's empty because the compiler automatically links with any iOS frameworks that your application uses, but the compiler doesn't know anything about the SQLite3 library, so we need to add it here.

Click the **+** button at the bottom of the linked frameworks list, and you'll be presented with a sheet that lists all available frameworks and libraries. Find *libsqlite3.dylib* in the list (or use the handy search field) and click the **Add** button. Note that there may be several other entries in that directory that start with *libsqlite3*. Be sure you select *libsqlite3.dylib*. It is an alias that always points to the latest version of the SQLite3 library.

Modifying the Persistence View Controller

Now we can write some more code. Select *ViewController.m* and make the following changes:

```objc
#import "ViewController.h"
#import <sqlite3.h>

@interface ViewController ()

@property (strong, nonatomic) IBOutletCollection(UITextField) NSArray *lineFields;

@end

@implementation ViewController

- (NSString *)dataFilePath {
    NSArray *paths = NSSearchPathForDirectoriesInDomains(
                          NSDocumentDirectory, NSUserDomainMask, YES);
    NSString *documentsDirectory = [paths objectAtIndex:0];
    return [documentsDirectory stringByAppendingPathComponent:@"data.sqlite"];
}

- (void)viewDidLoad
{
    [super viewDidLoad];
    // Do any additional setup after loading the view, typically from a nib.
    sqlite3 *database;
    if (sqlite3_open([[self dataFilePath] UTF8String], &database)
        != SQLITE_OK) {
        sqlite3_close(database);
        NSAssert(0, @"Failed to open database");
    }

    // Useful C trivia: If two inline strings are separated by nothing
    // but whitespace (including line breaks), they are concatenated into
    // a single string:
    NSString *createSQL = @"CREATE TABLE IF NOT EXISTS FIELDS "
                           "(ROW INTEGER PRIMARY KEY, FIELD_DATA TEXT);";
    char *errorMsg;
    if (sqlite3_exec (database, [createSQL UTF8String],
                      NULL, NULL, &errorMsg) != SQLITE_OK) {
        sqlite3_close(database);
        NSAssert(0, @"Error creating table: %s", errorMsg);
    }

    NSString *query = @"SELECT ROW, FIELD_DATA FROM FIELDS ORDER BY ROW";
    sqlite3_stmt *statement;
    if (sqlite3_prepare_v2(database, [query UTF8String],
                           -1, &statement, nil) == SQLITE_OK) {
        while (sqlite3_step(statement) == SQLITE_ROW) {
            int row = sqlite3_column_int(statement, 0);
            char *rowData = (char *)sqlite3_column_text(statement, 1);
```

```objc
            NSString *fieldValue = [[NSString alloc]
                                    initWithUTF8String:rowData];
            UITextField *field = self.lineFields[row];
            field.text = fieldValue;
        }
        sqlite3_finalize(statement);
    }
    sqlite3_close(database);

    UIApplication *app = [UIApplication sharedApplication];
    [[NSNotificationCenter defaultCenter]
     addObserver:self
        selector:@selector(applicationWillResignActive:)
            name:UIApplicationWillResignActiveNotification
          object:app];
}

- (void)applicationWillResignActive:(NSNotification *)notification
{
    sqlite3 *database;
    if (sqlite3_open([[self dataFilePath] UTF8String], &database)
        != SQLITE_OK) {
        sqlite3_close(database);
        NSAssert(0, @"Failed to open database");
    }
    for (int i = 0; i < 4; i++) {
        UITextField *field = self.lineFields[i];
        // Once again, inline string concatenation to the rescue:
        char *update = "INSERT OR REPLACE INTO FIELDS (ROW, FIELD_DATA) "
                       "VALUES (?, ?);";
        char *errorMsg = NULL;
        sqlite3_stmt *stmt;
        if (sqlite3_prepare_v2(database, update, -1, &stmt, nil)
            == SQLITE_OK) {
            sqlite3_bind_int(stmt, 1, i);
            sqlite3_bind_text(stmt, 2, [field.text UTF8String], -1, NULL);
        }
        if (sqlite3_step(stmt) != SQLITE_DONE) {
            NSAssert(0, @"Error updating table: %s", errorMsg);
        }
        sqlite3_finalize(stmt);
    }
    sqlite3_close(database);
}

- (void)didReceiveMemoryWarning
{
    [super didReceiveMemoryWarning];
    // Dispose of any resources that can be recreated.
}

@end
```

The first piece of new code to look at is in the viewDidLoad method. We begin by opening the database. If we hit a problem with opening the database, we close it and raise an assertion:

```
sqlite3 *database;
if (sqlite3_open([[self dataFilePath] UTF8String], &database)
    != SQLITE_OK) {
    sqlite3_close(database);
    NSAssert(0, @"Failed to open database");
}
```

Next, we need to make sure that we have a table to hold our data. We can use SQL CREATE TABLE to do that. By specifying IF NOT EXISTS, we prevent the database from overwriting existing data. If there is already a table with the same name, this command quietly completes without doing anything, so it's safe to call every time our application launches without explicitly checking to see if a table exists:

```
NSString *createSQL = @"CREATE TABLE IF NOT EXISTS FIELDS "
                       "(ROW INTEGER PRIMARY KEY, FIELD_DATA TEXT);";
char *errorMsg;
if (sqlite3_exec (database, [createSQL UTF8String],
                  NULL, NULL, &errorMsg) != SQLITE_OK) {
    sqlite3_close(database);
    NSAssert(0, @"Error creating table: %s", errorMsg);
}
```

Each row in the database table contains an integer and a string. The integer is the number of the row in the GUI from which the data was obtained (starting from zero), and the string is the content of the text field on that row. Finally, we need to load our data. We do this using an SQL SELECT statement. In this simple example, we create an SQL SELECT that requests all the rows from the database and ask SQLite3 to prepare our SELECT. We also tell SQLite3 to order the rows by the row number, so that we always get them back in the same order. Absent this, SQLite3 will return the rows in the order in which they are stored internally.

```
NSString *query = @"SELECT ROW, FIELD_DATA FROM FIELDS ORDER BY ROW";
sqlite3_stmt *statement;
if (sqlite3_prepare_v2(database, [query UTF8String],
                       -1, &statement, nil) == SQLITE_OK) {
```

Next, we step through each of the returned rows:

```
while (sqlite3_step(statement) == SQLITE_ROW) {
```

Now we grab the row number, store it in an int, and then grab the field data as a C string:

```
int row = sqlite3_column_int(statement, 0);
char *rowData = (char *)sqlite3_column_text(statement, 1);
```

Next, we set the appropriate field with the value retrieved from the database:

```
NSString *fieldValue = [[NSString alloc]
                        initWithUTF8String:rowData];
UITextField *field = self.lineFields[row];
field.text = fieldValue;
```

Finally, we close the database connection, and we're finished:

```
    }
    sqlite3_finalize(statement);
}
sqlite3_close(database);
```

Note that we close the database connection as soon as we're finished creating the table and loading any data it contains, rather than keeping it open the entire time the application is running. It's the simplest way of managing the connection; and in this little app, we can just open the connection those few times we need it. In a more database-intensive app, you might want to keep the connection open all the time.

The other changes we made are in the applicationWillResignActive: method, where we need to save our application data. Our application's data will look something like Table 13-1 when stored in the database table.

Table 13-1. Data Stored in the FIELDS Table of the Database

ROW	FIELD_DATA
0	Here's to the crazy ones.
1	The misfits. The rebels.
2	The troublemakers.
3	The round pegs in the square holes.

The applicationWillResignActive: method starts by once again opening the database.
To save the data, we loop through all four fields and issue a separate command to update each row of the database:

```
for (int i = 0; i < 4; i++) {
    UITextField *field = self.lineFields[i];
```

We craft an INSERT OR REPLACE SQL statement with two bind variables. The first represents the row that's being stored; the second is for the actual string value to be stored. By using INSERT OR REPLACE instead of the more standard INSERT, we don't need to worry about whether a row already exists:

```
char *update = "INSERT OR REPLACE INTO FIELDS (ROW, FIELD_DATA) "
               "VALUES (?, ?);";
```

Next, we declare a pointer to a statement, prepare our statement with the bind variables, and bind values to both of the bind variables:

```
sqlite3_stmt *stmt;
if (sqlite3_prepare_v2(database, update, -1, &stmt, nil)
    == SQLITE_OK) {
    sqlite3_bind_int(stmt, 1, i);
    sqlite3_bind_text(stmt, 2, [field.text UTF8String], -1, NULL);
}
```

Now we call `sqlite3_step` to execute the update, check to make sure it worked, and finalize the statement, ending the loop:

```
if (sqlite3_step(stmt) != SQLITE_DONE) {
    NSAssert(0, @"Error updating table: %s", errorMsg);
}
sqlite3_finalize(stmt);
```

Notice that we used an assertion here to check for an error condition. We use assertions rather than exceptions or manual error-checking because this condition should happen only if we, the developers, make a mistake. Using this assertion macro will help us debug our code, and it can be stripped out of our final application. If an error condition is one that a user might reasonably experience, you should probably use some other form of error checking.

> **Note**   There is one condition that could cause an error to occur in the preceding SQLite code that is not a programmer error. If the device's storage is completely full—to the extent that SQLite can't save its changes to the database—then an error will occur here, as well. However, this condition is fairly rare and will probably result in deeper problems for the user, outside the scope of our app's data. Our app probably wouldn't even launch successfully if the system were in that state. So we're going to just sidestep the issue entirely.

Once we're finished with the loop, we close the database:

```
sqlite3_close(database);
```

Why don't you compile and run the app? Enter some data and then press the iPhone simulator's **Home** button. Quit the simulator (to force the app to actually quit), and then relaunch the SQLite Persistence application. That data should be right where you left it. As far as the user is concerned, there's absolutely no difference between the various versions of this application; however, each version uses a very different persistence mechanism.

Using Core Data

The final technique we're going to demonstrate in this chapter is how to implement persistence using Apple's Core Data framework. Core Data is a robust, full-featured persistence tool. Here, we will show you how to use Core Data to re-create the same persistence you've seen in our Persistence application so far.

> **Note** For more comprehensive coverage of Core Data, check out *Pro iOS Persistence: Using Core Data* by Michael Privet and Robert Warner (Apress, 2014).

In Xcode, create a new project. Select the **Single View Application** template from the **iOS** section and click **Next**. Name the product *Core Data Persistence* and select **Universal** from the **Devices** control; but don't click the **Next** button just yet. If you look just below the **Devices** control, you'll see a check box labeled **Use Core Data**. There's a certain amount of complexity involved in adding Core Data to an existing project, so Apple has kindly provided an option with some application project templates to do much of the work for you.

Check the **Use Core Data** check box (see Figure 13-7), and then click the **Next** button. When prompted, choose a directory to store your project and then click **Create**.

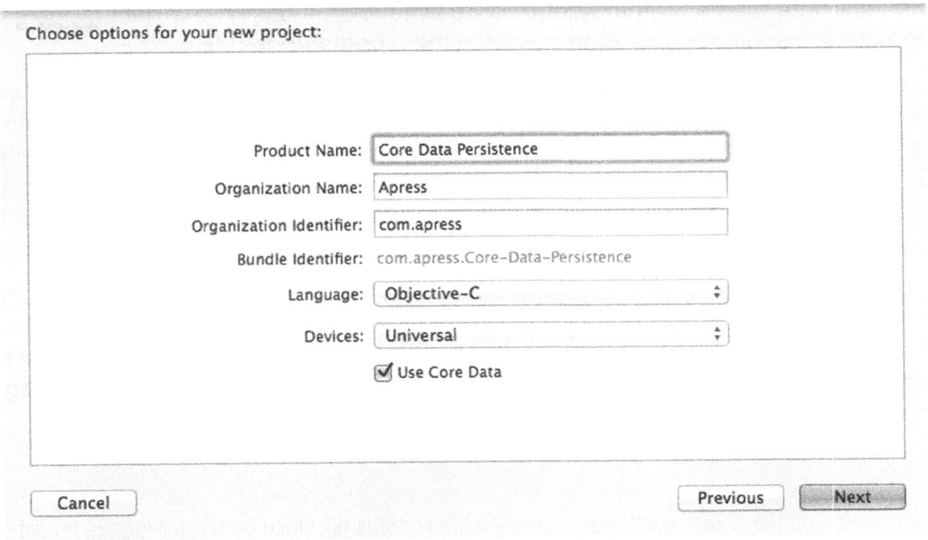

Figure 13-7. Some project templates, including Single View Application, offer the option to use Core Data for persistence

Before we move on to our code, let's take a look at the project window, which contains some new stuff. Expand the *Core Data Persistence* folder if it's closed (see Figure 13-8).

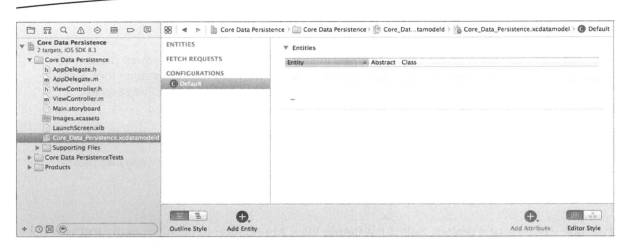

Figure 13-8. *Our project template with the files needed for Core Data. The Core Data model is selected, and the data model editor is shown in the editing pane*

Entities and Managed Objects

Most of what you see in the Project Navigator should be familiar: the application delegate and the image assets catalog. In addition, you'll find a file called *Core_Data_Persistence.xcdatamodeld*, which contains our data model. Within Xcode, Core Data lets us design our data models visually, without writing code, and stores that data model in the *.xcdatamodeld* file.

Single-click the *.xcdatamodeld* file now, and you will be presented with the **data model editor** (see the right side of Figure 13-8). The data model editor gives you two distinct views into your data model, depending on the setting of the **Editor Style** control in the lower-right corner of the project window. In Table mode, the mode shown in Figure 13-8, the elements that make up your data model will be shown in a series of editable tables. In Graph mode, you'll see a graphical depiction of the same elements. At the moment, both views reflect the same empty data model.

Before Core Data, the traditional way to create data models was to create subclasses of NSObject and conform them to NSCoding and NSCopying so that they could be archived, as we did earlier in this chapter. Core Data uses a fundamentally different approach. Instead of classes, you begin by creating **entities** here in the data model editor; and then, in your code, you create **managed objects** from those entities.

> **Note** The terms *entity* and *managed object* can be a little confusing, since both refer to data model objects. *Entity* refers to the description of an object. *Managed object* refers to actual concrete instances of that entity created at runtime. So, in the data model editor, you create entities; but in your code, you create and retrieve managed objects. The distinction between entities and managed objects is similar to the distinction between a class and instances of that class.

An entity is made up of properties. There are three types of properties:

- **Attributes**: An attribute serves the same function in a Core Data entity as an instance variable does in an Objective-C class. They both hold the data.

- **Relationships**: As the name implies, a relationship defines the relationship between entities. For example, to create a `Person` entity, you might start by defining a few attributes such as `hairColor`, `eyeColor`, `height`, and `weight`. You might also define address attributes, such as `state` and `zipCode`, or you might embed them in a separate `HomeAddress` entity. Using the latter approach, you would then create a relationship between a `Person` and a `HomeAddress`. Relationships can be **to-one** and **to-many**. The relationship from `Person` to `HomeAddress` is probably to-one, since most people have only a single home address. The relationship from `HomeAddress` to `Person` might be to-many, since there may be more than one `Person` living at that `HomeAddress`.

- **Fetched properties**: A fetched property is an alternative to a relationship. Fetched properties allow you to create a query that is evaluated at fetch time to see which objects belong to the relationship. To extend our earlier example, a `Person` object could have a fetched property called `Neighbors` that finds all `HomeAddress` objects in the data store that have the same ZIP code as the `Person`'s own `HomeAddress`. Due to the nature of how fetched properties are constructed and used, they are always one-way relationships. Fetched properties are also the only kind of relationship that lets you traverse multiple data stores.

Typically, attributes, relationships, and fetched properties are defined using Xcode's data model editor. In our Core Data Persistence application, we'll build a simple entity, so you can get a sense of how this all works together.

Key-Value Coding

In your code, instead of using accessors and mutators, you will use **key-value coding** to set properties or retrieve their existing values. Key-value coding may sound intimidating, but you've already used it quite a bit in this book. Every time we used `NSDictionary`, for example, we were using a form of key-value coding because every object in a dictionary is stored under a unique key value. The key-value coding used by Core Data is a bit more complex than that used by `NSDictionary`, but the basic concept is the same.

When working with a managed object, the key you will use to set or retrieve a property's value is the name of the attribute you wish to set. So, here's how to retrieve the value stored in the attribute called `name` from a managed object:

```
NSString *name = [myManagedObject valueForKey:@"name"];
```

Similarly, to set a new value for a managed object's property, do this:

```
[myManagedObject setValue:@"Gregor Overlander" forKey:@"name"];
```

Putting It All in Context

So where do these managed objects live? They live in something called a **persistent store**, also referred to as a **backing store**. Persistent stores can take several different forms. By default, a Core Data application implements a backing store as an SQLite database stored in the application's *Documents* directory. Even though your data is stored via SQLite, classes in the Core Data framework do all the work associated with loading and saving your data. If you use Core Data, you don't need to write any SQL statements like the ones you saw in the SQLite Persistence application. You just work with objects, and Core Data figures out what it needs to do behind the scenes.

SQLite isn't the only option Core Data has for storage. Backing stores can also be implemented as binary flat files or even stored in an XML format. Another option is to create an in-memory store, which you might use if you're writing a caching mechanism; however, it doesn't save data beyond the end of the current session. In almost all situations, you should just leave it as the default and use SQLite as your persistent store.

Although most applications will have only one persistent store, it is possible to have multiple persistent stores within the same application. If you're curious about how the backing store is created and configured, take a look at the file *AppDelegate.m* in your Xcode project. The Xcode project template we chose provided us with all the code needed to set up a single persistent store for our application.

Other than creating it (which is handled for you in your application delegate), you generally won't work with your persistent store directly. Rather, you will use something called a **managed object context**, often referred to as just a **context**. The context manages access to the persistent store and maintains information about which properties have changed since the last time an object was saved. The context also registers all changes with the **undo manager**, which means that you always have the ability to undo a single change or roll back all the way to the last time data was saved.

> **Note**   You can have multiple contexts pointing to the same persistent store, though most iOS applications will use only one.

Many Core Data method calls require an NSManagedObjectContext as a parameter or must be executed against a context. With the exception of more complicated, multithreaded iOS applications, you can just use the managedObjectContext property provided by your application delegate, which is a default context that is created for you automatically, also courtesy of the Xcode project template.

You may notice that in addition to a managed object context and a persistent store coordinator, the provided application delegate also contains an instance of NSManagedObjectModel. This class is responsible for loading and representing, at runtime, the data model you will create using the data model editor in Xcode. You generally won't need to interact directly with this class. It's used behind the scenes by the other Core Data classes, so they can identify which entities and properties you've defined in your data model. As long as you create your data model using the provided file, there's no need to worry about this class at all.

Creating New Managed Objects

Creating a new instance of a managed object is pretty easy, though not quite as straightforward as creating a normal object instance using alloc and init. Instead, you use the insertNewObjectFor EntityForName:inManagedObjectContext: factory method in a class called NSEntityDescription. NSEntityDescription's job is to keep track of all the entities defined in the app's data model and to let you create instances of those entities. This method creates and returns an instance representing a single entity in memory. It returns either an instance of NSManagedObject that is set up with the correct properties for that particular entity; or, if you've configured your entity to be implemented with a specific subclass of NSManagedObject, an instance of that class. Remember that entities are like classes. An entity is a description of an object and defines which properties a particular entity has.

To create a new object, do this:

```
NSManagedObject *thing = [NSEntityDescription
                    insertNewObjectForEntityForName:@"Thing"
                        inManagedObjectContext:context];
```

The method is called insertNewObjectForEntityForName:inManagedObjectContext: because, in addition to creating the object, it inserts the newly created object into the context and then returns that object. After this call, the object exists in the context, but is not yet part of the persistent store. The object will be added to the persistent store the next time the managed object context's save: method is called.

Retrieving Managed Objects

To retrieve managed objects from the persistent store, you'll use a **fetch request**, which is Core Data's way of handling a predefined query. For example, you might say, "Give me every Person whose eyeColor is blue."

After first creating a fetch request, you provide it with an NSEntityDescription that specifies the entity of the object or objects you wish to retrieve. Here is an example that creates a fetch request:

```
NSFetchRequest *request = [[NSFetchRequest alloc] init];
NSEntityDescription *entityDescr = [NSEntityDescription
    entityForName:@"Thing" inManagedObjectContext:context];
[request setEntity:entityDescr];
```

Optionally, you can also specify criteria for a fetch request using the NSPredicate class. A **predicate** is similar to the SQL WHERE clause and allows you to define the criteria used to determine the results of your fetch request. Here is a simple example of a predicate:

```
NSPredicate *pred =
    [NSPredicate predicateWithFormat:@"(name = %@)", nameString];
[request setPredicate: pred];
```

The predicate created by the first line of code tells a fetch request that, instead of retrieving all managed objects for the specified entity, get just those where the name property is set to the value currently stored in the nameString variable. So, if nameString is an NSString that holds the value @"Bob", we are telling the fetch request to bring back only managed objects that have a name property set to "Bob". This is a simple example, but predicates can be considerably more complex and can use Boolean logic to specify the precise criteria you might need in most any situation.

> **Note**   *Learn Objective-C on the Mac,* 2nd Edition, by Scott Knaster, Waqar Maliq, and Mark Dalrymple
> (Apress, 2012) has an entire chapter devoted to the use of NSPredicate.

After you've created your fetch request, provided it with an entity description, and optionally given it a predicate, you **execute** the fetch request using an instance method on NSManagedObjectContext:

```
NSError *error;
NSArray *objects = [context executeFetchRequest:request error:&error];
if (objects == nil) {
    // handle error
}
```

executeFetchRequest:error: will load the specified objects from the persistent store and return them in an array. If an error is encountered, you will get a nil array, and the error pointer you provided will point to an NSError object that describes the specific problem. If no error occurs, you will get a valid array, though it may not have any objects in it since it is possible that none meets the specified criteria. From this point on, any changes you make to the managed objects returned in that array will be tracked by the managed object context you executed the request against, and saved when you send that context a save: message.

The Core Data Application

Let's take Core Data for a spin now. First, we'll return our attention to Xcode and create our data model.

Designing the Data Model

Select *Core_Data_Persistence.xcdatamodel* to open Xcode's data model editor. The data model editing pane shows all the entities, fetch requests, and configurations that are contained within your data model.

> **Note**   The Core Data concept of **configurations** lets you define one or more named subsets of the entities
> contained in your data model, which can be useful in certain situations. For example, if you want to create a
> suite of apps that shares the same data model, but some apps shouldn't have access to everything (perhaps
> there's one app for normal users and another for administrators), this approach lets you do that. You can
> also use multiple configurations within a single app as it switches between different modes of operation.
> In this book, we're not going to deal with configurations at all; but since the list of configurations (including
> the single default configuration that contains everything in your model) is right there, staring you in the face
> beneath the entities and fetch requests, we thought it was worth a mention here.

As shown in Figure 13-8, those lists are empty now because we haven't created anything yet. Remedy that by clicking the plus icon labeled **Add Entity** in the lower-left corner of the editor pane. This will create a brand-new entity with the name *Entity* (see Figure 13-9).

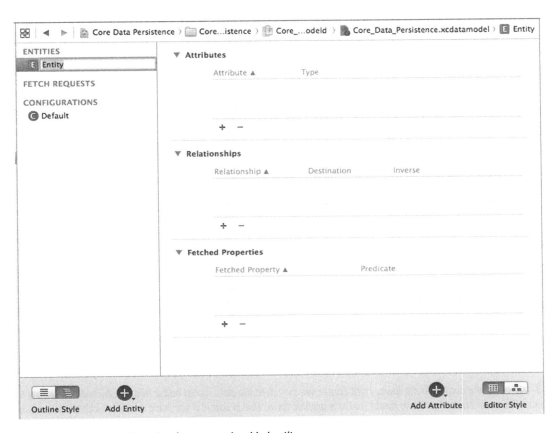

Figure 13-9. The data model editor, showing our newly added entity

As you build your data model, you'll probably find yourself switching between Table view and Graph view using the **Editor Style** control at the bottom right of the editing area. Switch to Graph view now. Graph view presents a little box representing our entity, which itself contains sections for showing the entity's attributes and relationships, also currently empty (see Figure 13-10). Graph view is really useful if your model contains multiple entities, because it shows a graphic representation of all the relationships between your entities.

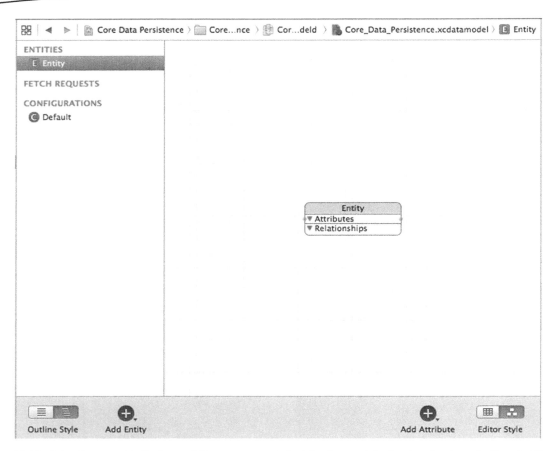

Figure 13-10. *Using the control in the lower-right corner, we switched the data model editor into Graph mode. Note that Graph mode shows the same entities as Table mode, just in a graphic form. This is useful if you have multiple entities with relationships between them*

Note   If you prefer working graphically, you can actually build your entire model in Graph view. We're going to stick with Table view in this chapter because it's easier to explain. When you're creating your own data models, feel free to work in Graph view if that approach suits you better.

Whether you're using Table view or Graph view for designing your data model, you'll almost always want to bring up the Core Data data model inspector. This inspector lets you view and edit relevant details for whatever item is selected in the data model editor—whether it's an entity, attribute, relationship, or anything else. You can browse an existing model without the data model inspector; but to really work on a model, you'll invariably need to use this inspector, much as you frequently use the Attributes Inspector when editing nib files.

Press ⌥⌘3 to open the data model inspector. At the moment, the inspector shows information about the entity we just added. The single entity in our model contains the data from one line on the GUI, so we'll call it *Line*. Change the **Name** field from *Entity* to *Line* (see Figure 13-11).

Figure 13-11. Using the data model inspector to change our entity's name to Line

If you're currently in Graph view, use the **Editor Style** control to switch to Table view now. Table view shows more details for each piece of the entity we're working on, so it's usually more useful than Graph view when creating a new entity. In Table view, most of the data model editor is taken up by the table showing the entity's attributes, relationships, and fetched properties. This is where we'll set up our entity.

Notice that at the lower right of the editing area, next to the Editor Style control, there's an icon containing a plus sign labeled **Add Attribute**. If you select your entity and then hold down the mouse button over this control, a pop-up menu will appear, allowing you to add an attribute, relationship, or fetched property to your entity (see Figure 13-12).

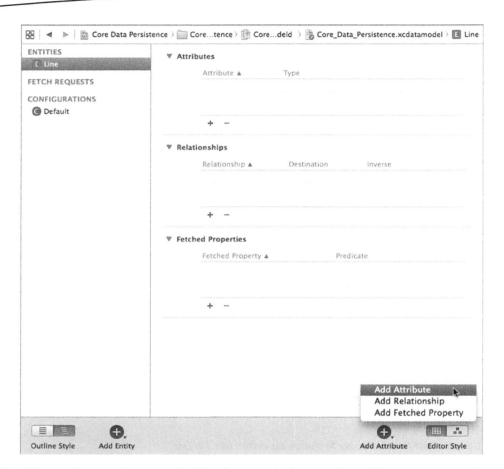

Figure 13-12. *With an entity selected, press and hold the right plus-sign icon to add an attribute, relationship, or fetched property to your entity*

> **Note**   Notice that you don't need to press and hold to add an attribute. You'll get the same result if you just click the plus icon. Shortcut!

Go ahead and use this technique to add an attribute to your Line entity. A new attribute, creatively named *attribute*, is added to the Attributes section of the table and selected. In the table, you'll see that not only is the row selected, but the attribute's name is selected as well. This means that immediately after clicking the plus sign, you can start typing the name of the new attribute without further clicking.

Change the new attribute's name from *attribute* to *lineNumber,* and click the pop-up next to the name to change its Type from *Undefined* to *Integer 16*. Doing so turns this attribute into one that will hold an integer value. We will be using this attribute to identify which of the managed object's four fields holds data. Since we have only four options, we selected the smallest integer type available.

Now direct your attention to the data model inspector, which is in the pane to the right of the editor area. Here, additional details can be configured. The check box below the **Name** field on the right, **Optional**, is selected by default. Click it to deselect it. We don't want this attribute to be optional—a line that doesn't correspond to a label on our interface is useless.

Selecting the **Transient** check box creates a transient attribute. This attribute is used to specify a value that is held by managed objects while the app is running, but is never saved to the data store. We do want the line number saved to the data store, so leave the **Transient** check box unchecked.

Selecting the **Indexed** check box will cause an index in the underlying SQL database to be created on the column that holds this attribute's data. Leave the **Indexed** check box unchecked. The amount of data is small, and we won't provide the user with a search capability; therefore, there's no need for an index.

Beneath that are more settings that allow us to do some simple data validation by specifying minimum and maximum values for the integer, a default value, and more. We won't be using any of these settings in this example.

Now make sure the Line entity is selected and click the **Add Attribute** control to add a second attribute. Change the name of your new attribute to *lineText* and change its Type to *String*. This attribute will hold the actual data from the text field. Leave the **Optional** check box checked for this one; it is altogether possible that the user won't enter a value for a given field.

> **Note**   When you change the Type to *String*, you'll notice that the inspector shows a slightly different set of options for setting a default value or limiting the length of the string. Although we won't be using any of those options for this application, it's nice to know they're there.

Guess what? Your data model is complete. That's all there is to it. Core Data lets you point and click your way to an application data model. Let's finish building the application so you can see how to use our data model from our code.

Creating the Persistence View

Select *ViewController.m* and make the following change:

```
#import "ViewController.h"

@interface ViewController ()

@property (strong, nonatomic) IBOutletCollection(UITextField) NSArray *lineFields;

@end
```

Save this file. Next, select *Main.storyboard* to edit the GUI in Interface Builder. Design the view and connect the outlet collection by following the instructions in the "Designing the Persistence Application View" section earlier in this chapter. You might also find it useful to refer back to Figure 13-5. Once your design is complete, save the storyboard file.

Now go back to *ViewController.m*, and make the following changes:

```objc
#import "ViewController.h"
#import "AppDelegate.h"

static NSString * const kLineEntityName = @"Line";
static NSString * const kLineNumberKey = @"lineNumber";
static NSString * const kLineTextKey = @"lineText";

@interface ViewController ()

@property (strong, nonatomic) IBOutletCollection(UITextField) NSArray *lineFields;

@end

@implementation ViewController

- (void)viewDidLoad
{
    [super viewDidLoad];
    // Do any additional setup after loading the view, typically from a nib.

    AppDelegate *appDelegate = [UIApplication sharedApplication].delegate;
    NSManagedObjectContext *context = [appDelegate managedObjectContext];
    NSFetchRequest *request = [[NSFetchRequest alloc]
                                initWithEntityName:kLineEntityName];

    NSError *error;
    NSArray *objects = [context executeFetchRequest:request error:&error];
    if (objects == nil) {
        NSLog(@"There was an error!");
        // Do whatever error handling is appropriate
    }

    for (NSManagedObject *oneObject in objects) {
        int lineNum = [[oneObject valueForKey:kLineNumberKey] intValue];
        NSString *lineText = [oneObject valueForKey:kLineTextKey];

        UITextField *theField = self.lineFields[lineNum];
        theField.text = lineText;
    }

    UIApplication *app = [UIApplication sharedApplication];
    [[NSNotificationCenter defaultCenter]
      addObserver:self
        selector:@selector(applicationWillResignActive:)
            name:UIApplicationWillResignActiveNotification
          object:app];
}
```

```objc
- (void)applicationWillResignActive:(NSNotification *)notification {
    AppDelegate *appDelegate = [UIApplication sharedApplication].delegate;
    NSManagedObjectContext *context = [appDelegate managedObjectContext];
    NSError *error;
    for (int i = 0; i < 4; i++) {
        UITextField *theField = self.lineFields[i];

        NSFetchRequest *request = [[NSFetchRequest alloc]
                                    initWithEntityName:kLineEntityName];
        NSPredicate *pred = [NSPredicate
                             predicateWithFormat:@"(%K = %d)", kLineNumberKey, i];
        [request setPredicate:pred];

        NSArray *objects = [context executeFetchRequest:request error:&error];
        if (objects == nil) {
            NSLog(@"There was an error!");
            // Do whatever error handling is appropriate
        }

        NSManagedObject *theLine = nil;
        if ([objects count] > 0) {
            theLine = [objects objectAtIndex:0];
        } else {
            theLine = [NSEntityDescription
                       insertNewObjectForEntityForName:kLineEntityName
                       inManagedObjectContext:context];
        }

        [theLine setValue:[NSNumber numberWithInt:i] forKey:kLineNumberKey];
        [theLine setValue:theField.text forKey:kLineTextKey];


    }
    [appDelegate saveContext];
}

- (void)didReceiveMemoryWarning
{
    [super didReceiveMemoryWarning];
    // Dispose of any resources that can be recreated.
}

@end
```

Now let's look at the `viewDidLoad` method, which needs to check whether there is any existing data in the persistent store. If there is, it should load the data and populate the fields with it. The first thing we do in that method is get a reference to our application delegate, which we then use to get the managed object context that was created for us:

```objc
AppDelegate *appDelegate = [UIApplication sharedApplication].delegate;
NSManagedObjectContext *context = [appDelegate managedObjectContext];
```

The next order of business is to create a fetch request and pass it the entity name, so it knows which type of objects to retrieve:

```
NSFetchRequest *request = [[NSFetchRequest alloc]
                             initWithEntityName:kLineEntityName];
```

Since we want to retrieve all Line objects in the persistent store, we do not create a predicate. By executing a request without a predicate, we're telling the context to give us every Line object in the store. We make sure we got back a valid array and log it if we didn't.

```
NSError *error;
NSArray *objects = [context executeFetchRequest:request error:&error];
if (objects == nil) {
    NSLog(@"There was an error!");
    // Do whatever error handling is appropriate
}
```

Next, we use fast enumeration to loop through the array of retrieved managed objects, pull the lineNum and lineText values from each managed object, and use that information to update one of the text fields on our user interface:

```
for (NSManagedObject *oneObject in objects) {
    int lineNum = [[oneObject valueForKey:kLineNumberKey] intValue];
    NSString *lineText = [oneObject valueForKey:kLineTextKey];

    UITextField *theField = self.lineFields[lineNum];
    theField.text = lineText;
}
```

Then, just as with all the other applications in this chapter, we register to be notified when the application is about to move out of the active state (either by being shuffled to the background or exited completely), so we can save any changes the user has made to the data:

```
UIApplication *app = [UIApplication sharedApplication];
[[NSNotificationCenter defaultCenter]
 addObserver:self
    selector:@selector(applicationWillResignActive:)
        name:UIApplicationWillResignActiveNotification
      object:app];
```

Let's look at applicationWillResignActive: next. We start out the same way as the previous method: by getting a reference to the application delegate and using that to get a pointer to our application's default context:

```
AppDelegate *appDelegate = [UIApplication sharedApplication].delegate;
NSManagedObjectContext *context = [appDelegate managedObjectContext];
```

After that, we go into a loop that executes four times, one time for each text field, and then get a reference to the correct field:

```
for (int i = 0; i < 4; i++) {
    UITextField *theField = self.lineFields[i];
```

Next, we create our fetch request for our Line entry. We need to find out if there's already a managed object in the persistent store that corresponds to this field, so we create a predicate that identifies the correct object for the field by using the index of the text field as the record key:

```
NSFetchRequest *request = [[NSFetchRequest alloc]
                        initWithEntityName:kLineEntityName];
NSPredicate *pred = [NSPredicate
            predicateWithFormat:@"(%K = %d)", kLineNumberKey, i];
[request setPredicate:pred];
```

Now we execute the fetch request against the context and check to make sure that objects is not nil. If it is nil, there was an error, and we should do whatever error checking is appropriate for our application. For this simple application, we're just logging the error and moving on:

```
NSArray *objects = [context executeFetchRequest:request error:&error];
if (objects == nil) {
    NSLog(@"There was an error!");
    // Do whatever error handling is appropriate
}
```

After that, we declare a pointer to an NSManagedObject and set it to nil. We do this because we don't know yet whether we're going to get a managed object from the persistent store or create a new one. To know this, we check if an object that matched our criteria was returned. If there is one, we load it. If there isn't one, we create a new managed object to hold this field's text:

```
NSManagedObject *theLine = nil;
if ([objects count] > 0) {
    theLine = [objects objectAtIndex:0];
} else {
    theLine = [NSEntityDescription
                insertNewObjectForEntityForName:kLineEntityName
                inManagedObjectContext:context];
}
```

Next, we use key-value coding to set the line number and text for this managed object:

```
[theLine setValue:[NSNumber numberWithInt:i] forKey:kLineNumberKey];
[theLine setValue:theField.text forKey:kLineTextKey];
```

Finally, once we're finished looping, we tell the context to save its changes:

```
[appDelegate saveContext];
```

That's it! Build and run the app to make sure it works. The Core Data version of your application should behave exactly the same as the previous versions.

It may seem that Core Data entails a lot of work; and, for a simple application like this, it doesn't offer much of an advantage. But in more complex applications, Core Data can substantially decrease the amount of time you spend designing and writing your data model.

Persistence Rewarded

You should now have a solid handle on four different ways of preserving your application data between sessions—five ways if you include the user defaults that you learned how to use in the previous chapter. We built an application that persisted data using property lists and modified the application to save its data using object archives. We then made a change and used the iOS's built-in SQLite3 mechanism to save the application data. Finally, we rebuilt the same application using Core Data. These mechanisms are the basic building blocks for saving and loading data in almost all iOS applications.

Chapter 14

Documents and iCloud

One of the biggest new features added to iOS in the past couple of years is Apple's iCloud service, which provides cloud storage services for iOS devices, as well as for computers running OS X. Most iOS users will probably encounter the iCloud device backup option immediately when setting up a new device or upgrading an old device to a more recent version of iOS. And they will quickly discover the advantages of automatic backup that doesn't even require the use of a computer.

Computerless backup is a great feature, but it only scratches the surface of what iCloud can do. What may be even a bigger feature of iCloud is that it provides app developers with a mechanism for transparently saving data to Apple's cloud servers with very little effort. You can make your apps save data to iCloud and have that data automatically transfer to any other devices that are registered to the same iCloud user. Users may create a document on their iPad and later view the same document on their iPhone or Mac without any intervening steps; the document just appears.

A system process takes care of making sure the user has a valid iCloud login and manages the file transfers, so you don't need to worry about networks or authentication. Apart from a small amount of app configuration, just a few small changes to your methods for saving files and locating available files will get you well on your way to having an iCloud-backed app.

One key component of the iCloud filing system is the UIDocument class. UIDocument takes a portion of the work out of creating a document-based app by handling some of the common aspects of reading and writing files. That way, you can spend more of your time focusing on the unique features of your app, instead of building the same plumbing for every app you create.

Whether you're using iCloud or not, UIDocument provides some powerful tools for managing document files in iOS. To demonstrate these features, the first portion of this chapter is dedicated to creating TinyPix, a simple document-based app that saves files to local storage. This is an approach that can work well for all kinds of iOS-based apps.

Later in this chapter, we'll show you how to iCloud-enable TinyPix. For that to work, you'll need to have one or more iCloud-connected iOS devices at hand. You'll also need a paid iOS developer account, so that you can install on devices. This is because apps running in the simulator don't have access to iCloud services.

Managing Document Storage with UIDocument

Anyone who has used a desktop computer for anything besides just surfing the Web has probably worked with a document-based application. From TextEdit to Microsoft Word to GarageBand to Xcode, any piece of software that lets you deal with multiple collections of data, saving each collection to a separate file, could be considered a document-based application. Often, there's a one-to-one correspondence between an on-screen window and the document it contains; however, sometimes (e.g., Xcode) a single window can display multiple documents that are all related in some way.

On iOS devices, we don't have the luxury of multiple windows, but plenty of apps can still benefit from a document-based approach. Now iOS developers have a little boost in making it work—thanks to the UIDocument class, which takes care of the most common aspects of document file storage. You won't need to deal with files directly (just URLs), and all the necessary reading and writing happens on a background thread, so your app can remain responsive even while file access is occurring. It also automatically saves edited documents periodically and whenever the app is suspended (such as when the device is shut down, the **Home** button is pressed, and so on), so there's no need for any sort of save button. All of this helps make your apps behave the way users expect their iOS apps to behave.

Building TinyPix

We're going to build an app called TinyPix that lets you edit simple 8 × 8 images, in glorious 1-bit color (see Figure 14-1)! For the user's convenience, each picture is blown up to the full screen size for editing. And, of course, we'll be using UIDocument to represent the data for each image.

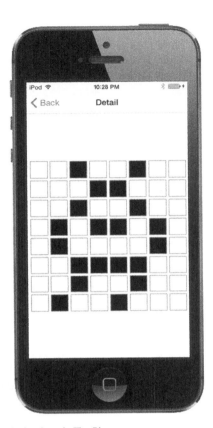

Figure 14-1. Editing an extremely low-resolution icon in TinyPix

Start off by creating a new project in Xcode. From the **iOS Application** section, select the **Master-Detail Application** template and then click **Next**. Name this new app *TinyPix* and set the **Devices** pop-up to *Universal*. Make sure the **Use Core Data** check box is unchecked. Now click **Next** again and choose the location to save your project.

In Xcode's Project Navigator, you'll see that your project contains files for AppDelegate, MasterViewController, and DetailViewController, as well as the *Main.storyboard* file. We'll make changes to all of these files and we will create a few new classes along the way, as well.

Creating TinyPixDocument

The first new class we're going to create is the document class that will contain the data for each TinyPix image that's loaded from file storage. Select the *TinyPix* folder in Xcode and press ⌘N to create a new file. From the **iOS** section, select **Cocoa Touch Class** and click **Next**. Enter **TinyPixDocument** in the **Class** field, enter **UIDocument** in the **Subclass of** field, and click **Next**. Finally, click **Create** to create the files.

Let's think about the public API of this class before we get into its implementation details. This class is going to represent an 8 × 8 grid of pixels, where each pixel consists of a single on or off value. So, let's give it a method that takes a pair of row and column indexes and returns a BOOL value. Let's also provide a method to set a specific state at a specified row and column, and as a convenience, another method that simply toggles the state at a particular place.

Select *TinyPixDocument.h* to edit the new class's header. Add the following bold lines:

```
#import <UIKit/UIKit.h>

@interface TinyPixDocument : UIDocument

// row and column range from 0 to 7
- (BOOL)stateAtRow:(NSUInteger)row column:(NSUInteger)column;
- (void)setState:(BOOL)state atRow:(NSUInteger)row column:(NSUInteger)column;
- (void)toggleStateAtRow:(NSUInteger)row column:(NSUInteger)column;

@end
```

Now switch over to *TinyPixDocument.m*, where we'll implement storage for our 8 × 8 grid, the methods defined in our public API, and the required UIDocument methods that will enable loading and saving our documents.

Let's start by defining the storage for our 8 × 8 bitmap data. We'll hold this data in an instance of NSMutableData, which lets us work directly with an array of byte data that is still contained inside an object, so that the usual Cocoa memory management will take care of freeing the memory when we're finished with it. Add this class extension to make it happen:

```
#import "TinyPixDocument.h"

@interface TinyPixDocument ()

@property (strong, nonatomic) NSMutableData *bitmap;

@end

@implementation TinyPixDocument
```

The UIDocument class has a designated initializer that all subclasses should use. This is where we'll create our initial bitmap. In true bitmap style, we're going to minimize memory usage by using a single byte to contain each row. Each bit in the byte represents the on/off value of a column index within that row. In total, our document contains just 8 bytes.

> **Note**   This section contains a small number of bitwise operations, as well as some C pointer and array manipulation. This is all pretty mundane for C developers; but if you don't have much C experience, it may seem puzzling or even impenetrable. In that case, feel free to simply copy and use the code provided (it works just fine). If you really want to understand what's going on, you may want to dig deeper into C itself, perhaps by adding a copy of *Learn C on the Mac* by Dave Mark (Apress, 2009) to your bookshelf.

Add this method to our document's implementation, placing it directly above the @end at the bottom of the file:

```
- (id)initWithFileURL:(NSURL *)url {
    self = [super initWithFileURL:url];
    if (self) {
        unsigned char startPattern[] = {
            0x01,
            0x02,
            0x04,
            0x08,
            0x10,
            0x20,
            0x40,
            0x80
        };

        self.bitmap = [NSMutableData dataWithBytes:startPattern length:8];
    }
    return self;
}
```

This starts off each bitmap with a simple diagonal pattern stretching from one corner to another.

Now, it's time to implement the methods that make up the public API we defined in the header. Let's tackle the method for reading the state of a single bit first. This simply grabs the relevant byte from our array of bytes, and then does a bit shift and an AND operation to determine whether the specified bit was set, returning YES or NO accordingly. Add this method above the @end:

```
- (BOOL)stateAtRow:(NSUInteger)row column:(NSUInteger)column {
    const char *bitmapBytes = [self.bitmap bytes];
    char rowByte = bitmapBytes[row];
    char result = (1 << column) & rowByte;
    if (result != 0) {
        return YES;
    } else {
        return NO;
    }
}
```

Next comes the **inverse**: a method that sets the value specified at a given row and column. Here, we once again grab the relevant byte for the specified row and do a bit shift. But this time, instead of using the shifted bit to examine the contents of the row, we use it to either set or unset a bit in the row. Add this method above the @end:

```
- (void)setState:(BOOL)state atRow:(NSUInteger)row column:(NSUInteger)column {
    char *bitmapBytes = [self.bitmap mutableBytes];
    char *rowByte = &bitmapBytes[row];

    if (state) {
        *rowByte = *rowByte | (1 << column);
    } else {
        *rowByte = *rowByte & ~(1 << column);
    }
}
```

Now, let's add a convenience method that lets outside code simply toggle a single cell:

```
- (void)toggleStateAtRow:(NSUInteger)row column:(NSUInteger)column {
    BOOL state = [self stateAtRow:row column:column];
    [self setState:!state atRow:row column:column];
}
```

Our document class requires two final pieces before it fits into the puzzle of a document-based app: methods for reading and writing. As we mentioned earlier, you don't need to deal with files directly. You don't even need to worry about the URL that was passed into the initWithFileURL: method earlier. All that you need to do is implement one method that transforms the document's data structure into an NSData object, ready for saving, and another that takes a freshly loaded NSData object and pulls the object's data structure out of it. Because our document's internal structure is already contained in an NSMutableData object, which is a subclass of NSData, these implementations are pleasingly simple. Add these two methods above the @end:

```
- (id)contentsForType:(NSString *)typeName error:(NSError **)outError {
    NSLog(@"saving document to URL %@", self.fileURL);
    return [self.bitmap copy];
}

- (BOOL)loadFromContents:(id)contents ofType:(NSString *)typeName
        error:(NSError **)outError {
    NSLog(@"loading document from URL %@", self.fileURL);
    self.bitmap = [contents mutableCopy];
    return true;
}
```

The first of these methods, contentsForType:error:, is called whenever our document is about to be saved to storage. It simply returns an immutable copy of our bitmap data, which the system will take care of storing later.

The second method, `loadFromContents:ofType:error:`, is called whenever the system has just loaded data from storage and wants to provide this data to an instance of our document class. Here, we just grab a mutable copy of the data that has been passed in. We've included some logging statements, just so you can see what's happening in the Xcode log later on.

Each of these methods allows you to do some things that we're ignoring in this app. They both provide a `typeName` parameter, which you could use to distinguish between different types of data storage that your document can load from or save to. They also have an `outError` parameter, which you could use to specify that an error occurred while copying data to or from your document's in-memory data structure. In our case, however, what we're doing is so simple that these aren't important concerns.

That's all we need for our document class. Sticking to MVC principles, our document sits squarely in the model camp, knowing nothing about how it's displayed. And thanks to the `UIDocument` superclass, the document is even shielded from most of the details about how it's stored.

Code Master

Now that we have our document class ready to go, it's time to address the first view that a user sees when running our app: the list of existing TinyPix documents, which is taken care of by the `MasterViewController` class. We need to let this class know how to grab the list of available documents, let the user choose an existing document for viewing or editing, and create and name a new document. When a document is created or chosen, it's then passed along to the detail controller for display.

Start by selecting *MasterViewController.m*. This file, generated as part of the Master–Detail application template, contains starter code for displaying an array of items. We're not going to use any of that, but instead do these things all on our own. Therefore, delete all the methods from the `@implementation` block and all the declarations in the class extension at the top. When you're done, you should have a clean slate that looks something like this:

```
#import "MasterViewController.h"
#import "DetailViewController.h"

@interface MasterViewController ()
@end

@implementation MasterViewController
@end
```

We'll also include a segmented control in our GUI, which will allow the user to choose a tint color that will be used as a highlight color for portions of the TinyPix GUI. Although this is not a particularly useful feature in and of itself, it will help demonstrate the iCloud mechanism, as the highlight color setting makes its way from the device on which you set it to another of your connected devices running the same app. The first version of the app will use the color as a local setting on each device. Later in the chapter, we'll add the code to make the color setting propagate through iCloud to the user's other devices.

To implement the color selection control, we'll add an outlet and an action to our code as well. We'll also add properties for holding onto a list of document file names and a pointer to the document the user has chosen. Make these changes to *MasterViewController.m*:

```
#import "MasterViewController.h"
#import "DetailViewController.h"
#import "TinyPixDocument.h"

@interface MasterViewController ()

@property (weak, nonatomic) IBOutlet UISegmentedControl *colorControl;
@property (strong, nonatomic) NSArray *documentFilenames;
@property (strong, nonatomic) TinyPixDocument *chosenDocument;

@end
```

Before we implement the table view methods and other standard methods that we need to deal with, we are going to write a couple of private utility methods. The first of these takes a file name, combines it with the file path of the app's *Documents* directory, and returns a URL pointing to that specific file. As you saw in Chapter 13, the *Documents* directory is a special location that iOS sets aside, one for each app installed on an iOS device. You can use it to store documents created by your app, and rest assured that those documents will be automatically included whenever users back up their iOS device, whether it's to iTunes or iCloud.

Add this method to the implementation, placing it directly above the @end at the bottom of the file:

```
- (NSURL *)urlForFilename:(NSString *)filename {
    NSFileManager *fm = [NSFileManager defaultManager];
    NSArray *urls = [fm URLsForDirectory:NSDocumentDirectory
                              inDomains:NSUserDomainMask];
    NSURL *directoryURL = urls[0];
    NSURL *fileURL = [directoryURL URLByAppendingPathComponent:filename];
    return fileURL;
}
```

Here we are using a method of the NSFileManager class to get a URL that maps to the application's *Documents* directory. This method works just like the NSSearchPathForDirectoriesInDomains() function that we used in Chapter 13, except that it returns an array of NSURL objects instead of strings, which is more convenient for the purposes of this method.

The second private method is a bit longer. It also uses the *Documents* directory, this time to search for files representing existing documents. The method takes the files it finds and sorts them by creation date, so that the user will see the list of documents sorted "blog-style" with the newest items first. The document file names are stashed away in the documentFilenames property, and then the table view (which we admittedly haven't yet dealt with) is reloaded. Add this method above the @end:

```
- (void)reloadFiles {
    NSArray *paths = NSSearchPathForDirectoriesInDomains(NSDocumentDirectory,
        NSUserDomainMask, YES);
    NSString *path = paths[0];
    NSFileManager *fm = [NSFileManager defaultManager];
```

```
NSError *dirError;
NSArray *files = [fm contentsOfDirectoryAtPath:path error:&dirError];
if (!files) {
    NSLog(@"Error listing files in directory %@: %@",
            path, dirError);
}
NSLog(@"found files: %@", files);

files = [files sortedArrayUsingComparator:
            ^NSComparisonResult(id filename1, id filename2) {
    NSDictionary *attr1 = [fm attributesOfItemAtPath:
                                [path stringByAppendingPathComponent:filename1]
                                                error:nil];
    NSDictionary *attr2 = [fm attributesOfItemAtPath:
                                [path stringByAppendingPathComponent:filename2]
                                                error:nil];
    return [attr2[NSFileCreationDate] compare: attr1[NSFileCreationDate]];
}];
self.documentFilenames = files;
[self.tableView reloadData];
}
```

Now, let's deal with our dear old friends, the table view data source methods. These should be pretty familiar to you by now. Add the following three methods above the @end:

```
- (NSInteger)numberOfSectionsInTableView:(UITableView *)tableView {
    return 1;
}

- (NSInteger)tableView:(UITableView *)tableView
        numberOfRowsInSection:(NSInteger)section {
    return [self.documentFilenames count];
}

- (UITableViewCell *)tableView:(UITableView *)tableView
        cellForRowAtIndexPath:(NSIndexPath *)indexPath {
    UITableViewCell *cell = [tableView dequeueReusableCellWithIdentifier:
                                @"FileCell"];

    NSString *path = self.documentFilenames[indexPath.row];
    cell.textLabel.text = path.lastPathComponent.stringByDeletingPathExtension;
    return cell;
}
```

These methods are based on the contents of the array stored in the documentFilenames property. The tableView:cellForForAtIndexPath: method relies on the existence of a cell attached to the table view with "FileCell" set as its identifier, so we must be sure to set that up in the storyboard a little later.

If not for the fact that we haven't touched our storyboard yet, the code we have now would almost be something we could run and see in action; however, with no preexisting TinyPix documents, we would have nothing to display in our table view. And so far, we don't have any way to create new documents, either. Also, we have not yet dealt with the color-selection control we're going to add. So, let's do a bit more work before we try to run our app.

The user's choice of highlight color will be used to immediately set a tint color for the segmented control. The UIView class has a tintColor property. When it's set for any view, the value applies to that view and will propagate down to all of its subviews. When we set the segmented control's tint color, we'll also store it in NSUserDefaults for later retrieval. Add these two methods above the @end:

```
- (IBAction)chooseColor:(id)sender {
    NSInteger selectedColorIndex = [(UISegmentedControl *)sender
                                    selectedSegmentIndex];
    [self setTintColorForIndex:selectedColorIndex];

    NSUserDefaults *prefs = [NSUserDefaults standardUserDefaults];
    [prefs setInteger:selectedColorIndex forKey:@"selectedColorIndex"];
    [prefs synchronize];
}
- (void)setTintColorForIndex:(NSInteger)selectedColorIndex {
    self.colorControl.tintColor = [TinyPixUtils getTintColorForIndex:selectedColorIndex];
}
```

The first method is triggered when the user changes the selection in the segmented control. It saves the selected index in the user defaults and passes it to the second method, which converts the index to a color and applies it to the segmented control. We'll need the code that does the conversion from index to color in the detail view controller as well, so it's implemented in a separate class. To create that class, press ⌘N to open the new file dialog. From the **iOS** section, select **Cocoa Touch Class** and click **Next**. Enter **TinyPixUtils** in the **Class** field, enter **NSObject** in the **Subclass of** field, and click **Next**. Finally, click **Create** to create the files.

The TinyPixUtils class will have a single method. Edit *TinyPixUtils.h* to add the declaration of that method:

```
#import <UIKit/UIKit.h>

@interface TinyPixUtils : NSObject

+ (UIColor *)getTintColorForIndex:(NSUInteger)index;

@end
```

Now switch over to *TinyPixUtils.m* to add the method implementation:

```
#import "TinyPixUtils.h"

@implementation TinyPixUtils

+ (UIColor *)getTintColorForIndex:(NSUInteger)index {
    UIColor *color = [UIColor redColor];
```

```
    switch (index) {
        case 0:
            color = [UIColor redColor];
            break;
        case 1:
            color =
            [UIColor colorWithRed:0 green:0.6 blue:0 alpha:1];
            break;
        case 2:
            color = [UIColor blueColor];
            break;
        default:
            break;
    }
    return color;
}
```

@end

We realize that we haven't yet set anything up in the storyboard, but we'll get there! First, we have some more work to do in *MasterViewController.m*. Start by adding an import for *TinyPixUtils.h*:

```
#import "MasterViewController.h"
#import "DetailViewController.h"
#import "TinyPixDocument.h"
#import "TinyPixUtils.h"

@interface MasterViewController ()
```

Now let's work on the viewDidLoad method. After calling the superclass's implementation, we'll start by adding a button to the right side of the navigation bar. The user will press this button to create a new TinyPix document. We'll also load the saved tint color from the user defaults and use it to set the tint color of the segmented control. We finish by calling the reloadFiles method that we implemented earlier.

Add this code to implement viewDidLoad:

```
- (void)viewDidLoad {
    [super viewDidLoad];

    UIBarButtonItem *addButton = [[UIBarButtonItem alloc]
        initWithBarButtonSystemItem:UIBarButtonSystemItemAdd
        target:self
        action:@selector(insertNewObject)];
    self.navigationItem.rightBarButtonItem = addButton;

    NSUserDefaults *prefs = [NSUserDefaults standardUserDefaults];
    NSInteger selectedColorIndex = [prefs integerForKey:@"selectedColorIndex"];
    [self setTintColorForIndex:selectedColorIndex];
    [self.colorControl setSelectedSegmentIndex:selectedColorIndex];

    [self reloadFiles];
}
```

As you'll see when you run the app for the first time, the segmented control's tint color starts out being red. That's because there's nothing stored in the user defaults yet, so the `integerForKey:` method returns 0, which the `setTintColorForIndex:` method interprets as red.

You may have noticed that, when we created the `UIBarButtonItem`, we told it to call the `insertNewObject` method when it's pressed. We haven't written that method yet, so let's do so now. Add this method above the @end:

```
- (void)insertNewObject {
    UIAlertController *alert =
        [UIAlertController alertControllerWithTitle:@"Choose File Name"
                  message: @"Enter a name for your new TinyPix document."
                  preferredStyle: UIAlertControllerStyleAlert];

    [alert addTextFieldWithConfigurationHandler:nil];
    UIAlertAction *cancelAction = [UIAlertAction actionWithTitle:@"Cancel"
            style:UIAlertActionStyleCancel handler:nil];
    UIAlertAction *createAction = [UIAlertAction actionWithTitle:@"Create"
            style:UIAlertActionStyleDefault handler:^(UIAlertAction *action) {
                UITextField *textField = (UITextField *)alert.textFields[0];
                [self createFileNamed:textField.text];
            }];
    [alert addAction:cancelAction];
    [alert addAction:createAction];

    [self presentViewController:alert animated:YES completion:nil];
}
```

This method uses the `UIAlertController` class to display an alert that includes a text-input field, a **Create** button, and a **Cancel** button. If the **Create** button is pressed, the responsibility of creating a new item instead falls to the method that the button's handler block calls when it's finished, which we'll also address now. Add this method above the @end:

```
- (void)createFileNamed:(NSString *)fileName {
    NSString *trimmedFileName = [fileName
        stringByTrimmingCharactersInSet:[NSCharacterSet whitespaceCharacterSet]];
    if (trimmedFileName.length > 0) {
        NSString *targetName = [NSString stringWithFormat:@"%@.tinypix",
                                trimmedFileName];
        NSURL *saveUrl = [self urlForFilename:targetName];
        self.chosenDocument =
            [[TinyPixDocument alloc] initWithFileURL:saveUrl];
        [self.chosenDocument saveToURL:saveUrl
                    forSaveOperation:UIDocumentSaveForCreating
                   completionHandler:^(BOOL success) {
                        if (success) {
                            NSLog(@"save OK");
                            [self reloadFiles];
                            [self performSegueWithIdentifier:@"masterToDetail"
                                                      sender:self];
```

```
                } else {
                    NSLog(@"failed to save!");
                }
            }];
    }
}
```

This method starts out simply enough. It strips leading and trailing whitespace characters from the name that it's passed. If the result is not empty, it then creates a file name based on the user's entry, a URL based on that file name (using the urlForFilename: method we wrote earlier), and a new TinyPixDocument instance using that URL.

What comes next is a little more subtle. It's important to understand here that just creating a new document with a given URL doesn't create the file. In fact, at the time that the initWithFileURL: is called, the document doesn't yet know if the given URL refers to an existing file or to a new file that needs to be created. We need to tell it what to do. In this case, we tell it to save a new file at the given URL with this code:

```
        [self.chosenDocument saveToURL:saveUrl
                    forSaveOperation:UIDocumentSaveForCreating
                    completionHandler:^(BOOL success) {
    .
    .
    .
        }];
```

Of interest is the purpose and usage of the block that is passed in as the last argument. The method we're calling, saveToURL:forSaveOperation:completionHandler:, doesn't have a return value to tell us how it all worked out. In fact, the method returns immediately after it's called, long before the file is actually saved. Instead, it starts the file-saving work, and later, when it's done, calls the block that we gave it, using the success parameter to let us know whether it succeeded. To make it all work as smoothly as possible, the file-saving work is actually performed on a background thread. The block we pass in, however, is executed on the thread that called saveToURL:forSaveOperation:completion Handler: in the first place. In this particular case, that means that the block is executed on the main thread, so we can safely use any facilities that require the main thread, such as UIKit. With that in mind, take a look again at what happens inside that block:

```
if (success) {
    NSLog(@"save OK");
    [self reloadFiles];
    [self performSegueWithIdentifier:@"masterToDetail"
            sender:self];
} else {
    NSLog(@"failed to save!");
}
```

This is the content of the block we passed in to the file-saving method, and it's called later, after the file operation is completed. We check to see if it succeeded; if so, we do an immediate file reload, and then initiate a segue to another view controller. This is an aspect of segues that we didn't cover in Chapter 9, but it's pretty straightforward.

The idea is that a segue in a storyboard file can have an identifier, just like a table view cell, and you can use that identifier to trigger a segue programmatically. In this case, we'll just need to remember to configure that segue in the storyboard when we get to it. But before we do that, let's add the last method this class needs, to take care of that segue. Insert this method above the @end:

```
- (void)prepareForSegue:(UIStoryboardSegue *)segue sender:(id)sender {
    UINavigationController *destination =
                    (UINavigationController *)segue.destinationViewController;
    DetailViewController *detailVC =
                    (DetailViewController *)destination.topViewController;
    if (sender == self) {
        // if sender == self, a new document has just been created,
        // and chosenDocument is already set.
        detailVC.detailItem = self.chosenDocument;
    } else {
        // find the chosen document from the tableview
        NSIndexPath *indexPath = [self.tableView indexPathForSelectedRow];
        NSString *filename = self.documentFilenames[indexPath.row];
        NSURL *docUrl = [self urlForFilename:filename];
        self.chosenDocument = [[TinyPixDocument alloc]
                                    initWithFileURL:docUrl];
        [self.chosenDocument openWithCompletionHandler:^(BOOL success) {
            if (success) {
                NSLog(@"load OK");
                detailVC.detailItem = self.chosenDocument;
            } else {
                NSLog(@"failed to load!");
            }
        }];
    }
}
```

This method has two clear paths of execution that are determined by the condition at the top. Remember from our discussion of storyboards in Chapter 9 that this method is called on a view controller whenever a segue is about to performed from that view controller. The sender parameter refers to the object that initiated the segue, and we use that to figure out just what to do here. If the segue is initiated by the programmatic method call we performed in the alert view delegate method, then sender will be equal to self, because that's the value of the sender argument in the performSegueWithIdentifier:sender: call in the createFileNamed: method. In that case, we know that the chosenDocument property is already set, and we simply pass its value to the destination view controller.

Otherwise, we know we're responding to the user touching a row in the table view, and that's where things get a little more complicated. That's the time to construct a URL (much as we did when creating a document), create a new instance of our document class, and try to open the file. You'll see that the method we call to open the file, openWithCompletionHandler:, works similarly to the save method we used earlier. We pass it a block that it will save for later execution. Just as with the file-saving method, the loading occurs in the background, and this block will be executed on the main thread when it's complete. At that point, if the loading succeeded, we pass the document along to the detail view controller.

Note that both of these methods use the key-value coding technique that we've used a few times before, letting us set the detailItem property of the segue's destination controller, even though we don't include its header. This will work out just fine for us, since DetailViewController—the detail view controller class created as part of the Xcode project—happens to include a property called detailItem right out of the box.

With the amount of code we now have in place, it's high time we configured the storyboard so that we can run our app and make something happen. Save your code and continue.

Initial Storyboarding

Select *Main.storyboard* in the Xcode Project Navigator and take a look at what's already there. You'll find scenes for a split view controller, two navigation controllers, the master view controller, and the detail view controller (see Figure 14-2). All of our work will be with the master and detail view controllers.

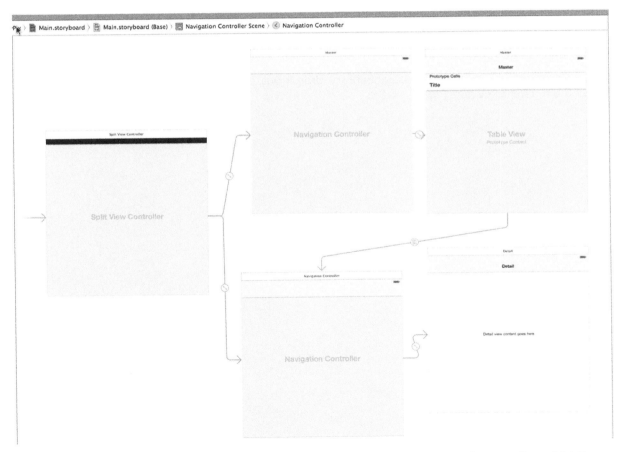

Figure 14-2. The TinyPix storyboard, showing split view controller, navigation controllers, master view controller, and detail view controller

Let's start by dealing with the master view controller scene. This is where the table view showing the list of all our TinyPix documents is configured. By default, this scene's table view is configured to use dynamic cells instead of static cells. We want our table view to get its contents from the data source methods we implemented, so this default setting is just what we want. We do need to configure the cell prototype though, so select it, and open the Attributes Inspector. Change the cell's **Identifier** from *Cell* to *FileCell*. This will let the data source code we wrote earlier access the table view cell.

We also need to create the segue that we're triggering in our code. Do this by Control-dragging from the master view controller's icon (a yellow circle at the top of its scene or the **Master** icon under Master Scene in the Document Outline) over to the Navigation Controller for the detail view, and then selecting **Show Detail** from the storyboard segues menu.

You'll now see two segues that seem to connect the two scenes. By selecting each of them, you can tell where they're coming from. Selecting one segue highlights the whole master scene; selecting the second one highlights just the table view cell. Select the segue that highlights the whole scene (i.e., the segue that you just created), and use the Attributes Inspector to set its **Identifier**, which is currently empty, to *masterToDetail*.

The final touch needed for the master view controller scene is to let the user pick which color will be used to represent an "on" point in the detail view. Instead of implementing some kind of comprehensive color picker, we're just going to add a segmented control that will let the user pick from a set of predefined colors.

Find a **Segmented Control** in the object library, drag it out, and place it in the navigation bar at the top of the master view (see Figure 14-3).

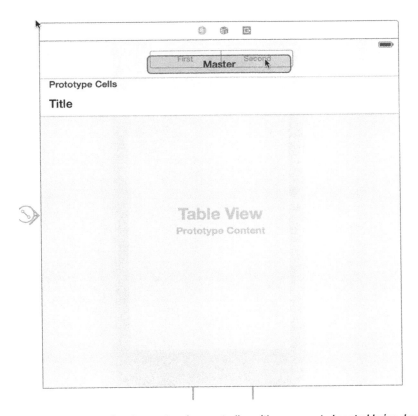

Figure 14-3. The TinyPix storyboard, showing the master view controller with a segmented control being dropped on the controller's navigation bar

Make sure the segmented control is selected and then open the Attributes Inspector. In the **Segmented Control** section at the top of the inspector, use the stepper control to change the number of Segments from *2* to *3*. Next, double-click the title of each segment in turn, changing them to *Red*, *Green*, and *Blue*, respectively. After setting those titles, click one of the resizing handles for the segmented control to make it fill out to the right width.

Next, Control-drag from the segmented control to the icon representing the master controller (the yellow circle labeled *Master* above the controller in the storyboard, or the Document Outline icon labeled *Master* under Master Scene) and select the **chooseColor:** method. Then Control-drag from the master controller back to the segmented control, and select the **colorControl** outlet.

We've finally reached a point where we can run the app and see all our hard work brought to life! Run your app. You'll see it start up and display an empty table view with a segmented control at the top and a plus (+) button in the upper-right corner (see Figure 14-4).

Figure 14-4. The TinyPix app when it first appears. Click the plus icon to add a new document. You'll be prompted to name your new TinyPix document. At the moment, all the detail view does is display the document name in a label

Hit the **+** button, and the app will ask you to name the new document. Give it a name, tap **Create**, and you'll see the app transition to the detail display, which is, well, under construction right now. All the default implementation of the detail view controller does is display the description of its detailItem in a label. Of course, there's more information in the console view in Xcode. It's not much, but it's something!

Tap the **Back** button to return to the master list, where you'll see the item you added. Go ahead and create one or two more items to see that they're correctly added to the list. Finally, head back to Xcode because we've got more work to do!

Creating TinyPixView

Our next order of business is the creation of a view class to display our grid and let the user edit it. Select the *TinyPix* folder in the Project Navigator, and press ⌘N to create a new file. In the **iOS Source** section, select **Cocoa Touch Class** and click **Next**. Name the new class *TinyPixView* and choose **UIView** in the **Subclass of** pop-up. Click **Next**, verify that the save location is OK, and click **Create**.

> **Note** The implementation of our view class includes some drawing and touch handling that we haven't covered yet. Rather than bog down this chapter with too many details about these topics, we're just going to quickly show you the code. We'll cover details about drawing with Core Graphics in Chapter 16, and responding to touches and drags in Chapter 18.

Select *TinyPixView.h* and make the following changes:

```
#import <UIKit/UIKit.h>

@class TinyPixDocument;

@interface TinyPixView : UIView

@property (strong, nonatomic) TinyPixDocument *document;

@end
```

All we're doing here is adding a property, so that the controller can pass along the document.

Now switch over to *TinyPixView.m*, where we have some more substantial work ahead of us. Start by adding this class extension at the top of the file:

```
#import "TinyPixView.h"
#import "TinyPixDocument.h"

typedef struct {
    NSUInteger row;
    NSUInteger column;
} GridIndex;

@interface TinyPixView ()

@property (assign, nonatomic) CGSize lastSize;
@property (assign, nonatomic) CGRect gridRect;
@property (assign, nonatomic) CGSize blockSize;
@property (assign, nonatomic) CGFloat gap;
@property (assign, nonatomic) GridIndex selectedBlockIndex;

@end

@implementation TinyPixView

    •
    •
    •
```

Here, we defined a C struct called GridIndex as a handy way to deal with row/column pairs. We also defined a class extension with some properties that we'll need to use later.

A `UIView` subclass is usually initialized by calling its `initWithFrame:` method, which is its default initializer. However, since this class is going to be loaded from a storyboard, it will instead be initialized using the `initWithCoder:` method. We'll implement both of these methods, making each call a third method that initializes our properties. Add the following code to *TinyPixView.m*:

```objc
- (id)initWithFrame:(CGRect)frame {
    self = [super initWithFrame:frame];
    if (self) {
        // Initialization code
        [self commonInit];
    }
    return self;
}

- (id)initWithCoder:(NSCoder *)aDecoder {
    self = [super initWithCoder:aDecoder];
    if (self) {
        [self commonInit];
    }
    return self;
}

- (void)commonInit{
    [self calculateGridForSize:self.bounds.size];
    _selectedBlockIndex.row = NSNotFound;
    _selectedBlockIndex.column = NSNotFound;
}
```

The `calculateGridForSize:` method figures out how large the cells in the color grid should be, based on the size of `TinyPixView`. Calculating the grid size allows us to use the same application with screens of different sizes, and also handles the case where the size of the view changes when the device is rotated. Add the implementation of the `calculateGridForSize:` method to *TinyPixView.m*:

```objc
- (void)calculateGridForSize:(CGSize)size {
    CGFloat space = MIN(size.width, size.height);
    _gap = space/57;
    CGFloat cellSide = 6 * _gap;
    _blockSize = CGSizeMake(cellSide, cellSide);
    _gridRect = CGRectMake((size.width - space)/2,
                           (size.height - space)/2, space, space);
}
```

The idea behind this method is to make the grid fill either the full width or the full height of the view, whichever is the smaller, and to center it along the longer axis. To do that, we calculate the size of each cell, plus the gaps between the cells, by dividing the smaller dimension of the view by 57. Why 57? Well, we want to have space for eight cells and we want each cell to be six times the size of the intercell gap. Given that we need gaps between each pair of cell, plus a gap at the start and end of each row or column, that effectively means we need space for $(6 \times 8) + 9 = 57$ gaps. Once we have the gap size, we get the size of each cell (by multiplying by 6). We use that information to set the value of the `blockSize` property, which represents the size of each cell, and the `gridRect` property, which corresponds to the region within the view in which the grid cells will actually be drawn.

Now let's take a look at the drawing routines. We override the standard UIView drawRect: method, use that to simply walk through all the blocks in our grid, and then call another method that will draw each cell block. Add the following bold code and don't forget to remove the comment marks around the drawRect: method:

```
/*
// Only override drawRect: if you perform custom drawing.
// An empty implementation adversely affects performance during animation.
- (void)drawRect:(CGRect)rect
{
    // Drawing code
    if (!_document) return;

    CGSize size = self.bounds.size;
    if (!CGSizeEqualToSize(size, self.lastSize)) {
        self.lastSize = size;
        [self calculateGridForSize:size];
    }

    for (NSUInteger row = 0; row < 8; row++) {
        for (NSUInteger column = 0; column < 8; column++) {
            [self drawBlockAtRow:row column:column];
        }
    }
}
*/
```

Before we draw the cells, we compare the current size of the view to the value in the lastSize property, and if it's different, we call calculateGridForSize:. This will happen when the view is first drawn and any time it changes size, which will most likely be when the device is rotated.

Now add the code that draws the block for each cell in the grid:

```
- (void)drawBlockAtRow:(NSUInteger)row column:(NSUInteger)column {
    CGFloat startX = _gridRect.origin.x + _gap
                    + (_blockSize.width + _gap) * (7 - column) + 1;
    CGFloat startY = _gridRect.origin.y + _gap
                    + (_blockSize.height + _gap) * row + 1;
    CGRect blockFrame = CGRectMake(startX, startY,
                            _blockSize.width, _blockSize.height);
    UIColor *color = [_document stateAtRow:row column:column] ?
            [UIColor blackColor] : [UIColor whiteColor];
    [color setFill];
    [self.tintColor setStroke];
    UIBezierPath *path = [UIBezierPath bezierPathWithRect:blockFrame];
    [path fill];
    [path stroke];
}
```

This code uses the grid origin and the cell size and gap values set by the `calculateGridForSize:` method to figure out where each cell should be, and then draws it using the current tint color for the outline, and either black or white for the interior fill, depending on whether the cell should be filled or not. The methods that are used for drawing will be explained in Chapter 16.

Finally, we add a set of methods that respond to touch events by the user. Both `touchesBegan:withEvent:` and `touchesMoved:withEvent:` are standard methods that every `UIView` subclass can implement to capture touch events that happen within the view's frame. We'll discuss these methods in detail in Chapter 19. Our implementation of these two methods uses two other methods we're adding here to calculate a grid location based on a touch location and to toggle a specific value in the document. Again, these methods use the values set by the `calculateGridForSize:` method to decide whether a touch falls within a grid cell or not. Add these four methods at the bottom of the file, just above the @end:

```objc
- (GridIndex)touchedGridIndexFromTouches:(NSSet *)touches {
    GridIndex result;
    result.row = -1;
    result.column = -1;
    UITouch *touch = [touches anyObject];
    CGPoint location = [touch locationInView:self];
    if (CGRectContainsPoint(_gridRect, location)) {
        location.x -= _gridRect.origin.x;
        location.y -= _gridRect.origin.y;
        result.column = 8 - (location.x * 8.0 / _gridRect.size.width);
        result.row = location.y * 8.0 / _gridRect.size.height;
    }
    return result;
}

- (void)toggleSelectedBlock {
    if (_selectedBlockIndex.row != -1 && _selectedBlockIndex.column != -1) {
        [_document toggleStateAtRow:_selectedBlockIndex.row
                             column:_selectedBlockIndex.column];
        [[_document.undoManager prepareWithInvocationTarget:_document]
         toggleStateAtRow:_selectedBlockIndex.row column:_selectedBlockIndex.column];
        [self setNeedsDisplay];
    }
}

- (void)touchesBegan:(NSSet *)touches withEvent:(UIEvent *)event {
    self.selectedBlockIndex = [self touchedGridIndexFromTouches:touches];
    [self toggleSelectedBlock];
}

- (void)touchesMoved:(NSSet *)touches withEvent:(UIEvent *)event {
    GridIndex touched = [self touchedGridIndexFromTouches:touches];
    if (touched.row != _selectedBlockIndex.row
            || touched.column != _selectedBlockIndex.column) {
        _selectedBlockIndex = touched;
        [self toggleSelectedBlock];
    }
}
```

Sharp-eyed readers may have noticed that the `toggleSelectedBlock` method does something a bit special. After calling the document's `toggleStateAtRow:column:` method to change the value of a particular grid point, it does something more. Let's take another look:

```
- (void)toggleSelectedBlock {
    if (_selectedBlockIndex.row != -1 && _selectedBlockIndex.column != -1) {
        [_document toggleStateAtRow:_selectedBlockIndex.row
                             column:_selectedBlockIndex.column];
        [[_document.undoManager prepareWithInvocationTarget:_document]
              toggleStateAtRow:_selectedBlockIndex.row
              column:_selectedBlockIndex.column];
        [self setNeedsDisplay];
    }
}
```

The call to `_document.undoManager` returns an instance of `NSUndoManager`. We haven't dealt with this directly anywhere else in this book, but `NSUndoManager` is the structural underpinning for the undo/redo functionality in both iOS and OS X. The idea is that anytime the user performs an action in the GUI, you use `NSUndoManager` to leave a sort of breadcrumb by "recording" a method call that will undo what the user just did. `NSUndoManager` will store that method call on a special undo stack, which can be used to backtrack through a document's state whenever the user activates the system's undo functionality.

The way it works is that the `prepareWithInvocationTarget:` method returns a proxy object to which you can send any message, and the message will be packed up with the target and pushed onto the undo stack. So, while it may look like you're calling `toggleStateAtRow:column:` twice in a row, the second time it's not being called but instead is just being queued up for later potential use. This kind of spectacularly dynamic behavior is an area where Objective-C really stands out in comparison to static languages such as C++, where techniques such as letting one object act as a proxy to another or packing up a method invocation for later use have no language support and are nearly impossible (and therefore many tasks, such as building undo support, can be quite tedious).

So, why are we doing this? We haven't been giving any thought to undo/redo issues up to this point, so why now? The reason is that registering an undoable action with the document's `NSUndoManager` marks the document as "dirty" and ensures that it will be saved automatically at some point in the next few seconds. The fact that the user's actions are also undoable is just icing on the cake, at least in this application. In an app with a more complex document structure, allowing document-wide undo support can be hugely beneficial.

Save your changes. Now that our view class is ready to go, let's head back to the storyboard to configure the GUI for the detail view.

Storyboard Detailing

Select *Main.storyboard*, find the detail scene, and take a look at what's there right now.

All the GUI contains is a label ("Detail view content goes here"), which is the one that contained the document's description when you ran the app earlier. That label isn't particularly useful, so select the label in the detail view controller and press the **Delete** key to remove it.

Use the object library to find a **UIView** and drag it into the detail view. Position and size it so that it fills the entire area below the title bar (see Figure 14-5).

Figure 14-5. *We replaced the label in the detail view with another view, centered in its containing view. The view becomes somewhat invisible while dragging, but here you can see that it's partly covering the dashed lines that appear when you drag it to the center of the view*

Switch over to the Identity Inspector, so we can change this UIView instance into an instance of our custom class. In the **Custom Class** section at the top of the inspector, select the **Class** pop-up list and choose **TinyPixView**. Now open the Attributes Inspector and change the **Mode** setting to *Redraw*. This causes TinyPixView to redraw itself when its size changes. This is necessary because the position of the grid inside the view depends on the size of the view itself, which changes when the device is rotated. At this point, the view hierarchy for the Detail Scene should look like Figure 14-6.

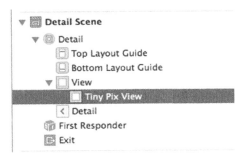

Figure 14-6. The detail view scene's view hierarchy

Before we go on, we need to adjust the auto layout constraints for the new view. We want it to fill the available area in the detail view. So, in the Document Outline, Control-drag from TinyPixView to its parent view and release the mouse. Hold down the **Shift** key and in the pop-up, select **Leading Space to Container Margin**, **Trailing Space to Container Margin**, **Top Space to Top Layout Guide**, and **Bottom Space to Bottom Layout Guide**, and then click outside the pop-up to apply the constraints.

Now we need to wire up the custom view to our detail view controller. We haven't prepared an outlet for our custom view yet, but that's OK since Xcode's drag-to-code feature will do that for us.

Activate the Assistant Editor. A text editor should slide into place alongside the GUI editor, displaying the contents of *DetailViewController.m*. If it's showing you anything else, use the jump bar at the top of the text editor to make *DetailViewController.m* come into view.

To make the connection, Control-drag from the **TinyPixView** icon in the Document Outline to the code, releasing the drag in the class extension at the top of the file. In the pop-up window that appears, make sure that Connection is set to *Outlet*, name the new outlet *pixView*, and click the **Connect** button.

You should see that making that connection has added this line to *DetailViewController.m*:

```
@property (weak, nonatomic) IBOutlet TinyPixView *pixView;
```

One thing it didn't add, however, is any knowledge of our custom view class to the source code. Let's take care of that by adding this line toward the top of *DetailViewController.m*:

```
#import "DetailViewController.h"
#import "TinyPixView.h"

@interface DetailViewController ()
```

Now let's modify the configureView method. This isn't a standard UIViewController method. It's just a private method that the project template included in this class as a convenient spot to put code that needs to update the view after anything changes. Since we're not using the description label, we delete the line that sets that. Next, we add a bit of code to pass the chosen document along to our custom view and tell it to redraw itself by calling setNeedsDisplay:

```
- (void)configureView
{
    // Update the user interface for the detail item.

    if (self.detailItem) {
        self.detailDescriptionLabel.text = [self.detailItem description];
        self.pixView.document = self.detailItem;
        [self.pixView setNeedsDisplay];
    }
}
```

Next, we need to arrange for the tint color to be applied to the TinyPixView. We need to do this both when the view is first loaded and whenever the tint color is changed. We know that we can get the initial tint color from the user defaults, so let's add a method that gets the value saved there, converts it to a UIColor, and applies it to the TinyPixView. The conversion requires the TinyPixUtils class that we created earlier, so first add an import for that class at the top of the file:

```
#import "DetailViewController.h"
#import "TinyPixView.h"
#import "TinyPixUtils.h"
```

Next, add this method somewhere in the body of the class:

```
- (void)updateTintColor {
    NSUserDefaults *prefs = [NSUserDefaults standardUserDefaults];
    NSInteger selectedColorIndex = [prefs integerForKey:@"selectedColorIndex"];
    UIColor *tintColor = [TinyPixUtils getTintColorForIndex:selectedColorIndex];
    self.pixView .tintColor = tintColor;
    [self.pixView setNeedsDisplay];
}
```

We need to call this method to set the initial tint color when the view is first loaded. We also need to call it when the tint changes. How will we know that's happened? When the tint color is changed, the new value is saved in the user defaults. You can find out that something in the user defaults has changed by registering an observer for the NSUserDefaultsDidChangeNotification notification with the default notification center. Add the following code to the viewDidLoad method:

```
- (void)viewDidLoad {
    [super viewDidLoad];
    // Do any additional setup after loading the view, typically from a nib.
    [self configureView];
    [self updateTintColor];
    [[NSNotificationCenter defaultCenter] addObserver:self
        selector:@selector(onSettingsChanged:)
        name:NSUserDefaultsDidChangeNotification object:nil];
}
```

Now, when anything in the user defaults changes, the onSettingsChanged: method is called. When this happens, we need to set the new tint color, in case it's changed. Add the implementation of this method above the @end in the class:

```
- (void)onSettingsChanged:(NSNotification *)notification {
    [self updateTintColor];
}
```

Having added a notification observer, we have to remove it before the class is deallocated. We can do this by overriding the view's dealloc method:

```
- (void)dealloc {
    [[NSNotificationCenter defaultCenter] removeObserver:self
                name:NSUserDefaultsDidChangeNotification object:nil];
}
```

We're nearly finished with this class, but we need to make one more change. Remember when we mentioned the autosaving that takes place when a document is notified that some editing has occurred, triggered by registering an undoable action? The save normally happens within about 10 seconds after the edit occurs. Like the other saving and loading procedures we described earlier in this chapter, it happens in a background thread, so that normally the user won't even notice. However, that works only as long as the document is still around.

With our current setup, there's a risk that when the user hits the **Back** button to go back to the master list, the document instance will be deallocated without any save operation occurring, and the user's latest changes will be lost. To make sure this doesn't happen, we need to add some code to the viewWillDisappear: method to close the document as soon as the user navigates away from the detail view. Closing a document causes it to be automatically saved, and again, the saving occurs on a background thread. In this particular case, we don't need to do anything when the save is done, so we pass in nil instead of a block:

Add this viewWillDisappear: method:

```
- (void)viewWillDisappear:(BOOL)animated {
    [super viewWillDisappear:animated];
    UIDocument *doc = self.detailItem;
    [doc closeWithCompletionHandler:nil];
}
```

And with that, this version of our first truly document-based app is ready to try out! Fire it up and bask in the glory. You can create new documents, edit them, flip back to the list, and then select another document (or the same document), and it all just works. Experiment with changing the tint color and verify that it is properly saved and restored when you stop and restart the app. If you open the Xcode console while doing this, you'll see some output each time a document is loaded or saved. Using the autosaving system, you don't have direct control over just when saves occur (except for when closing a document), but it can be interesting to watch the logs just to get a feel for when they happen.

Adding iCloud Support

You now have a fully working document-based app, but we're not going to stop here. We promised you iCloud support in this chapter, and it's time to deliver!

Modifying TinyPix to work with iCloud is pretty straightforward. Considering all that's happening behind the scenes, this requires a surprisingly small number of changes. We'll need to make some revisions to the method that loads the list of available files and the method that specifies the URL for loading a new file, but that's about it.

Apart from the code changes, we will also need to deal with some additional administrative details. Apple allows an app to save to iCloud only if it contains an embedded provisioning profile that is configured to allow iCloud usage. This means that to add the iCloud support to our app, you must have a paid iOS developer membership and have installed your developer certificate. It also works only with actual devices, not the simulator, so you'll need to have at least one iOS device registered with iCloud to run the new iCloud-backed TinyPix. With two devices, you'll have even more fun, as you can see how changes made on one device propagate to the other.

Creating a Provisioning Profile

First, you need to create an iCloud-enabled provisioning profile for TinyPix. This used to require a lot of convoluted steps on Apple's developer web site, but nowadays Xcode makes it easy. In the Project Navigator, select the **TinyPix** item at the top, and then click the **Capabilities** tab in the editing area. You should see something like what's shown in Figure 14-7.

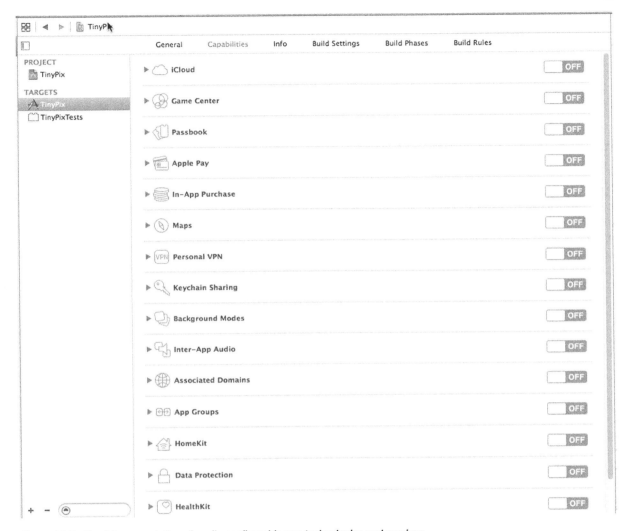

Figure 14-7. Xcode's presentation of easily configurable app technologies and services

The list of capabilities shown in Figure 14-7 can all be configured directly in Xcode, all without needing to go to a web site, create and download provisioning profiles, and so on. Before you can do this, you need to give your app a unique App ID. If you used the version of the project that's in the source code download, the App ID is com.apress.BID. This App ID is already registered, so you won't be able to use it. Select the **General** tab and use a different prefix in the **Bundle Identifier** field. To change the App ID to com.myCo, for example, you would set the Bundle Identifier as shown in Figure 14-8.

Figure 14-8. Changing the application's bundle ID

Of course, you should use a value that's unique to you rather than com.myCo. Now switch back to the **Capabilities** tab. For TinyPix, we want to enable iCloud, the first capability listed, so click the disclosure triangle next to the cloud icon. Here you'll see some information about what this capability is for. Click the switch at the right to turn it on. Xcode will then communicate with Apple's servers to configure the provisioning profile for this app. This will require you to log in with your Apple ID, and it obviously requires you to be connected to the Internet. After it's enabled, click to turn on the **Key-value storage** and **iCloud Documents** check boxes, as shown in Figure 14-9.

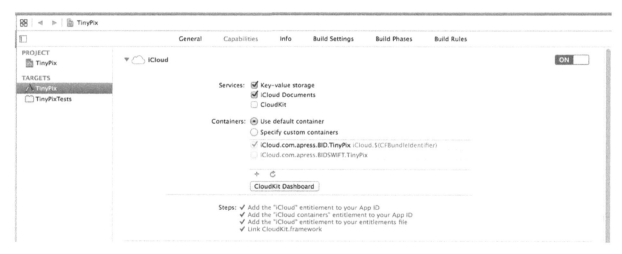

Figure 14-9. The app is now configured to use iCloud. This simple configuration let us remove several pages from this chapter, which probably ends up saving the life of a tree or two. Thanks, Apple!

You're finished! Your app now has the necessary permissions to access iCloud from your code. The rest is a simple matter of programming.

How to Query

Select *MasterViewController.m* so that we can start making changes for iCloud. The biggest change is going to be the way we look for available documents. In the first version of TinyPix, we used NSFileManager to see what's available on the local file system. This time, we're going to do things a little differently. Here, we will fire up a special sort of query to look for documents.

Start by adding a pair of properties in the class extension: one to hold a pointer to an ongoing query and the other to hold the list of all the documents the query finds.

```
@interface MasterViewController ()

@property (weak, nonatomic) IBOutlet UISegmentedControl *colorControl;
@property (strong, nonatomic) NSArray *documentFilenames;
@property (strong, nonatomic) TinyPixDocument *chosenDocument;
@property (strong, nonatomic) NSMetadataQuery *query;
@property (strong, nonatomic) NSMutableArray *documentURLs;

@end
```

Now, let's look at the new file-listing method. Remove the entire reloadFiles method and replace it with this:

```
- (void)reloadFiles {
    NSFileManager *fileManager = [NSFileManager defaultManager];
    // passing nil is OK here, matches first entitlement
    NSURL *cloudURL = [fileManager URLForUbiquityContainerIdentifier:nil];
    NSLog(@"got cloudURL %@", cloudURL);  // returns nil in simulator
    if (cloudURL != nil) {
        self.query = [[NSMetadataQuery alloc] init];
        _query.predicate = [NSPredicate predicateWithFormat:@"%K like '*.tinypix'",
                            NSMetadataItemFSNameKey];
        _query.searchScopes = [NSArray arrayWithObject:
                                NSMetadataQueryUbiquitousDocumentsScope];
        [[NSNotificationCenter defaultCenter]
                addObserver:self
                selector:@selector(updateUbiquitousDocuments:)
                name:NSMetadataQueryDidFinishGatheringNotification
                object:nil];
        [[NSNotificationCenter defaultCenter]
                addObserver:self
                selector:@selector(updateUbiquitousDocuments:)
                name:NSMetadataQueryDidUpdateNotification
                object:nil];
        [_query startQuery];
    }
}
```

There are some new things here that are definitely worth mentioning. The first is seen in this line:

```
NSURL *cloudURL = [fileManager URLForUbiquityContainerIdentifier:nil];
```

That's a mouthful, for sure. Ubiquity? What are we talking about here? When it comes to iCloud, a lot of Apple's terminology for identifying resources in iCloud storage includes words like "ubiquity" and "ubiquitous" to indicate that something is omnipresent—accessible from any device using the same iCloud login credentials.

In this case, we're asking the file manager to give us a base URL that will let us access the iCloud directory associated with a particular **container identifier**. A container identifier is normally a string containing your company's unique bundle seed ID and the application identifier. The container identifier is used to pick one of the iCloud entitlements contained within your app. Passing nil here is a shortcut that just means "give me the first one in the list." Since our app contains only one checked item in that list (which you can see listed under "Containers" at the bottom of Figure 14-9), that shortcut suits our needs perfectly.

After that, we create and configure an instance of NSMetadataQuery:

```
self.query = [[NSMetadataQuery alloc] init];
_query.predicate = [NSPredicate predicateWithFormat:@"%K like '*.tinypix'",
                    NSMetadataItemFSNameKey];
_query.searchScopes = [NSArray arrayWithObject:
                    NSMetadataQueryUbiquitousDocumentsScope];
```

The NSMetaDataQuery class was originally written for use with the Spotlight search facility on OS X, but it's now doing extra duty as a way to let iOS apps search iCloud directories. We give the query a predicate, which limits its search results to include only those with the correct sort of file name, and we give it a search scope that limits it to look just within the *Documents* folder in the app's iCloud storage. Next, we set up some notifications to let us know when the query is complete, and then we initiate the query:

```
[[NSNotificationCenter defaultCenter]
        addObserver:self
        selector:@selector(updateUbiquitousDocuments:)
        name:NSMetadataQueryDidFinishGatheringNotification
        object:nil];
[[NSNotificationCenter defaultCenter]
        addObserver:self
        selector:@selector(updateUbiquitousDocuments:)
        name:NSMetadataQueryDidUpdateNotification
        object:nil];
[_query startQuery];
```

Now we need to implement the method that those notifications call when the query is done. Add this method just below the reloadFiles method:

```
- (void)updateUbiquitousDocuments:(NSNotification *)notification {
    self.documentURLs = [NSMutableArray array];
    self.documentFilenames = [NSMutableArray array];
```

```
NSLog(@"updateUbiquitousDocuments, results = %@", self.query.results);
NSArray *results = [self.query.results sortedArrayUsingComparator:
    ^NSComparisonResult(id obj1, id obj2) {
    NSMetadataItem *item1 = obj1;
    NSMetadataItem *item2 = obj2;
    return [[item2 valueForAttribute:NSMetadataItemFSCreationDateKey]
            compare:
            [item1 valueForAttribute:NSMetadataItemFSCreationDateKey]];
}];

for (NSMetadataItem *item in results) {
    NSURL *url = [item valueForAttribute:NSMetadataItemURLKey];
    [self.documentURLs addObject:url];
    [(NSMutableArray *)_documentFilenames addObject:[url lastPathComponent]];
}

[self.tableView reloadData];
}
```

The query's results contain a list of NSMetadataItem objects, from which we can get items like file URLs and creation dates. We use this to sort the items by date, and then grab all the URLs for later use.

Save Where?

The next change is to the urlForFilename: method, which once again is completely different. Here we're using a ubiquitous URL to create a full path URL for a given file name. We insert "Documents" in the generated path as well, to make sure we're using the app's *Documents* directory. Delete the old method and replace it with this new one:

```
- (NSURL *)urlForFilename:(NSString *)filename {
    // be sure to insert "Documents" into the path
    NSURL *baseURL = [[NSFileManager defaultManager]
                    URLForUbiquityContainerIdentifier:nil];
    NSURL *pathURL = [baseURL URLByAppendingPathComponent:@"Documents"];
    NSURL *destinationURL = [pathURL URLByAppendingPathComponent:filename];
    return destinationURL;
}
```

Now, build and run your app on an actual iOS device (not the simulator). If you've run the previous version of the app on that device, you'll find that any TinyPix masterpieces you created earlier are now nowhere to be seen. This new version ignores the local *Documents* directory for the app and relies completely on iCloud. However, you should be able to create new documents and find that they stick around after quitting and restarting the app. Moreover, you can even delete the TinyPix app from your device entirely, run it again from Xcode, and find that all your iCloud-saved documents are available at once. If you have an additional iOS device configured with the same iCloud user, use Xcode to run the app on that device, and you'll see all the same documents appear there, as well! It's pretty sweet. You can also find these documents in the iCloud section of your iOS device's Settings app (look under **Storage ➤ Manage Storage ➤ TinyPix**), as well as the iCloud section of your Mac's System Preferences app if you're running OS X 10.8 or later.

Storing Preferences on iCloud

We can "cloudify" one more piece of functionality with just a bit of effort. iOS's iCloud support includes a class called NSUbiquitousKeyValueStore, which works a lot like NSUserDefaults; however, its keys and values are stored in the cloud. This is great for application preferences, login tokens, and anything else that doesn't belong in a document, but could be useful when shared among all of a user's devices.

In TinyPix, we'll use this feature to store the user's preferred highlight color. That way, instead of needing to be configured on each device, the user sets the color once, and it shows up everywhere. Here's the plan of action:

▨   Whenever the user changes the tint color, we'll save the new value in NSUserDefaults and we'll also save it in the NSUbiquitousKeyValueStore, which will make it available to instances of the application on other devices.

▨   We'll register to be notified of changes in the NSUbiquitousKeyValueStore. When we're notified of a change, we'll get the new tint color value. At this point, we need to update the segmented control and the tint color used by the master view controller and the drawing color in the detail view controller. Rather than do this directly, we'll just save the new tint color in NSUserDefaults. Changing NSUserDefaults causes a notification to be generated. The detail view controller is already observing this notification, so it will update itself automatically. We're going to make some small changes to the master view controller so that it does the same thing.

It's important to be aware that updates to NSUbiquitousKeyValueStore do not propagate immediately to other devices, and, in fact, if a device is not connected to iCloud for any reason, it won't see the update until it next connects. So don't expect changes to be seen immediately.

Let's start by registering to receive change notifications from the iCloud key-value store. Open *AppDelegate.m* and add the following code to the application:didFinishLaunchingWithOptions: method:

```
- (BOOL)application:(UIApplication *)application didFinishLaunchingWithOptions:(NSDictionary *)
launchOptions {
    // Override point for customization after application launch.
    UISplitViewController *splitViewController =
        (UISplitViewController *)self.window.rootViewController;
    UINavigationController *navigationController =
        [splitViewController.viewControllers lastObject];
    navigationController.topViewController.navigationItem.leftBarButtonItem =
        splitViewController.displayModeButtonItem;
    splitViewController.delegate = self;

    // Register for notification of iCloud key-value changes
    [[NSNotificationCenter defaultCenter] addObserver:self
        selector:@selector(iCloudKeysChanged:)
        name:NSUbiquitousKeyValueStoreDidChangeExternallyNotification
        object:nil];
```

```
// Start iCloud key-value updates
[[NSUbiquitousKeyValueStore defaultStore] synchronize];
[self updateUserDefaultsFromICloud];

    return YES;
}
```

The first new line of code arranges for the application delegate's iCloudKeysChanged: method to be called when an NSUbiquitousKeyValueStoreDidChangeExternallyNotification occurs—that is, when iCloud notifies a change in any of the application's key/value pairs. The synchronize method causes local changes to the NSUbiquitousKeyValueStore to be written to iCloud in the background and notification of remote updates to start. The updateUserDefaultsFromICloud method, which you'll see shortly, gets the current state of the selected tint color from the iCloud key-value store, if it's set, and stores it in the local user defaults, so that it will be used immediately.

Next, add the implementation of the iCloudKeysChanged: and updateUserDefaultsFromCloud methods:

```
- (void)iCloudKeysChanged:(NSNotification *)notification {
    [self updateUserDefaultsFromICloud];
}

- (void)updateUserDefaultsFromICloud {
    NSDictionary *values = [[NSUbiquitousKeyValueStore defaultStore] dictionaryRepresentation];
    if ([values valueForKey:@"selectedColorIndex"] != nil) {
        NSUInteger selectedColorIndex = (NSUInteger)[[NSUbiquitousKeyValueStore defaultStore]
        longLongForKey:@"selectedColorIndex"];
        NSUserDefaults *prefs = [NSUserDefaults standardUserDefaults];
        [prefs setInteger:selectedColorIndex forKey:@"selectedColorIndex"];
        [prefs synchronize];
    }
}
```

When a notification occurs, we use the longLongForKey: method to get the new selected tint color index from the key store. The API is very similar to that of NSUserDefaults, but there is no method to store an integer value, so we treat the tint color index as a long long instead. Once we have the value, we simply copy it to the NSUserDefaults and synchronize the change, so that a notification is generated. We already know that the detail view controller will update itself when it receives this notification. Next, we need to change the master view controller so that it does the same. Back in *MasterViewController.m*, start by registering the controller to be notified of NSUserDefaults changes in its viewDidLoad method:

```
    [self reloadFiles];

    [[NSNotificationCenter defaultCenter] addObserver:self
            selector:@selector(onSettingsChanged:)
            name:NSUserDefaultsDidChangeNotification object:nil];
}
```

Next, add the onSettingsChanged: method:

```
- (void)onSettingsChanged:(NSNotification *)notification {
    NSUserDefaults *prefs = [NSUserDefaults standardUserDefaults];
    NSInteger selectedColorIndex = [prefs integerForKey:@"selectedColorIndex"];
    [self setTintColorForIndex:selectedColorIndex];
    self.colorControl.selectedSegmentIndex = selectedColorIndex;
}
```

This method updates the tint color of the segmented control using the same method that's called when the user taps one of its segments, but it gets the color index from NSUserDefaults instead of from the control.

Finally, when the user changes the tint color, we need to save the new index in the iCloud key-value store. Make the following changes to the chooseColor: method to take care of this:

```
- (IBAction)chooseColor:(id)sender {
    NSInteger selectedColorIndex = [(UISegmentedControl *)sender
                                    selectedSegmentIndex];
    [self setTintColorForIndex:selectedColorIndex];

    NSUserDefaults *prefs = [NSUserDefaults standardUserDefaults];
    [prefs setInteger:selectedColorIndex forKey:@"selectedColorIndex"];
    [prefs synchronize];
    [[NSUbiquitousKeyValueStore defaultStore]
            setLongLong:selectedColorIndex
            forKey:@"selectedColorIndex"];
    [[NSUbiquitousKeyValueStore defaultStore] synchronize];
}
```

That's it! You can now run the app on multiple devices configured for the same iCloud user and will see that setting the color on one device results in the new color appearing on the other device soon afterward. Piece of cake!

What We Didn't Cover

We now have the basics of an iCloud-enabled, document-based application up and running, but there are a few more issues that you may want to consider. We're not going to cover these topics in this book; but if you're serious about making a great iCloud-based app, you'll want to think about these areas:

- Documents stored in iCloud are prone to conflicts. What happens if you edit the same TinyPix file on several devices at once? Fortunately, Apple has already thought of this and provides some ways to deal with these conflicts in your app. It's up to you to decide whether you want to ignore conflicts, try to fix them automatically, or ask the user to help sort out the problem. For full details, search for a document titled "Resolving Document Version Conflicts" in the Xcode documentation viewer.

▪ Apple recommends that you design your application to work in a completely offline mode in case the user isn't using iCloud for some reason. It also recommends that you provide a way for a user to move files between iCloud storage and local storage. Sadly, Apple doesn't provide or suggest any standard GUI for helping a user manage this, and current apps that provide this functionality, such as Apple's iWork apps, don't seem to handle it in a particularly user-friendly way. See Apple's "Managing the Life Cycle of a Document" in the Xcode documentation for more on this.

▪ Apple supports using iCloud for Core Data storage and even provides a class called `UIManagedDocument` that you can subclass if you want to make that work. See the `UIManagedDocument` class reference for more information. This architecture is a lot more complex and problematic than normal iCloud document storage. Apple has taken steps to improve things in recent versions of iOS, but it's still not perfectly smooth, so look before you leap.

What's up next? In Chapter 15, we'll take you through the process of making sure your apps work properly in a multithreaded, multitasking environment.

Grand Central Dispatch, Background Processing, and You

If you've ever tried your hand at multithreaded programming, in any environment, chances are you've come away from the experience with a feeling of dread, terror, or worse. Fortunately, technology marches on, and Apple has come up with a new approach that makes multithreaded programming much easier. This approach is called **Grand Central Dispatch**, and we'll get you started using it in this chapter. We'll also dig into the multitasking capabilities of iOS, showing you how to adjust your applications to play nicely in this new world and work even better than before.

Grand Central Dispatch

One of the biggest challenges developers face today is to write software that can perform complex actions in response to user input while remaining responsive, so that the user isn't constantly kept waiting while the processor does some behind-the-scenes task. If you think about it, that challenge has been with us all along; and in spite of the advances in computing technology that bring us faster CPUs, the problem persists. If you want evidence, you need look no further than your nearest computer screen. Chances are that the last time you sat down to work at your computer, at some point, your workflow was interrupted by a spinning mouse cursor of some kind or another.

So why does this continue to vex us, given all the advances in system architecture? One part of the problem is the way that software is typically written: as a sequence of events to be performed in order. Such software can scale up as CPU speeds increase, but only to a certain point. As soon as the program gets stuck waiting for an external resource, such as a file or a network connection, the entire sequence of events is effectively paused. All modern operating systems now allow the use of multiple threads of execution within a program, so that even if a single thread is stuck waiting for a specific event, the other threads can keep going. Even so, many developers see multithreaded programming as something of a black art and shy away from it.

Fortunately, Apple has some good news for anyone who wants to break up their code into simultaneous chunks without too much hands-on intimacy with the system's threading layer.

This good news is Grand Central Dispatch (GCD). It provides an entirely new API for splitting up the work your application needs to do into smaller chunks that can be spread across multiple threads and, with the right hardware, multiple CPUs.

Much of this new API is accessed using **blocks**, another Apple innovation that adds a sort of anonymous in-line function capability to C and Objective-C. Blocks have a lot in common with similar features in languages such as Ruby and Lisp, and they can provide interesting new ways to structure interactions between different objects while keeping related code closer together in your methods.

Introducing SlowWorker

As a platform for demonstrating how GCD works, we'll create an application called SlowWorker, which consists of a simple interface driven by a single button and a text view. Click the button, and a synchronous task is immediately started, locking up the app for about ten seconds. Once the task completes, some text appears in the text view (see Figure 15-1).

Figure 15-1. *The SlowWorker application hides its interface behind a single button. Click the button, and the interface hangs for about ten seconds while the application does its work*

Start by using the Single View Application template to make a new application in Xcode, as you've done many times before. Name this one *SlowWorker*, set **Devices** to **Universal**, click **Next** to **save** your project, and so on. Next, make the following additions to *ViewController.m*:

```objc
#import "ViewController.h"

@interface ViewController ()

@property (weak, nonatomic) IBOutlet UIButton *startButton;
@property (weak, nonatomic) IBOutlet UITextView *resultsTextView;

@end
```

This simply defines a couple of outlets to the two objects visible in our GUI.

Now continue by adding the following code in bold inside the @implementation section:

```objc
@implementation ViewController

- (NSString *)fetchSomethingFromServer
{
    [NSThread sleepForTimeInterval:1];
    return @"Hi there";
}

- (NSString *)processData:(NSString *)data
{
    [NSThread sleepForTimeInterval:2];
    return [data uppercaseString];
}

- (NSString *)calculateFirstResult:(NSString *)data
{
    [NSThread sleepForTimeInterval:3];
    return [NSString stringWithFormat:@"Number of chars: %lu",
            (unsigned long)[data length]];
}

- (NSString *)calculateSecondResult:(NSString *)data
{
    [NSThread sleepForTimeInterval:4];
    return [data stringByReplacingOccurrencesOfString:@"E"
                                           withString:@"e"];
}
```

```
- (IBAction)doWork:(id)sender
{
    self.resultsTextView.text = @"";
    NSDate *startTime = [NSDate date];
    NSString *fetchedData = [self fetchSomethingFromServer];
    NSString *processedData = [self processData:fetchedData];
    NSString *firstResult = [self calculateFirstResult:processedData];
    NSString *secondResult = [self calculateSecondResult:processedData];
    NSString *resultsSummary = [NSString stringWithFormat:
                                    @"First: [%@]\nSecond: [%@]", firstResult,
                                    secondResult];
    self.resultsTextView.text = resultsSummary;
    NSDate *endTime = [NSDate date];
    NSLog(@"Completed in %f seconds",
        [endTime timeIntervalSinceDate:startTime]);
}
```
.
.
.

As you can see, the work of this class (such as it is) is split up into a number of small chunks. This code is just meant to simulate some slow activities, and none of those methods really do anything time-consuming at all. To make things interesting, each method contains a call to the sleepForTimeInterval: class method in NSThread, which simply makes the program (specifically, the thread from which the method is called) effectively pause and do nothing at all for the given number of seconds. The doWork: method also contains code at the beginning and end to calculate the amount of time it took for all the work to be done.

Now open *Main.storyboard* and drag a **Button** and a **Text View** into the empty View window, laying things out as shown in Figure 15-2. To set the auto layout constraints, start by selecting the **Start Working** button, then select **Editor ➤ Align ➤ Horizontal Center in Container** in the menu bar. Next, Control-drag from the button to the top of the View window, release the mouse and select **Top Space to Top Layout Guide**. To complete the constraints for this button, Control-drag from the button down to the text view, release the mouse, and select **Vertical Spacing**. To fix the position and size of the text view, Control-drag from it to the View window. Release the mouse and, when the pop-up appears, hold down the **Shift** key and select **Leading Space to Container Margin**, **Trailing Space to Container Margin**, and **Bottom Space to Bottom Layout Guide**, and then click **outside the pop-up to apply the constraints**. That completes the auto layout constraints for this application.

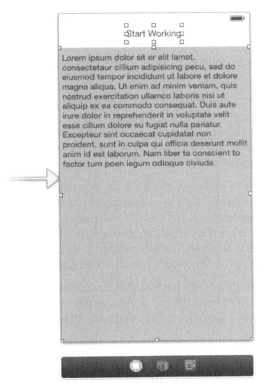

Figure 15-2. *The SlowWorker interface consists of a button and a text view. Be sure to uncheck the Editable check box for the text view and delete all of its text*

Control-drag from **File's Owner** to connect the view controller's two outlets (i.e., the startButton and resultsTextView instance variables) to the button and the text view.

Next, Control-drag from the button to the view controller's doWork: method so that it's called when the button is pressed. Finally, select the text view, use the Attributes Inspector to uncheck the **Editable** check box (it's in the upper-right corner), and delete the default text from the text view.

Save your work, and then select **Run**. Your app should start up, and pressing the button will make it work for about ten seconds (the sum of all those sleep amounts) before showing you the results. During your wait, you'll see that the **Start Working** button fades visibly, never turning back to its normal color until the "work" is done. Also, until the work is complete, the application's view is unresponsive. Tapping anywhere on the screen has no effect. In fact, the only way you can interact with your application during this time is by tapping the home button to switch away from it. This is exactly the state of affairs we want to avoid!

In this particular case, the wait is not too bad, since the application appears to be hung for just a few seconds; however, if your app regularly hangs this way for much longer, using it will be a frustrating experience. In the worst of cases, the operating system may actually kill your app if it's unresponsive for too long. In any case, you'll end up with some unhappy users—and maybe even some ex-users!

Threading Basics

Before we start implementing solutions, let's go over some concurrency basics. This is far from a complete description of threading in iOS or threading in general. We just want to explain enough for you to understand what we're doing in this chapter.

Most modern operating systems (including, of course, iOS) support the notion of threads of execution. Each process can contain multiple threads, which all run concurrently. If there's just one processor core, the operating system will switch between all executing threads, much like it switches between all executing processes. If more than one core is available, the threads will be distributed among them, just as processes are.

All threads in a process share the same executable program code and the same global data. Each thread can also have some data that is exclusive to the thread. Threads can make use of a special structure called a **mutex** (short for *mutual exclusion*) or a lock, which can ensure that a particular chunk of code can't be run by multiple threads at once. This is useful for ensuring correct outcomes when multiple threads access the same data simultaneously, by locking out other threads when one thread is updating a value (in what's called a **critical section** of your code).

A common concern when dealing with threads is the idea of code being **thread-safe**. Some software libraries are written with thread concurrency in mind and have all their critical sections properly protected with mutexes. Some code libraries aren't thread-safe.

For example, in Cocoa Touch, the Foundation framework (containing basic classes appropriate for all sorts of Objective-C programming, such as NSString, NSArray, and so on) is generally considered to be thread-safe. However, the UIKit framework (containing the classes specific to building GUI applications, such as UIApplication, UIView and all its subclasses, and so on) is, for the most part, not thread-safe. This means that in a running iOS application, all method calls that deal with any UIKit objects should be executed from within the same thread, which is commonly known as the **main thread**. If you access UIKit objects from another thread, all bets are off! You are likely to encounter seemingly inexplicable bugs (or, even worse, you won't experience any problems, but some of your users will be affected by them after you ship your app).

By default, the main thread is where all the action of your iOS app occurs (e.g., dealing with actions triggered by user events). Thus, for simple applications, it's nothing you need to worry about. Action methods triggered by a user are already running in the main thread. Up to this point in the book, our code has been running exclusively on the main thread, but that's about to change.

Tip   A lot has been written about thread safety, and it's well worth your time to dig in and try to digest as much of it as you can. One great place to start is Apple's own documentation. Take a few minutes and read through this page (it will definitely help):

http://developer.apple.com/library/ios/documentation/Cocoa/Conceptual/
Multithreading/ThreadSafetySummary/ThreadSafetySummary.html

Units of Work

The problem with the threading model described earlier is that, for the average programmer, writing error-free, multithreaded code is nearly impossible. This is not meant as a critique of our industry or of the average programmer's abilities; it's simply an observation. The complex interactions you must account for in your code when synchronizing data and actions across multiple threads are really just too much for most people to tackle. Imagine that 5% of all people have the capacity to write software at all. Only a small fraction of those 5% are really up to the task of writing heavy-duty multithreaded applications. Even people who have done it successfully will often advise others to not follow their example!

Fortunately, all hope is not lost. It is possible to implement some concurrency without too much low-level thread-twisting. Just as we have the ability to display data on the screen without directly poking bits into video RAM and to read data from disk without interfacing directly with disk controllers, we can also leverage software abstractions that let us run our code on multiple threads without requiring us to do much directly with the threads.

The solutions that Apple encourages us to use are centered on the ideas of splitting up long-running tasks into units of work and putting those units into queues for execution. The system manages the queues for us, executing units of work on multiple threads. We don't need to start and manage the background threads directly, and we are freed from much of the bookkeeping that's usually involved in implementing multithreaded applications; the system takes care of that for us.

GCD: Low-Level Queuing

This idea of putting units of work into queues that can be executed in the background, with the system managing the threads for you, is really powerful and greatly simplifies many development situations where concurrency is needed. GCD made its debut on OS X several years ago, providing the infrastructure to do just that. A couple of years later, this technology came to the iOS platform as well.

GCD puts some great concepts—units of work, painless background processing, and automatic thread management—into a C interface that can be used not only with Objective-C, but also with C , C++, and, of course, Swift. To top things off, Apple has made its implementation of GCD open source, so it can be ported to other Unix-like operating systems, as well.

One of the key concepts of GCD is the **queue**. The system provides a number of predefined queues, including a queue that's guaranteed to always do its work on the main thread. It's perfect for the non-thread-safe UIKit! You can also create your own queues—as many as you like. GCD queues are strictly first-in, first-out (FIFO). Units of work added to a GCD queue will always be started in the order they were placed in the queue. That said, they may not always finish in the same order, since a GCD queue will automatically distribute its work among multiple threads, if possible.

GCD has access to a pool of threads that are reused throughout the lifetime of the application, and it will try to maintain a number of threads that's appropriate for the machine's architecture. It will automatically take advantage of a more powerful machine by utilizing more processor cores when it has work to do. Until recently, iOS devices were all single-core, so this wasn't much of an issue. But now that all iOS devices released in the past few years feature multicore processors, GCD is becoming truly useful.

Becoming a Blockhead

Along with GCD, Apple has added a bit of new syntax to the C language itself (and, by extension, Objective-C and C++) to implement a language feature called **blocks** (also known as **closures** or **lambdas** in some other languages), which are really important for getting the most out of GCD. The idea behind a block is to let a particular chunk of code be treated like any other C-language type. A block can be assigned to a variable, passed as an argument to a function or method, and (unlike most other types) executed. In this way, blocks can be used as an alternative to the delegate pattern in Objective-C or to callback functions in C.

Much like a method or function, a block can take one or more parameters and specify a return value. To declare a block variable, you use the caret (^) symbol along with some additional parenthesized bits to declare parameters and return types. To define the block itself, you do roughly the same, but follow it up with the actual code defining the block wrapped in curly braces:

```
// Declare a block variable "loggerBlock" with no parameters
// and no return value.
void (^loggerBlock)(void);

// Assign a block to the variable declared above.  A block without parameters
// and with no return value, like this one, needs no "decorations" like the use
// of void in the preceding variable declaration.
loggerBlock = ^{ NSLog(@"I'm just glad they didn't call it a lambda"); };

// Execute the block, just like calling a function.
loggerBlock();  // this produces some output in the console
```

If you've done much C programming, you may recognize that this is similar to the concept of a function pointer in C. However, there are a few critical differences. Perhaps the biggest difference—the one that's the most striking when you first see it—is that blocks can be defined in-line in your code. You can define a block right at the point where it's going to be passed to another method or function.

Another big difference is that a block can access all variables available in the scope of its creation. By default, the block "captures" any variable you access this way. It duplicates the value into a new variable with the same name, leaving the original intact. Objective-C objects are automatically sent a retain message (and later, when the block is done, a release, effectively giving strong semantics to the variable inside the block) while scalar values such as int and float are simply copied. However, you can make an outside variable "read/write" by prepending the storage qualifier __block before its declaration. Note that there are two underscores before block, not just one. Or, if you want to pass in an object pointer with weak semantics, you can preface it with it with __weak:

```
// define a variable that can be changed by a block
__block int a = 0;

// define a block that tries to modify a variable in its scope
void (^sillyBlock)(void) = ^{ a = 47; };

// check the value of our variable before calling the block
NSLog(@"a == %d", a); // outputs "a == 0"
```

```
// execute the block
sillyBlock();

// check the values of our variable again, after calling the block
NSLog(@"a == %d", a); // outputs "a == 47"
```

As mentioned previously, blocks really shine when used with GCD, which lets you take a block and add it to a queue in a single step. When you do this with a block that you define immediately at that point, rather than a block stored in a variable, you have the added advantage of being able to see the relevant code directly in the context where it's being used.

Improving SlowWorker

To see how blocks work, let's revisit SlowWorker's doWork: method. It currently looks like this:

```
- (IBAction)doWork:(id)sender
{
    self.resultsTextView.text = @"";
    NSDate *startTime = [NSDate date];
    NSString *fetchedData = [self fetchSomethingFromServer];
    NSString *processedData = [self processData:fetchedData];
    NSString *firstResult = [self calculateFirstResult:processedData];
    NSString *secondResult = [self calculateSecondResult:processedData];
    NSString *resultsSummary = [NSString stringWithFormat:
                                @"First: [%@]\nSecond: [%@]", firstResult,
                                secondResult];
    self.resultsTextView.text = resultsSummary;
    NSDate *endTime = [NSDate date];
    NSLog(@"Completed in %f seconds",
          [endTime timeIntervalSinceDate:startTime]);
}
```

We can make this method run entirely in the background by wrapping all the code in a block and passing it to a GCD function called dispatch_async. This function takes two parameters: a GCD queue and a block to assign to the queue. Make these two changes to your copy of doWork:. Be sure to add the closing brace and parenthesis at the end of the method:

```
- (IBAction)doWork:(id)sender
{
    NSDate *startTime = [NSDate date];
    dispatch_queue_t queue =
        dispatch_get_global_queue(DISPATCH_QUEUE_PRIORITY_DEFAULT, 0);
    dispatch_async(queue, ^{
        NSString *fetchedData = [self fetchSomethingFromServer];
        NSString *processedData = [self processData:fetchedData];
        NSString *firstResult = [self calculateFirstResult:processedData];
        NSString *secondResult = [self calculateSecondResult:processedData];
        NSString *resultsSummary = [NSString stringWithFormat:
                                    @"First: [%@]\nSecond: [%@]", firstResult,
                                    secondResult];
```

```
        self.resultsTextView.text = resultsSummary;
        NSDate *endTime = [NSDate date];
        NSLog(@"Completed in %f seconds",
              [endTime timeIntervalSinceDate:startTime]);
    });
}
```

The first line grabs a preexisting global queue that's always available, using the `dispatch_get_global_queue()` function. That function takes two arguments: the first lets you specify a priority, and the second is currently unused and should always be 0. If you specify a different priority in the first argument, such as `DISPATCH_QUEUE_PRIORITY_HIGH` or `DISPATCH_QUEUE_PRIORITY_LOW`, you will actually get a different global queue, which the system will prioritize differently. For now, we'll stick with the default global queue.

The queue is then passed to the `dispatch_async()` function, along with the block of code that comes after. GCD takes that entire block and puts it on the queue, from where it will be scheduled to run on a background thread and executed one step at a time, just as when it was running in the main thread.

Note that we define a variable called `startTime` just before the block is created, and then use its value at the end of the block. Intuitively, this doesn't seem to make sense because, by the time the block is executed, the `doWork:` method has exited, so the `NSDate` instance that the `startTime` variable is pointing to should already be released! This is a crucial point of block usage: if a block accesses any variables from "the outside" during its execution, then some special setup happens when the block is created, allowing the block access to those variables. The values contained by such variables will either be duplicated (if they are plain C types such as `int` or `float`) or retained (if they are pointers to objects) so that the values they contain can be used inside the block. When `dispatch_async` is called in the second line of `doWork:`, and the block shown in the code is created, `startTime` is actually sent a `retain` message, the return value of which is assigned to what is essentially a new immutable variable with the same name (`startTime`) inside the block.

The `startTime` variable needs to be immutable inside the block, so that code inside the block can't accidentally mess with a variable that's defined outside the block. If that were allowed all the time, it would just be confusing for everyone. Sometimes, however, you actually do want to let a block write to a value defined on the outside, and that's where the __block storage qualifier (which we mentioned a couple of pages ago) comes in handy. If __block is used to define a variable, then it is directly available to any and all blocks that are defined within the same scope. An interesting side effect of this is that __block-qualified variables are not duplicated or retained when used inside a block.

Don't Forget That Main Thread

Getting back to the project at hand, there's one problem here: UIKit thread-safety. Remember that messaging any GUI object from a background thread, including our `resultsTextView`, is a no-no. In fact, it you run the example now, you'll get an exception after about ten seconds, when the block tries to update the text view. Fortunately, GCD provides a way to deal with this, too. Inside the block, we can call another dispatching function, passing work back to the main thread! We do this by once again calling dispatch_async(), this time passing in the queue returned by the dispatch_get_main_queue() function. This always gives us the special queue that lives on the main thread, ready to execute blocks that require the use of the main thread. Make one more change to your version of doWork:

```
- (IBAction)doWork:(id)sender
{
    self.resultsTextView.text = @"";
    NSDate *startTime = [NSDate date];
    dispatch_queue_t queue =
        dispatch_get_global_queue(DISPATCH_QUEUE_PRIORITY_DEFAULT, 0);
    dispatch_async(queue, ^{
        NSString *fetchedData = [self fetchSomethingFromServer];
        NSString *processedData = [self processData:fetchedData];
        NSString *firstResult = [self calculateFirstResult:processedData];
        NSString *secondResult = [self calculateSecondResult:processedData];
        NSString *resultsSummary = [NSString stringWithFormat:
                                    @"First: [%@]\nSecond: [%@]", firstResult,
                                    secondResult];
        dispatch_async(dispatch_get_main_queue(), ^{
            self.resultsTextView.text = resultsSummary;
        });
        NSDate *endTime = [NSDate date];
        NSLog(@"Completed in %f seconds",
              [endTime timeIntervalSinceDate:startTime]);
    });
}
```

Giving Some Feedback

If you build and run your app at this point, you'll see that it now seems to work a bit more smoothly, at least in some sense. The button no longer gets stuck in a highlighted position after you touch it, which perhaps leads you to tap again, and again, and so on. If you look in Xcode's console log, you'll see the result of each of those taps, but only the results of the last tap will be shown in the text view.

What we really want to do is enhance the GUI so that, after the user presses the button, the display is immediately updated in a way that indicates that an action is underway. We also want the button disabled while the work is in progress. We'll do this by adding a UIActivityIndicatorView to our display. This class provides the sort of spinner seen in many applications and web sites. Start by declaring it in the class extension at the top of *ViewController.m*:

```
@interface ViewController ()

@property (weak, nonatomic) IBOutlet UIButton *startButton;
@property (weak, nonatomic) IBOutlet UITextView *resultsTextView;
@property (weak, nonatomic) IBOutlet UIActivityIndicatorView *spinner;

@end
```

Next, open *Main.Storyboard*, locate an **Activity Indicator** View in the library, and drag it into our view, next to the button (see Figure 15-3). You'll need to add layout constraints to fix the activity indicator's position relative to the button. One way to do this is to Control-drag from the button to the activity indicator and select **Horizontal Spacing** from the pop-up menu to fix the horizontal separation between them, then Control-drag again and select **Center Y** to make sure that their centers remain vertically aligned.

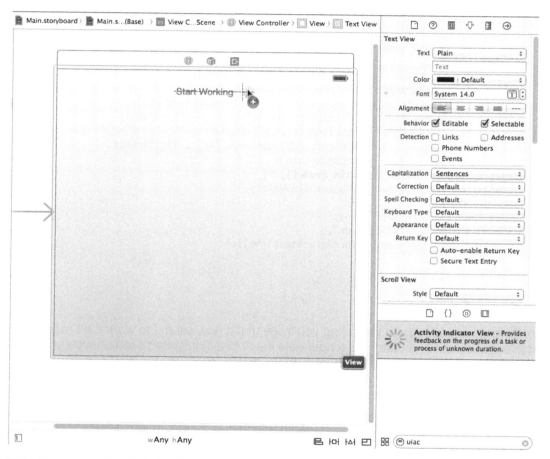

Figure 15-3. Dragging an activity indicator view into our main view in Interface Builder

With the activity indicator spinner selected, use the Attributes Inspector to check the **Hides When Stopped** check box so that our spinner will appear only when we tell it to start spinning (no one wants an unspinning spinner in their GUI).

Next, Control-drag from the **View Controller** icon to the spinner and connect the spinner outlet. Save your changes.

Now open *ViewController.m*. Here, we'll first work on the doWork: method a bit, adding a few lines to manage the appearance of the button and the spinner when the user taps the button and when the work is done. We'll first set the button's enabled property to NO, which prevents it from registering any taps and also shows that the button is disabled by making its text gray and somewhat transparent. Next, we get the spinner moving by calling its setAnimated: method. At the end of the block, we re-enable the button and stop the spinner, which causes it to disappear again:

```
- (IBAction)doWork:(id)sender
{
    self.resultsTextView.text = @"";
    NSDate *startTime = [NSDate date];
    self.startButton.enabled = NO;

    [self.spinner startAnimating];
    dispatch_queue_t queue =
        dispatch_get_global_queue(DISPATCH_QUEUE_PRIORITY_DEFAULT, 0);
    dispatch_async(queue, ^{
        NSString *fetchedData = [self fetchSomethingFromServer];
        NSString *processedData = [self processData:fetchedData];
        NSString *firstResult = [self calculateFirstResult:processedData];
        NSString *secondResult = [self calculateSecondResult:processedData];
        NSString *resultsSummary = [NSString stringWithFormat:
                                    @"First: [%@]\nSecond: [%@]", firstResult,
                                    secondResult];
        dispatch_async(dispatch_get_main_queue(), ^{
            self.resultsTextView.text = resultsSummary;
            self.startButton.enabled = YES;
            [self.spinner stopAnimating];
        });
        NSDate *endTime = [NSDate date];
        NSLog(@"Completed in %f seconds",
              [endTime timeIntervalSinceDate:startTime]);
    });
}
```

Build and run the app, and press the button. That's more like it, eh? Even though the work being done takes a few seconds, the user isn't just left hanging. The button is disabled and looks the part, as well. Also, the animated spinner lets the user know that the app hasn't actually hung and can be expected to return to normal at some point.

Concurrent Blocks

So far, so good, but we're not quite finished yet! The sharp-eyed among you will notice that, after going through these motions, we still haven't really changed the basic sequential layout of our algorithm (if you can even call this simple list of steps an algorithm). All that we're doing is moving a chunk of this method to a background thread and then finishing up in the main thread.
The Xcode console output proves it: this work takes ten seconds to run, just as it did at the outset. The 900-pound gorilla in the room is that calculateFirstResult: and calculateSecondResult: don't need to be performed in sequence, and doing them concurrently could give us a substantial speedup.

Fortunately, GCD has a way to accomplish this by using what's called a **dispatch group**. All blocks that are dispatched asynchronously within the context of a group, via the dispatch_group_async() function, are set loose to execute as fast as they can, including being distributed to multiple threads for concurrent execution, if possible. We can also use dispatch_group_notify() to specify an additional block that will be executed when all the blocks in the group have been run to completion.

Make the following changes to your copy of doWork:. Again, make sure you get that trailing bit of curly brace and parenthesis:

```
- (IBAction)doWork:(id)sender
{
    self.resultsTextView.text = @"";
    NSDate *startTime = [NSDate date];
    self.startButton.enabled = NO;
    self.startButton.alpha = 0.5f;
    [self.spinner startAnimating];
    dispatch_queue_t queue =
        dispatch_get_global_queue(DISPATCH_QUEUE_PRIORITY_DEFAULT, 0);
    dispatch_async(queue, ^{
        NSString *fetchedData = [self fetchSomethingFromServer];
        NSString *processedData = [self processData:fetchedData];
        NSString *firstResult = [self calculateFirstResult:processedData];
        NSString *secondResult = [self calculateSecondResult:processedData];
        __block NSString *firstResult;
        __block NSString *secondResult;
        dispatch_group_t group = dispatch_group_create();
        dispatch_group_async(group, queue, ^{
            firstResult = [self calculateFirstResult:processedData];
        });
        dispatch_group_async(group, queue, ^{
            secondResult = [self calculateSecondResult:processedData];
        });
        dispatch_group_notify(group, queue, ^{
            NSString *resultsSummary = [NSString stringWithFormat:
                                        @"First: [%@]\nSecond: [%@]",
                                        firstResult,
                                        secondResult];
```

```
            dispatch_async(dispatch_get_main_queue(), ^{
                self.resultsTextView.text = resultsSummary;
                self.startButton.enabled = YES;
                self.startButton.alpha = 1;
                [self.spinner stopAnimating];
            });
            NSDate *endTime = [NSDate date];
            NSLog(@"Completed in %f seconds",
                    [endTime timeIntervalSinceDate:startTime]);
        });
    });
}
```

One complication here is that each of the `calculate` methods returns a value that we want to grab, so we must first create the variables using the `__block` storage modifier. This ensures the values set inside the blocks are made available to the code that runs later.

With this in place, build and run the app again. You'll see that your efforts have paid off. What was once a ten-second operation now takes just seven seconds, thanks to the fact that we're running both of the calculations simultaneously.

Obviously, our contrived example gets the maximum effect because these two "calculations" don't actually do anything but cause the thread they're running on to sleep. In a real application, the speedup would depend on what sort of work is being done and which resources are available. The performance of CPU-intensive calculations is helped by this technique only if multiple CPU cores are available, and it will get better almost for free as more cores are added to future iOS devices. Other uses, such as fetching data from multiple network connections at once, would see a speed increase even with just one CPU.

As you can see, GCD is not a panacea. Using GCD won't automatically speed up every application. But by carefully applying these techniques at those points in your app where speed is essential, or where you find that your application feels like it's lagging in its responses to the user, you can easily provide a better user experience, even in situations where you can't improve the real performance.

Background Processing

Another important technology for handling concurrency is background processing. This allows your apps to run in the background—in some circumstances, even after the user has pressed the home button.

This functionality should not be confused with the true multitasking that modern desktop operating systems now feature, where all the programs you launch remain resident in the system RAM until you explicitly quit them. iOS devices still have too little RAM to be able to pull that off very well. Instead, this background processing is meant to allow applications that require specific kinds of system functionality to continue to run in a constrained manner when they are in the background. For instance, if you have an app that plays an audio stream from an Internet radio station, iOS will let that app continue to run, even if the user switches to another app. Beyond that, it will even provide standard pause and volume controls in the iOS control center (the translucent control panel that appears when you swipe up from the bottom of the screen) while your app is playing audio.

Assume you're creating an app that does one of the following things: plays audio even when the user is running another app, requests continuous location updates, responds to a special type of push request telling it to load new data from a server, or implements Voice over IP (VoIP) to let users send and receive phone calls on the Internet. In each of these cases, you can declare this situation in your app's *Info.plist* file, and the system will treat your app in a special way. This usage, while interesting, is probably not something that most readers of this book will be tackling, so we're not going to delve into it here.

Besides running apps in the background, iOS also includes the ability to put an app into a suspended state after the user presses the home button. This state of suspended execution is conceptually similar to putting your Mac into sleep mode. The entire working memory of the application is held in RAM; it just isn't executed while suspended. As a result, switching back to such an application is lightning-fast. This isn't limited to special applications. In fact, it is the default behavior of any app you build with Xcode (though this can be disabled by another setting in the *Info.plist* file). To see this in action, open your device's Mail application and drill down into a message. Next, press the home button, open the Notes application, and select a note. Now double-tap the home button and switch back to Mail. You'll see that there's no perceptible lag; it just slides into place as if it had been running all along.

For most applications, this sort of automatic suspending and resuming is all you're likely to need. However, in some situations, your app may need to know when it's about to be suspended and when it has just been awakened. The system provides ways of notifying an app about changes to its execution state via the UIApplication class, which has a number of delegate methods and notifications for just this purpose. We'll show you how to use them later in this chapter.

When your application is about to be suspended, one thing it can do, regardless of whether it's one of the special backgroundable application types, is request a bit of additional time to run in the background. The idea is to make sure your app has enough time to close any open files, network resources, and so on. We'll give you an example of this in a bit.

Application Life Cycle

Before we get into the specifics of how to deal with changes to your app's execution state, let's talk a bit about the various states in its life cycle:

- **Not Running**: This is the state that all apps are in on a freshly rebooted device. An application that has been launched at any point after the device is turned on will return to this state only under specific conditions:
  - If its *Info.plist* includes the UIApplicationExitsOnSuspend key (with its value set to YES)
  - If it was previously Suspended and the system needs to clear out some memory
  - If it crashes while running

- **Active**: This is the normal running state of an application when it's displayed on the screen. It can receive user input and update the display.

- **Background**: In this state, an app is given some time to execute some code, but it can't directly access the screen or get any user input. All apps enter this state briefly when the user presses the home button; most of them quickly move on to the Suspended state. Apps that want to do any sort of background processing stay in this state until they're made Active again.

- **Suspended**: A Suspended app is frozen. This is what happens to normal apps after their brief stint in the Background state. All the memory the app was using while it was active is held just as it was. If the user brings the app back to the Active state, it will pick up right where it left off. On the other hand, if the system needs more memory for whichever app is currently Active, any Suspended apps may be terminated (and placed back into the Not Running state) and their memory freed for other use.

- **Inactive**: An app enters the Inactive state only as a temporary rest stop between two other states. The only way an app can stay Inactive for any length of time is if the user is dealing with a system prompt (such as those shown for an incoming call or SMS message) or if the user has locked the screen. This state is basically a sort of limbo.

State-Change Notifications

To manage changes between these states, `UIApplication` defines a number of methods that its delegate can implement. In addition to the delegate methods, `UIApplication` also defines a matching set of notification names (see Table 15-1). This allows other objects besides the app delegate to register for notifications when the application's state changes.

Table 15-1. Delegate Methods for Tracking Your Application's Execution State and Their Corresponding Notification Names

Delegate Method	Notification Name
`application:didFinishLaunchingWithOptions:`	`UIApplicationDidFinishLaunchingNotification`
`applicationWillResignActive:`	`UIApplicationWillResignActiveNotification`
`applicationDidBecomeActive:`	`UIApplicationDidBecomeActiveNotification`
`applicationDidEnterBackground:`	`UIApplicationDidEnterBackgroundNotification`
`applicationWillEnterForeground:`	`UIApplicationWillEnterForegroundNotification`
`applicationWillTerminate:`	`UIApplicationWillTerminateNotification`

Note that each of these methods is directly related to one of the running states: Active, Inactive, and Background. Each delegate method is called (and each notification posted) in only one of those states. The most important state transitions are between Active and other states. Some transitions, like from Background to Suspended, occur without any notice whatsoever. Let's go through these methods and discuss how they're meant to be used.

The first of these, `application:didFinishLaunchingWithOptions:`, is one you've already seen many times in this book. It's the primary way of doing application-level coding directly after the app has launched. There is a similar method called `application:willFinishLaunchingWithOptions:` that's called first and which is intended for applications that use the view controller-based state saving feature). That method is not listed here because it's not associated with a state change.

The next two methods, `applicationWillResignActive:` and `applicationDidBecomeActive:`, are both used in a number of circumstances. If the user presses the home button, `applicationWillResignActive:` will be called. If the user later brings the app back to the foreground, `applicationDidBecomeActive:` will be called. The same sequence of events occurs if the user receives a phone call. To top it all off, `applicationDidBecomeActive:` is also called when the application launches for the first time! In general, this pair of methods brackets the movement of an application from the Active state to the Inactive state. They are good places to enable and disable any animations, in-app audio, or other items that deal with the app's presentation to the user. Because of the multiple situations where `applicationDidBecomeActive:` is used, you may want to put some of your app initialization code there instead of in `application:didFinishLaunchingWithO ptions:`. Note that you should not assume in `applicationWillResignActive:` that the application is about to be sent to the background; it may just be a temporary change that ends up with a move back to the Active state.

After those methods come `applicationDidEnterBackground:` and `applicationWillEnterForeground:`, which have a slightly different usage area: dealing with an app that is definitely being sent to the background. `applicationDidEnterBackground:` is where your app should free all resources that can be re-created later, save all user data, close network connections, and so on. This is also the spot where you can request more time to run in the background if you need to, as we'll demonstrate shortly. If you spend too much time doing things in `applicationDidEnterBackground:`—more than about five seconds—the system will decide that your app is misbehaving and terminate it. You should implement `applicationWillEnterForeground:` to re-create whatever was torn down in `applicationDidEnterBackground:`, such as reloading user data, reestablishing network connections, and so on. Note that when `applicationDidEnterBackground:` is called, you can safely assume that `applicationWillResignActive:` has also been recently called. Likewise, when `applicationWillEnterForeground:` is called, you can assume that `applicationDidBecomeActive:` will soon be called, as well.

Last in the list is `applicationWillTerminate:`, which you'll probably use seldom, if ever. It is called only if your application is already in the background and the system decides to skip suspension for some reason and simply terminate the app.

Now that you have a basic theoretical understanding of the states an application transitions between, let's put this knowledge to the test with a simple app that does nothing more than write a message to Xcode's console log each time one of these methods is called. We'll then manipulate the running app in a variety of ways, just as a user might, and see which transitions occur. To get the most out of this example, you'll need an iOS device. If you don't have one, you can use the simulator and skip over the parts that require a device.

Creating State Lab

In Xcode, create a new project based on the Single View Application template and name it *State Lab*.
Initially at least, this app won't display anything but the default gray screen it's born with.
Later, we'll make it do something more interesting, but for now, all the output it's going to generate
will end up in the Xcode console instead. The *AppDelegate.m* file already contains all the methods
we're interested in. We just need to add some logging, as shown in bold. Note that we've also
removed the comments from these methods, just for the sake of brevity:

```objc
#import "AppDelegate.h"

#import "ViewController.h"

@implementation AppDelegate

- (BOOL)application:(UIApplication *)application didFinishLaunchingWithOptions:(NSDictionary *)
launchOptions
{
    NSLog(@"%@", NSStringFromSelector(_cmd));
    return YES;
}

- (void)applicationWillResignActive:(UIApplication *)application
{
    NSLog(@"%@", NSStringFromSelector(_cmd));
}

- (void)applicationDidEnterBackground:(UIApplication *)application
{
    NSLog(@"%@", NSStringFromSelector(_cmd));
}

- (void)applicationWillEnterForeground:(UIApplication *)application
{
    NSLog(@"%@", NSStringFromSelector(_cmd));
}

- (void)applicationDidBecomeActive:(UIApplication *)application
{
    NSLog(@"%@", NSStringFromSelector(_cmd));
}

- (void)applicationWillTerminate:(UIApplication *)application
{
    NSLog(@"%@", NSStringFromSelector(_cmd));
}

@end
```

You may be wondering about that NSLog call we're using in all these methods. Objective-C provides a handy built-in variable called _cmd that always contains the selector of the current method. A **selector**, in case you need a refresher, is simply Objective-C's way of referring to a method. The NSStringFromSelector function returns an NSString representation of a given selector. Our usage here simply gives us a shortcut for outputting the current method name without needing to retype it or copy and paste it.

Exploring Execution States

Now build and run the app. The simulator will appear and launch our application. Switch back to Xcode and take a look at the console (**View ➤ Debug Area ➤ Activate Console**), where you should see something like this:

```
2014-06-26 19:12:36.953 State Lab[12751:70b] application:didFinishLaunchingWith
Options:
2014-06-26 19:12:36.957 State Lab[12751:70b] applicationDidBecomeActive:
```

Here, you can see that the application has successfully launched and been moved into the Active state. Now go back to the simulator and press the home button (which you'll have to do by selecting **Hardware ➤ Home** from the simulator's menu or ⇧⌘H on the keyboard), and you should see the following in the console:

```
2014-06-26 19:13:10.378 State Lab[12751:70b] applicationWillResignActive:
2014-06-26 19:13:10.386 State Lab[12751:70b] applicationDidEnterBackground:
```

These two lines show the app actually transitioning between two states: it first becomes Inactive, and then goes to Background. What you can't see here is that the app also switches to a third state: Suspended. Remember that you do not get any notification that this has happened; it's completely outside your control. Note that the app is still live in some sense, and Xcode is still connected to it, even though it's not actually getting any CPU time. Verify this by tapping the app's icon to relaunch it, which should produce this output:

```
2014-06-26 19:13:55.739 State Lab[12751:70b] applicationWillEnterForeground:
2014-06-26 19:13:55.739 State Lab[12751:70b] applicationDidBecomeActive:
```

There you are, back in business. The app was previously Suspended, is woken up to Inactive, and then ends up Active again. So, what happens when the app is really terminated? Tap the home button again, and you'll see this:

```
2014-06-26 19:14:35.035 State Lab[12751:70b] applicationWillResignActive:
2014-06-26 19:14:35.036 State Lab[12751:70b] applicationDidEnterBackground:
```

Now double-tap the home button (i.e., press ⇧⌘HH—you need to press the **H** key twice). The sideways-scrolling screen of apps should appear. Press and swipe upward on the State Lab screenshot until it flies offscreen, killing the application. What happens? You may be surprised to see that none of our NSLog calls print anything to the console. Instead, the app hangs in *main.m* on the call to the UIMainApplication function with the error message "Thread 1: signal SIGKILL". Click the **Stop** button in the upper-left corner of Xcode, and now State Lab is truly and completely terminated.

As it turns out, the `applicationWillTerminate:` method isn't normally called when the system is moving an app from the Suspended to Not Running state. When an app is Suspended, whether the system decides to dump it to reclaim memory or you manually force-quit it, the app simply vanishes and doesn't get a chance to do anything. The `applicationWillTerminate:` method is called only if the app being terminated is in the Background state. This can occur, for instance, if your app is actively running in the Background state, using system resources in one of the predefined ways (audio playback, GPS usage, and so on) and is force-quit either by the user or by the system. In the case we just explored with State Lab, the app was in the Suspended state, not Background, and was therefore terminated immediately without any notification.

> **Tip**   Do not rely on the `applicationWillTerminate:` method being called to save the state of your application—do this in `applicationDidEnterBackground:` instead.

There's one more interesting interaction to examine here. It's what happens when the system shows an alert dialog, temporarily taking over the input stream from the app and putting it into an Inactive state. This state can be readily triggered only when running on a real device instead of the simulator, using the built-in Messages app. Messages, like many other apps, can receive messages from the outside and display them in several ways.

To see how these are set up, run the Settings app on your device, choose Notifications from the list, and then select the Messages app from the list of apps. The hot "new" way to show messages, which debuted way back in iOS 5, is called **Banners**. This works by showing a small banner overlaid at the top of the screen, which doesn't need to interrupt whatever app is currently running. What we want to show is the bad old Alerts method, which makes a modal panel appear in front of the current app, requiring a user action. Under the heading **ALERT STYLE WHEN UNLOCKED**, select **Alerts**, so that the Messages app turns back into the kind of pushy jerk that users of iOS 4 and earlier always had to deal with.

Now back to your computer. In Xcode, use the pop-up at the upper left to switch from the simulator to your device, and then hit the **Run** button to build and run the app on your device. Now all you need to do is send a message to your device from the outside. If your device is an iPhone, you can send it an SMS message from another phone. If it's an iPod touch or an iPad, you're limited to Apple's own iMessage communication, which works on all iOS devices, as well as OS X in the Messages app. Figure out what works for your setup, and send your device a message via SMS or iMessage. When your device displays the system alert showing the incoming message, this will appear in the Xcode console:

```
2014-06-26 00:04:28.295 State Lab[16571:60b] applicationWillResignActive:
```

Note that our app didn't get sent to the background. It's in the Inactive state and can still be seen behind the system alert. If this app were a game or had any video, audio, or animations running, this is where we would probably want to pause them.

Press the **Close** button on the alert, and you'll get this:

```
2014-06-26 00:05:23.830 State Lab[16571:60b] applicationDidBecomeActive:
```

Now let's see what happens if you decide to reply to the message instead. Send another message to your device, generating this:

```
2013-11-18 00:05:55.487 State Lab[16571:60b] applicationWillResignActive:
```

This time, hit **Reply**, which switches you over to the Messages app, and you should see the following flurry of activity:

```
2014-06-26 00:06:10.513 State Lab[16571:60b] applicationDidBecomeActive:
2014-06-26 00:06:11.137 State Lab[16571:60b] applicationWillResignActive:
2014-06-26 00:06:11.140 State Lab[16571:60b] applicationDidEnterBackground:
```

Interesting! Our app quickly becomes Active, becomes Inactive again, and finally goes to Background (and then, silently, Suspended).

Using Execution State Changes

So, what should we make of all this? Based on what we've just demonstrated, it seems like there's a clear strategy to follow when dealing with these state changes.

Active ➤ Inactive

Use applicationWillResignActive:/UIApplicationWillResignActiveNotification to "pause" your app's display. If your app is a game, you probably already have the ability to pause the gameplay in some way. For other kinds of apps, make sure no time-critical demands for user input are in the works because your app won't be getting any user input for a while.

Inactive ➤ Background

Use applicationDidEnterBackground:/UIApplicationDidEnterBackgroundNotification to release any resources that don't need to be kept around when the app is backgrounded (such as cached images or other easily reloadable data) or that wouldn't survive backgrounding anyway (such as active network connections). Getting rid of excess memory usage here will make your app's eventual Suspended snapshot smaller, thereby decreasing the risk that your app will be purged from RAM entirely. You should also use this opportunity to save any application data that will help your users pick up where they left off the next time your app is relaunched. If your app comes back to the Active state, normally this won't matter; however, in case it's purged and must be relaunched, your users will appreciate starting off in the same place.

Background ➤ Inactive

Use applicationWillEnterForeground:/UIApplicationWillEnterForeground to undo anything you did when switching from Inactive to Background. For example, here you can reestablish persistent network connections.

Inactive ➤ Active

Use applicationDidBecomeActive:/UIApplicationDidBecomeActive to undo anything you did when switching from Active to Inactive. Note that, if your app is a game, this probably does not mean dropping out of pause straight to the game; you should let your users do that on their own. Also keep in mind that this method and notification are used when an app is freshly launched, so anything you do here must work in that context, as well.

There is one special consideration for the **Inactive ➤ Background** transition. Not only does it have the longest description in the previous list, but it's also probably the most code- and time-intensive transition in applications because of the amount of bookkeeping you may want your app to do. When this transition is underway, the system won't give you the benefit of an unlimited amount of time to save your changes here. It gives you about five seconds. If your app takes longer than that to return from the delegate method (and handle any notifications you've registered for), then your app will be summarily purged from memory and pushed into the Not Running state! If this seems unfair, don't worry because there is a reprieve available. While handling that delegate method or notification, you can ask the system to perform some additional work for you in a background queue, which buys you some extra time. We'll demonstrate that technique in the next section.

Handling the Inactive State

The simplest state change your app is likely to encounter is from Active to Inactive, and then back to Active. You may recall that this is what happens if your iPhone receives an SMS message while your app is running and displays it for the user. In this section, we're going to make State Lab do something visually interesting so that you can see what happens if you ignore that state change. Next, we'll show you how to fix it.

We'll also add a UILabel to our display and make it move using Core Animation, which is a really nice way of animating objects in iOS.

Start by adding a UILabel as an instance variable and property in *ViewController.m*:

```
#import "ViewController.h"

@interface ViewController ()

@property (strong, nonatomic) UILabel *label;

@end
```

Now let's set up the label when the view loads. Add the bold lines shown here to the viewDidLoad method:

```
- (void)viewDidLoad
{
    [super viewDidLoad];
    // Do any additional setup after loading the view, typically from a nib.
    CGRect bounds = self.view.bounds;
    CGRect labelFrame = CGRectMake(bounds.origin.x, CGRectGetMidY(bounds) - 50,
                                   bounds.size.width, 100);
```

```
    self.label = [[UILabel alloc] initWithFrame:labelFrame];
    self.label.font = [UIFont fontWithName:@"Helvetica" size:70];
    self.label.text = @"Bazinga!";
    self.label.textAlignment = NSTextAlignmentCenter;
    self.label.backgroundColor = [UIColor clearColor];
    [self.view addSubview:self.label];
}
```

It's time to set up some animation. We'll define two methods: one to rotate the label to an upside-down position and one to rotate it back to normal:

```
- (void)rotateLabelDown
{
    [UIView animateWithDuration:0.5
            animations:^{
                self.label.transform = CGAffineTransformMakeRotation(M_PI);
            }
            completion:^(BOOL finished){
                [self rotateLabelUp];
            }];
}

- (void)rotateLabelUp
{
    [UIView animateWithDuration:0.5
            animations:^{
                self.label.transform = CGAffineTransformMakeRotation(0);
            }
            completion:^(BOOL finished){
                [self rotateLabelDown];
            }];
}
```

This deserves a bit of explanation. UIView defines a class method called animateWithDuration: animations:completion:, which sets up an animation. Any animatable attributes that we set within the animations block don't have an immediate effect on the receiver. Instead, Core Animation will smoothly transition that attribute from its current value to the new value we specify. This is what's called an **implicit animation**, and it is one of the main features of Core Animation. The final completion block lets us specify what will happen after the animation is complete. Note carefully the syntax of this block:

```
completion:^(BOOL finished){
        [self rotateLabelDown];
}];
```

The code in bold is the signature of the block—it says that the block is called with a single boolean argument and returns nothing. The argument has a value of true if the animation completed normally, false if it was cancelled. In this example, we don't make any use of this argument.

So, each of these methods sets the label's `transform` property to a particular rotation angle, specified in radians, and uses the completion block to call the other method, so the text will continue to animate back and forth forever.

Finally, we need to set up a way to kick-start the animation. For now, we'll do this by adding this line at the end of `viewDidLoad`:

```
[self rotateLabelDown];
```

Now, build and run the app. You should see the *Bazinga!* label rotate back and forth (see Figure 15-4).

Figure 15-4. The State Lab application doing its label rotating magic

To test the **Active ➤ Inactive** transition, you really need to once again run this on an actual iPhone and send an SMS message to it from elsewhere. Unfortunately, there's no way to simulate this behavior in any version of the iOS simulator that Apple has released so far. If you don't yet have the ability to build and install on a device or don't have an iPhone, you won't be able to try this for yourself. In that case, please follow along as best you can!

Build and run the app on an iPhone, and see that the animation is running along. Now send an SMS message to the device. When the system alert comes up to show the message, you'll see that the animation keeps on running! That may be slightly comical, but it's probably irritating for a user. We will use application state transition notifications to stop our animation when this occurs.

Our controller class will need to have some internal state to keep track of whether it should be animating at any given time. For this purpose, let's add an ivar to *ViewController.m*. Because this simple BOOL doesn't need to be accessed by any outside classes, we skip the header and add it to the @implementation section:

```
@implementation ViewController {
    BOOL animate;
}
```

As you've seen, changes in the application state are notified to the application delegate, but since our class isn't the application delegate, we can't just implement the delegate methods and expect them to work. Instead, we sign up to receive notifications from the application when its execution state changes. Do this by adding the following code to the end of the viewDidLoad method in *ViewController.m*:

```
NSNotificationCenter *center = [NSNotificationCenter defaultCenter];
[center addObserver:self
        selector:@selector(applicationWillResignActive)
            name:UIApplicationWillResignActiveNotification
          object:nil];
[center addObserver:self
        selector:@selector(applicationDidBecomeActive)
            name:UIApplicationDidBecomeActiveNotification
          object:nil];
```

This sets up these two notifications, so each will call a method in our class at the appropriate time. Define these methods anywhere you like inside the @implementation block:

```
- (void)applicationWillResignActive
{
    NSLog(@"VC: %@", NSStringFromSelector(_cmd));
    animate = NO;
}

- (void)applicationDidBecomeActive
{
    NSLog(@"VC: %@", NSStringFromSelector(_cmd));
    animate = YES;
    [self rotateLabelDown];
}
```

This snippet includes the same method logging as before, just so you can see where the methods occur in the Xcode console. We added the preface "VC: " to distinguish this call from the NSLog() calls in the delegate (VC is for view controller). The first of these methods just turns off the animate flag. The second turns the flag back on, and then actually starts up the animations again. For that first method to have any effect, we need to add some code to check the animate flag and keep on animating only if it's enabled:

```
- (void)rotateLabelUp
{
    [UIView animateWithDuration:0.5
            animations:^{
                self.label.transform = CGAffineTransformMakeRotation(0);
            }
            completion:^(BOOL finished){
                if (animate) {
                    [self rotateLabelDown];
                }
            }];
}
```

We added this to the completion block of rotateLabelUp (and only there) so that our animation will stop only when the text is right-side up.

Finally, since we are now starting the animation when the application becomes active, and this happens right after it is launched, we no longer need the call rotateLabelDown in viewDidLoad, so delete it:

```
- (void)viewDidLoad {
    [self rotateLabelDown];

    NSNotificationCenter *center = [NSNotificationCenter defaultCenter];
}
```

Now build and run the app again, and you should see that it's animating as before. Once again, send an SMS message to your iPhone. This time, when the system alert appears, you'll see that the animation in the background stops as soon as the text is right-side up. Tap the **Close** button, and the animation starts back up.

Now you've seen what to do for the simple case of switching from Active to Inactive and back. The bigger task, and perhaps the more important one, is dealing with a switch to the background and then back to foreground.

Handling the Background State

As mentioned earlier, switching to the Background state is pretty important to ensure the best possible user experience. This is the spot where you'll want to discard any resources that can easily be reacquired (or will be lost anyway when your app goes silent) and save information about your app's current state, all without occupying the main thread for more than five seconds.

To demonstrate some of these behaviors, we're going to extend State Lab in a few ways. First, we're going to add an image to the display so that we can later show you how to get rid of the in-memory image. Then we're going to show you how to save some information about the app's state, so we can easily restore it later. Finally, we'll show you how to make sure these activities aren't taking up too much main thread time by putting all this work into a background queue.

Removing Resources When Entering the Background

Start by adding *smiley.png* from the *15 – Image* folder in the book's source archive to your project's *State Lab* folder. Be sure to enable the check box that tells Xcode to copy the file to your project directory. Don't add it to the *Images.xcassets* asset catalog because that would provide automatic caching, which would interfere with the specific resource management we're going to implement.

Now let's add properties for both the image and an image view to *ViewController.m*:

```
@interface ViewController ()

@property (strong, nonatomic) UILabel *label;
@property (strong, nonatomic) UIImage *smiley;
@property (strong, nonatomic) UIImageView *smileyView;

@end
```

Next, set up the image view and put it on the screen by modifying the viewDidLoad method, as shown here:

```
- (void)viewDidLoad
{
    [super viewDidLoad];
    // Do any additional setup after loading the view, typically from a nib.
    CGRect bounds = self.view.bounds;
    CGRect labelFrame = CGRectMake(bounds.origin.x, CGRectGetMidY(bounds) - 50,
                                   bounds.size.width, 100);
    self.label = [[UILabel alloc] initWithFrame:labelFrame];
    self.label.font = [UIFont fontWithName:@"Helvetica" size:70];
    self.label.text = @"Bazinga!";
    self.label.textAlignment = NSTextAlignmentCenter;
    self.label.backgroundColor = [UIColor clearColor];

    // smiley.png is 84 x 84
    CGRect smileyFrame = CGRectMake(CGRectGetMidX(bounds) - 42,
                                    CGRectGetMidY(bounds)/2 - 42,
                                    84, 84);
    self.smileyView = [[UIImageView alloc] initWithFrame:smileyFrame];
    self.smileyView.contentMode = UIViewContentModeCenter;
    NSString *smileyPath = [[NSBundle mainBundle] pathForResource:@"smiley"
                                                           ofType:@"png"];
    self.smiley = [UIImage imageWithContentsOfFile:smileyPath];
    self.smileyView.image = self.smiley;
```

```
[self.view addSubview:self.smileyView];

[self.view addSubview:self.label];

NSNotificationCenter *center = [NSNotificationCenter defaultCenter];
[center addObserver:self
           selector:@selector(applicationWillResignActive)
               name:UIApplicationWillResignActiveNotification
             object:nil];
[center addObserver:self
           selector:@selector(applicationDidBecomeActive)
               name:UIApplicationDidBecomeActiveNotification
             object:nil];
}
```

Build and run the app, and you'll see the incredibly happy-looking smiley face toward the top of your screen (see Figure 15-5).

***Figure 15-5.** The State Lab application doing its label-rotating magic with the addition of a smiley icon*

Next, press the home button to switch your app to the background, and then tap its icon to launch it again. You'll see that when the app resumes, the label starts rotating again, as expected. All seems well, but in fact, we're not yet optimizing system resources as well as we could.

Remember that the fewer resources we use while our app is Suspended, the lower the risk that iOS will terminate our app entirely. By clearing any easily re-created resources from memory when we can, we increase the chance that our app will stick around and therefore relaunch super-quickly.

Let's see what we can do about that smiley face. We would really like to free up that image when going to the Background state and re-create it when coming back from the Background state. To do that, we'll need to add two more notification registrations inside `viewDidLoad`:

```
[center addObserver:self
          selector:@selector(applicationDidEnterBackground)
              name:UIApplicationDidEnterBackgroundNotification
            object:nil];
[center addObserver:self
          selector:@selector(applicationWillEnterForeground)
              name:UIApplicationWillEnterForegroundNotification
            object:nil];
```

And we want to implement the two new methods:

```
- (void)applicationDidEnterBackground
{
    NSLog(@"VC: %@", NSStringFromSelector(_cmd));
    self.smiley = nil;
    self.smileyView.image = nil;
}

- (void)applicationWillEnterForeground
{
    NSLog(@"VC: %@", NSStringFromSelector(_cmd));
    NSString *smileyPath = [[NSBundle mainBundle] pathForResource:@"smiley"
                                                           ofType:@"png"];
    self.smiley = [UIImage imageWithContentsOfFile:smileyPath];
    self.smileyView.image = self.smiley;
}
```

Build and run the app, and repeat the same steps of backgrounding your app and switching back to it. You should see that, from the user's standpoint, the behavior appears to be about the same. If you want to verify for yourself that this is really happening, comment out the contents of the `applicationWillEnterForeground` method, and then build and run the app again. You'll see that the image really does disappear.

Saving State When Entering the Background

Now that you've seen an example of how to free up some resources when entering the Background state, it's time to think about saving state. Remember that the idea is to save information relevant to what the user is doing, so that if your application is later dumped from memory, users can still pick up right where they left off the next time they return.

The kind of state we're talking about here is really application-specific, not view-specific. Do not confuse this with saving and restoring the locations of views or which screen of your application the user was looking at when it was last active—for that, iOS provides the state saving and restoration mechanism, which you can read about in the *iOS App Programming Guide* on Apple's web site (https://developer.apple.com/library/ios/documentation/iphone/conceptual/iphoneosprogrammingguide/StatePreservation/StatePreservation.html). Here, we're thinking about things like user preferences in applications for which you do not want to implement a separate settings bundle. Using the same NSUserDefaults API that we introduced you to in Chapter 12, you can quickly and easily save preferences from within the application and read them back later. Of course, if your application is not visually complex or you don't want to use the state saving and restoration mechanism, you can save information that will allow you to restore its visual state in the user preferences, too.

The State Lab example is too simple to have real user preferences, so let's take a shortcut and add some application-specific state to its one and only view controller. Add a property called index in *ViewController.m*, along with a segmented control:

```
#import "ViewController.h"

@interface ViewController ()

@property (strong, nonatomic) UILabel *label;
@property (strong, nonatomic) UIImage *smiley;
@property (strong, nonatomic) UIImageView *smileyView;
@property (assign, nonatomic) NSInteger index;
@property (strong, nonatomic) UISegmentedControl *segmentedControl;

@end
```

We're going to allow the user to set the value of this property using a segmented control and we're going to save it in the user defaults. We're then going to terminate and relaunch the application, to demonstrate that we can recover the value of the property.
Next, move to the middle of the viewDidLoad method, where you'll create the segmented control, and add it to the view:

```
    .
    .
    .
    self.smileyView.image = self.smiley;

    self.segmentedControl = [[UISegmentedControl alloc] initWithItems:
                              [NSArray arrayWithObjects: @"One", @"Two", @"Three", @"Four", nil]] ;
    self.segmentedControl.frame = CGRectMake(bounds.origin.x + 20,
                                     50, bounds.size.width - 40, 30);
        [self.segmentedControl addTarget:self action:@selector(selectionChanged:)
        forControlEvents:UIControlEventValueChanged];

    [self.view addSubview:self.segmentedControl];
    [self.view addSubview:self.smileyView];
    [self.view addSubview:self.label];
    .
```

We also used the addTarget:action:forControlEvents: method to connect the segmented control to the selectionChanged: method, which we need to have called when the selected segment changes. Add the implementation of this method anywhere in the body of the *ViewController.m* file:

```
- (void)selectionChanged:(UISegmentedControl *)sender {
    self.index = sender.selectedSegmentIndex;
}
```

Now whenever the user changes the selected segment, the value of the index property will be updated.

Build and run the app. You should see the segmented control and be able to click its segments to select them one at a time. As you do so, the value of the index property will change, although you can't actually see this happening. Background your app again by clicking the home button, bring up the taskbar (by double-clicking the home button) and kill your app, and then relaunch it. When the application restarts, the index property will have a value of zero again and there will be no selected segment. That's what we need to fix next.

Saving the value of the index property is simple enough; we just need one line of code to the end of the applicationDidEnterBackground method in *ViewController.m*:

```
- (void)applicationDidEnterBackground
{
    NSLog(@"VC: %@", NSStringFromSelector(_cmd));
    self.smiley = nil;
    self.smileyView.image = nil;
    [[NSUserDefaults standardUserDefaults] setInteger:self.index forKey:@"index"];
}
```

But where should we restore the property value and use it to configure the segmented control? The inverse of this method, applicationWillEnterForeground, isn't what we want. When that method is called, the app has already been running, and the setting is still intact. Instead, we need to access this when things are being set up after a new launch, which brings us back to the viewDidLoad method. Add the bold lines shown here to that method:

```
.
    [self.view addSubview:self.label];

    self.index = [[NSUserDefaults standardUserDefaults] integerForKey:@"index"];
    self.segmentedControl.selectedSegmentIndex = self.index;
.
```

When the application is being launched for the first time, there will not be a value saved in the user defaults. In this case, the integerForKey: method returns the value zero, which happens to be the correct initial value for the index property. If you wanted to use a different initial value, you could do so by registering it as the default value for the index key, as described in "Registering Default Values" in Chapter 12.

Now build and run the app. You'll notice a difference immediately—the first segment in the segmented control is preselected, because its selected segment index was set in the viewDidLoad method. Now touch a segment, and then do the full background-kill-restart dance. There it is—the index value has been restored and, as a result, the correct segment in the segmented control is now selected!

Obviously, what we've shown here is pretty minimal, but the concept can be extended to all kinds of application states. It's up to you to decide how far you want to take it in order to maintain the illusion for the users that your app was always there, just waiting for them to come back!

Requesting More Backgrounding Time

Earlier, we mentioned the possibility of your app being dumped from memory if moving to the Background state takes too much time. For example, your app may be in the middle of doing a file transfer that it would really be a shame not to finish; however, trying to hijack the applicationDidEnterBackground method to make it complete the work there, before the application is really backgrounded, isn't really an option. Instead, you should use applicationDidEnterBackground as a platform for telling the system that you have some extra work you would like to do, and then start up a block to actually do it. Assuming that the system has enough available RAM to keep your app in memory while the user does something else, the system will oblige you and keep your app running for a while.

We'll demonstrate this, not with an actual file transfer, but with a simple sleep call. Once again, we'll be using our new acquaintances GCD and blocks to make the contents of our applicationDidEnterBackground method run in a separate queue.

In *ViewController.m*, modify the applicationDidEnterBackground method as follows:

```
- (void)applicationDidEnterBackground
{
    NSLog(@"VC: %@", NSStringFromSelector(_cmd));
    self.smiley = nil;
    self.smileyView.image = nil;
    [[NSUserDefaults standardUserDefaults] setInteger:self.index forKey:@"index"];
    UIApplication *app = [UIApplication sharedApplication];

    __block UIBackgroundTaskIdentifier taskId = [app beginBackgroundTaskWithExpirationHandler:^{
        NSLog(@"Background task ran out of time and was terminated.");
        [app endBackgroundTask:taskId];
    }];

    if (taskId == UIBackgroundTaskInvalid) {
        NSLog(@"Failed to start background task!");
        return;
    }
```

```
    dispatch_async(dispatch_get_global_queue(DISPATCH_QUEUE_PRIORITY_DEFAULT, 0),
    ^{
        NSLog(@"Starting background task with %f seconds remaining",
                app.backgroundTimeRemaining);
        self.smiley = nil;
        self.smileyView.image = nil;

        // simulate a lengthy (25 seconds) procedure
        [NSThread sleepForTimeInterval:25];

        NSLog(@"Finishing background task with %f seconds remaining",
                app.backgroundTimeRemaining);
        [app endBackgroundTask:taskId];
    });
}
```

Let's look through this code piece by piece. First, we grab the shared UIApplication instance, since we'll be using it several times in this method. And then comes this:

```
UIBackgroundTaskIdentifier taskId
        = [app beginBackgroundTaskWithExpirationHandler:^{
    NSLog(@"Background task ran out of time and was terminated.");
    [app endBackgroundTask:taskId];
}];
```

With the call to beginBackgroundTaskWithExpirationHandler:, we're basically telling the system that we need more time to accomplish something, and we promise to let it know when we're finished. The block we give as a parameter may be called if the system decides that we've been going way too long anyway and decides to stop our background task. The call to beginBackgroundTaskWithExpirationHandler: returns an identifier that we save in the local variable taskId for later use. This variable has the __block qualifier so that its current value can be read from both of the blocks that are created in this code. Without this qualifier, the value of the variable would be captured by the expiration handler (the first code block) when that block is created. This is at the point that the beginBackgroundTaskWithExpirationHandler: method is called, which is before its return value has been assigned to taskId! That would mean that if the expiration handler were ever invoked, it would pass an undefined value to the endBackgroundTask: method.

Note that the block we gave ended with a call to endBackgroundTask:, passing along taskId. That tells the system that we're finished with the work for which we previously requested extra time. It's important to balance each call to beginBackgroundTaskWithExpirationHandler: with a matching call to endBackgroundTask: so that the system knows when we've completed the work.

> **Note** Depending on your computing background, the use of the word *task* here may evoke associations with what we usually call a *process*, consisting of a running program that may contain multiple threads, and so on. In this case, try to put that out of your mind. The use of *task* in this context really just means "something that needs to get done." Any task you create here is running within your still-executing app.

Next, we do this:

```
if (taskId == UIBackgroundTaskInvalid) {
    NSLog(@"Failed to start background task!");
    return;
}
```

If our earlier call to beginBackgroundTaskWithExpirationHandler: returned the special value UIBackgroundTaskInvalid, which means the system is refusing to grant us any additional time. In that case, you could try to do the quickest part of whatever needs doing anyway and hope that it completes quickly enough that your app won't be terminated before it's finished. This was more likely to be an issue when running on older devices, such as the iPhone 3G, that didn't support multitasking. In this example, however, we're just letting it slide.

Next comes the interesting part where the work itself is actually done:

```
dispatch_async(dispatch_get_global_queue(DISPATCH_QUEUE_PRIORITY_DEFAULT, 0),
^{
    NSLog(@"Starting background task with %f seconds remaining",
        app.backgroundTimeRemaining);
    self.smiley = nil;
    self.smileyView.image = nil;

    // simulate a lengthy (25 seconds) procedure
    [NSThread sleepForTimeInterval:25];

    NSLog(@"Finishing background task with %f seconds remaining",
        app.backgroundTimeRemaining);
    [app endBackgroundTask:taskId];
});
```

All this does is take the same work our method was doing in the first place and place it in a background queue. Notice, though, that the code that uses NSUserDefaults to save state has not been moved into the block. That's because it's important to save that state whether or not iOS grants the application additional time to run when it moves into the background. At the end of the block, we call endBackgroundTask: to let the system know that we're finished.

With that in place, build and run the app, and then background your app by pressing the home button. Watch the Xcode console, as well as the status bar at the bottom of the Xcode window. You'll see that this time, your app stays running (you don't get the "Debugging terminated" message in the status bar), and after 25 seconds, you will see the final log in your output. A complete run of the app up to this point should give you console output along these lines:

```
2014-06-27 01:30:08.194 State Lab[12158:70b] application:didFinishLaunchingWith
Options:
2014-06-27 01:30:08.209 State Lab[12158:70b] applicationDidBecomeActive:
2014-06-27 01:30:08.210 State Lab[12158:70b] VC: applicationDidBecomeActive
2014-06-27 01:30:17.010 State Lab[12158:70b] applicationWillResignActive:
2014-06-27 01:30:17.011 State Lab[12158:70b] VC: applicationWillResignActive
2014-06-27 01:30:17.018 State Lab[12158:70b] applicationDidEnterBackground:
```

```
2014-06-27 01:30:17.019 State Lab[12158:70b] VC: applicationDidEnterBackground
2014-06-27 01:30:17.021 State Lab[12158:3a03] Starting background task with
179.988868 seconds remaining
2014-06-27 01:30:42.027 State Lab[12158:3a03] Finishing background task with
154.986797 seconds remaining
```

As you can see, the system is much more generous with time when doing things in the background than it is in the main thread of your app. Following this procedure can really help you out if you have any ongoing tasks to deal with.

Note that we used only a single background task identifier; but in practice, you use as many as you need. For example, if you have multiple network transfers happening at Background time and you need to complete them, you can create a background task for each and allow them to continue running in a background queue. So, you can easily allow multiple operations to run in parallel during the available time. Also consider that the task identifier for each background task is a normal C-language value (not an object). Apart from being stored in a local __block variable, it can also be stored as an instance variable if that better suits your class design.

Grand Central Dispatch, Over and Out

This has been a pretty heavy chapter, with a lot of new concepts thrown your way. Not only have you learned about a complete new feature set that Apple added to the C language, but you've also discovered a new conceptual paradigm for dealing with concurrency without worrying about threads. We also demonstrated some techniques for making sure your apps play nicely in the multitasking world of iOS. Now that we've gotten some of this heavy stuff out of the way, let's move on to the next chapter, which focuses on drawing. Pencils out, let's draw!

Chapter 16

Drawing with Core Graphics

Every application we've built so far has been constructed from views and controls that are part of the UIKit framework. You can do a lot with UIKit, and a great many applications can be constructed using only its predefined objects. Some visual elements, however, can't be fully realized without going beyond what the UIKit stock components offer.

For example, sometimes an application needs to be able to do custom drawing. Fortunately, iOS includes the Core Graphics framework, which allows us to do a wide array of drawing tasks. In this chapter, we'll explore this powerful graphics environment. We'll also build sample applications that demonstrate key features of Core Graphics and explain its main concepts.

Paint the World

One of the main components of Core Graphics is a set of APIs called **Quartz 2D**. This is a collection of functions, data types, and objects designed to let you draw directly into a view or an image in memory. Quartz 2D treats the view or image that is being drawn into as a virtual canvas. It follows what's called a **painter's model**, which is just a fancy way of saying that the drawing commands are applied in much the same way that paint is applied to a canvas.

If a painter paints an entire canvas red, and then paints the bottom half of the canvas blue, the canvas will be half red and half either blue or purple (blue if the paint is opaque; purple if the paint is semitransparent). Quartz 2D's virtual canvas works the same way. If you paint the whole view red, and then paint the bottom half of the view blue, you'll have a view that's half red and half either blue or purple, depending on whether the second drawing action was fully opaque or partially transparent. Each drawing action is applied to the canvas on top of any previous drawing actions.

Quartz 2D provides a variety of line, shape, and image drawing functions. Though easy to use, Quartz 2D is limited to two-dimensional drawing.

Now that you have a general idea of Quartz 2D, let's try it out. We'll start with the basics of how Quartz 2D works, and then build a simple drawing application with it.

The Quartz 2D Approach to Drawing

When using Quartz 2D (Quartz for short), you'll usually add the drawing code to the view doing the drawing. For example, you might create a subclass of UIView and add Quartz function calls to that class's drawRect: method. The drawRect: method is part of the UIView class definition and is called every time a view needs to redraw itself. If you insert your Quartz code in drawRect:, that code will be called, and then the view will redraw itself.

Quartz 2D's Graphics Contexts

In Quartz, as in the rest of Core Graphics, drawing happens in a **graphics context**, usually referred to simply as a **context**. Every view has an associated context. You retrieve the current context, use that context to make various Quartz drawing calls, and let the context worry about rendering your drawing onto the view. You can think of this context as a sort of canvas. The system provides you with a default context where the contents will appear on the screen. However, it's also possible to create a context of your own for doing drawing that you don't want to appear immediately, but to save for later or use for something else. We're going to be focusing mainly on the default context, which you can acquire with this line of code:

```
CGContextRef context = UIGraphicsGetCurrentContext();
```

> **Note**   Core Graphics is a C-language API, so you'll see a lot of C syntax in the code examples in this chapter.

Once you've defined your graphics context, you can draw into it by passing the context to a variety of Core Graphics drawing functions. For example, this sequence will create a **path** describing a simple line, and then draw that path:

```
CGContextSetLineWidth(context, 4.0);
CGContextSetStrokeColorWithColor(context, [UIColor redColor].CGColor);
CGContextMoveToPoint(context, 10.0, 10.0);
CGContextAddLineToPoint(context, 20.0, 20.0);
CGContextStrokePath(context);
```

The first call specifies that any subsequent drawing commands that create the current path should be performed with a brush that is 4 points wide. Think of this as selecting the size of the brush you're about to paint with. Until you call this function again with a different number, all lines will have a width of 4 points when drawn. You then specify that the stroke color should be red. In Core Graphics, two colors are associated with drawing actions:

- The **stroke color** is used in drawing lines and for the outline of shapes.
- The **fill color** is used to fill in shapes.

A context has a sort of invisible pen associated with it that does the line drawing. As drawing commands are executed, the movements of this pen form a path. When you call CGContextMoveToPoint(), you lift the virtual pen and move to the location you specify, without actually drawing anything. Whatever operation comes next, it will do its work relative to the point to which you moved the pen. In the earlier example, for instance, we first moved the pen to (10, 10). The next function call added a line from the current pen location (10, 10) to the specified location (20, 20), which became the new pen location.

When you draw in Core Graphics, you're not drawing anything you can actually see—at least not immediately. You're creating a path, which can be a shape, a line, or some other object; however, it contains no color or other features to make it visible. It's like writing in invisible ink. Until you do something to make it visible, your path can't be seen. So, the next step is to call the CGContextStrokePath() function, which tells Quartz to draw the path you've constructed. This function will use the line width and the stroke color we set earlier to actually color (or "paint") the path and make it visible.

The Coordinate System

In the previous chunk of code, we passed a pair of floating-point numbers as parameters to CGContextMoveToPoint() and CGContextLineToPoint(). These numbers represent positions in the Core Graphics coordinate system. Locations in this coordinate system are denoted by their x and y coordinates, which we usually represent as (x, y). The upper-left corner of the context is (0, 0). As you move down, y increases. As you move to the right, x increases.

In the previous code snippet, we drew a diagonal line from (10, 10) to (20, 20), which would look like the one shown in Figure 16-1.

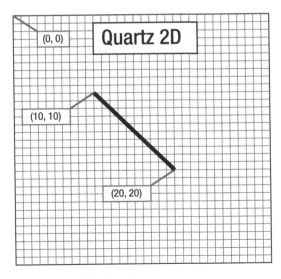

Figure 16-1. Drawing a line using Quartz 2D's coordinate system

The coordinate system is one of the gotchas in drawing with Quartz on iOS because its vertical component is flipped from what many graphics libraries use and from the traditional Cartesian coordinate system (introduced by René Descartes in the 17th century). In other systems, such as OpenGL, or even the OS X version of Quartz, (0, 0) is in the lower-left corner; and as the y coordinate increases, you move toward the top of the context or view, as shown in Figure 16-2.

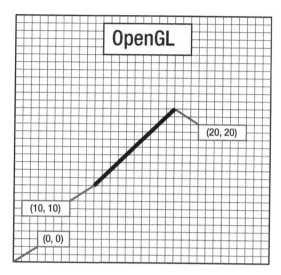

Figure 16-2. *In many graphics libraries, including OpenGL, drawing from (10, 10) to (20, 20) would produce a line that looks like this instead of the line in Figure 16-1*

To specify a point in the coordinate system, some Quartz functions require two floating-point numbers as parameters. Other Quartz functions ask for the point to be embedded in a CGPoint, a struct that holds two floating-point values: x and y. To describe the size of a view or other object, Quartz uses CGSize, a struct that also holds two floating-point values: width and height. Quartz also declares a data type called CGRect, which is used to define a rectangle in the coordinate system. A CGRect contains two elements: a CGPoint called origin, with x and y values that identify the top left of the rectangle; and a CGSize called size, which identifies the width and height of the rectangle.

Specifying Colors

An important part of drawing is color, so understanding the way colors work on iOS is critical. UIKit provides an Objective-C class that represents a color: UIColor. You can't use a UIColor object directly in Core Graphic calls. However, UIColor is just a wrapper around CGColor (which is what the Core Graphic functions require) and you can retrieve a CGColor reference from a UIColor instance by using its CGColor property, as we showed earlier, in this code snippet:

```
CGContextSetStrokeColorWithColor(context, [UIColor redColor].CGColor);
```

We created a UIColor instance using a convenience method called redColor, and then retrieved its CGColor property and passed that into the function.

A Bit of Color Theory for Your iOS Device's Display

In modern computer graphics, any color displayed on the screen has its data stored in some way based on something called a **color model**. A color model (sometimes called a **color space**) is simply a way of representing real-world color as digital values that a computer can use. One common way to represent colors is to use four components: red, green, blue, and alpha. In Quartz, each of these values is represented as CGFloat (which is a 4-byte floating-point value on 32-bit systems and an 8-byte value on 64-bit systems). These values should always contain a value between 0.0 and 1.0.

> **Note**   A floating-point value that is expected to be in the range 0.0 to 1.0 is often referred to as a **clamped floating-point variable**, or sometimes just a **clamp**.

The red, green, and blue components are fairly easy to understand, as they represent the **additive primary colors**, or the **RGB color model** (see Figure 16-3). If you add together the light of these three colors in equal proportions, the result will appear to the eye as either white or a shade of gray, depending on the intensity of the light mixed. Combining the three additive primaries in different proportions gives you a range of different colors, referred to as a **gamut**.

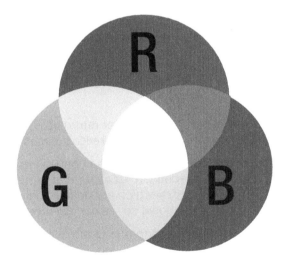

Figure 16-3. A simple representation of the additive primary colors that make up the RGB color model

In grade school, you probably learned that the primary colors are red, yellow, and blue. These primaries, which are known as the **historical subtractive primaries**, or the **RYB color model**, have little application in modern color theory and are almost never used in computer graphics. The color gamut of the RYB color model is much more limited than the RGB color model, and it also doesn't lend itself easily to mathematical definition. As much as we hate to tell you that your wonderful third-grade art teacher, Mrs. Smedlee, was wrong about anything—well, in the context of computer graphics, she was. For our purposes, the primary colors are red, green, and blue, not red, yellow, and blue.

In addition to red, green, and blue, Quartz uses another color component, called **alpha**, which represents how transparent a color is. When drawing one color on top of another color, alpha is used to determine the final color that is drawn. With an alpha of 1.0, the drawn color is 100% opaque and obscures any colors beneath it. With any value less than 1.0, the colors below will show through and mix with the color above. If the alpha is 0.0, then this color will be completely invisible and whatever is behind it will show through completely. When an alpha component is used, the color model is sometimes referred to as the **RGBA color model,** although technically speaking, the alpha isn't really part of the color; it just defines how the color will interact with other colors when it is drawn.

Other Color Models

Although the RGB model is the most commonly used in computer graphics, it is not the only color model. Several others are in use, including the following:

- Hue, saturation, value (HSV)
- Hue, saturation, lightness (HSL)
- Cyan, magenta, yellow, black (CMYK), which is used in four-color offset printing
- Grayscale

To make matters even more confusing, there are different versions of some of these models, including several variants of the RGB color space.

Fortunately, for most operations, we don't need to worry about the color model that is being used. We can just call CGColor on our UIColor objects, and in most cases, Core Graphics will handle any necessary conversions.

Color Convenience Methods

UIColor has a large number of convenience methods that return UIColor objects initialized to a specific color. In our previous code sample, we used the redColor method to initialize a color to red.

Fortunately, the UIColor instances created by most of these convenience methods all use the RGBA color model. The only exceptions are the predefined UIColors that represent grayscale values—such as blackColor, whiteColor, and darkGrayColor—which are defined only in terms of white level and alpha. In our examples here, we're not using those, so we can assume RGBA for now.

If you need more control over color, instead of using one of those convenience methods based on the name of the color, you can create a color by specifying all four of the components. Here's an example:

```
UIColor *red = [UIColor colorWithRed:1.0 green:0.0 blue:0.0 alpha:1.0];
```

Drawing Images in Context

Quartz allows you to draw images directly into a context. This is another example of an Objective-C class (UIImage) that you can use as an alternative to working with a Core Graphics data structure (CGImage). The UIImage class contains methods to draw its image into the current context. You'll need to identify where the image should appear in the context using either of the following techniques:

- By specifying a CGPoint to identify the image's upper-left corner
- By specifying a CGRect to frame the image, resized to fit the frame, if necessary

You can draw a UIImage into the current context, like so:

```
UIImage *image; // assuming this exists and points at a UIImage instance
CGPoint drawPoint = CGPointMake(100.0, 100.0);
[image drawAtPoint:drawPoint];
```

Drawing Shapes: Polygons, Lines, and Curves

Quartz provides a number of functions to make it easier to create complex shapes. To draw a rectangle or a polygon, you don't need to calculate angles, draw lines, or do any math at all. You can just call a Quartz function to do the work for you. For example, to draw an ellipse, you define the rectangle into which the ellipse needs to fit and let Core Graphics do the work:

```
CGRect theRect = CGRectMake(0, 0, 100, 100);
CGContextAddEllipseInRect(context, theRect);
CGContextDrawPath(context, kCGPathFillStroke);
```

You use similar methods for rectangles. Quartz also provides methods that let you create more complex shapes, such as arcs and Bezier paths.

> **Note**   We won't be working with complex shapes in this chapter's examples. To learn more about arcs and Bezier paths in Quartz, check out the *Quartz 2D Programming Guide* in the iOS Dev Center at http://developer.apple.com/documentation/GraphicsImaging/Conceptual/drawingwithquartz2d/ or in Xcode's online documentation.

Quartz 2D Tool Sampler: Patterns, Gradients, and Dash Patterns

Quartz offers quite an impressive array of tools. For example, Quartz supports filling polygons not only with solid colors, but also with gradients. And in addition to drawing solid lines, it can also use an assortment of dash patterns. Take a look at the screenshots in Figure 16-4, which are from Apple's QuartzDemo sample code, to see a sampling of what Quartz can do for you.

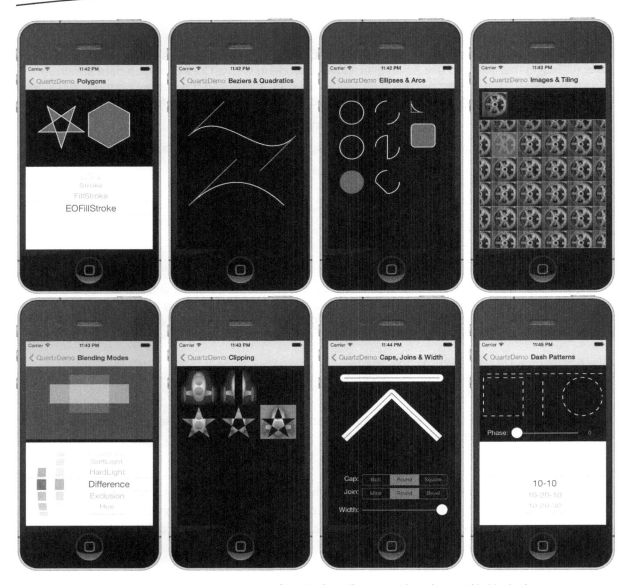

Figure 16-4. Some examples of what Quartz 2D can do, from the QuartzDemo sample project provided by Apple

Now that you have a basic understanding of how Quartz works and what it is capable of doing, let's try it out.

The QuartzFun Application

Our next application is a simple drawing program (see Figure 16-5). We're going to build this application using Quartz to give you a real feel for how the concepts we've been describing fit together.

Figure 16-5. Our chapter's simple drawing application in action

The application features a bar across the top and one across the bottom, each with a segmented control. The control at the top lets you change the drawing color, and the one at the bottom lets you change the shape to be drawn. When you touch and drag, the selected shape will be drawn in the selected color. To minimize the application's complexity, only one shape will be drawn at a time.

Setting Up the QuartzFun Application

In Xcode, create a new project using the Single View Application template and call it *QuartzFun*. The template has already provided us with an application delegate and a view controller. We're going to be executing our custom drawing in a custom view, so we need to also create a subclass of UIView where we'll do the drawing by overriding the drawRect: method.

With the *QuartzFun* folder selected (the folder that currently contains the app delegate and view controller files), press ⌘N to bring up the new file assistant, and then select Cocoa Touch Class from the iOS section. Name the new class *QuartzFunView* and make it a subclass of `UIView`.

We're going to define some constants, as we've done in previous projects; but this time, our constants will be needed by more than one class. We'll create a header file just for the constants.

Select the QuartzFun group again and press ⌘N to bring up the new file assistant. Select the Header File template from the iOS section, and name the file *Constants.h*.

We have two more files to go. If you look at Figure 16-5, you can see that we offer an option to select a random color. UIColor doesn't have a method to return a random color, so we'll need to write code to do that. We could put that code into our controller class, but because we're savvy Objective-C programmers, we'll put it into a category on `UIColor`.

Again, select the *QuartzFun* folder and press ⌘N to bring up the new file assistant. Select Objective-C File from the iOS heading and hit Next. When prompted, name the file Random, set the File Type to Category and the Class to UIColor, then press Next and save the file in the project folder.

Creating a Random Color

Let's tackle the category first. Add the following lines to *UIColor+Random.h*, replacing everything that's currently in the file:

```
#import <UIKit/UIKit.h>

@interface UIColor (Random)
+ (UIColor *)randomColor;
@end
```

Now, switch over to *UIColor+Random.m* and add this code:

```
#import <Foundation/Foundation.h>
#import "UIColor+Random.h"

@implementation UIColor (Random)

+ (UIColor *)randomColor {
    CGFloat red = (CGFloat)(arc4random() % 256)/255;
    CGFloat blue = (CGFloat)(arc4random() % 256)/255;
    CGFloat green = (CGFloat)(arc4random() % 256)/255;
    return [UIColor colorWithRed:red green:green blue:blue alpha:1.0f];
}

@end
```

This is fairly straightforward. For each color component, we use the `arc4random()` function to generate a random floating point number. Each component of the color needs to be between 0.0 and 1.0, so we take the remainder after dividing the random value by 256, which gives us a number in the range 0 to 255, and then divide by 255. Why 255? Quartz 2D on iOS supports 256 different intensities for each of the color components, so using the number 255 ensures that we have a chance to randomly select any one of them. Finally, we use those three random components to create a new color. We set the alpha value to 1.0 so that all generated colors will be opaque.

Defining Application Constants

Next, we'll define constants for each of the options that the user can select using the segmented controllers. Single-click *Constants.h* and replace everything in the file with the following code:

```
typedef NS_ENUM(NSInteger, ShapeType) {
    kLineShape = 0,
    kRectShape,
    kEllipseShape,
    kImageShape
};

typedef NS_ENUM(NSInteger, ColorTabIndex) {
    kRedColorTab = 0,
    kBlueColorTab,
    kYellowColorTab,
    kGreenColorTab,
    kRandomColorTab
};
```

To make our code more readable, we've declared two enumerated types using `typedef` and the `NS_ENUM` macro. One will represent the shape options available in our application; the other will represent the various color options available. The values these constants hold correspond to the segments of the two segmented controls we'll create in our application.

Implementing the QuartzFunView Skeleton

Since we're going to do our drawing in a subclass of `UIView`, let's set up that class with everything it needs, except for the actual code to do the drawing, which we'll add later. Single-click *QuartzFunView.h* and add the following code at the top:

```
#import <UIKit/UIKit.h>
#import "Constants.h"

@interface QuartzFunView : UIView

@property (assign, nonatomic) ShapeType shapeType;
@property (assign, nonatomic) BOOL useRandomColor;
@property (strong, nonatomic) UIColor *currentColor;

@end
```

First, we import the *Constants.h* header we just created so we can use our enumeration values. We then declare three properties—a ShapeType property to keep track of the shape that the user wants to draw, a boolean that will be used to keep track of whether the user is requesting a random color, and a UIColor property to keep track of the currently chosen color.

Switch over to *QuartzFunView.m*; we have several changes we need to make in this file. For starters, import the *UIColor+Random.h* header so that we can generate random colors by adding this line near the top, just below the other import:

```
#import "UIColor+Random.h"
```

Next, we need to create the class extension and add three more properties to it:

```
#import "UIColor+Random.h"

@interface QuartzFunView ()

@property (assign, nonatomic) CGPoint firstTouchLocation;
@property (assign, nonatomic) CGPoint lastTouchLocation;
@property (strong, nonatomic) UIImage *image;

@end
```

The first two properties will track the user's finger as it drags across the screen. We'll store the location where the user first touches the screen in firstTouchLocation and we store the location of the user's finger while dragging and when the drag ends in lastTouchLocation. Our drawing code will use these two variables to determine where to draw the requested shape. The image property holds the image to be drawn on the screen when the user selects the rightmost toolbar item on the bottom toolbar (see Figure 16-6). These properties are in the class extension and not in the *QuartzFunView.h* file because they are for internal use only, so are not a part of the view's public API.

Figure 16-6. Using QuartzFun to draw a UIImage

Now on to the implementation itself. The template gave us a method called initWithFrame:, but we won't be using that. Keep in mind that object instances in nibs and storyboards are stored as archived objects, which is the same mechanism we used in Chapter 13 to archive our objects. As a result, when an object instance is loaded from a nib or a storyboard, neither init nor initWithFrame: is ever called. Instead, initWithCoder: is used, so this is where we need to add any initialization code. In our case, we'll set the initial color value to red, initialize useRandomColor to NO, and load the image file that we're going to draw later in the chapter. Delete the existing stub implementation of initWithFrame: and replace it with the following method:

```
- (id)initWithCoder:(NSCoder*)coder {
    if (self = [super initWithCoder:coder]) {
        _currentColor = [UIColor redColor];
        _useRandomColor = NO;
        _image = [UIImage imageNamed:@"iphone"] ;
    }
    return self;
}
```

After `initWithCoder:`, we need to add a few more methods to respond to the user's touches. After `initWithCoder:`, insert the following three methods:

```
#pragma mark - Touch Handling

- (void)touchesBegan:(NSSet *)touches withEvent:(UIEvent *)event {
    if (self.useRandomColor) {
        self.currentColor = [UIColor randomColor];
    }
    UITouch *touch = [touches anyObject];
    self.firstTouchLocation = [touch locationInView:self];
    self.lastTouchLocation = [touch locationInView:self];
    [self setNeedsDisplay];
}

- (void)touchesEnded:(NSSet *)touches withEvent:(UIEvent *)event {
    UITouch *touch = [touches anyObject];
    self.lastTouchLocation = [touch locationInView:self];

    [self setNeedsDisplay];
}

- (void)touchesMoved:(NSSet *)touches withEvent:(UIEvent *)event {
    UITouch *touch = [touches anyObject];
    self.lastTouchLocation = [touch locationInView:self];

    [self setNeedsDisplay];
}
```

These three methods are inherited from `UIView`, which in turn inherits them from `UIView`'s parent, `UIResponder`. They can be overridden to find out where the user is touching the screen. They work as follows:

- `touchesBegan:withEvent:` is called when the user's finger first touches the screen. In that method, we change the color if the user has selected a random color using the new `randomColor` method we added to `UIColor` earlier. After that, we store the current location so that we know where the user first touched the screen, and we indicate that our view needs to be redrawn by calling `setNeedsDisplay` on `self`.

- `touchesMoved:withEvent:` is continuously called while the user is dragging a finger on the screen. All we do here is store the new location in `lastTouchLocation` and indicate that the screen needs to be redrawn.

- `touchesEnded:withEvent:` is called when the user lifts the finger off the screen. Just as in the `touchesMoved:withEvent:` method, all we do is store the final location in the `lastTouchLocation` variable and indicate that the view needs to be redrawn.

Don't worry if you don't fully understand the rest of the code here. We'll get into the details of working with touches and the specifics of the `touchesBegan:withEvent:`, `touchesMoved:withEvent:`, and `touchesEnded:withEvent:` methods in Chapter 18.

We'll come back to this class once we have our application skeleton up and running. That drawRect: method, which is currently commented out, is where we will do this application's real work, and we haven't written that yet. Let's finish setting up the application before we add our drawing code.

Creating and Connecting Outlets and Actions

Before we can start drawing, we need to add the segmented controls to our GUI, and then hook up the actions and outlets. Single-click *Main.storyboard* to set these things up.

The first order of business is to change the class of the view. In the document outline, expand the items for the scene and for the view controller it contains, and then single-click the View item. Press ⇧⌘3 to bring up the identity inspector and change the class from *UIView* to *QuartzFunView*.

Now use the object library to find a segmented control and drag it to the top of the view, just below the status bar. Place it somewhere near the center, as shown in Figure 16-7. You don't need to be too accurate with this because we'll shortly add a layout constraint that will center it.

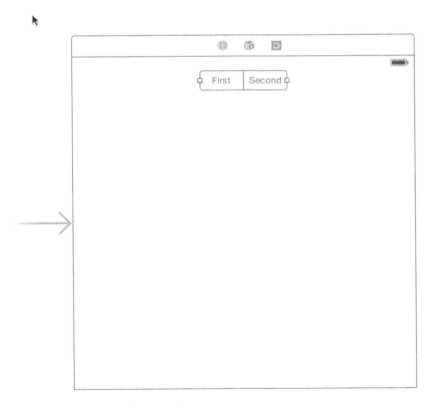

Figure 16-7. Adding a segmented control for color selection

With the segmented control selected, bring up the Attributes Inspector and change the number of segments from *2* to *5*. Double-click each segment in turn, changing its label to (from left to right) *Red*, *Blue*, *Yellow*, *Green*, and *Random*, in that order. Now let's apply layout constraints. In the Document Outline, Control-drag from the segmented control item to the Quartz Fun View item, release the mouse and select Top Space to Top Layout Guide. Repeat the Control-drag operation and, this time, select Center Horizontally in Container. So far, we've pinned the segmented control horizontally and vertically—all that remains is to set its size. Click the Pin button at the bottom of the editing area, click the Width check box and enter **290**, as shown in Figure 16-8. Click Add 1 constraint. In the Document Outline, select the View Controller icon, and then back in the storyboard editor, click the Resolve Auto Layout Issues button (the one to the right of the Pin button) and select Update Frames. The segmented control should now be properly sized and positioned.

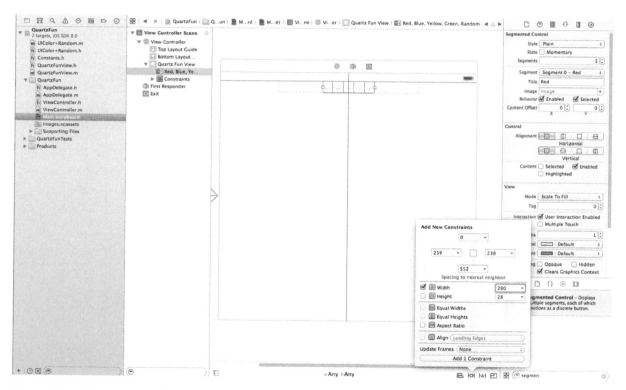

Figure 16-8. Setting the size of the color selection segmented control

Bring up the assistant editor, if it's not already open, and select *ViewController.m* from the jump bar. Now Control-drag from the segmented control in the Document Outline to the *ViewController.m* file on the right, into the space between the @interface and @end lines near the top that delineate the class extension. When your cursor is between the @interface and @end declarations, release the mouse to create a new outlet. Name the new outlet *colorControl*, and leave all the other options at their default values.

Next, let's add an action. With *ViewController.m* still open in the assistant editor, select *Main. storyboard* again and Control-drag from the segmented control over to the view controller file, directly above the @end declaration at the bottom. This time, change the connection type to *Action* and the name to *changeColor*. The pop-up should default to using the Value Changed event, which is what we want. You should also set the type to *UISegmentedControl*.

Now let's add a second segmented control. This one will be used to choose the shape to be drawn. Drag a segmented control from the library and drop it near the bottom of the view. Select the segmented control in the Document Outline, bring up the Attributes Inspector, and change the number of segments from *2* to *4*. Now double-click each segment and change the titles of the four segments to *Line*, *Rect*, *Ellipse*, and *Image*, in that order. Now we need to add layout constraints to fix the size and position of the control, just like we did with the color selection control. Here's the sequence of steps that you need:

1. In the Document Outline, Control-drag from the new segmented control item to the Quartz Fun View item, release the mouse, and select Bottom Space to Bottom Layout Guide.

2. Control-drag again and select Center Horizontally in Container.

3. Click the Pin button at the bottom of the editing area, and then click the Width check box and enter **220**. Click Add 1 constraint.

4. In the Document Outline, select the View Controller icon, and then back in the editor, click the Resolve Auto Layout Issues button and select Update Frames.

Once you've done that, open *ViewController.m* in the assistant editor again, and then Control-drag from the new segmented control over to just above the @end line in *ViewController.m* to create an action. Change the connection type to *Action*, name the action *changeShape*, and change the type to *UISegmentedControl*.

The storyboard should now look like Figure 16-9. Our next task is to implement the action methods.

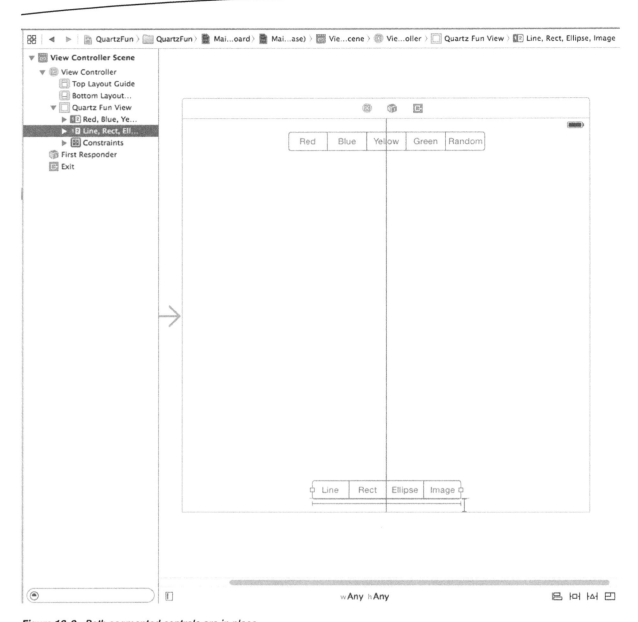

Figure 16-9. Both segmented controls are in place

Implementing the Action Methods

Save the storyboard and feel free to close the assistant editor. Now select *ViewController.m*. The first thing we need to do is to import our constants file, so that we have access to our enumeration values. We'll also be interacting with our custom view, so we need to import its header as well. At the top of the file, immediately below the existing import statement, add the following lines of code:

```
#import "Constants.h"
#import "QuartzFunView.h"
```

Next, look for the stub implementation of changeColor: that Xcode created for you and add the following code to it:

```
- (IBAction)changeColor:(UISegmentedControl *)sender {
    QuartzFunView *funView = (QuartzFunView *)self.view;
    ColorTabIndex index = [sender selectedSegmentIndex];
    switch (index) {
        case kRedColorTab:
            funView.currentColor = [UIColor redColor];
            funView.useRandomColor = NO;
            break;
        case kBlueColorTab:
            funView.currentColor = [UIColor blueColor];
            funView.useRandomColor = NO;
            break;
        case kYellowColorTab:
            funView.currentColor = [UIColor yellowColor];
            funView.useRandomColor = NO;
            break;
        case kGreenColorTab:
            funView.currentColor = [UIColor greenColor];
            funView.useRandomColor = NO;
            break;
        case kRandomColorTab:
            funView.useRandomColor = YES;
            break;
        default:
            break;
    }
}
```

This is pretty straightforward. We simply look at which segment was selected and create a new color based on that selection to serve as our current drawing color. After that, we set the currentColor property so that our class knows which color to use when drawing, unless random color has been selected. In that case, we set the useRandomColor property to YES and a new color will be chosen each time the user starts a new drawing action (you'll find in this code in the touchesBegan:withEvent: method, which we added a few pages ago. Since all the drawing code will be in the view itself, we don't need to do anything else in this method.

Next, look for the existing implementation of changeShape: and add the following code to it:

```
- (IBAction)changeShape:(UISegmentedControl *)sender {
    [(QuartzFunView *)self.view setShapeType:[sender
                            selectedSegmentIndex]];
    self.colorControl.hidden = [sender selectedSegmentIndex] == kImageShape;
}
```

In this method, all we do is set the shape type based on the selected segment of the control. Do you recall the ShapeType enum? The four elements of the enum correspond to the four toolbar segments at the bottom of the application view. We set the shape to be the same as the currently selected segment, and we also hide or show the color selection control based on whether the Image segment was selected.

Make sure that everything is in order by compiling and running your app. You won't be able to draw shapes on the screen yet, but the segmented controls should work; and when you tap the Image segment in the bottom control, the color controls should disappear.

Now that we have everything working, let's do some drawing.

Adding Quartz 2D Drawing Code

We're ready to add the code that does the drawing. We'll draw a line, some shapes, and an image. We're going to work incrementally, adding a small amount of code and then running the app to see what that code does.

Drawing the Line

Let's do the simplest drawing option first: drawing a single line. Select *QuartzFunView.m* and replace the commented-out drawRect: method with this one:

```
- (void)drawRect:(CGRect)rect {
    CGContextRef context = UIGraphicsGetCurrentContext();
    CGContextSetLineWidth(context, 2.0);
    CGContextSetStrokeColorWithColor(context, self.currentColor.CGColor);

    switch (self.shapeType) {
        case kLineShape:
            CGContextMoveToPoint(context,
                                    self.firstTouchLocation.x,
                                    self.firstTouchLocation.y);
            CGContextAddLineToPoint(context,
                                    self.lastTouchLocation.x,
                                    self.lastTouchLocation.y);
            CGContextStrokePath(context);
            break;
        case kRectShape:
            break;
        case kEllipseShape:
            break;
        case kImageShape:
            break;
        default:
            break;
    }
}
```

We start things off by retrieving a reference to the current context, so we know where to draw:

```
CGContextRef context = UIGraphicsGetCurrentContext();
```

Next, we set the line width to 2.0, which means that any line that we stroke will be 2 points wide:

```
CGContextSetLineWidth(context, 2.0);
```

After that, we set the color for stroking lines. Since UIColor has a CGColor property, which is what this function needs, we use that property of our currentColor property to pass the correct color on to this function.

```
CGContextSetStrokeColorWithColor(context, self.currentColor.CGColor);
```

We use a switch to jump to the appropriate code for each shape type. As we mentioned earlier, we'll start off with the code to handle kLineShape, get that working, and then we'll add code for each shape in turn as we make our way through this example:

```
switch (self.shapeType) {
    case kLineShape:
```

To draw a line, we tell the graphics context to create a path starting at the first place the user touched. Remember that we stored that value in the touchesBegan:withEvents: method, so it will always reflect the starting point of the most recent touch or drag:

```
CGContextMoveToPoint(context,
                     self.firstTouchLocation.x,
                     self.firstTouchLocation.y);
```

Next, we draw a line from that spot to the last spot the user touched. If the user's finger is still in contact with the screen, lastTouchLocation contains the finger's current location. If the user is no longer touching the screen, lastTouchLocation contains the location of the user's finger when it was lifted off the screen:

```
CGContextAddLineToPoint(context,
                        self.lastTouchLocation.x,
                        self.lastTouchLocation.y);
```

This function doesn't actually draw the line—it just adds it to the context's current path. To make the line appear on the screen, we need to stroke the path. This function will stroke the line we just drew, using the color and width we set earlier:

```
CGContextStrokePath(context);
```

After that, we finish the switch statement:

```
    break;
case kRectShape:
    break;
case kEllipseShape:
    break;
case kImageShape:
    break;
default:
    break;
}
```

And that's it for now. At this point, you should be able to compile and run the app once more. The Rect, Ellipse, and Shape options won't work, but you should be able to draw lines just fine using any of the color choices (see Figure 16-10).

Figure 16-10. *The line-drawing part of our application is now complete. Here, we are drawing using the color red*

Drawing the Rectangle and Ellipse

Let's write the code to draw the rectangle and the ellipse at the same time, since Quartz implements both of these objects in basically the same way. Add the following bold code to your existing drawRect: method:

```
- (void)drawRect:(CGRect)rect {
    CGContextRef context = UIGraphicsGetCurrentContext();

    CGContextSetLineWidth(context, 2.0);
    CGContextSetStrokeColorWithColor(context, self.currentColor.CGColor);
```

```
CGContextSetFillColorWithColor(context, self.currentColor.CGColor);
CGRect currentRect = CGRectMake(self.firstTouchLocation.x,
                                self.firstTouchLocation.y,
                                self.lastTouchLocation.x -
                                self.firstTouchLocation.x,
                                self.lastTouchLocation.y -
                                self.firstTouchLocation.y);

    switch (self.shapeType) {
        case kLineShape:
            CGContextMoveToPoint(context,
                                 self.firstTouchLocation.x,
                                 self.firstTouchLocation.y);
            CGContextAddLineToPoint(context,
                                    self.lastTouchLocation.x,
                                    self.lastTouchLocation.y);
            CGContextStrokePath(context);
            break;
        case kRectShape:
        CGContextAddRect(context, currentRect);
        CGContextDrawPath(context, kCGPathFillStroke);
            break;
        case kEllipseShape:
        CGContextAddEllipseInRect(context, currentRect);
        CGContextDrawPath(context, kCGPathFillStroke);
            break;
        case kImageShape:
            break;
        default:
            break;
    }
}
```

Because we want to paint both the outline of the ellipse and the rectangle and to fill their interiors, we add a call to set the fill color using currentColor:

```
CGContextSetFillColorWithColor(context, self.currentColor.CGColor);
```

Next, we declare a CGRect variable. We do this here because both the rectangle and ellipse are drawn based on a rectangle. We'll use currentRect to hold the rectangle described by the user's drag. Remember that a CGRect has two members: size and origin. A function called CGRectMake() lets us create a CGRect by specifying the x, y, width, and height values, so we use that to make our rectangle.

The code to create the rectangle is pretty straightforward. We use the point stored in firstTouchLocation to create the origin. Next, we figure out the size by getting the difference between the two x values and the two y values. Note that, depending on the direction of the drag, one or both size values may end up with negative numbers, but that's OK. A CGRect with a negative size will simply be rendered in the opposite direction of its origin point (to the left for a negative width; upward for a negative height):

```
CGRect currentRect = CGRectMake(self.firstTouchLocation.x,
                                self.firstTouchLocation.y,
                                self.lastTouchLocation.x -
                                self.firstTouchLocation.x,
                                self.lastTouchLocation.y -
                                self.firstTouchLocation.y);
```

Once we have this rectangle defined, drawing either a rectangle or an ellipse is as easy as calling two functions: one to draw the rectangle or ellipse in the CGRect we defined, and the other to stroke and fill it:

```
case kRectShape:
    CGContextAddRect(context, currentRect);
    CGContextDrawPath(context, kCGPathFillStroke);
    break;
case kEllipseShape:
    CGContextAddEllipseInRect(context, currentRect);
    CGContextDrawPath(context, kCGPathFillStroke);
    break;
```

Compile and run your application. Try out the Rect and Ellipse tools to see how you like them. Don't forget to change colors, including using a random color.

Drawing the Image

For our last trick, let's draw an image. The *16 – Image* folder contains two images named *iphone.png* and *iphone@2x.png* that you can add to your project's *Images.xcassets* item—create an image set called iphone and drop both images into it. Now add the following code to your drawRect: method:

```
- (void)drawRect:(CGRect)rect {
    CGContextRef context = UIGraphicsGetCurrentContext();

    CGContextSetLineWidth(context, 2.0);
    CGContextSetStrokeColorWithColor(context, self.currentColor.CGColor);

    CGContextSetFillColorWithColor(context, _currentColor.CGColor);
    CGRect currentRect = CGRectMake(self.firstTouchLocation.x,
                                    self.firstTouchLocation.y,
                                    self.lastTouchLocation.x -
                                    self.firstTouchLocation.x,
                                    self.lastTouchLocation.y -
                                    self.firstTouchLocation.y);
```

```
switch (self.shapeType) {
    case kLineShape:
        CGContextMoveToPoint(context,
                                self.firstTouchLocation.x,
                                self.firstTouchLocation.y);
        CGContextAddLineToPoint(context,
                                    self.lastTouchLocation.x,
                                    self.lastTouchLocation.y);
        CGContextStrokePath(context);
        break;
    case kRectShape:
        CGContextAddRect(context, currentRect);
        CGContextDrawPath(context, kCGPathFillStroke);
        break;
    case kEllipseShape:
        CGContextAddEllipseInRect(context, currentRect);
        CGContextDrawPath(context, kCGPathFillStroke);
        break;
    case kImageShape: {
        CGFloat horizontalOffset = self.image.size.width / 2;
        CGFloat verticalOffset = self.image.size.height / 2;
        CGPoint drawPoint = CGPointMake(self.lastTouchLocation.x -
                                horizontalOffset,
                                self.lastTouchLocation.y -
                                verticalOffset);
        [self.image drawAtPoint:drawPoint];
        break;
    }
    default:
        break;
    }
}
```

Note Notice that, in the switch statement, we added curly braces around the code following case kImageShape:. That's because the compiler has a problem with variables declared in the first line after a case statement. These curly braces are our way of telling the compiler to stop complaining. We could also have declared horizontalOffset before the switch statement, but our chosen approach keeps the related code together.

First, we calculate the center of the image, since we want the image drawn centered on the point where the user last touched. Without this adjustment, the image would be drawn with the upper-left corner at the user's finger, also a valid option. We then make a new CGPoint by subtracting these offsets from the x and y values in lastTouchLocation:

```
CGFloat horizontalOffset = self.image.size.width / 2;
CGFloat verticalOffset = self.image.size.height / 2;
CGPoint drawPoint = CGPointMake(self.lastTouchLocation.x -
                                horizontalOffset,
                                self.lastTouchLocation.y -
                                verticalOffset);
```

Now we tell the image to draw itself. This line of code will do the trick:

```
[self.image drawAtPoint:drawPoint];
```

Build and run the application, select Image from the segmented control and check that you can place an image on the drawing canvas.

Optimizing the QuartzFun Application

Our application does what we want, but we should consider a bit of optimization. In our little application, you won't notice a slowdown; however, in a more complex application that is running on a slower processor, you might see some lag.

The problem occurs in *QuartzFunView.m*, in the methods touchesMoved:withEvent: and touchesEnded:withEvent:. Both methods include this line of code:

```
[self setNeedsDisplay];
```

Obviously, this is how we tell our view that something has changed and that it needs to redraw itself. This code works, but it causes the entire view to be erased and redrawn, even if only a tiny bit has changed. We do want to erase the screen when we get ready to drag out a new shape, but we don't want to clear the screen several times a second as we drag out our shape.

Rather than forcing the entire view to be redrawn many times during our drag, we can use setNeedsDisplayInRect: instead. setNeedsDisplayInRect: is a UIView method that marks just one rectangular portion of a view's region as needing redisplay. By using this method, we can be more efficient by marking only the part of the view that is affected by the current drawing operation as needing to be redrawn.

We need to redraw, not just the rectangle between firstTouchLocation and lastTouchLocation, but any part of the screen encompassed by the current drag. If the user touched the screen and then scribbled all over, but we redrew only the section between firstTouchLocation and lastTouchLocation, then we would leave a lot of stuff drawn on the screen by the previous redraw that we don't want to remain.

The solution is to keep track of the entire area that has been affected by a particular drag in a CGRect instance variable. In touchesBegan:withEvent:, we reset that instance variable to just the point where the user touched. Then, in touchesMoved:withEvent: and touchesEnded:withEvent:, we use a Core Graphics function to get the union of the current rectangle and the stored rectangle, and we store the resulting rectangle. We also use it to specify which part of the view needs to be redrawn. This approach gives us a running total of the area impacted by the current drag.

At the moment, we calculate the current rectangle in the drawRect: method for use in drawing the ellipse and rectangle shapes. We'll move that calculation into a new method, so that it can be used in all three places without repeating code. Ready? Let's do it.

Make the following changes at the top of *QuartzFunView.m*:

```
@interface QuartzFunView ()

@property (assign, nonatomic) CGPoint firstTouchLocation;
@property (assign, nonatomic) CGPoint lastTouchLocation;
@property (strong, nonatomic) UIImage *image;
@property (readonly, nonatomic) CGRect currentRect;
@property (assign, nonatomic) CGRect redrawRect;

@end
```

We declare a CGRect called redrawRect that we will use to keep track of the area that needs to be redrawn. We also declare a read-only property called currentRect, which will return the rectangle that we were previously calculating in drawRect:. Add the accessor method for the currentRect property, at the end of the file:

```
- (CGRect)currentRect {
    return CGRectMake (self.firstTouchLocation.x,
                       self.firstTouchLocation.y,
                       self.lastTouchLocation.x - self.firstTouchLocation.x,
                       self.lastTouchLocation.y - self.firstTouchLocation.y);

}
```

Now, in the drawRect: method, change all references to currentRect to self.currentRect, so that the code uses that new accessor we just created. Next, delete the lines of code where we calculated currentRect:

```
- (void)drawRect:(CGRect)rect {
    CGContextRef context = UIGraphicsGetCurrentContext();

    CGContextSetLineWidth(context, 2.0);
    CGContextSetStrokeColorWithColor(context, self.currentColor.CGColor);

    CGContextSetFillColorWithColor(context, self.currentColor.CGColor);

    CGRect currentRect = CGRectMake(self.firstTouchLocation.x,
                                    self.firstTouchLocation.y,
                                    self.lastTouchLocation.x -
                                    self.firstTouchLocation.x,
                                    self.lastTouchLocation.y -
                                    self.firstTouchLocation.y);
```

```
    switch (self.shapeType) {
        case kLineShape:
            CGContextMoveToPoint(context,
                                 self.firstTouchLocation.x,
                                 self.firstTouchLocation.y);
            CGContextAddLineToPoint(context,
                                    self.lastTouchLocation.x,
                                    self.lastTouchLocation.y);
            CGContextStrokePath(context);
            break;
        case kRectShape:
            CGContextAddRect(context, self.currentRect);
            CGContextDrawPath(context, kCGPathFillStroke);
            break;
        case kEllipseShape:
            CGContextAddEllipseInRect(context, self.currentRect);
            CGContextDrawPath(context, kCGPathFillStroke);
            break;
        case kImageShape: {
            CGFloat horizontalOffset = self.image.size.width / 2;
            CGFloat verticalOffset = self.image.size.height / 2;
            CGPoint drawPoint = CGPointMake(self.lastTouchLocation.x -
                                            horizontalOffset,
                                            self.lastTouchLocation.y -
                                            verticalOffset);
            [self.image drawAtPoint:drawPoint];
            break;
        }
        default:
            break;
    }
}
```

We also need to make some changes to touchesEnded:withEvent: and touchesMoved:withEvent:. We will recalculate the space impacted by the current operation and use that to indicate that only a portion of our view needs to be redrawn. Replace the existing touchesEnded:withEvent: and touchesMoved:withEvent: methods with these new versions:

```
- (void)touchesEnded:(NSSet *)touches withEvent:(UIEvent *)event {
    UITouch *touch = [touches anyObject];
    self.lastTouchLocation = [touch locationInView:self];

    if (self.shapeType == kImageShape) {
        CGFloat horizontalOffset = self.image.size.width / 2;
        CGFloat verticalOffset = self.image.size.height / 2;
        self.redrawRect = CGRectUnion(self.redrawRect,
                                      CGRectMake(self.lastTouchLocation.x -
                                                 horizontalOffset,
                                                 self.lastTouchLocation.y -
                                                 verticalOffset,
                                                 self.image.size.width,
                                                 self.image.size.height));
```

```
    } else {
        self.redrawRect = CGRectUnion(self.redrawRect, self.currentRect);
    }
    self.redrawRect = CGRectInset(self.redrawRect, -2.0, -2.0);
    [self setNeedsDisplayInRect:self.redrawRect];
}

- (void)touchesMoved:(NSSet *)touches withEvent:(UIEvent *)event {
    UITouch *touch = [touches anyObject];
    self.lastTouchLocation = [touch locationInView:self];

    if (self.shapeType == kImageShape) {
        CGFloat horizontalOffset = self.image.size.width / 2;
        CGFloat verticalOffset = self.image.size.height / 2;
        self.redrawRect = CGRectUnion(self.redrawRect,
                                      CGRectMake(self.lastTouchLocation.x -
                                                 horizontalOffset,
                                                 self.lastTouchLocation.y -
                                                 verticalOffset,
                                                 self.image.size.width,
                                                 self.image.size.height));
    } else {
        self.redrawRect = CGRectUnion(_redrawRect, self.currentRect);
    }
    [self setNeedsDisplayInRect:self.redrawRect];
}
```

Also add the following line to the touchesBegan:withEvent: method:

```
- (void)touchesBegan:(NSSet *)touches withEvent:(UIEvent *)event {
    if (self.useRandomColor) {
        self.currentColor = [UIColor randomColor];
    }
    UITouch *touch = [touches anyObject];
    self.firstTouchLocation = [touch locationInView:self];
    self.lastTouchLocation = [touch locationInView:self];

    self.redrawRect = CGRectZero;

    [self setNeedsDisplay];
}
```

Build and run the application again to see the final result. You probably won't see any difference, but with only a few additional lines of code, we reduced the amount of work necessary to redraw our view by getting rid of the need to erase and redraw any portion of the view that hasn't been affected by the current drag. Being kind to your iOS device's precious processor cycles like this can make a big difference in the performance of your applications, especially as they get more complex.

> **Note**   If you're interested in a more in-depth exploration of Quartz 2D topics, you might want to take a look at *Beginning iPad Development for iPhone Developers: Mastering the iPad SDK* by Jack Nutting, Dave Wooldridge, and David Mark (Apress, 2010). This book covers a lot of Quartz 2D drawing. All the drawing code and explanations in that book apply to the iPhone as well as the iPad.

Drawing to a Close

In this chapter, we've really just scratched the surface of the drawing capabilities built into iOS. You should feel pretty comfortable with Quartz 2D now; and with some occasional references to Apple's documentation, you can probably handle most any drawing requirement that comes your way.

Now it's time to level up your graphics skills even further! Chapter 17 will introduce you to the Sprite Kit framework, introduced in iOS 7, which lets you do blazingly-fast bitmap rendering for creating games or other fast-moving, interactive content.

Getting Started with Sprite Kit

In iOS 7, Apple introduced Sprite Kit, a framework for the high-performance rendering of 2D graphics. That sounds a bit like Core Graphics and Core Animation, so what's new here? Well, unlike Core Graphics (which is focused on drawing graphics using a painter's model) or Core Animation (which is focused on animating attributes of GUI elements), Sprite Kit is focused on a different area entirely: video games! Sprite Kit is built on top of OpenGL, a technology present in many computing platforms that allows modern graphics hardware to write graphics bitmaps into a video buffer at incredible speeds. With Sprite Kit, you get the great performance characteristics of OpenGL, but without needing to dig into the depths of OpenGL coding.

This is Apple's first foray into the graphical side of game programming in the iOS era. It was released for iOS 7 and OS X 10.9 (Mavericks) at the same time, and it provides the same API on both platforms, so that apps written for one can be easily ported to the other. Although Apple has never before supplied a framework quite like Sprite Kit, it has clear similarities to various open source libraries such as Cocos2D. If you've used Cocos2D or something similar in the past, you'll feel right at home.

Sprite Kit does not implement a flexible, general-purpose drawing system like Core Graphics. There are no methods for drawing paths, gradients, or filling spaces with color. Instead, what you get is a **scene graph** (analogous to UIKit's view hierarchy); the ability to transform each graph node's position, scale, and rotation; and the ability for each node to draw itself. Most drawing occurs in an instance of the SKSprite class (or one of its subclasses), which represents a single graphical image ready for putting on the screen.

In this chapter, we're going to use Sprite Kit to build a simple shooting game called *TextShooter*. Instead of using premade graphics, we're going to build our game objects with pieces of text, using a subclass of SKSprite that is specialized for just this purpose. Using this approach, you won't need to pull graphics out of a project library or anything like that. The app we make will be simple in appearance, but easy to modify and play with.

Simple Beginnings

Let's get the ball rolling. In Xcode, press ⌘N or select **File ➤ New ➤ File...** and choose the **Game** template from the iOS section. Press **Next**, name your project *TextShooter*, set Devices to *Universal* and Game Technology to *SpriteKit*, and create the project. While you're here, it's worth looking briefly at the other available technology choices. OpenGL ES and Metal (the latter of which is new in iOS 8) are low-level graphics APIs that give you almost total control over the graphics hardware, but are much more difficult to use than Sprite Kit. Whereas Sprite Kit is a 2D API, SceneKit (also new in iOS 8) is a toolkit that you can use to build 3D graphics applications. After you've read this chapter, it's worth checking out the SceneKit documentation at `https://developer.apple.com/library/prerelease/ios/documentation/SceneKit/Reference/SceneKit_Framework/index.html` if you have any interest in 3D game programming.

If you run the TextShooter project now, you'll see the default Sprite Kit application, which is shown in Figure 17-1. Initially, you'll just see the "Hello, World" text. To make things slightly (but only slightly) more interesting, touch the screen to add some rotating spaceships. Over the course of this chapter, we'll replace everything in this template and progressively build up a simple application of our own.

Figure 17-1. *The default Sprite Kit app in action. Some text is displayed in the center of the screen, and each tap on the screen puts a rotating graphic of a fighter jet at that location*

Now let's take a look at the project that Xcode created. You'll see it has a pretty standard-looking AppDelegate class and a small view controller class called GameViewController that does some initial configuration of an SKView object. This object, which is loaded from the application's storyboard, is the view that will display all our Sprite Kit content. Here's the code from the GameViewController viewDidLoad method that initializes the SKView:

```
- (void)viewDidLoad
{
    [super viewDidLoad];

    // Configure the view.
    SKView * skView = (SKView *)self.view;
    skView.showsFPS = YES;
    skView.showsNodeCount = YES;
    skView.ignoresSiblingOrder = YES;

    // Create and configure the scene.
    GameScene *scene = [GameScene nodeWithFileNamed:@"GameScene"];
    scene.scaleMode = SKSceneScaleModeAspectFill;

    // Present the scene.
    [skView presentScene:scene];
}
```

The first few lines get the SKView instance from the storyboard and configure it to show some performance characteristics while the game is running. Sprite Kit applications are constructed as a set of **scenes**, represented by the SKScene class. When developing with Sprite Kit, you'll probably make a new SKScene subclass for each visually distinct portion of your app. A scene can represent a fast-paced game display with dozens of objects animating around the screen, or something as simple as a start menu. We'll see multiple uses of SKScene in this chapter. The template generates an initially empty scene in the shape of a class called GameScene.

The relationship between SKView and SKScene has some parallels to the UIViewController classes we've been using throughout this book. The SKView class acts a bit like UINavigationController, in the sense that it is sort of a blank slate that simply manages access to the display for other controllers. At this point, things start to diverge, however. Unlike UINavigationController, the top-level objects managed by SKView aren't UIViewController subclasses. Instead, they're subclasses of SKScene, which knows how to manage a graph of objects that can be displayed, acted upon by the physics engine, and so on.

The next part of the viewDidLoad method creates the initial scene:

```
// Create and configure the scene.
GameScene *scene = [GameScene nodeWithFileNamed:@"GameScene"];
```

There are two ways to create a scene—you can manually allocate and initialize an instance programmatically, or you can load one from a **Sprite Kit scene file**. The Xcode template takes the latter approach—it generates a Sprite Kit scene file called *GameScene.sks* containing an archived copy of an SKScene object. SKScene, like most of the other Sprite Kit classes, conforms to the NSCoder protocol, which we discussed in Chapter 13. The *GameScene.sks* file is just a standard archive, which you can read and write using the NSKeyedUnarchiver and NSKeyedArchiver classes. Usually, though, you'll use the SKScene nodeWithFileNamed: method, which loads the SKScene from the archive for you and initializes it as an instance of the concrete subclass on which it is invoked—in this case, the archived SKScene data is used to initialize the GameScene object.

You may be wondering why the template code goes to the trouble of loading an empty scene object from the scene file when it could have just created one. The reason is the Xcode **Sprite Kit Level Designer**, which lets you design a scene much like you construct a user interface in Interface Builder. Having designed your scene, you save it to the scene file and run your application again. This time, of course, the scene is not empty and you should see the design that you created in the Level Designer. Having loaded the initial scene, you are at liberty to programmatically add additional elements to it. We'll be doing a lot of that in this chapter. Alternatively, if you don't find the Level Designer useful, you can build all your scenes completely in code.

If you select the *GameScene.sks* file in the Project Navigator, Xcode opens it in the Level Designer, as shown in Figure 17-2.

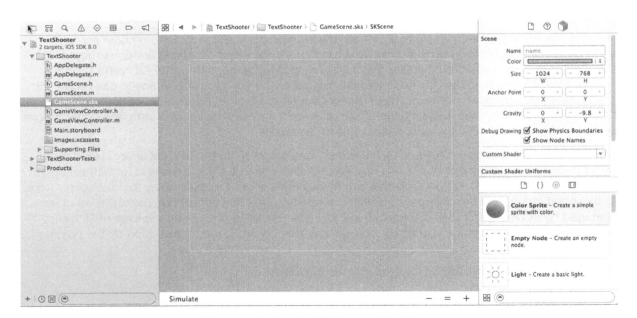

Figure 17-2. The Xcode Sprite Kit Level Designer, showing the initially empty GameScene

The scene is displayed in the editor area—right now, it's just an empty yellow rectangle on a gray background. To the right of it is the **SKNode Inspector**, which you can use to set properties of the node that's selected in the editor. Sprite Kit scene elements are all nodes—instances of the SKNode class. SKScene itself is a subclass of SKNode. Here, the SKScene node is selected, so the SKNode Inspector is displaying its properties. Below the inspector, in the bottom right, is the usual Xcode Object Library, which is automatically filtered to show only the types of objects you can add to a Sprite Kit scene. You design your scene by dragging objects from here and dropping them onto the editor.

> **Tip**   You may be wondering why the method used to load the scene is from the scene file called nodeWithFileNamed: and not sceneWithFileNamed:. Although the template code only uses this method to load the initial scene, it can actually load any Sprite Kit node, which means you can archive a node to a file and load it back later. In fact, you can use the Level Designer to create a scene consisting of a single node that you can save and load into the scene graph later. This allows you to design complex nodes without having to write any code.

Now let's go back and finish up our discussion of the viewDidLoad method.

```
scene.scaleMode = SKSceneScaleModeAspectFill;

// Present the scene.
[skView presentScene:scene];
```

These two lines of code set the scene's scale mode and make the scene visible. Let's talk about those two things in reverse order. In order for a scene and its content to be visible and active, it must be presented by an SKView. To present a scene, you call the SKView's presentScene: method. An SKView can display only one scene at a time, so calling this method when there's already a presented scene causes the new scene to immediately replace the old one. If you are switching from one scene to another, you should probably prefer to use the presentScene:transition: method, which animates the scene change. You'll see examples of this later in the chapter. In this case, since we are making the initial scene visible, there is nothing to transition from, so it's acceptable to use the presentScene: method.

Now let's talk about the scene's scaleMode property. If you look back at Figure 17-2, you'll see that the default scene in the Level Designer is 1024 points wide and 768 points high—the same as the size of an iPad screen. That's all well and good if you plan to run your game only in landscape mode on an iPad, but what about portrait mode, or other screen sizes, like on the iPhone? How should you adapt the scene for the size of the screen that your application is running on? There is no simple answer to that question. There are four different ways to adjust the size of the scene when it's presented in an SKView, corresponding to the four values of the SKSceneScaleMode enumeration. To see what each scale mode does, let's create another Sprite Kit project and experiment with it. Using the same steps as before, create a Sprite Kit project, call it *ResizeModes*, and select the *GameScene.sks* file in the Project Navigator. At this point, your Xcode window should look like Figure 17-2.

In the Object Library, locate a *Label* node and drag it into the center of the scene. In the SKNode Inspector, use the **Text**, field to change the label's text to *Center*. Drag another label to the bottom left of the scene, placing it carefully so that it's exactly in the corner of the scene. Change its `text` property to *Bottom Left*. Drag a third label to the top right of the scene and change its text to *Top Right*. Drag a couple more labels to the top and bottom of the scene and name them *Top* and *Bottom*, respectively. You can change the colors and fonts associated with the labels to make the text more visible, if necessary. When you're done, you should have something like the scene shown in Figure 17-3.

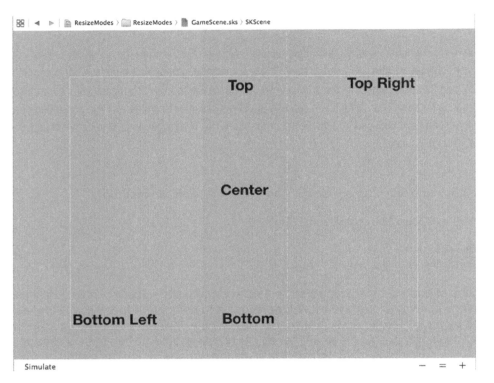

Figure 17-3. Using the Sprite Kit Level Designer to add nodes to a scene

> **Tip**   If you can't see all of the scene in the Editor area, you can use the -/=/+ buttons at the bottom right of the Editor to zoom out until you have enough of the scene in view to work comfortably with it.

Select *GameScene.m* in the Project Navigator and delete the `didMoveToView:` method. This method contains the code that adds the "Hello, World" label to the scene, which we don't need. Next, select *GameViewController.m* and locate the line of code in the `viewDidLoad` method that sets the `scaleMode` of the SKScene object. As you can see, it's initially set to `SKSceneScaleModeAspectFill`. Run the application on an iPhone simulator (or device) with this scale mode set, and then edit the code and run it three more times, using the values `SKSceneScaleModeAspectFit`, `SKSceneScaleModeFill`, and `SKSceneScaleModeResizeFill`. The results are shown in Figure 17-4.

SKSceneScaleModeAspectFill   SKSceneScaleModeAspectFit   SKSceneScaleModeFill   SKSceneScaleModeResizeFill

Figure 17-4. Comparing the four scene rescale modes

Here's what these modes do:

- SKSceneScaleModeAspectFill resizes the scene so that it fills the screen while preserving its aspect (width-to-height ratio). As you can see in Figure 17-4, this mode ensures that every pixel of the SKView is covered, but loses part of the scene—in this case, the scene has been cropped on the left and right. The content of the scene is also scaled, so the text is smaller than in the original scene, but its position relative to the scene is preserved.

- SKSceneScaleModeAspectFit also preserves the scene's aspect ratio, but ensures that the whole scene is visible. The result is a letter-box view, with parts of the SKView visible above and below the scene content.

- SKSceneScaleModeFill scales the scene along both axes so that it exactly fits the view. This ensures that everything in the scene is visible, but since the aspect ratio of the original scene is not preserved, there may be unacceptable distortion of the content. Here, you can see that the text has been horizontally compressed.

- Finally, SKSceneScaleModeResizeFill places the bottom-left corner of the scene in the bottom-left corner of the view and leaves it at its original size.

Which of these rescale modes is best for you depends on the needs of your application. If none of them work, there are two other possibilities. First, you can elect to support a fixed set of screen sizes, create an individual design tailored to each of them, store it in its own *.sks* file, and load the scene from the correct file when it's needed. Secondly, you can simply create the scene in code, make it the same size as the SKView in which it's being presented, and populate it with nodes programmatically. This only works if your game doesn't depend on the exact relative positions of its elements. To illustrate how this approach works, we'll use it for the TextShooter application.

Initial Scene Customization

Open the TextShooter project and select the GameScene class. We don't need most of the code that the Xcode template generated for us, so let's remove it. First, delete the entire didMoveToView: method. This method is called whenever the scene is presented in an SKView and it is typically used to make last-minute changes to the scene before it becomes visible. Next, take away most of the touchesBegan:withEvent: method, leaving just the for loop and the first line of code it contains. At this point, your GameScene class should look like the following (the compiler will warn that location is an unused variable—don't worry about that, because we'll fix it later):

```
@implementation GameScene

-(void)touchesBegan:(NSSet *)touches withEvent:(UIEvent *)event {
    /* Called when a touch begins */

    for (UITouch *touch in touches) {
        CGPoint location = [touch locationInNode:self];
    }
}

-(void)update:(CFTimeInterval)currentTime {
    /* Called before each frame is rendered */
}

@end
```

Since we're not going to load our scene from *GameScene.sks*, we need a method that will create a scene for us, with some initial content. We'll also need to add properties for the current game-level number, the number of lives the player has, and a flag to let us know whether the level is finished. Add the following bold lines to *GameScene.h*:

```
@interface GameScene : SKScene

@property (assign, nonatomic) NSUInteger levelNumber;
@property (assign, nonatomic) NSUInteger playerLives;
@property (assign, nonatomic) BOOL finished;

+ (instancetype)sceneWithSize:(CGSize)size levelNumber:(NSUInteger)levelNumber;
- (instancetype)initWithSize:(CGSize)size levelNumber:(NSUInteger)levelNumber;

@end
```

Now switch over to *GameScene.m*, where we'll implement the two new methods that we just declared. Add the following code in the implementation section of the file:

```
+ (instancetype)sceneWithSize:(CGSize)size levelNumber:(NSUInteger)levelNumber {
    return [[self alloc] initWithSize:size levelNumber:levelNumber];
}

- (instancetype)initWithSize:(CGSize)size {
    return [self initWithSize:size levelNumber:1];
}

- (instancetype)initWithSize:(CGSize)size levelNumber:(NSUInteger)levelNumber {
    if (self = [super initWithSize:size]) {
        _levelNumber = levelNumber;
        _playerLives = 5;

        self.backgroundColor = [SKColor whiteColor];

        SKLabelNode *lives = [SKLabelNode labelNodeWithFontNamed:@"Courier"];
        lives.fontSize = 16;
        lives.fontColor = [SKColor blackColor];
        lives.name = @"LivesLabel";
        lives.text = [NSString stringWithFormat:@"Lives: %lu",
                        (unsigned long)_playerLives];
        lives.verticalAlignmentMode = SKLabelVerticalAlignmentModeTop;
        lives.horizontalAlignmentMode = SKLabelHorizontalAlignmentModeRight;
        lives.position = CGPointMake(self.frame.size.width,
                                        self.frame.size.height);
        [self addChild:lives];

        SKLabelNode *level = [SKLabelNode labelNodeWithFontNamed:@"Courier"];
        level.fontSize = 16;
        level.fontColor = [SKColor blackColor];
        level.name = @"LevelLabel";
        level.text = [NSString stringWithFormat:@"Level: %lu",
                        (unsigned long)_levelNumber];
        level.verticalAlignmentMode = SKLabelVerticalAlignmentModeTop;
        level.horizontalAlignmentMode = SKLabelHorizontalAlignmentModeLeft;
        level.position = CGPointMake(0, self.frame.size.height);
        [self addChild:level];
    }
    return self;
}
```

The first method, `sceneWithSize:levelNumber:`, gives us a factory method that will work as a shorthand for creating a level and setting its level number at once. In the second method, `initWithSize:`, we override the class's default initializer, passing control to the third method (and passing along a default value for the level number). That third method in turn calls the designated initializer from its superclass's implementation. This may seem like a roundabout way of doing things, but it's a common pattern when you want to add new initializers to a class while still using the class's designated initializer.

The third method we added, `initWithSize:levelNumber:`, is where we set up the basic configuration of our level scene. First, we set the values of a couple of instance variables from the parameters that were passed in. Second, we set the scene's background color. Note that we're using a class called `SKColor` instead of `UIColor` here. In fact, `SKColor` isn't really a class at all; it's a sort of alias that can be used in place of either `UIColor` for an iOS app or `NSColor` for an OS X app. This allows us to port games between iOS and OS X a little more easily.

After that, we create two instances of a class called `SKLabelNode`. This is a handy class that works somewhat like a `UILabel`, allowing us to add some text to the scene and letting us choose a font, set a text value, and specify some alignments. We create one label for displaying the number of lives at the upper right of the screen and another that will show the level number at the upper left of the screen. Look closely at the code that we use to position these labels. Here is the code that sets the position of the lives label:

```
lives.position = CGPointMake(self.frame.size.width,
                             self.frame.size.height);
```

If you think about the points we're passing in as the position for this label, you may be surprised to see that we're passing in the scene's height. In UIKit, positioning anything at the height of a `UIView` would put it at the bottom of that view; but in Scene Kit, the y axis is flipped—the coordinate origin is at the bottom left of the scene and the y axis points upward. As a result, the maximum value of the scene's height is a position at the top of the screen instead. What about the label's x coordinate? We're setting that to be the width of the view. If you did that with a `UIView`, the view would be positioned just off the right side of the screen. That doesn't happen here, because we also did this:

```
lives.horizontalAlignmentMode = SKLabelHorizontalAlignmentModeRight;
```

Setting the `horizontalAlignmentMode` property of the `SKLabelNode` to `SKLabelHorizontal AlignmentModeRight` moves the point of the label node that's used to position it (it's actually a property called `position`) to the right of the text. Since we want the text to be right justified on the screen, we therefore need to set the x coordinate of the `position` property to be the width of the scene. By contrast, the text in the `level` label is left-aligned and we position it at the left edge of the scene by setting its x coordinate to zero:

```
level.horizontalAlignmentMode = SKLabelHorizontalAlignmentModeLeft;
level.position = CGPointMake(0, self.frame.size.height);
```

You'll also see that we gave each label a name. This works similar to a tag or identifier in other parts of UIKit, and it will let us retrieve those labels later by asking for them by name.

Now select *GameViewController.m* and make the following changes to the viewDidLoad method:

```
- (void)viewDidLoad
{
    [super viewDidLoad];

    // Configure the view.
    SKView * skView = (SKView *)self.view;
    skView.showsFPS = YES;
    skView.showsNodeCount = YES;
    skView.ignoresSiblingOrder = YES;

    // Create and configure the scene.
    GameScene *scene = [GameScene nodeWithFileNamed:@"GameScene"];
    scene.scaleMode = SKSceneScaleModeAspectFill;

    GameScene *scene = [GameScene sceneWithSize:self.view.frame.size
                                    levelNumber:1];

    // Present the scene.
    [skView presentScene:scene];
}
```

Instead of loading the scene from the scene file, we're using the sceneWithSize:levelNumber: method that we just added to GameScene to create and initialize the scene and make it the same size as the SKView. Since the view and scene are the same size, there is no longer any need to set the scene's scaleMode property, so we can remove the line of code that does that.

At the bottom of *GameViewController.m*, you'll see the following method that the template included for us:

```
- (BOOL)prefersStatusBarHidden {
    return YES;
}
```

Returning YES from this method makes the iOS status bar disappear while our game is running, which is usually what you want for action games like this. Now run the game and you'll see that we have a very basic structure in place, as shown in Figure 17-5.

Figure 17-5. Our game doesn't have much fun factor right now, but at least it has a high frame rate!

Tip   The node count and frame rate at the bottom right of the scene are useful for debugging, but you don't want them to be there when you release your game! You can switch them off by setting the showsFPS and showsNodeCount properties of the SKView to NO in the viewDidLoad method of GameViewController. There are some other SKView properties that let you get more debugging information—refer to the API documentation for the details.

Player Movement

Now it's time to add a little interactivity. We're going to make a new class that represents a player. It will know how to draw itself using internal components, as well as how to move to a new location in a nicely animated way. Next, we'll insert an instance of the new class into the scene and write some code to let the player move the object around by touching the screen.

Every object that's going to be part of our scene must be a subclass of SKNode. Thus, you'll use Xcode's **File** menu to create a new Cocoa Touch class named `PlayerNode` that's a subclass of SKNode. In the nearly empty *PlayerNode.m* file that's created, add the following methods:

```
- (instancetype)init {
    if (self = [super init]) {
        self.name = [NSString stringWithFormat:@"Player %p", self];
        [self initNodeGraph];
    }
    return self;
}

- (void)initNodeGraph {
    SKLabelNode *label = [SKLabelNode labelNodeWithFontNamed:@"Courier"];
    label.fontColor = [SKColor darkGrayColor];
    label.fontSize = 40;
    label.text = @"v";
    label.zRotation = M_PI;
    label.name = @"label";

    [self addChild:label];

}
```

Our `PlayerNode` doesn't display anything itself, because a plain SKNode has no way to do any drawing of its own. Instead, the `init` method sets up a subnode that will do the actual drawing. This subnode is another instance of SKLabelNode, just like the one we created for displaying the level number and the number of lives remaining. SKLabelNode is a subclass of SKNode that *does* know how to draw itself. Another such subclass is SKSpriteNode. We're not setting a position for the label, which means that its position is coordinate (0, 0). Just like views, each SKNode lives in a coordinate system that is inherited from its parent object. Giving this node a zero position means that it will appear on-screen at the `PlayerNode` instance's position. Any non-zero values would effectively be an offset from that point.

We also set a rotation value for the label, so that the lowercase letter "v" it contains will be shown upside-down. The name of the rotation property, `zRotation`, may seem a bit surprising; however, it simply refers to the z axis of the coordinate space in use with Sprite Kit. You only see the x and y axes on screen, but the z axis is useful for ordering items for display purposes, as well as for rotating things around. The values assigned to `zRotation` need to be in radians instead of degrees, so we assign the value `M_PI`, which is equivalent to the mathematical value π. Since π radians are equal to 180°, this is just what we want.

Adding the Player to the Scene

Now switch back to *GameScene.m*. Here, we're going to add an instance of `PlayerNode` to the scene. Start off by importing the new class's header and adding a property inside a new class extension:

```
#import "GameScene.h"
#import "PlayerNode.h"
```

```
@interface GameScene ()

@property (strong, nonatomic) PlayerNode *playerNode;

@end
```

Continue by adding the following bold code near the end of the initWithSize:levelNumber: method. Be sure to put it before the return self and before the right curly brace above it:

```
        [self addChild:level];
        _playerNode = [PlayerNode node];
        _playerNode.position = CGPointMake(CGRectGetMidX(self.frame),
                                  CGRectGetHeight(self.frame) * 0.1);

        [self addChild:_playerNode];
    }
    return self;
}
```

If you build and run the app now, you should see that the player appears near the lower middle of the screen, as shown in Figure 17-6.

Figure 17-6. *An upside-down "v" to the rescue!*

Handling Touches: Player Movement

Next, we're going to put some logic back into the touchesBegan:withEvent: method, which we earlier left nearly empty. Insert the bold lines shown here in *GameScene.m* (you'll get a compiler error when you add this code—we'll fix it shortly):

```
- (void)touchesBegan:(NSSet *)touches withEvent:(UIEvent *)event {
    /* Called when a touch begins */

    for (UITouch *touch in touches) {
        CGPoint location = [touch locationInNode:self];
        if (location.y < CGRectGetHeight(self.frame) * 0.2 ) {
            CGPoint target = CGPointMake(location.x,
                                         self.playerNode.position.y);
            [self.playerNode moveToward:target];
        }
    }
}
```

The preceding snippet uses any touch location in the lower fifth of the screen as the basis of a new location toward which you want the player node to move. It also tells the player node to move toward it. The compiler complains because we haven't defined the player node's moveToward: method yet. So, start by declaring the method in *PlayerNode.h*, like this:

```
#import <SpriteKit/SpriteKit.h>

@interface PlayerNode : SKNode

// returns duration of future movement
- (void)moveToward:(CGPoint)location;

@end
```

Next, switch over to *PlayerNode.m* and add the following implementation:

```
- (void)moveToward:(CGPoint)location {
    [self removeActionForKey:@"movement"];

    CGFloat distance = PointDistance(self.position, location);
    CGFloat screenWidth = [UIScreen mainScreen].bounds.size.width;
    CGFloat duration = 2.0 * distance / screenWidth;

    [self runAction:[SKAction moveTo:location duration:duration]
          withKey:@"movement"];
}
```

We'll skip the first line for now, returning to it shortly. This method compares the new location to the current position and figures out the distance and the number of pixels to move. Next, it figures out how much time the movement should take, using a numeric constant to set the speed of the overall movement. Finally, it creates an SKAction to make the move happen. SKAction is a part of Sprite Kit that knows how to make changes to nodes over time, letting you easily animate a node's position, size, rotation, transparency, and more. In this case, we are telling the player node to run a simple movement action over a particular duration, and then assigning that action to the key @"movement." As you see, this key is the same as the key used in the first line of this method to remove an action. We started off this method by removing any existing action with the same key, so that the user can tap several locations in quick succession without spawning a lot of competing actions trying to move in different ways!

Geometry Calculations

Now you'll notice that we've introduced another problem, because Xcode can't find any function called PointDistance(). This is one of several simple geometric functions that our app will use to perform calculations using points, vectors, and floats. Let's put this in place now. Use Xcode to make a new file, this time a Header File from the iOS section. Name it *Geometry.h* and give it the following content:

```
#ifndef TextShooter_Geometry_h
#define TextShooter_Geometry_h

// Takes a CGVector and a CGFLoat.
// Returns a new CGFloat where each component of v has been multiplied by m.
static inline CGVector VectorMultiply(CGVector v, CGFloat m) {
    return CGVectorMake(v.dx * m, v.dy * m);
}

// Takes two CGPoints.
// Returns a CGVector representing a direction from p1 to p2.
static inline CGVector VectorBetweenPoints(CGPoint p1, CGPoint p2) {
    return CGVectorMake(p2.x - p1.x, p2.y - p1.y);
}

// Takes a CGVector.
// Returns a CGFloat containing the length of the vector, calculated using
// Pythagoras' theorem.
static inline CGFloat VectorLength(CGVector v) {
    return sqrtf(powf(v.dx, 2) + powf(v.dy, 2));
}

// Takes two CGPoints. Returns a CGFloat containing the distance between them,
// calculated with Pythagoras' theorem.
static inline CGFloat PointDistance(CGPoint p1, CGPoint p2) {
    return sqrtf(powf(p2.x - p1.x, 2) + powf(p2.y - p1.y, 2));
}

#endif
```

These are simple implementations of some common operations that are useful in many games: multiplying vectors, creating vectors pointing from one point to another, and calculating distances. To let the code use these, just add the following import near the top of *PlayerNode.m*:

```
#import "Geometry.h"
```

Now build and run the app. After the player's ship appears, tap anywhere in the bottom portion of the screen to see that the ship slides left or right to reach the point you tapped. You can tap again before the ship reaches its destination, and it will immediately begin a new animation to move toward the new spot. That's fine, but wouldn't it be nice if the player's ship were a bit livelier in its motion?

Wobbly Bits

Let's give the ship a bit of a wobble as it moves by adding another animation. Add the bold lines to PlayerNode's moveToward: method.

```
- (void)moveToward:(CGPoint)location {
    [self removeActionForKey:@"movement"];
    [self removeActionForKey:@"wobbling"];

    CGFloat distance = PointDistance(self.position, location);
    CGFloat pixels = [UIScreen mainScreen].bounds.size.width;
    CGFloat duration = 2.0 * distance / pixels;

    [self runAction:[SKAction moveTo:location duration:duration]
            withKey:@"movement"];

    CGFloat wobbleTime = 0.3;
    CGFloat halfWobbleTime = wobbleTime * 0.5;
    SKAction *wobbling = [SKAction
                sequence:@[[SKAction scaleXTo:0.2 duration:halfWobbleTime],
                           [SKAction scaleXTo:1.0
                                 duration:halfWobbleTime]
                          ]];
    NSUInteger wobbleCount = duration / wobbleTime;

    [self runAction:[SKAction repeatAction:wobbling count:wobbleCount]
            withKey:@"wobbling"];
}
```

What we just did is similar to the movement action we created earlier, but it differs in some important ways. For the basic movement, we simply calculated the movement duration, and then created and ran a movement action in a single step. This time, it's a little more complicated. First, we define the time for a single "wobble" (the ship may wobble multiple times while moving, but will wobble at a consistent rate throughout). The wobble itself consists of first scaling the ship along the x axis (i.e., its width) to 2/10ths of its normal size, and then scaling it back to it to its full size. Each of these is a single action that is packed together into another kind of action called a **sequence**, which performs all the actions it contains one after another. Next, we figure out how many times this wobble can happen during the duration of the ship's travel and wrap the wobbling sequence inside a repeat action, telling it how many complete wobble cycles it should execute. And, as before, we start the method by canceling any previous wobbling action, since we wouldn't want competing wobblers.

Now run the app, and you'll see that the ship wobbles pleasantly when moving back and forth. It kind of looks like it's walking!

Creating Your Enemies

So far so good, but this game is going to need some enemies for our players to shoot at. Use Xcode to make a new Cocoa Touch class called EnemyNode, using SKNode as the parent class. We're not going to give the enemy class any real behavior just yet, but we will give it an appearance. We'll use the same technique that we used for the player, using text to build the enemy's body. Surely, there's no text character more intimidating than the letter X, so our enemy will be a letter X... made of lowercase Xs! Try not to be scared just thinking about that as you add these methods to *EnemyNode.m*:

```
- (instancetype)init {
    if (self = [super init]) {
        self.name = [NSString stringWithFormat:@"Enemy %p", self];
        [self initNodeGraph];
    }
    return self;
}

- (void)initNodeGraph {
    SKLabelNode *topRow = [SKLabelNode
                            labelNodeWithFontNamed:@"Courier-Bold"];
    topRow.fontColor = [SKColor brownColor];
    topRow.fontSize = 20;
    topRow.text = @"x x";
    topRow.position = CGPointMake(0, 15);
    [self addChild:topRow];

    SKLabelNode *middleRow = [SKLabelNode
                            labelNodeWithFontNamed:@"Courier-Bold"];
    middleRow.fontColor = [SKColor brownColor];
    middleRow.fontSize = 20;
    middleRow.text = @"x";
    [self addChild:middleRow];

    SKLabelNode *bottomRow = [SKLabelNode
                            labelNodeWithFontNamed:@"Courier-Bold"];
    bottomRow.fontColor = [SKColor brownColor];
    bottomRow.fontSize = 20;
    bottomRow.text = @"x x";
    bottomRow.position = CGPointMake(0, -15);
    [self addChild:bottomRow];
}
```

There's nothing much new there; we're just adding multiple "rows" of text by shifting the y value for each of their positions.

Putting Enemies in the Scene

Now let's make some enemies appear in the scene by making some changes to *GameScene.m*. First, add the bold lines shown here, near the top:

```
#import "GameScene.h"
#import "PlayerNode.h"
#import "EnemyNode.h"

@interface GameScene ()

@property (strong, nonatomic) PlayerNode *playerNode;
@property (strong, nonatomic) SKNode *enemies;

@end
```

We imported the header for our new enemy class and we added a new property for holding all the enemies that will be added to the level. You might think that we'd use an NSMutableArray for this, but it turns out that using a plain SKNode is perfect for the job. SKNode can hold any number of child nodes. And since we need to add all the enemies to the scene anyway, we may as well hold them all in an SKNode for easy access.

The next step is to create the spawnEnemies method, as shown here:

```
- (void)spawnEnemies {
    NSUInteger count = log(self.levelNumber) + self.levelNumber;
    for (NSUInteger i = 0; i < count; i++) {
        EnemyNode *enemy = [EnemyNode node];
        CGSize size = self.frame.size;
        CGFloat x = arc4random_uniform(size.width * 0.8)
                    + (size.width * 0.1);
        CGFloat y = arc4random_uniform(size.height * 0.5)
                    + (size.height * 0.5);
        enemy.position = CGPointMake(x, y);
        [self.enemies addChild:enemy];
    }
}
```

Finally, add these lines near the end of the initWithSize:levelNumber: method to create an empty enemies node, and then call the spawnEnemies method:

```
[self addChild:_playerNode];
_enemies = [SKNode node];
[self addChild:_enemies];
[self spawnEnemies];
```

Since we added the enemies node to the scene, any child enemy nodes we add to the enemies node will also appear in the scene.

Now run the app, and you'll see a dreadful enemy placed randomly in the upper portion of the screen (see Figure 17-7). Don't you wish you could shoot it?

Figure 17-7. *I'm sure you'll agree that the X made of Xs just needs to be shot*

Start Shooting

It's time to implement the next logical step in the development of this game: letting the player attack the enemies. We want the player to be able to tap anywhere in the upper 80% of the screen to shoot a bullet at the enemies. We're going to use the **physics engine** included in Sprite Kit both to move our player's bullets and to let us know when a bullet collides with an enemy.

But first, what is this thing we call a physics engine? Basically, a physics engine is a software component that keeps track of multiple physical objects (commonly referred to as **bodies**) in a world, along with the forces that are acting upon them. It also makes sure that everything moves in a realistic way. It can take into account the force of gravity, handle collisions between objects (so that objects don't occupy the same space simultaneously), and even simulate physical characteristics like friction and bounciness.

It's important to understand that a physics engine is typically separate from a graphics engine. Apple provides convenient APIs to let us work with both, but they are essentially separate. It's common to have objects in your display, such as our labels that show the current level number and remaining lives, that are completely separate from the physics engine. And it's possible to create objects that have a physics body, but don't actually display anything at all.

Defining Your Physics Categories

One of the things that the Sprite Kit physics engine lets us do is to assign objects to several distinct **physics categories**. A physics category has nothing to do with Objective-C categories. Instead, a physics category is a way to group related objects so that the physics engine can handle collisions between them in different ways. In this game, for example, we'll create three categories: one for enemies, one for the player, and one for player missiles. We definitely want the physics engine to concern itself with collisions between enemies and player missiles, but we probably want it to ignore collisions between player missiles and the player itself. This is easy to set up using physics categories.

So, let's create the categories we're going to need. Press ⌘**N** to bring up the new file assistant, choose **Header File** from the iOS section, and press **Next**. Give the new header file the name *PhysicsCategories.h* and save it, and then add the following code to it:

```
#ifndef TextShooter_PhysicsCategories_h
#define TextShooter_PhysicsCategories_h

typedef NS_OPTIONS(uint32_t, PhysicsCategory) {
    PlayerCategory        = 1 << 1,
    EnemyCategory         = 1 << 2,
    PlayerMissileCategory = 1 << 3
};

#endif
```

Here we declared three category constants. Note that the categories work as a bitmask, so each of them must be a power of two. We can easily do this by bit-shifting. These are set up as a bitmask in order to simplify the physics engine's API a little bit. With bitmasks, we can logically *OR* several values together. This enables us to use a single API call to tell the physics engine how to deal with collisions between many different layers. We'll see this in action soon.

Creating the BulletNode Class

Now that we've laid some groundwork, let's create some bullets so we can start shooting.

Create a new Cocoa Touch class called `BulletNode`, once again using `SKNode` as its superclass. Start in the header file, where you'll declare the two public methods this class will have:

```
#import <SpriteKit/SpriteKit.h>

@interface BulletNode : SKNode

+ (instancetype)bulletFrom:(CGPoint)start toward:(CGPoint)destination;
- (void)applyRecurringForce;

@end
```

The first method is a factory method for creating new instances of the class. The second is one that you'll need to call from your scene each frame, to tell the bullet to move. Now switch over to *BulletNode.m* to start implementing this class.

The first thing we're going to do is import a header for our special geometry functions and physics categories. The second step is to add a class extension with a single property, which will contain this bullet's thrust vector:

```
#import "BulletNode.h"
#import "PhysicsCategories.h"
#import "Geometry.h"

@interface BulletNode ()

@property (assign, nonatomic) CGVector thrust;

@end
```

Next, we implement an init method. Like other init methods in this application, this is where we create the object graph for our bullet. This will consist of a single dot. While we're at it, let's also configure physics for this class by creating and configuring an SKPhysicsBody instance and attaching it to self. In the process, we tell the new body what category it belongs to and which categories should be checked for collisions with this object.

```
@implementation BulletNode

- (instancetype)init {
    if (self = [super init]) {
        SKLabelNode *dot = [SKLabelNode labelNodeWithFontNamed:@"Courier"];
        dot.fontColor = [SKColor blackColor];
        dot.fontSize = 40;
        dot.text = @".";
        [self addChild:dot];

        SKPhysicsBody *body = [SKPhysicsBody bodyWithCircleOfRadius:1];
        body.dynamic = YES;
        body.categoryBitMask = PlayerMissileCategory;
        body.contactTestBitMask = EnemyCategory;
        body.collisionBitMask = EnemyCategory;
        body.mass = 0.01;

        self.physicsBody = body;
        self.name = [NSString stringWithFormat:@"Bullet %p", self];
    }
    return self;
}
```

Applying Physics

Next, we'll create the factory method that creates a new bullet and gives it a thrust vector that the physics engine will use to propel the bullet toward its target:

```
+ (instancetype)bulletFrom:(CGPoint)start toward:(CGPoint)destination {
    BulletNode *bullet = [[self alloc] init];

    bullet.position = start;

    CGVector movement = VectorBetweenPoints(start, destination);
    CGFloat magnitude = VectorLength(movement);
    if (magnitude == 0.0f) return nil;

    CGVector scaledMovement = VectorMultiply(movement, 1 / magnitude);

    CGFloat thrustMagnitude = 100.0;
    bullet.thrust = VectorMultiply(scaledMovement, thrustMagnitude);

    return bullet;
}
```

The basic calculations are pretty simple. We first determine a movement vector that points from the start location to the destination, and then we determine its magnitude (length). Dividing the movement vector by its magnitude produces a normalized **unit vector**, a vector that points in the same direction as the original, but is exactly one unit long (a unit, in this case, is the same as a "point" on the screen—e.g., two pixels on a Retina device, one pixel on older devices). Creating a unit vector is very useful because we can multiply that by a fixed magnitude (in this case, 100) to determine a uniformly powerful thrust vector, no matter how far away the user tapped the screen.

The final piece of code we need to add to this class is this method, which applies thrust to the physics body. We'll call this once per frame, from inside the scene:

```
- (void)applyRecurringForce {
    [self.physicsBody applyForce:self.thrust];
}
```

Adding Bullets to the Scene

Now switch over to *GameScene.m* to add bullets to the scene itself. For starters, import the header for the new class near the top. Next, add another property to contain all bullets in a single SKNode, just as you did earlier for enemies:

```
#import "GameScene.h"
#import "PlayerNode.h"
#import "EnemyNode.h"
#import "BulletNode.h"

@interface GameScene ()
```

```
@property (strong, nonatomic) PlayerNode *playerNode;
@property (strong, nonatomic) SKNode *enemies;
@property (strong, nonatomic) SKNode *playerBullets;

@end
```

Find the section of the initWithSize:levelNumber: method where you previously added the enemies. That's the place to set up the playerBullets node, too.

```
[self spawnEnemies];
_playerBullets = [SKNode node];
[self addChild:_playerBullets];
```

Now we're ready to code the actual missile launches. Add this else clause to the touchesBegan:withEvent: method, so that all taps in the upper part of the screen shoot a bullet instead of moving the ship:

```
- (void)touchesBegan:(NSSet *)touches withEvent:(UIEvent *)event {
    for (UITouch *touch in touches) {
        CGPoint location = [touch locationInNode:self];
        if (location.y < CGRectGetHeight(self.frame) * 0.2 ) {
            CGPoint target = CGPointMake(location.x,
                                         self.playerNode.position.y);
            [self.playerNode moveToward:target];

        } else {
            BulletNode *bullet = [BulletNode
                                      bulletFrom:self.playerNode.position
                                      toward:location];
            [self.playerBullets addChild:bullet];
        }
    }
}
```

That adds the bullet, but none of the bullets we add will actually move unless we tell them to by applying thrust every frame. Our scene already contains an empty method called update:. This method is called each frame, and that's the perfect place to do any game logic that needs to occur in each frame. Rather than updating all our bullets right in that method, however, we put that code in a separate method that we call from the update: method:

```
- (void)update:(CFTimeInterval)currentTime {
    [self updateBullets];
}


- (void)updateBullets {
    NSMutableArray *bulletsToRemove = [NSMutableArray array];
    for (BulletNode *bullet in self.playerBullets.children) {
        // Remove any bullets that have moved off-screen
        if (!CGRectContainsPoint(self.frame, bullet.position)) {
```

```
        // mark bullet for removal
        [bulletsToRemove addObject:bullet];
        continue;
    }
    // Apply thrust to remaining bullets
    [bullet applyRecurringForce];
  }
  [self.playerBullets removeChildrenInArray:bulletsToRemove];
}
```

Before telling each bullet to apply its recurring force, we also check whether each bullet is still on-screen. Any bullet that's gone off-screen is put into a temporary array; and then, at the end, those are swept out of the playerBullets node. Note that this two-stage process is necessary because the for loop at work in this method is iterating over all children in the playerBullets node. Making changes to a collection while you're iterating over it is never a good idea, and it can easily lead to a crash.

Now build and run the app, and you'll see that, in addition to moving the player's ship, you can make it shoot missiles upward by tapping on the screen (see Figure 17-8). Neat!

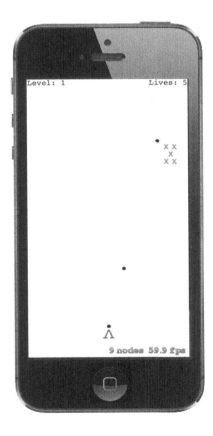

Figure 17-8. Shooting up a storm!

Attacking Enemies with Physics

A couple of important gameplay elements are still missing from our game. The enemies never attack us, and we can't yet get rid of the enemies by shooting them. Let's take care of the latter right now. We're going to set things up so that shooting an enemy has the effect of dislodging it from the spot where it's currently fixed on the screen. This feature will use the physics engine for all the heavy lifting, and it will involve making changes to PlayerNode, EnemyNode, and GameScene.

For starters, let's add physics bodies to our nodes that don't already have them. Start with *EnemyNode.m*, adding this #import statement near the top:

```
#import "PhysicsCategories.h"
```

Next, add the following line to the init method:

```
- (instancetype)init {
    if (self = [super init]) {
        self.name = [NSString stringWithFormat:@"Enemy %p", self];
        [self initNodeGraph];
        [self initPhysicsBody];
    }
    return self;
}
```

Now add the code to really set up the physics body. This is pretty similar to what you did earlier for the PlayerBullet class:

```
- (void)initPhysicsBody {
    SKPhysicsBody *body = [SKPhysicsBody bodyWithRectangleOfSize:
                                CGSizeMake(40, 40)];
    body.affectedByGravity = NO;
    body.categoryBitMask = EnemyCategory;
    body.contactTestBitMask = PlayerCategory|EnemyCategory;
    body.mass = 0.2;
    body.angularDamping = 0.0f;
    body.linearDamping = 0.0f;
    self.physicsBody = body;
}
```

Then select *PlayerNode.m*, where you're going to do a pretty similar set of things. First, add the following #import near the top:

```
#import "PhysicsCategories.h"
```

Follow up by adding the bold line shown here to the init method:

```
- (instancetype)init {
    if (self = [super init]) {
        self.name = [NSString stringWithFormat:@"Player %p", self];
        [self initNodeGraph];
        [self initPhysicsBody];
    }
    return self;
}
```

Finally, add the new initPhysicsBody method:

```
- (void)initPhysicsBody {
    SKPhysicsBody *body = [SKPhysicsBody bodyWithRectangleOfSize:
                              CGSizeMake(20, 20)];
    body.affectedByGravity = NO;
    body.categoryBitMask = PlayerCategory;
    body.contactTestBitMask = EnemyCategory;
    body.collisionBitMask = 0;

    self.physicsBody = body;
}
```

At this point, you can run the app and see that your bullets now have the ability to knock enemies into space. However, you'll also see there's a problem here. When you start the game and then send the lone enemy hurtling into space, you're stuck! This is probably a good time to add level management to the game.

Finishing Levels

We need to enhance GameScene so that it knows when it's time to move to the next level. It can figure this out simply enough by looking at the number of available enemies. If it finds that there aren't any on-screen, then the level is over, and the game should transition to the next.

Keeping Tabs on the Enemies

Begin by adding this updateEnemies method. It works a lot like the updateBullets method added earlier:

```
- (void)updateEnemies {
    NSMutableArray *enemiesToRemove = [NSMutableArray array];
    for (SKNode *node in self.enemies.children) {
        // Remove any enemies that have moved off-screen
        if (!CGRectContainsPoint(self.frame, node.position)) {
            // mark enemy for removal
            [enemiesToRemove addObject:node];
            continue;
        }
    }
    if ([enemiesToRemove count] > 0) {
        [self.enemies removeChildrenInArray:enemiesToRemove];
    }
}
```

That takes care of removing each enemy from the level's enemies array each time one goes off-screen. Now let's modify the update: method, telling it to call updateEnemies, as well as a new method we haven't yet implemented:

```
- (void)update:(CFTimeInterval)currentTime {
    /* Called before each frame is rendered */
    if (self.finished) return;

    [self updateBullets];
    [self updateEnemies];
    [self checkForNextLevel];
}
```

We started out that method by checking the finished property. Since we're about to add code that can officially end a level, we want to be sure that we don't keep doing additional processing after the level is complete! Then, just as we're checking each frame to see if any bullets or enemies have gone off-screen, we're going to call checkForNextLevel each frame to see if the current level is complete. Let's add this method:

```
- (void)checkForNextLevel {
    if ([self.enemies.children count] == 0) {
        [self goToNextLevel];
    }
}
```

Transitioning to the Next Levels

The checkForNextLevel method in turn calls another method we haven't yet implemented. The goToNextLevel method marks this level as finished, displays some text on the screen to let the player know, and then starts the next level:

```
- (void)goToNextLevel {
    self.finished = YES;

    SKLabelNode *label = [SKLabelNode labelNodeWithFontNamed:@"Courier"];
    label.text = @"Level Complete!";
    label.fontColor = [SKColor blueColor];
    label.fontSize = 32;
    label.position = CGPointMake(self.frame.size.width * 0.5,
                                 self.frame.size.height * 0.5);
    [self addChild:label];

    GameScene *nextLevel = [[GameScene alloc]
                            initWithSize:self.frame.size
                            levelNumber:self.levelNumber + 1];
    nextLevel.playerLives = self.playerLives;
    [self.view presentScene:nextLevel
    transition:[SKTransition flipHorizontalWithDuration:1.0]];
}
```

The second half of the goToNextLevel method creates a new instance of GameScene and gives it all the start values it needs. It then tells the view to present the new scene, using a transition to smooth things over. The SKTransition class lets us pick from a variety of transition styles. Run the app and complete a level to see what this one looks like (see Figure 17-9).

Figure 17-9. *Here you see a snapshot taken during the end-of-level screen-flipping transition*

The transition in use here makes it looks like we're flipping a card over its horizontal axis, but there are plenty more to choose from! See the documentation or header file for SKTransition to see more possibilities. We'll use a couple more variations later in this chapter.

Customizing Collisions

Now we've got a game that you can really play. You can clear level after level by knocking enemies upward off the screen. That's OK, but there's really not much challenge! We mentioned earlier that having enemies attack the player is one piece of missing gameplay, and now it's time to make that happen. We're going to make things a little harder by making the enemies fall down when they're bumped, either from being hit by a bullet or from being touched by another enemy. We also want to make it so that being hit by a falling enemy takes a life away from the player. You also may have noticed that after a bullet hits an enemy, the bullet squiggles its way around the enemy and continues on its upward trajectory, which is pretty weird. We're going to tackle all these things by implementing a collision-handling routine in *GameScene.m*.

The method for handling detected collisions is a delegate method for the SKPhysicsWorld class. Our scene has a physics world by default, but we need to set it up a little bit before it will tell us anything. For starters, it's good to let the compiler know that we're going to implement a delegate protocol, so let's add this declaration to the class extension declaration near the top of the *GameScene.m* file:

```
@interface GameScene () <SKPhysicsContactDelegate>
```

We still need to configure the world a bit (giving it a slightly less cruel amount of gravity) and tell it who its delegate is. To do so, we add these bold lines near the end of the initWithSize:levelNumber: method:

```
self.physicsWorld.gravity = CGVectorMake(0, -1);
self.physicsWorld.contactDelegate = self;
```

Now that we've set the physics world's contactDelegate to be the GameScene, we can implement the relevant delegate method. The core of the method looks like this:

```
- (void)didBeginContact:(SKPhysicsContact *)contact {
    if (contact.bodyA.categoryBitMask == contact.bodyB.categoryBitMask) {
        // Both bodies are in the same category
        SKNode *nodeA = contact.bodyA.node;
        SKNode *nodeB = contact.bodyB.node;

        // What do we do with these nodes?
    } else {
        SKNode *attacker = nil;
        SKNode *attackee = nil;

        if (contact.bodyA.categoryBitMask > contact.bodyB.categoryBitMask) {
            // Body A is attacking Body B
            attacker = contact.bodyA.node;
            attackee = contact.bodyB.node;
        } else {
            // Body B is attacking Body A
            attacker = contact.bodyB.node;
            attackee = contact.bodyA.node;
        }
        if ([attackee isKindOfClass:[PlayerNode class]]) {
            self.playerLives--;
        }
        // What do we do with the attacker and the attackee?
    }
}
```

Go ahead and add that method, but if you look at it right now, you'll see that it doesn't really do much yet. In fact, the only concrete result of that method is to reduce the number of player lives each time a falling enemy hits the player's ship. But the enemies aren't falling yet!

The idea behind this implementation is to look at the two colliding objects and to figure out whether they are of the same category (in which case, they are "friends" to one another) or if they are of different categories. If they are of different categories, we have to determine who is attacking whom. If you look at the order of the categories declared in *PhysicsCategories.h*, you'll see that they are specified in order of increased "attackyness": Player nodes can be attacked by Enemy nodes, which in turn can be attacked by PlayerMissile nodes. That means that we can use a simple greater-than comparison to figure out who is the "attacker" in this scenario.

For the sake of simplicity and modularity, we don't really want the scene to decide how each object should react to being attacked by an enemy or bumped by another object. It's much better to build those details into the affected node classes themselves. But, as you see in the method we've got, the only thing we're sure of is that each side has an SKNode instance. Rather than coding up a big chain of if-else statements to ask each node which SKNode subclass it belongs to, we can use regular polymorphism to let each of our node classes handle things in its own way. In order for that to work, we have to add methods to SKNode, with default implementations that do nothing, and let our subclasses override them where appropriate. This calls for a category! Not a Sprite Kit physics category this time, but a genuine Objective-C @category definition.

Adding a Category to SKNode

To add a category to SKNode, right-click the *TextShooter* folder in Xcode's Project Navigator and choose **New File...** from the pop-up menu. From the assistant's iOS/Source section, choose **Objective-C File**, and then click **Next**. Give it a File name of *Extra*, select **Category** as the File Type, and choose SKNode as the class to which the category is being added. Now click **Next** again and create the files. Select the category header file *SKNode+Extra.h* and add the bold method declarations shown here:

```
#import <SpriteKit/SpriteKit.h>

@interface SKNode (Extra)

- (void)receiveAttacker:(SKNode *)attacker contact:(SKPhysicsContact *)contact;
- (void)friendlyBumpFrom:(SKNode *)node;

@end
```

Switch over to the matching *.m* file and enter the following empty definitions:

```
#import "SKNode+Extra.h"

@implementation SKNode (Extra)

- (void)receiveAttacker:(SKNode *)attacker contact:(SKPhysicsContact *)contact {
    // default implementation does nothing
}

- (void)friendlyBumpFrom:(SKNode *)node {
    // default implementation does nothing
}

@end
```

Now head back over to *GameScene.m* to finish up its part of the collision handling. Start by adding a new header at the top:

```
#import "GameScene.h"
#import "PlayerNode.h"
#import "EnemyNode.h"
#import "BulletNode.h"
#import "SKNode+Extra.h"
```

Next, go back to the didBeginContact: method, where you'll add the bits that actually do some work:

```
- (void)didBeginContact:(SKPhysicsContact *)contact {
    if (contact.bodyA.categoryBitMask == contact.bodyB.categoryBitMask) {
        // Both bodies are in the same category
        SKNode *nodeA = contact.bodyA.node;
        SKNode *nodeB = contact.bodyB.node;

        // What do we do with these nodes?
        [nodeA friendlyBumpFrom:nodeB];
        [nodeB friendlyBumpFrom:nodeA];
    } else {
        SKNode *attacker = nil;
        SKNode *attackee = nil;

        if (contact.bodyA.categoryBitMask > contact.bodyB.categoryBitMask) {
            // Body A is attacking Body B
            attacker = contact.bodyA.node;
            attackee = contact.bodyB.node;
        } else {
            // Body B is attacking Body A
            attacker = contact.bodyB.node;
            attackee = contact.bodyA.node;
        }
        if ([attackee isKindOfClass:[PlayerNode class]]) {
            self.playerLives--;
        }
        // What do we do with the attacker and the attackee?
        [attackee receiveAttacker:attacker contact:contact];
        [self.playerBullets removeChildrenInArray:@[attacker]];
        [self.enemies removeChildrenInArray:@[attacker]];
    }
}
```

All we added here were a few calls to our new methods. If the collision is "friendly fire," such as two enemies bumping into each other, we'll tell each of them that it received a friendly bump from the other. Otherwise, after figuring out who attacked whom, we tell the attackee that it's come under attack from another object. Finally, we remove the attacker from whichever of the playerBullets or enemies nodes it may be in. We tell each of those nodes to remove the attacker, even though it can only be in one of them, but that's OK. Telling a node to remove a child it doesn't have isn't an error—it just has no effect.

Adding Custom Collision Behavior to Enemies

Now that all that's in place, we can implement some specific behaviors for our nodes by overriding the category methods we added to SKNode.

Select *EnemyNode.m*. At the top of the file, add an import of *Geometry.h*:

```
#import "PhysicsCategories.h"
#import "Geometry.h"

@implementation EnemyNode
```

Next, add the following two methods:

```
- (void)friendlyBumpFrom:(SKNode *)node {
    self.physicsBody.affectedByGravity = YES;
}

- (void)receiveAttacker:(SKNode *)attacker contact:(SKPhysicsContact *)contact {
    self.physicsBody.affectedByGravity = YES;
    CGVector force = VectorMultiply(attacker.physicsBody.velocity,
                                    contact.collisionImpulse);
    CGPoint myContact = [self.scene convertPoint:contact.contactPoint
                                          toNode:self];
    [self.physicsBody applyForce:force
                         atPoint:myContact];
}
```

The first of those, `friendlyBumpFrom:`, simply turns on gravity for the affected enemy. So, if one enemy is in motion and bumps into another, the second enemy will suddenly notice gravity and start falling downward.

The `receiveAttacker:contact:` method, which is called if the enemy is hit by a bullet, first turns on gravity for the enemy. However, it also uses the contact data that was passed in to figure out just where the contact occurred and applies a force to that point, giving it an extra push in the direction that the bullet was fired.

Showing Accurate Player Lives

Run the game, and you'll see that you can shoot at enemies to knock them down. You'll also see that any other enemies bumped into by a falling enemy will fall, as well.

Note   At the start of each level, the world performs one step of its physics simulation to make sure that there aren't physics bodies overlapping each other. This will produce an interesting side effect at higher levels, since there will be an increasing chance that multiple randomly placed enemies will occupy overlapping spaces. Whenever that happens, the enemies will be immediately shifted so they no longer overlap, and our collision-handling code will be triggered, which subsequently turns on gravity and lets them fall! This behavior wasn't anything we planned on when we started building this game, but it turns out to be a happy accident that makes higher levels progressively more difficult, so we're letting physics run its course!

If you let enemies hit you as they fall, the number of player lives decreases, but… hey wait, it just shows 5 all the time! The Lives display is set up when the level is created, but it's never updated after that. Fortunately, this is easily fixed by implementing the setPlayerLives: setter in *GameScene.m* instead of using the automatically synthesized setter, like this:

```
- (void)setPlayerLives:(NSUInteger)playerLives  {
    _playerLives = playerLives;
    SKLabelNode *lives = (id)[self childNodeWithName:@"LivesLabel"];
    lives.text = [NSString stringWithFormat:@"Lives: %lu",
                  (unsigned long)_playerLives];
}
```

The preceding snippet uses the name we previously associated with the label (in the initWithSize:level: method) to find the label again and set a new text value. Play the game again, and you'll see that, as you let enemies rain down on your player, the number of lives will decrease to zero. And then the game doesn't end. After the next hit, you end up with a very large number of lives indeed, as you can see in Figure 17-10.

Figure 17-10. That's a lot of lives

So what's going on here? Well, we are using an unsigned integer to hold the number of lives. And when you're using unsigned integers and dip below zero, you sort of wrap around that zero boundary and end up with the maximum allowed unsigned integer value instead!

The reason this problem appears is really because we haven't written any code to detect the end of the game; that is, the point in time when the number of player lives hits zero. We'll do that soon, but first let's make our on-screen collisions a bit more stimulating.

Spicing Things Up with Particles

One of the nice features of Sprite Kit is the inclusion of a particle system. Particle systems are used in games to create visual effects simulating smoke, fire, explosions, and more. Right now, whenever our bullets hit an enemy or an enemy hits the player, the attacking object simply blinks out of existence. Let's make a couple of particle systems to improve this situation!

Start out by pressing ⌘N to bring up the new file assistant. Select the **iOS/Resource** section on the left, and then choose **SpriteKit Particle File** on the right. Click **Next**, and on the following screen choose the **Spark** particle template. Click **Next** again and name this file *MissileExplosion.sks*.

Your First Particle

You'll see that Xcode creates the particle file and also adds a new resource called *spark.png* to the project. At the same time, the entire Xcode editing area switches over to the new particle file, showing you a huge, animated exploding thing.

We don't want something quite this extravagant and enormous when our bullets hit enemies, so let's reconfigure this thing. All the properties that define this particle's animation are available in the SKNode Inspector, which you can bring up by pressing **Opt-Cmd-7**. Figure 17-11 shows both the massive explosion and the inspector.

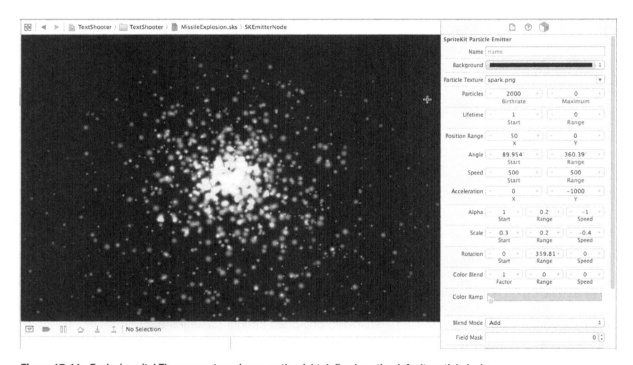

Figure 17-11. Explosion city! The parameters shown on the right define how the default particle looks

Now, for our bullet hit, let's make it a much smaller explosion. It will have a whole different set of parameters, all of which you configure right in the inspector. First, fix the colors to match what our game looks like by clicking the small color well in the Color Ramp at the bottom and setting it to black. Next, change the Background color to white and change the Blend Mode to *Alpha*. Now you'll see that the flaming fountain has turned all inky.

The rest of the parameters are all numeric. Change them one at a time, setting them all as shown in Figure 17-12. At each step of the way, you'll see the particle effect change until it eventually reaches its target appearance.

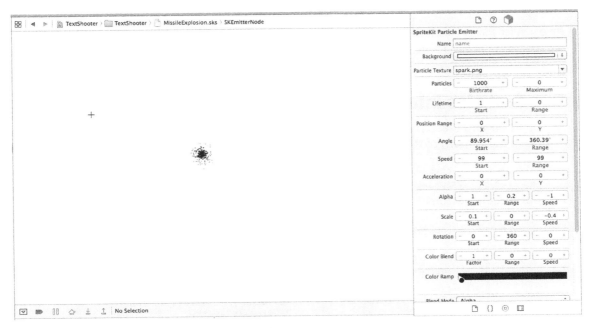

Figure 17-12. This is the final missile explosion particle effect we want

Now make another particle system, once again using the Spark template. Name this one *EnemyExplosion.sks* and set its parameters as shown in Figure 17-13.

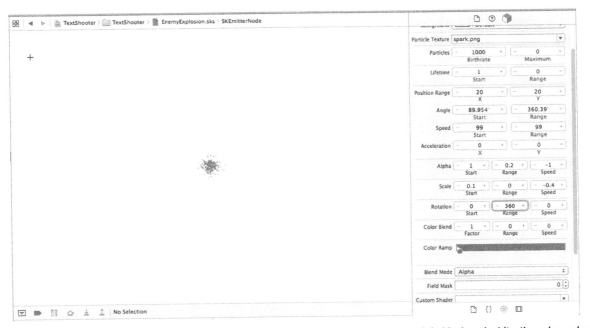

Figure 17-13. Here's the enemy explosion we want to create. In case you're seeing this book in black and white, the color we've chosen in the Color Ramp at the bottom is deep red

> **Note**   After adding the second particle file, you may find two copies of the file spark.png in the Project
> Navigator and a warning in the Activity View. Fix this by right-clicking on one of the files and selecing Delete.

Putting Particles into the Scene

Now let's start putting these particles to use. Switch over to *EnemyNode.m* and add the bold code
shown here to the bottom of the receiveAttacker:contact: method:

```
- (void)receiveAttacker:(SKNode *)attacker contact:(SKPhysicsContact *)contact {
    self.physicsBody.affectedByGravity = YES;
    CGVector force = VectorMultiply(attacker.physicsBody.velocity,
                                    contact.collisionImpulse);
    CGPoint myContact = [self.scene convertPoint:contact.contactPoint
                                          toNode:self];
    [self.physicsBody applyForce:force
                    atPoint:myContact];

    NSString *path = [[NSBundle mainBundle] pathForResource:@"MissileExplosion"
                                            ofType:@"sks"];
    SKEmitterNode *explosion = [NSKeyedUnarchiver unarchiveObjectWithFile:path];
    explosion.numParticlesToEmit = 20;
    explosion.position = contact.contactPoint;
    [self.scene addChild:explosion];
}
```

Run the game, shoot some enemies, and you'll see a nice little explosion where each bullet hits an
enemy, as shown in Figure 17-14.

Figure 17-14. *Bullets smash nicely after impact*

Nice! Now let's do something similar for those times an enemy smashes into a player's ship. Select *PlayerNode.m* and add this method:

```
- (void)receiveAttacker:(SKNode *)attacker contact:(SKPhysicsContact *)contact {
    NSString *path = [[NSBundle mainBundle] pathForResource:@"EnemyExplosion"
                                                     ofType:@"sks"];
    SKEmitterNode *explosion =
           [NSKeyedUnarchiver unarchiveObjectWithFile:path];
    explosion.numParticlesToEmit = 50;
    explosion.position = contact.contactPoint;
    [self.scene addChild:explosion];
}
```

Play again, and you'll see a nice red splat every time an enemy hits the player, as shown in Figure 17-15.

Figure 17-15. Ouch!

These changes are pretty simple, but they improve the feel of the game substantially. Now when things collide, you have visual c.uences and can see that something happened.

The End Game

As we mentioned before, we currently have a small problem in the game. When the number of lives hits zero, we need to end the game. What we'll do is create a new scene class to transition to when the game is over. You've seen us do a scene transition before, when moving from one level to the next. This will be similar, but with a new class.

So, create a new iOS/Cocoa Touch class. Use SKScene as the parent class and name the new class GameOverScene.

We'll start with a very simple implementation that just displays "Game Over" text and does nothing more. We'll accomplish this by adding this code to the @implementation in *GameOverScene.m*:

```
- (instancetype)initWithSize:(CGSize)size {
    if (self = [super initWithSize:size]) {
        self.backgroundColor = [SKColor purpleColor];
        SKLabelNode *text = [SKLabelNode labelNodeWithFontNamed:@"Courier"];
```

```
        text.text = @"Game Over";
        text.fontColor = [SKColor whiteColor];
        text.fontSize = 50;
        text.position = CGPointMake(self.frame.size.width * 0.5,
                                    self.frame.size.height * 0.5);
        [self addChild:text];
    }
    return self;
}
```

Now let's switch back to *GameScene.m*. We'll need to import the header for the new scene at the top:

```
#import "GameScene.h"
#import "PlayerNode.h"
#import "EnemyNode.h"
#import "BulletNode.h"
#import "SKNode+Extra.h"
#import "GameOverScene.h"
```

The basic action of what to do when the game ends is defined by a new method called `triggerGameOver`. Here, we show both an extra explosion and kick off a transition to the new scene we just created:

```
- (void)triggerGameOver {
    self.finished = YES;

    NSString *path = [[NSBundle mainBundle] pathForResource:@"EnemyExplosion"
                                                     ofType:@"sks"];
    SKEmitterNode *explosion =
                [NSKeyedUnarchiver unarchiveObjectWithFile:path];
    explosion.numParticlesToEmit = 200;
    explosion.position = _playerNode.position;
    [self addChild:explosion];
    [_playerNode removeFromParent];

    SKTransition *transition =
                [SKTransition doorsOpenVerticalWithDuration:1.0];
    SKScene *gameOver = [[GameOverScene alloc] initWithSize:self.frame.size];
    [self.view presentScene:gameOver transition:transition];
}
```

Next, create this new method that will check for the end of the game, call `triggerGameOver` if it's time, and return either YES to indicate the game ended or NO to indicate that it's still on:

```
- (BOOL)checkForGameOver {
    if (self.playerLives == 0) {
        [self triggerGameOver];
        return YES;
    }
    return NO;
}
```

Finally, add a check to the existing update: method. It checks for the game-over state and only checks for a potential next-level transition if the game is still going. Otherwise, there's a risk that the final enemy on a level could take the player's final life and trigger two scene transitions at once!

```
- (void)update:(CFTimeInterval)currentTime {
    if (self.finished) return;

    [self updateBullets];
    [self updateEnemies];
    if (![self checkForGameOver]) {
        [self checkForNextLevel];
    }
}
```

Now run the game again, let falling enemies damage your ship five times, and you'll see the Game Over screen, as shown in Figure 17-16.

Figure 17-16. That's it, man. Game over, man—game over

At Last, a Beginning: Create a StartScene

This leads us to another problem: What do we do after the game is over? We could allow the player to tap to restart the game; but while thinking of that, a thought crossed my mind. Shouldn't this game have some sort of start screen, so the player isn't immediately thrust into a game at launch time? And shouldn't the game-over screen lead you back there? Of course, the answer to both questions is yes! Go ahead and create another new iOS/Cocoa Touch class, once again using SKScene as the superclass, and this time naming it StartScene.

We're going to make a super-simple start scene here. All it will do is display some text and start the game when the user taps anywhere. Add all the bold code shown here to *StartScene.m* to complete this class:

```objc
#import "StartScene.h"
#import "GameScene.h"

@implementation StartScene

- (instancetype)initWithSize:(CGSize)size {
    if (self = [super initWithSize:size]) {
        self.backgroundColor = [SKColor greenColor];

        SKLabelNode *topLabel = [SKLabelNode labelNodeWithFontNamed:@"Courier"];
        topLabel.text = @"TextShooter";
        topLabel.fontColor = [SKColor blackColor];
        topLabel.fontSize = 48;
        topLabel.position = CGPointMake(self.frame.size.width * 0.5,
                                self.frame.size.height * 0.7);
        [self addChild:topLabel];

        SKLabelNode *bottomLabel = [SKLabelNode labelNodeWithFontNamed:
                                @"Courier"];
        bottomLabel.text = @"Touch anywhere to start";
        bottomLabel.fontColor = [SKColor blackColor];
        bottomLabel.fontSize = 20;
        bottomLabel.position = CGPointMake(self.frame.size.width * 0.5,
                                self.frame.size.height * 0.3);
        [self addChild:bottomLabel];

    }
    return self;
}

- (void)touchesBegan:(NSSet *)touches withEvent:(UIEvent *)event {
    SKTransition *transition = [SKTransition doorwayWithDuration:1.0];
    SKScene *game = [[GameScene alloc] initWithSize:self.frame.size];
    [self.view presentScene:game transition:transition];
}

@end
```

Now go back to *GameOverScene.m*, so we can make the game-over scene perform a transition to the start scene. Add this header import:

```
#import "GameOverScene.h"
#import "StartScene.h"
```

And then add the following code:

```
- (void)didMoveToView:(SKView *)view {
    dispatch_after(
            dispatch_time(DISPATCH_TIME_NOW, (int64_t)(3.0 * NSEC_PER_SEC)),
            dispatch_get_main_queue(), ^{
        SKTransition *transition = [SKTransition flipVerticalWithDuration:1.0];
        SKScene *start = [[StartScene alloc] initWithSize:self.frame.size];
        [self.view presentScene:start transition:transition];
    });
}
```

As you saw earlier, the didMoveToView: method is called on any scene after it's been put in place in a view. Here, we simply trigger a three-second pause, followed by a transition back to the start scene.

There's just one more piece of the puzzle to make all our scenes transition to each other as they should. We need to change the app startup procedure so that, instead of jumping right into the game, it shows us the start screen instead. This takes us back to *GameViewController.m*, where we first import the header for our start scene:

```
#import "GameViewController.h"
#import "GameScene.h"
#import "StartScene.h"
```

Then, in the viewDidLoad method, we just replace the code to create one scene class with another:

```
// Create and configure the scene.
GameScene *scene =
        [GameScene sceneWithSize:self.view.frame.size levelNumber:1];
SKScene * scene = [StartScene sceneWithSize:skView.bounds.size];
```

Now give it a whirl! Launch the app, and you'll be greeted by the start scene. Touch the screen, play the game, die a lot, and you'll get to the game-over scene. Wait a few seconds, and you're back to the start screen, as shown in Figure 17-17.

Figure 17-17. *Finally, we made it to the start screen!*

A Sound Is Worth a Thousand Pictures

We've been working on a video game, and video games are known for being noisy, but ours is completely silent! Fortunately, Sprite Kit contains audio playback code that's extremely easy to use. In the *17 – Sound Effects* folder in the source code for this chapter, you'll find the prepared audio files: *enemyHit.wav*, *gameOver.wav*, *gameStart.wav*, *playerHit.wav*, and *shoot.wav*. Drag all of them into Xcode's Project Navigator.

Note   These sound effects were created using the excellent, open source CFXR application (available from `https://github.com/nevyn/cfxr`). If you need quirky little sound effects, CFXR is hard to beat!

Now we'll bake in easy playback for each of these sound effects. Start with *BulletNode.m*, adding the bold code to the end of the bulletFrom:toward: method, just before the return line:

```
[bullet runAction:[SKAction playSoundFileNamed:@"shoot.wav"
                          waitForCompletion:NO]];
```

Next, switch over *to EnemyNode.m*, adding these lines to the end of the receiveAttacker:contact: method:

```
[self runAction:[SKAction playSoundFileNamed:@"enemyHit.wav"
                        waitForCompletion:NO]];
```

Now do something extremely similar in *PlayerNode.m*, adding these lines to the end of the receiveAttacker:contact: method:

```
[self runAction:[SKAction playSoundFileNamed:@"playerHit.wav"
                        waitForCompletion:NO]];
```

Those are enough in-game sounds to satisfy for the moment. Go ahead and run the game at this point to try them out. I think you'll agree that the simple addition of particles and sounds gives the game a much better feel.

Now let's just add some effects for starting the game and ending the game. In *StartScene.m*, add these lines at the end of the touchesBegan:withEvent: method:

```
[self runAction:[SKAction playSoundFileNamed:@"gameStart.wav"
                        waitForCompletion:NO]];
```

And finally, add these lines to the end of the triggerGameOver method in *GameScene.m*:

```
[self runAction:[SKAction playSoundFileNamed:@"gameOver.wav"
                        waitForCompletion:NO]];
```

Now when you play the game, you'll be inundated by comforting bleeps and bloops, just like when you were a kid! Or maybe when your parents were kids. Or your grandparents! Just trust me, all the games used to sound pretty much like this.

Making the Game a Little Harder: Force Fields

One of the more interesting new features added to Sprite Kit in iOS 8 is the ability to place force fields in a scene. A force field has a type, a location, a region in which it takes effect, and several other properties that specify how it behaves. The idea is that the field perturbs the motion of objects as they move through its region. There are various standard force fields that you can use, just by creating and configuring an instance and adding it to a scene. If you are feeling ambitious, you can even create custom force fields. For a list of the standard force fields and their behaviors, which include gravity fields, electric and magnetic fields, and turbulence, look at the API documentation for the SKFieldNode class.

To make our game a little more challenging, we're going to add some radial gravity fields to the scene. Radial gravity fields act like a large mass concentrated at a point. As an object moves through the region of a radial gravity field, it will be deflected toward it (or away from it, if you want to configure it that way), much like a meteor passing close enough to the Earth would be as it flies past. We're going to arrange for our gravity fields to act on missiles, so that you won't always be able to directly aim at an enemy and be sure of hitting it. Let's get started.

First, we need to add a new category to *PhysicsCategories.h*. Make the following change in that file, not forgetting to add the comma at the end of the definition of `PlayerMissileCategory`:

```
typedef NS_OPTIONS(uint32_t, PhysicsCategory) {
    PlayerCategory        = 1 << 1,
    EnemyCategory         = 1 << 2,
    PlayerMissileCategory = 1 << 3,
    GravityFieldCategory  = 1 << 4
};
```

A field acts on a node if the `fieldBitMask` in the node's physics body has any category in common with the field's `categoryBitMask`. By default, a physics body's `fieldBitMask` has all categories set. Since we don't want enemies to be affected by the gravity field, we need to clear its `fieldBitMask` by adding the following code in *EnemyNode.m*:

```
- (void)initPhysicsBody {
    SKPhysicsBody *body = [SKPhysicsBody bodyWithRectangleOfSize:
                            CGSizeMake(40, 40)];
    body.affectedByGravity = NO;
    body.categoryBitMask = EnemyCategory;
    body.contactTestBitMask = PlayerCategory|EnemyCategory;
    body.mass = 0.2;
    body.angularDamping = 0.0f;
    body.linearDamping = 0.0f;
    body.fieldBitMask = 0;
    self.physicsBody = body;
}
```

Make a similar change in *PlayerNode.m*:

```
- (void)initPhysicsBody {
    SKPhysicsBody *body = [SKPhysicsBody bodyWithRectangleOfSize:
                            CGSizeMake(20, 20)];
    body.affectedByGravity = NO;
    body.categoryBitMask = PlayerCategory;
    body.contactTestBitMask = EnemyCategory;
    body.collisionBitMask = 0;
    body.fieldBitMask = 0;
    self.physicsBody = body;
}
```

The missile nodes will respond to the gravity field even if we don't do anything, since their physics nodes have all field categories set by default, but it's cleaner if we make this explicit, so make the following change in *BulletNode.m*:

```
- (instancetype)init {
    if (self = [super init]) {
        SKLabelNode *dot = [SKLabelNode labelNodeWithFontNamed:@"Courier"];
        dot.fontColor = [SKColor blackColor];
        dot.fontSize = 40;
        dot.text = @".";
        [self addChild:dot];

        SKPhysicsBody *body = [SKPhysicsBody bodyWithCircleOfRadius:1];
        body.dynamic = YES;
        body.categoryBitMask = PlayerMissileCategory;
        body.contactTestBitMask = EnemyCategory;
        body.collisionBitMask = EnemyCategory;
        body.fieldBitMask = GravityFieldCategory;
        body.mass = 0.01;

        self.physicsBody = body;
        self.name = [NSString stringWithFormat:@"Bullet %p", self];
    }
    return self;
}
```

The rest of the changes are going to be in the file *GameScene.m*. We're going to add three gravity fields centered at random points just below the center of the scene. As we did with the missiles and enemies, we'll add the force field nodes to a parent node that we'll then add to the scene. Add the definition of the parent node to the class extension of GameScene:

```
@interface GameScene () <SKPhysicsContactDelegate>

@property (strong, nonatomic) PlayerNode *playerNode;
@property (strong, nonatomic) SKNode *enemies;
@property (strong, nonatomic) SKNode *playerBullets;
@property (strong, nonatomic) SKNode *forceFields;

@end
```

At the end of the initWithSize:level: method, add code to allocate the forceFields node, add it to the scene, and create the actual force field nodes:

```
_playerBullets = [SKNode node];
[self addChild:_playerBullets];

_forceFields = [SKNode node];
[self addChild:_forceFields];
[self createForceFields];

self.physicsWorld.gravity = CGVectorMake(0, -1);
self.physicsWorld.contactDelegate = self;
```

Finally, add the implementation of the createForceFields method:

```
- (void)createForceFields {
    static int fieldCount = 3;
    CGSize size = self.frame.size;
    float sectionWidth = size.width/fieldCount;
    for (NSUInteger i = 0; i < fieldCount; i++) {
        CGFloat x = i * sectionWidth + arc4random_uniform(sectionWidth);
        CGFloat y = arc4random_uniform(size.height * 0.25)
                    + (size.height * 0.25);

        SKFieldNode *gravityField = [SKFieldNode radialGravityField];
        gravityField.position = CGPointMake(x, y);
        gravityField.categoryBitMask = GravityFieldCategory;
        gravityField.strength = 4;
        gravityField.falloff = 2;
        gravityField.region = [[SKRegion alloc]
                initWithSize:CGSizeMake(size.width * 0.3, size.height * 0.1)];
        [self.forceFields addChild:gravityField];

        SKLabelNode *fieldLocationNode =
                [SKLabelNode labelNodeWithFontNamed:@"Courier"];
        fieldLocationNode.fontSize = 16;
        fieldLocationNode.fontColor = [SKColor redColor];
        fieldLocationNode.name = @"GravityField";
        fieldLocationNode.text = @"*";
        fieldLocationNode.position = CGPointMake(x, y);
        [self.forceFields addChild:fieldLocationNode];
    }
}
```

All force fields are represented by instances of the SKFieldNode class. For each type of field, the SKFieldNode class has a factory method that lets you create a node of that field's type. Here, we use the radialGravityFieldNode method to create three instances of a radial gravity field and we place them in a band just below the center of the scene. The strength and falloff properties control how strong the gravity field is and how rapidly it diminishes with the distance from the field node. A falloff value of 2 makes the force proportional to the inverse square of the distance between the field node and the affected object, just like in the real world. A positive force makes the field node attract the other object. Experiment with different strength values, including negative ones, to see how the effect varies. We also create three SKLabelNodes at the same positions as the gravity force fields, so that the player can see where they are. That's all we need to do. Build and run the app and watch what happens when your bullets fly close to one of the red asterisks in the scene!

Game On

Although TextShooter may be simple in appearance, the techniques you've learned in this chapter form the basis for all sorts of game development using Sprite Kit. You've learned how to organize your code across multiple node classes, group objects together using the node graph, and more. You've also been given a taste of what it's like to build this sort of game one feature at a time, discovering each step along the way. Of course, we're not showing you all of our own missteps made along the way—this book is already over 700 pages long without that—but even counting those, this app really was built from scratch, in roughly the order shown in this chapter, in just a few short hours.

Once you get going, Sprite Kit allows you to build up a lot of structure in a short amount of time. As you've seen, you can use text-based sprites if you don't have images handy. And if you want to swap them out for real graphics later, it's no problem. One early reader even pointed out a middle path: "Instead of plain old ASCII text in the strings in your source code, you can insert emoji characters by using Apple's Character Viewer input source." Accomplishing this is left as an exercise to the reader!

Chapter 18

Taps, Touches, and Gestures

The screens of the iPhone, iPod touch, and iPad—with their crisp, bright, touch-sensitive display—are truly things of beauty and masterpieces of engineering. The multitouch screen common to all iOS devices is one of the key factors in the platform's tremendous usability. Because the screen can detect multiple touches at the same time and track them independently, applications are able to detect a wide range of gestures, giving the user power that goes beyond the interface.

Suppose you are in the Mail application staring at a long list of junk e-mail that you want to delete. You can tap each one individually, tap the trash icon to delete it, and then wait for the next message to download, deleting each one in turn. This method is best if you want to read each message before you delete it.

Alternatively, from the list of messages, you can tap the **Edit** button in the upper-right corner, tap each e-mail row to mark it, and then hit the **Trash** button to delete all marked messages. This method is best if you don't need to read each message before deleting it. Another alternative is to swipe across a message in the list from right to left. That gesture produces a **More** button and a **Trash** button for that message. Tap the **Trash** button, and the message is deleted.

This example is just one of the countless gestures that are made possible by the multitouch display. You can pinch your fingers together to zoom out while viewing a picture or reverse-pinch to zoom in. On the home screen, you can long-press an icon to turn on "jiggly mode," which allows you to delete applications from your iOS device.

In this chapter, we're going to look at the underlying architecture that lets you detect gestures. You'll learn how to detect the most common gestures, as well as how to create and detect a completely new gesture.

Multitouch Terminology

Before we dive into the architecture, let's go over some basic vocabulary. First, a **gesture** is any sequence of events that happens from the time you touch the screen with one or more fingers until you lift your fingers off the screen. No matter how long it takes, as long as one or more fingers remain against the screen, you are still within a gesture (unless a system event, such as an incoming phone call, interrupts it). Note that Cocoa Touch doesn't expose any class or structure that represents a gesture. In some sense, a gesture is a verb, and a running app can watch the user input stream to see if one is happening.

A gesture is passed through the system inside a series of **events**. Events are generated when you interact with the device's multitouch screen. They contain information about the touch or touches that occurred.

The term **touch** refers to a finger being placed on the screen, dragging across the screen, or being lifted from the screen. The number of touches involved in a gesture is equal to the number of fingers on the screen at the same time. You can actually put all five fingers on the screen, and as long as they aren't too close to each other, iOS can recognize and track them all. Now there aren't many useful five-finger gestures, but it's nice to know the iOS can handle one if necessary. In fact, experimentation has shown that the iPad can handle up to 11 simultaneous touches! This may seem excessive, but could be useful if you're working on a multiplayer game, in which several players are interacting with the screen at the same time.

A **tap** happens when you touch the screen with a finger and then immediately lift your finger off the screen without moving it around. The iOS device keeps track of the number of taps and can tell you if the user double-tapped, triple-tapped, or even 20-tapped. It handles all the timing and other work necessary to differentiate between two single-taps and a double-tap, for example.

A **gesture recognizer** is an object that knows how to watch the stream of events generated by a user and recognize when the user is touching and dragging in a way that matches a predefined gesture. The UIGestureRecognizer class and its various subclasses can help take a lot of work off your hands when you want to watch for common gestures. This class nicely encapsulates the work of looking for a gesture and can be easily applied to any view in your application.

In the first part of this chapter, you'll see the events that are reported when the user touches the screen with one or more fingers, and how to track the movement of fingers on the screen. You can use these events to handle gestures in a custom view or in your application delegate. Next, we'll look at some of the gesture recognizers that come with the iOS SDK, and finally, you'll see how to build your own gesture recognizer.

The Responder Chain

Since gestures are passed through the system inside events, and events are passed through the **responder chain**, you need to have an understanding of how the responder chain works in order to handle gestures properly. If you've worked with Cocoa for Mac OS X, you're probably familiar with the concept of a responder chain, as the same basic mechanism is used in both Cocoa and Cocoa Touch. If this is new material, don't worry; we'll explain how it works.

Responding to Events

Several times in this book, we've mentioned the first responder, which is usually the object with which the user is currently interacting. The first responder is the start of the responder chain, but it's not alone. There are always other responders in the chain as well. In a running application, the responder chain is a changing set of objects that are able to respond to user events. Any class that has UIResponder as one of its superclasses is a **responder**. UIView is a subclass of UIResponder, and `UIControl` is a subclass of `UIView`, so all views and all controls are responders. `UIViewController` is also a subclass of `UIResponder`, meaning that it is a responder, as are all of its subclasses, such as `UINavigationController` and `UITabBarController`. Responders, then, are so named because they respond to system-generated events, such as screen touches.

If a responder doesn't handle a particular event, such as a gesture, it usually passes that event up the responder chain. If the next object in the chain responds to that particular event, it will usually consume the event, which stops the event's progression through the responder chain. In some cases, if a responder only partially handles an event, that responder will take an action and forward the event to the next responder in the chain. That's not usually what happens, though. Normally, when an object responds to an event, that's the end of the line for the event. If the event goes through the entire responder chain and no object handles the event, the event is then discarded.

Let's take a more specific look at the responder chain. An event first gets delivered to the `UIApplication` object, which in turn passes it to the application's `UIWindow`. The `UIWindow` handles the event by selecting an initial responder. The initial responder is chosen as follows:

- In the case of a touch event, the `UIWindow` object determines the view that the user touched, and then offers the event to any gesture recognizers that are registered for that view or any view higher up the view hierarchy. If any gesture recognizer handles the event, it goes no further. If not, the initial responder is the touched view and the event will be delivered to it.

- For an event generated by the user shaking the device (which we'll say more about in Chapter 20) or from a remote control device, the event is delivered to the first responder.

If the initial responder doesn't handle the event, it passes the event to its parent view, if there is one, or to the view controller if the view is the view controller's view. If the view controller doesn't handle the event, it continues up the responder chain through the view hierarchy of its parent view controller, if it has one.

If the event makes it all the way up through the view hierarchy without being handled by a view or a controller, the event is passed to the application's window. If the window doesn't handle the event, the `UIApplication` object will pass it to the application delegate, if the delegate is a subclass of `UIResponder` (which it normally is if you create your project from one of Apple's application templates). Finally, if the app delegate isn't a subclass of `UIResponder` or doesn't handle the event, then the event goes gently into the good night.

This process is important for a number of reasons. First, it controls the way gestures can be handled. Let's say a user is looking at a table and swipes a finger across a row of that table. What object handles that gesture?

If the swipe is within a view or control that's a subview of the table view cell, that view or control will get a chance to respond. If it doesn't respond, the table view cell gets a chance. In an application like Mail, in which a swipe can be used to delete a message, the table view cell probably needs to look at that event to see if it contains a swipe gesture. Most table view cells don't respond to gestures, however. If they don't respond, the event proceeds up to the table view, and then up the rest of the responder chain until something responds to that event or it reaches the end of the line.

Forwarding an Event: Keeping the Responder Chain Alive

Let's take a step back to that table view cell in the Mail application. We don't know the internal details of the Apple Mail application; however, let's assume that the table view cell handles the delete swipe and only the delete swipe. That table view cell must implement the methods related to receiving touch events (discussed shortly) so that it can check to see if that event could be interpreted as part of a swipe gesture. If the event matches a swipe that the table view is looking for, then the table view cell takes an action, and that's that; the event goes no further.

If the event doesn't match the table view cell's swipe gesture, the table view cell is responsible for forwarding that event manually to the next object in the responder chain. If it doesn't do its forwarding job, the table and other objects up the chain will never get a chance to respond, and the application may not function as the user expects. That table view cell could prevent other views from recognizing a gesture.

Whenever you respond to a touch event, you need to keep in mind that your code doesn't work in a vacuum. If an object intercepts an event that it doesn't handle, it needs to pass it along manually. One way to do this is to call the same method on the next responder. Here's a bit of fictional code:

```
- (void)respondToFictionalEvent:(UIEvent *)event {
    if ([self shouldHandleEvent:event]) {
        [self handleEvent:event];
    } else {
        [[self nextResponder] respondToFictionalEvent:event];
    }
}
```

Notice that we call the same method on the next responder. That's how to be a good responder-chain citizen. Fortunately, most of the time, methods that respond to an event also consume the event. However, it's important to know that if that's not the case, you need to make sure the event is passed along to the next link in the responder chain.

The Multitouch Architecture

Now that you know a little about the responder chain, let's look at the process of handling gestures. As we've indicated, gestures are passed along the responder chain, embedded in events. This means that the code to handle any kind of interaction with the multitouch screen needs to be contained in an object in the responder chain. Generally, that means we can choose to either embed that code in a subclass of UIView or embed the code in a UIViewController.

So, does this code belong in the view or in the view controller?

If the view needs to do something to itself based on the user's touches, the code probably belongs in the class that defines that view. For example, many control classes, such as UISwitch and UISlider, respond to touch-related events. A UISwitch might want to turn itself on or off based on a touch. The folks who created the UISwitch class embedded gesture-handling code in the class so the UISwitch can respond to a touch.

Often, however, when the gesture being processed affects more than the object being touched, the gesture code really belongs in the relevant view controller class. For example, if the user makes a gesture touching one row that indicates that all rows should be deleted, the gesture should be handled by code in the view controller. The way you respond to touches and gestures in both situations is exactly the same, regardless of the class to which the code belongs.

The Four Touch Notification Methods

Four methods are used to notify a responder about touches. When the user first touches the screen, the system looks for a responder that has a method called touchesBegan:withEvent:. To find out when the user first begins a gesture or taps the screen, implement this method in your view or your view controller. Here's an example of what that method might look like:

```
- (void)touchesBegan:(NSSet *)touches withEvent:(UIEvent *)event  {
    NSUInteger numTaps = [[touches anyObject] tapCount];
    NSUInteger numTouches = [event.allTouches count];

    // Do something here.
}
```

This method (and each of the touch-related methods) is passed an NSSet instance called touches and an instance of UIEvent, which has a property called allTouches that is another set of touches. Here's a simple description of what these two sets of touches contain:

- The allTouches property contains one UITouch object for each finger that is currently pressed against the screen, whether or not that finger is currently moving.

- The NSSet passed as the touches argument contains one UITouch object for each finger that has just been added or removed from the screen or which has just moved or stopped moving. In other words, it tells you what changed between this call and the last time one of your touch notification methods was called.

Each time a finger touches the screen for the first time, a new UITouch object is allocated to represent that finger and added to the set that is delivered in the allTouches property of each UIEvent. All future events that report activity for that same finger will contain the same UITouch instance in both the allTouches set and in the touches argument (although in the latter case, it will not be present if there is no activity to report for that finger), until that finger is removed from the screen. Thus, to track the activity of any given finger, you need to monitor its UITouch object.

You can determine the number of fingers currently pressed against the screen by getting a count of the objects in allTouches. If the event reports a touch that is part of a series of taps by any given finger, you can get the tap count from the tapCount property of the UITouch object for that finger. If there's only one finger touching the screen, or if you don't care which finger you ask about, you can quickly get a UITouch object to query by using the anyObject method of NSSet. In the preceding example, a numTaps value of 2 tells you that the screen was tapped twice in quick succession by at least one finger. Similarly, a numTouches value of 2 tells you the user has two fingers touching the screen.

Not all of the objects in touches or allTouches may be relevant to the view or view controller in which you've implemented this method. A table view cell, for example, probably doesn't care about touches that are in other rows or that are in the navigation bar. You can get the touches that fall within a particular view from the event:

```
NSSet *myTouches = [event touchesForView:self.view];
```

Every UITouch represents a different finger, and each finger is located at a different position on the screen. You can find out the position of a specific finger using the UITouch object. It will even translate the point into the view's local coordinate system if you ask it to:

```
CGPoint point = [touch locationInView:self.view];
```

You can get notified while the user is moving fingers across the screen by implementing touchesMoved:withEvent:. This method is called multiple times during a long drag, and each time it is called, you will get another set of touches and another event. In addition to being able to find out each finger's current position from the UITouch objects, you can also discover the previous location of that touch, which is the finger's position the last time either touchesMoved:withEvent: or touchesBegan:withEvent: was called.

When any of the user's fingers is removed from the screen, another method, touchesEnded:withEvent:, is invoked. When this method is called, you know that the user is finished with a gesture.

There's one final touch-related method that responders might implement. It's called touchesCancelled:withEvent:, and it is called if the user is in the middle of a gesture when something happens to interrupt it, like the phone ringing. This is where you can do any cleanup you might need so you can start fresh with a new gesture. When this method is called, touchesEnded:withEvent: will not be called for the current gesture.

OK, enough theory—let's see some of this in action.

The TouchExplorer Application

We're going to build a little application that will give you a better feel for when the four touch-related responder methods are called. In Xcode, create a new project using the Single View Application template. Enter **TouchExplorer** as the Product Name and select **Universal** from the Devices pop-up.

TouchExplorer will print messages to the screen that indicate the touch and tap count every time a touch-related method is called (see Figure 18-1).

Figure 18-1. *The TouchExplorer application*

> **Note**   Although the applications in this chapter will run on the simulator, you won't be able to see all the
> available multitouch functionality unless you run them on a real iOS device. If you have a paid membership in
> Apple's iOS Developer Program, you have the ability to run the programs you write on your device of choice.
> The Apple web site does a great job of walking you through the process of getting everything you need to
> prepare to connect Xcode to your device.

We need three labels for this application: one to indicate which method was last called, another
to report the current tap count, and a third to report the number of touches. Single-click
ViewController.m and add three outlets to the class extension at the top of the file:

```
#import "ViewController.h"

@interface ViewController ()
```

```
@property (weak, nonatomic) IBOutlet UILabel *messageLabel;
@property (weak, nonatomic) IBOutlet UILabel *tapsLabel;
@property (weak, nonatomic) IBOutlet UILabel *touchesLabel;
```

@end

Now select *Main.storyboard* to edit the GUI. You'll see the usual empty view contained in all new projects of this kind. Drag a label onto the view, using the blue guidelines to place the label toward the upper-left corner of the view. Hold down the **Option** key and drag two more labels out from the original, spacing them one below the other. This leaves you with three labels (see Figure 18-1). Feel free to play with the fonts and colors if you're feeling a bit like Picasso.

Now we need to set the auto layout constraints for the labels. In the Document Outline, Control-drag from the first label to the main view and release the mouse. Hold down the **Shift** key and select **Top Space to Top Layout Guide** and **Leading Space to Container Margin**, and then click outside the pop-up with the mouse. Do the same for the other three labels.

The next step is to connect the labels to their outlets. Control-drag from the **View Controller** icon to each of the three labels, connecting the top one to the **messageLabel** outlet, the middle one to the **tapsLabel** outlet, and the last one to the **touchesLabel** outlet.

Finally, double-click each label and press the **Delete** key to get rid of its text.

Next, single-click either the background of the view you've been working on or the **View** icon in the Document Outline, and then bring up the Attributes Inspector (see Figure 18-2). On the Inspector, go to the View section and make sure that both **User Interaction Enabled** and **Multiple Touch** are checked. If **Multiple Touch** is not checked, your controller class's touch methods will always receive one and only one touch, no matter how many fingers are actually touching the phone's screen.

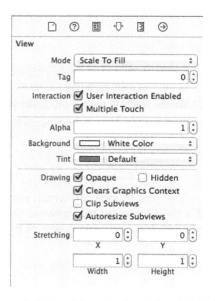

Figure 18-2.   In the View attributes, make sure both User Interaction Enabled and Multiple Touch are checked

When you're finished, switch back *ViewController.m* and add the following code to the class's @implementation section:.

```objc
@implementation ViewController

- (void)viewDidLoad
{
    [super viewDidLoad];
    // Do any additional setup after loading the view, typically from a nib.
}

- (void)didReceiveMemoryWarning
{
    [super didReceiveMemoryWarning];
    // Dispose of any resources that can be recreated.
}

- (void)updateLabelsFromTouches:(NSSet *)touches {
    NSUInteger numTaps = [[touches anyObject] tapCount];
    NSString *tapsMessage = [[NSString alloc]
                              initWithFormat:@"%ld taps detected", (unsigned long)numTaps];
    self.tapsLabel.text = tapsMessage;

    NSUInteger numTouches = [touches count];
    NSString *touchMsg = [[NSString alloc] initWithFormat:
                          @"%ld touches detected", (unsigned long)numTouches];
    self.touchesLabel.text = touchMsg;
}

#pragma mark - Touch Event Methods
- (void)touchesBegan:(NSSet *)touches withEvent:(UIEvent *)event {
    self.messageLabel.text = @"Touches Began";
    [self updateLabelsFromTouches:event.allTouches];
}

- (void)touchesCancelled:(NSSet *)touches withEvent:(UIEvent *)event {
    self.messageLabel.text = @"Touches Cancelled";
    [self updateLabelsFromTouches: event.allTouches];
}

- (void)touchesEnded:(NSSet *)touches withEvent:(UIEvent *)event {
    self.messageLabel.text = @"Touches Ended.";
    [self updateLabelsFromTouches: event.allTouches];
}

- (void)touchesMoved:(NSSet *)touches withEvent:(UIEvent *)event {
    self.messageLabel.text = @"Drag Detected";
    [self updateLabelsFromTouches: event.allTouches];
}

@end
```

In this controller class, we implement all four of the touch-related methods we discussed earlier. Each one sets messageLabel so the user can see when each method has been called. Next, all four of them call updateLabelsFromTouches: to update the other two labels. The updateLabelsFromTouches: method gets the tap count from one of the touches, figures out the number of fingers touch the screen by looking at the count property of the set of touches that it receives, and updates the labels with that information.

Compile and run the application. If you're running in the simulator, try repeatedly clicking the screen to drive up the tap count. You should also try clicking and holding down the mouse button while dragging around the view to simulate a touch and drag.

You can emulate a two-finger pinch in the iOS simulator by holding down the **Option** key while you click with the mouse and drag. You can also simulate two-finger swipes by first holding down the **Option** key to simulate a pinch, moving the mouse so the two dots representing virtual fingers are next to each other, and then holding down the **Shift** key (while still holding down the **Option** key). Pressing the **Shift** key will lock the position of the two fingers relative to each other, enabling you to do swipes and other two-finger gestures. You won't be able to do gestures that require three or more fingers, but you can do most two-finger gestures on the simulator using combinations of the **Option** and **Shift** keys.

If you're able to run this program on a device, see how many touches you can get to register at the same time. Try dragging with one finger, followed by two fingers, and then three. Try double- and triple-tapping the screen, and see if you can get the tap count to go up by tapping with two fingers.

Play around with the TouchExplorer application until you feel comfortable with what's happening and with the way that the four touch methods work. When you're ready, continue on to see how to detect one of the most common gestures: the swipe.

The Swipes Application

The application we're about to build does nothing more than detect swipes, both horizontal and vertical. If you swipe your finger across the screen from left to right, right to left, top to bottom, or bottom to top, the app will display a message across the top of the screen for a few seconds, informing you that a swipe was detected (see Figure 18-3).

Figure 18-3. *The Swipes application will detect both vertical and horizontal swipes*

Using Touch Events to Detect Swipes

Detecting swipes is relatively easy. We're going to define a minimum gesture length in pixels, which is how far the user needs to swipe before the gesture counts as a swipe. We'll also define a variance, which is how far from a straight line our user can veer and still have the gesture count as a horizontal or vertical swipe. A diagonal line generally won't count as a swipe, but one that's just a little off from horizontal or vertical will.

When the user touches the screen, we'll save the location of the first touch in a variable. We'll then check as the user's finger moves across the screen to see if it reaches a point where it has gone far enough and straight enough to count as a swipe. There's actually a built-in gesture recognizer that does exactly this, but we're going to use what we've learned about touch events to make one of our own. Let's build it.

Create a new project in Xcode using the Single View Application template, set Devices to *Universal*, and name the project *Swipes*.

Single-click *ViewController.m* and add the following code to the class extension near the top:

```
#import "ViewController.h"

@interface ViewController ()

@property (weak, nonatomic) IBOutlet UILabel *label;
@property (nonatomic) CGPoint gestureStartPoint;

@end
```

This code declares an outlet for our one label and a variable to hold the first spot the user touches.

Select *Main.storyboard* to open it for editing. Make sure that the view controller's view is set so **User Interaction Enabled** and **Multiple Touch** are both checked using the Attributes Inspector, and drag a label from the library and drop it in the upper portion of the View window. Set the text alignment to center and feel free to play with the other text attributes to make the label easier to read. In the Document Outline, Control-drag from the label to the view, release the mouse, hold down **Shift** and select **Top Space to Top Layout Guide** and **Center Horizontally in Container**, and then click outside the pop-up with the mouse. Control-drag from the **View Controller** icon to the label and connect it to the **label** outlet. Finally, double-click the label and delete its text.

Then switch over to *ViewController.m* and add the bold code shown here:

```
static CGFloat const kMinimumGestureLength = 25;
static CGFloat const kMaximumVariance      = 5;

@implementation ViewController

- (void)viewDidLoad
{
    [super viewDidLoad];
    // Do any additional setup after loading the view, typically from a nib.
}

- (void)didReceiveMemoryWarning
{
    [super didReceiveMemoryWarning];
    // Dispose of any resources that can be recreated.
}

#pragma mark - Touch Handling

- (void)touchesBegan:(NSSet *)touches withEvent:(UIEvent *)event {
    UITouch *touch = [touches anyObject];
    self.gestureStartPoint = [touch locationInView:self.view];
}

- (void)touchesMoved:(NSSet *)touches withEvent:(UIEvent *)event {
    UITouch *touch = [touches anyObject];
    CGPoint currentPosition = [touch locationInView:self.view];
```

```
    CGFloat deltaX = fabsf(self.gestureStartPoint.x - currentPosition.x);
    CGFloat deltaY = fabsf(self.gestureStartPoint.y - currentPosition.y);

    if (deltaX >=kMinimumGestureLength && deltaY <= kMaximumVariance) {
        self.label.text = @"Horizontal swipe detected";
        dispatch_after(dispatch_time(DISPATCH_TIME_NOW, 2 * NSEC_PER_SEC),
                      dispatch_get_main_queue(),
                      ^{ self.label.text = @""; });
    } else if (deltaY >=kMinimumGestureLength &&
              deltaX <= kMaximumVariance){
        self.label.text = @"Vertical swipe detected";
        dispatch_after(dispatch_time(DISPATCH_TIME_NOW, 2 * NSEC_PER_SEC),
                      dispatch_get_main_queue(),
                      ^{ self.label.text = @""; });
    }
}
@end
```

Let's start with the touchesBegan:withEvent: method. All we do there is grab any touch from the touches set and store its touch point. We're primarily interested in single-finger swipes right now, so we don't worry about how many touches there are; we just grab one of them:

```
UITouch *touch = [touches anyObject];
self.gestureStartPoint = [touch locationInView:self.view];
```

We're using the UITouch objects in the touches argument instead of the ones in the UIEvent because we're interested in tracking changes as they happen, not in the overall state of all of the active touches.

In the next method, touchesMoved:withEvent:, we do the real work. First, we get the current position of the user's finger:

```
UITouch *touch = [touches anyObject];
CGPoint currentPosition = [touch locationInView:self.view];
```

After that, we calculate how far the user's finger has moved both horizontally and vertically from its starting position. fabsf() is a function from the standard C math library that returns the absolute value of a float. This allows us to subtract one from the other without needing to worry about which is the higher value:

```
CGFloat deltaX = fabsf(self.gestureStartPoint.x - currentPosition.x);
CGFloat deltaY = fabsf(self.gestureStartPoint.y - currentPosition.y);
```

Once we have the two deltas, we check to see if the user has moved far enough in one direction without having moved too far in the other to constitute a swipe. If that's true, we set the label's text to indicate whether a horizontal or vertical swipe was detected. We also use the GCD dispatch_async() function to erase the text after it has been on the screen for 2 seconds. That way, the user can practice multiple swipes without needing to worry whether the label is referring to an earlier attempt or the most recent one:

```
if (deltaX >=kMinimumGestureLength && deltaY <= kMaximumVariance) {
    self.label.text = @"Horizontal swipe detected";
    dispatch_after(dispatch_time(DISPATCH_TIME_NOW, 2 * NSEC_PER_SEC),
                    dispatch_get_main_queue(),
                    ^{ self.label.text = @""; });
} else if (deltaY >=kMinimumGestureLength &&
        deltaX <= kMaximumVariance){
    self.label.text = @"Vertical swipe detected";
    dispatch_after(dispatch_time(DISPATCH_TIME_NOW, 2 * NSEC_PER_SEC),
                    dispatch_get_main_queue(),
                    ^{ self.label.text = @""; });
}
```

Go ahead and compile and run the application. If you find yourself clicking and dragging with no visible results, be patient. Click and drag straight down or straight across until you get the hang of swiping.

Automatic Gesture Recognition

The procedure we just used for detecting a swipe wasn't too bad. All the complexity is in the touchesMoved:withEvent: method, and even that wasn't all that complicated. But there's an even easier way to do this. iOS includes a class called UIGestureRecognizer, which eliminates the need for watching all the events to see how fingers are moving. You don't use UIGestureRecognizer directly, but instead create an instance of one of its subclasses, each of which is designed to look for a particular type of gesture, such as a swipe, pinch, double-tap, triple-tap, and so on.

Let's see how to modify the Swipes app to use a gesture recognizer instead of our hand-rolled procedure. As always, you might want to make a copy of your *Swipes* project folder and start from there.

Start by selecting *ViewController.m* and deleting both the touchesBegan:withEvent: and touchesMoved:withEvent: methods. That's right, you won't need them. Next, add a couple of new methods in their place:

```
- (void)reportHorizontalSwipe:(UIGestureRecognizer *)recognizer {
    self.label.text = @"Horizontal swipe detected";
    dispatch_after(dispatch_time(DISPATCH_TIME_NOW, 2 * NSEC_PER_SEC),
                        dispatch_get_main_queue(),
                        ^{ self.label.text = @""; });
}

- (void)reportVerticalSwipe:(UIGestureRecognizer *)recognizer {
    self.label.text = @"Vertical swipe detected";
    dispatch_after(dispatch_time(DISPATCH_TIME_NOW, 2 * NSEC_PER_SEC),
                        dispatch_get_main_queue(),
                        ^{ self.label.text = @""; });
}
```

These methods implement the actual "functionality" (if you can call it that) that's provided by the swipe gestures, just as the touchesMoved:withEvent: did previously. Now add the new code shown here to the viewDidLoad method:

```
- (void)viewDidLoad
{
    [super viewDidLoad];
    // Do any additional setup after loading the view, typically from a nib.
    UISwipeGestureRecognizer *vertical = [[UISwipeGestureRecognizer alloc]
                        initWithTarget:self action:@selector(reportVerticalSwipe:)];
    vertical.direction = UISwipeGestureRecognizerDirectionUp |
                        UISwipeGestureRecognizerDirectionDown;
    [self.view addGestureRecognizer:vertical];

    UISwipeGestureRecognizer *horizontal = [[UISwipeGestureRecognizer alloc]
                        initWithTarget:self action:@selector(reportHorizontalSwipe:)];
    horizontal.direction = UISwipeGestureRecognizerDirectionLeft |
                        UISwipeGestureRecognizerDirectionRight;
    [self.view addGestureRecognizer:horizontal];
}
```

All we're doing here is creating two gesture recognizers—one that will detect vertical movement and another to detect horizontal movement. When one of them recognizes its configured gesture, it will call either the reportVerticalSwipe: or the reportHorizontalSwipe: method and we'll set the label's text appropriately. There you have it! To sanitize things even further, you can also delete the declaration of the gestureStartPoint property and the two constant values from *ViewController.m*. Now build and run the application to try out the new gesture recognizers!

In terms of total lines of code, there's not much difference between these two approaches for a simple case like this. But the code that uses gesture recognizers is undeniably simpler to understand and easier to write. You don't need to give even a moment's thought to the issue of calculating a finger's movement over time because that's already done for you by the UISwipeGestureRecognizer. And better yet, Apple's gesture recognition system is extendable, which means that if your application requires really complex gestures that aren't covered by any of Apple's recognizers, you can make your own, and keep the complex code (along the lines of what we saw earlier) tucked away in the recognizer class instead of polluting your view controller code. We'll build an example of just such a thing later in this chapter. Meanwhile, run the application and you'll see that it behaves just like the previous version.

Implementing Multiple Swipes

In the Swipes application, we worried about only single-finger swipes, so we just grabbed any object out of the touches set to figure out where the user's finger was during the swipe. This approach is fine if you're interested in only single-finger swipes, the most common type of swipe used.

But what if you want to handle two- or three-finger swipes? In the earliest versions of this book, we dedicated about 50 lines of code, and a fair amount of explanation, to achieving this by tracking multiple UITouch instances across multiple touch events. Now that we have gesture recognizers, this is a solved problem. A UISwipeGestureRecognizer can be configured to recognize any number of simultaneous touches. By default, each instance expects a single finger, but you can configure it to look for any number of fingers pressing the screen at once. Each instance responds only to the exact number of touches you specify, so what we'll do is create a whole bunch of gesture recognizers in a loop.

Make another copy of your *Swipes* project folder.

Edit *ViewController.m* and modify the viewDidLoad method, replacing it with the one shown here:

```
- (void)viewDidLoad
{
    [super viewDidLoad];
    // Do any additional setup after loading the
    // view, typically from a nib.
    for (NSUInteger touchCount = 1; touchCount <= 5; touchCount++) {
        UISwipeGestureRecognizer *vertical;
        vertical = [[UISwipeGestureRecognizer alloc]
                    initWithTarget:self action:@selector(reportVerticalSwipe:)];
        vertical.direction = UISwipeGestureRecognizerDirectionUp |
                            UISwipeGestureRecognizerDirectionDown;
        vertical.numberOfTouchesRequired = touchCount;
        [self.view addGestureRecognizer:vertical];

        UISwipeGestureRecognizer *horizontal;
        horizontal = [[UISwipeGestureRecognizer alloc]
                    initWithTarget:self action:@selector(reportHorizontalSwipe:)];
        horizontal.direction = UISwipeGestureRecognizerDirectionLeft |
                            UISwipeGestureRecognizerDirectionRight;
        horizontal.numberOfTouchesRequired = touchCount;
        [self.view addGestureRecognizer:horizontal];
    }
}
```

Note that in a real application, you might want different numbers of fingers swiping across the screen to trigger different behaviors. You can easily do that using gesture recognizers, simply by having each of them call a different action method.

Now all we need to do is change the logging by adding a method that gives us a handy description of the number of touches, and then using that in the reporting methods, as shown here. Add this method toward the bottom of the ViewController class, just above the two swipe-reporting methods:

```
- (NSString *)descriptionForTouchCount:(NSUInteger)touchCount {
    switch (touchCount) {
        case 1:
            return @"Single";
        case 2:
            return @"Double";
        case 3:
            return @"Triple";
        case 4:
            return @"Quadruple";
```

```
        case 5:
            return @"Quintuple";
        default:
            return @"";
    }
}
```

Next, modify the two swipe-reporting methods as shown:

```
- (void)reportHorizontalSwipe:(UIGestureRecognizer *)recognizer {
    self.label.text = @"Horizontal swipe detected";
    self.label.text = [NSString stringWithFormat:@"%@ Horizontal swipe detected",
                        [self descriptionForTouchCount:[recognizer numberOfTouches]]];
    dispatch_after(dispatch_time(DISPATCH_TIME_NOW, 2 * NSEC_PER_SEC),
                    dispatch_get_main_queue(),
                    ^{ self.label.text = @""; });
}

- (void)reportVerticalSwipe:(UIGestureRecognizer *)recognizer {
    self.label.text = @"Vertical swipe detected";
    self.label.text = [NSString stringWithFormat:@"%@ Vertical swipe detected",
                        [self descriptionForTouchCount:[recognizer numberOfTouches]]];
    dispatch_after(dispatch_time(DISPATCH_TIME_NOW, 2 * NSEC_PER_SEC),
                    dispatch_get_main_queue(),
                    ^{ self.label.text = @""; });
}
```

Compile and run the app. You should be able to trigger double- and triple-swipes in both directions, yet still be able to trigger single-swipes. If you have small fingers, you might even be able to trigger a quadruple- or quintuple-swipe.

> **Tip**   In the simulator, if you hold down the **Option** key, a pair of dots, representing a pair of fingers, will appear. Get them close together, and then hold down the **Shift** key. This will keep the dots in the same position relative to each other, allowing you to move the pair of fingers around the screen. Now click and drag down the screen to simulate a double-swipe. Cool!

With a multiple-finger swipe, one thing to be careful of is that your fingers aren't too close to each other. If two fingers are very close to each other, they may register as only a single touch. Because of this, you shouldn't rely on quadruple- or quintuple-swipes for any important gestures because many people will have fingers that are too big to do those swipes effectively. Also, on the iPad some four- and five-finger gestures are turned on by default at the system level for switching between apps and going to the home screen. These can be turned off in the Settings app, but you're probably better off just not using such gestures in your own apps.

Detecting Multiple Taps

In the TouchExplorer application, we printed the tap count to the screen, so you've already seen how easy it is to detect multiple taps. It's not quite as straightforward as it seems, however, because often you will want to take different actions based on the number of taps. If the user triple-taps, you get notified three separate times. You get a single-tap, a double-tap, and finally a triple-tap. If you want to do something on a double-tap but something completely different on a triple-tap, having three separate notifications could cause a problem, since you will first receive notification of a double-tap, and then a triple-tap. Unless you write your own clever code to take this into account, you'll wind up doing both actions.

Fortunately, the engineers at Apple anticipated this situation, and they provided a mechanism to let multiple gesture recognizers play nicely together, even when they're faced with ambiguous inputs that could seemingly trigger any of them. The basic idea is that you place a restriction on a gesture recognizer, telling it to not trigger its associated method unless some other gesture recognizer fails to trigger its own method.

That seems a bit abstract, so let's make it real. Tap gestures are recognized by the UITapGestureRecognizer class. A tap recognizer can be configured to do its thing when a particular number of taps occur. Imagine that we have a view for which we want to define distinct actions that occur when the user taps once or double-taps. You might start off with something like the following:

```
UITapGestureRecognizer *singleTap = [[UITapGestureRecognizer alloc]
                               initWithTarget:self
                               action:@selector(doSingleTap)];
singleTap.numberOfTapsRequired = 1;
[self.view addGestureRecognizer:singleTap];

UITapGestureRecognizer *doubleTap = [[UITapGestureRecognizer alloc]
                               initWithTarget:self
                               action:@selector(doDoubleTap)];
doubleTap.numberOfTapsRequired = 2;
[self.view addGestureRecognizer:doubleTap];
```

The problem with this piece of code is that the two recognizers are unaware of each other, and they have no way of knowing that the user's actions may be better suited to another recognizer. If the user double-taps the view in the preceding code, the doDoubleTap method will be called, but the doSingleMethod will also be called—twice!—once for each tap.

The way around this is to create a failure requirement. We tell singleTap that it should trigger its action only if doubleTap doesn't recognize and respond to the user input by adding this single line:

```
[singleTap requireGestureRecognizerToFail:doubleTap];
```

This means that, when the user taps once, singleTap doesn't do its work immediately. Instead, singleTap waits until it knows that doubleTap has decided to stop paying attention to the current gesture (that is, the user didn't tap twice). We're going to build on this further with our next project.

In Xcode, create a new project with the Single View Application template. Call this new project *TapTaps* and use the Devices pop-up to choose **Universal**.

This application will have four labels: one each that informs us when it has detected a single-tap, double-tap, triple-tap, and quadruple-tap (see Figure 18-4).

Figure 18-4. The TapTaps application detects up to four sequential taps

We need outlets for the four labels, and we also need separate methods for each tap scenario to simulate what we would have in a real application. We'll also include a method for erasing the text fields. Open *ViewController.m* and make the following changes to the class interface near the top:

```
#import "ViewController.h"

@interface ViewController ()

@property (weak, nonatomic) IBOutlet UILabel *singleLabel;
@property (weak, nonatomic) IBOutlet UILabel *doubleLabel;
@property (weak, nonatomic) IBOutlet UILabel *tripleLabel;
@property (weak, nonatomic) IBOutlet UILabel *quadrupleLabel;

@end
```

Save the file and select *Main.storyboard* to edit the GUI. Once you're there, add four labels to the view from the library and arrange them one above the other. In the Attributes Inspector, set the text alignment for each label to *Center*. In the Document Outline, Control-drag from the top label to its parent view and release the mouse. Hold down **Shift** and select **Top Space to Top Layout Guide** and **Center Horizontally in Container**, and then click outside the pop-up with the mouse. Do the same for the other three labels to set their auto layout constraints. When you're finished, Control-drag from the **View Controller** icon to each label and connect each one to *singleLabel*, *doubleLabel*, *tripleLabel*, and *quadrupleLabel*, respectively. Finally, make sure you double-click each label and press the **Delete** key to get rid of any text.

Now select *ViewController.m* and make the following code changes:

```
@implementation ViewController

- (void)viewDidLoad
{
    [super viewDidLoad];
    // Do any additional setup after loading the view, typically from a nib.
    UITapGestureRecognizer *singleTap =
            [[UITapGestureRecognizer alloc] initWithTarget:self
                                            action:@selector(singleTap)];
    singleTap.numberOfTapsRequired = 1;
    singleTap.numberOfTouchesRequired = 1;
    [self.view addGestureRecognizer:singleTap];

    UITapGestureRecognizer *doubleTap =
            [[UITapGestureRecognizer alloc] initWithTarget:self
                                            action:@selector(doubleTap)];
    doubleTap.numberOfTapsRequired = 2;
    doubleTap.numberOfTouchesRequired = 1;
    [self.view addGestureRecognizer:doubleTap];
    [singleTap requireGestureRecognizerToFail:doubleTap];

    UITapGestureRecognizer *tripleTap =
            [[UITapGestureRecognizer alloc] initWithTarget:self
                                            action:@selector(tripleTap)];
    tripleTap.numberOfTapsRequired = 3;
    tripleTap.numberOfTouchesRequired = 1;
    [self.view addGestureRecognizer:tripleTap];
    [doubleTap requireGestureRecognizerToFail:tripleTap];

    UITapGestureRecognizer *quadrupleTap =
            [[UITapGestureRecognizer alloc] initWithTarget:self
                                            action:@selector(quadrupleTap)];
    quadrupleTap.numberOfTapsRequired = 4;
    quadrupleTap.numberOfTouchesRequired = 1;
    [self.view addGestureRecognizer:quadrupleTap];
    [tripleTap requireGestureRecognizerToFail:quadrupleTap];
}
```

```objc
- (void)didReceiveMemoryWarning
{
    [super didReceiveMemoryWarning];
    // Dispose of any resources that can be recreated.
}

- (void)singleTap {
    self.singleLabel.text = @"Single Tap Detected";
    dispatch_after(dispatch_time(DISPATCH_TIME_NOW, 2 * NSEC_PER_SEC),
                   dispatch_get_main_queue(),
                   ^{ self.singleLabel.text = @""; });
}

- (void)doubleTap {
    self.doubleLabel.text = @"Double Tap Detected";
    dispatch_after(dispatch_time(DISPATCH_TIME_NOW, 2 * NSEC_PER_SEC),
                   dispatch_get_main_queue(),
                   ^{ self.doubleLabel.text = @""; });
}

- (void)tripleTap {
    self.tripleLabel.text = @"Triple Tap Detected";
    dispatch_after(dispatch_time(DISPATCH_TIME_NOW, 2 * NSEC_PER_SEC),
                   dispatch_get_main_queue(),
                   ^{ self.tripleLabel.text = @""; });
}

- (void)quadrupleTap {
    self.quadrupleLabel.text = @"Quadruple Tap Detected";
    dispatch_after(dispatch_time(DISPATCH_TIME_NOW, 2 * NSEC_PER_SEC),
                   dispatch_get_main_queue(),
                   ^{ self.quadrupleLabel.text = @""; });
}

@end
```

The four tap methods do nothing more in this application than set one of the four labels and use dispatch_async() to erase that same label after 2 seconds.

The interesting part of this is what occurs in the viewDidLoad method. We start off simply enough, by setting up a tap gesture recognizer and attaching it to our view:

```objc
UITapGestureRecognizer *singleTap =
        [[UITapGestureRecognizer alloc] initWithTarget:self
                                        action:@selector(singleTap)];
singleTap.numberOfTapsRequired = 1;
singleTap.numberOfTouchesRequired = 1;
[self.view addGestureRecognizer:singleTap];
```

Note that we set both the number of taps (touches in the same position, one after another) required to trigger the action and touches (number of fingers touching the screen at the same time) to 1. After that, we set another tap gesture recognizer to handle a double-tap:

```
UITapGestureRecognizer *doubleTap =
        [[UITapGestureRecognizer alloc] initWithTarget:self
                                  action:@selector(doubleTap)];
doubleTap.numberOfTapsRequired = 2;
doubleTap.numberOfTouchesRequired = 1;
[self.view addGestureRecognizer:doubleTap];
[singleTap requireGestureRecognizerToFail:doubleTap];
```

This is pretty similar to the previous code, right up until that last line, in which we give singleTap some additional context. We are effectively telling singleTap that it should trigger its action only in case some other gesture recognizer—in this case, doubleTap—decides that the current user input isn't what it's looking for.

Let's think about what this means. With those two tap gesture recognizers in place, a single tap in the view will immediately make singleTap think, "Hey, this looks like it's for me." At the same time, doubleTap will think, "Hey, this looks like it *might* be for me, but I'll need to wait for one more tap." Because singleTap is set to wait for doubleTap's "failure," it doesn't send its action method right away; instead, it waits to see what happens with doubleTap.

After that first tap, if another tap occurs immediately, doubleTap says, "Hey, that's mine all right," and it fires its action. At that point, singleTap will realize what happened and give up on that gesture. On the other hand, if a particular amount of time goes by (the amount of time that the system considers to be the maximum length of time between taps in a double-tap), doubleTap will give up, and singleTap will see the failure and finally trigger its event.

The rest of the method goes on to define gesture recognizers for three and four taps, and at each point it configures one gesture to be dependent on the failure of the next:

```
UITapGestureRecognizer *tripleTap =
        [[UITapGestureRecognizer alloc] initWithTarget:self
                                  action:@selector(tripleTap)];
tripleTap.numberOfTapsRequired = 3;
tripleTap.numberOfTouchesRequired = 1;
[self.view addGestureRecognizer:tripleTap];
[doubleTap requireGestureRecognizerToFail:tripleTap];

UITapGestureRecognizer *quadrupleTap =
        [[UITapGestureRecognizer alloc] initWithTarget:self
                                  action:@selector(quadrupleTap)];
quadrupleTap.numberOfTapsRequired = 4;
quadrupleTap.numberOfTouchesRequired = 1;
[self.view addGestureRecognizer:quadrupleTap];
[tripleTap requireGestureRecognizerToFail:quadrupleTap];
```

Note that we don't need to explicitly configure every gesture to be dependent on the failure of each of the higher tap-numbered gestures. That multiple dependency comes about naturally as a result of the chain of failure established in our code. Since singleTap requires the failure of doubleTap,

doubleTap requires the failure of tripleTap, and tripleTap requires the failure of quadrupleTap. By extension, singleTap requires that all of the others fail.

Compile and run the app. Whether you single-, double-, triple-, or quadruple-tap, you should see only one label displayed at the end of the sequence. After about a second and a half, the label will clear itself and you can try again.

Detecting Pinch and Rotation

Another common gesture is the two-finger pinch. It's used in a number of applications (e.g., Mobile Safari, Mail, and Photos) to let you zoom in (if you pinch apart) or zoom out (if you pinch together).

Detecting pinches is really easy, thanks to UIPinchGestureRecognizer. This one is referred to as a **continuous gesture recognizer** because it calls its action method over and over again during the pinch. While the gesture is underway, the recognizer goes through a number of states. When the gesture is recognized, the recognizer is in state UIGestureRecognizerStateBegan and its scale property is set to an initial value of 1.0; for the rest of the gesture, the state is UIGestureRecognizerStateChanged and the scale value goes up and down, relative to how far the user's fingers move from the start. We're going to use the scale value to resize an image. Finally, the state changes to UIGestureRecognizerStateEnded.

Another common gesture is the two-finger rotation. This is also a continuous gesture recognizer and is named UIRotationGestureRecognizer. It has a rotation property that is 0.0 by default when the gesture begins, and then changes from 0.0 to 2.0*PI as the user rotates her fingers. In the next example, we'll use both pinch and rotation gestures.

Create a new project in Xcode, again using the Single View Application template, and call this one *PinchMe*. First, drag and drop the beautiful *yosemite-meadows.png* image from the *18 - Image* folder in the example source code archive (or some other favorite photo of yours) into your project's *Images.xcassets*. Expand the *PinchMe* folder, single-click *ViewController.h*, and make the following change:

```
#import <UIKit/UIKit.h>

@interface ViewController : UIViewController <UIGestureRecognizerDelegate>

@end
```

The big change here is that we make ViewController conform to the UIGestureRecognizerDelegate protocol in order to allow several gesture recognizers to recognize gestures simultaneously.

Now bounce over to *ViewController.m* and make the following changes:

```
#import "ViewController.h"

@interface ViewController ()

@property (strong, nonatomic) UIImageView *imageView;

@end
```

```objc
@implementation ViewController
CGFloat scale, previousScale;
CGFloat rotation, previousRotation;

- (void)viewDidLoad
{
    [super viewDidLoad];
    // Do any additional setup after loading the view, typically from a nib.
    previousScale = 1;

    UIImage *image = [UIImage imageNamed:@"yosemite-meadows"];
    self.imageView = [[UIImageView alloc] initWithImage:image];
    self.imageView.userInteractionEnabled = YES;
    self.imageView.center = self.view.center;
    [self.view addSubview:self.imageView];

    UIPinchGestureRecognizer *pinchGesture =
            [[UIPinchGestureRecognizer alloc]
                                     initWithTarget:self action:@selector(doPinch:)];
    pinchGesture.delegate = self;
    [self.imageView addGestureRecognizer:pinchGesture];

    UIRotationGestureRecognizer *rotationGesture =
            [[UIRotationGestureRecognizer alloc]
                                     initWithTarget:self action:@selector(doRotate:)];
    rotationGesture.delegate = self;
    [self.imageView addGestureRecognizer:rotationGesture];
}

- (BOOL)gestureRecognizer:(UIGestureRecognizer *)gestureRecognizer
                shouldRecognizeSimultaneouslyWithGestureRecognizer:
                            (UIGestureRecognizer *)otherGestureRecognizer {
    return YES;
}

- (void)transformImageView {
    CGAffineTransform t = CGAffineTransformMakeScale(scale * previousScale,
                                                     scale * previousScale);
    t = CGAffineTransformRotate(t, rotation + previousRotation);
    self.imageView.transform = t;
}

- (void)doPinch:(UIPinchGestureRecognizer *)gesture {
    scale = gesture.scale;
    [self transformImageView];
    if (gesture.state == UIGestureRecognizerStateEnded) {
        previousScale = scale * previousScale;
        scale = 1;
    }
}
```

```
- (void)doRotate:(UIRotationGestureRecognizer *)gesture {
    rotation = gesture.rotation;
    [self transformImageView];
    if (gesture.state == UIGestureRecognizerStateEnded) {
        previousRotation = rotation + previousRotation;
        rotation = 0;
    }
}

- (void)didReceiveMemoryWarning
{
    [super didReceiveMemoryWarning];
    // Dispose of any resources that can be recreated.
}

@end
```

First, we define four instance variables for the current and previous scale and rotation. The previous values are the values from a previously triggered and ended gesture recognizer; we need to keep track of these values as well because the UIPinchGestureRecognizer for scaling and UIRotationGestureRecognizer for rotation will always start at the default positions of 1.0 scale and 0.0 rotation:

```
@implementation ViewController {
CGFloat scale, previousScale;
CGFloat rotation, previousRotation;
```

Next, in viewDidLoad, we begin by creating a UIImageView to pinch and rotate, load our Yosemite image into it, and center it in the main view. We must remember to enable user interaction on the image view because UIImageView is one of the few UIKit classes that have user interaction disabled by default.

```
UIImage *image = [UIImage imageNamed:@"yosemite-meadows"];
self.imageView = [[UIImageView alloc] initWithImage:image];
self.imageView.userInteractionEnabled = YES;
self.imageView.center = self.view.center;
[self.view addSubview:self.imageView];
```

Next, we set up a pinch gesture recognizer and a rotation gesture recognizer, and we tell them to notify us when their gestures are recognized via the doPinch: and doRotation: methods, respectively. We tell both to use self as their delegate:

```
UIPinchGestureRecognizer *pinchGesture =
        [[UIPinchGestureRecognizer alloc]
                         initWithTarget:self action:@selector(doPinch:)];
pinchGesture.delegate = self;
[self.imageView addGestureRecognizer:pinchGesture];

UIRotationGestureRecognizer *rotationGesture =
        [[UIRotationGestureRecognizer alloc]
                         initWithTarget:self action:@selector(doRotate:)];
rotationGesture.delegate = self;
[self.imageView addGestureRecognizer:rotationGesture];
```

In the gestureRecognizer:shouldRecognizeSimultaneoslyWithGestureRecognizer: method (which is the only method from the UIGestureRecognizerDelegate protocol that we need to implement) we always return YES to allow our pinch and rotation gestures to work together; otherwise, the gesture recognizer that starts first would always block the other:

```
- (BOOL)gestureRecognizer:(UIGestureRecognizer *)gestureRecognizer
        shouldRecognizeSimultaneouslyWithGestureRecognizer:
                (UIGestureRecognizer *)otherGestureRecognizer {
    return YES;
}
```

Next, we implement a helper method for transforming the image view according to the current scaling and rotation from the gesture recognizers. Notice that we multiply the scale by the previous scale. We also add to the rotation with the previous rotation. This allows us to adjust for pinch and rotation that has been done previously when a new gesture starts from the default 1.0 scale and 0.0 rotation.

```
- (void)transformImageView {
    CGAffineTransform t = CGAffineTransformMakeScale(scale * previousScale,
                                                     scale * previousScale);
    t = CGAffineTransformRotate(t, rotation + previousRotation);
    self.imageView.transform = t;
}
```

Finally we implement the action methods that take the input from the gesture recognizers and update the transformation of the image view. In both doPinch: and doRotate:, we first extract the new scale or rotation values. Next, we update the transformation for the image view. And finally, if the gesture recognizer reports that its gesture has ended by having a state equal to UIGestureRecognizerStateEnded, we store the current correct scale or rotation values, and then reset the current scale or rotation values to the default 1.0 scale or 0.0 rotation:

```
- (void)doPinch:(UIPinchGestureRecognizer *)gesture {
    scale = gesture.scale;
    [self transformImageView];
    if (gesture.state == UIGestureRecognizerStateEnded) {
        previousScale = scale * previousScale;
        scale = 1;
    }
}

- (void)doRotate:(UIRotationGestureRecognizer *)gesture {
    rotation = gesture.rotation;
    [self transformImageView];
    if (gesture.state == UIGestureRecognizerStateEnded) {
        previousRotation = rotation + previousRotation;
        rotation = 0;
    }
}
```

And that's all there is to pinch and rotation detection. Compile and run the app to give it a try. As you do some pinching and rotation, you'll see the image change in response (see Figure 18-5). If you're on the simulator, remember that you can simulate a pinch by holding down the **Option** key and clicking and dragging in the simulator window using your mouse.

Figure 18-5. The PinchMe application detects the pinch and rotation gesture

Defining Custom Gestures

You've now seen how to detect the most commonly used gestures. The real fun begins when you start defining your own custom gestures! You've already learned how to use a few of UIGestureRecognizer's subclasses, so now it's time to learn how to create your own gestures, which can be easily attached to any view you like.

Defining a custom gesture is a little trickier than using one of the standard ones. You've already mastered the basic mechanism, and that wasn't too difficult. The tricky part is being flexible when defining what constitutes a gesture.

Most people are not precise when they use gestures. Remember the variance we used when we implemented the swipe, so that even a swipe that wasn't perfectly horizontal or vertical still counted? That's a perfect example of the subtlety you need to add to your own gesture definitions.

If you define your gesture too strictly, it will be useless. If you define it too generically, you'll get too many false positives, which will frustrate the user. In a sense, defining a custom gesture can be hard because you must be precise about a gesture's imprecision. If you try to capture a complex gesture like, say, a figure eight, the math behind detecting the gesture is also going to get quite complex.

The CheckPlease Application

In our sample, we're going to define a gesture shaped like a check mark (see Figure 18-6).

Figure 18-6. An illustration of our check-mark gesture

What are the defining properties of this check-mark gesture? Well, the principal one is that sharp change in angle between the two lines. We also want to make sure that the user's finger has traveled a little distance in a straight line before it makes that sharp angle. In Figure 18-6, the legs of the check mark meet at an acute angle, just under 90 degrees. A gesture that required exactly an 85-degree angle would be awfully hard to get right, so we'll define a range of acceptable angles.

Create a new project in Xcode using the Single View Application template and call the project *CheckPlease*. In this project, we're going to need to do some fairly standard analytic geometry to calculate such things as the distance between two points and the angle between two lines. Don't worry if you don't remember much geometry; we've provided you with functions that will do the calculations for you.

Look in the *18 – CheckPlease Utils* folder for two files called *CGPointUtils.h* and *CGPointUtils.c*. Drag both of these files to the CheckPlease group of your project. Feel free to use the utility functions in these files your own applications. Next, go to the *18 – Image* folder and drag the image file *CheckImage.png* to the *Image.xcassets* folder in your project.

In Xcode, press ⌘N to bring up the new file assistant and in the iOS section, choose **Cocoa Touch Class**. Name the new class *CheckMarkRecognizer* and make it a subclass of UIGestureRecognizer. Now select *CheckMarkRecognizer.m* in the Project Navigator and make the following changes:

```
#import "CheckMarkRecognizer.h"
#import "CGPointUtils.h"
#import <UIKit/UIGestureRecognizerSubclass.h>

static CGFloat const kMinimumCheckMarkAngle  =  50;
static CGFloat const kMaximumCheckMarkAngle  = 135;
static CGFloat const kMinimumCheckMarkLength =  10;

@implementation CheckMarkRecognizer {
    CGPoint lastPreviousPoint;
    CGPoint lastCurrentPoint;
    CGFloat lineLengthSoFar;
}

@end
```

After importing *CGPointUtils.h*, the file we mentioned earlier, we import a special header file called *UIGestureRecognizerSubclass.h*, which contains declarations that are intended for use only by a UIGestureRecognizer subclass. The important thing this does is to make the gesture recognizer's state property writable. That's the mechanism our subclass will use to affirm that the gesture we're watching was successfully completed.

Next, we define the parameters that we use to decide whether the user's finger-squiggling matches our definition of a check mark. You can see that we've defined a minimum angle of 50 degrees and a maximum angle of 135 degrees. This is a pretty broad range; depending on your needs, you might decide to restrict the angle. We experimented a bit with this and found that our practice check-mark gestures fell into a fairly broad range, which is why we chose a relatively large tolerance here. We were somewhat sloppy with our check-mark gestures, and so we expect that at least some of our users will be, as well. As a wise man once said, "Be rigorous in what you produce and tolerant in what you accept."

Now we declare three instance variables: lastPreviousPoint, lastCurrentPoint, and lineLengthSoFar. Each time we're notified of a touch, we're given the previous touch point and the current touch point. Those two points define a line segment. The next touch adds another segment. We store the previous touch's previous and current points in lastPreviousPoint and lastCurrentPoint, which gives us the previous line segment. We can then compare that line segment to the current touch's line segment. Comparing these two line segments can tell us whether we're still drawing a single line or if there's a sharp enough angle between the two segments that we're actually drawing a check mark.

Remember that every UITouch object knows its current position in the view, as well as its previous position in the view. In order to compare angles, however, we need to know the line that the previous two points made, so we need to store the current and previous points from the last time the user touched the screen. We'll use these two variables to store those two values each time this method is called, so that we have the ability to compare the current line to the previous line and check the angle.

We also declare an instance variable to keep a running count of how far the user has dragged the finger. If the finger hasn't traveled at least 10 pixels (the value defined in kMinimumCheckMarkLength), it doesn't matter whether the angle falls in the correct range. If we didn't require this distance, we would receive a lot of false positives.

The CheckPlease Touch Methods

Next, add these two methods to handle touch events sent to the gesture recognizer:

```
- (void)touchesBegan:(NSSet *)touches withEvent:(UIEvent *)event {
    [super touchesBegan:touches withEvent:event];
    UITouch *touch = [touches anyObject];
    CGPoint point = [touch locationInView:self.view];
    lastPreviousPoint = point;
    lastCurrentPoint = point;
    lineLengthSoFar = 0.0;
}

- (void)touchesMoved:(NSSet *)touches withEvent:(UIEvent *)event {
    [super touchesMoved:touches withEvent:event];
    UITouch *touch = [touches anyObject];
    CGPoint previousPoint = [touch previousLocationInView:self.view];
    CGPoint currentPoint = [touch locationInView:self.view];
    CGFloat angle = angleBetweenLines(lastPreviousPoint,
                                      lastCurrentPoint,
                                      previousPoint,
                                      currentPoint);
    if (angle >=kMinimumCheckMarkAngle && angle <= kMaximumCheckMarkAngle
        && lineLengthSoFar > kMinimumCheckMarkLength) {
        self.state = UIGestureRecognizerStateRecognized;
    }
    lineLengthSoFar += distanceBetweenPoints(previousPoint, currentPoint);
    lastPreviousPoint = previousPoint;
    lastCurrentPoint = currentPoint;
}
```

You'll notice that each of these methods first calls the superclass's implementation—something we haven't previously done in any of our touch methods. We need to do this in a UIGestureRecognizer subclass so that our superclass can have the same amount of knowledge about the events as we do. Now let's move on to the code itself.

In touchesBegan:withEvent:, we determine the point that the user is currently touching and store that value in lastPreviousPoint and lastCurrentPoint. Since this method is called when a gesture begins, we know there is no previous point to worry about, so we store the current point in both. We also reset the length of the line we're tracking to 0.

In touchesMoved:withEvent:, we calculate the angle between the line from the current touch's previous position to its current position and the line between the two points stored in the lastPreviousPoint and lastCurrentPoint instance variables. Once we have that angle, we check to see if it falls within our range of acceptable angles and check to make sure that the user's finger has traveled far enough before making that sharp turn. If both of those are true, we set the gesture recognizer state to UIGestureRecognizerStateRecognized to show that we've identified a check-mark gesture. Next, we calculate the distance between the touch's position and its previous position, add that to lineLengthSoFar, and replace the values in lastPreviousPoint and lastCurrentPoint with the two points from the current touch, so we'll have them next time through this method.

Now that we have a gesture recognizer of our own to try out, it's time to connect it to a view, just as we did with the others we used. Switch over to *ViewController.m* and add the following bold code to the top of the file:

```
#import "ViewController.h"
#import "CheckMarkRecognizer.h"

@interface ViewController ()

@property (weak, nonatomic) IBOutlet UIImageView *imageView;

@end
```

Here, we simply import the header for the gesture recognizer we defined, and then add an outlet to an image view that we'll use to inform the user when we've detected a check-mark gesture.

Select *Main.storyboard* to edit the GUI. Add an **Image View** from the library to the view, dropping it somewhere near its center and resize it so that it covers the whole view. In the Document Outline, Control-drag from the **Image View** to the main view, release the mouse, hold down **Shift** and select **Leading Space to Container Margin**, **Trailing Space to Container Margin**, **Top Space to Top Layout Guide**, and **Bottom Space to Bottom Layout Guide**, and then click outside the pop-up with the mouse. Select the image view in the Document Outline and, in the Attributes Inspector, set the Mode property to *Center* and the Image property to *CheckImage*. Finally, Control-drag from the **View Controller** icon to the image view to connect it to the **imageView** outlet.

Now switch back to *ViewController.m* and add the following code to the @implementation section:

```
@implementation ViewController

- (void)doCheck:(CheckMarkRecognizer *)check {
    self.imageView.hidden = NO;
    dispatch_after(dispatch_time(DISPATCH_TIME_NOW, 2 * NSEC_PER_SEC),
                   dispatch_get_main_queue(),
                   ^{ self.imageView.hidden = YES; });
}
```

This gives us an action method to connect our recognizer to. When the gesture is recognized, the image view will be made visible, which will make the check mark appear. Shortly afterward, the image will be hidden again.

Next, edit the `viewDidLoad` method, adding the following lines, which connect an instance of our new recognizer to the view and ensure that the image view (and hence the check mark) is initially hidden:

```
- (void)viewDidLoad
{
    [super viewDidLoad];
    // Do any additional setup after loading the view, typically from a nib.
    CheckMarkRecognizer *check = [[CheckMarkRecognizer alloc]
                             initWithTarget:self
                                     action:@selector(doCheck:)];
    [self.view addGestureRecognizer:check];
    self.imageView.hidden = YES;
}
```

Compile and run the app, and try out the gesture.

When defining new gestures for your own applications, make sure you test them thoroughly. If you can, also have other people test them for you, as well. You want to make sure that your gesture is easy for the user to do, but not so easy that it gets triggered unintentionally. You also need to make sure that you don't conflict with other gestures used in your application. A single gesture should not count, for example, as both a custom gesture and a pinch.

Garçon? Check, Please!

You should now understand the mechanism iOS uses to tell your application about touches, taps, and gestures. You also learned how to detect the most commonly used iOS gestures, and even got a taste of how you might go about defining your own custom gestures. The iOS user interface relies on gestures for much of its ease of use, so you'll want to have these techniques at the ready for most of your iOS development.

When you're ready to move on, turn the page, and we'll tell you how to figure out where in the world you are using Core Location.

Chapter 19

Where Am I? Finding Your Way with Core Location and Map Kit

Every iOS device has the ability to determine where in the world it is using a framework called **Core Location**. iOS also includes a framework called **Map Kit** that lets you easily create a live interactive map showing any locations you like, including, of course, the user's location. In this chapter, we'll get you started using both of these frameworks.

Core Location can actually leverage three technologies to do this: GPS, cell ID location, and Wi-Fi Positioning Service (WPS). GPS is the most accurate of the three technologies, but it is not available on first-generation iPhones, iPod touches, or Wi-Fi-only iPads. In short, any device with at least a 3G data connection also contains a GPS unit. GPS reads microwave signals from multiple satellites to determine the current location.

Note Technically, Apple uses a version of GPS called **Assisted GPS**, also known as A-GPS. A-GPS uses network resources to help improve the performance of stand-alone GPS. The basic idea is that the telephony provider deploys services on its network that mobile devices will automatically find and collect some data from. This allows a mobile device to determine its starting location much more quickly than if it were relying on the GPS satellites alone.

Cell ID location lookup gives a rough approximation of the current location based on the physical location of the cellular base station that the device is currently in contact with. Since each base station can cover a fairly large area, there is a fairly large margin of error here. Cell ID location lookup requires a cell radio connection, so it works only on the iPhone (all models, including the very first) and any iPad with a 3G data connection.

The WPS option uses the media access control (MAC) addresses from nearby Wi-Fi access points to make a guess at your location by referencing a large database of known service providers and the areas they service. WPS is imprecise and can be off by many miles.

All three methods put a noticeable drain on the battery, so keep that in mind when using Core Location. Your application shouldn't poll for location any more often than is absolutely necessary. When using Core Location, you have the option of specifying a desired accuracy. By carefully specifying the absolute minimum accuracy level you need, you can prevent unnecessary battery drain.

The technologies that Core Location depends on are hidden from your application. We don't tell Core Location whether to use GPS, triangulation, or WPS. We just tell it how accurate we would like it to be, and it will decide from the technologies available to it which is best for fulfilling our request.

The Location Manager

The Core Location API is actually fairly easy to use. The main class we'll work with is CLLocationManager, usually referred to as the **location manager**. To interact with Core Location, you need to create an instance of the location manager, like this:

```
CLLocationManager *locationManager = [[CLLocationManager alloc] init];
```

This creates an instance of the location manager, but it doesn't actually start polling for your location. You must create an object that conforms to the CLLocationManagerDelegate protocol and assign it as the location manager's delegate. The location manager will call delegate methods when location information becomes available or changes. The process of determining location may take some time—even a few seconds.

Setting the Desired Accuracy

After you set the delegate, you also want to set the desired accuracy. As we mentioned, don't specify a degree of accuracy any greater than you absolutely need. If you're writing an application that just needs to know which state or country the phone is in, don't specify a high level of precision. Remember that the more accuracy you demand of Core Location, the more juice you're likely to use. Also, keep in mind that there is no guarantee that you will get the level of accuracy you have requested.

Here's an example of setting the delegate and requesting a specific level of accuracy:

```
locationManager.delegate = self;
locationManager.desiredAccuracy = kCLLocationAccuracyBest;
```

The accuracy is set using a CLLocationAccuracy value, a type that's defined as a double. The value is in meters, so if you specify a desiredAccuracy of 10, you're telling Core Location that you want it to try to determine the current location within 10 meters, if possible. Specifying kCLLocationAccuracyBest (as we did previously) or specifying kCLLocationAccuracyBestForNavigation (where it uses other sensor data as well) tells Core Location to use the most accurate method that's currently available. In addition, you can also use kCLLocationAccuracyNearestTenMeters, kCLLocationAccuracyHundredMeters, kCLLocationAccuracyKilometer, and kCLLocationAccuracyThreeKilometers.

Setting the Distance Filter

By default, the location manager will notify the delegate of any detected change in the device's location. By specifying a **distance filter**, you are telling the location manager not to notify you of every change, but instead to notify you only when the location changes by more than a certain amount. Setting up a distance filter can reduce the amount of polling your application does.

Distance filters are also set in meters. Specifying a distance filter of 1000 tells the location manager not to notify its delegate until the iPhone has moved at least 1,000 meters from its previously reported position. Here's an example:

```
locationManager.distanceFilter = 1000.;
```

If you ever want to return the location manager to the default setting, which applies no filter, you can use the constant kCLDistanceFilterNone, like this:

```
locationManager.distanceFilter = kCLDistanceFilterNone;
```

Just as when specifying the desired accuracy, you should take care to avoid getting updates any more frequently than you really need them; otherwise, you waste battery power. A speedometer app that's calculating the user's velocity based on the user's location will probably want to have updates as quickly as possible, but an app that's going to show the nearest fast-food restaurant can get by with a lot fewer updates.

Getting Permission to Use Location Services

Before your application can use location services, you need to get the user's permission to do so. Core Location offers several different services, some of which can be used even when your application is in the background—in fact, you can even request to have your application launched when certain events happen while it is not running. Depending on what your application does, it may be enough to request permission to access location services only while the user is using your application, or it might need to always be able to use the service. When writing an application, you need to decide which type of permission it requires and you need to make the request before initiating the services that you need. You'll see how to do this in the course of creating the example application for this chapter.

Starting the Location Manager

When you're ready to start polling for location, and after you request from the user to access location services, you tell the location manager to start. It will go off and do its thing and then call a delegate method when it has determined the current location. Until you tell it to stop, it will continue to call your delegate method whenever it senses a change that exceeds the current distance filter.

Here's how you start the location manager:

```
[locationManager startUpdatingLocation];
```

Using the Location Manager Wisely

If you need to determine the current location only and you don't need continuous updates, you should have your location delegate stop the location manager as soon as it gets the information your application requires. If you need to poll, make sure you stop polling as soon as you possibly can. Remember that as long as you are getting updates from the location manager, you are putting a strain on the user's battery.

To tell the location manager to stop sending updates to its delegate, call stopUpdatingLocation, like this:

```
[locationManager stopUpdatingLocation];
```

The Location Manager Delegate

The location manager delegate must conform to the CLLocationManagerDelegate protocol, which defines several methods, all of them optional. One of these methods is called by the location manager when the availability of user authorization to use location services changes, another when it has determined the current location or when it detects a change in location. Yet another method is called when the location manager encounters an error. We'll implement all of these delegate methods in our app.

Getting Location Updates

When the location manager wants to inform its delegate of the current location, it calls the locationManager:didUpdateLocations: method. This method takes two parameters:

- ▧ The first parameter is the location manager that called the method.

- ▧ The second parameter is an array of CLLocation objects that describe the current location of the device and perhaps a few previous locations. If several location updates occur in a short period of time, they may be reported all at once with a single call to this method. In any case, the most recent location is always the last item in this array.

Getting Latitude and Longitude Using CLLocation

Location information is passed from the location manager using instances of the CLLocation class. This class has six properties that might be of interest to your application:

- ▧ coordinate
- ▧ horizontalAccuracy
- ▧ altitude
- ▧ verticalAccuracy
- ▧ floor
- ▧ timestamp

The latitude and longitude are stored in a property called `coordinate`. To get the latitude and longitude in degrees, do this:

```
CLLocationDegrees latitude = theLocation.coordinate.latitude;
CLLocationDegrees longitude = theLocation.coordinate.longitude;
```

The `CLLocation` object can also tell you how confident the location manager is in its latitude and longitude calculations. The `horizontalAccuracy` property describes the radius of a circle (in meters, like all Core Location measurements) with the `coordinate` as its center. The larger the value in `horizontalAccuracy`, the less certain Core Location is of the location. A very small radius indicates a high level of confidence in the determined location.

You can see a graphic representation of `horizontalAccuracy` in the Maps application (see Figure 19-1). The circle shown in Maps uses `horizontalAccuracy` for its radius when it detects your location. The location manager thinks you are at the center of that circle. If you're not, you're almost certainly somewhere inside the circle. A negative value in `horizontalAccuracy` is an indication that you cannot rely on the values in `coordinate` for some reason.

Figure 19-1. The Maps application uses Core Location to determine your current location. The outer circle is a visual representation of the horizontal accuracy

The CLLocation object also has a property called altitude that can tell you how many meters above (or below) sea level you are:

```
CLLocationDistance altitude = theLocation.altitude;
```

Each CLLocation object maintains a property called verticalAccuracy that is an indication of how confident Core Location is in its determination of altitude. The value in altitude could be off by as many meters as the value in verticalAccuracy. If the verticalAccuracy value is negative, Core Location is telling you it could not determine a valid altitude.

The floor property gives the floor within the building in which the user is located. This value is only valid in buildings that are able to provide the information, so you should not rely on its availability.

CLLocation objects also have a timestamp that tells when the location manager made the location determination.

In addition to these properties, CLLocation has a useful instance method that will let you determine the distance between two CLLocation objects. The method is called distanceFromLocation: and it returns a value of type CLLocationDistance, which is just a double, so you can use it in arithmetic calculations, as you'll see in the application we're about to create. Here's how you use this method:

```
CLLocationDistance distance = [fromLocation distanceFromLocation:toLocation];
```

The preceding line of code will return the distance between two CLLocation objects: fromLocation and toLocation. This distance value returned will be the result of a great-circle distance calculation that ignores the altitude property and calculates the distance as if both points were at sea level. For most purposes, a great-circle calculation will be more than sufficient; however, if you do want to take altitude into account when calculating distances, you'll need to write your own code to do it.

> **Note** If you're not sure what's meant by *great-circle distance*, you might want to think back to geography class and the notion of a *great-circle route*. The idea is that the shortest distance between any two points on the earth's surface will be found along a path that would, if extended, go the entire way around the earth: a "great circle." The most obvious great circles are perhaps the ones you've seen on maps: the equator and the longitudinal lines. However, such a circle can be found for any two points on the surface of the earth. The calculation performed by CLLocation determines the distance between two points along such a route, taking the curvature of the earth into account. Without accounting for that curvature, you would end up with the length of a straight line connecting the two points, which isn't much use, since that line would invariably go straight through some amount of the earth itself!

Error Notifications

If Core Location needs to report an error to your application, it will call a delegate method named locationManager:didFailWithError:. One possible cause of an error is that the user denied access to location services, in which case the method will be called with the error code kCLErrorDenied. Another commonly encountered error code supported by the location manager is kCLErrorLocationUnknown, which indicates that Core Location was unable to determine the location but that it will keep trying. While a kCLErrorLocationUnknown error indicates a problem that may be temporary, kCLErrorDenied and other errors may indicate that your application will not be able to access Core Location any time during the remainder of the current session.

> **Note**   The simulator has no way to determine your current location, but you can choose one (such as Apple's HQ, which is the default) or set your own, from the simulator's Debug ➤ Location menu.

Trying Out Core Location

Let's build a small application to detect your device's current location and the total distance traveled while the program has been running. You can see what the first version of our application will look like in Figure 19-2.

Figure 19-2. The WhereAmI application in action

In Xcode, create a new project using the Single View Application template and call it *WhereAmI*. When the project window opens, select *ViewController.m* and make the following changes:

```
#import "ViewController.h"
#import <CoreLocation/CoreLocation.h>

@interface ViewController () <CLLocationManagerDelegate>

@property (strong, nonatomic) CLLocationManager *locationManager;
@property (strong, nonatomic) CLLocation *previousPoint;
@property (assign, nonatomic) CLLocationDistance totalMovementDistance;
@property (weak, nonatomic) IBOutlet UILabel *latitudeLabel;
@property (weak, nonatomic) IBOutlet UILabel *longitudeLabel;
@property (weak, nonatomic) IBOutlet UILabel *horizontalAccuracyLabel;
@property (weak, nonatomic) IBOutlet UILabel *altitudeLabel;
@property (weak, nonatomic) IBOutlet UILabel *verticalAccuracyLabel;
@property (weak, nonatomic) IBOutlet UILabel *distanceTraveledLabel;

@end
```

First, notice that we've included the Core Location header file. Core Location is not part of either UIKit or Foundation, so we need to include the header files manually. Next, we conform this class to the CLLocationManagerDelegate method, so that we can receive location information from the location manager.

Then, we declare a CLLocationManager pointer, which will be used to hold a pointer to the instance of the Core Location Manager we're going create. We also declare a pointer to a CLLocation, which we will set to the location of the last update we received from the location manager. This way, each time the user moves far enough to trigger an update, we'll be able to add the latest movement distance to our running total, which we'll keep in the totalMovementDistance property.

The remaining properties are outlets that will be used to update labels on the user interface.

Now select *Main.storyboard* and let's start creating the GUI. First, expand the view controller hierarchy in the Document Outline, select the view item and change its name to *Main View*, and then in the Attributes Inspector, change its background color to light gray. Next, drag a UIView from the object library, drop it onto the existing view, and then position and size it so that it covers the bottom half of the Main View. Make sure that the bottom, left, and right sides of the view exactly match those of the gray view. You are aiming to create something like the arrangement shown in Figure 19-2, where the view that you just dropped is the one at the bottom of the figure with the white background.

In the Document Outline, select the view that you just added and change its name to *Lower View*. Control-drag from the Lower View to Main View and release the mouse. In the pop-up menu that appears, hold down the Shift key and click Leading Space to Container Margin, Trailing Space to Container Margin, and Bottom Space to Bottom Layout Guide. This pins the Lower View in place, but does not yet set its height. To fix that, with the Lower View still selected in the Document Outline, click the Pin button. In the pop-up, select the Height check box and set the height to **166**, set Update Frames to Items of New Constraint, and then press Add 1 Constraint to set the height. That should do the job.

Next, we'll create the rightmost column of labels shown in Figure 19-2. Drag a label from the object library and drop it a little way below the top of the Lower View. Resize it to a width of about 80 points and move it so that it is close to the right edge of the view. Option-drag a copy of this label downward five times to create a stack of labels, as shown in Figure 19-2. Now let's fix the labels' sizes and positions relative to the Lower View.

Starting with the topmost label in the Document Outline, Control-drag from that label to Lower View. Release the mouse. Hold down the Shift key and select Top Space to Container Margin and Trailing Space to Container Margin, and then click anywhere else with the mouse to close the pop-up. To set the label's size, click the Pin button to open the Add New Constraints pop-up menu, click the Width and Height check boxes, enter **80** as the width and **21** as the height (if they are not already set), and click Add 2 Constraints. You have now fixed the size and position of the top label. If you select the label in the storyboard editor, you should see the constraints shown on the left in Figure 19-3. Repeat the same procedure for the other five labels.

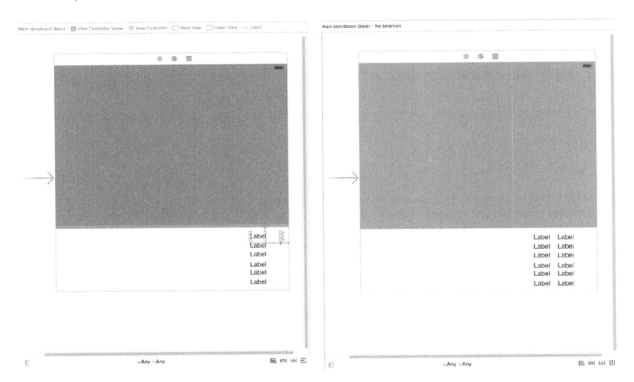

Figure 19-3. Preparing the labels that will show location information

Next, we'll add the second column of labels. Drag a label from the object library and place it to the left of the topmost label, leaving a small horizontal gap between them. Drag the left side of the label so that it almost reaches the left edge of Lower View, and then in the Attributes Inspector, set the Alignment so that the label text is right-aligned. Make five copies of this label by Option-dragging downward, aligning each of them with the corresponding label on the right, to make the left column shown on the right in Figure 19-3.

Select the top label in the left column and Control-drag from its left side to the left side of Lower View. Release the mouse and, in the context menu, select Leading Space to Container Margin. Next, Control-drag from the same label to the matching label in the right-hand column. Release the mouse to open the context menu, hold down the Shift key, select Horizontal Spacing and Baseline, and then click outside the context menu with the mouse. Do the same for the other five labels in the left column. Finally, select the View Controller icon in the Document Outline, click the Resolve Auto Layout Issues button, and select Update Frames, if it's enabled. Any orange warning indications should disappear and the lower part of the screen should look like the right side in Figure 19-3.

We are almost there! We now need to connect the labels in the right column to the outlets in the view controller. Open *ViewController.m* in the assistant editor and Control-drag from the top label in the right column to the outlet called `latitudeLabel` in the view controller. Release the mouse to connect the outlet. Control-drag from the second label to `longitudeLabel` to connect the second outlet, from the third label to `horizontalAccuracyLabel`, from the fourth to `altitudeLabel`, from the fifth to `verticalAccuracyLabel`, and from the bottom label to `distanceTraveledLabel`. You have now connected all six outlets.

Finally, clear the text from all of the labels in the right column and change the text of the labels in the left column to match that shown in Figure 19-2; the top label's text should be *Latitude:*, the next one down should be *Longitude:*, and so on.

Now let's write the code to display some useful information in all those labels. Select *ViewController.m* and insert the following lines in `viewDidLoad` to configure the location manager:

```
- (void)viewDidLoad
{
    [super viewDidLoad];

    self.locationManager = [[CLLocationManager alloc] init];
    self.locationManager.delegate = self;
    self.locationManager.desiredAccuracy = kCLLocationAccuracyBest;
    [self.locationManager requestWhenInUseAuthorization];
}
```

We allocate and initialize a `CLLocationManager` instance, assign our controller class as the delegate, set the desired accuracy to the best available, and then request permission to use the location service while the user is using our application. This is sufficient authorization for the purposes of this example. To use some of the more advanced features of Core Location, which are beyond the scope of this book, you will probably need to request permission to use Core Location at any time by calling the `requestAlwaysAuthorization` method instead.

> **Note** In this simple example, the request for authorization is made as the application starts up, but Apple recommends that, in a real application, you should delay making the request until you actually need to use location services. The reason for this is that the user is more likely to agree if it's obvious why you need access to the device's location, based on operation that has been requested, than if an application, probably one that the user has just installed, requests permission as soon as it launches.

The first time this application runs, iOS will display an alert asking the user whether your application should be allowed to use your location. You need to supply a short piece of text that iOS will include in the alert pop-up, explaining why your application needs to know the user's location. Open the *info.plist* file and add the text you'd like to have displayed under the key NSLocationWhenInUseUsageDescription (if you need to request permission to use location services even when the application is not actively being used, the text should be added under the key NSLocationAlwaysUsageDescription instead). For the purposes of this example, use something like "The application needs to know your location to update your position on a map".

> **Caution**   In earlier versions of iOS, supplying text to qualify the permission request was optional. As of iOS 8, it is mandatory. If you don't supply any text, the permission request will not be made.

If you run the application now, you'll see that iOS uses your text in the permission request, as shown in Figure 19-4.

Figure 19-4. Prompting the user for permission to use location services

This prompt appears only once in the lifetime of the application. Whether or not the user allows your application to use location services, this request will never be made again, no matter how many times the application is run. That's not to say that the user can't change his mind about this, of course. We'll say more about that in the upcoming "Changing Location Service Permissions" section. As far as testing is concerned, rerunning the application from Xcode has no effect on the user's saved response—to get a clean state for testing, you have to delete the application from the simulator or device. If you do that, iOS will prompt for permission again when you reinstall and relaunch the application. For now, reply "Allow" to the prompt and let's continue writing our application.

You probably noticed that the viewDidLoad method did not call the location manager's startUpdatingLocation method immediately after calling requestWhenInUseAuthorization. There is, in fact, no point in doing so, because the authorization process does not take place immediately. At some point after viewDidLoad returns, the location manager delegate's locationManager:didChangeAuthorizationStatus: method will be called with the application's authorization status. This may be the result of the user's reply to the permission request pop-up, or it may be the saved authorization state from when the application last executed. Either way, this method is an ideal place to start listening for location updates, assuming you are authorized to. Add the following implementation of this method to the *ViewController.m* file:

```
- (void)locationManager:(CLLocationManager *)manager
        didChangeAuthorizationStatus:(CLAuthorizationStatus)status {
    NSLog(@"Authorization status changed to %d", status);
    switch (status) {
    case kCLAuthorizationStatusAuthorizedAlways:
    case kCLAuthorizationStatusAuthorizedWhenInUse:
        [self.locationManager startUpdatingLocation];
        break;

    case kCLAuthorizationStatusNotDetermined:
    case kCLAuthorizationStatusRestricted:
    case kCLAuthorizationStatusDenied:
        [self.locationManager stopUpdatingLocation];
        break;
    }
}
```

This code starts listening for location updates if authorization was granted, and stops listening if it was not. Since we don't start listening unless we have authorization, what's the point of calling stopUpdatingLocation if we didn't get permission? That's a good question. The reason this code is required is because the user can give your application permission to use Core Location and then later revoke it. In that case, we need to stop listening for updates. For more on this, see "Changing Location Service Permissions" later in this chapter.

If your application tries to use location services when it doesn't have permission to do so, or if an error occurs at any time, the location manager calls its delegate's locationManager:didFailWithError: method. Let's add an implementation of that method to the view controller:

```
- (void)locationManager:(CLLocationManager *)manager
        didFailWithError:(NSError *)error {
    NSString *errorType = error.code == kCLErrorDenied ? @"Access Denied"
            : [NSString stringWithFormat:@"Error %ld", (long)error.code, nil];
```

```
    UIAlertController *alertController =
      [UIAlertController alertControllerWithTitle:@"Location Manager Error"
                        message:errorType
                        preferredStyle:UIAlertControllerStyleAlert];
    UIAlertAction *okAction = [UIAlertAction actionWithTitle:@"OK"
                                  style:UIAlertActionStyleCancel handler:nil];
    [alertController addAction:okAction];
    [self presentViewController:alertController animated:YES completion:nil];
}
```

For the purposes of this example, when an error occurs, we just alert the user. In a real application, you would use a more meaningful error message and clean up the application state as required.

Using Location Manager Updates

Now that we've dealt with getting permission to use the user's location, let's do something with that information. Insert this implementation of the delegate's locationManager:didUpdateLocation: method at the end of the @implementation block:

```
- (void)locationManager:(CLLocationManager *)manager
            didUpdateLocations:(NSArray *)locations {
    CLLocation *newLocation = [locations lastObject];
    NSString *latitudeString = [NSString stringWithFormat:@"%g\u00B0",
                                newLocation.coordinate.latitude];
    self.latitudeLabel.text = latitudeString;

    NSString *longitudeString = [NSString stringWithFormat:@"%g\u00B0",
                                  newLocation.coordinate.longitude];
    self.longitudeLabel.text = longitudeString;

    NSString *horizontalAccuracyString = [NSString stringWithFormat:@"%gm",
                                          newLocation.horizontalAccuracy];
    self.horizontalAccuracyLabel.text = horizontalAccuracyString;

    NSString *altitudeString = [NSString stringWithFormat:@"%gm",
                                newLocation.altitude];
    self.altitudeLabel.text = altitudeString;

    NSString *verticalAccuracyString = [NSString stringWithFormat:@"%gm",
                                        newLocation.verticalAccuracy];
    self.verticalAccuracyLabel.text = verticalAccuracyString;

    if (newLocation.verticalAccuracy < 0 ||
        newLocation.horizontalAccuracy < 0) {
        // invalid accuracy
        return;
    }
```

```
    if (newLocation.horizontalAccuracy > 100 ||
        newLocation.verticalAccuracy > 50) {
        // accuracy radius is so large, we don't want to use it
        return;
    }

    if (self.previousPoint == nil) {
        self.totalMovementDistance = 0;
    } else {
        NSLog(@"movement distance: %f",
                [newLocation distanceFromLocation:self.previousPoint]);
        self.totalMovementDistance +=
                [newLocation distanceFromLocation:self.previousPoint];
    }
    self.previousPoint = newLocation;

    NSString *distanceString = [NSString stringWithFormat:@"%gm",
                                self.totalMovementDistance];
    self.distanceTraveledLabel.text = distanceString;

}
```

The first thing we do in the delegate method is to update the first five labels in the second column of Figure 19-2 with values from the CLLocation objects passed in the locations argument. The locations array could contain more than one location update, but use the last entry, which always represents the most recent information.

> **Note**   Both the longitude and latitude are displayed in formatting strings containing the cryptic-looking \u00B0. This is the hexadecimal value of the Unicode representation of the degree symbol (°). It's never a good idea to put anything other than ASCII characters directly in a source code file, but including the hex value in a string is just fine, and that's what we've done here.

Next, we check the accuracy of the values that the location manager gives us. High accuracy values indicate that the location manager isn't quite sure about the location, while negative accuracy values indicate that the location is actually invalid. However, some devices do not have the hardware required to determine vertical position. On these devices, and on the simulator, the verticalAccuracy property will always be –1, so we don't exclude position reports that have this value.

These accuracy values are in meters and indicate the radius of a circle from the location we're given, meaning that the true location could be anywhere in that circle. Our code checks to see whether these values are acceptably accurate; if not, it simply returns from this method rather than doing anything more with garbage data:

```
if (newLocation.horizontalAccuracy < 0) {
    // invalid accuracy
    return;
}
```

```
if (newLocation.horizontalAccuracy > 100 ||
    newLocation.verticalAccuracy > 50) {
    // accuracy radius is so large, we don't want to use it
    return;
}
```

Next, we check whether previousPoint is nil. If it is, then this update is the first valid one we've gotten from the location manager, so we zero out the distanceFromStart property. Otherwise, we add the latest location's distance from the previous point to the total distance. In either case, we update previousPoint to contain the current location:

```
if (self.previousPoint == nil) {
    self.totalMovementDistance = 0;
} else {
    self.totalMovementDistance += [newLocation
                         distanceFromLocation:self.previousPoint];
}
self.previousPoint = newLocation;
```

After that, we populate the final label with the total distance that we've traveled from the start point. While this application runs, if the user moves far enough for the location manager to detect the change, the Distance Traveled: field will be continually updated with the distance the user has moved since the application started:

```
NSString *distanceString = [NSString stringWithFormat:@"%gm",
                         self.totalMovementDistance];
self.distanceTraveledLabel.text = distanceString;
```

And there you have it. Core Location is fairly straightforward and easy to use.

Compile and run the application, and then try it. If you have the ability to run the application on your iPhone or iPad, try going for a drive with the application running, and watch the values change as you drive. Um, actually, it's better to have someone else do the driving!

Visualizing Your Movement on a Map

What we've done so far is pretty neat, but wouldn't it be nice if we could visualize our travel on a map? Fortunately, iOS includes the Map Kit framework to help us out here. Map Kit utilizes the same back-end services that Apple's Maps app uses, which means it's fairly robust and improving all the time. It contains a view class that presents a map, and it responds to user gestures just as you'd expect of any modern mapping app. This view also lets us insert annotations for any locations we want to show up on our map, which by default show up as "pins" that can be touched to reveal some more info. We're going to extend our WhereAmI app to display the user's starting position and current position on a map.

Select *ViewController.m* and add the following near the top to import the Map Kit framework headers:

```
#import <MapKit/MapKit.h>
```

Now add a new property declaration for the Map View that will display the user's location below the others in the class extension:

```
@property (weak, nonatomic) IBOutlet MKMapView *mapView;
```

Now select *Main.storyboard* to edit the view. Drag a Map View from the object library and drop it onto the user interface. Resize the Map View so that it covers the whole screen, including the Lower View and all of its labels, and then choose Editor ➤ Arrange ➤ Send to Back to move the Map View behind Lower View. In the Document Outline, Control-drag from the Map View to the Main View and, in the context menu, hold down the Shift key and select Leading Space to Container Margin, Trailing Space to Container Margin, Top Space to Top Layout Guide, and Bottom Space to Bottom Layout Guide, and then click outside the context menu with the mouse.

The Map View is now locked in place, but the bottom part of it is obscured. We can fix that by making Lower View partly transparent. To do that, select Lower View in the Document Outline, open the Attributes Inspector, click the Background color editor and, in the pop-up that appears, choose Other… to open a color chooser. Select a white background and move the Opacity slider to about 70%. Finally, Control-drag from the Map View to the `mapView` property in *ViewController.m* to connect the outlet.

Now that these preliminaries are in place, it's time to write a little code that will make the map do some work for us. Before dealing with the code required in the view controller, we need to set up a sort of model class to represent our starting point. *MKMapView* is built as the View part of an MVC (Model-View-Controller) architecture, and it works best if we have distinct classes to represent markers on the map. We can pass model objects off to the map view, and it will query them for coordinates, a title, and so on, using a protocol defined in the Map Kit framework.

Press ⌘N to bring up the new file assistant, and in the iOS section, choose Cocoa Touch Class. Name the class *Place* and make it a subclass of NSObject. Select *Place.h* and modify it as shown next. You need to import the Map Kit header, specify a protocol that the new class conforms to, and add some properties:

```
#import <Foundation/Foundation.h>
#import <MapKit/MapKit.h>

@interface Place : NSObject <MKAnnotation>

@property (copy, nonatomic) NSString *title;
@property (copy, nonatomic) NSString *subtitle;
@property (assign, nonatomic) CLLocationCoordinate2D coordinate;

@end
```

This is a fairly "dumb" class that acts solely as a holder for these properties. We don't even need to touch the *.m* file here! In a real-world example, you may have real model classes that need to be shown on a map as an annotation, and the `MKAnnotation` protocol lets you add this capability to any class of your own without messing up any existing class hierarchies.

Select *ViewController.m* and get started by importing the header for the new class:

```
#import "Place.h"
```

Now add the following two lines to the `locationManager:didChangeAuthorizationStatus:` method:

```
- (void)locationManager:(CLLocationManager *)manager
        didChangeAuthorizationStatus:(CLAuthorizationStatus)status {
    NSLog(@"Authorization status changed to %d", status);
    switch (status) {
    case kCLAuthorizationStatusAuthorizedAlways:
    case kCLAuthorizationStatusAuthorizedWhenInUse:
        [self.locationManager startUpdatingLocation];
        self.mapView.showsUserLocation = YES;
        break;

    case kCLAuthorizationStatusNotDetermined:
    case kCLAuthorizationStatusRestricted:
    case kCLAuthorizationStatusDenied:
        [self.locationManager stopUpdatingLocation];
        self.mapView.showsUserLocation = NO;
        break;
    }
}
```

The Map View's `showsUserLocation` property does just what you probably imagine: it saves us the hassle of manually moving a marker around as the user moves by automatically drawing one for us. It uses Core Location to get the user's location and it works only if your application is authorized for that, so we enable the property when we are told that we have permission to use Core Location, and disable it again if we lose permission.

Now let's revisit the `locationManager:didUpdateLocations:` method. We've already got some code in there that notices the first valid location data we receive and establishes our start point. We're also going to allocate a new instance of our `Place` class. We set its properties, giving it a location. We also add a title and subtitle that we want to appear when a marker for this location is displayed. Finally, we pass this object off to the map view.

We also create an instance of `MKCoordinateRegion`, a struct included in Map Kit that lets us tell the view which section of the map we want it to display. `MKCoordinateRegion` uses our new location's coordinates and a pair of distances in meters (100, 100) that specify how wide and tall the displayed map portion should be. We pass this off to the map view as well, telling it to animate the change. All of this is done by adding the bold lines shown here:

```
if (self.previousPoint == nil) {
    self.totalMovementDistance = 0;

    Place *start = [[Place alloc] init];
    start.coordinate = newLocation.coordinate;
    start.title = @"Start Point";
    start.subtitle = @"This is where we started!";
```

```
    [self.mapView addAnnotation:start];
    MKCoordinateRegion region;
    region = MKCoordinateRegionMakeWithDistance(newLocation.coordinate,
                                            100, 100);
    [self.mapView setRegion:region animated:YES];
} else {
    self.totalMovementDistance += [newLocation
                            distanceFromLocation:self.previousPoint];
}
self.previousPoint = newLocation;
```

So now we've told the map view that we have an annotation (i.e., a visible placemark) that we want the user to see. But how should it be displayed? Well, the map view figures out what sort of view to display for each annotation by asking its delegate. In a more complex app, that would work for us. But in this example we haven't made ourselves a delegate, simply because it's not necessary for our simple use case. Unlike UITableView, which requires its data source to supply cells for display, MKMapView has a different strategy: if it's not provided with annotation views by a delegate, it simply displays a default sort of view represented by a red "pin" on the map that reveals some more information when touched. Neat!

There's one final thing you need to do—enable your application to use Map Kit. To do this, select the project in the Project Navigator and then select the WhereAmI target. At the top of editor area, select Capabilities, locate the Maps section, and move the selector switch on the right from OFF to ON. Now build and run your app, and you'll see the map view load. As soon as it gets valid position data, you'll see it scroll to the right location, drop a pin at your starting point, and mark your current location with a glowing blue dot (see Figure 19-5). Not bad for a few dozen lines of code!

Figure 19-5. *The red pin marks our starting location, and the blue dot shows how far we've gotten—in this case, no distance at all!*

Changing Location Service Permissions

When your application runs for the first time, you hope the user will give it permission to use location services. Whether you get permission or not, you can't assume that nothing will change. The user can grant or revoke location permission via the Settings app. You can test this on the simulator. Launch the app and grant yourself permission to use Core Location (if you've previously denied permission, you'll need to remove and reinstall the app first). You should see your location on the map. Now go to the Settings app and choose Privacy ➤ Location. At the top of the screen is a switch that turns location services on or off. Turn the switch to OFF and go back to your application. You'll see that the map no longer shows your position. That's because the location manager called the locationManager: didChangeAuthorizationStatus: method with authorization code kCLAuthorizationStatusDenied, in response to which the application stops receiving position updates and tells Map Kit to stop tracking the user's position. Now go back to the Settings app, re-enable Core Location, and come back to your application; you'll find that it's tracking your position again.

Switching Location Services off is not the only way for the user to change your app's ability to use Core Location. Go back to the Settings app. Below the switch that enables Location Services, you'll see a list of all the apps that are using it, including WhereAmI, as shown on the left in Figure 19-6. Clicking the application name takes you to another page where you can allow or deny access to your application, which you can see on the right in Figure 19-6. At the moment, the application can use location services while the user is using the app. If you click Never, that permission is revoked, as you can prove by returning to the application again. This demonstrates that it's important to code the application so that it can detect and respond properly to changes in its authorization status.

Figure 19-6. *Changing Core Location access permission for the WhereAmI app*

Wherever You Go, There You Are

That's the end of our introduction to Core Location and Map Kit. There is quite a lot more to be discovered about both of these frameworks. Here are just a few of the highlights:

- Instead of closely tracking the user's location using the `startUpdatingLocation` method, applications that need less positional accuracy and/or less frequent updates, such as Weather apps, can use the Significant Location Updates service. You should use this service if at all possible, because it can significantly reduce power consumption.

- On devices that have a magnetometer, Core Location can report the user's heading. If the device also has a GPS, it can report the direction in which the user is moving.

- Core Location can report when the user enters or leaves application-defined geographical regions (defined as a circle of a given radius and center) or when the application is in the vicinity of an iBeacon.

- You can convert between the coordinates reported by Core Location and a user-friendly placemark object and vice versa, using the Geocoding service. In addition to this, Map Kit includes an API that lets you search for locations by name or address.

- New in iOS 8, Core Location monitors the user's movement and can determine when the user stops for a period of time at a location. When this happens, the user is assumed to be "visiting" that location. Your application can receive notification when the user arrives at and departs from a visited location.

The best source of information for all of these features is Apple's *Location and Maps Programming Guide*.

Although the underlying technologies are quite complex, Apple has provided simple interfaces that hide most of the complexity, making it quite easy to add location-related and mapping features to your applications so that you can tell where the users are, notice when they move, and mark their location (and any other locations) on a map.

And speaking of moving, when you're ready, proceed directly to the next chapter so that we can play with the iPhone's built-in accelerometer.

Chapter 20

Whee! Gyro and Accelerometer!

One of the coolest features of the iPhone, iPad, and iPod touch is the built-in accelerometer—the tiny device that lets iOS know how the device is being held and if it's being moved. iOS uses the accelerometer to handle autorotation, and many games use it as a control mechanism. The accelerometer can also be used to detect shakes and other sudden movement. This capability was extended even further with the introduction of the iPhone 4, which was the first iPhone to include a built-in gyroscope to let developers determine the angle at which the device is positioned around each axis. The gyro and accelerometer are now standard fare on all new iPads and iPod touches. In this chapter, we're going to introduce you to the use of the Core Motion framework to access the gyro and accelerometer values in your application.

Accelerometer Physics

An **accelerometer** measures both acceleration and gravity by sensing the amount of inertial force in a given direction. The accelerometer inside your iOS device is a three-axis accelerometer. This means that it is capable of detecting either movement or the pull of gravity in three-dimensional space. In other words, you can use the accelerometer to discover not only how the device is currently being held (as autorotation does), but also to learn if it's laying on a table and even whether it's face down or face up.

Accelerometers give measurements in g-forces (*g* for gravity), so a value of 1.0 returned by the accelerometer means that 1 g is sensed in a particular direction, as in these examples:

- If the device is being held still with no movement, there will be approximately 1 g of force exerted on it by the pull of the earth.

- If the device is being held perfectly upright, in portrait orientation, it will detect and report about 1 g of force exerted on its y axis.

- If the device is being held at an angle, that 1 g of force will be distributed along different axes depending on how it is being held. When held at a 45-degree angle, the 1 g of force will be split roughly equally between two of the axes.

Sudden movement can be detected by looking for accelerometer values considerably larger than 1 g. In normal usage, the accelerometer does not detect significantly more than 1 g on any axis. If you shake, drop, or throw your device, the accelerometer will detect a greater amount of force on one or more axes. (Please do not drop or throw your own iOS device to test this theory, unless you are looking for an excuse to upgrade to the newest model!)

Figure 20-1 shows a graphic representation of the three axes used by the accelerometer. Notice that the accelerometer uses the more standard convention for the y coordinate, with increases in y indicating upward force, which is the opposite of Quartz 2D's coordinate system (discussed in Chapter 16). When you are using the accelerometer as a control mechanism with Quartz 2D, you need to translate the y coordinate. When working with Sprite Kit, which is more likely when you are using the accelerometer to control animation, no translation is required.

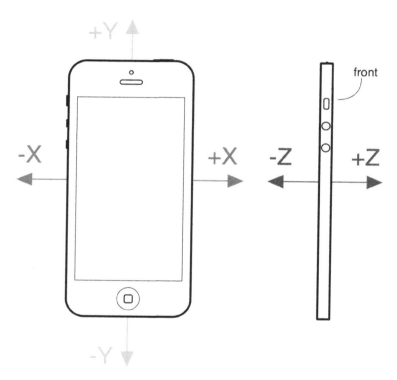

Figure 20-1. *The iPhone accelerometer's axes in three dimensions. The front view of an iPhone on the left shows the x and y axes. The side view on the right shows the z axis*

Don't Forget Rotation

We mentioned earlier that all current devices include a gyroscope sensor, allowing you to read values describing the device's rotation around its axes.

If the difference between the gyroscope and the accelerometer seems unclear, consider an iPhone lying flat on a table. If you begin to turn the phone around while it's lying flat, the accelerometer values won't change. That's because the forces bent on moving the phone—in this case, just the force of gravity pulling straight down the z axis—aren't changing. (In reality, things are a bit fuzzier than that, and the action of your hand bumping the phone will surely trigger a small amount of accelerometer action.) During that same movement, however, the device's rotation values will change—particularly the z-axis rotation value. Turning the device clockwise will generate a negative value, and turning it counterclockwise gives a positive value. Stop turning, and the z-axis rotation value will go back to zero.

Rather than registering an absolute rotation value, the gyroscope tells you about changes to the device's rotation as they happen. You'll see how this works in this chapter's first example, coming up shortly.

Core Motion and the Motion Manager

Accelerometer and gyroscope values are accessed using the Core Motion framework. This framework provides, among other things, the CMMotionManager class, which acts as a gateway for all the values describing how the device is being moved by its user. Your application creates an instance of CMMotionManager and then puts it to use in one of two modes:

- It can execute some code for you whenever motion occurs.

- It can hang on to a perpetually updated structure that lets you access the latest values at any time.

The latter method is ideal for games and other highly interactive applications that need to be able to poll the device's current state during each pass through the game loop. We'll show you how to implement both approaches.

Note that the CMMotionManager class isn't actually a singleton, but your application should treat it like one. You should create only one of these per app, using the normal alloc and init methods. So, if you need to access the motion manager from several places in your app, you should probably create it in your application delegate and provide access to it from there.

Besides the CMMotionManager class, Core Motion also provides a few other classes, such as CMAccelerometerData and CMGyroData, which are simple containers through which your application can access raw accelerometer and gyroscope information; and CMDeviceMotion, a class that combines accelerometer and gyroscope measurements together with attitude information—that is, whether the device is lying flat, tilting upward or to the left, and so on. We'll be using the CMDeviceMotion class in the examples in this chapter.

Event-Based Motion

We mentioned that the motion manager can operate in a mode where it executes some code for you each time the motion data changes. Most other Cocoa Touch classes offer this sort of functionality by letting you connect to a delegate that gets a message when the time comes, but Core Motion does things a little differently.

Instead of using a set of delegate methods to let us know what happens, `CMMotionManager` lets you pass in a block to execute whenever motion occurs. We've already used blocks a couple of times in this book, and now you're going to see another application of this technique.

Use Xcode to create a new Single View Application project named *MotionMonitor*. This will be a simple app that reads both accelerometer data, gyroscope data (if available), and attitude information, and then displays the information on the screen.

> **Note**   The applications in this chapter do not function on the simulator because the simulator has no accelerometer. Aw, shucks.

Now select the *ViewController.m* file and make the following changes:

```
#import "ViewController.h"

@interface ViewController ()

@property (weak, nonatomic) IBOutlet UILabel *gyroscopeLabel;
@property (weak, nonatomic) IBOutlet UILabel *accelerometerLabel;
@property (weak, nonatomic) IBOutlet UILabel *attitudeLabel;

@end
```

This provides us with outlets to three labels where we'll display the information. Nothing much needs to be explained here, so just go ahead and save your changes.

Next, open *Main.storyboard* in Interface Builder. In the Document Overview, expand the view controller and rename its view to *Main View*. Now drag out a **Label** from the library into the view. Resize the label to make it run from the left side of the screen to the right, resize it to be about one-third the height of the entire view, and then align the top of the label to the top blue guideline. Now open the Attributes Inspector and change the Lines field from *1* to *0*. The Lines attribute is used to specify the number of lines of text that may appear in the label, and it provides a hard upper limit. If you set it to 0, no limit is applied, and the label can contain as many lines as you like.

Next, drag a second label from the library and drop it directly below the first one. Align its top with the bottom of the first label and align its sides with the left and right edges of the screen. Resize it to be about the same height as the first label. You don't need to be too exact with this since we will be using auto layout to control the final height of the labels. Drag out a third label, placing it with its top edge along the bottom edge of the second label, and then resize it so that its bottom edge is along the bottom edge of the screen, and align its sides to the left and right edges of the screen. Set the Lines attribute for both labels to 0.

Now let's fix the positions and sizes of the three labels. In the Document Overview, Control-drag from the top label to Main View and release the mouse. In the context menu, hold down the **Shift** key and select **Leading Space to Container Margin**, **Top Space to Top Layout Guide**, and Trailing Space to Container Margin, and then click outside the context menu with the mouse. Control-drag from the second label to the Main View. In the context menu, hold down **Shift** and select **Leading Space to Container Margin** and **Trailing Space to Container Margin**, and then click outside the context menu with the mouse. Control-drag from the third label to Main View, and this time, holding down **Shift**, select **Leading Space to Container Margin**, **Bottom Space to Bottom Layout Guide**, and **Trailing Space to Container Margin**.

Now that all three labels are pinned to the edges of Main View, let's link them to each other. Control-drag from the second label to the first label and select **Vertical Spacing** from the pop-up menu. Control-drag from the second label to the third label and do the same. Finally, we need to ensure that the labels have the same height. To do this, hold down the **Shift** key and click all three labels so that they are all selected. Click the **Pin** button and, in the pop-up, click the **Equal Heights** check box and press **Add 2 Constraints**. Click the **Resolve Auto Layout Issues** button and then click **Update All Frames in View Controller**. If this item is not available, select the **View Controller** icon in the Document Outline and try again.

That completes the layout; now let's connect the labels to their outlets. Open *ViewController.m* in the assistant editor, and then Control-drag from the top label to gyroscopeLabel and connect the outlet. Do the same with the second label, connecting it to accelerometerLabel and the third label, which should be linked to attituteLabel. Finally, double-click each of the labels and delete the existing text.

This simple GUI is complete, so save your work and get ready for some coding.

Next, select *ViewController.m*. Now comes the interesting part. Add the following content:

```
#import "ViewController.h"
#import <CoreMotion/CoreMotion.h>

@interface ViewController ()

@property (weak, nonatomic) IBOutlet UILabel *gyroscopeLabel;
@property (weak, nonatomic) IBOutlet UILabel *accelerometerLabel;
@property (weak, nonatomic) IBOutlet UILabel *attitudeLabel;

@property (retain, nonatomic) CMMotionManager *motionManager;
@property (retain, nonatomic) NSOperationQueue *queue;

@end

@implementation ViewController

- (void)viewDidLoad
{
    [super viewDidLoad];
    // Do any additional setup after loading the view, typically from a nib.

    self.motionManager = [[CMMotionManager alloc] init];
```

```objc
    self.queue = [[NSOperationQueue alloc] init];
    if (self.motionManager.deviceMotionAvailable) {
        self.motionManager.deviceMotionUpdateInterval = 0.1;
        [self.motionManager startDeviceMotionUpdatesToQueue:self.queue
                        withHandler:^(CMDeviceMotion *motion, NSError *error) {
            CMRotationRate rotationRate = motion.rotationRate;
            CMAcceleration gravity = motion.gravity;
            CMAcceleration userAcc = motion.userAcceleration;
            CMAttitude *attitude = motion.attitude;

            NSString *gyroscopeText = [NSString stringWithFormat:
                            @"Rotation Rate:\n----------------\n"
                            "x: %+.2f\ny: %+.2f\nz: %+.2f\n",
                            rotationRate.x, rotationRate.y, rotationRate.z];
            NSString *acceleratorText = [NSString stringWithFormat:
                            @"Acceleration:\n--------------\n"
                            "Gravity x: %+.2f\t\tUser x: %+.2f\n"
                            "Gravity y: %+.2f\t\tUser y: %+.2f\n"
                            "Gravity z: %+.2f\t\tUser z: %+.2f\n",
                            gravity.x, userAcc.x, gravity.y,
                            userAcc.y, gravity.z,userAcc.z];
            NSString *attitudeText = [NSString stringWithFormat:
                            @"Attitude:\n----------\n"
                            "Roll: %+.2f\nPitch: %+.2f\nYaw: %+.2f\n",
                            attitude.roll, attitude.pitch, attitude.yaw];

            dispatch_async(dispatch_get_main_queue(), ^{
                self.gyroscopeLabel.text = gyroscopeText;
                self.accelerometerLabel.text = acceleratorText;
                self.attitudeLabel.text = attitudeText;
            });
        }];
    }
}

- (void)didReceiveMemoryWarning
{
    [super didReceiveMemoryWarning];
    // Dispose of any resources that can be recreated.
}

@end
```

First, we import the header file for working with the Core Motion framework and add two additional properties to the class extension:

```
@interface ViewController ()

@property (weak, nonatomic) IBOutlet UILabel *gyroscopeLabel;
@property (weak, nonatomic) IBOutlet UILabel *accelerometerLabel;
@property (weak, nonatomic) IBOutlet UILabel *attitudeLabel;

@property (strong, nonatomic) CMMotionManager *motionManager;
@property (strong, nonatomic) NSOperationQueue *queue;

@end
```

Next, in the `viewDidLoad` method, we add the code to request device motion updates and update the labels with the gyroscope, accelerometer, and attitude readings as we get them.

Thanks to the power of blocks, it's all really simple and cohesive. Instead of putting parts of the functionality in delegate methods, you can define behaviors in blocks to see a behavior in the same method where it's being configured. Let's take this apart a bit. We start off with this:

```
self.motionManager = [[CMMotionManager alloc] init];
self.queue = [[NSOperationQueue alloc] init];
```

This code first creates an instance of `CMMotionManager`, which we'll use to monitor motion events. The code then creates an operation queue, which is simply a container for work that needs to be done.

> **Caution** The motion manager wants to have a queue in which it will put the bits of work to be done, as specified by the blocks you will give it, each time an event occurs. It would be tempting to use the system's default queue for this purpose, but the documentation for `CMMotionManager` explicitly warns not to do this! The concern is that the default queue could end up chock-full of these events and have a hard time processing other crucial system events as a result.

The next step is to start requesting device motion updates. We first check to make sure the device actually has the required equipment to provide motion information. All handheld iOS devices released so far do, but it's worth checking in case some future device doesn't. Next, we set the time interval we want between updates, specified in seconds. Here, we're asking for a tenth of a second. Note that setting this doesn't guarantee that we'll receive updates at precisely that speed. In fact, that setting is really a cap, specifying the best rate the motion manager will be allowed to give us. In reality, it may update less frequently than that:

```
if (self.motionManager.deviceMotionAvailable) {
    self.motionManager.deviceMotionUpdateInterval = 0.1;
```

Next, we tell the motion manager to start reporting device motion updates. We pass in the block that defines the work that will be done each time an update occurs and the queue where the block will be queued for execution. Remember that a block always starts off with a caret (^), followed by a parentheses-wrapped list of arguments that the block expects to be populated when it's executed (in this case, a CMDeviceMotion object that contains the most recent motion data and potentially an error to alert us of trouble), and finishes with a curly brace section that contains the code to be executed:

```
[self.motionManager startDeviceMotionUpdatesToQueue:self.queue
    withHandler:^(CMDeviceMotion *motion, NSError *error) {
```

What follows is the content of the block. It creates strings based on the current motion values and pushes them into the labels. We can't do that directly here because UIKit classes like UILabel usually work well only when accessed from the main thread. Due to the way this code will be executed, from within an NSOperationQueue, we simply don't know the specific thread in which we'll be executing. So, we use the dispatch_async() function to pass control to the main thread before setting the labels' text properties.

The gyroscope values are accessed through the rotationRate property of the CMDeviceMotion object that was passed into the block. The rotationRate property is of type CMRotationRate, which is just a simple struct containing three float values that represent the rotation rates around the x, y, and z axes. The accelerometer data is a little more complex, since Core Motion reports two different values—the acceleration due to gravity and any additional acceleration caused by forces applied by the user. You get these values from the gravity and userAcceleration properties, which are both of type CMAcceleration. CMAccelaration is another simple struct that holds the accelerations along the x, y, and z axes. Finally, the device attitude is reported in the attitude property, which is of type CMAttitude. We'll discuss this further when we run the application.

Before trying out the application, there is one more thing to do. We are going to be moving and rotating the device in various ways to see how the values in the CMDeviceMotion structure correlate to what's happening to the device. While we're doing this, we don't want autorotation to kick in. To prevent this, select the project in the Project Navigator, select the **MotionMonitor** target, and then the **General** tab. In the Device Orientation section under Deployment Info, select **Portrait** and make sure that the other three orientations are not selected. This locks the application to Portrait orientation only.

Now build and run your app on whatever iOS device you have, and then try it out (see Figure 20-2).

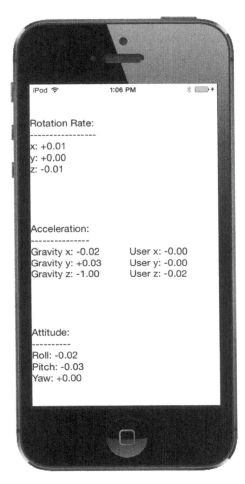

Figure 20-2. MotionMonitor running on an iPhone. Unfortunately, you'll get no useful information if you run this app in the simulator

As you tilt your device around in different ways, you'll see how the rotation rate, accelerometer, and attitude values adjust to each new position and will hold steady as long as you hold the device steady. Whenever the device is standing still, no matter which orientation it is in, the rotation values will hover around zero. As you rotate the device, you'll see that the rotation values change, depending on how you turn it around its various axes. The values will always move back to zero when you stop moving the device. We'll look more closely at all of the results shortly.

Proactive Motion Access

You've seen how to access motion data by passing CMMotionManager blocks to be called as motion occurs. This kind of event-driven motion handling can work well enough for the average Cocoa app, but sometimes it doesn't quite fit an application's particular needs. Interactive games, for example, typically have a perpetually running loop that processes user input, updates the state of the game, and redraws the screen. In such a case, the event-driven approach isn't such a good fit, since you would need to implement an object that waits for motion events, remembers the latest positions from each sensor as they're reported, and is ready to report the data back to the main game loop when necessary.

Fortunately, CMMotionManager has a built-in solution. Instead of passing in blocks, we can just tell it to activate the sensors using the startDeviceMotionUpdates method. Once we do so, we can simply read the values any time we want, directly from the motion manager!

Let's change our MotionMonitor app to use this approach, just so you can see how it works. Start by making a copy of your *MotionMonitor* project folder.

Note You'll find a completed version of this project in the *20 – MonitorMotion2* folder in the example source code.

Close the open Xcode project and open the one from the new copy instead, heading straight to *ViewController.m*. The first step is to remove the queue property and add a new property, a pointer to an NSTimer that will trigger all our display updates:

```
#import "ViewController.h"
#import <CoreMotion/CoreMotion.h>

@interface ViewController ()

@property (weak, nonatomic) IBOutlet UILabel *gyroscopeLabel;
@property (weak, nonatomic) IBOutlet UILabel *accelerometerLabel;
@property (weak, nonatomic) IBOutlet UILabel *attitudeLabel;

@property (strong, nonatomic) CMMotionManager *motionManager;
@property (strong, nonatomic) NSOperationQueue *queue;
@property (strong, nonatomic) NSTimer *updateTimer;

@end
```

Next, get rid of most of the viewDidLoad method that we had before and replace it with this simpler version:

```
- (void)viewDidLoad
{
    [super viewDidLoad];
    // Do any additional setup after loading the view, typically from a nib.
    self.motionManager = [[CMMotionManager alloc] init];
}
```

We're going to use a timer to collect motion data directly from the motion manager every tenth of a second instead of having it delivered to a code block. We want our timer—and the motion manager itself—to be active only during a small window of time, when the view is actually being displayed. That way, we keep the usage of our main game loop to a bare minimum. We can accomplish this by implementing the viewWillAppear: and viewDidDisappear: methods, as shown here:

```
- (void)viewWillAppear:(BOOL)animated {
    [super viewWillAppear:animated];
    if (self.motionManager.deviceMotionAvailable) {
        self.motionManager.deviceMotionUpdateInterval = 0.1;
        [self.motionManager startDeviceMotionUpdates];
        self.updateTimer = [NSTimer
                        scheduledTimerWithTimeInterval:0.1
                        target:self
                        selector:@selector(updateDisplay)
                        userInfo:nil
                        repeats:YES];
    }
}

- (void)viewDidDisappear:(BOOL)animated {
    [super viewDidDisappear:animated];
    if (self.motionManager.deviceMotionAvailable) {
        [self.motionManager stopDeviceMotionUpdates];
        [self.updateTimer invalidate];
        self.updateTimer = nil;
    }
}
```

The code in viewWillAppear: calls the motion manager's startDeviceMotionUpdates method to start it off device motion information, then creates a new timer and schedules it to fire once every tenth of a second, calling the updateDisplay method, which we haven't created yet. Add this method just below viewDidDisappear:

```
- (void)updateDisplay {
    CMDeviceMotion *motion = self.motionManager.deviceMotion;
    if (motion != nil) {
        CMRotationRate rotationRate = motion.rotationRate;
        CMAcceleration gravity = motion.gravity;
        CMAcceleration userAcc = motion.userAcceleration;
        CMAttitude *attitude = motion.attitude;

        NSString *gyroscopeText = [NSString stringWithFormat:
                        @"Rotation Rate:\n----------------\n"
                        "x: %+.2f\ny: %+.2f\nz: %+.2f\n",
                        rotationRate.x, rotationRate.y, rotationRate.z];
```

```
        NSString *acceleratorText = [NSString stringWithFormat:
                            @"Acceleration:\n--------------\n"
                            "Gravity x: %+.2f\t\tUser x: %+.2f\n"
                            "Gravity y: %+.2f\t\tUser y: %+.2f\n"
                            "Gravity z: %+.2f\t\tUser z: %+.2f\n",
                            gravity.x, userAcc.x, gravity.y,
                            userAcc.y, gravity.z,userAcc.z];
        NSString *attitudeText = [NSString stringWithFormat:
                            @"Attitude:\n----------\n"
                            "Roll: %+.2f\nPitch: %+.2f\nYaw: %+.2f\n",
                            attitude.roll, attitude.pitch, attitude.yaw];

        dispatch_async(dispatch_get_main_queue(), ^{
            self.gyroscopeLabel.text = gyroscopeText;
            self.accelerometerLabel.text = acceleratorText;
            self.attitudeLabel.text = attitudeText;
        });
    }
}
```

This is a copy of the code from the closure in the previous version of this example, except that the CMDeviceMotion object is obtained directly from the motion manager. Notice the check for nil; this is required because the timer may fire before the motion manager has acquired its first data sample.

Build and run the app on your device, and you should see that it behaves exactly like the first version. Now you've seen two ways of accessing motion data. Use whichever suits your application best.

Gyroscope and Attitude Results

The gyroscope measures the rate at which the device is rotating about the x, y, and z axes. Refer to Figure 20-1 to see how the axes relate to the body of the device. First, lay the device flat on a table. While it's not moving, all three rotation rates will be close to zero and you'll see that the roll, pitch, and yaw values are also close to zero. Now gently rotate the device clockwise. As you do, you'll see that the rotation rate around the z axis becomes negative. The faster you rotate the device, the larger the absolute value of the rotation rate will be. When you stop rotating, the rotation rate will return to zero, but the yaw does not. The yaw represents the angle through which the device has been rotated about the z axis from its initial rest position. If you rotate the device clockwise, the yaw will increase through negative values until the device is 180° from its rest position, when its value will be around –3. If you continue to rotate the device clockwise, the yaw will jump to a value slightly larger than +3 and then decrease to zero as you rotate it back to its initial position. If you start by rotating counterclockwise, the same thing happens, except that the yaw is initially positive. The yaw angle is actually measured in radians, not degrees. A rotation of 180° is the same as a rotation by π radians, which is why the maximum yaw value is about 3 (since π is a little larger than 3.14).

With the device flat on the table again, hold the top edge and rotate it upward, leaving the base on the table. This is a rotation around the x axis, so you'll see the x rotation rate increase through positive values until you hold the device steady, at which point it returns to zero. Now look at the pitch value. It has increased by an amount that depends on the angle through which you have lifted the top edge of the device. If you lift the device all the way to the vertical, the pitch value will be around 1.5. Like yaw, pitch is measured in radians, so when the device is vertical, it has rotated through 90°, or $\pi/2$ radians, which is a little over 1.5. If you lay the device flat again and repeat—but this time lift the bottom edge and leave the top on the table, you are performing a counterclockwise rotation about the x axis and you'll see a negative rotation rate and a negative pitch.

Finally, with the device flat on the table again, lift its left edge, leaving the right edge on the table. This is a rotation about the y axis and you'll see this reflect in the y-axis rotation rate. You can get the total rotation angle at any point from the roll value. It will be about 1.5 (actually $\pi/2$) radians when the device is standing upright on its right edge and it will increase all the way to π radians if you turn it on its face; although, of course, you'll need a glass table to be able to see this.

In summary, use the rotation rates to see how fast the device is rotating about each axis and the yaw, pitch, and roll values to get its current total rotation about these axes, relative to its starting orientation.

Accelerometer Results

We mentioned earlier that the iPhone's accelerometer detects acceleration along three axes, and it provides this information using two CMAcceleration structs. Each CMAcceleration has an x, y, and z field, each of which holds a floating-point value. A value of 0 means that the accelerometer detects no movement on that particular axis. A positive or negative value indicates force in one direction. For example, a negative value for y indicates that a downward pull is sensed, which is probably an indication that the phone is being held upright in portrait orientation. A positive value for y indicates some force is being exerted in the opposite direction, which could mean the phone is being held upside down or that the phone is being moved in a downward direction. The CMDeviceMotion object separately reports the acceleration along each axis due to gravity and any additional forces caused by the user. For example, if you hold the device flat, you'll see that gravity value is close to −1 along the z axis and the user acceleration components are all close to zero. Now if you quickly raise the device, keeping it level, you'll see that the gravity values remain about the same, but there is positive user acceleration along the z axis. For some applications, it is useful to have separate gravity and user acceleration values, while for others, you need the total acceleration, which you can get by adding together the components of the gravity and userAcceleration properties of the CMDeviceMotion object.

Keeping the diagram in Figure 20-1 in mind, let's look at some accelerometer results (see Figure 20-3). This figure shows the reported acceleration due to gravity while the device is in a given attitude and not moving. Note that in real life you will almost never get values this precise, as the accelerometer is sensitive enough to sense even tiny amounts of motion, and you will usually pick up at least some tiny amount of force on all three axes. This is real-world physics, not high-school physics.

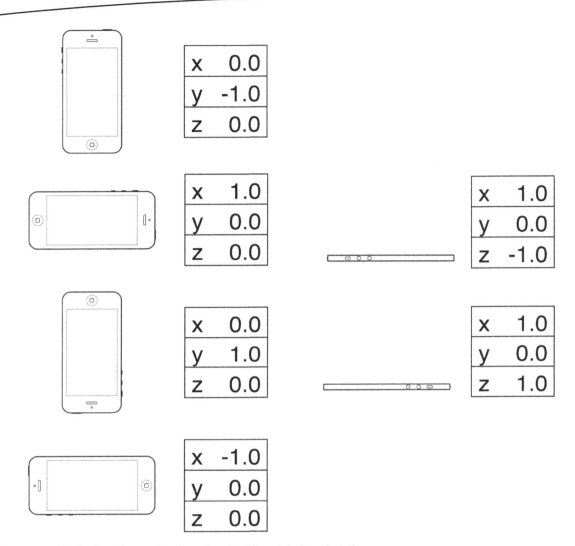

Figure 20-3. *Idealized gravity acceleration values for different device orientations*

The most common usage of the accelerometer in third-party applications is probably as a controller for games. We'll create a program that uses the accelerometer for input a little later in the chapter, but first we'll look at another common accelerometer use: detecting shakes.

Detecting Shakes

Like a gesture, a shake can be used as a form of input to your application. For example, the drawing program GLPaint, which is one of Apple's iOS sample code projects, lets users erase drawings by shaking their iOS device, sort of like an Etch A Sketch.

Detecting shakes is relatively trivial. All it requires is checking for an absolute value of user acceleration on one of the axes that is greater than a set threshold. During normal usage, it's not uncommon for one of the three axes to register values up to around 1.3 g, but getting values much higher than that generally requires intentional force. The accelerometer seems to be unable to register values higher than around 2.3 g (at least in our experience), so you don't want to set your threshold any higher than that.

To detect a shake, you could check for an absolute value greater than 1.5 for a slight shake and 2.0 for a strong shake, by adding code like this to the motion manager callback block in the MotionMonitor example:

```
CMAcceleration userAcc = motion.userAcceleration;
if (fabsf(userAcc.x) > 2.0
        || fabsf(userAcc.y) > 2.0
        || fabsf(userAcc.z) > 2.0) {
    // Do something here...
}
```

This code would detect any movement on any axis that exceeded two g-forces.

Baked-In Shaking

There's actually another, much simpler way to check for shakes—one that's baked right into the responder chain. Remember back in Chapter 18 when we implemented methods like touchesBegan:withEvent: to detect touches? Well, iOS also provides three similar responder methods for detecting motion:

- When motion begins, the motionBegan:withEvent: method is sent to the first responder and then on through the responder chain, as discussed in Chapter 18.

- When the motion ends, the motionEnded:withEvent: method is sent to the first responder.

- If the phone rings, or some other interrupting action happens during the shake, the motionCancelled:withEvent: message is sent to the first responder.

The first argument to each of these methods is an event subtype, one of which is UIEventSubtypeMotionShake. This means that you can actually detect a shake without using CMMotionManager directly. All you need to do is override the appropriate motion-sensing methods in your view or view controller, and they will be called automatically when the user shakes the phone. Unless you specifically need more control over the shake gesture, you should use the baked-in motion detection rather than the manual method described previously. However, we thought we would show you the basics of the manual method in case you ever do need more control.

Now that you have the basic idea of how to detect shakes, we're going to break your phone.

Shake and Break

Okay, we're not really going to break your phone, but we'll write an application that detects shakes, and then makes your phone look and sound as if it broke as a result of the shake.

When you launch the application, the program will display a picture that looks like the iPhone home screen (see Figure 20-4). Shake the phone hard enough, though, and your poor phone will make a sound that you never want to hear coming out of a consumer electronics device. What's more, your screen will look like the one shown in Figure 20-5. Why do we do these evil things? Not to worry. You can reset the iPhone to its previously pristine state by touching the screen.

Figure 20-4. The ShakeAndBreak application looks innocuous enough. . .

Figure 20-5. . . . but handle it too roughly and—oh no!

Create a new project in Xcode using the Single View Application template. Make sure that the device type is set to *iPhone*—unlike most of the other examples in this book, this one only works on iPhone because the images are of the correct size for an iPhone 5 screen. Of course, it's easy to extend this project to iPad if you create additional images. Call the new project *ShakeAndBreak*. In the *20 – Images and Sounds* folder of the example source code, we've provided the two images and the sound file you need for this application. In *Images.xcassets*, create an image set called *home* and drag *home.png* into it, and then create another image set called *homebroken* and drag *homebroken.png*, into it. Drag *glass.wav* to your project.

Now let's start creating our view controller. We're going to need to create an outlet to point to an image view so that we can change the displayed image. Single-click *ViewController.m* and add the following property declaration to the class extension:

```
#import "ViewController.h"

@interface ViewController ()

@property (weak, nonatomic) IBOutlet UIImageView *imageView;

@end
```

Save the file. Now select *Main.storyboard* to edit the file in Interface Builder and drag an **Image View** over from the library to the view in the layout area. The image view should automatically resize to take up the full window, so just place it so that it sits perfectly within the window. In the Document Overview, Control-drag from the Image View to its parent View, hold down **Shift**, and in the context menu, select **Leading Space to Container Margin**, **Trailing Space to Container Margin**, **Top Space to Top Layout Guide**, and **Bottom Space to Bottom Layout Guide**, and then click outside the context menu with the mouse to lock the size and position of the image view. Finally, Control-drag from the **View Controller** icon to the **image view** and select the imageView outlet, and then save the storyboard.

Next, go back to the *ViewController.m* file. We're going to add some additional properties for both of the images we're going to display, to track whether we're showing the broken image. We're also adding an audio player object that we'll use to play our breaking glass sound. The following bold lines go near the top of the file:

```
#import "ViewController.h"
#import <AVFoundation/AVFoundation.h>

@interface ViewController ()

@property (weak, nonatomic) IBOutlet UIImageView *imageView;
@property (strong, nonatomic) UIImage *fixed;
@property (strong, nonatomic) UIImage *broken;
@property (assign, nonatomic) BOOL brokenScreenShowing;
@property (strong, nonatomic) AVAudioPlayer *crashPlayer;

@end
```

Add the following code to the viewDidLoad method:

```
@implementation ViewController

- (void)viewDidLoad
{
    [super viewDidLoad];
    // Do any additional setup after loading the view, typically from a nib.
```

```
NSURL *url = [[NSBundle mainBundle] URLForResource:@"glass"
                                      withExtension:@"wav"];

NSError *error = nil;
self.crashPlayer = [[AVAudioPlayer alloc] initWithContentsOfURL:url
                                                 error:&error];
if (!self.crashPlayer) {
    NSLog(@"Audio Error! %@", error.localizedDescription);
}

self.fixed = [UIImage imageNamed:@"home"];
self.broken = [UIImage imageNamed:@"homebroken"];

self.imageView.image = self.fixed;
}
```

At this point, we've created an NSURL object pointing to our sound file and initialized an instance of AVAudioPlayer, a class that will simply play the sound. After a quick sanity check to make sure the audio player was set up correctly, we loaded both images we need to use and put the first one in place. Next, add the following new method:

```
- (void)motionEnded:(UIEventSubtype)motion withEvent:(UIEvent *)event {
    if (!self.brokenScreenShowing && motion == UIEventSubtypeMotionShake) {
        self.imageView.image = self.broken;
        [self.crashPlayer play];
        self.brokenScreenShowing = YES;
    }
}
```

This method will be called whenever a shake happens. After checking to make sure the broken screen isn't already showing and that the event we're looking at really is a shake event, the method shows the broken image and plays our shattering noise.

The last method is one you should already be familiar with by now. It's called when the screen is touched. All we need to do in that method is set the image back to the unbroken screen and set brokenScreenShowing back to NO:

```
- (void)touchesBegan:(NSSet *)touches withEvent:(UIEvent *)event {
    self.imageView.image = self.fixed;
    self.brokenScreenShowing = NO;
}
```

Compile and run the application, and take it for a test shake. For those of you who don't have the ability to run this application on your iOS device, you can still give this a try. The simulator does not simulate the accelerometer hardware, but it does include a menu item that simulates the shake event, so this will work with the simulator, too.

Go have some fun with it. When you're finished, come on back, and you'll see how to use the accelerometer as a controller for games and other programs.

Accelerometer As Directional Controller

Instead of using buttons to control the movement of a character or object in a game, developers often use an accelerometer to accomplish this task. In a car-racing game, for example, twisting the iOS device like a steering wheel might steer your car, while tipping it forward might accelerate, and tipping it back might brake.

Exactly how you use the accelerometer as a controller will vary greatly, depending on the specific mechanics of the game. In the simplest cases, you might just take the value from one of the axes, multiply it by a number, and add that to one of the coordinates of the controlled objects. In more complex games where physics are modeled more realistically, you would need to make adjustments to the velocity of the controlled object based on the values returned from the accelerometer.

The one tricky aspect of using the accelerometer as a controller is that the delegate method is not guaranteed to call back at the interval you specify. If you tell the motion manager to read the accelerometer 60 times a second, all that you can say for sure is that it won't update more than 60 times a second. You're not guaranteed to get 60 evenly spaced updates every second. So, if you're doing animation based on input from the accelerometer, you must keep track of the time that passes between updates and factor that into your equations to determine how far objects have moved.

Rolling Marbles

For our next trick, we're going to let you move a sprite around the iPhone's screen by tilting the phone. This is a very simple example of using the accelerometer to receive input. We'll use Quartz 2D to handle our animation.

> **Note**   As a general rule, when you're working with games and other programs that need smooth animation, you'll probably want to use Sprite Kit or OpenGL ES. We're using Quartz 2D in this application for the sake of simplicity and to reduce the amount of code that's unrelated to using the accelerometer.

In this application, as you tilt your iPhone, the marble will roll around as if it were on the surface of a table (see Figure 20-6). Tip it to the left, and the ball will roll to the left. Tip it farther, and it will move faster. Tip it back, and it will slow down, and then start going in the other direction.

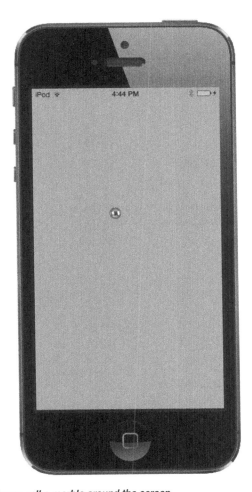

Figure 20-6. The Ball application lets you roll a marble around the screen

In Xcode, create a new project using the Single View Application template. Set the device type to *Universal* and call the project *Ball*. In the *20 – Images and Sounds* folder in the example source code, you'll find an image called *ball.png*. Create an image set called *ball* in *Images.xcassets* and drag *ball.png* into it.

Next, select the Ball project in the Project Navigator, and then the **General** tab of the Ball target. In the Device Orientation section under Deployment Info, select **Portrait** and deselect all of the other check boxes, as you did for the MotionMonitor application earlier in this chapter. This disables the default interface orientation changes; we want to roll our ball and not change the interface orientation as we move our device around.

Now single-click the *Ball* folder and select **File ➤ New ➤ File**. . . . Select **Cocoa Touch Class** from the iOS section, and click **Next**. Make the new class a subclass of UIView and name it *BallView*, and then click **Create**. We'll get back to editing this class a little later.

Select *Main.storyboard* to edit the file in Interface Builder. Single-click the **View** icon and use the identity inspector to change the view's class from *UIView* to *BallView*. Next, switch to the Attributes Inspector and change the view's **Background** to **Light Gray Color**. Finally, save the storyboard.

Now it's time to edit *ViewController.m*. Add the following lines at the top of the file:

```
#import "ViewController.h"
#import "BallView.h"
#import <CoreMotion/CoreMotion.h>

#define kUpdateInterval     (1.0f / 60.0f)

@interface ViewController ()
@property (strong, nonatomic) CMMotionManager *motionManager;
@property (strong, nonatomic) NSOperationQueue *queue;
@end

@implementation ViewController
```

Next, populate viewDidLoad with this code:

```
- (void)viewDidLoad
{
    [super viewDidLoad];
    // Do any additional setup after loading the view, typically from a nib.
    self.motionManager = [[CMMotionManager alloc] init];
    self.queue = [[NSOperationQueue alloc] init];
    self.motionManager.deviceMotionUpdateInterval = kUpdateInterval;
    __weak ViewController *weakSelf = self;
    [self.motionManager startDeviceMotionUpdatesToQueue:self.queue
                    withHandler: ^(CMDeviceMotion *motionData, NSError *error) {
            BallView *ballView = (BallView *)weakSelf.view;
            [ballView setAcceleration:motionData.gravity];
            dispatch_async(dispatch_get_main_queue(), ^{
                [ballView update];
            });
    }];

}
```

> **Note**   After entering this code, you will see an error as a result of BallView not being complete. We're doing the bulk of our work in the BallView class, and it's up next.

The viewDidLoad method here is similar to some of what we've done elsewhere in this chapter. The main difference is that we are using a much higher update interval of 60 times per second. In the block that we tell the motion manager to execute when there are accelerometer updates to report, we pass the acceleration object along to our view. We then call a method named update, which updates the position of the ball in the view based on acceleration and the amount of time that has passed since the last update. Since that block can be executed on any thread, and the methods belonging to UIKit objects (including UIView) can be safely used only from the main thread, we once again force the update method to be called in the main thread.

Writing the Ball View

Select *BallView.h*. Here, you'll need to import the Core Motion header file and add the property that our controller will use to pass along an acceleration value and a method that it will call to update the ball's position:

```
#import <UIKit/UIKit.h>
#import <CoreMotion/CoreMotion.h>

@interface BallView : UIView

@property (assign, nonatomic) CMAcceleration acceleration;

- (void)update;

@end
```

Switch over to *BallView.m* and add a class extension with the following code near the top:

```
#import "BallView.h"

@interface BallView ()

@property (strong, nonatomic) UIImage *image;
@property (assign, nonatomic) CGPoint currentPoint;
@property (assign, nonatomic) CGPoint previousPoint;
@property (assign, nonatomic) CGFloat ballXVelocity;
@property (assign, nonatomic) CGFloat ballYVelocity;

@end
```

Let's look at the properties and talk about what we're doing with each of them. The first is a UIImage that will point to the sprite that we'll be moving around the screen:

```
UIImage *image;
```

After that, we keep track of two CGPoint variables. The currentPoint property will hold the current position of the ball. We'll also keep track of the last point where we drew the sprite. That way, we can build an update rectangle that encompasses both the new and old positions of the ball, so that it is drawn at the new spot and erased at the old one:

```
CGPoint    currentPoint;
CGPoint    previousPoint;
```

We also have two variables to keep track of the ball's current velocity in two dimensions. Although this isn't going to be a very complex simulation, we do want the ball to move in a manner similar to a real ball. We'll calculate the ball movement in the next section. We'll get acceleration from the accelerometer and keep track of velocity on two axes with these variables.

```
CGFloat ballXVelocity;
CGFloat ballYVelocity;
```

Now let's write the code to draw and move the ball around the screen. First, add the following methods at the beginning of the @implementation section in *BallView.m*:

```
@implementation BallView

- (void)commonInit {
    self.image = [UIImage imageNamed:@"ball"];
    self.currentPoint = CGPointMake((self.bounds.size.width / 2.0f) +
                                    (self.image.size.width / 2.0f),
                                    (self.bounds.size.height / 2.0f) +
                                    (self.image.size.height / 2.0f));
}

- (id)initWithCoder:(NSCoder *)coder  {
    self = [super initWithCoder:coder];
    if (self) {
        [self commonInit];
    }
    return self;
}

- (id)initWithFrame:(CGRect)frame {
    self = [super initWithFrame:frame];
    if (self) {
        [self commonInit];
    }
    return self;
}
```

Both the initWithCoder: and the initWithFrame: methods call our commonInit method. Our view that is created in a storyboard file will be initialized with the initWithCoder: method. We call the commonInit method from both initializer methods so that our view class can safely be created both from code and from a nib file. This is a nice thing to do for any view class that may be reused, such as this fancy ball rolling view.

Now uncomment the commented-out `drawRect:` method and give it this simple implementation:

```
- (void)drawRect:(CGRect)rect
{
    // Drawing code
    [self.image drawAtPoint:self.currentPoint];
}
```

Next, add these methods to the end of the class:

```
#pragma mark -

- (void)setCurrentPoint:(CGPoint)newPoint {
    self.previousPoint = self.currentPoint;
    _currentPoint = newPoint;

    if (self.currentPoint.x < 0) {
        _currentPoint.x = 0;
        self.ballXVelocity = 0;
    }
    if (self.currentPoint.y < 0){
        _currentPoint.y = 0;
        self.ballYVelocity = 0;
    }
    if (self.currentPoint.x > self.bounds.size.width - self.image.size.width) {
        _currentPoint.x = self.bounds.size.width - self.image.size.width;
        self.ballXVelocity = 0;
    }
    if (self.currentPoint.y >
        self.bounds.size.height - self.image.size.height) {
        _currentPoint.y = self.bounds.size.height - self.image.size.height;
        self.ballYVelocity = 0;
    }

    CGRect currentRect =
    CGRectMake(self.currentPoint.x, self.currentPoint.y,
               self.currentPoint.x + self.image.size.width,
               self.currentPoint.y + self.image.size.height);
    CGRect previousRect =
    CGRectMake(self.previousPoint.x, self.previousPoint.y,
               self.previousPoint.x + self.image.size.width,
               self.currentPoint.y + self.image.size.width);
    [self setNeedsDisplayInRect:CGRectUnion(currentRect, previousRect)];
}

- (void)update {
    static NSDate *lastUpdateTime = nil;

    if (lastUpdateTime != nil) {
        NSTimeInterval secondsSinceLastDraw =
            [[NSDate date] timeIntervalSinceDate:lastUpdateTime];
```

```
            self.ballYVelocity = self.ballYVelocity -
                               (self.acceleration.y * secondsSinceLastDraw);
            self.ballXVelocity = self.ballXVelocity +
                               (self.acceleration.x * secondsSinceLastDraw);

            CGFloat xAccel = secondsSinceLastDraw * self.ballXVelocity * 500;
            CGFloat yAccel = secondsSinceLastDraw * self.ballYVelocity * 500;

            self.currentPoint = CGPointMake(self.currentPoint.x + xAccel,
                                            self.currentPoint.y + yAccel);
    }
    // Update last time with current time
    lastUpdateTime = [[NSDate alloc] init];
}

@end
```

Calculating Ball Movement

Our drawRect: method couldn't be much simpler. We just draw the image we loaded in commonInit: at the position stored in currentPoint. The currentPoint accessor is a standard accessor method. The setCurrentPoint: mutator is another story, however.

The first things we do in setCurrentPoint: are to store the old currentPoint value in previousPoint and assign the new value to currentPoint:

```
self.previousPoint = self.currentPoint;
self.currentPoint = newPoint;
```

Next, we do a boundary check. If either the x or y position of the ball is less than 0 or greater than the width or height of the screen (accounting for the width and height of the image), then the acceleration in that direction is stopped:

```
if (self.currentPoint.x < 0) {
    _currentPoint.x = 0;
    self.ballXVelocity = 0;
}
if (self.currentPoint.y < 0){
    _currentPoint.y = 0;
    self.ballYVelocity = 0;
}
if (self.currentPoint.x > self.bounds.size.width - self.image.size.width) {
    _currentPoint.x = self.bounds.size.width - self.image.size.width;
    self.ballXVelocity = 0;
}
if (self.currentPoint.y >
    self.bounds.size.height - self.image.size.height) {
    _currentPoint.y = self.bounds.size.height - self.image.size.height;
    self.ballYVelocity = 0;
}
```

> **Tip** Do you want to make the ball bounce off the walls more naturally, instead of just stopping? It's easy enough to do. Just change the two lines in setCurrentPoint: that currently read self.ballXVelocity = 0; to **self.ballXVelocity = - (self.ballXVelocity / 2.0);**. And change the two lines that currently read self.ballYVelocity = 0; to **self.ballYVelocity = - (self.ballYVelocity / 2.0);**. With these changes, instead of killing the ball's velocity, we reduce it in half and set it to the inverse. Now the ball has half the velocity in the opposite direction.

After that, we calculate two CGRects based on the size of the image. One rectangle encompasses the area where the new image will be drawn, and the other encompasses the area where it was last drawn. We'll use these two rectangles to ensure that the old ball is erased at the same time the new one is drawn:

```
CGRect currentRect =
CGRectMake(self.currentPoint.x, self.currentPoint.y,
            self.currentPoint.x + self.image.size.width,
            self.currentPoint.y + self.image.size.height);
CGRect previousRect =
CGRectMake(self.previousPoint.x, self.previousPoint.y,
            self.previousPoint.x + self.image.size.width,
            self.currentPoint.y + self.image.size.width);
```

Finally, we create a new rectangle that is the union of the two rectangles we just calculated and feed that to setNeedsDisplayInRect: to indicate the part of our view that needs to be redrawn:

```
[self setNeedsDisplayInRect:CGRectUnion(currentRect, previousRect)];
```

The last substantive method in our class is update, which is used to figure out the correct new location of the ball. This method is called from the accelerometer method of its controller class after it feeds the view the new acceleration object. The first thing this method does is to declare a static NSDate variable that will be used to keep track of how long it has been since the last time the update method was called. The first time through this method, when lastUpdateTime is nil, we don't do anything because there's no point of reference. Because the updates are happening about 60 times a second, no one will ever notice a single missing frame:

```
static NSDate *lastUpdateTime = nil;

if (lastUpdateTime != nil) {
```

Every other time through this method, we calculate how long it has been since the last time this method was called. The NSDate instance returned by [NSDate date] represents the current time. By asking it for the time interval since lastUpdateDate, we get a number representing the number of seconds between the current time and lastUpdateTime:

```
NSTimeInterval secondsSinceLastDraw =
    [[NSDate date] timeIntervalSinceDate:lastUpdateTime];
```

Next, we calculate the new velocity in both directions by adding the current acceleration to the current velocity. We multiply acceleration by `secondsSinceLastDraw` so that our acceleration is consistent across time. Tipping the phone at the same angle will always cause the same amount of acceleration:

```
self.ballYVelocity = self.ballYVelocity -
                        (self.acceleration.y * secondsSinceLastDraw);
self.ballXVelocity = self.ballXVelocity +
                        (self.acceleration.x * secondsSinceLastDraw);
```

After that, we figure out the actual change in pixels since the last time the method was called based on the velocity. The product of velocity and elapsed time is multiplied by 500 to create movement that looks natural. If we didn't multiply it by some value, the acceleration would be extraordinarily slow, as if the ball were stuck in molasses:

```
CGFloat xDelta = secondsSinceLastDraw * self.ballXVelocity * 500;
CGFloat yDelta = secondsSinceLastDraw * self.ballYVelocity * 500;
```

Once we know the change in pixels, we create a new point by adding the current location to the calculated acceleration and assign that to `currentPoint`. By using `self.currentPoint`, we use that accessor method we wrote earlier, rather than assigning the value directly to the instance variable:

```
self.currentPoint = CGPointMake(self.currentPoint.x + xDelta,
                                self.currentPoint.y + yDelta);
```

That ends our calculations, so all that's left is to update `lastUpdateTime` with the current time:

```
lastUpdateTime = [[NSDate alloc] init];
```

Before you build the app, add the Core Motion framework using the technique mentioned earlier. Once it's added, go ahead and build and run the app.

If all went well, the application will launch, and you should be able to control the movement of the ball by tilting the phone. When the ball gets to an edge of the screen, it should stop. Tip the phone back the other way, and it should start rolling in the other direction. Whee!

Rolling On

Well, we've certainly had some fun in this chapter with physics and the amazing iOS accelerometer and gyro. We created a great April Fools' prank, and you got to see the basics of using the accelerometer as a control device. The possibilities for applications using the accelerometer and gyro are nearly as endless as the universe. So now that you have the basics down, go create something cool and surprise us!

When you feel up to it, we're going to get into using another bit of iOS hardware: the built-in camera.

Chapter 21

The Camera and Photo Library

By now, it should come as no surprise to you that the iPhone, iPad, and iPod touch have a built-in camera and a nifty application called **Photos** to help you manage all those awesome pictures and videos you've taken. What you may not know is that your programs can use the built-in camera to take pictures. Your applications can also allow the user to select from among and view the media already stored on the device. We'll look at both of these abilities in this chapter.

Using the Image Picker and UIImagePickerController

Because of the way iOS applications are sandboxed, applications ordinarily can't get access to photographs or other data that live outside their own sandboxes. Fortunately, both the camera and the media library are made available to your application by way of an **image picker**.

Using the Image Picker Controller

As the name implies, an image picker is a mechanism that lets you select an image from a specified source. When this class first appeared in iOS, it was used only for images. Nowadays, you can use it to capture video as well.

Typically, an image picker will use a list of images and/or videos as its source (see the left side of Figure 21-1). You can, however, specify that the picker use the camera as its source (see the right side of Figure 21-1).

Figure 21-1. An image picker in action. Users are presented with a list of images (left). Once an image is selected, it can be moved and scaled (right). And, yeah, sometimes my camera roll is just pictures of Clumsy Ninja. I blame my children for this

The image picker interface is implemented by way of a controller class called `UIImagePickerController`. You create an instance of this class, specify a delegate (as if you didn't see that coming), specify its image source and whether you want the user to pick an image or a video, and then present it. The image picker will take control of the device to let the user select a picture or video from the existing media library. Or, the user can take a new picture or video with the camera. Once the user makes a selection, you can give the user an opportunity to do some basic editing, such as scaling or cropping an image, or trimming away a bit of a video clip. All of that behavior is implemented by the `UIImagePickerController`, so you really don't need to do much heavy lifting here.

Assuming the user doesn't press Cancel, the image or video that the user either captures or selects from the library will be delivered to your delegate. Regardless of whether the user selects a media file or cancels, your delegate is responsible for dismissing the `UIImagePickerController` so that the user can return to your application.

Creating a UIImagePickerController is extremely straightforward. You just create an instance the way you would with most classes. There is one catch, however: not every iOS device has a camera. Older iPod touches were the first examples of this, and the first-generation iPad is the latest. However, more such devices may roll off Apple's assembly lines in the future. Before you create an instance of UIImagePickerController, you need to check to see whether the device your app is currently running on supports the image source you want to use. For example, before letting the user take a picture with the camera, you should make sure the program is running on a device that has a camera. You can check that by using a class method on UIImagePickerController, like this:

```
if ([UIImagePickerController isSourceTypeAvailable:
    UIImagePickerControllerSourceTypeCamera]) {
```

In this example, we're passing UIImagePickerControllerSourceTypeCamera to indicate that we want to let the user take a picture or shoot a video using the built-in camera. The method isSourceTypeAvailable: returns YES if the specified source is currently available. We can specify two other values in addition to UIImagePickerControllerSourceTypeCamera:

- UIImagePickerControllerSourceTypePhotoLibrary specifies that the user should pick an image or video from the existing media library. That image will be returned to your delegate.

- UIImagePickerControllerSourceTypeSavedPhotosAlbum specifies that the user will select the image from the library of existing photographs, but that the selection will be limited to the camera roll. This option will run on a device without a camera, where it is less useful but still allows you to select any screenshots you have taken.

After making sure that the device your program is running on supports the image source you want to use, launching the image picker is relatively easy:

```
UIImagePickerController *picker = [[UIImagePickerController alloc] init];
picker.delegate = self;
picker.sourceType = UIImagePickerControllerSourceTypeCamera;
picker.cameraDevice = UIImagePickerControllerCameraDeviceFront;
[self presentViewController:picker animated:YES completion:nil];
```

> **Tip**   On a device that has more than one camera, you can select which one to use by setting the cameraDevice property to UIImagePickerControllerCameraDeviceFront or UIImagePickerControllerCameraDeviceRear. To find out whether a front or rear camera is available, use the same constants with the isCameraDeviceAvailable: method.

After we have created and configured the UIImagePickerController, we use a method that our class inherited from UIView called presentViewController:animated:completion: to present the image picker to the user.

Implementing the Image Picker Controller Delegate

To find out when the user has finished using the image picker, you need to implement the UIImagePickerControllerDelegate protocol. This protocol defines two methods: imagePickerContro ller:didFinishPickingMediaWithInfo: and imagePickerControllerDidCancel:.

The imagePickerController:didFinishPickingMediaWithInfo: method is called when the user has successfully captured a photo or video, or selected an item from the media library. The first argument is a pointer to the UIImagePickerController that you created earlier. The second argument is an NSDictionary instance that will contain the chosen photo or the URL of the chosen video, as well as optional editing information if you enabled editing in the image picker controller (and if the user actually did some editing). That dictionary will contain the original, unedited image stored under the key UIImagePickerControllerOriginalImage. Here's an example of a delegate method that retrieves the original image:

```
- (void)imagePickerController:(UIImagePickerController *)picker
            didFinishPickingMediaWithInfo:(NSDictionary *)info {
    UIImage *selectedImage = info[UIImagePickerControllerEditedImage];
    UIImage *originalImage = info[UIImagePickerControllerOriginalImage];

    // do something with selectedImage and originalImage

    [picker dismissViewControllerAnimated:YES completion:nil];
}
```

The editingInfo dictionary will also tell you which portion of the entire image was chosen during editing by way of an NSValue object stored under the key UIImagePickerControllerCropRect. You can convert this NSValue instance into a CGRect, like so:

```
NSValue *cropValue = info[UIImagePickerControllerCropRect];
CGRect cropRect = [cropValue CGRectValue];
```

After this conversion, cropRect will specify the portion of the original image that was selected during the editing process. If you do not need this information, you can just ignore it.

> **Caution**   If the image returned to your delegate comes from the camera, that image will not be stored in the photo library automatically. It is your application's responsibility to save the image, if necessary.

The other delegate method, imagePickerControllerDidCancel:, is called if the user decides to cancel the process without capturing or selecting any media. When the image picker calls this delegate method, it's just notifying you that the user is finished with the picker and didn't choose anything.

Both of the methods in the UIImagePickerControllerDelegate protocol are marked as optional, but they really aren't, and here is why: modal views like the image picker must be told to dismiss themselves. As a result, even if you don't need to take any application-specific actions when the user cancels an image picker, you still need to dismiss the picker. At a bare minimum, your `imagePickerControllerDidCancel:` method will need to look like this for your program to function correctly:

```
- (void)imagePickerControllerDidCancel:(UIImagePickerController *)picker {
    [picker dismissViewControllerAnimated:YES completion:NULL];
}
```

Road Testing the Camera and Library

In this chapter, we're going to build an application that lets the user take a picture or shoot some video with the camera. Or, the user can select something from the photo library, and then display the selection on the screen (see Figure 21-2). If the user is on a device without a camera, we will hide the **New Photo or Video** button and allow selection only from the photo library.

Figure 21-2. The Camera application in action

Designing the Interface

Create a new project in Xcode using the Single View Application template, naming the application *Camera*. The first order of business is to add a couple of outlets to this application's view controller. We need one to point to the image view so that we can update it with the image returned from the image picker. We'll also need an outlet to point to the **New Photo or Video** button so that we can hide the button if the device doesn't have a camera.

We also need two action methods: one for the **New Photo or Video** button and one that lets the user select an existing picture from the photo library.

Expand the *Camera* folder so that you can get to all the relevant files. Select *ViewController.m* and add the following protocol conformance declarations and properties to the class extension:

```
#import "ViewController.h"

@interface ViewController ()
<UIImagePickerControllerDelegate, UINavigationControllerDelegate>

@property (weak, nonatomic) IBOutlet UIImageView *imageView;
@property (weak, nonatomic) IBOutlet UIButton *takePictureButton;

@end
```

The first thing you might notice is that we've actually conformed our class to two different protocols: UIImagePickerControllerDelegate and UINavigationControllerDelegate. Because UIImagePickerController is a subclass of UINavigationController, we must conform our class to both of these protocols. The methods in UINavigationControllerDelegate are optional, and we don't need either of them to use the image picker; however, we do need to conform to the protocol, or the compiler will give us a warning later on.

The other thing you might notice is that, while we'll be dealing with an instance of UIImageView for displaying a chosen image, we don't have anything similar for displaying a chosen video. UIKit doesn't include any publicly available class like UIImageView that works for showing video content, so we'll have to show video using another technique instead. When we get to that point, we will use an instance of MPMoviePlayerController, grabbing its view property and inserting it into our view hierarchy. This is a highly unusual way of using any view controller, but it's actually an Apple-approved technique to show video inside a view hierarchy.

We're also going to add two action methods that we want to connect our buttons to. For now, we'll just create empty implementations so that Interface Builder can see them. We'll fill in the actual code later:

```
- (IBAction)shootPictureOrVideo:(UIButton *)sender {
}

- (IBAction)selectExistingPictureOrVideo:( UIButton *)sender {
}
```

Save your changes and select *Main.storyboard* to edit the GUI in Interface Builder.

The layout we're going to build for this application is very simple—just an image view and two buttons. The finished layout is shown in Figure 21-3. Use this as a guide as you work.

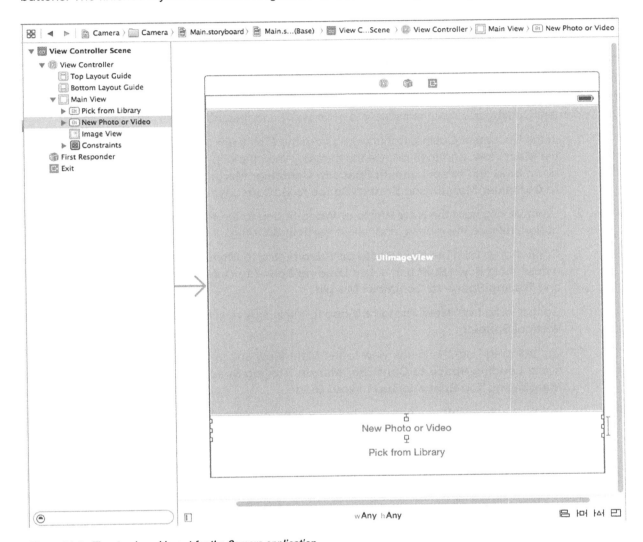

Figure 21-3. The storyboard layout for the Camera application

Drag two **Button**s from the library to the window labeled **View**. Place them one above the other, aligning the bottom button with the bottom blue guideline. Double-click the top button and give it a title of *New Photo or Video*. Now double-click the bottom button and give it a title of *Pick from Library*. Next, drag an **Image View** from the library and place it above the buttons. Expand the image view to take up the entire space of the view above the buttons, as shown earlier in Figure 21-2. In the Attributes Inspector, change the image view's background to black and set its **Mode** to **Aspect Fit**, which will cause it to resize images so that they fit within its bounds, but maintain their original aspect ratio.

Now Control-drag from the **View Controller** icon to the image view and select the **imageView** outlet. Drag again from **View Controller** to the **New Photo or Video** button and select the **takePictureButton** outlet.

Next, select the **New Photo or Video** button and bring up the connections inspector. Drag from the **Touch Up Inside** event to **View Controller** and select the **shootPictureOrVideo:** action. Now click the **Pick from Library** button, drag from the **Touch Up Inside** event in the connections inspector to View Controller, and select the **selectExistingPictureOrVideo:** action.

The final step, as usual, is to add auto layout constraints. Start by expanding the view controller in the Document Outline, and rename its view to *Main View*, and then add constraints as follows:

1. In the Document Outline, Control-drag from the **Pick from Library** button to the **Main View**, and then release the mouse. When the pop-up appears, hold down **Shift** and select **Leading Space to Container Margin**, **Trailing Space to Container Margin**, and **Bottom Space to Bottom Layout Guide**.

2. Control-drag from the **New Photo or Video** button to the **Pick from Library** button, release the mouse, and select **Vertical Spacing**.

3. Control-drag from the **New Photo or Video** button to **Main View**, release the mouse, hold down **Shift** and select **Leading Space to Container Margin** and **Trailing Space to Container Margin**.

4. Control-drag from **New Photo or Video** to the image view and select **Vertical Spacing**.

5. Control-drag from the image view to the **Main View** and use the **Shift** key to select **Leading Space to Container Margin**, **Trailing Space to Container Margin**, and **Top Space to Top Layout Guide**.

6. Hold down the **Shift** key and click both the **New Photo or Video button and** the **Pick from Library** button to select them, and then click the **Pin** button below the storyboard editor. In the pop-up, check the **Width** check box and press **Add 2 Constraints**, as shown in Figure 21-4.

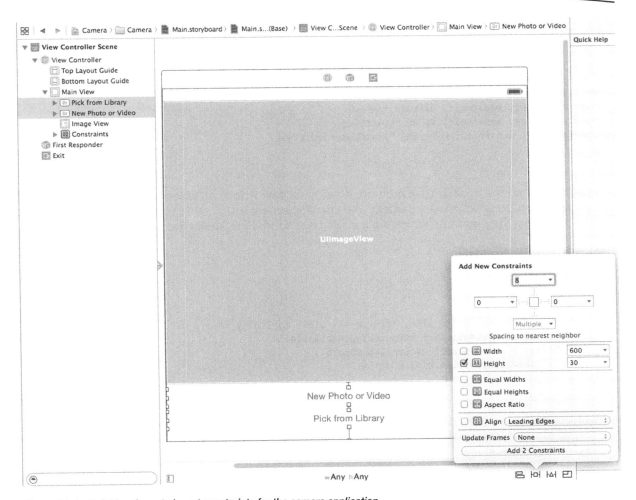

Figure 21-4. Finishing the auto layout constraints for the camera application

All of the layout constraints are now in place, so save your changes.

Implementing the Camera View Controller

Select *ViewController.m*, where we have some more changes to make. Since we're going to allow users to optionally capture a video, we need a property for an `MPMoviePlayerController` instance. Two more properties keep track of the last selected image and video, along with a string to determine whether a video or image was the last thing chosen. We also need to import a few additional headers to make this all work. Add the bold lines shown here:

```
#import "ViewController.h"
#import <MediaPlayer/MediaPlayer.h>
#import <MobileCoreServices/UTCoreTypes.h>
```

```
@interface ViewController ()
<UIImagePickerControllerDelegate, UINavigationControllerDelegate>

@property (weak, nonatomic) IBOutlet UIImageView *imageView;
@property (weak, nonatomic) IBOutlet UIButton *takePictureButton;
@property (strong, nonatomic) MPMoviePlayerController *moviePlayerController;
@property (strong, nonatomic) UIImage *image;
@property (strong, nonatomic) NSURL *movieURL;
@property (copy, nonatomic) NSString *lastChosenMediaType;

@end
```

Now let's enhance the viewDidLoad method, hiding the **New Photo or Video** button if the device we're running on does not have a camera. We also implement the viewDidAppear: method, having it call the updateDisplay method, which we'll implement soon. First, make these changes:

```
@implementation ViewController

- (void)viewDidLoad
{
    [super viewDidLoad];
    // Do any additional setup after loading the view, typically from a nib.
    if (![UIImagePickerController isSourceTypeAvailable:
          UIImagePickerControllerSourceTypeCamera]) {
        self.takePictureButton.hidden = YES;
    }
}

- (void)viewDidAppear:(BOOL)animated {
    [super viewDidAppear:animated];
    [self updateDisplay];
}

- (void)didReceiveMemoryWarning
{
    [super didReceiveMemoryWarning];
    // Dispose of any resources that can be recreated.
}
```

It's important to understand the distinction between the viewDidLoad and viewDidAppear: methods. The former is called only when the view has just been loaded into memory. The latter is called every time the view is displayed, which happens both at launch and whenever we return to our controller after showing another full-screen view, such as the image picker.

Next up are three utility methods, the first of which is the updateDisplay method. It is called from the viewDidAppear: method, which is called both when the view is first created and again after the user picks an image or video and dismisses the image picker. Because of this dual usage, it needs to make a few checks to see what's what and set up the GUI accordingly. Add this code toward the bottom of the file:

```
- (void)updateDisplay {
    if ([self.lastChosenMediaType isEqual:(NSString *)kUTTypeImage]) {
        self.imageView.image = self.image;
        self.imageView.hidden = NO;
        self.moviePlayerController.view.hidden = YES;
    } else if ([self.lastChosenMediaType isEqual:(NSString *)kUTTypeMovie]) {
        if (self.moviePlayerController == nil) {
            self.moviePlayerController = [[MPMoviePlayerController alloc]
                                    initWithContentURL:self.movieURL];
            UIView *movieView = self.moviePlayerController.view;
            movieView.frame = self.imageView.frame;
            movieView.clipsToBounds = YES;
            [self.view addSubview:movieView];
            [self setMoviePlayerLayoutConstraints];
        } else {
            self.moviePlayerController.contentURL = self.movieURL;
        }
        self.imageView.hidden = YES;
        self.moviePlayerController.view.hidden = NO;
        [self.moviePlayerController play];
    }
}
```

This method shows the correct view based on the type of media that the user selected—the image view for a photograph and the movie player for a movie. The image view is always present, but the movie player is created and added to the user interface only when the user picks a movie for the first time. When we add the movie player, we need to ensure that it occupies the same space as the image view and we need to add layout constraints that ensure that remains the case even if the device is rotated. Here's the code that adds the layout constraints:

```
- (void)setMoviePlayerLayoutConstraints {
    UIView *moviePlayerView = self.moviePlayerController.view;
    UIView *takePictureButton = self.takePictureButton;
    moviePlayerView.translatesAutoresizingMaskIntoConstraints = NO;
    NSDictionary *views =
        NSDictionaryOfVariableBindings(moviePlayerView, takePictureButton);
    [self.view addConstraints:[NSLayoutConstraint constraintsWithVisualFormat:
            @"H:|[moviePlayerView]|" options:0 metrics:nil views:views]];
    [self.view addConstraints:[NSLayoutConstraint constraintsWithVisualFormat:
            @"V:|[moviePlayerView]-0-[takePictureButton]" options:0 metrics:nil
            views:views]];
}
```

The horizontal constraints tie the movie player to the left and right sides of the main view, and the vertical constraints link it to the top of the main view and the top of the **New Photo or Video** button.

The final utility method, `pickMediaFromSource:`, is the one that both of our action methods call. This method is pretty simple. It just creates and configures an image picker, using the passed-in `sourceType` to determine whether to bring up the camera or the media library. We do so by adding this code toward the bottom of the file:

```
- (void)pickMediaFromSource:(UIImagePickerControllerSourceType)sourceType {
    NSArray *mediaTypes = [UIImagePickerController
                            availableMediaTypesForSourceType:sourceType];
    if ([UIImagePickerController
        isSourceTypeAvailable:sourceType] && [mediaTypes count] > 0) {
        UIImagePickerController *picker =
                    [[UIImagePickerController alloc] init];
        picker.mediaTypes = mediaTypes;
        picker.delegate = self;
        picker.allowsEditing = YES;
        picker.sourceType = sourceType;
        [self presentViewController:picker animated:YES completion:NULL];
    } else {
        UIAlertController *alertController = [UIAlertController
                    alertControllerWithTitle:@"Error accessing media"
                            message:@"Unsupported media source."
                            preferredStyle:UIAlertControllerStyleAlert];
        UIAlertAction *okAction = [UIAlertAction actionWithTitle:@"OK"
                                style:UIAlertActionStyleCancel handler:nil];
        [alertController addAction:okAction];
        [self presentViewController:alertController animated:YES
            completion:nil];
    }
}
```

Next, implement the following action methods that we declared in the header:

```
- (IBAction)shootPictureOrVideo:(id)sender {
    [self pickMediaFromSource:UIImagePickerControllerSourceTypeCamera];
}

- (IBAction)selectExistingPictureOrVideo:(id)sender {
    [self pickMediaFromSource:UIImagePickerControllerSourceTypePhotoLibrary];
}
```

Each of these simply calls out to the `pickMediaFromSource:` method, passing in a constant defined by `UIImagePickerController` to specify where the picture or video should come from.

Now it's finally time to implement the delegate methods for the picker view:

```
#pragma mark - Image Picker Controller delegate methods

- (void)imagePickerController:(UIImagePickerController *)picker
        didFinishPickingMediaWithInfo:(NSDictionary *)info {
    self.lastChosenMediaType = info[UIImagePickerControllerMediaType];
```

```
    if ([self.lastChosenMediaType isEqual:(NSString *)kUTTypeImage]) {
        self.image = info[UIImagePickerControllerEditedImage];
    } else if ([self.lastChosenMediaType isEqual:(NSString *)kUTTypeMovie]) {
        self.movieURL = info[UIImagePickerControllerMediaURL];
    }
    [picker dismissViewControllerAnimated:YES completion:NULL];
}

- (void)imagePickerControllerDidCancel:(UIImagePickerController *)picker {
    [picker dismissViewControllerAnimated:YES completion:NULL];
}
```

The first delegate method checks to see whether a picture or video was chosen, makes note of the selection, and then dismisses the modal image picker. If the image is larger than the available space on the screen, it will be resized by the image view when it's displayed, because we set the image view's content mode to Aspect Fit when we created it. The second delegate method is called when the user cancels the image picking process and just dismisses the image picker.

That's all you need to do. Compile and run the app. If you're running on the simulator, you won't have the option to take a new picture, but will only be able to choose from the photo library—as if you had any photos in your simulator's photo library! If you have the opportunity to run the application on a real device, go ahead and try it. You should be able to take a new picture or movie, and zoom in and out of the picture using the pinch gestures. The first time the app needs to access the user's photos on iOS, the user will be asked to allow this access; this is a privacy feature that was added back in iOS 6 to make sure that apps aren't sneakily grabbing photos without users' consent.

After choosing or taking a photo, if you zoom in and pan around before hitting the **Use Photo** button, the cropped image will be the one returned to the application in the delegate method.

It's a Snap!

Believe it or not, that's all there is to letting your users take pictures with the camera so that the pictures can be used by your application. You can even let the user do a small amount of editing on that image if you so choose.

In the next chapter, we're going to look at reaching a larger audience for your iOS applications by making them oh-so-easy to translate into other languages. *Êtes-vous prêt? Tournez la page et allez directement. Allez, allez!*

Chapter 22

Application Localization

At the time of this writing, iOS devices are available in more than 90 different countries, and that number will continue to increase over time. You can now buy and use an iPhone on every continent except Antarctica. The iPad and iPod touch are also sold all over the world and are nearly as ubiquitous as the iPhone.

If you plan on releasing applications through the App Store, your potential market is considerably larger than just people in your own country who speak your own language. Fortunately, iOS has a robust **localization** architecture that lets you easily translate your application (or have it translated by others) into, not only multiple languages, but even into multiple dialects of the same language. Do you want to provide different terminology to English speakers in the United Kingdom than you do to English speakers in the United States? No problem.

That is, localization is no problem if you've written your code correctly. Retrofitting an existing application to support localization is much harder than writing your application that way from the start. In this chapter, we'll show you how to write your code so it is easy to localize, and then we'll go about localizing a sample application.

Localization Architecture

When a nonlocalized application is run, all of the application's text will be presented in the developer's own language, also known as the **development base language**.

When developers decide to localize their applications, they create a subdirectory in their application bundle for each supported language. Each language's subdirectory contains a subset of the application's resources that were translated into that language. Each subdirectory is called a **localization project**, or **localization folder**. Localization folder names always end with the *.lproj* extension.

In the iOS Settings application, the user has the ability to set the device's preferred language and region format. For example, if the user's language is English, available regions might be the United States, Australia, and Hong Kong—all regions in which English is spoken.

When a localized application needs to load a resource—such as an image, property list, or nib—the application checks the user's language and region, and then looks for a localization folder that matches that setting. If it finds one, it will load the localized version of the resource instead of the base version.

For users who select French as their iOS language and Switzerland as their region, the application will look first for a localization folder named *fr-CH.lproj*. The first two letters of the folder name are the ISO country code that represents the French language. The two letters following the underscore are the ISO code that represents Switzerland.

If the application cannot find a match using the two-letter code, it will look for a match using the language's three-letter ISO code. In our example, if the application is unable to find a folder named *fr-CH.lproj*, it will look for a localization folder named *fre-CH* or *fra-CH*.

All languages have at least one three-letter code. Some have two three-letter codes: one for the English spelling of the language and another for the native spelling. Some languages have only two-letter codes. When a language has both a two-letter code and a three-letter code, the two-letter code is preferred.

> **Note**   You can find a list of the current ISO country codes on the ISO web site (`www.iso.org/iso/country_codes.htm`). Both the two- and three-letter codes are part of the ISO 3166 standard.

If the application cannot find a folder that is an exact match, it will then look for a localization folder in the application bundle that matches just the language code without the region code. So, staying with our French-speaking person from France, the application next looks for a localization folder called *fr.lproj*. If it doesn't find a language folder with that name, it will look for *fre.lproj* and then *fra.lproj*. If none of those is found, it checks for *French.lproj*. The last construct exists to support legacy Mac OS X applications; generally speaking, you should avoid it.

If the application doesn't find a language folder that matches either the language/region combination or just the language, it will use the resources from the development base language. If it does find an appropriate localization folder, it will always look there first for any resources that it needs. If you load a UIImage using `imageNamed:`, for example, the application will look first for an image with the specified name in the localization folder. If it finds one, it will use that image. If it doesn't, it will fall back to the base language resource.

If an application has more than one localization folder that matches—for example, a folder called *fr-CH.lproj* and one called *fr.lproj*—it will look first in the more specific match, which is *fr-CH.lproj* if the user has selected Swiss French as their preferred language. If it doesn't find the resource there, it will look in *fr.lproj*. This gives you the ability to provide resources common to all speakers of a language in one language folder, localizing only those resources that are impacted by differences in dialect or geographic region.

You should choose to localize only those resources that are affected by language or country. For example, if an image in your application has no words and its meaning is universal, there's no need to localize that image.

Strings Files

What do you do about string literals and string constants in your source code? Consider this source code from Chapter 19:

```
UIAlertController *alertController =
  [UIAlertController alertControllerWithTitle:@"Location Manager Error"
                      message:errorType
                      preferredStyle:UIAlertControllerStyleAlert];
UIAlertAction *okAction = [UIAlertAction actionWithTitle:@"OK"
                            style:UIAlertActionStyleCancel handler:nil];
[alertController addAction:okAction];
[self presentViewController:alertController animated:YES completion:nil];
```

If you've gone through the effort of localizing your application for a particular audience, you certainly don't want to be presenting alerts written in the development base language. The answer is to store these strings in special text files called **strings files**.

What's in a Strings File?

Strings files are nothing more than Unicode text files that contain a list of string pairs, each identified by a comment. Here is an example of what a strings file might look like in your application:

```
/* Used to ask the user his/her first name */
"LABEL_FIRST_NAME" = "First Name";

/* Used to get the user's last name */
"LABEL_LAST_NAME" = "Last Name";

/* Used to ask the user's birth date */
"LABEL_BIRTHDAY" = "Birthday";
```

The values between the /* and the */ characters are just comments for the translator. They are not used in the application, and you could skip adding them, though they're a good idea. The comments give context, showing how a particular string is being used in the application.

You'll notice that each line is in two parts, separated by an equal sign. The string on the left side of the equal sign acts as a key, and it will always contain the same value, regardless of language. The value on the right side of the equal sign is the one that is translated to the local language. So, the preceding strings file, localized into French, might look like this:

```
/* Used to ask the user his/her first name */
"LABEL_FIRST_NAME " = "Prénom";

/* Used to get the user's last name */
"LABEL_LAST_NAME" = "Nom de famille";

/* Used to ask the user's birth date */
"LABEL_BIRTHDAY" = "Anniversaire";
```

The Localized String Macro

You won't actually create the strings file by hand. Instead, you'll get the localized versions of the strings that you need by using the NSLocalizedString macro. Once your source code is final and ready for localization, Xcode will search all your code files for occurrences of this macro, pulling out all the unique strings and embedding them in a file that you can send to a translator, or add the translations yourself. Once that's done, you'll have Xcode import the updated file and use its content to create the localized string files for the languages for which you have provided translations.

Let's see how the first part of this process works. First, here's a traditional string declaration:

```
NSString *myString = @"First Name";
```

To make this string localizable, do this instead:

```
NSString *myString = NSLocalizedString(@"LABEL_FIRST_NAME",
    @"Used to ask the user his/her first name");
```

The NSLocalizedString macro takes two parameters:

■ The first parameter is a key that will be used to look for the localized string. If there is no localization that contains text for the key, the application will use the key as the localized text.

■ The second parameter is used as a comment to explain how the text is being used. The comment will appear in the file sent to the translator and in the localized strings file after import.

NSLocalizedString looks in the application bundle inside the appropriate localization folder for a strings file named *Localizable.strings*. If it does not find the file, it returns its first parameter, which is the key for the text that was required.

If NSLocalizedString finds the strings file, it searches the file for a line that matches its first parameter. In the preceding example, NSLocalizedString will search the strings file for the string "LABEL_FIRST_NAME". If it doesn't find a match in the localization folder that matches the user's language settings, it will then look for a strings file in the base language and use the value there. If there is no strings file, it will just use the first parameter you passed to the NSLocalizedString macro.

You could use the base language text as the key for the NSLocalizedString macro because it returns the key if no matching localized text can be found. This would make the preceding example look like this:

```
NSString *myString = NSLocalizedString(@"First Name",
    @"Used to ask the user his/her first name");
```

However, this approach is not recommended for two reasons. First, it is unlikely that you will come up with the perfect text for your app on your first try. Going back and changing all keys in the strings files is cumbersome and error-prone, which means that you will most likely end up with keys that do not match what is used in the app, anyway. The second reason is that, by clearly using uppercase keys, you can immediately notice if you have forgotten to localize any text when you run the app just by looking at it.

Now that you have an idea of how the localization architecture and the strings file work, let's take a look at localization in action.

Real-World iOS: Localizing Your Application

We're going to create a small application that displays the user's current **locale**. A locale (an instance of NSLocale) represents both the user's language and region. It is used by the system to determine which language to use when interacting with the user, as well as how to display dates, currency, and time information, among other things. After we create the application, we will then localize it into other languages. You'll learn how to localize storyboard files, strings files, images, and even your application's display name.

You can see what our application is going to look like in Figure 22-1. The name across the top comes from the user's locale. The ordinals down the left side of the view are static labels, and their values will be set by localizing the storyboard file. The words down the right side, and the flag image at the bottom of the screen, will all be chosen in our app's code at runtime based on the user's preferred language.

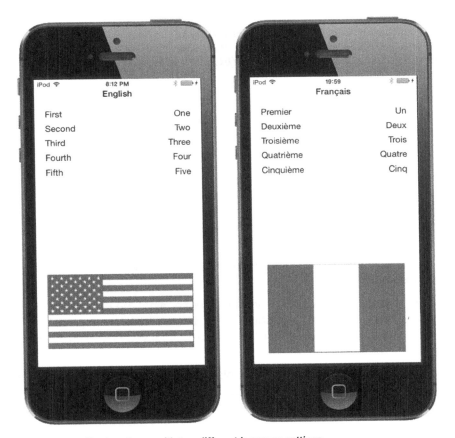

Figure 22-1. The LocalizeMe application shown with two different language settings

Let's hop right into it.

Setting Up LocalizeMe

Create a new project in Xcode using the Single View Application template and call it *LocalizeMe*.

If you look in the folder *22 – Images* in the example source code, you'll find a pair of images named *flag_usa.png* and *flag_france.png*. In Xcode, select the *Images.xcassets* item, and then drag both *flag_usa.png* and *flag_france.png* into it.

Now let's add some label outlets to the project's view controller. We need to create one outlet for the blue label across the top of the view, another for the image view that will show a flag, and an outlet collection for all the words down the right-hand side (see Figure 22-1). Select *ViewController.m* and make the following changes:

```
#import "ViewController.h"

@interface ViewController ()

@property (weak, nonatomic) IBOutlet UILabel *localeLabel;
@property (weak, nonatomic) IBOutlet UIImageView *flagImageView;
@property (strong, nonatomic) IBOutletCollection(UILabel) NSArray *labels;

@end
```

Now select *Main.storyboard* to edit the GUI in Interface Builder. In the Document Outline, expand the view controller and change the name of its view to *Main View*. Drag a **Label** from the library, dropping it at the top of the view, aligned with the top blue guideline. Resize the label so that it takes the entire width of the view, from edge to edge. With the label selected, open the Attributes Inspector. Look for the **Font** control and click the small **T** icon it contains to bring up a small font-selection pop-up. Click **System Bold** to make the title label stand out a bit from the rest. Next, use the Attributes Inspector to set the text alignment to centered. You can also use the font selector to make the font size larger if you wish. As long as **Autoshrink** is set to **Minimum Font Size** in the object Attributes Inspector, the text will be resized if it gets too long to fit.

With your label in place, Control-drag from the **View Controller** icon to this new label, and then select the **localeLabel** outlet.

Next, drag five more **Label**s from the library and put them against the left margin using the blue guideline, one above the other (again, see Figure 22-1). Double-click the top one and change its text from *Label* to *First*. Repeat this procedure with the other four labels, changing the text to the words *Second*, *Third*, *Fourth*, and *Fifth*.

Drag another five labels from the library, this time placing them against the right margin. Change the text alignment using the object Attributes Inspector so that they are right-aligned, and then increase the width of the labels so that they stretch from the right blue guideline to about the middle of the view. Control-drag from **View Controller** to each of the five new labels, connecting each one to the labels outlet collection, and making sure to connect them in the right order from top to bottom.

Drag an **Image View** from the library over to the bottom part of the view, so that it touches the bottom and left blue guidelines. In the Attributes Inspector, select **flag_usa** for the view's Image attribute and resize the image horizontally to stretch from blue guideline to blue guideline, and vertically so that it is about a third of the height of the user interface. In the Attributes Inspector, change the Mode attribute from its current value to *Aspect Fit*. Not all flags have the same aspect ratio, and we want to make sure the localized versions of the image look right. Selecting this option will cause the image view to resize any images that it displays so they fit, but it will also maintain the correct aspect ratio (ratio of height to width). Now Control-drag from the view controller to this image view and select the **flagImageView** outlet.

To complete the user interface, we need to set the auto layout constraints. Starting with the label at the top, Control-drag from it to Main View in the Document Outline, press the **Shift** key, select **Leading Space to Container Margin**, **Trailing Space to Container Margin**, and **Top Space to Top Layout Guide**, and then **click outside the popup with the mouse**.

Next, we'll fix the positions of each of the five rows of labels. Control-drag from the label with the text *First* to Main View in the Document Outline, select both **Leading Space to Container Margin** and **Top Space to Top Layout Guide**, and **click outside the popup with the mouse**. Control-drag from the label to the label on the same row to its right and select **Baseline**, and then Control-drag horizontally from the label on the right to Main View in the Document Outline and select **Trailing Space to Container Margin**.

You have now positioned the top row of labels. Do exactly the same thing for the other four rows. Finally, select all of the five labels on the right by holding down the **Shift** key while clicking them with the mouse, and then **Editor ➤ Size to Fit Content**. You can now clear the text from each of these labels, since we will be setting it programmatically.

To fix the position and size of the flag, Control-drag from the flag label to Main View in the Document Outline, select **Leading Space to Container Margin**, **Trailing Space to Container Margin**, and **Bottom Space to Bottom Layout Guide**, and then **click outside the popup with the mouse**. With the flag label still selected, click the **Pin** button, check the **Height** check box in the pop-up, and then press **Add 1 Constraint**. You have now added all of the auto layout constraints that we need.

Save your storyboard, and then switch to *ViewController.m* and add the following code to the viewDidLoad method:

```objectivec
- (void)viewDidLoad
{
    [super viewDidLoad];
    // Do any additional setup after loading the view, typically from a nib.
    NSLocale *locale = [NSLocale currentLocale];
    NSString *currentLangID = [[NSLocale preferredLanguages] objectAtIndex:0];
    NSString *displayLang = [locale displayNameForKey:NSLocaleLanguageCode
                                                value:currentLangID];
    NSString *capitalized = [displayLang capitalizedStringWithLocale:locale];
    self.localeLabel.text = capitalized;

    [self.labels[0] setText:NSLocalizedString(@"LABEL_ONE", @"The number 1")];
    [self.labels[1] setText:NSLocalizedString(@"LABEL_TWO", @"The number 2")];
    [self.labels[2] setText:NSLocalizedString(@"LABEL_THREE",
                                              @"The number 3")];
    [self.labels[3] setText:NSLocalizedString(@"LABEL_FOUR", @"The number 4")];
    [self.labels[4] setText:NSLocalizedString(@"LABEL_FIVE", @"The number 5")];

    NSString *flagFile = NSLocalizedString(@"FLAG_FILE", @"Name of the flag");
    self.flagImageView.image = [UIImage imageNamed:flagFile];
}
```

The first thing we do in this code is get an NSLocale instance that represents the user's current locale. This instance tells us both the user's language and region preferences, as set in the device's Settings application:

```
NSLocale *locale = [NSLocale currentLocale];
```

Next, we grab the user's preferred language. This gives us a two-character code, such as "en" or "fr", or a string like "fr_CH" for a regional language variant:

```
NSString *currentLangID = [[NSLocale preferredLanguages] objectAtIndex:0];
```

The next line of code might need a bit of explanation. NSLocale works somewhat like a dictionary. It can give you a whole bunch of information about the current user's locale, including the name of the currency and the expected date format. You can find a complete list of the information that you can retrieve in the NSLocale API reference.

In this next line of code, we're using a method called displayNameForKey:value: to retrieve the actual name of the chosen language, translated into the language of the current locale itself. The purpose of this method is to return the value of the item we've requested in a specific language.

The display name for the French language, for example, is *français* in French, but *French* in English. This method gives you the ability to retrieve data about any locale, so that it can be displayed appropriately for all users. In this case, we want the display name of the user's preferred language in the language currently being used, which is why we pass currentLangID as the second argument. This string is a two-letter language code, similar to the one we used earlier to create our language projects. For an English speaker, it would be *en*; and for a French speaker, it would be *fr*:

```
NSString *displayLang = [locale displayNameForKey:NSLocaleLanguageCode
                                            value:currentLangID];
```

The name we get back from this is going to be something like "English" or "français"—and it will only be capitalized if language names are always capitalized in the user's preferred language. That's the case in English, but not so in French. We want the name capitalized for displaying as a title, however. Fortunately, NSString has methods for capitalizing strings, including one that will capitalize a string according to the rules of a given locale! Let's use that to turn "français" into "Français":

```
NSString *capitalized = [displayLang capitalizedStringWithLocale:locale];
```

Once we have the display name, we use it to set the top label in the view:

```
self.localeLabel.text = capitalized;
```

Next, we set the five other labels to the numbers 1 through 5, spelled out in our development base language. We use the NSLocalizedString() macro to get the text for these labels, passing it the key and a comment indicating what each word is. You can just pass an empty string if the words are obvious, as they are here; however, any string you pass in the second argument will be turned into a comment in the strings file, so you can use this comment to communicate with the person doing your translations:

```
[self.labels[0] setText:NSLocalizedString(@"LABEL_ONE", @"The number 1")];
[self.labels[1] setText:NSLocalizedString(@"LABEL_TWO", @"The number 2")];
[self.labels[2] setText:NSLocalizedString(@"LABEL_THREE",
                                          @"The number 3")];
[self.labels[3] setText:NSLocalizedString(@"LABEL_FOUR", @"The number 4")];
[self.labels[4] setText:NSLocalizedString(@"LABEL_FIVE", @"The number 5")];
```

Finally, we do another string lookup to find the name of the flag image to use and populate our image view with the named image:

```
NSString *flagFile = NSLocalizedString(@"FLAG_FILE", @"Name of the flag");
self.flagImageView.image = [UIImage imageNamed:flagFile];
```

Let's run our application now.

Trying Out LocalizeMe

You can use either the simulator or a device to test LocalizeMe. Once the application launches, it should look like Figure 22-2.

Figure 22-2. *The language running under the authors' base language. The application is set up for localization, but it is not yet localized*

Because we used the NSLocalizedString macros instead of static strings, we are now ready for localization. However, we are not localized yet, as is glaringly obvious from the uppercase labels in the right column and the lack of a flag image at the bottom. If you use the Settings application on the simulator or on your iOS device to change to another language or region, the results look essentially the same, except for the label at the top of the view (see Figure 22-3).

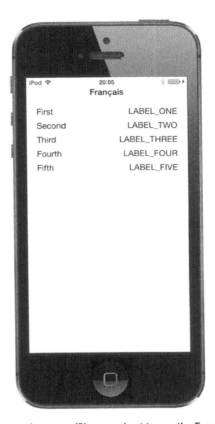

Figure 22-3. The nonlocalized application running on an iPhone and set to use the French language

Localizing the Project

Now let's localize the project. In Xcode's Project Navigator, single-click **LocalizeMe**, click the **LocalizeMe** project (not one of the targets) in the editing area, and then select the **Info** tab for the project.

Look for the Localizations section in the **Info** tab. You'll see that it shows one localization, which is for your development language—in my case, that's English. This localization is usually referred to as the **base** localization and it's added automatically when Xcode creates a project. We want to add French, so click the plus (+) button at the bottom of the Localizations section and select **French (fr)** from the pop-up list that appears (see Figure 22-4).

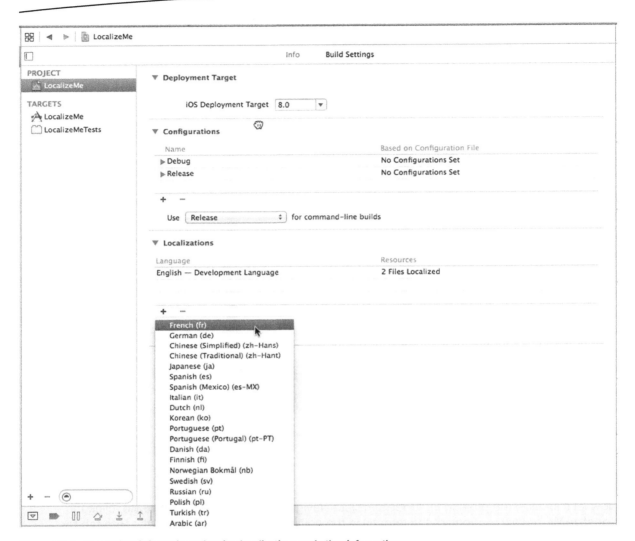

Figure 22-4. The project info settings showing localizations and other information

Next, you will be asked to choose all existing localizable files that you want to localize and which existing localization you want the new French localization to start from (see Figure 22-5). Sometimes when you add a new language, it is advantageous to start with the files for the new language based on those for another one for which you already have a localization; for example, to create a Swiss French localization in a project that's already been translated into French (as we will, later in this chapter), you would almost certainly prefer to use the existing French localization as the start point instead of your base language, and you would do this by selecting **French** as the Reference Language when you add the Swiss French localization. Right now, though, are only two files to be localized and one choice of starting point language (your base language), so just leave everything as it is and click **Finish**.

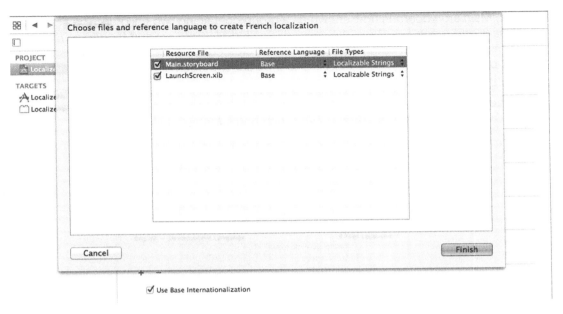

Figure 22-5. *Choosing the files for localization*

Now that you've added a French localization, take a look at the Project Navigator. Notice that the *Main.storyboard* file now has a disclosure triangle next to it, as if it were a group or folder. Expand it and take a look (see Figure 22-6).

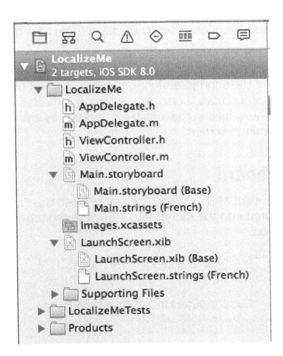

Figure 22-6. *Localizable files have a disclosure triangle and a child value for each language or region you add*

In our project, *Main.storyboard* is now shown as a group containing two children. The first is called *Main.Storyboard* and tagged as *Base*; the second is called *Main.strings* and tagged as *French*. The Base version was created automatically when you created the project, and it represents your development base language The same applies to the LaunchScreen.xib file.

These files actually live in two different folders: one called *Base.lproj* and one called *fr.lproj*. Go to the Finder and open the *LocalizeMe* folder within your *LocalizeMe* project folder. In addition to all your project files, you should see folders named *Base.lproj* and *fr.lproj* (see Figure 22-7).

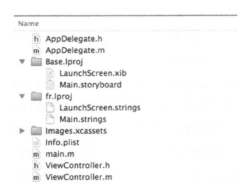

Figure 22-7. From the outset, our Xcode project included a Base language project folder (Base.lproj). When we chose to make a file localizable, Xcode created a language folder (fr.lproj) for the language we selected

Note that the *Base.lproj* folder was there all along, with its copy of *Main.storyboard* inside it. When Xcode finds a resource that has exactly one localized version, it displays it as a single item. As soon as a file has two or more localized versions, Xcode displays them as a group.

When you asked Xcode to create the French localization, it created a new localization folder in your project called *fr.lproj* and placed in it strings files that contain values extracted from *Base.lproj/Main.storyboard* and Base.lproj/LaunchScreen.xib. Instead of duplicating both files, Xcode just extracts every text string from them and creates strings files ready for localization. When the app is compiled and run, the values in the localized strings files are pulled in to replace the values in the storyboard and launch screen.

Localizing the Storyboard

In Xcode's Project Navigator, select *Main.strings (French)* to open the French strings file, the contents of which will be injected into the storyboard shown to French speakers. You'll see something like the following text:

```
/* Class = "IBUILabel"; text = "Second"; ObjectID = "4Cx-kj-ksN"; */
"4Cx-kj-ksN.text" = "Second";

/* Class = "IBUILabel"; text = "First"; ObjectID = "KBK-Xn-YPP"; */
"KBK-Xn-YPP.text" = "First";
```

```
/* Class = "IBUILabel"; text = "Label"; ObjectID = "VDB-gc-4Rh"; */
"VDB-gc-4Rh.text" = "Label";

/* Class = "IBUILabel"; text = "Third"; ObjectID = "ekY-67-m9W"; */
"ekY-67-m9W.text" = "Third";

/* Class = "IBUILabel"; text = "Fourth"; ObjectID = "fcA-Mg-z4f"; */
"fcA-Mg-z4f.text" = "Fourth";

/* Class = "IBUILabel"; text = "Fifth"; ObjectID = "zsr-qF-ry6"; */
"zsr-qF-ry6.text" = "Fifth";
```

Each of the pairs of lines represents a string that was found in the storyboard. The comment tells you the class of the object that contained the string, the original string itself, and a unique identifier for each object (which will probably be different in your copy of this file). The line after the comment is where you actually want to change the value on the right-hand side. You'll see that some of these are ordinals such as *First*; those come from the labels on the left of Figure 22-3, all of which were given names in the storyboard. The entry with the name *Label* is for the title label, which we set programmatically, so you don't need to localize it.

Prior to iOS 8, the usual practice was to localize the storyboard by directly editing this file. With iOS 8, you can still do that if you choose, but if you plan to use a professional translator, it's likely to be more convenient to have them translate the storyboard text and the strings in your code at the same time. For that reason, Apple has made it possible to collect all of the strings that need to be translated into one file per language that you can send to your translator. If you plan to use that approach, you would leave the storyboard strings file alone and proceed to the next step, which is described in the next section. However, it's still possible to modify the storyboard strings file and, if you do so, those changes would not be lost should you need to have your translator make changes or localize additional text. So, just on this occasion, let's localize the storyboard strings in the old-fashioned way. To do so, locate the text for the labels *First*, *Second*, *Third*, *Fourth*, and *Fifth*, and then change the string to the right of the equal sign to *Premier*, *Deuxième*, *Troisième*, *Quatrième*, and *Cinquième*, respectively. Finally, save the file.

Your storyboard is now localized in French. Compile and run the program. If you've already changed your Settings to the French language, you should see your translated labels on the left. Otherwise, go into the Settings app, switch to French, and then launch the app from Xcode again. For those folks who are a bit unsure about how to make those changes, we'll walk you through it.

In the simulator or on your device, go to the Settings application, select the **General** row, and then select the row labeled **Language and Region**. From here, you'll be able to change your language preferences (see Figure 22-8).

Figure 22-8. Changing the language

Touch **iPhone Language** to reveal the list of languages into which iOS has been localized, and then find and select the entry for French (which appears in French, as *Français*). Press **Done**, and then confirm that you want the device language to be changed. This will cause the device to do a partial reboot, which will take a few seconds. Now run the app again and you'll see that the labels on the left side are showing the localized French text (see Figure 22-9). However, the flag and right column of text are still wrong. We'll take care of those in the next section.

Figure 22-9. *The application has been partially translated into French*

Generating and Localizing a Strings File

In Figure 22-9, the words on the right side of the view are still in SHOUT_ALL_CAPS style because we haven't translated them yet; what you are seeing are they keys that NSLocalizedString is using to look for the localized texts. In order to localize those, we need to first extract the key and comment strings from the code. It used to be necessary to either do this by hand, or use a command-line tool call genstrings to scan through your source code. As I mentioned earlier, in iOS 8, Apple has made it much easier to extract the text that needs to be localized from your project and put it all in one file for each language—so let's see how that works.

In the Project Navigator, select your project, and then, in the editor, select either the project or one of its targets. Now choose **Editor ➤ Export for Localization…** from the menu. This opens a dialog where you choose which languages you want to localize and where the files for each language should be written. Select a suitable location for the file (for example, in the project's root directory), ensure that **Existing Translations** and the check box for **French** are both selected, and then press **Save**. Xcode will create a file called fr.xliff in the location that you chose. If you plan to use a third-party service to translate your application's text, it's likely that they can work with XLIFF files; all you should need to do is send them this file, have them update it with the translated strings and re-import it into Xcode. For now, though, we are going to do the translation ourselves.

Open the *fr.xliff* file. You'll see that it contains a lot of XML. It breaks down into three different sections that contain the strings from the storyboard, the strings that Xcode found in your source code, and a number of localizable values from your application's *Info.plist* file. We'll talk about why you need to localize entries from *Info.plist* later in the chapter. For now, let's translate the text that comes from the application's code. Look through the file and you'll find that text embedded in some XML that looks like this:

```
<file original="LocalizeMe/Localizable.strings"
      source-language="en" datatype="plaintext"
      target-language="fr">
  <header>
    <tool tool-id="com.apple.dt.xcode" tool-name="Xcode"
          tool-version="6.1" build-num="6A1027"/>
  </header>
  <body>
    <trans-unit id="FLAG_FILE">
      <source>FLAG_FILE</source>
      <note>Name of the flag</note>
    </trans-unit>
    <trans-unit id="LABEL_FIVE">
      <source>LABEL_FIVE</source>
      <note>The number 5</note>
    </trans-unit>
    <trans-unit id="LABEL_FOUR">
      <source>LABEL_FOUR</source>
      <note>The number 4</note>
    </trans-unit>
    <trans-unit id="LABEL_ONE">
      <source>LABEL_ONE</source>
      <note>The number 1</note>
    </trans-unit>
    <trans-unit id="LABEL_THREE">
      <source>LABEL_THREE</source>
      <note>The number 3</note>
    </trans-unit>
    <trans-unit id="LABEL_TWO">
      <source>LABEL_TWO</source>
      <note>The number 2</note>
    </trans-unit>
  </body>
</file>
```

You can see that there is a `<trans-unit>` element for each string that needs to be translated into French. Each of them contains a `<source>` element with the original text and a `<note>` element that contains the comment from the `NSLocalizedString` macro in the source code. Professional translators have software tools that present the information in this file and allow them to enter the translations. We, on the other hand, are going to do it manually by adding `<target>` elements containing the French text, like this:

```
<file original="LocalizeMe/Localizable.strings"
        source-language="en" datatype="plaintext"
        target-language="fr">
  <header>
    <tool tool-id="com.apple.dt.xcode" tool-name="Xcode"
            tool-version="6.1" build-num="6A1027"/>
  </header>
  <body>
    <trans-unit id="FLAG_FILE">
      <source>FLAG_FILE</source>
      <note>Name of the flag</note>
      <target>flag_france</target>
    </trans-unit>
    <trans-unit id="LABEL_FIVE">
      <source>LABEL_FIVE</source>
      <note>The number 5</note>
      <target>Cinq</target>
    </trans-unit>
    <trans-unit id="LABEL_FOUR">
      <source>LABEL_FOUR</source>
      <note>The number 4</note>
      <target>Quatre</target>
    </trans-unit>
    <trans-unit id="LABEL_ONE">
      <source>LABEL_ONE</source>
      <note>The number 1</note>
      <target>Un</target>
    </trans-unit>
    <trans-unit id="LABEL_THREE">
      <source>LABEL_THREE</source>
      <note>The number 3</note>
      <target>Trois</target>
    </trans-unit>
    <trans-unit id="LABEL_TWO">
      <source>LABEL_TWO</source>
      <note>The number 2</note>
      <target>Deux</target>
    </trans-unit>
  </body>
</file>
```

If you haven't already translated the storyboard strings, you can do that too. You'll find them in a separate block of <trans-unit> elements, which are easy to find because of the comments that include the links to the labels from which the text came. On the other hand, if you have done the translations already, you'll find that Xcode included them in the XLIFF file:

```
<trans-unit id="ORM-IQ-8n2.text">
    <source>Third</source>
    <target>Troisième</target>
    <note>Class = "IBUILabel"; text = "Third"; ObjectID = "ORM-IQ-8n2";</note>
</trans-unit>
<trans-unit id="48p-R8-5Ug.text">
    <source>Fourth</source>
    <target>Quatrième</target>
    <note>Class = "IBUILabel"; text = "Fourth"; ObjectID = "48p-R8-5Ug";</note>
</trans-unit>
```

Save your translations and now let's import the results back into Xcode. On the menu, choose **Editor ➤ Import Localizations**, navigate to your file, and open it. Xcode will show you a list of keys for which you have not yet provided translations—these come from the *Info.plist* file and we'll take care of them later. For now, just press **Import** to complete the import process. If you look under Supporting Files in the Project Navigator, you'll see that two files have been added—*InfoPlist.strings* and *Localizable.strings*. Open *Localizable.strings* and you'll see that it contains the French translations of the strings that Xcode extracted from *ViewController.m*:

```
/* Name of the flag */
"FLAG_FILE" = "flag_france";

/* The number 5 */
"LABEL_FIVE" = "Cinq";

/* The number 4 */
"LABEL_FOUR" = "Quatre";

/* The number 1 */
"LABEL_ONE" = "Un";

/* The number 3 */
"LABEL_THREE" = "Trois";

/* The number 2 */
"LABEL_TWO" = "Deux";
```

Now compile and run the app. You should see the labels on the right-hand side translated into French (see Figure 22-1); and at the bottom of the screen, you should now see the French flag, as shown on the right in Figure 22-1.

So are we done yet? Not quite. Use the Settings app to switch back to English and rerun the app. You'll see the unlocalized version of the app shown in Figure 22-2. To make the app work in English, we have to localize it for English. To do that, select **Editor ➤ Export for Localization…** from the menu, but this time choose **Development Language Only**, and then press **Save**. This creates a file called en.xliff, where we'll add the localizations for English. Edit the file and make the following changes:

```
<file original="LocalizeMe/Localizable.strings"
      source-language="en" datatype="plaintext">
  <header>
    <tool tool-id="com.apple.dt.xcode" tool-name="Xcode"
          tool-version="6.1" build-num="6A1027"/>
  </header>
  <body>
    <trans-unit id="FLAG_FILE">
      <source>FLAG_FILE</source>
      <note>Name of the flag</note>
      <target>flag_usa</target>
    </trans-unit>
    <trans-unit id="LABEL_FIVE">
      <source>LABEL_FIVE</source>
      <note>The number 5</note>
      <target>Five</target>
    </trans-unit>
    <trans-unit id="LABEL_FOUR">
      <source>LABEL_FOUR</source>
      <note>The number 4</note>
      <target>Four</target>
    </trans-unit>
    <trans-unit id="LABEL_ONE">
      <source>LABEL_ONE</source>
      <note>The number 1</note>
      <target>One</target>
    </trans-unit>
    <trans-unit id="LABEL_THREE">
      <source>LABEL_THREE</source>
      <note>The number 3</note>
      <target>Three</target>
    </trans-unit>
    <trans-unit id="LABEL_TWO">
      <source>LABEL_TWO</source>
      <note>The number 2</note>
      <target>Two</target>
    </trans-unit>
  </body>
</file>
```

Import these changes back into Xcode using **Editor ➤ Import Localizations**. Xcode creates a folder called *en.lproj* and adds to it files called *InfoPlist.strings*, *Localizable.strings*, and *Main.strings* that contain the English localization. What you have added is the reference to the image file for the flag and the text to replace the keys used in the NSLocalizedString() function calls in the code. Now if you run the app with English as your selected language, you'll see the correct English text and the US flag.

> **Note**   You may find that Xcode is not able to import the development language localizations. A bug has been filed for this problem but, at the time of writing, it remains open. You can temporarily fix the problem by editing the *en.xliff* file, finding every `<file>` element and adding a `target-language` attribute to it, with a value of en. There should be five places where you need to make a change. Here's an example of an element that's been modified, with the change highlighted in bold:
>
> `<file original="LocalizeMe/Info.plist" source-language="en" datatype="plaintext"` **`target-language="en">`**
>
> Save the file and import it—all should now be well.

There's one more step that you need to take. Switch the simulator to a language that's not French or English—say, Spanish—and run the application again. You'll get the same unlocalized result that you saw when running in English before we added the English localization. That's because when the user's language does not match any of the available localizations, the base localization is used, but we haven't supplied the text strings and flag file to be used in this case. There's a quick solution to this—we can use the English localization to create the base localization. In the Project Navigator, select the file that contains the English variant of *Localizable.strings*, and then in the File Inspector, under Localization, click the **Base** check box to select it. Xcode creates a copy of Localizable.strings for the base localization. If you now run the app with Spanish as the active language, it will look just the same as it does in English, which is better than the incomplete version shown in Figure 22-2.

The requirement to provide the flag image file name and the text strings for the base localization arises because we chose not to use localized text as the keys for NSLocalizedString. Had we done something like this, the English text would appear in the user interface for any language for which there is no localization, even if we didn't provide a base localization:

```
[self.labels[0] setText:NSLocalizedString(@"One", @"The number 1")];
[self.labels[1] setText:NSLocalizedString(@"Two", @"The number 2")];
[self.labels[2] setText:NSLocalizedString(@"Three", @"The number 3")];
[self.labels[3] setText:NSLocalizedString(@"Four", @"The number 4")];
[self.labels[4] setText:NSLocalizedString(@"Five", @"The number 5")];
NSString *flagFile = NSLocalizedString(@"flag_usa", @"Name of the flag");
```

While this is perfectly legal, the downside is that if you need to change any of the English text strings, you are also changing the key used to look up the strings for all of the other languages, so you will need to manually update all of the localized *.strings* files so that they use the new key.

Previewing Localizations in Xcode

You have probably realized by now that switching languages on your iOS device or on the simulator takes a lot of time. Well, the good news is that you don't actually need to do that every time you make changes to your code or localized strings, because Xcode 6 lets you preview your app's localizations in the Preview Assistant! To see how this works, select *Main.storyboard*, and then in the Assistant Editor, select **Preview** from the jump bar at the top and choose your storyboard. You'll see your application in its base localization. In the bottom right of the Preview Assistant, you'll see a button that lets you choose which of your localizations you'd like a preview of, as shown on the left in Figure 22-10.

Figure 22-10. Previewing localizations in Xcode

Select **French** and you'll see the application as it would appear to a French user, without ever leaving Xcode. Well, almost. In this case, the labels on the right are not populated and the flag has not changed. That's because we set those elements from our application code, which is beyond Xcode's power to figure out. For most purposes, however, it's likely that previewing the app like this as you design and localize it will save you a lot of time.

Localizing the App Display Name

We want to show you one final piece of localization that is commonly used: localizing the app name that's visible on the home screen and elsewhere. Apple does this for several of the built-in apps, and you might want to do so, as well.

The app name used for display is stored in your app's *Info.plist* file, which you'll find in the Supporting Files group in the Project Navigator. Select this file for editing, and you'll see that one of the items it contains, *Bundle display name*, is currently set to *${PRODUCT_NAME}*.

In the syntax used by *Info.plist* files, anything starting with a dollar sign is subject to variable substitution. In this case, it means that when Xcode compiles the app, the value of this item will be replaced with the name of the product in this Xcode project, which is the name of the app itself. This is where we want to do some localization, replacing *${PRODUCT_NAME}* with the localized name for each language. However, as it turns out, this doesn't quite work out as simply as you might expect.

The *Info.plist* file is sort of a special case, and it isn't meant to be localized. Instead, if you want to localize the content of *Info.plist*, you need to make localized versions of a file named *InfoPlist.strings*. Before you can do that, you need to create a Base version of that file. If you followed the steps in the previous section to localize the app, you'll already have English and French versions of this file that are empty. If you don't have these files, you can add one as follows:

1. Select **File ➤ New ➤ File...**, and then in the iOS section, choose **Resource** followed by **Strings File**. Press **Next**, name the file *InfoPlist.strings*, assign it to the Supporting Files group in the LocalizeMe project, and create it.

2. Select the new file and, in the File Inspector, press **Localize**. In the dialog box that appears, have the file moved to the English localization, and then, back in the File Inspector, check the check box for **French** under **Localizations**. You should now see copies of this file for both French and English in the Project Navigator.

We need to add a line to each localized copy of this file to define the display name for the app. In the *Info.plist* file, we were shown the display name associated with a dictionary key called *Bundle display name*; however, that's not the real key name! It's merely an Xcode nicety, trying to give us a more friendly and readable name. The real name is `CFBundleDisplayName`, which you can verify by selecting *Info.plist*, right-clicking anywhere in the view, and then selecting **Show Raw Keys/Values**. This shows you the true names of the keys in use.

So, select the English localization of *InfoPlist.strings* and either add or modify the following line:

```
"CFBundleDisplayName" = "Localize Me";
```

This key may already exist if you followed the localization steps for English, because it's inserted as part of the process of importing an XLIFF file. In fact, another way to localize your app's name is to add the translation to the XLIFF file in the same way as we did for the other texts that we needed to translate—just look for the entry for `CFBundleDisplayName` and add a `<trans>` element with the translated name. Similarly, select the French localization of the *InfoPlist.strings* file and edit it to give the app a proper French name:

```
"CFBundleDisplayName" = "Localisez Moi";
```

Build and run the app, and then press the **Home** button to get back to the launch screen. And of course, switch the device or simulator you're using to French if it's currently running in English. You should see the localized name just underneath the app's icon, but sometimes it may not appear immediately. iOS seems to cache this information when a new app is added, but it doesn't necessarily change it when an existing app is replaced by a new version—at least not when Xcode is doing the replacing. So, if you're running in French and you don't see the new name—don't worry. Just delete the app from the launch screen, go back to Xcode, and then build and run the app again.

Now our application is fully localized for both French and English.

Adding Another Localization

To wrap up, we're going to add another localization to our application. This time, we'll localize it to Swiss French, which is a regional variation of French with language code *fr-CH*. The reason I chose this language is that, at least at the time of writing, it is not one of the languages for which iOS has a specific localization. Nevertheless, you can still localize your app to Swiss French and run it on your iOS device.

The basic principle is the same as before—in fact, now that you have done this once, it should go much faster this time. Start by selecting the project in the Project Navigator, and then select the project itself in the editor, followed by the **Info** tab. In the Localizations section, press + to add a new language. You won't see Swiss French in the menu, so scroll down and select **Other**. This opens a submenu with a very large number of languages to choose from—fortunately, they are in alphabetical order. If you scroll down, you will eventually find **French (Switzerland)**, so select it. In the dialog that appears (which looks like Figure 22-5), change the Reference Language for all of the listed files to *French*, and then click **Finish**. Now if you look at the Project Navigator, you'll see that you have Swiss French versions of the storyboard, localizable strings, and *InfoPlist.strings* files. To demonstrate that this localization is distinct from the French one, open the Swiss French version of *InfoPlist.strings* and change the bundle name to this:

```
"CFBundleDisplayName" = "Swiss Localisez Moi";
```

Now build and run the application. Switch to the Settings application and go to Language & Region. As I said earlier, you won't find Swiss French in the list of iPhone Languages. Instead, click **Other Languages** and scroll down (or search) until you find **French (Switzerland)**, and then select it and press **Done**. This will bring up an action sheet in which you will be asked if you prefer Swiss French or your current language. Select **Swiss French** and let iOS reset itself. You should now see that our application is called *Swiss Localisez Moi* (in fact, you won't see the whole name, because it's too long, but you get the point ;-)).

Auf Wiedersehen

If you want to maximize sales of your iOS application, you'll probably want to localize it as much as possible. Fortunately, the iOS localization architecture makes easy work of supporting multiple languages, and even multiple dialects of the same language, within your application. As you saw in this chapter, nearly any type of file that you add to your application can be localized.

Even if you don't plan on localizing your application, you should get in the habit of using `NSLocalizedString` instead of just using static strings in your code. With Xcode's Code Sense feature, the difference in typing time is negligible. And, should you ever want to translate your application, your life will be much, much easier. Going back late in the project to find all text strings that should be localized is a boring and error-prone process, which you can avoid with a little effort in advance.

And on that note, we have now reached the end of our travels together, so it's time for us to say *sayonara, au revoir, auf wiedersehen, avtío, arrivederci, hej då, до свидания*, and *adiós*.

The programming language and frameworks we've worked within this book are the end result of more than 25 years of evolution. And Apple engineers are feverishly working round the clock, thinking of that next, cool, new thing. The iOS platform has just begun to blossom. There is so much more to come.

By making it through this book, you've built yourself a sturdy foundation. You have a solid knowledge of Objective-C, Cocoa Touch, and the tools that bring these technologies together to create incredible new iPhone, iPod touch, and iPad applications. You understand the iOS software architecture—the design patterns that make Cocoa Touch sing. In short, you're ready to chart your own course. We are so proud!

We sure are glad you came along on this journey with us. We wish you the best of luck and hope that you enjoy programming iOS as much as we do.

Index

Q

Get the eBook for only $10!

Now you can take the weightless companion with you anywhere, anytime. Your purchase of this book entitles you to 3 electronic versions for only $10.

This Apress title will prove so indispensible that you'll want to carry it with you everywhere, which is why we are offering the eBook in 3 formats for only $10 if you have already purchased the print book.

Convenient and fully searchable, the PDF version enables you to easily find and copy code—or perform examples by quickly toggling between instructions and applications. The MOBI format is ideal for your Kindle, while the ePUB can be utilized on a variety of mobile devices.

Go to www.apress.com/promo/tendollars to purchase your companion eBook.

Lightning Source UK Ltd.
Milton Keynes UK
UKOW07f1916260815

257583UK00004B/244/P

Eat to Beat Arthritis

Eat to Beat Arthritis

Over 60 recipes and a self-treatment plan to transform your life

Marguerite Patten, O.B.E. *and*
Jeannette Ewin, Ph.D.

TED SMART

This edition produced for

The Book People Ltd,
Hall Wood Avenue,
Haydock, St Helens
WA11 9UL

Thorsons
An Imprint of HarperCollins*Publishers*
77–85 Fulham Palace Road
Hammersmith, London W6 8JB

The Thorsons website address is: www.thorsons.com

Published by Thorsons 2001

10 9 8 7 6 5 4 3 2 1

© Marguerite Patten and Jeannette Ewin 2001

Marguerite Patten and Jeannette Ewin assert the moral
right to be identified as the authors of this work

A catalogue record of this book is
available from the British Library

ISBN 0 00 765783 8

Printed and bound in Malaysia by
Times Publishing Ltd

Contents

Preface

Marguerite Patten, O.B.E., a well-known and highly respected food writer, and Jeannette Ewin, Ph.D., a health journalist with an international following, have joined forces to create an eating plan that can help you beat the pain and distress of arthritis. The *Eat to Beat Arthritis* Diet, and everything you need to know about how it can change your life, is contained in this book.

Arthritis has been compared to being locked in a prison: its symptoms bar you from living the way you wish. In this book you will learn how to break lifestyle habits that have shackled you to pain. The pages that follow contain the latest information about food supplements that fight the causes and symptoms of arthritis. You will also learn how to listen to your own body, and understand what it is telling you about the food you eat.

The *Eat to Beat Arthritis* Diet is based on a selection of foods and supplements that help your body fight the pain of crippling disease. Unlike other diets you may have tried in the past, it allows you to enjoy appetizing and satisfying meals while you chart the dietary course towards wellbeing. Using foods recommended in the *Eat to Beat Arthritis* Diet, Marguerite Patten has developed over 60 delicious recipes that can be enjoyed by everyone – not just those suffering from arthritis. Unlike the recipes you may have tried in some health-related cookery books, the dishes described here are full of appealing flavour and texture.

Working on this book was a labour of love for Marguerite, as she personally knows how arthritis can affect one's life. Her search for a means of controlling this painful illness had been long and hard, and included both acupuncture and chiropractic treatments. When these failed, her doctor said surgery on a severely arthritic hip was the only answer. Faced with family and professional responsibilities, Marguerite's response was, 'Sorry. I haven't the time right now.' With hope of finding an answer to her advancing illness in some other form of therapy, she turned for help to the subject she knows best: food. By changing her diet she changed her life, and in this book she not only provides clear instructions about how to cook the appropriate foods, but also shares the secrets of her own story.

Reading every health and diet book she could find that focused on the perplexing problem of arthritis, Marguerite came across an international bestseller: *A Doctor's Proven New Home Cure for Arthritis*, by Dr Giraud W. Campbell. Here was a healing diet that incorporated foods she enjoyed eating. The prescribed therapy was strict, but manageable. She gave it a try and within weeks experienced a dramatic and clinically recognizable improvement in her condition.

Over the years since her introduction to Dr Campbell's book, much has been learned about how diets work and why certain nutrient supplements help control this debilitating illness. To share her personal experience, and to expand what she had learned about diet and arthritis, Marguerite Patten teamed up with a friend and nutritionist, Dr Jeannette Ewin. Taking their lead from Dr Campbell's book, they developed the *Eat to Beat Arthritis* Diet. This sensible and healthy way to enjoy good food combines Marguerite's decades of experience developing tasty and sure-fire recipes, with Jeannette's insight into the interactions between food, nutrition and health. As a side benefit, those who follow their advice will soon find they not only gain control over pain, but also enjoy a greater feeling of wellbeing.

PART ONE

You Can Beat Arthritis!

CHAPTER 1

You can beat arthritis!

During an awards ceremony, American comedian Jack Benny reportedly said:
'Thank you for this honour, but I don't know what I did to deserve it. Then again,
I have arthritis, and I don't know what I did to deserve that either.'

If – like Jack Benny – you suffer from arthritis, you know it is no laughing matter. Pain can
dominate your life, and its effects are insidious. You don't sleep well at night because your joints
hurt. Backache plagues you while you are in bed. Knees and hips ache when you get out of bed.
Slowly, you begin to feel depressed by the lack of sleep. During the day you begin avoiding
exercise. Taking a walk, swinging a golf club, or doing everyday household chores cause
discomfort and pain and, as a result, you find yourself moving less. Muscles that were once firm
and strong begin to weaken from lack of use. Not burning off calories as quickly as you once did,
you find yourself gaining a bit of weight. The problem of wakeful nights becomes compounded
because the exercise you now avoid is an important part of getting the body ready for sleep. Over
time, arthritis begins to dominate your life, and you find yourself in a slow physical and
emotional cycle of decline.

   The above scenario is not inevitable, however. You can prevent it happening to you. By
changing your diet and lifestyle, it is possible to regain a sense of physical and mental wellbeing.
Arthritis leads to negative changes in your life: The *Eat to Beat Arthritis* Diet is your guide to the
positive changes needed to overcome them.

   Unfortunately, many arthritis sufferers never find a way of overcoming the debilitating
symptoms of the disease. They may seek help from their doctor, and find that the medication
they are prescribed causes unpleasant side effects such as stomach pain. Others try various forms
of alternative therapy only to find them ineffective. In the end, they all too often submit. After
all, they may reason, everyone who reaches a certain age must suffer from some form of aches or
pains. As time goes by, their condition gets worse. All too soon the activities they once enjoyed –
like playing with the grandchildren, gardening, or keeping up with a favourite hobby – cause too
much pain to bear.

   Don't give in to arthritis. By learning to select and enjoy the foods that uniquely suit you,
and by following the lifestyle advice in this book, you can continue enjoying life. Think positive.
Be positive. Make the changes that release you from the negative cycle of arthritis.

The *Eat to Beat Arthritis* Diet is based on a simple, three-part strategy to healing and health:

* Know your enemy (in this case – arthritis);
* Know how to defeat your enemy (gain control over arthritis in seven weeks); and
* Enjoy life.

The details of this strategy are outlined in the chapters that follow, but here is a brief summary of what is involved.

Know your enemy

Strip away the mystery of arthritis by understanding what it is and why it occurs. When an illness is diagnosed and given a name by a doctor, it has power. It is the unknown, and we are its victims. By learning something about an illness, or disease, and why it makes us suffer, we gain control. Knowledge replaces doubt, and hope replaces fear.

The basic facts outlined in Chapter 2 demystify arthritis. More detailed information is presented in the section of the book called 'Questions and answers about arthritis'. Additional help is also provided by a glossary, a selection of good food tips and a list of helpful resources (this includes a number of websites for those of you with access to the internet).

Know how to defeat your enemy (gain control over arthritis in seven weeks)

This book is your guide to seven weeks that can change your life. Once you understand an illness, you can build a strategy to defeat it. If its total defeat is not possible, you can still find ways to minimize its symptoms and learn to live a brighter, fuller life.

In the early parts of this book you will learn how to alter your diet and lifestyle to break the negative cycle of arthritis. You will discover why good nutrition can rebuild failing tissues, block pain and revitalize aching joints. It will also become clear why certain foods should be avoided, and how everyday favourites – like tomatoes and aubergines (eggplants) – can cause joint pain and swelling.

You are unique, and your requirement for food is unique. Not only do you need to know which foods you should eat, but how they can be balanced to help you live a full and active life – despite having arthritis. This is explained in Chapter 3, where you will find an outline of the basic rules of nutrition, and information about how the substances in food affect your health. The basic rules of nutrition hold for everyone, but the amounts of individual nutrients you require for optimum health are not the same as those needed by others.

During the seven weeks of this diet, you will learn how to listen to your body and recognize when specific foods are doing harm. Simply by avoiding all foods containing wheat and all drinks containing caffeine, many arthritis suffers find their lives changed forever.

If all this is beginning to sound a bit too restrictive – take heart! In Part Two you will find a long list of foods you *can* eat. And to help you enjoy a delicious (and very modern) approach to cooking with these ingredients, Marguerite Patten has devised over 60 easy-to-prepare recipes.

Marguerite's recipes are a vital part of this book. In them she not only explains what to cook and how, but also shares her own experience with the diet. Day by day, step by step, she takes you through the diet and discusses why she chose one ingredient over another. These personal insights give invaluable information and encouragement as you begin to experiment with a style of cooking that is fresh and tasty as well as healing and healthy.

Enjoy life

This is the third proclamation of the *Eat to Beat Arthritis* Diet. Unfortunately there are no simple recipes to help you with this part of the programme. Some suggestions are offered later on, but no one can prescribe what is best for *you*. Just remember:

* The glass of life is half full – *not* half empty.
* Smiling has been scientifically shown to have a positive effect on mood and the sensation of pain.
* Exercise relaxes you, loosens joints and muscles, and helps lay the groundwork for a good night's sleep.

Know your enemy

(understanding arthritis and its causes)

The costly epidemic of arthritis

'People ignore arthritis both as public and personal health problems because it doesn't kill you.' So said Chad Helmick, a medical epidemiologist at the Center for Disease Control and Prevention in the United States. He continued: 'But what they don't realize is that as Americans work and live longer, arthritis can affect their quality of life and eventually lead to disability.' According to the *FDA Consumer* (May–June 2000), who quoted Dr Helmick, the current annual cost of arthritis to the U.S. economy is nearly $65 billion – a sum large enough to have about the same impact as a moderate recession.

Arthritis can strike at any age, and the number of arthritis sufferers increases each year. During a person's lifetime, arthritis is more likely to restrict activity than cancer, diabetes or heart disease. World-wide, arthritis inflicts a terrible cost. In the United States alone, currently about 42 million people are afflicted by chronic forms of arthritis: according to the Center for Disease Control, that number will rise to 60 million by 2020. More than 11 million of those people will be crippled badly enough to be classified as disabled. And the U.S. is not an exceptional case – the social and economic impact of arthritis in the United States is mirrored throughout the Western world.

Why should more people suffer from arthritis today than in the past? And why do various forms of arthritis appear to be increasing at a greater rate in Westernized countries than in the rest of the world? Many experts believe the answer must be related to our lifestyle and diet.

When you consider the vast amount of money spent on medication to treat the symptoms of arthritis, and on surgical repair of crippled hips and knees, you get some idea just how much could be saved if people would eat and live according to the simple rules suggested here.

Arthritis comes in many forms

The word 'arthritis' refers to any process that causes inflammation of joints and surrounding tissues. Depending on which expert you believe, there are between one and two hundred different conditions that can be classified as 'arthritis'. Some of these are common (osteoarthritis, rheumatoid arthritis and gout), while others are relatively rare (ankylosing spondylitis and systemic lupus erythematosis are examples). In *Eat to Beat Arthritis* we focus on those types of arthritis that affect the most people, although the anti-inflammation diet described here will help almost everyone.

Two key words need explanation: 'inflammation' and 'joint'.

Inflammation is a natural process in which the body's immune system reacts to infection, injury or any abnormal form of irritation. The area of inflammation becomes red, swollen and abnormally warm. When inflammation takes place around a site of infection or injury its role is to kill any invading organisms and speed up the removal of debris from dead bacteria (or viruses) and tissue. In other words, inflammation is a healthy part of the normal healing process. Unfortunately, there are times when the immune system mistakes the body's own normal tissues for the 'enemy', and attacks them. This is known as an auto-immune reaction. The immune system may also attack parts of the body where concentrations of abnormal substances occur – such as joints in which bony nodules form after injury; or in places where abnormal deposits of uric acid form, as is the case in gout.

Inflammation is the real culprit in arthritis, so the diet described in this book is designed to help control inflammation. Even if you are on medication for your condition, changing the way you eat will help break the painful bonds of inflamed joints and tissues.

A *joint* is a place, or 'join', in the body where bones meet. Some joints are stationary, or fused, and have no motion; the joints between bone in the skull are examples. Other joints may allow a limited degree of motion, such as those in the fingers and toes, while others allow extensive motion. Hip joints are a good example of a place where there can be considerable movement at the place where bones meet.

As a general rule joints are formed from fibrous tissue, a pad of cartilage at the end of each bone within the joint, a thin lining of synovial membrane (which secretes a thin lubricating fluid into the joint to aid its motion) and, sometimes, a ligament, or strong band of fibrous tissue binding the bones together. Ligaments are also found supporting other parts of the body, including some internal organs.

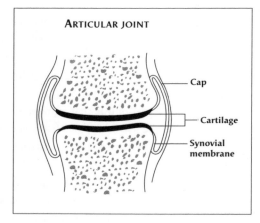

ARTICULAR JOINT

Cap

Cartilage

Synovial membrane

OSTEOARTHRITIS

Almost everyone suffers from some degree of osteoarthritis. The older you get the more likely it is that injury or constant use has damaged one or more of your joints, and osteoarthritis has set in. Many athletes suffer this form of arthritis at a fairly early age owing to injury to cartilage and the bones within much-used joints, such as the knee. In less athletic people the pain experienced in knees, hands and hips by the time they reach retirement age is as a result of simple wear and tear on the internal structure of joints. In both cases, cartilage can wear so thin the ends of bones become exposed within joints. This causes pain and inflammation. To make matters worse, bony nodules may collect in osteoarthritic joints, adding to the pain and inflammation. And as anyone who suffers from pain knows, it can be mentally exhausting as well as physically debilitating.

Medical treatment for osteoarthritis usually involves analgesics (painkillers) and – in some cases – drugs that support the body's attempts to rebuild damaged cartilage. Most of these drugs not only effectively reduce pain, they also reduce inflammation. The problem is that many analgesics (including aspirin and ibuprofen) cause stomach irritation that can lead to bleeding, and they do nothing to help rebuild worn tissue. During the past decade research has shown that there are natural compounds that support the rebuilding of damaged cartilage: *glucosamine* holds the greatest promise at present. You can learn more about this healing compound on page 154.

Rheumatoid arthritis

The stiffness, pain, swelling and loss of function associated with rheumatoid arthritis results from inflammation of the lining that secretes lubricating fluid into joints. The disease can affect other parts of the body, but treatment is most often sought for the condition when it involves joints. In most cases this form of arthritis affects the same joint on both sides of the body: both knees, or both hips, or the knuckles of both forefingers. In severe cases deformity and loss of function result.

The medications used to treat rheumatoid and osteoarthritis are similar, and are selected to block pain and reduce inflammation. However, there is strong evidence that certain foods, such as oily fish, and food supplements, such as fish oil, help reduce the causes of the inflammation without endangering the delicate lining of the stomach.

More information about rheumatoid arthritis can be found on page 151.

Gout

Gout is frequently lampooned as a rich man's illness, associated with too much fine wine and fatty food. In fact it strikes people from all walks of life: beggar and king. It can be very painful, and it is common to hear sufferers describe how they cannot bear to have even the weight of a bed-sheet rest on an affected toe. (Big toes are frequent victims of this illness.) Mercifully, gout is far less common than either osteoarthritis or rheumatoid arthritis.

Gout is caused when too much uric acid collects in the blood. Uric acid is a by-product of normal metabolism, and it is usually collected and discarded from the body by the kidneys in urine. However, when the kidneys are not functioning normally, or when the diet contains an excess of certain foods, blood levels can rise to the point where the excess uric acid crystallizes in joints, the kidneys, or even the soft tissue of the ear. These stone-like residues cause pain, damage surrounding tissues, and trigger the biological processes that lead to inflammation.

There are medications to help gout suffers, but diet is a vital part of controlling the build-up of uric acid in the blood, and reducing or eliminating inflammation.

For more about gout, see page 152.

CHAPTER 3

Know how to combat your enemy
(seven weeks that will change your life)

The power to heal is within you. Given the right nutritional building blocks, adequate rest, exercise and a pollution-free environment, the human body has remarkable powers of restoration and self-healing. The *Eat to Beat Arthritis* Diet is all about harnessing these elements to your advantage.

Food is the answer

No diet should promise overnight success. Healing takes time. If you suffer from arthritis you need to eat foods, and take food supplements, that calm the inflammatory processes that cause pain. You also need to consume those nutrients that the body needs to build new and healthy tissues, such as cartilage in joints.

Think of it this way. Your body is made entirely of the foods you eat. In an ideal world, what you eat would exactly match what your body needs to function at its best. But this is not an ideal world. Stress, illness, lifestyle changes and the natural processes of bearing children all place demands on your body that require a specific blend of nutrients. For example, smoking increases the body's need for vitamin C, and you can cope with stress better if your diet is rich in foods containing B vitamins.

Using the advice in this book you will learn how to select those foods that provide the unique blend of nutrients your body needs for healing. You will also learn how the right foods can help you combat damaging and painful inflammation. Also highlighted is the importance of identifying foods to which you may be sensitive. Once you know what are the right foods for you, you can then go on to prepare delicious dishes using these ingredients. Best of all, you can read Marguerite Patten's excellent advice on using and living with this diet. When you know what suits your body best, and you have experienced the rewards from changing your eating habits to improve your arthritis, you will find that you can relax from time to time and allow yourself some flexibility in what you eat. Marguerite explains how she balances her lifestyle with the diet and allows herself the occasional treat. The trick is just to enjoy yourself, then reinstate the *Eat to Beat Arthritis* Diet as soon as you can afterwards and you'll soon be back to your best.

A schedule for success

Once you begin this diet you will probably experience an improvement in your condition during the first week: but there is more to come! Give yourself at least six weeks before you judge its total benefits to you. Eating plans that promise much faster results are not really being fair. It takes time for your body to heal. The full programme is explained in the next section, but here is a brief week-by-week summary of the diet, followed by an explanation of how it works:

Week zero – *Listening to your body*
* Learn about yourself by keeping records of what you eat and when your symptoms appear.
* As the first step towards controlling pain, eliminate coffee, cola drinks, tea and other sources of caffeine from your diet.
* If you smoke cigarettes, this is the time to stop.

Week one – *Cleansing and detoxifying your body*
* After a one-day fast, begin a diet of foods that help heal and rebuild the body.
* Eliminate all foods containing wheat, rye, oats, and all sources of gluten from your diet.
* Eliminate alcohol from your diet.
* Supplements containing fish oil and vitamin E are added to your healing routine, as is a Health Drink that you make at home.

Week two – *Stabilizing your body*
* The routine of foods and supplements started during Week One continues. (By this time, many people experience significant relief from the pain and inflammation of arthritis.)

Weeks three through six – *The elimination diet*
* During these four weeks, you will introduce various foods and food groups into your diet to test their effect on your arthritis.
* Up to now you have enjoyed a diet based on a limited number of ingredients. To live in the real world of work and family, that list of foods needs to be expanded.
* The benefits of the diet by now include a greater sense of wellbeing, and improved skin and hair texture.

Week seven and forever – *Enjoy life*

Week zero – Getting to know yourself

This period is a preparation for the life-changes to come. By keeping a daily chart of when and where you experience pain, what you eat, how well you sleep, and when and how you exercise, you will have a snapshot of how well you are taking care of your body. Make no changes during this week (with the exception of giving up caffeine). Just listen to your body. You will continue to keep these charts throughout the first six weeks of the diet, because they will provide information about how your body is reacting to change.

It may be tempting to skip this week's activities. Forget any such ideas. This may be the most valuable week of the diet, because it provides the information you need to monitor your progress towards a life of less pain and greater mobility. Keeping notes for anything shorter than a week will give you a false picture, because your life activities have a pattern – and they run from Sunday through to Saturday.

If you smoke, use this time to consider how you plan to remove this pollutant from your body. As you will learn in the next chapter, smoking adds to the problems that increase the pain of arthritis.

Week one – Cleansing and detoxifying your body

Work begins here. During these seven days you will lower the level of harmful substances in the body through fasting, avoiding specific foods, and drinking adequate amounts of fluids. The charts you keep will begin to show early benefits of the diet.

Week two – Stabilizing your body

By the end of Week One you will be eating a very healthy, although somewhat restricted diet. This is the Basic Arthritis Diet. By following the same eating plan during the second week of the diet, you will stabilize your metabolism and remove any traces of reaction from foods you have eaten in the past. You are allowing your body to rest. (Do not worry about having to eat bland and uninteresting food – the recipes Marguerite Patten provides further on in the book are full of flavour.)

Weeks three to six – Expanding your food vocabulary

Now is the time to expand the variety of foods you eat. In this section, guidance is provided on how to test specific foods for their effect on your level of joint pain and discomfort. You may be surprised by the results. Foods you have enjoyed for years – and that you have been told are good for you – may be just the ones that stimulate an inflammatory reaction in your joints.

Week seven and forever – How to live a little and still maintain control over pain

Once you know which foods present problems, and how to detoxify your body on the Basic Arthritis Diet, you can try breaking the rules. But remember: once you break the rules you must return to them as quickly as possible.

CHAPTER 4

Changing your lifestyle

As you change your diet, and learn about yourself by using a self-assessment chart, you should consider other ways to improve your health. In addition to changing your diet and giving up smoking (see box below), there are other ways you can change your lifestyle and help control the painful and crippling effects of arthritis:

1 Control your weight
2 Enjoy gentle exercise
3 Get adequate sleep
4 Learn to relax
5 Have a good laugh

Control your weight

Extra pounds place excess wear and tear on joints and ligaments. Hundreds of diet plans exist to help you lose weight: ignore them all. The healthiest and most important step towards eliminating unnecessary fat from your body is to eat a balanced diet in moderation, and become more active. Using the *Eat to Beat Arthritis* Diet as your guide, choose foods that suit you best and enjoy them in small portions until your weight has reached an ideal level.

Serve yourself whenever possible (other people always give you more than you need), and only put on your plate what you intend to eat. Do not have second helpings. If you would usually take two tablespoons of peas, take only one. If you usually enjoy a full bowl of soup,

If you smoke, try to stop. The health evidence against smoking tobacco is overwhelming. Smokers dislike hearing people drone on about this, but the effects of smoke on your body are worth keeping in mind when you are committed to improving your health. As all those massively expensive anti-smoking campaigns tell us, the link between smoking and certain forms of cancer is obvious, but smoking causes other damage as well. There is evidence that the damaging levels of free radicals released in the body by cigarette smoke increases inflammation, and thus increases the level of pain associated with arthritis.

ladle out half a bowl as your diet portion. For the good health of your heart and vascular system, cut the amount of butter and animal fat in your diet to the smallest possible amounts, and use only half the oil you would usually use on salads and in cooking. Eat smaller portions and eat more slowly to enjoy the full flavour of your food. There are two exceptions to the rule on eating less. Among the foods you will enjoy on the *Eat to Beat Arthritis* Diet are liver and a nutritious Health Drink. Do not reduce your intake of either of these foods. (Gout sufferers must eliminate the liver, however. See page 45.)

If you are trying to lose weight, it is essential to add some extra exercise to your daily routine to burn off unwanted calories. Housework and walking to the shops are not enough.

Enjoy gentle exercise

Many of the causes of joint and muscle pain and discomfort should be eliminated or reduced by following the *Eat to Beat Arthritis* Diet. However, you also need to keep active to keep your body at its best, especially if you need to lose weight.

The choice of exercise activities is rich and varied. All you need to do is choose one and give it a try. If your first choice does not suit you, try another, and another, until you find one that you enjoy. Add at least three exercise sessions to your weekly routine. Include gentle stretching at both the start and conclusion of each session. No matter how old or unfit you are, visit the local gym and see if they offer anything that would interest you. Alternatively, contact local community and church groups to see if they offer activities that would get your blood pumping. You'll be surprised by the variety of activities available. For example, line dancing seems to be all the rage for every age these days, and some of the less strenuous martial arts both strengthen the body and calm the mind.

Remember, talk with your doctor before beginning any new exercise or sporting activity. He or she will probably applaud your decision to get out and get moving.

Good forms of exercise include walking, swimming and stretching. Gardening is also valuable exercise as it promotes joint health by stretching and placing gentle pressure on muscles surrounding joints in the arms, legs, hips and back.

Pain may be increased when you first start exercising, but you will soon 'work through' that as your stiff joints regain their flexibility. Exercise unlocks stiff joints and tissues. How many times have you heard someone say, 'I was so stiff this morning I thought I wouldn't be able to get out of bed; but once I got moving everything was fine.' You have probably had this same experience, and know that movement is a large part of keeping stiff limbs and muscles active.

To conquer the pain of arthritis, you should gently and repeatedly move the joints and tissues that hurt. By doing so, you strengthen the muscles that support the tissues, stimulate normal bone growth, and stimulate the circulation to the inflamed area. Remember, if you reduce your level of daily activity because you are afraid of the pain and discomfort that accompanies movement, you are going to lose more muscle strength and fail to stimulate normal bone growth.

Yoga and Pilates are two excellent exercise disciplines. Both stretch and strengthen muscles, but in their elementary forms neither one pushes or pulls muscles into extreme positions or activity. As relaxation is a principle goal in the practice of yoga, it has special value for arthritis sufferers. Yoga originated in India about three thousand years ago, and is based on physical control and relaxation. The practice has become increasingly popular over the past several decades, and many forms of movement and self-training have evolved. To learn more about yoga, visit your local library for books on the subject. Also, shop around to see what programmes are available in your area. Yoga is often offered in community and adult education centres.

Pilates is a form of exercise and body control developed by Joseph Pilates in the early 1900s. Born in Germany in 1880, Pilates was sickly and frail as a child, and as a result became obsessed by physical fitness. By the time the Great War broke out in Europe, Pilates was in England, teaching detectives self-defence. As a German, he was interned for the duration of the conflict. While in the camp he devised a regime of exercises for his fellow internees that maintained their health and fitness level while they were held in confinement. Not one of these people died during the influenza outbreak of 1918, and Pilates often claimed this was due to the exercise programme he developed. (There may be some truth in this, as we now know that exercise strengthens the immune system.)

After the war Joseph Pilates returned to Germany and began working with dancers and others who sought perfection in body form, flexibility and balance. When asked to begin work with the German army, Pilates refused and fled to America. On the boat he met a nursery teacher whom he later married. Together they established a fitness studio in New York, where dancers, athletes and members of top society soon became his clients. His devoted followers have included Martha Graham, Gregory Peck, Katherine Hepburn, Jodi Foster, Michael Crawford, Joan Collins and Sigourney Weaver. Tennis professional Pat Cash and world champion ice skating star Kristi Yamaguchi are among the athletes who have profited from Joseph Pilates' teaching. His methods are now taught around the world.

The Pilates method differs from other fitness programmes in the way the exercises are approached. Like yoga, it binds the activities of the mind with those of the body, making the mental perception of the body as important as physical movement. As in yoga, the three main elements of each exercise are relaxation, control and co-ordination. Pilates differs from yoga in one important way, however: the Girdle of Strength, that is the internal cage of muscles that supports and holds the body's internal organs in place, is tightened and used in every exercise practised. So too are the multifidous muscles, which stabilize the lumbar spine. By building power and flexibility into these often overlooked muscle groups, Pilates uniquely contributes to the physical fitness of sufferers of innumerable physical ailments and injuries.

For more about Pilates and how it can help you, browse in your local library and bookshop for more information. Also contact community and fitness centres to see what they have to offer in the way of basic courses.

Get adequate sleep

Insomnia affects the ability to concentrate and increases the awareness of pain and discomfort. If you have trouble sleeping, you are not alone. According to the Mayo Clinic in Rochester, Minnesota, more than 100 million people in the United States do not get a good night's sleep on a regular basis. Tired people have slower reaction times, are less productive and are less likely to interact with others in a positive manner. Like everyone else, arthritis sufferers should do all they can to maximize their chances of sleeping for eight hours a night. Here are some tips on what you can do to help you deal with this insidious problem.

First, however, what is insomnia? According to the Mayo Clinic, in the United States, these are some signs to watch out for:

* It takes longer than 30 minutes to fall asleep
* You wake several times during the night
* You wake up feeling muddled and tired
* You fall asleep during meetings and daytime events
* You are forgetful.

Dr Peter Hauri, Director of the Mayo Clinic Insomnia Program, suggests that answers to the following questions may help determine why you have sleep problems:

* Do you feel anxious when you are getting ready for bed?
* Do you argue with your spouse or partner in bed?
* Do you worry about the next day's tasks when you are trying to fall asleep?
* Do you keep checking the time on a bedside clock?
* Do you sleep better on holiday, or at a friend's house, than when you are in your own bed at home?
* Do you try to force yourself to go to sleep?

If you answered 'yes' to any of these questions you should take action.

Dr John W. Shepard Jr, M.D., Medical Director of the Mayo Clinic Sleep Disorders Center, has offered the following tips on how to get the full eight hours of sleep we all need each night. Remember, however, that what works for one person may not work for another. Try one or two of the following suggestions at a time until you find the combination that is right for you.

* Avoid caffeine and nicotine. Both are addictive stimulants that can interfere with sleep. (Remember that on the *Eat to Beat Arthritis* Diet, neither caffeine nor cigarettes are permitted.)
* Exercise, preferably in the afternoon.
* Watch what you eat and drink. Fatty and spicy foods may cause heartburn that disturbs sleep.
* Avoid drinking alcohol before going to bed; it may cause you to snore or get up during the night. (You should be avoiding it anyway while on the *Eat to Beat Arthritis* diet.)
* If you must have a midnight snack, eat foods rich in the amino acid L-tryptophan, which triggers the release of serotonin in the brain. Good snacks include a glass of milk (warm or cold, as you prefer) or a tuna or turkey sandwich.

- Make sure the room is cool before going to bed, but have enough bedding to keep your body warm. Warm hands and feet encourage sleep.
- Avoid naps. Save your sleep for night-time.
- Enjoy stillness. Leave the radio and television off. If external noises disturb you use earplugs.
- Use your bed only for sleeping and sex. Watch television somewhere else.
- Set a sleep schedule. Try to go to bed and get up at the same time each day. Remember that a lazy Sunday morning in bed after a night out can mean a restless night ahead.
- Do not fret if you cannot go to sleep immediately. After a time, get up and do something else, like reading a good book. Then try again.

Learn to relax

Learn to unwind and let the world pass by. Use techniques like yoga and meditation to help release you from internal tension.

A hot bath or shower will relax you. Gently massage the area around inflamed joints. Try using herbal bath products that make you relax.

Many people who are disabled or slowed in their daily activities by pain become obsessive about what they *cannot* do. If this sounds familiar, then concentrate on what you *can* do, and do not be afraid to ask others for help to take care of the rest. It isn't easy, but it is necessary. If, for example, you are used to keeping your home and garden immaculate and can no longer do so, you need to admit that this is the case and take steps to reduce or spread the load. Decide which chores can be reduced in frequency, which can be turned over to someone else and which can simply be ignored. You may have ironed your bed linen – even your underwear – for many years but is it really necessary?

Have a good laugh

Laughter and a positive attitude are powerful medicines to be taken in large and frequent doses. When someone is in pain or discomfort they have a tendency to turn emotionally inwards. Before they know what has happened, the pain is worse. And as the pain gets worse, they withdraw into themselves. Laughter brings out the best in people. Let it lift you when those aching joints are getting you down.

To brighten your spirit:
- Enjoy films and videos that you know will make you laugh, even if you have seen them before. Read a book with a positive message. Better still, read a book of jokes or amusing short stories. I know a lovely elderly gentleman who reads Harry Potter to forget his gouty feet.
- Call a friend who makes you laugh. Avoid all talk of illness and pain; just enjoy a good chat.
- Write a letter to someone you love. Tell them about all the funny and happy things that you can remember happening during the past week.

PART TWO

The Facts About Arthritis and Diet

CHAPTER 1

About arthritis

The aim in this part of the book is to get you started on the *Eat to Beat Arthritis* Diet. After basic information about arthritis in several of its more common forms you will read about food and diet, and how they affect inflammatory illnesses.

Coming from 'arthron', the Greek word for joint, *arthritis* literally means 'inflammation of the joint'. It may surprise you to know that about 200 different illnesses, all causing degeneration of joints and soft tissues, are classified as arthritis. Millions of people around the world suffer from some form of this illness, and in the United Kingdom one quarter of all visits to the doctor relate to its symptoms.

Although there are a surprising number of different types of arthritis, the great majority of people suffer from either *osteoarthritis* or *rheumatoid arthritis*. Both rheumatoid and osteoarthritis vary in their degree of severity, ranging from very mild discomfort to crippling. As you would expect, those with milder forms of these conditions will experience a greater degree of healing on this diet than those who have already suffered a major deterioration of joints. However, everyone should improve, and many will experience a return to normal activity.

Osteoarthritis is due to 'wear and tear' on joints, and most people beyond the age of 65 are affected to some degree. Athletes, or people involved in vocations that repeatedly use one or more joints – such as dancers and typists – may begin suffering from signs of arthritis at a relatively young age. Osteoarthritis may co-exist with other forms of arthritis, especially rheumatoid arthritis. It frequently occurs in the weight-bearing joints of the knees, hips and feet. Bony lumps, called 'nodes' sometimes form on the ends of finger bones, causing a gnarled, enlarged appearance. Stress, wear and tear can also cause slow deterioration of the discs between the spinal vertebrae, leading to pain and stiffness in the neck and back.

Heat and redness around an affected joint is common, and cold packs help dull the sensation of pain during the early part of an attack. Warm packs relax muscles surrounding joints, and are effective after acute pain has subsided. Remove warm packs after 10 minutes.

Rheumatoid arthritis is a chronic inflammatory disease involving the immune system. About three times as many women as men are affected. It is thought that some factor in the environment triggers an abnormal immune response in the joints. Many experts agree that specific foods may trigger inflammation. Unfortunately, not every case of rheumatoid arthritis responds to the same stimulus, and it is necessary to identify the specific food, or foods, that affect an individual.

Rheumatoid arthritis begins gradually with aching and stiffness. At first it may involve only one joint, but soon spreads to others, tending to affect the same joint on both sides of the body. Small lumps under the skin may appear around the elbows. Sufferers may get very tired, but experience a great deal of difficulty sleeping. A minority of sufferers will experience other symptoms, including skin rash and ulceration, enlargement of lymph nodes, and inflammation of tissues around the lungs and heart.

Bearing all this information in mind, just how does the *Eat to Beat Arthritis* Diet work?' Its success relies on three objectives. The first is to eliminate from the diet all foods that trigger, or aggravate, abnormal inflammation in the joints and tissues. The second is to reduce the symptoms by supplying the body with nutrients known to strike at the stiffness, swelling and aching caused by inflammation. Many scientists believe that free radicals are a primary factor in causing inflammation, and foods used in the diet are rich sources of natural antioxidants that block inflammation. The third objective is to supply, through both food and dietary supplements, substances that help rebuild the internal components of joints destroyed by wear and tear.

Now that you know how the diet works, the following chapter will explain which foods are best for success.

Gout is a form of arthritis caused by a build-up of waste products in the blood. For more detailed information about it turn to page 152. For more detailed information on all forms of arthritis turn to pages 150–152.

CHAPTER 2

Food, supplements and medication

'People are more easily convinced of the power of magic, than convinced of the healing power of nutrition.'

The above statement – one I often use to open seminars – is, sadly, very true. Yet you *can* halt the pain of arthritis by changing the way you eat. In most cases, the difference will be so great it will change your life forever. All that is required for this transformation is the knowledge of which foods to avoid and which to enjoy, and a commitment to staying on the diet long enough to experience its benefits. Once you have experienced the improvement it brings about you will be very reluctant to return to your old ways. The path to success is not easy, however. You will be giving up foods and drinks that are part of most people's daily lives – for example, coffee, alcohol, bacon, bread and sugary sweets. These changes will be easier if you understand why they are necessary. Use this book as your guide, and you will soon find that you feel better, look better and no longer crave the foods that trigger the pain that once overshadowed your life.

Several years ago a group of women attending a community meeting about nutrition were asked for a show of hands as to how many agreed with the statement: *eliminating a single food from the diet can change a person's health.* Less than a third agreed. During the discussion that followed, some people were slightly amused by the question: after all, they ate a 'healthy' diet, how could that do them harm? When asked to describe a 'healthy diet', it was generally agreed that a healthy diet consisted of foods they 'had always eaten'. In fact, none of us eats 'what we have always eaten'. Differences in food production and processing – along with changing cultural influences – have subtly reshaped both the content and nutritional value of the food we eat. A healthy diet entails eating a high proportion of fresh fruits and vegetables, pulses, grains and nuts, and a modest amount of meat.

Many consumers are confused by all the dietary advice provided in the media these days. What should we listen to: old advice that we have followed for years; or new opinions still untested by time? Listen to both, and then ask yourself which makes good sense. If promises made for a wonder food sound too good to be true, they probably are. If someone tells you that a special diet will help control an illness, ask why and how it works. That is why you should take time to read all the information in this book, rather than just trying the recipes. You need to become familiar with your enemy in order to beat it.

Do eggs dangerously increase levels of blood cholesterol? The answer to this question is an example of how conflicting information about the health value of a food arises. Until the medical community became convinced that high levels of blood cholesterol were a significant risk factor in coronary artery disease, eggs were looked upon as a safe and healthy food, ideal for all the family – including infants and the infirm. Then came the theory that the cholesterol contained in foods, such as egg yolk, increases the level of blood cholesterol. As a result, people were advised to reduce their intake of eggs to as few as two per week. Recently, scientific research has established that the cholesterol contained in eggs has very little effect on blood cholesterol: saturated fats, such as those found in red meat, are the culprits. Eggs contain a far lower percentage of saturated fat than a portion of cheese of equal weight and, when enjoyed in moderation, they are an easy-to-eat food, high in the protein and vitamins our bodies need. Produced by free-range hens fed on grain and free of infection, eggs are a welcomed part of breakfast, lunch or dinner. You will see in Parts Three and Four that eggs are very much a part of the *Eat to Beat Arthritis* Diet.

Basic nutrition

Food is the essential link between your body and the rest of the living world. For optimum health, there is no substitute for a diet based on leafy vegetables, root vegetables, fruits, nuts, seeds, grains and various forms of meat. *Eat food in a form as close to its natural state as possible: fresh, raw or lightly cooked, unsalted and without artificial flavours, colours and preservatives.* That way, you will be giving your body the nutrients it requires.

Plants contain natural compounds that have healing properties. Ginger, for example, is not only a good source of B-vitamins, magnesium and zinc, but also contains a substance that helps control nausea. Chilli peppers contain a substance that fights pain. (More examples are found on page 26.) So to get the most from your diet, include a wide range of foods from plants, and vary what you eat.

A balanced diet contains a healthy combination of carbohydrates, proteins and fats. It may surprise you to know that international experts recommend a diet containing about 50 per cent carbohydrate, 30 per cent fat and 20 per cent protein. The healthiest carbohydrates come from grains, root vegetables and fruits. Sources of protein should be as low-fat as possible. Red meat (muscle) and full-fat milk products are high in saturated fats, which should be limited to no more than 10 per cent of the total calories consumed. Organ meats such as liver and kidney are relatively low in saturated fats, as are tofu and other plant-protein products.

It is widely believed that fats are bad for us, and that all fats should form a minimal part of a healthy diet. This is not true. Our bodies need fat, and deficiencies in certain fats lead to illness. Fats are a compact source of stored energy. They also aid the absorption of vitamins A, D and E from the gut, and form important parts of cell membranes, hormones and messenger molecules in the body. For good health, enjoy oils obtained from plants, and oily fish. These provide healing substances that people suffering from arthritis need to help fight pain. More is said about this when the omega-3 fatty acids, like those found in fish oil, are discussed. (See pages 153 and 162.)

If you are a vegetarian, ensure you eat at least one meal a day that *combines* grain and one or more pulses; for example, rice and beans. All the amino acids (protein building blocks) needed by the human body are found in plants, but not in the combination required by the human body. The amino acids we must obtain from our diet are called essential amino acids, and must be supplied in the same meal. More in-depth information can be found on page 161.

Vegetarians may not benefit from this diet as much as people who eat meat because they will not benefit from the healing properties of liver.

Foods that harm

Things we eat may cause harm in several ways:

* Some may contain a toxic substance that, eaten in excess, can create metabolic problems in your body.
* Some may trigger an allergic reaction.
* Some may cause food sensitivity.
* Some may aggravate inflammation.

Here are some examples:

Arthritis sufferers, and people concerned about the health of their bones, should be aware that rhubarb contains oxalic acid, which inhibits the body's ability to absorb calcium and iron from other foods. (The acid is concentrated in the leaves, which are poisonous and should never be eaten.) Rhubarb aggravates gout and rheumatoid arthritis, and may even cause an attack if eaten in excess. It may also increase the risk of kidney stones in some patients. If you cook rhubarb, do not use aluminium pans, as the acid juice dissolves aluminium from the surface, leaving it in the food for you to eat. Aluminium may be harmful to the body. Rhubarb is not the only plant containing oxalic acid. Smaller amounts are found in spinach, sorrel and chocolate.

Certain foods can trigger an allergic reaction – some people are allergic to nuts, for example. Seafood, especially lobster and prawns, may also cause problems.

This is a good opportunity to talk about the difference between an *allergic reaction* and *food sensitivity* (also known as *food intolerance*). These two conditions are frequently confused.

An *allergic reaction* is a serious matter that has immediate consequences. It is caused when the body's immune system has built up antibodies to one or more substances in a particular food. Symptoms include hives (urticaria), severe breathing difficulty, rash, swelling of the tongue and throat, and – in extreme cases – shock and death. Tingling of the lips and mouth after eating a particular food is a sign that an allergy to a particular food may be developing. If you experience such a response to a specific food, obviously it is prudent to avoid it.

Food sensitivity, or *intolerance*, is far less dramatic, but can cause serious symptoms that may vary from person to person. Migraine headaches, nausea, indigestion, eczema, stomach upset and hyperactivity have all been linked with food sensitivity. Symptoms do not appear with the speed seen in allergic reactions, and it is frequently difficult to identify the exact cause of the problem. In order to identify which food is causing the symptoms, an elimination diet is usually necessary.

For a few days the sufferer is placed on a diet based on foods known to cause little, if any, intolerance. This gives the body time to rid itself of substances that may be causing the problem. Following this rest period, other foods are introduced one at a time. Most will cause no recurrence of symptoms, and thereafter can be safely added to the diet. As more foods are introduced, almost inevitably one new item will cause symptoms to reappear. When this occurs, the culprit (or one of them) has been identified and the person on the exclusion diet will know to avoid that food in the future.

The *Eat to Beat Arthritis* Diet includes an elimination diet that should help you identify your sensitivity to foods that can trigger, or increase, the painful inflammation of arthritis.

Certain foods known to cause sensitivity are eliminated from the *Eat to Beat Arthritis* Diet. These are:

1 ALL PRODUCTS MADE WITH WHEAT AND OTHER GRAINS CONTAINING THE PROTEIN GLUTEN (RYE, BARLEY AND OATS)

More is said about this later (see page 34). For the moment, however, you need only be aware that gluten is often the cause of health problems ranging from migraine headaches to coeliac disease – a debilitating condition characterized by diarrhoea, bloating, and even anaemia. Coeliac disease can cause serious problems in some people, and even mimic the symptoms of certain forms of cancer.

Cutting out gluten will improve your general health and nutritional status. It will also help control the inflammation that causes much of the pain of arthritis.

2 ALL FOOD AND DRINK CONTAINING CAFFEINE

Some experts believe that caffeine increases the swelling and pain of inflammation. Many people find that removing this one source of trouble from their diet dramatically improves their life.

3 ALL PROCESSED FOODS, INCLUDING SALTED AND PRESERVED MEATS

Removing processed foods from your diet may seem daunting, but the rewards are great. You will be eliminating major sources of additives and unnatural chemicals from your body. You will be choosing not to eat foods that have been milled, stewed, or baked to the point that all the precious nutrients they once contained have been removed. And you will be leaving room in your diet for foods that are full of natural flavour and nutrition.

If you have gouty arthritis, the problem of diet becomes more complicated because liver and all other forms of offal should be avoided.

Foods that heal

How can something as basic as food heal? How can it be true that simply by changing the content of your dinner plate you can beat illness and heal damaged tissues?

Nothing in your body is static. Every moment of every day billions of cells are in constant change. They form, fill with molecules that conduct the chemical processes of life, and eventually die. It is said that over the course of seven years every molecule in the body is replaced. What we eat, and therefore supply to the body to reconstruct itself, determines its health and strength in the future.

When illness or injury damages the body, eating foods rich in the nutrients needed to replace and rebuild tissues promotes healing. When arthritis is present the nutrients most needed are protein; the B-vitamins, plus folic acid and biotin; vitamins C, E, B12, and D; the minerals selenium, manganese, iron, calcium and zinc; and certain specific fats known as omega-3 fatty acids.

The foods rich in these nutrients that form the basis of the *Eat to Beat Arthritis* Diet are:

Liver: polyunsaturated fats, vitamin A, vitamin B2 (riboflavin), vitamin B3 (niacin), vitamin B5 (pantothenic acid), vitamin B12 (cobalamin), folic acid, biotin, selenium, copper

Kidney: vitamin A, vitamin B2 (riboflavin), selenium, copper

Milk and dairy products: calcium, zinc

Black treacle (molasses): calcium, magnesium, zinc, iron

Brewers' yeast: vitamin B1 (thiamin), vitamin B5 (pantothenic acid), vitamin B12 (cobalamin), folic acid, biotin, copper, magnesium, zinc

Oily fish: omega-3 essential fatty acids, vitamin A,

Vegetable oils: vitamin E, omega-3 essential fatty acids

Nuts and seeds: vitamin E, manganese, magnesium, copper, (omega-3 fatty acids are found in walnuts)

Fresh fruit and vegetables: vitamin C, manganese

(More about healing foods can be found on pages 26 and 146.)

People with gout should enjoy celery and cherries several times a week. Both are thought to contain compounds that help the body eliminate uric acid. Celery also contains an anti-inflammatory substance.

Most of these nutrients play numerous roles in human metabolism. It is unnecessary to know all the details, but the following list identifies the specific role that makes them appropriate for arthritis sufferers:

Vitamin A is needed for normal function of the immune system, and the control of inflammation.

B-vitamins help maintain a healthy nervous system and fight depression.

Vitamin C is needed to build collagen required for healthy tissues, including tendons and joints; it is also a strong antioxidant and fights damage by free radicals.

Folic acid is needed for the normal absorption of other nutrients from the gut.

Vitamin D plays a vital role in normal formation of bone.

Vitamin E helps fight the oxidation of essential fatty acids in the body, thus reducing the symptoms of inflammation.

Selenium is a strong antioxidant and helps protect against free-radical damage.

Magnesium is an important component of bone.

Manganese is vital for the normal formation of tissues in joints and bone.

Zinc is essential for a normal immune system.

Copper is needed for normal connective tissue and bones; it also helps protect against damage caused by free radicals and acts as an anti-inflammatory agent.

Omega-3 fatty acids (as found in fish oil, hemp oil and walnuts) help control the inflammation, swelling and pain of arthritis.

The *Eat to Beat Arthritis* Diet recommends including frequent servings of offal such as liver, sweetbreads, heart and tripe. These are low-fat sources of protein that supply all the amino acids needed for healthy tissue. Sweetbreads contain useful amounts of important minerals, but not in quantities as large as those found in liver and kidney. Tripe and heart are good sources of low-fat protein, but contain smaller amounts of healing nutrients.

The BSE crisis in Europe forced the removal of many fine products from the market, and sweetbreads are among them. Very few stores now stock them, but a few organic meat producers have earned the right to sell these delicious morsels again. They are expensive, but when cooked correctly are delicious delicacies.

People with osteoarthritis will benefit significantly from eating foods rich in vitamin B12. The best source of these nutrients are the healthy bacteria in your own gut, but food sources are also available: liver and other animal proteins are a rich source, and play an important role in the *Eat to Beat Arthritis* Diet. If you are a vegetarian, vitamin B12 will be difficult for you to obtain from your diet. Plant sources include mushrooms and parsley. Certain fermented foods, such as tempeh and fermented black beans, contain a high bacterial count that insures they are a good source of vitamin B12.

Dietary supplements and medications

The past ten years have seen a considerable increase in the number of medications available to treat all forms of arthritis. (The more frequently used of these are discussed on pages 152–153.) Although many people find these a primary avenue of relief from arthritis, they all carry some risk of side effects. The NSAIDS (non-steroidal anti-inflammatory drugs) can irritate the lining of the stomach and in some cases can cause ulcers when used over a long period. Commonly used NSAIDS include aspirin and ibuprofen. Treating arthritic symptoms by altering your dietary habits carries none of these risks.

The following dietary supplements have been shown to have special healing properties that counter the effects of both rheumatoid and osteoarthritis:

Vitamin E is one of the most powerful natural antioxidants identified to date. It works best when combined with vitamin C and the mineral selenium, both of which are well known for their antioxidant properties. Scientific studies have shown that people with rheumatoid arthritis have lower blood levels of antioxidants than others, and there is growing interest in what this means for the treatment of the disease. In a controlled study of osteoarthritis patients with knee and hip joint problems, 400mg of vitamin E was shown to be as effective in controlling symptoms as 50mg of Diclofenac, a medication classified as an NSAID. The effects of the NSAID were faster, but it produced more side effects than vitamin E. As pain relief over time was comparable, vitamin E was thought to be the treatment of choice.

Another study showed that rheumatoid arthritis patients treated with vitamin E had less pain and improved symptoms when treated over a three-month period. Vitamin E can be taken in large quantities with little risk of side effects.

Fish oil supplements are an important source of omega-3 essential fatty acids, and part of the *Eat to Beat Arthritis* Diet. You can read more about this subject on page 153. If you are a vegetarian, or cannot tolerate fish oil, try flaxseed oil instead. This is another rich source of omega-3 fatty acids, although they are in their original plant form, and have not been through the metabolic processes that produce the DHA and EPA fatty acids known to be deposited in the flesh of oily fish. These specific fatty acids are necessary for the body's production of small hormone-like molecules with strong anti-inflammatory properties, known as prostaglandins. Many people suffering from inflammatory illnesses experience dramatic effects when they supplement their diets with a fish or flaxseed oil supplement.

For maximum benefit:

✤ Do not mix fish oil and other fatty acid supplements. Take omega-6 supplements (evening primrose oil or borage oil) at a different time of day.

✤ Make sure you take a vitamin E supplement, as this protects the omega-acids.

✤ Keep any opened bottles of supplements in the refrigerator or other cool place.

Note: there is a difference between *fish oil* and *fish liver oil*. Liver oils contain substantial quantities of vitamin A, which is stored in your liver and can be toxic if taken in large amounts. If you are setting out on this diet, it is recommended that you use *fish oil* supplements.

Flaxseed oil is the richest known source of omega-3 fatty acids, and also contains substantial amounts of omega-6 fatty acids. It also contains plant chemicals known as *lignins*, which are plant estrogens that help control the body's estrogen level. Lignins are also believed to have other biological effects, including anti-viral and anti-bacterial activities.

Glucosamine and *chondroitin* are naturally occurring substances in the body that act as a building block in many tissues. Of the two, better curative effects have been demonstrated by glucosamine than by chondroitin, so it is suggested that this is the supplement of choice. Sometimes called the 'basement membrane builder', glucosamine is an essential substance in manufacturing and maintaining the ligaments, tendons, cartilage and synovial fluid found in joints. More detailed information on glucosamine and how it is thought to work can be found on page 154.

PART THREE

The Eat to Beat
Arthritis Diet

CHAPTER 1

The basics

What is the *Eat to Beat Arthritis* diet?

Since the 1930s, scientists have been aware of a possible link between rheumatoid arthritis and food allergies. Some scientists went so far as to suggest that symptoms of rheumatoid arthritis could be completely controlled by dietary changes.

Max Warmbrand, a naturopathic doctor who practised up until the mid-1970s, advocated a very low-fat diet in the treatment of both rheumatoid and osteoarthritis. In addition he told his patients to avoid eating all red meat, eggs, dairy foods, sugar, chemicals and processed foods. Six months were required before improvement was noticeable, he claimed. The diet seemed to work for a few people, but not others.

In 1979, Giraud W. Campbell wrote A *Doctor's Proven New Home Cure for Arthritis*, a book that helped millions of people break the bonds of this crippling disease. Using the information available at that time, he prescribed a strict regime that called for raw fruits and vegetables, hearty amounts of lightly cooked organ meats (liver, kidney, sweetbread, brain, heart and tripe), and daily doses of unpasteurized milk, nutrient-rich black treacle (molasses) and brewers' yeast. The diet began with a brief period of fasting, during which the body was freed of toxins from previous poor eating habits. He instructed his readers to shun all drinks containing caffeine, and cautioned against all processed foods – including canned and frozen items. If you followed this somewhat Spartan plan, you could end the pain of arthritis in seven days, he claimed.

The science of nutrition has changed greatly over the past several decades, and we know more about how and why you can control illness through diet. The *Eat to Beat Arthritis* Diet therefore builds on the Campbell diet, but also uses new information and a more modern approach to food and dietary supplements. At the same time, it recognizes some of the realities of modern life. For example, not all frozen foods are taboo: frozen peas, sweetcorn and spinach are very useful items in any kitchen. Soaking and cooking dried pulses such as chickpeas (garbanzo beans) takes hours; so canned ones, well rinsed to remove any salt and sugar, are allowed as an alternative.

This book also recognizes that more than seven days are needed to fully achieve benefits from recommended changes in food choices. Here, you will follow a gradual process that is tailored to your unique needs. The foundations of the *Eat To Beat Arthritis* Diet are:

- Finding the right balance of foods for your body.
- Knowing how to tell when a specific food is making the symptoms of arthritis worse.

The initial programme spans seven weeks. In the first week you keep a diary of your pain and stiffness and also record your intake of food and drink. You then learn to eliminate the specific foods that aggravate (or even cause) a flare-up of arthritis, and how to make this a diet you can use for life. You will also be encouraged to try new foods that you may have otherwise passed by.

While you remain on the *Eat to Beat Arthritis* Diet you will notice that you feel better. Depending on the severity of your condition you will find that pain will disappear, or diminish in severity. These are not the only exciting benefits you will enjoy from changing your eating habits. Selecting the right foods strengthens your body and enhances its metabolic activities. You will begin enjoying improved general health, stronger nails and hair and younger-looking skin. You will suffer from fewer colds and other infections. You may even find that you lose some of the excess weight that may be contributing to your joint pain and stiffness.

Rediscovering the way to eat

You are now ready to focus your attention on one of life's great pleasures: food. What comes next will change your life forever. Previous sections of this book have covered three main topics:
- The causes and symptoms of several forms of arthritis.
- The links between good nutrition and healing.
- The role plant and other natural substances play in controlling pain and inflammation.

Armed with this knowledge, read the remainder of this book before you begin the diet. As you read, keep these principles in mind:

THERE ARE NO QUICK FIXES
If you follow this diet exactly, you will begin to feel better within days, but the full extent of healing will take longer. Diets promising remarkable cures often disappoint. If you really want to change the way you feel, and improve your health, you must be patient and give your body time to heal.

THIS IS A DIET FOR LIFE
A diet must be both practical and flexible, or you will find it boring and impossible. Once you have gone through a full seven-week cycle of the diet plan, you can occasionally bend the rules a little. In the chapter that follows, Marguerite discusses her flexible approach to the diet.

WHILE YOU ARE ON THIS DIET, ENJOY EATING
A partial list of the foods and ingredients you can incorporate into meals appears on pages 37–43. I call it a *partial* list because it cannot include every fruit, vegetable and fish from around the world. When you begin your new eating plan, take time to taste new varieties of fresh food.

Have you tried the sweet, orange flesh of Sharon fruit? For a fantastic dessert, scoop out the flesh of chilled, ripe Sharon fruit and serve in small glass bowls. No sugar needed for this treat! On the more substantial side, have you enjoyed the delicate flavour of firm-textured steaks of escolar (mock sea bass), caught off the coast of South America? Or tasted barracuda fillets? If not, a treat or two awaits you.

The culinary arts are based on a rich palate of fruit, vegetables, meat, seafood, nuts, grains, seeds, herbs and spices. Combined in different ways by different cultures, these ingredients produce dishes with an endless variety of flavours and textures. The *Eat to Beat Arthritis* Diet actually sets very few restrictions on your enjoyment of this wonderful diversity.

THERE ARE CERTAIN FOODS AND DRINKS YOU MUST ABANDON
These are listed on pages 33–36. Don't let this put you off. Give your body a chance. Following the diet carefully for at least seven weeks should reduce the symptoms of arthritis and improve your general health, so it will be worth the sacrifice.

THERE ARE CERTAIN FOODS YOU MUST EAT
These are listed on page 24. Be faithful to these foods: they contain the healing nutrients your body needs. Include raw fruits and vegetables in your diet as often as possible.

THERE ARE CERTAIN DIETARY SUPPLEMENTS YOU MUST TAKE
Many of you will already be using supplements containing fish oil and vitamin E. The *Eat to Beat Arthritis* Diet also includes black treacle (molasses), brewers' yeast, and further suggests that you use supplements containing the mineral selenium (see page 157) and glucosamine, a naturally occurring substance that forms part of normal joint cartilage (see page 154).

DRINK WATER
This sounds simple enough, but you would be surprised how many people fail to drink enough water to fully flush waste products from their bodies. You need 1 ½–2 litres/2 ½–3 pints/1½–2 quarts, drunk in small amounts throughout the day. This can include fruit juice and milk, but no caffeine drinks. Filtered water and fresh tap water are recommended, or still bottled water (not carbonated).

CHOOSE NATURAL AND ORGANIC FOODS
Avoid all foods contaminated with pesticides, additives, artificial sweeteners, preservatives, and anything else nature did not intend you to eat. Choose organic foods as far as your budget and their availability allow.

ENJOY YOUR FOOD RAW OR LIGHTLY COOKED
Prolonged frying, boiling and baking destroy important nutrients and damage delicate molecules. Microwave cooking is quick and easy, and actually increases the availability of some nutrients in food. (There is no evidence that it 'denatures' food, as some people believe.)

If all this sounds a bit daunting, do not despair! You have a friend to talk you through it. In Part Four, along with the recipes she has developed for this book, Marguerite Patten gives you an insight into her own experiences on the diet, and answers practical questions about enjoying food and controlling pain.

The basic anti-arthritis diet: food and drink you must avoid

The first group to avoid is not only foods and drinks containing unnatural substances, but those that may have been contaminated by the environment in which they were grown or raised. The second group to avoid is food and drink known to cause food sensitivities, or to be potentially toxic to your body. The main offenders in both groups are detailed below.

ALCOHOLIC BEVERAGES

Do your body a favour and eliminate this damaging substance from your diet. Here are a few facts to consider:

❦ If you have ever suffered from a blinding hangover, you know that alcohol is toxic. Even in small amounts it can disrupt the natural biological functions of the liver, kidneys and heart. Large amounts can cause permanent damage.

❦ People who suffer from gout know that drinking alcohol can bring on an attack.

❦ The beneficial effects of certain medications – including antibiotics – are reduced by the consumption of alcohol.

❦ High alcohol intake increases the risk of certain cancers and heart disease.

❦ During pregnancy, alcohol can cause the growing foetus harm.

❦ Alcohol can increase depression and feelings of aggression. It is hard to stay on a diet – or any other health regime – when you lack self control or are in an irritable mood.

How can you have any kind of social life without enjoying a drink with your friends? Pubs and bars no longer look down on paying customers who ask for a glass of still mineral water on the rocks. In the right glass, it can look very drinkable indeed! Alternatively, try a glass of grape juice and pretend it is wine.

BEVERAGES CONTAINING CAFFEINE (COFFEE, COLA DRINKS AND TEA)

Coffee may be your favourite morning pick-me-up, but it plays nasty tricks on your body. It has been shown to increase inflammation, making an attack of arthritis worse. It can cause insomnia, robbing you of much-needed sleep. It can increase the rate at which minerals are lost from bone, escalating the possibility of osteoporosis. In large amounts it can cause heart palpitations and tremors of the hands. It also stimulates the secretion of stomach acid: if you suffer from heartburn it may be due to the coffee you drink. Coffee is addictive if taken frequently over a long period of time, so when you give it up don't be surprised if you experience some withdrawal symptoms for a day or two. Headaches are the most common problem.

All drinks containing caffeine create these problems to some degree. Remove all cola drinks, coffee and tea from your diet and you will soon find yourself free of some unpleasant symptoms you probably never associated with caffeine. Consider the following:

* Excessive amounts of caffeine increase the risk of osteoporosis in later life. This is particularly pertinent to women, who are far more prone to the condition than men.
* There is evidence that certain ways of brewing coffee increase the risk of heart disease.
* Caffeine is thought to increase blood cholesterol levels.
* Caffeine can make you jittery and tense, and alter your normal blood sugar levels.
* Migraine headaches can be triggered by caffeine.
* Caffeine acts as a mild diuretic. You are wrong if you think that all that coffee you drink helps satisfy your daily requirement for fluids – it does just the opposite. It draws precious water from your body and works the kidneys hard at the same time.

Many people find it harder to give up coffee than wine and spirits. Experts believe you can become 'hooked' on caffeine, and anyone who has gone off the brown stuff 'cold-turkey' will know how true this is. For this reason, we suggest you give up caffeinated drinks before you actually begin the diet.

A word about tea: it is off the *Eat to Beat Arthritis* Diet during the first two weeks, but then you can try a cup a day to see if your body will tolerate it. Tea contains certain powerful plant compounds with antioxidant and healing properties. A *single cup* of black or green tea each day may do you more good than harm.

ALL FOODS MADE FROM GRAINS CONTAINING GLUTEN (WHEAT, RYE, BARLEY AND OATS)

For many people, simply eliminating gluten from their diet has changed their lives. It can do the same for you. Gluten is one of the most common causes of food allergies and sensitivities. It is a protein in plants that the human body does not use. However, because gluten gives food a nice texture, and a smooth, shiny appearance, it is used extensively by the food industry in the production of everything from baked products to stock cubes. Check everything you buy to make sure it does not contain gluten.

Sensitivities to gluten take many forms, including migraine, joint swelling and coeliac disease – characterized by dramatic diarrhoea and weight loss. Hair-like projections (the *villi*) absorb nutrients from food passing through the small intestine and transfers them into the bloodstream. Gluten can affect the *villi* by causing them to lie flat. This makes them less effective, thus restricting the amount of nutrients being absorbed the body. When this happens the person will become malnourished, no matter how much he or she may eat.

SUGAR

Although links have been suggested between high sugar intake and increased risks of diabetes, heart disease and certain types of cancer, none have been proven. What is certain, however, is that purified sugar gives you little more than empty calories that are easily converted to fat.

Arthritis pain is made worse when unnecessary weight is placed on joints. So is sugar worth it?

Sugar also causes tooth decay and, by satisfying your hunger, discourages you from eating the complex carbohydrates (see page 161) needed to maintain a healthy blood sugar level.

Do not use artificial sweeteners. Natural substitutes for sugar are listed on page 37. Enjoy these instead, safe in the knowledge you are increasing your intake of beneficial nutrients.

CANNED AND PROCESSED FOODS

Just read the contents label on a can of soup or a packet of cake and you will see how many artificial ingredients are added to most processed food. Preservatives, artificial colours and artificial flavours are *not* part of the natural chemical composition of the human body. In addition, the nutrient content of many processed foods has been lowered during processing. So, with few exceptions, avoid canned and processed foods.

Many experts recommend the elimination of all canned and frozen foods. We do not agree. There are times when practicality and good sense must come into play. For example, made properly, houmous is a very good food. Few people make it for themselves because dried chickpeas (garbanzo beans) take forever to cook. Why not use canned ones, well washed and drained, to make your own? It's much better than being tempted by a store-bought variety or simply avoiding this nutritious dish.

Likewise, there are frozen foods that are at least as high in nutrients and as free from chemical residues as any you can buy in the fresh vegetable section of the supermarket. Best bets are frozen peas, corn (maize), spinach and beans. All these are usually frozen without the addition of any preservatives or other chemicals. (The very best, of course, come from your own organic garden, but few of us can enjoy such luxury.)

SMOKED, PICKLED AND CURED FOODS

For thousands of years, humans have used these methods to preserve food during months of plenty in order to ward off starvation in times of want. They are unnecessary today because we have other ways of maintaining our food supply. However, because we like the taste of preserved foods – such as smoked salmon, pickled cucumber and bacon – preserved foods continue to play a large role in our diet. Unfortunately, these foods have drawbacks. All contain chemicals that are not naturally found in the human body, some of which carry potential danger. Both smoking and curing introduce chemicals into food that are known to be harmful and may be linked with certain forms of cancer.

MEAT FROM FACTORY-FARMED ANIMALS

As the demand for food increases around the world, farmers are increasingly turning to the chemical industry for help. Hormones and antibiotics are used to increase growth rates, while chemicals are utilized to enhance animal health and cleanliness. As a result, food yields have increased dramatically over the past few decades. Careful health controls are in place to make sure that residues from these practices are held within 'safe' limits. But what are 'safe' limits?

One of the basic aims of this diet is to eliminate as many unnatural substances from the body as possible. So whenever possible, choose food that contains no – or at best low – levels of chemical residues. Press your local supermarkets to sell organic meat; increased demand will bring down the price.

NON-ORGANIC FRUITS AND VEGETABLES

Everything said about chemicals and meat is appropriate here. Carefully peel and wash all fresh fruits and vegetables not organically grown. To aid the release of dirt and chemical residue from grapes and berries place them in a glass bowl containing 3-4 tablespoons of vinegar to 1 litre (1 quart) of water; allow to stand for five minutes; rinse well and dry.

SEAFOOD CAUGHT IN INLAND STREAMS

Fish and shellfish are the best sources of protein you can have, and there are many varieties to choose from. But you must pick those that live in the deep waters of the seas and oceans.

The amount of industrial, agricultural and sewage pollution that finds its way into the waters of our once sparkling-clean streams and waterways means that pollution is a fact of life. Even in remote areas, environmentalists are finding increased levels of toxic substances. Some inshore waters are also affected – hardly surprising when effluent is pumped straight into them. Ask surfing enthusiasts about water pollution and you will hear gruesome details of contamination. All this, in turn, pollutes the fish we eat through the food they eat.

So choose fish from the sea or deep, clean Scottish lochs, and avoid adding your own body to the list of living organisms fouled by the waste in our water. Enjoy cod, bass, fresh tuna and game fish such as swordfish. If this sounds expensive, remember that your body requires no more than four or five ounces of protein a day. Smaller portions of fine fish makes sense.

The sad fact is that even our oceans are also slowly becoming polluted. Where will we go next for clean food?

The basic anti-arthritis diet: food and drink you can enjoy

Those of you who suffer from gout should follow this advice, but avoid eating liver, kidney, spinach, sardines, shellfish, game, turkey, asparagus and rhubarb.

DRINKS

Fruit juice (see box below)

Fruit 'smoothies' (fruit, sometimes combined with milk or yoghurt, put through a blender)

Milk (the base of your daily Health Drink, see page 49)

Tea (for the first two weeks drink only herbal tea. After that one cup of black or green tea a day is allowed)

Water (cool, freshly filtered water, tap water or still bottled water)

SWEETENERS

Black treacle (molasses)*

Honey (organic)

Cactus syrup

Maple syrup

Date syrup (yummy!)

Puréed fruit* (apricot purée makes a wonderful sauce, or can be served with yoghurt as a tasty dessert)

Concentrated fruit juices (organic and free of preservatives)

*Black treacle (molasses) is an important ingredient in the *Eat to Beat Arthritis* Diet, as it is a healthy source of calcium, magnesium and phosphate, all of which are needed for healthy bones. It is also rich in iron, copper and zinc, and contains traces of several B-vitamins.

*Puréed *dried* fruits are an excellent source of nutrients. Dried apricots are especially good because they contain: beta-carotene (a powerful antioxidant and the substance your body needs to make vitamin A); fibre needed for a healthy digestive system; B-vitamins used during metabolism and functioning of the nervous system. (Apricots are also an excellent source of folic acid, a member of the B-complex, which is vital for the production of blood cells and the normal development of the foetal nervous system. Recent evidence suggests that it is also needed for a healthy heart.)

BAKED GOODS AND PASTA

You can enjoy all baked goods and pasta made with organic, *gluten-free* flour. There are some excellent products on the market, but also try making your own. Do not simply substitute gluten-free flour for that specified in standard recipes; use recipes tried and tested on the product. And, if you plan to use a bread machine, make certain your recipe and ingredients specify that they are appropriate for that purpose.

OILS AND FATS

Butter*

Canola (rapeseed) *oil**

Corn oil*

Groundnut (peanut) *oil* (unless there is evidence of an allergy)

Olive oil*

Safflower oil

Fruit juice is a delicious part of this diet. Buy a juicer and make your own, or use concentrates prepared with no preservatives. Ask your health-food store to stock brands made from organically grown fruit. Recent years have seen some excellent products come on to the market.

*Soya oil**
Sunflower oil *
Sesame seed oil
Walnut oil

***Butter** is an enjoyable source of flavour in food. Used in small amounts it can make a world of difference. Remember, however, that it is a saturated fat, which should make up no more than 10 per cent of your total caloric intake. Also, it contains traces of milk protein. Some people sensitive to cows' milk may find it causes phlegm or other symptoms. Clarified butter can be a substitute.

***Olive oil** is an excellent ingredient for dressing salads and vegetables, and for cooking. It is a rich source of the fat we need in greatest quantity: oleic acid, a monounsaturated fat. Olive oil is low in saturated fats, and contains antioxidants and plant compounds that have been shown to have healing properties. Choose a good-quality olive oil, even though the price may seem high. There are several grades of olive oil on the market: extra-virgin is the most expensive. It is worth the money, however, because it

has been subjected to the least mechanical processing. Dr. Robert Owen and colleagues at the Division of Toxicology and Cancer Research Factors, German Cancer Research Centre, Heidelberg, have recently stated that the unique blend of compounds in olive oil giving it health-promoting properties are lost during processing.

***Sunflower oil, safflower oil, corn oil, canola (rapeseed) oil* and *soya oil** are all sources of essential fatty acids needed for good health. Do not overheat them as their delicate molecular structure is damaged by high temperatures. Keep all oils in a cool dark place, and discard if they begin to have a strange fishy smell; this means they are rancid.

FRUITS

Avoid canned fruits unless there is no alternative, because canning removes

nutrients found in fresh products. Rinse well before using to remove any additives and contaminates from cans. Even then, limit your intake. For example, canned pineapple is permitted, but infrequently. Frozen fruit is fine as long as it does not contain added sugar or preservatives.

Apples – in all their delicious varieties

Apricots – loaded with vitamins and minerals. Fresh are best, but you can also enjoy dried ones provided they are prepared with no preservative

Avocados – include this delicious fruit in your anti-arthritis diet whenever possible

Bananas – a great source of energy and nutrients

Berries – strawberries, raspberries, loganberries, blueberries, cranberries, blackberries, currants (red and black), gooseberries and anything else that falls into

---

Note: this list does not include citrus fruit. This is because many people are surprised to find that their arthritis symptoms greatly improve when they eliminate oranges, lemons, limes and grapefruit from their diet. You will read more about this later. For now, just remember that citrus fruit is not part of the Basic Anti-arthritis Diet.

this category. Many berries contain phytochemicals with natural antiviral and anti-bacterial properties, so they give your body an extra edge when fighting off infection

Cherries – another red fruit loaded with natural healing substances for your body

Currants

Figs – great flavour and highly nutritious. Fresh are best

Grapes – red or black are best, as they contain more natural antioxidants, but white ones will do

Guava

Kiwi fruit

Mangoes – sweet, smooth, and an excellent source of vitamins

Melons – a versatile low-calorie food that can be used in salads, main courses, desserts and even soups!

Papaya (*paw-paw*)

Peaches – excellent source of flavour and nutrients. Fresh are best

Pears – fresh are best

Plums

Prunes

Raisins

Sultanas

VEGETABLES
Beetroot (beet)
Broad beans (fava beans)
Broccoli

Brussels sprouts
Cabbage – all forms
Cardoon
Carrot
Cassava
Cauliflower
Celery – gout sufferers should include celery in their diet at least three times a week
Chard
Chicory
Chives
Courgettes (zucchini)
Cress
Cucumbers
Endive
Fennel
Garden peas
Garlic
Globe artichoke
Green beans
Horseradish
Jerusalem artichokes
Kale
Kohlrabi
Leeks
Lemongrass
Lettuce – all types
Lima beans
Lotus root

Mangetout (snow peas)
Marrow
Mushrooms
Okra
Olives
Onions
Pak choi
Plantain
Parsley – parsley is considered a vegetable here because it is so rich in nutrients
Parsnips
Peas, garden
Pumpkin
Radishes
Shallots
Sea vegetables – including agar-agar, carragheen, dulse, kelp, nori (laver) and wakame
Sorrel
Spinach
Squash – summer and winter
Spring onions (scallions, green onions)
Swede (rutabaga)
Sweetcorn (corn on the cob)
Sweet potato
Swiss chard
Turnips
Yam (yellow and cush-cush)

You will notice that several very popular vegetables are missing: tomatoes, potatoes, peppers and aubergines (eggplants). This is because they are all members of the nightshade family of plants, and cause food sensitivities in some people. Leave these off the menu during the first two weeks of the diet. You may be able to reintroduce them later if you prove not to be sensitive to them.

Water chestnuts
Watercress

PULSES (LEGUMES)
These foods can be enjoyed
fresh, canned, frozen or dried.
Canned are often preferable
as they are easy to use and
will have been well cooked
(this applies especially to
kidney beans as they contain
toxins which must be
removed by rapid boiling).
However, you must drain
and rinse them well.
People with gout should avoid
pulses as they contain purines.
Beans of all kinds:
aduki, borlotti (pinto), broad
(fava), brown, butter,
cannellini, flageolet, ful
medames, haricot (navy), red
and *black kidney*
Blackeyed peas
Chickpeas (garbanzo beans)
Lentils – red, green and brown
Mung beans
Peas, whole and split
Soya beans (all foods made
of soya are rich in plant
chemicals that help protect
the body against cancer and
heart disease)

GRAINS
Amaranth and *Quinoa* – two
grains from South America
with a high protein content
Buckwheat – not a type of
wheat, but seeds from a

plant in the rhubarb family
Corn (maize)
Millet – an excellent source
of vegetable protein
Rice - brown is preferable
to white as it contains more
nutrients
Wild rice – not a true rice,
but seeds from a North
American grass

SUBSTITUTES FOR WHEAT FLOUR INCLUDE:
Arrowroot (ground)
Buckwheat flour
Cornflour (cornstarch)
Corn meal (maize meal)
Gram flour – ground
chickpeas (garbanzo beans)
Potato flour – check for
sensitivity before using this
Rice flour
Soya flour

NUTS AND SEEDS
NUTS
Almonds
Brazil nuts
Pine (pignolia) nuts
Walnuts

SEEDS
Alfalfa
Fennel
Linseed
Mustard
Pumpkin seeds
Sesame seeds
Sunflower seeds

HERBS AND SPICES
You can eat as many herbs
and spices as you like.
There are none that will
harm you when eaten in
moderate quantities, and
many contain healing and
nutritious substances that
are a welcome part of a
healthy diet.

EGGS AND DAIRY FOODS
Forget the terrible things you
have read about eggs in the
past. Research has shown
they make little difference to
blood cholesterol, but are an
excellent source of nutrition.
Just make sure they are fresh
and from a source you trust.
Organic eggs are best; failing
these buy ones from free-
range grain-fed chickens.

Grains: gluten is a major cause of food sensitivity. Wheat,
rye, barley and oats should be completely avoided.
However, as grains are the main source of B-vitamins and
minerals, forming an important part of a balanced diet,
you need to find gluten-free alternatives.

Vary your menu by trying quail and duck eggs in addition to hen's eggs.

Some people find eggs constipating, but this is usually due to lack of sufficient high-fibre foods. If you are eating the amount of fruit and vegetables specified in the diet you should have no problems.

Dairy foods are excellent sources of calcium and protein, which are both needed for healthy bones. Cheeses and yoghurt of all kinds are good for you, but remember:

❀ Yoghurt should be unsweetened – add honey, date syrup or fruit if necessary.

❀ Avoid processed cheeses such as spreads, Gruyère triangles and low-fat types. Keep to natural cheeses, such as Cheddar, feta, Edam and full-fat cottage cheese.

❀ Dairy products are rich in saturated fat, and therefore should not be the major source of protein in your diet.

❀ When Dr Giraud Campbell wrote his diet, in the late 1970s, food contamination was a far less significant problem than it is today. He recommended drinking a glass of unpasteurized milk each day: we do not. Drink full-fat pasteurized milk from a reliable source. Some people are allergic to cows' milk – excessive phlegm and coughing are common symptoms. If you think you may be susceptible, eliminate cows' milk from your diet for two days, substituting soya milk, or pasteurized goats' or ewes' milk.

FISH AND SHELLFISH

All deep-water fish, including:

Abalone
Anchovy
Barracuda (becune, sea pike)
Bass
Bluefish
Bonito
Bream
Brill (britt, kite, pearl)
Cockles (arkshell)
Cod
Coley (coalfish, pollock, saithe)
Conger eel
Clams
Crabs
Croaker (black drum, queenfish, sea drum, weakfish)
Cuttlefish
Dogfish (flake, huss, rigg, tope)
Dolphinfish (dorade, dorado, lampuka, mahi-mahi) – these are not dolphins

Flying fish
Grey mullet
Grouper
Gurnard
Haddock
Hake
Halibut
Herring
John Dory (tila pia)
Langoustine (Dublin bay prawns)
Lemon sole (lemon fish, lemon dab)
Lobster
Monkfish (anglerfish)
Mussels
Octopus
Oysters
Pompano
Prawns
Redfish (berghuilt, Norway haddock, ocean perch, red perch, rose fish)
Red mullet
Red snapper
Salmon (wild is preferable, but is very expensive and may not be readily available. Farmed salmon is acceptable so long as it comes from deep Scottish lochs)
Scabbard (espada, sabre fish)
Scallops
Sea bream (porgy, scup)
Shark
Shrimp
Skate
Sole
Squid (calamar)

Swordfish
Tuna – not canned
Turbot
Whiting

✤ Enjoy the roe from any of the above. If the budget allows, salmon roe and caviar are excellent sources of nutrients. Unfortunately, people with gout should avoid all fish roe (eggs) because they are high in purines.

✤ Avoid smoked or commercially salted fish.

✤ Gout sufferers should ask their doctors if it is okay for them to eat shellfish and anchovy.

OFFAL (ORGAN MEAT, VARIETY MEAT)

Offal is a general term used to describe the internal organs of an animal, and includes liver, kidney, heart, brain, tripe and sweetbreads (the pancreas and thymus gland). These form an important part of this diet. Liver is the most nutritious offal, and is an excellent source of many important nutrients needed to heal tissues and control the symptoms of arthritis. Since the BSE outbreak in Europe, brain is no longer recommended.

Unfortunately, people with gout should avoid eating all types of offal because of its high purine content.

LIVER

This highly nutritious meat is the most important food in the *Eat to Beat Arthritis* Diet. Try including it in your menu at least three times a week. Liver is rich in vitamin A, pyridoxine (vitamin B6), cobalamin (vitamin B12), riboflavin (vitamin B2), niacin, folate and biotin; also the minerals iron, selenium, zinc, molybdenum and copper. It is also a good source of pantothenic acid (vitamin B5), calciferol (vitamin D), and co-enzyme Q10.

Do not overcook liver, as some of the more delicate nutrients will be lost. It is also much nicer to eat when it has just turned colour and is still soft – not grey and hard.

KIDNEYS

Kidneys are less rich in nutrients than liver, but still rank among the best. Kidney is a rich source of riboflavin, biotin, vitamin B2, vitamin B12, iron and niacin. It also contains useful amounts

of the minerals zinc, selenium and molybdenum. It also contains useful amounts of vitamin A.

HEARTS

These are a rich source of choline and inositol. These substances help prevent fatty degeneration of the liver, and choline is part of the chemical complex involved in the transmission of nerve impulses.

SWEETBREADS

This delicious food is the thymus gland and pancreas taken from calves, lambs and pigs. Considered by many to be a great delicacy, they may be both hard to find and expensive. Sweetbreads are an excellent source of zinc, several of the B-vitamins, and minerals.

TRIPE

Tripe is the muscular part of the stomach, and an excellent source of almost fat-free protein. However, it has few of the nutrients for which liver and kidneys are prized. If you do not like it, skip it.

GAME ANIMALS

If cooked well, wild game – rabbit, hare, venison and wild boar – are delicious alternatives to the usual forms of meat.

FARMED MEAT

All cuts of beef, lamb, pork, veal, kid and goat are acceptable – though you should always try to buy organic meat. If this is not possible, purchase from sources where you know that only the minimum amount of antibiotics, hormones and other foreign substances are used in raising the animals and preparing them for market.

Remember, however, that red meat is a rich source of saturated fat, which should be kept to a minimum on a healthy diet.

POULTRY AND GAME BIRDS (DOMESTIC – ORGANIC)

Chicken (avoid capons)
Duck
Goose
Turkey (because of its high level of purines, this meat should be avoided by people with gout)

Wild game birds are often preferable to poultry, unless the latter is organically produced.

GAME BIRDS

Guinea fowl
Grouse
Quail
Partridge
Pheasant
Pigeon
Snipe
Squab
Wild duck
Woodcock

Avoid all forms of cured, processed and salted meats, including bacon, ham, sausages and salami.

Vegetarians should turn to pages 22 and 161, where they will find advice on obtaining the essential amino acids that are normally provided in the diet through eating meat.

CHAPTER 2

The seven-week diet plan

Read this chapter carefully before you begin. You may also find it useful to read Part Four, in which Marguerite Patten recounts her experience on the diet, and gives tips on how to succeed.

Seven weeks may seem like a long time, but it is a worthwhile investment in your health. The aims of the diet plan are:

❋ To become more aware of what you eat, and identify the pattern of your pain and discomfort (Week Zero).

❋ To introduce high-nutrient foods and food supplements that will reduce inflammation and encourage healing in joints and surrounding tissues (Week One).

❋ To give your body an opportunity to rid itself of the effects of foods to which you are sensitive (Weeks One and Two).

❋ To eliminate from your diet any foods that may increase joint inflammation (Weeks One to Seven).

Not everyone responds at the same rate. Some people take longer to notice an improvement than others. Full benefits from this plan depend on which type of arthritis you have, and your body's sensitivity to specific foods. Soon after you begin this diet plan, you should feel better and have less pain. It may be tempting to rest on one's laurels then, and not continue with the full seven-week plan. Please give your body time to heal and adjust to this new plan of foods and supplements, and stay with the diet for the full seven weeks to receive its full benefit.

Week zero

Unlike most diets, where you just plunge right in, this one involves taking time to prepare yourself for the changes you are about to undertake. Knowing yourself – your feelings and your body – is the keystone to improving your health.

Too many of us begin diets with good intentions and high expectations, but lack a realistic view of what lies ahead. It is human nature to want a quick fix when in pain or ill. We expect changes in ourselves to take place overnight. When that does not happen, we get discouraged. We may stick to a diet for weeks, or even months, but slowly old habits creep back. However, if you can actually see improvements, by recording your body's response to your new eating habits, you are more likely to stay the course.

If you smoke, seriously consider ridding yourself of this addiction. Along with being a cause of cancer and a predisposing factor in heart disease, it speeds up the ageing process and damages tissues – including those found in joints. Give it up!

During this week of preparation there are two aims:

* To better understand your pain and discomfort, and your dietary habits, by using a self-assessment diary.
* To eliminate all caffeine and caffeine-like substances from your body.

Let us deal with this second aim first. 'Why', you may ask, 'begin eliminating anything from my diet before Week One?' The answer is simple: caffeine increases the pain of inflammation; it is also mildly addictive. Too much caffeine can cause jittery feelings, and add to aggressive behaviour and even tremors.

People who drink four or five cups of coffee – or fewer very strong cups – each day find they experience headaches, tiredness and irritability when they stop. These symptoms can be mild, or surprisingly uncomfortable. They may appear a few hours after you stop drinking caffeine – or not at all. As you *must* eliminate caffeine from your diet, it is best to deal with this beast before tackling other foods and drinks that may be causing you trouble. You will be delighted by the effect this has on your body. Joint pain frequently dramatically improves. A feeling of calm, and being in control, often sets in. You will sleep better, look better and feel better. What better reasons could there be for giving up something your body does not need, and that ultimately increases your pain?

The other aim for Week Zero, better understanding of your pain and discomfort, and your dietary habits, is achieved by using a self-assessment diary. Draw out a basic format and fill it in meticulously – see sample forms on the following pages.

WARNING!

If you know you have gout, *do not* eat liver, kidney, heart, sweetbreads or tripe. Offal is high in purines, which should be avoided. Poultry and pulses are also high in purines. For protein in your diet, substitute game, pork, lamb, deep-water fish and soya products such as tofu.
Add high-quality multivitamin and multimineral supplements to your diet regime to replace the natural nutrients you would otherwise obtain from liver and other organ meats. Make certain the mineral supplement contains selenium.

SAMPLE SELF-ASSESSMENT FORM		
WEEK ZERO, DAY 3 **TIME**	**WEEK ZERO** **MEALS, SNACKS AND DRINKS**	**PAIN AND DISCOMFORT** **LOCATION, SEVERITY (1–5)**
7 A.M.–10 A.M.		
10 A.M.–1 P.M.		
1 P.M.–5 P.M.		
5 P.M.–12 MIDNIGHT		
MIDNIGHT–7 A.M.		

SAMPLE COMPLETED SELF-ASSESSMENT FORM

WEEK ZERO, DAY 3 TIME	WEEK ZERO MEALS, SNACKS AND DRINKS	PAIN AND DISCOMFORT LOCATION, SEVERITY (1–5)
7 A.M.–10 A.M.	Wheat toast with butter 2 fried eggs with bacon Coffee, milk and sugar Orange juice – 8fl oz (1 cup)	Stiff knee and back on rising (3) Knee worse late morning (4)
10 A.M.–1 P.M.	Coffee and biscuit – 11.00 Note: coffee should have been eliminated from the diet by this time	Knee red and painful after walking dog (5)
1 P.M.–5 P.M.	Lunch – tuna and tomato sandwich with cola drink Chocolate bar Herbal tea with milk and sugar Scone with butter and jam	Hip hurt after lunch (3) Lay down to rest
5 P.M.–12 MIDNIGHT	Dinner – roast chicken, potato and gravy, peas and carrots Herbal tea and cake for dessert	Hip very sore (5) Took hot shower to relax it
MIDNIGHT–7 A.M.	Glass of water before bedtime	Could not sleep Pain in hip and knee (3)

Week One – the elimination diet

To begin this all-important part of the plan, organize your self-assessment diary for the week. Make a commitment to yourself that you will record details of how you feel and what you eat each day. These notes form the picture that will show how you are progressing.

REMEMBER:

* Eliminate all wheat, rye and barley from your diet. For now, do not eat oats in any form.
* Say goodbye to caffeinated drinks: coffee, tea, cola and chocolate.
* Say goodbye to all alcoholic beverages.
* Eat food raw when possible. Otherwise cook it lightly to maintain maximum nutrients.
* Drink 4–5 glasses of fresh water each day.
* If you are sensitive to cows' milk, drink goats', ewes' or soya milk instead.
* Eliminate all processed foods from your diet.
* Eliminate all sugar and artificial sweeteners from your food.
* For now, *do not* eat citrus fruit, asparagus, all red meat, tomatoes, aubergine (eggplant), all forms of peppers, and 'true' potatoes (sweet potatoes and yams are permitted).

Until you reach Weeks Three to Six, avoid eating all foods containing high levels of oxalic acid: rhubarb, cranberry, plum, chard, beet greens and spinach.

DAY ONE

A day of fasting is a good way to begin an elimination diet. This should be a time to pamper yourself – so stay warm, rest, and sip cool, fresh water. If you get terribly light headed, sip a glass of fruit juice. *Remember:* citrus fruit and tomatoes are off your diet for now, so choose peach, mango, grape or cherry juice. This is the only day you can skip the Health Drink.

DAY TWO

Today you can eat three light meals all based on raw fruit and vegetables. One of these should contain some liver. Sautéed liver and onions are always a treat.

Beginning on Day 2, take capsules containing the equivalent of 1 gram of fish oil, or take 2 tablespoons of cod liver oil each day. Fish oil is the better choice. All fish liver oils are rich in vitamins A and D, which accumulate in the liver and can be toxic in large quantities. Fish oil does not carry this risk. If you take these supplements with food they are less likely to 'repeat' on you. *If you have diabetes, or are on any medication that thins the blood, please ask your doctor before adding this supplement to your daily diet.*

Health Drink

On Day 2 add your daily Health Drink. Mix 225ml/8fl oz/1 cup of whole, pasteurized milk with 1 tablespoon of dried brewers' yeast and 1 tablespoon of black treacle (molasses). You may find that mixing these ingredients in a blender with a small banana makes a more palatable drink. Do not use bakers' yeast; use only brewers' yeast, and avoid unpasteurized milk.

DAY THREE

The same as day two but add seafood from deep-water sources. It is also suggested that on Day 3 you add 400 i.u. of vitamin E to your diet. The anti-ageing benefits of this vitamin not only support healthy joints, but also protect the heart.

DAYS FOUR, FIVE, SIX AND SEVEN

The same as the above. Each day enjoy one meal containing seafood and one based on an organ meat.

At the end of Week One, find a comfortable chair, put your feet up, and have a long look at your self-assessment diary. Have you noticed any changes in the level of discomfort or pain you are experiencing? If you suffer from joint stiffness, is it about the same as at the beginning of Week Zero? Does it occur at the same times during the day, or has this changed? Make a few notes to summarize any changes, and add a sentence or two about how you feel about the diet.

Constipation: for good health you should avoid constipation and straining when having a bowel movement. Some other diet books, including that written by Giraud Campbell, recommend colon cleansing, or enemas; we do not. The only function of the colon is to absorb water and salts from the digestive residue carried through the system by the gut. Bacteria and waste materials accumulated during digestion are naturally eliminated by the muscular contractions of a healthy colon. Many medical doctors treating digestive illnesses do not recommend colon cleansing because it disrupts the functions of the lower bowel.

To avoid constipation and straining, drink 8–10 glasses of water every day and follow the *Eat to Beat Arthritis* Diet. The wide selection of fresh fruits and vegetables you enjoy will supply at least the 20–30 grams of natural fibre you need each day for a healthy digestive system.

Week Two – resting your body

Continue the diet you followed on days 4, 5, 6 and 7 of Week One.

Do not forget the Health Drink of milk, black treacle (molasses) and brewers' yeast.

Remember to take the recommended amounts of fish oil and vitamin E.

If you have experienced little or no improvement thus far, and are drinking cows' milk and/or eating cheese made from cows' milk, eliminate these products from your diet. Substitute goats', ewes' or soya milk.

At the end of Week Two, reassess your pain and stiffness. Write down a summary of your experience, and also record how you are feeling on the diet. Have you lost a bit of unwanted weight? How is your skin? Some people find that by this time their skin has a fresher look and they have fewer blemishes.

SOME THINGS ARE NOT FOREVER – ELIMINATING FOOD SENSITIVITIES AND ALLERGIES

By eliminating the most common causes of food sensitivity during the first two weeks of the *Eat to Beat Arthritis Diet*, your body has been refreshed. Unfortunately, some of your favourite foods may be missing from your table during this process. Cooking without any potatoes, tomatoes or peppers can be difficult, but the results will make the effort worthwhile. Delicious recipes and tips to help get you through this phase of the diet are provided in Part Four. Do not despair. You need not give up all these foods forever. From the beginning of Week Three you can begin testing various foods to see how your body responds.

Weeks Three to Seven – learning to expand your food vocabulary

Now that your body has been resting on an allergen-free diet for two weeks you have reached the time when you can come to grips with how it reacts to specific foods known to cause problems. Because it takes three days to test each food, or food group, this takes some time, but the results are well worth it. Remember to have your Health Drink each day.

The process of testing your sensitivity to a food is simple:

* Add a new food, or group of foods, to your diet by using it in some wonderful dish you enjoy. Have it for lunch or dinner. Keep notes in your self-assessment diary of any twinges you may have.
* The following day, have the same food again – perhaps prepared in another way. Are there any new twinges of discomfort? Or, is your stiffness worse, or about the same?
* Go back to the Basic Arthritis Diet for a day, and see how you feel. If your arthritis has shown no signs of getting worse at the end of the third day you can be fairly certain that the food you have reintroduced is not making your arthritis worse. Add it to the list of foods you can eat, and enjoy!
* Go on to the next food, or food group, listed below, and use the same three-day test to see how your body responds. Continue until you have covered the entire list.

Remember that *allergies* and *sensitivities* are not the same. If you begin to feel a tingling feeling around your mouth soon after eating a specific food – such as lobster – you are probably allergic to it. Symptoms may get worse, and you may experience swelling in your mouth, or shortness of breath. If this occurs, seek medical help at once. In their most extreme form, food allergies can lead to anaphylactic shock and death. Other allergy symptoms are eczema, asthma, and hives (urticaria). If any food gives you a hint of these symptoms *eliminate it from your diet at once and for good.*

IT IS IMPORTANT THAT YOU TEST FOODS IN THE ORDER LISTED BELOW

1 All dairy food made from cows' milk, known as bovine products. Cows' milk is not well tolerated by many people because they are unable to digest the protein in milk and cream. Physical symptoms include inflamed and swollen joints, and phlegm. If you develop a cough a few hours after breakfast, do not be surprised. What may appear to be an on-coming cold could be a reaction to the milk you poured on your morning cereal.

   If you find you experience symptoms at this stage, check to see if you can tolerate cheese and yoghurt. Eliminate milk and cream from your diet for 48 hours, and then try only yoghurt and cheese. The protein in these products has been altered by natural processes, and is more easily digested.

2 All citrus fruits: oranges, tangerines, satsumas, clementines, lemons, limes, grapefruit and kumquats. (This includes your morning glass of orange juice! Some people find that the simple elimination of orange juice dramatically reduces joint pain.)

3 Foods high in oxalic acid: spinach, rhubarb, cranberries, plums, chard and beet greens. (If you have gout, don't even test yourself for these foods: eliminate them from your diet now and forever.)

4 Asparagus. (Asparagus is high in purines and should be avoided by those with gout.)

5 Cheese made from buffalo milk (authentic mozzarella). Sensitivity to products made from cows' milk (bovine milk) may mean you are also allergic to buffalo milk. But if you find you are not affected, then this is a great food to include in Mediterranean dishes.

6 Nuts, with the exception of almonds, walnuts and pine (pignolia) nuts, which are part of the Basic Anti-arthritis Diet.

7 Nightshade vegetables: tomatoes, aubergine (eggplant), peppers and 'true' potatoes. These should be the last test foods in your arthritis diet plan. The substances they contain, which are mildly toxic in some people, take a long time to work their way through the body.
   If pain reoccurs go back to Week One and begin again.

PART FOUR

The Recipes

Contents

Introducing the diet

The facts and recipes that follow give you all the information you need to make a success of this particular diet. I state 'particular diet' because there are many regimes you could follow to try and alleviate the effects of arthritis. This is the diet that brought me relief some years ago and still prevents my arthritis bothering me.

MARGUERITE PATTEN

WHY DID I CHOOSE THIS DIET?

Because it seemed to me to fit in with my food preferences. I could have decided on a dairy-free diet but I discarded that – I am too fond of cheese and other dairy foods. I like vegetarian dishes but was very disinclined to give up meat, poultry, game and fish.

I read of the extraordinary success achieved by people who followed Dr Giraud W. Campbell's advice, so in 1993 I began my dietary fight against this affliction.

DID I FIND IT DIFFICULT TO KEEP TO THE RULES?

In 1993, when I read through the essential information, I must confess I felt it would be very difficult to follow the diet. However, when I began eating the recommended foods I found it very possible, and as soon as I began to feel a definite improvement in my mobility and a reduction in pain, I knew I was on the right lines. I did not enjoy giving up tea and coffee but discovered many other drinks instead (see page 57).

The diet made me realize how much wheat we eat nowadays – for we enjoy pasta and couscous as well as bread, biscuits, cakes and many other things made with flour.

I love citrus fruits, but I had to forego those for a time, together with alcohol. By 2000, when I began work on my part of this book, many more facts had been discovered about foods that may well affect arthritis, including those vegetables in the nightshade group (outlined on page 39), so these are omitted in the initial meals.

FOR HOW LONG DID I FOLLOW THE INITIAL DIET IN 1993?

I kept to the strict rules for three weeks, then in the fourth week, when I was so much better, I introduced the thing I missed most – oranges. I ate them sparingly and was fine. It was only when I started to have them 'ad lib' that I noticed I had more pain – so that taught me to be careful about citrus fruits.

When writing this book I went back on the diet for a week – it did me good. I followed it implicitly for the second week but introduced tomatoes and had them every day – no adverse effect. I then went on to include aubergines (eggplants), peppers and potatoes – again I was fine. In my case vegetables in the nightshade family do not affect my arthritis.

Do I follow a strict diet all the time?

No, I do not. I could not do my job as a cookery writer, which entails testing, cooking and eating a wide variety of foods, if I ate a strictly limited range of ingredients. Over the years I have found the foods I need to avoid on a regular basis, and adjust my intake accordingly.

In my case I am better if I eat a restricted amount of wheat, so I avoid this entirely where possible. If I do have toast for breakfast, I try not to eat pasta or anything else made with wheat for the rest of the day.

I avoid tea, coffee and wine. From time to time, when I am with friends, I have the odd cup or glass. I enjoy that, but never drink any more that day. I need to curb my love of tall glasses of fresh orange juice. I still drink it, but in much smaller amounts.

Those are **my** results, but **yours** may well be different. The important thing is for **you** to take charge of what you eat, note the results and then act accordingly.

I eat a large amount of fresh fruit and vegetables. I try to buy good-quality organic foods. I do avoid most convenience foods, except for testing purposes. Finally, I treat the foods Jeannette Ewin says should be avoided with respect, and rarely eat them.

Do I ever return to the diet?

Yes, if I have a bad patch then I go back to the strict diet for a few days. When I say a bad patch I mean odd niggles of pain – nothing like as bad as in the pre-1993 days.

I always try and have liver, kidneys or sweetbreads once a week. As I enjoy these foods it is no hardship. Also, I try and keep physically active and watch my weight. After spending a long time at my desk I then try to spend an hour or so gardening or walking to compensate for this.

Do I take supplements?

I have taken cod-liver oil since 1993. Since 2000 I have been buying it combined with fish oils, and take the strong one-a-day capsules.

I drink 300ml/10fl oz/1¼ cups of pasteurized milk every day. The original diet suggests stirring brewers' yeast and black treacle (molasses) into this to make a health drink. I hated it, so I take the brewers' yeast as tablets and a spoonful of black treacle before the milk.

I have never taken any medical tablets, but you must follow your doctor's advice on that matter.

Is my arthritis completely cured?

No. I still have stiffness climbing stairs, but I can live a perfectly normal life, generally without any pain whatsoever. Before I began the diet in 1993 I was badly disabled and had terrible pain.

What would my advice be to anyone who has the first twinge of arthritis?

I would follow the advice in this book, and change to gluten-free bread and breakfast cereals.

The menus

The menus that follow are a guide for the first weeks of your arthritis diet. It is essential to follow the advice from Jeannette Ewin as to the foods to include, and those to avoid, during this initial period.

You can change around the dishes for various days to suit yourself but it is important to include the amount of liver and/or kidney suggested, together with the Health Drink of milk, brewers' yeast and black treacle (molasses) (see page 49).

When you read the menus it may seem an excessive amount of food is being recommended. Remember, while you are finding out just what foods could affect your arthritis, you have to avoid familiar things such as bread, pasta and potatoes, together with ready-prepared breakfast cereals and porridge. These are satisfying and sustaining so you need other foods to take their place. If you have overlooked root vegetables such as celeriac, parsnips, turnips and sweet potatoes in the past include plenty of these in salads and as cooked vegetables. Polenta (which comes from maize) is another satisfying food. You will find a recipe for cooking this on page 113.

Gluten-free breads and pasta are readily available in supermarkets so you could use these from time to time.

If you do feel pangs of hunger do not rush to the biscuit tin, for most biscuits are based upon wheat, oats or other grains. Choose a favourite fruit instead.

I have suggested you include a banana as part of your breakfast each morning, as it is very satisfying. If, by chance, you have no time for a more elaborate meal do at least eat the banana.

What can I drink?

If you are a lover of tea and coffee you will be somewhat unhappy at the thought that these must be avoided completely during the initial stages of your diet. In fact you may well find that your arthritis is better if you avoid or limit these beverages at all times. What can take their place?

Water: you need to drink as much as possible, so make this your first priority. Drink tap or filtered water. Still bottled water is fine, but not carbonated.

Commercial fruit juices: the most readily-available ones are apple (there is a wonderful selection of organic and pure apple juice), grape juice and pineapple juice. Do not drink any form of citrus fruit juice, or tomato juice. Look out for other interesting pure fruit juices.

Home-made fruit and vegetable juices: juice extractors have become very inexpensive and you may find it worthwhile purchasing one so you can make your own juices and have the fun of combining fruits and vegetables to create a range of drinks. These are wonderfully health-giving but do not enjoy them at the expense of *eating* fresh fruits and vegetables – you need these to add fibre to your diet.

Herb teas: look around in specialist shops and supermarkets and you will find an unbelievable range. You can also make your own herb teas from fresh herbs. Even if you do not grow these you can get them in garden centres and supermarkets. Choose those grown in pots, so you have them really freshly-grown, and look for organically grown ones. Wash well in cold water before using.

My favourites are mint and lemon balm. Pick a number of leaves, put them into the cup or mug, crush slightly with a spoon, then add the boiling water. Both of these make refreshing cold teas too. Infuse the leaves in the boiling water, then chill well before straining.

Milk: this is one of the main ingredients of the Health Drink recommended on page 49, but extra milk can be used to make milk shakes (now often known as smoothies) in the liquidizer. Simply blend the milk with fresh fruits of your choice. These become a food as well as a drink and can take the place of a dessert.

There are recommendations about various types of milk on page 41. This information is important if you are allergic to cows' milk.

The first seven days of the diet

I have not given specific vegetables and fruits for these will vary according to the season of the year. Just serve an ample selection at each main meal. But do check the advice on the vegetables and fruits to avoid during this time (see page 39).

Try and eat a good breakfast. If you are not a breakfast eater then have fruit mid-morning. Undoubtedly you will miss drinking tea and coffee at first but you will find alternative suggestions given above.

The main meal could be taken at midday or in the evening, and the lighter meal for lunch or supper. Some of the salads will be suitable as packed meals for workers.

DAY 1	No meals	Just drink plenty of water Work out how you will cope with this. You may decide to have a day of leisure – rest and read a special book – or you may find it better to plan so much activity that you have no time to think about food.
DAY 2	**Breakfast**	Selection of fresh fruits, including a banana
	Main meal	Liver with Mixed Herbs (see page 90) with vegetables Fresh fruit
	Light meal	Selection of fresh fruits
DAY 3	**Breakfast**	Boiled egg or Millet Porridge (see page 141) Banana
	Main meal	Country Lambs' Kidneys (see page 95) with vegetables Fresh fruit
	Light meal	Seafood Stir-fry (see page 80) Fresh fruit

Day 4	**Breakfast**	Poached Herring Roes (see page 86) Banana
	Main meal	Chicken Liver Risotto (see page 92) with vegetables Fresh fruit
	Light meal	Grilled Goat's Cheese Salad (see page 124) Fresh fruit
Day 5	**Breakfast**	Poached egg on Corn Bread toast (see page 143) Banana
	Main meal	Grilled Fish with Cucumber Sauce (see pages 76 and 108) with vegetables Fresh fruit
	Light meal	Creamy Liver Pâté with Sweetcorn Salad (see pages 64 and 123) Fresh fruit
Day 6	**Breakfast**	Speedy Blinis (see page 139) filled with goat's cheese Banana
	Main meal	Liver Stir-fry (see page 81) with vegetables Fresh fruit
	Light meal	Grilled Spiced Sardines (see page 85) Fresh fruit
Day 7	**Breakfast**	Savoury Omelette (see page 114) or Millet Muesli (see page 141) Banana
	Main meal	Roast Chicken with Almond Relish (see pages 102 and 112) with vegetables Fresh fruit
	Light meal	Liver and Herb Salad (see page 125) Fresh fruit

The second seven days of the diet

If you are happy to, you can repeat the dishes recommended for the first seven days. Alternatively, follow the change of menus I have provided below for the second week. Although most dishes are different from those in Week One they are still based on the essential foods: liver, or a suitable alternative, and fish, plus fresh fruits and vegetables in season.

If you have seen a real improvement in your arthritis then follow the advice on pages 50–51 and start to introduce new foods gradually. If there is only very little improvement then I suggest you keep to the basic diet for this second week. Add a soup if you want to make the main meal more sustaining. Always include a selection of vegetables.

Day 8	Breakfast	Scrambled egg on Corn Bread toast (see page 143)
		Banana
	Main meal	Liver Soufflé (see page 94) with vegetables
		Fresh fruit
	Light meal	Lentil Soup (see page 70)
		Roquefort cheese and salad
		Fresh fruit
Day 9	Breakfast	Sautéed Cod's Roe (see page 87)
		Banana
	Main meal	Creamed Sweetbreads (see page 96) with vegetables
		Fresh fruit
	Light meal	Lentil and Pine (Pignolia) Nut Salad (see page 128)
		Fresh fruit
Day 10	Breakfast	Mushroom Omelette (see page 115)
		Banana
	Main meal	Fish Véronique (see page 75) with vegetables
		Fresh fruit
	Light meal	Creamy Liver Pâté with Sweet Potato Salad (pages 64 and 127)
		Fresh fruit
Day 11	Breakfast	Sautéed Kidneys (see page 95)
		Banana
	Main meal	Grilled Fish with Pesto Sauce (pages 76 and 109) with vegetables
		Fresh fruit
	Light meal	Bean and Walnut Salad (see page 129)
		Fresh fruit

DAY 12	Breakfast	Boiled egg and Blinis (see page 138) Banana
	Main meal	Grilled Liver with Cucumber Coulis (see pages 89 and 108) with vegetables Fresh fruit
	Light meal	Thai Fish Cakes (see page 84) with vegetables Fresh fruit
DAY 13	Breakfast	Kedgeree (see page 79) Banana
	Main meal	Quail with Blueberry Sauce (see page 105) with vegetables Fresh fruit
	Light meal	Sautéed Liver (see page 90) with a **mixed** salad Fresh fruit
DAY 14	Breakfast	Avocado moistened with apple or grape juice or Millet Muesli (see page 141) Banana
	Main meal	**SPECIAL PARTY BUFFET** (to show everyone that the diet is interesting as well as beneficial) Chicken and Almond Soup (page 71) Cucumber and Seafood Dip (see page 66) Golden Roquefort Dip (see page 67) Mushroom and Liver Salad (see page 126) Fresh fruit
	Light meal	Beetroot Soup (see page 69) Garlic Mushrooms (see page 120) and a mixed salad Fresh fruit Note: in addition to the recipes covering the initial two weeks of the diet you will find a further wide selection enabling you to continue eating in a way that will maintain your good health.

Following the recipes

THE INGREDIENTS

The ingredients used in the recipes follow Jeannette Ewin's recommendations about the kinds of foods to eat to combat arthritis. As you will have read on pages 33–36 there are certain foods that it is advisable to omit during the first weeks of the diet, but these may be reintroduced gradually, so you can ascertain just what does – or does not – affect your arthritis.

Whatever foods you buy try to ensure they are organic, and therefore free from pesticides, and that they are as fresh as possible. In a few instances you may choose to buy canned foods to save a long cooking time (as in the case of dried beans). Read the labels carefully to avoid brands that contain additives; drain and wash well.

✽ Wash all fruits, vegetables, fish, meat, etc. well before using them.

✽ If you wish to use nuts make certain no-one is allergic to these.

MEASURING THE INGREDIENTS

The ingredients for each recipe are given in metric, imperial and American measures so they are easy to follow. All spoon measures are level.

✽ A metric teaspoon is equivalent to 5ml.

✽ A metric tablespoon is equivalent to 15ml.

✽ American teaspoons are similar in size to metric and imperial ones.

✽ American tablespoons are slightly smaller than metric and imperial tablespoons, so an allowance for this is made in the American column. Where tablespoons are mentioned in the method, the American equivalent is given in brackets.

✽ An American cup is the equivalent of 226.8ml (8fl oz).

✽ Metric measures are adjusted slightly to give amounts that are easy to measure or weigh.

✽ Always follow one set of measurements and not a mixture.

OVEN SETTINGS

The oven settings are given for electricity and gas but in case any readers have cookers without settings the following information will be helpful.

DESCRIPTION	CELSIUS (°C)	FAHRENHEIT (°F)	GAS MARK (No)
very cool	110–130	225–250	¼–½
cool/slow	140–150	275–300	1–2
warm	160–170	325	3
moderate	180	350	4
moderately hot	190	375	5
fairly hot	200	400	6
hot	220	425	7
very hot	230–240	450–475	8–9

A fan oven or fan-assisted (convection) oven should be set at a slightly lower temperature than an ordinary oven. A general recommendation is given in the recipes but it is wise to check with your manufacturer's handbook too.

Using a microwave oven

In some recipes it is suggested you could use a microwave oven. As these vary a great deal according to the output and the model, check the food from time to time during the cooking process.

It is advisable to allow a few minutes' standing time after the food comes out of the microwave before serving.

Seasoning

It is recommended that sea salt is used, for this contains valuable minerals.

Pepper, like all spices, deteriorates with storage, especially when ready-ground, therefore it is wise to buy small amounts of whole peppercorns and use these in a pepper mill so they are ground each time you need pepper. Most recipes state black pepper but occasionally you will see white mentioned. This is where the dish is light in colour and therefore white pepper is a better choice.

Quantities in the recipes

Most dishes are planned to serve all the family, generally assumed to be four people. This is because everyone will benefit from the healthy food and I hope they will find the dishes enjoyable as well as nutritious.

Obviously people not suffering from arthritis can add extra ingredients, such as tomatoes and potatoes, etc. to the basic dish if they wish to.

In a few fish recipes, in omelettes, and most liver recipes quantities are given for one person only. In the case of liver, there are two reasons for this. First: not everyone has to eat the regular quantity of liver given in the initial diet – although they may wish to do so. Second: cooked liver does not improve by being kept waiting, so if members of the family are likely to be a little late, it is better to cook it for each person separately. Fortunately the cooking times and method are quick and easy, so that should not be a problem.

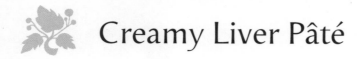

Creamy Liver Pâté

The addition of cream in the recipe below gives a more mellow taste to the liver so that it will appeal to most people – even those who are not over-fond of this meat. It is a good basic recipe which can be varied in many ways: you can make it with calves' liver, lambs' liver or chicken livers.

When cooking liver (pages 88–91) you could increase the quantity and mince or process some, then add a little cream and/or melted butter with a crushed garlic clove and chopped herbs to turn it into a very quickly prepared pâté.

Ingredients

SERVES 6–8 AS A STARTER OR 4 AS PART OF A MAIN COURSE

METRIC (IMPERIAL)		AMERICAN
2 teaspoons	olive oil	2 teaspoons
2	small shallots or spring onions (scallions), chopped	2
450g (1 lb)	liver, sliced	1 lb
115g (4oz)	pork, preferably from fillet	¼ lb
2 teaspoons	finely chopped sage leaves	2 teaspoons
2	small eggs, beaten	2
3 tablespoons	meat stock (bouillon) (see page 68)	3¾ tablespoons
150ml (5fl oz)	double (heavy) cream	⅔ cup
to taste	sea salt and freshly ground black pepper	to taste
1 teaspoon	prepared English or Dijon mustard	1 teaspoon

Method

1 Preheat the oven to 160°C/325°F/Gas Mark 3 or 150°C for a fan (convection) oven. Grease a 900ml (1½ pint) terrine tin or ovenproof container.

2 Heat the olive oil, then add the shallots or spring onions. Turn in the oil for about 4 minutes, then mix with the liver and pork.

3 Put the mixture through a mincer or into a food processor and mince (grind) or chop to the desired texture. If you require a very smooth texture do this twice. If you are using a food processor be careful that you do not over-process, for this makes the meat sticky. Mix in the remaining ingredients.

4 Spoon into the prepared container and press firmly down (this helps the pâté to turn out well). Cover with a lid or foil.

5 Stand in a tin half filled with warm water (a bain-marie) and cook for 1½ hours. Allow to cool, then turn out and serve portions with salad. As you cannot have ordinary toast while on the initial diet, rice cakes are a good accompaniment.

Variations

※ For a pâté with a stronger taste omit the cream and use 6 (7½) extra tablespoons of stock.

※ If you have discovered that you can eat citrus fruits, add 2 teaspoons of finely grated lemon zest to give extra flavour to the mixture.

※ *Millet Liver Pâté:* millet gives an interesting taste and texture to the pâté and also adds extra food value. Take the 3 (3¾) tablespoons stock given in the recipe, heat to boiling point and pour over 3 (3¾) tablespoons of millet. Allow to stand for at least 10 minutes, then add to the other ingredients after they have been minced (ground) or placed in the food processor, see step 3. Continue
as in the recipe.

Freezing: pâtés tend to lose much of their smooth texture in freezing – they become drier and crumbly. This mixture can be frozen for up to 2 weeks without being spoiled.

Cucumber and Seafood Dip

If you find eating salads regularly quite difficult then try combining salad ingredients with an interesting dip. This can be served in a bowl surrounded by a selection of crudités (raw salad ingredients), or you can spoon individual portions of the dip into small bowls and arrange the crudités on a plate. The following could be served as part of a party buffet or as a first course, light lunch or supper dish.

Ingredients

METRIC (IMPERIAL)		AMERICAN
4 tablespoons	cucumber, peeled and grated	5 tablespoons
225g (8oz)	crabmeat	½ lb
175g (6oz)	peeled prawns (shelled shrimp), finely chopped	1 cup
3 tablespoons	Mayonnaise (see page 111)	3¾ tablespoons
1 tablespoon	lemon grass stalk, finely chopped	1 tablespoon
1 tablespoon	finely chopped fennel bulb	1¼ tablespoons
to taste	sea salt and freshly ground black pepper	to taste
to bind	yoghurt	to bind
	For the crudités	
	sticks of carrot, celery, cucumber and courgette (zucchini)	

Method

1 Combine all the ingredients except the yoghurt. Mix well so you have a thick, smooth consistency.
2 Gradually add enough yoghurt to give a mixture like thick whipped cream. Taste and adjust the seasoning.

Variations

❋ If you find you can have a certain amount of citrus fruits use lemon juice instead of lemon grass.

❋ Flavour the mixture with chopped fresh herbs such as mint, thyme or rosemary.

❋ Sticks of red, green and yellow (bell) peppers are ideal crudités, if you find you are not allergic to nightshade vegetables.

❋ *Avocado and Seafood Dip:* substitute the flesh from 1 large or 2 small avocados for the cucumber.

Do not freeze

Golden Roquefort Dip

This is a dip you can make while on the initial diet. Based on delicious Roquefort cheese, sweetcorn and eggs, it is both nutritious and appetizing. Serve it with crudités, as on page 66, and rice cakes. These are obtainable from most health food stores and supermarkets.

Ingredients

SERVES 4–6

METRIC (IMPERIAL)		AMERICAN
1	corn cob	1
to taste	sea salt and freshly ground black pepper	to taste
2	large eggs, hard-boiled (hard-cooked)	2
175g (6oz)	Roquefort cheese, crumbled	1 cup
3 tablespoons	Mayonnaise (see page 111)	3¾ tablespoons
2 tablespoons	finely chopped spring onions (scallions) or chives	2½ tablespoons
to bind	double (heavy) cream or yoghurt	to bind
to taste	few drops balsamic or other vinegar, optional crudités as page 66	to taste

Method

1 Strip away the outer leaves from the corn cob and put the cob into boiling water. Do not add salt at this stage as it tends to prevent the corn becoming tender; add a little towards the end of the cooking time.

2 Strip the kernels from the cob into a bowl; season lightly.

3 Remove the shells from the eggs and chop the whites and yolks separately. Mix the whites with the sweetcorn, cheese, mayonnaise and spring onions or chives.

4 Gradually stir in enough cream or yoghurt to give the dip the consistency of whipped cream. Taste and add a little vinegar if desired.

5 Spoon into a suitable bowl or bowls and top with the chopped egg yolks just before serving. Surround with crudités and rice cakes.

Variations

* When you are introducing other foods into the diet you could use Stilton, Gorgonzola or other blue cheeses instead of Roquefort.

* Finely chopped sun-dried tomatoes add both flavour and colour but avoid these for the first two weeks of the diet.

Do not freeze

Making Stock

Several recipes in this book mention stock (bouillon). This is the liquid that will give the dish a really good flavour. It is possible to purchase ready-prepared stocks in various convenient forms (cube, liquid or powder). However, during the initial stages of your diet you are trying to avoid ready-made products, so it is sensible to make your own stock. The conventional method of making stock is given below, but you could also use a microwave or a covered casserole in the oven for this purpose.

If it is not possible to make stock, buy additive-free stock cubes or powders.

In each of the recipes below the amount of stock made will be about 600ml (1 pint/2½ cups). After cooking, strain the stock through a fine sieve.

Chicken Stock

Simmer the carcass of a cooked chicken with 1 or 2 chopped onions, 1 chopped carrot and 1 or 2 chopped celery sticks in 1.5 litres (2½ pints/4¼ cups) of water. Add sprigs of thyme, 1 or 2 fresh bay leaves, sea salt and freshly ground black pepper. Allow it to simmer for 1¼–1½ hours. To give a stronger-tasting stock add a portion of uncooked chicken.

Fish Stock

This is made by simmering the heads, skins and bones of fish and/or the shells of seafood like lobster or prawns. Put about 450g (1 lb) of fish trimmings into a pan with 900ml (1½ pints/3¾ cups) of water. Add 1 chopped onion, 1 chopped carrot, 1 chopped celery stick, a good sprig of chervil or parsley, a sprig of thyme, sea salt and freshly ground black pepper. Simmer for 25–30 minutes and strain after cooking.

Meat Stock

Use about 450g (1 lb) of beef or lamb bones*, together with similar vegetables, herbs and seasonings to those used in the recipe for Chicken Stock. You will obtain a richer flavour and colour if the bones and vegetables are first browned in a pan in a small amount of oil. Allow 1.8 litres (3 pints) or 7½ cups of water and simmer for at least 2 hours.

* Uncooked bones make a stronger-flavoured stock but bones from cooked meat can be used.

Vegetable Stock

Use about 450g (1 lb) of mixed vegetables to 1.2 litres (2 pints/5 cups) of water. Add herbs that will give the appropriate flavour to the dishes in which the stock will be used. Season lightly with sea salt and freshly ground black pepper. The cooking time will vary according to the size of the vegetables. If finely chopped, allow about 30 minutes; 40 minutes if in larger pieces. Do not overcook.

Freezing: allow the stock to cool then remove any fat from the top of the liquid. Pack into suitable containers; allow 2cm (¾ inch) headroom as stock expands when frozen.

Beetroot Soup

If you have a sweet tooth include plenty of beetroot (beets) in your salads as it has a wonderful natural sweetness. It is also an excellent vegetable to serve hot, or to make into a soup. This soup is equally good hot or cold.

Ingredients

SERVES 4

METRIC (IMPERIAL)		AMERICAN
1 medium	red (mild) onion, finely chopped	1 medium
600ml (1 pint)	chicken or vegetable stock (bouillon) (see page 68)	2½ cups
225g (8oz)	cooked beetroot (weight when peeled and chopped)	½ lb
300ml (10fl oz)	yoghurt	1¼ cups
to taste	sea salt and freshly ground black pepper	to taste
	To garnish	
	chopped watercress leaves	

Method

1 Put the onion and stock into a saucepan, bring just to the boil, then lower the heat and simmer for 10 minutes.

2 Add the beetroot, then liquidize the mixture.

3 *To serve hot*: bring the soup just to boiling point then whisk in the yoghurt and heat gently; do not allow to boil again. Season to taste. Garnish and serve.

To serve cold: chill the liquidized mixture well and whisk in the yoghurt and seasoning just before serving. Garnish and serve.

Variation

Increase the amount of watercress leaves and liquidize some of these with the beetroot mixture.

Do not freeze

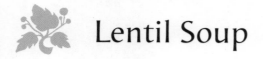

Lentil Soup

I use the small split orange lentils for this soup as they give it a good colour. They need no soaking and become tender quite quickly, so do not overcook the soup as you need to retain the fresh flavour.

Ingredients

METRIC (IMPERIAL)		AMERICAN
1½ tablespoons	sunflower oil	scant 2 tablespoons
2	medium onions, finely chopped	2
1	garlic clove, chopped	1
2	small carrots, thinly sliced	2
600ml (1 pint)	water	2½ cups
225g (8oz)	lentils	1 cup
1	small dessert apple, peeled, cored and finely chopped	1
	bouquet garni (bunch of parsley, sage, thyme and coriander tied with cotton)	
to taste	sea salt and freshly ground black pepper	to taste
1 tablespoon	cornflour (cornstarch)	1¼ tablespoons
300ml (10fl oz) or as required	milk	1¼ cups or as required
	To garnish	
	chopped parsley or coriander (cilantro)	

Method

1 Heat the oil in a large saucepan, add the onions and cook gently for 5 minutes. Stir in the garlic and carrots and cook for another 2 minutes.

2 Pour the water into the saucepan and bring to the boil. Add the lentils, apple, bouquet garni and seasoning to taste.

3 Bring the liquid back to the boil, stir briskly, then lower the heat and cover the pan. Simmer gently for 45 minutes. Remove the bouquet garni.

4 Mix the cornflour with the milk, pour into the saucepan and stir over a low heat until the mixture thickens.

5 Pour the soup into a liquidizer or food processor and process until very smooth. Return to the saucepan and heat. If it is a little too thick add more milk. Taste and adjust the seasoning.

6 Serve the soup topped with a generous amount of parsley or coriander.

Freezing: cook to the end of step 5, cool then pack and freeze. Remember to leave 2cm (¾ inch) headroom in the container.

Chicken and Almond Soup

Almonds were traditionally used as a thickening instead of flour, so this tasty soup fits well into the basic diet.

Ingredients

SERVES 4

METRIC (IMPERIAL)		AMERICAN
1	small onion, chopped	1
900ml (1½ pints)	chicken stock (bouillon) (see page 68)	3¾ cups
1	chicken breast	1
to taste	sea salt and freshly ground black pepper	to taste
50g (2oz)	ground almonds	½ cup
	To garnish	
2	small eggs, hard-boiled (hard-cooked)	2
2 tablespoons	chopped parsley	2½ tablespoons

Method

1 Put the onion, stock and chicken breast into a saucepan, season lightly, then cover the pan and simmer for 30 minutes.
2 Stir in the ground almonds, then tip the soup into a liquidizer or food processor. Process to a smooth purée.
3 Return to the pan and reheat gently. Meanwhile, shell the eggs and chop the whites and yolks separately. Stir the whites into the soup.
4 Pour the soup into individual soup bowls and top with the chopped egg yolks and parsley.

Variation
A little double (heavy) cream can be stirred into the soup just before serving.

Freezing: the soup can be frozen at the end of step 2.

Indonesian Chicken Soup

This is so filling it could be described as a meal in a soup. It is also packed with flavour. Leave out the canned water chestnuts while you are on the strict diet and use pine (pignolia) nuts or chopped, blanched almonds instead to give an interesting texture. Omit the lime juice if avoiding citrus fruits.

Ingredients

SERVES 4–6

METRIC (IMPERIAL)		AMERICAN
2 tablespoons	groundnut or sunflower oil	2½ tablespoons
2	medium onions, finely chopped	2
2	garlic cloves, finely chopped	2
1 tablespoon	grated root ginger	1¼ tablespoons
2	chicken breasts, finely chopped	2
1.2 litres (2 pints)	chicken stock (bouillon) (see page 68)	5 cups
1 tablespoon	thinly sliced lemon grass	1¼ tablespoons
150ml (5fl oz)	coconut milk	⅔ cup
2	canned water chestnuts, finely diced, optional – see above	2
to taste	sea salt and freshly ground black pepper	to taste
50g (2oz)	fresh bean sprouts	1 cup
1 tablespoon	lime juice, optional – see above	1¼ tablespoons
2 tablespoons	chopped coriander (cilantro)	2½ tablespoons

Method

1 Heat the oil in a saucepan, add the onions and cook for 5 minutes, then stir in the garlic, ginger and chicken. Continue stirring over a moderate heat for a further 5 minutes.
2 Add the stock and lemon grass, bring to the boil, then lower the heat, cover the pan and simmer for 10 minutes.
3 Pour in the coconut milk and add the water chestnuts, a little seasoning and the bean sprouts. Simmer for 3–4 minutes then stir in the lime juice and half the coriander. Adjust the seasoning and serve topped with the remaining coriander.

Variation

To make an even more sustaining soup, top with chopped hard-boiled (hard-cooked) eggs as well as coriander.

Do not freeze

Liver and Mushroom Soup

This soup can be made within a very short time if you have the chicken stock (bouillon) available. The method of making this is given on page 68.

Ingredients

METRIC (IMPERIAL)		AMERICAN
1 litre (1¾ pints)	chicken stock (bouillon) (see page 68)	scant 4½ cups
1 medium bunch	spring onions (scallions)	1 medium bunch
350g (12oz)	mushrooms (can be mixed types), wiped	¾ lb
to taste	sea salt and freshly ground black pepper	to taste
175g (6oz)	cooked liver (see page 89), finely diced	¾ cup
	To garnish	
2 tablespoons	chopped coriander (cilantro)	2½ tablespoons

Method

1 Pour the chicken stock into a saucepan. Remove the green ends from the spring onions and add the white bulbs to the pan with the whole mushrooms.
2 Bring the stock to the boil, add a little seasoning, then lower the heat and cover the pan. Simmer steadily for 20 minutes. Remove from the heat and add the liver.
3 Ladle the soup into a liquidizer or food processor. Process to a smooth purée.
4 Return to the pan, check the seasoning and add a little more if required. Bring just to the boil, then pour into individual soup bowls, garnish with the coriander and serve.

Variation
Kidney and Mushroom Soup: use the same amount of kidneys (cooked as on page 95) instead of liver.

Freezing: the soup can be frozen at the end of step 3. Remember to leave 2cm (¾ inch) headroom.

Cod with Pineapple and Cucumber

This dish is perfect for those avoiding citrus fruits, as its refreshing flavour is provided not by lemon or lime but by pineapple. The quantities are for a single person. If cooking for more people wrap each portion of fish separately.

Ingredients
SERVES 1

METRIC (IMPERIAL)		AMERICAN
1 teaspoon	olive oil	1 teaspoon
50g (2oz)	cucumber, peeled and thinly sliced	½ cup
3 teaspoons	chopped mint	3 teaspoons
to taste	sea salt and freshly ground black pepper	to taste
2 slices	fresh pineapple, 2cm (¾ inch) thick	2 slices
1 portion	cod cutlet, 2.5cm (1 inch) thick	1 portion

Method

1 Preheat the oven to 190°C/375°F/Gas Mark 5 or 180°C for a fan (convection) oven. Cut a square of foil sufficiently large to envelop the ingredients, and brush the middle with the oil.
2 Place half the cucumber on the foil, then add half the mint and a little seasoning.
3 Cut away the outer skin and centre hard core from the pineapple and place one ring over the cucumber. Add the fish.
4 Cover the fish with the second ring of pineapple then with the remaining cucumber, mint and more seasoning. Fold the foil to enclose the ingredients.
5 Place on a baking sheet and cook for 30 minutes. Open the foil carefully, as steam builds up inside. Serve with a crisp salad or lightly cooked vegetables.

Variations
❋ Use 4 teaspoons of finely chopped lemon grass instead of, or with, the mint.
❋ Cod is becoming increasingly scarce so you may want to use another white fish such as haddock.

Do not freeze

Fish Véronique

This is a version of one of the great classic fish dishes. Originally it was based upon sole, but plaice or whiting are good alternatives. The fish needs to be filleted and then skinned. Use the bones and skin to make your fish stock (bouillon) (see page 68). The classic fish recipes almost invariably use wine with fish stock, so I have substituted a little pure grape juice.

Ingredients

SERVES 4

METRIC (IMPERIAL)		AMERICAN
150g (5oz)	black or white grapes	scant 1 cup
4 large or 8 small	fish fillets, without skin and bones	4 large or 8 small
300ml (10fl oz)	fish stock (bouillon) (see page 68)	1¼ cups
2 tablespoons	grape juice	2½ tablespoons
to taste	sea salt and freshly ground white pepper	to taste
	For the sauce	
25g (1oz)	butter	2 tablespoons
15g (½ oz)	cornflour (cornstarch)	1 tablespoon
150ml (5fl oz)	double (heavy) cream	⅔ cup
	To garnish	
	black and/or white grapes	
	fennel leaves	

Method

1 Preheat the oven to 200°C/400°F/Gas Mark 6 or 190°C for a fan (convection) oven.

2 If the grapes are seedless just slit them so the juice will run out during cooking. If they contain seeds halve the grapes and remove them. The grapes could be peeled but this is not essential.

3 Place the grapes on the fillets of fish, then roll up to enclose the fruit. Secure with wooden cocktail sticks (tooth picks) and lay in a large ovenproof dish.

4 Mix the fish stock and grape juice, pour over the fish and add a little seasoning. Cover the dish and bake for 25 minutes or until the fish is just tender. Carefully lift the fillets on to another dish, cover and keep hot.

5 Strain 250ml (8fl oz/1 cup) of the stock from the dish.

6 Heat the butter in a small saucepan, stir in the cornflour, then gradually add the fish liquid and whisk as the mixture comes to the boil and thickens. Stir in the cream and continue stirring until smooth; season to taste.

7 Remove the cocktail sticks and coat the fish with the sauce. Garnish with grapes and fennel leaves. Rings of cooked fennel bulb and broccoli florets are good accompaniments.

Do not freeze

Grilled Fish

Grilling (broiling) is a very healthy way of cooking fish. Only a small amount of fat is required, just enough to keep the fish beautifully moist as it cooks. Because grilling is a fast method of cooking, the fish retains maximum flavour and a moist texture. Always preheat the grill before putting the fish under it.

I do not specify the choice of fish in the first menus but leave that to you. Do not be too conservative in your choice. As well as white fish, such as sole, plaice, cod and halibut, remember good oily fish, like salmon (not in the initial diet) herring and trout; and the modern favourites, fresh tuna and swordfish. Always buy the freshest fish possible.

Ingredients

SERVES 4

METRIC (IMPERIAL)		AMERICAN
4 portions	fish	4 portions
to taste	sea salt and freshly ground white or black pepper	to taste
50g (2oz)	butter, melted; or olive oil	¼ cup
	To garnish	
	Cucumber Sauce (see page 108)	
	parsley and watercress	

Method

1 Preheat the grill (broiler) well. Wash the fish thoroughly in cold water and pat dry with paper towels. To save the grill pan picking up fishy flavours line it with foil (discard after cooking).

2 Season the fish and also add seasoning to the butter. Brush the foil with a very little butter, place the fish on top and brush the top of the fish with butter.

3 Cook thin fillets of fish for 4–5 minutes and do not turn them over. Cook thicker fish fillets and cutlets for 8–10 minutes; turn halfway through the cooking time and brush with more seasoned butter. Whole fish or solid fish slices (often known as steaks) may need up to 15 minutes. Cook these on a fairly high heat on each side, reducing it slightly for the last few minutes.

4 Check that the fish is cooked by piercing the thickest part with the tip of a knife; the flesh should look opaque, not translucent. Garnish and serve.

Flavouring Fish

* White fish is best with the more delicate flavourings. As you are not using lemon or lime juice at the beginning of the diet, substitute crushed and chopped lemon grass or chopped lemon balm leaves. Parsley and other herbs, such as fennel, dill or coriander (cilantro) all blend well with white fish. If you find you are not allergic to citrus fruits then be generous with lime, lemon and orange zest and juice.

* White fish also goes well with the flavour of bananas. Fry fillets of fish in a little butter and oil with some sliced bananas. Add finely chopped chives as well as seasoning.

* Oily fish can have more robust flavourings such as grated root ginger, chilli powder, garlic and various kinds of mustard.

* Meaty fish like tuna and swordfish are best marinated before cooking.

  To make a marinade for 4 portions of fish:

1 Mix together 2 (2½) tablespoons olive oil, 2 teaspoons sesame seed oil, 2 (2½) tablespoons balsamic vinegar, 1 crushed garlic clove, sea salt and freshly ground black pepper.

2 Place the fish in the marinade and leave for 1 hour. Do not leave for any longer or the marinade may make the fish over-tender.

3 Lift the fish out of the marinade, drain well and grill as instructed opposite. Baste with the marinade during cooking.

Do not freeze

Herbed Baked Fish

Do not be sparing with the fresh herbs used in this dish. They add a splendid flavour to any white fish, and also to fresh salmon.

Ingredients

SERVES 4

METRIC (IMPERIAL)		AMERICAN
2 tablespoons	olive oil	2½ tablespoons
6–8	small courgettes (zucchini), thinly sliced	6–8
1 large bunch	spring onions (scallions), chopped	1 large bunch
2 tablespoons	chopped parsley	2½ tablespoons
1 tablespoon	chopped coriander (cilantro)	1¼ tablespoon
1 tablespoon	chopped basil	1¼ tablespoon
3 tablespoons	fish stock (bouillon) (see page 68)	3¾ tablespoons
4 portions	white fish or salmon	4 portions

Method

1 Brush a large ovenproof dish with a little of the oil. Arrange the courgettes in a neat layer in the dish, then top with the spring onions, half the herbs and half the stock.

2 Place the fish on top and cover with the remaining stock, then the last of the herbs. Finally, spoon the remaining oil evenly over the ingredients. Cover the dish with a lid or foil.

3 Preheat the oven to 190°C/375°F/Gas Mark 5 or 180°C for a fan (convection) oven. Bake thin fillets of fish for 15–20 minutes and thicker cutlets for 25–30 minutes.

4 Serve with a crisp green salad.

Do not freeze

Kedgeree

Although it is famous as a breakfast dish, kedgeree could be served at any time of the day. Its association with India is indicated by the optional use of a small amount of curry powder. The version below is different from the classic one, for that is based upon smoked haddock and, as you will have read, smoked or salted fish and meats of all kinds should be avoided. That does not make this kedgeree less interesting, but gives you more scope to be imaginative in your choice of fish. I have suggested cod in the main recipe but given further suggestions too.

Kedgeree is practical for breakfast as the rice and fish are already cooked, so it is simply a matter of putting these together. Cook the rice in your favourite way and poach the cod in seasoned water. To give the weight of cooked rice in the recipe you need about 115g (4oz) or a good ½ cup of raw rice.

Ingredients

SERVES 4

METRIC (IMPERIAL)		AMERICAN
2	large eggs	2
50g (2oz)	butter	¼ cup
1 teaspoon or to taste	curry powder, optional	1 teaspoon or to taste
350g (12oz)	cooked long grain rice, preferably brown	good 2 cups
350g (12oz)	cooked cod, free from bones and skin, broken into large flakes	¾ lb
2 tablespoons	single (light) cream or milk	2½ tablespoons
to taste	sea salt and cayenne pepper	to taste

Method

1 Hard-boil (hard-cook) the eggs. Shell them, then chop the yolks and whites separately.

2 Heat the butter in a saucepan, stir in the curry powder, if using, then add the rice and fish together with the cream or milk. Stir over a medium heat until piping hot.

3 Add the egg white and any seasoning required. Spoon on to a large hot dish or individual plates and garnish with the egg yolk.

Variations

❋ Often fried onion rings were added with the egg yolks as a garnish but they are less suitable for breakfast time.

❋ *Scallop Kedgeree:* lightly fry 6–8 large (king) scallops, then slice thinly and use instead of cooked fish. Save this dish until after the initial diet.

❋ Use any other firm fish, such as halibut or monkfish.

❋ Chopped fresh parsley or thyme can be added to give flavour and colour to the dish.

Do not freeze

Seafood Stir-fry

This is an excellent way of cooking a complete meal in a large frying pan (skillet) or wok. The vegetables should be young and cut into small pieces so they cook quickly and the fish sufficiently firm in texture not to break up with stirring. Makes of soy sauce vary, so check that you are using a brand that does not include a lot of additives. The quality of the stock (bouillon) makes a lot of difference to the success of the dish.

For the first part of the diet use all white fish and no prawns (shrimp). Defrost and dry frozen cooked prawns so that they are firm when added to the pan.

Ingredients

SERVES 4

METRIC (IMPERIAL)		AMERICAN
3 teaspoons	cornflour (cornstarch)	3 teaspoons
to taste	sea salt and freshly ground white pepper	to taste
450–675g (1–1½ lb)	firm white fish, such as monkfish, cut into narrow strips, free from skin and bone	1–1½ lb
2 tablespoons	sunflower or groundnut oil	2½ tablespoons
115g (4oz)	mangetout (snow peas)	¼ lb
115g (4oz)	baby sweetcorn, halved	¼ lb
2 or 3	young carrots, cut into narrow strips	2 or 3
150ml (5fl oz)	fish stock (bouillon) (see page 68)	⅔ cup
1 tablespoon	rice vinegar	1¼ tablespoons
2 teaspoons	soy sauce	2 teaspoons
1 teaspoon	grated root ginger, optional	1 teaspoon
1 teaspoon, or to taste	honey	1 teaspoon, or to taste
175g (6oz)	peeled prawns (shrimp)	1 cup

Method

1 Put half the cornflour, with a little seasoning, on to a plate. Add the fish strips and stir around gently until dusted with the cornflour.

2 Heat the oil in a large frying pan (skillet) or wok. Add the coated fish and sauté for about 3 minutes or until delicately brown on the outside. Lift out of the pan with a fish slice or perforated spoon and place on a plate.

3 Stir in the vegetables and continue stirring over the heat for about 5 minutes or until nearly cooked. They should retain a firm texture.

4 Mix the remaining cornflour with the stock, vinegar, soy sauce, ginger and honey. Pour into the pan and stir until the mixture forms a sauce. Return the white fish to the pan and stir over a moderate heat until tender. Add the prawns together with any seasoning required. Heat for 1–2 minutes and serve with cooked brown rice.

Variations

* Add other vegetables, such as florets of cauliflower or broccoli or tender green beans – these could be cut into 5cm (2 inch) lengths.

* *Chicken Stir-fry:* use strips of uncooked chicken instead of fish. Coat, then cook for about 5 minutes at step 2. Prawns may be an unusual accompaniment to chicken but they blend well together so these could be included. If the prawns are omitted use 450g (1 lb) of chicken breast or leg meat – weight without skin and bones. Use chicken stock instead of fish stock (see page 68).

* *Liver Stir-fry:* use chicken livers instead of strips of fish. You will need about 450g (1 lb) to serve four people. Do not coat with cornflour, simply season very lightly, then sauté for 2 minutes at step 2. Continue as in the recipe but exclude the prawns. Broccoli, shiitake mushrooms, asparagus tips and baby courgettes are particularly good with the liver instead of mangetout, sweetcorn and carrots. Stir-fry the vegetables first then add to the liver when it is almost cooked. Use meat or chicken stock instead of fish stock (see page 68).

Do not freeze

Mussels in Cream Sauce

Green-lipped mussels have become well known as one of the foods that may benefit people suffering from arthritis. Sadly these are not found throughout the world but only in New Zealand. However, they are exported, both fresh or pre-cooked and frozen. Ordinary mussels are more readily available and make a nutritious and very appetizing dish.

Ingredients

SERVES 4

METRIC (IMPERIAL)		AMERICAN
2 litres (3½ pints)	fresh mussels	8½ cups
1–2	garlic cloves, chopped (optional)	1–2
1	medium onion, finely chopped	1
1 small bunch	parsley	1 small bunch
250ml (8fl oz)	water	1 cup
to taste	sea salt and black pepper	to taste
1–2	lemon grass stalks, chopped	1–2
300ml (10fl oz)	double (heavy) cream	1¼ cups
	To garnish	
2 tablespoons	chopped parsley	2½ tablespoons
1 tablespoon	chopped coriander (cilantro)	1 tablespoon

Method

1 Wash the mussels in plenty of cold water to remove the grit. If you have managed to obtain green-lipped mussels there is virtually no grit on them. Pull or cut away the small weed (the beard) you may find on some of the shells.

2 Check carefully for any mussels that are open. Tap them firmly, and if the shells fail to close discard them.

3 Put the mussels, garlic (if using), onion, bunch of parsley and water into a large saucepan. Add a very little seasoning, then the lemon grass.

4 Heat steadily for 4–5 minutes or until the shells are open. Do not overcook for that toughens the flesh. Strain, reserving the liquid.

5 Check carefully again and if any mussels remain closed discard them. For this dish the mussels can be removed from the shells.

6 Heat the strained liquid, add the cream, bring to simmering point and heat slowly, stirring, until thickened. Put in the mussels and cook for 2 minutes only. Taste and adjust the seasoning. Top with the chopped parsley and coriander and serve with cooked rice and a selection of vegetables or a salad.

Variations

* If using ready-cooked, frozen, green-lipped mussels defrost at room temperature, then remove from the shells. These mussels are larger than the more familiar type so you need fewer. Use fish stock (see page 68) or water and heat this with the mussel shells and ingredients given in step 3 for 5 minutes, strain and continue with steps 5 and 6.
* If you find you can include citrus fruit in your diet add a little lemon juice to the liquid instead of, or as well as, lemon grass. If you are eating tomatoes add 2 (2½) tablespoons finely diced sun-dried tomatoes at step 6.
* Instead of straining the stock at step 4 simply remove the bunch of parsley and retain the chopped ingredients.

Do not freeze

Thai Fish Cakes

This recipe uses a small amount of prepared curry paste so it should be made when you have completed your initial diet. Any firm white fish is suitable for this dish.

Ingredients

SERVES 4

METRIC (IMPERIAL)		AMERICAN
350g (12oz)	firm white fish (weight without bones or skin)	¾ lb
2 teaspoons	vegetable oil	2 teaspoons
1	shallot or small onion, chopped	1
1	garlic clove	1
1 teaspoon	Thai green curry paste	1 teaspoon
2 tablespoons, or as required	fish stock (bouillon) (see page 68)	2½ tablespoons, or as required
1 tablespoon	chopped coriander (cilantro)	1¼ tablespoons
1	egg, whisked	1
to taste	sea salt and freshly ground black pepper	to taste
1 tablespoon, or as required	cornflour (cornstarch)	1¼ tablespoons, or as required
	For coating and frying	
1 tablespoon	cornflour (cornstarch)	1¼ tablespoons
2 tablespoons	vegetable oil	2½ tablespoons

Method

1 Process the fish lightly (over-processing makes the cakes rubbery) and put on one side. Heat the oil in a frying pan (skillet), add the shallot or onion and garlic and fry gently for 4 minutes.

2 Stir in the curry paste, blend with the other ingredients and heat for 1 minute. Stir in the fish and mix well. Gradually add enough fish stock plus the coriander and egg to give a fairly soft mixture; season to taste.

3 Stir in enough cornflour to make the mixture easy to handle. Do not be too generous with the cornflour. If the mixture is a little over-soft chill for a time in the refrigerator. The fish cakes should never be too dry.

4 Put the coating cornflour on to a plate and mix with a little salt and pepper. Form the fish mixture into about 12 balls, or round cakes if more convenient, then roll in the cornflour. It is easier to fry them if they are chilled for a short time.

5 Heat the oil and fry the fish cakes for 5 minutes, turning them until evenly browned.

Freezing: do not freeze for longer than 2 weeks. The fish cakes tend to lose their moist texture.

Grilled Spiced Sardines

Fresh sardines are both plentiful and delicious. They make a very good light meal served with a salad or lightly cooked vegetables. Choose really plump fish and use as soon as possible after purchase.

Ingredients

METRIC (IMPERIAL)		AMERICAN
12	large fresh sardines	12
50g (2oz)	butter	¼ cup
¼ teaspoon or to taste	chilli powder	¼ teaspoon or to taste
¼ teaspoon	ground cumin	¼ teaspoon
2 tablespoons	finely chopped coriander (cilantro)	2½ tablespoons
2 tablespoons	chopped parsley	2½ tablespoons
2 teaspoons	balsamic or sherry vinegar	2 teaspoons
1 tablespoon	sunflower oil	1¼ tablespoons
to taste	sea salt and freshly ground black pepper	to taste
	To garnish	
	coriander (cilantro) leaves	

Method

1 Cut off the sardine heads, then split along the stomach of each fish and open out until flat; carefully remove the intestines. If you wish you can take out the backbones (see below). Rinse in cold water and dry well.

2 Mix the butter with the chilli powder, cumin, coriander, parsley and vinegar. Spread over the inside of each fish then fold so the fish look whole again.

3 Preheat the grill (broiler) and place a sheet of foil over the grid. Brush the foil and the fish with the oil and season to taste.

4 Cook for about 10 minutes. There is no need to turn the fish. Garnish and serve hot.

Variations

* Allow 1 large or 2 small herrings per person instead of the sardines. You will need double the amount of filling for herrings.
* Use cayenne pepper instead of chilli powder.
* To bone the fish: turn the split fish skin side uppermost, run your finger down the backbone very firmly, turn over and you will find you can gently lift away the backbone.

Do not freeze

Poached Herring Roes

Herring roes, especially the soft kind, are exceptionally easy to digest, and make a nourishing dish for breakfast or for a light snack. Their creamy texture makes them especially good served on toast.

Ingredients

METRIC (IMPERIAL)		AMERICAN
450g (1 lb)	soft herring roes	1 lb
4 tablespoons	milk	5 tablespoons
25g (1oz)	butter	2 tablespoons
to taste	sea salt and freshly ground white pepper	to taste
	To garnish	
	paprika or cayenne pepper	

Method

1 The herring roes can be cooked in a saucepan but they keep a better shape, and look more attractive, if they are cooked between two plates.

2 Dry the roes well on paper towels. Arrange in a single layer on a large heat-proof plate. Add the milk, butter and a little seasoning.

3 Place the plate over a saucepan of boiling water, cover with a second plate and cook for 10–12 minutes or until the flesh is opaque.

4 Lift from the liquid and serve topped with a dusting of paprika or cayenne. Toasted Corn Bread (see page 143) or Blinis (see page 138) are good accompaniments.

Variation

Put the ingredients into a saucepan, bring the milk to the boil, lower the heat and cook for 8–10 minutes. Serve as above.

Do not freeze

Sautéed Cod's Roe

Cod's roe is most nutritious and can be used in many ways. Most fish counters sell it already cooked, so it simply needs frying, but if you have to buy it uncooked see step 1 below.

Ingredients

METRIC (IMPERIAL)		AMERICAN
450g (1 lb)	cod's roe	1 lb
to taste	sea salt and freshly ground white pepper	to taste
50g (2oz)	butter	¼ cup
1 tablespoon	sunflower or groundnut oil	1¼ tablespoons

Method

1 If the roe is uncooked place it in a steamer with a little seasoning. Cover and cook over boiling water for 10–15 minutes, until the roe loses its translucent appearance.

2 Cool slightly, then remove the outer skin and cut the roe into slices.

3 Heat the butter and oil in a large frying pan (skillet) and heat the slices for 2 minutes. Turn them over and cook for the same time on the second side. Serve hot. Fried or grilled (broiled) mushrooms are a good accompaniment.

Freezing: the uncooked cod's roe can be frozen.

Enjoying Liver

As you will see from the initial menus, calves' or lambs' liver is an essential part of the diet and should be eaten regularly. It should be a most enjoyable meat, full of flavour, moist and tender. Here are a few tips to insure that you achieve this.

✳ If you find the flavour slightly too strong for your taste marinate the slices for one person in 3–4 tablespoons of milk before cooking. Leave for 30 minutes, then remove the liver and dry it well on paper towels. The milk, which reduces the strong taste, can be heated with seasoning and chopped herbs, thickened with cornflour and served as a sauce.
Note: this step is not suitable for kosher diets.

✳ Never overcook liver. This does not make it more tender; on the contrary it makes it hard and dry. It cooks extremely quickly, so I never do it in the microwave. Neither do I flour it before cooking. I find this tends to harden the outside; and of course while following the diet you should omit a flour coating in any form of cooking.

✳ If you are serving other ingredients, such as onions, as an accompaniment to liver, cook them first and keep them warm, *then* cook the liver. *Never* keep liver waiting on the hot pan, as it will continue to cook; serve it immediately.

As you will see from the following recipes there are many ingredients that blend well with liver. Do try them, for they make a pleasant change. The liver recipes covering the first 14 days of the diet are very simple, as they use just the recommended ingredients. After you have discovered which foods do, and do not, affect your arthritis you can become more adventurous.

Grilled Liver

Grilling (broiling) is one good way of cooking liver. It is also the way of preparing liver as required by Jewish dietary laws – see under Variations.

Ingredients

METRIC (IMPERIAL)		AMERICAN
2	slices of calves' liver, about 1cm (⅓ inch) thick	2
1 tablespoon	butter, melted or olive oil	1¼ tablespoons
to taste	sea salt and freshly ground black pepper	to taste

Method

1 Wash the liver in cold water, then dry thoroughly on paper towels.

2 Preheat the grill (broiler) and spread a piece of foil over the wire grid. Place the liver slices on this, brush with the butter or oil and season lightly.

3 Cook for about 1 minute only, then turn over, brush with the remaining butter or oil and season again. Cook for the same time on the second side; remove immediately and serve at once.

Variations

* The butter or oil can be flavoured with a little ground ginger or grated ginger root or with ground cinnamon or chilli powder.

* Finely grated lemon or orange zest are other good additions (if you are sure these do not affect your arthritis).

* This is also a good method of cooking lambs' and chicken livers.

* Jewish dietary recommendations: grilling (broiling) is the method recommended for preparing all kinds of liver. The slices should first be lightly scored so the blood runs out, laid on foil in a special grill pan, sprinkled with kitchen salt and grilled as above. Butter or oil is not used. It is essential to take this step before cooking the liver in other ways. Always discard the foil.

Do not freeze

Sautéed Liver

Calves' liver is the ideal choice but as this is more expensive than lambs' liver you may choose to fry that instead. Cut lambs' liver even thinner than recommended for calves' liver. Do not forget chicken livers, as they are equally good when fried. As liver is so important in this initial attack on arthritis do spoil yourself and choose the meat that pleases you most. I have not specified the weight of liver; you can judge this for yourself. Buy two fairly large slices.

Liver is very lean, so you should be fairly generous with the amount of fat used.

Ingredients

SERVES 1

METRIC (IMPERIAL)		AMERICAN
2	slices of calves' liver, about 1cm (⅓ inch) thick	2
to taste	sea salt and freshly ground black pepper	to taste
25g (1oz)	butter	2 tablespoons
2 teaspoons	sunflower oil	2 teaspoons

Method

1 Wash the liver in cold water, dry thoroughly on paper towels and season lightly.
2 Heat the butter and oil in a large frying pan (skillet). Fry the liver for about 1 minute, then turn over and fry for the same time on the second side. Remove immediately and serve at once.

Variations

✻ Lambs' liver and chicken livers may need another ½–1 minute's cooking on either side to suit the tastes of some people.

✻ *Liver with Mixed Herbs:* add 2 (2½) tablespoons of mixed coarsely chopped herbs to the butter and oil before frying the liver. A good selection would be sage, chervil or parsley, chives and tarragon. If you want to use one herb only sage leaves are a very good choice.

✻ *Gravy to serve with liver:* the ideal time to make this is when the liver is cooked on one side only. Have ready a teaspoon of cornflour (cornstarch) mixed with 175ml (6fl oz/ ¾ cup) of chicken or vegetable stock (bouillon). Pour over the liver in the frying pan, turn the meat over and stir briskly as the gravy thickens and the liver finishes cooking. You could also add 1 or 2 teaspoons of prepared English or Dijon mustard to the pan. Instead of all stock you could use half stock and half single (light) cream.

✻ *Liver with Avocado:* halve, stone and peel a small avocado, then cut the flesh into neat slices. Sprinkle these with a little cider vinegar or rice vinegar (or lemon juice if you are happy with citrus fruit). Fry briefly in the butter and oil, then move to one side of the pan and fry the liver.

* *Liver with Kiwi Fruit:* wash and dry the liver as in step 1, place on a plate and cover with thin slices of peeled kiwi fruit. Leave for an hour, then fry the fruit and liver together. The acidity of kiwi fruit flavours and tenderizes liver. It is particularly good with chicken livers or lambs' liver.

* *Liver and Onions:* if preparing this dish for several people it is almost easier to work with two frying pans. If using one frying pan for one person this is the method to use. Heat a good tablespoon of oil in a pan and fry 1 medium to large thinly sliced onion – the slices should be pulled apart to form rings. Cook these fairly slowly, adding a little seasoning as you do so. To give a slightly caramelized taste to the onion stir in a teaspoon of honey or sugar. When the onions are tender put on to a well-heated dish and keep hot in the oven, or move to one side of the frying pan while frying the liver.

Do not freeze

Chicken Liver Risotto

This is one of the best-known Italian rice dishes. The classic name is Risotto alla Finanziera. To avoid overcooking the livers do not add them at the beginning of the cooking period. Risotto (medium grain) rice is easily obtainable; the most common one is called arborio. It may sound troublesome to add the hot liquid gradually but this is essential to achieve the desired moist texture. If you have difficulty finding fresh chicken livers buy frozen ones; defrost and dry them well.

You will find cooked rice is an excellent accompaniment to many main dishes instead of potatoes, which are one of the nightshade vegetables you have to avoid during the initial steps of the diet. Choose organic brown rice whenever possible.

Ingredients

Serves 4

METRIC (IMPERIAL)		AMERICAN
2 tablespoons	olive oil	2½ tablespoons
1	medium onion, finely chopped	1
1 or 2	garlic cloves, finely chopped	1 or 2
350g (12oz)	arborio or other risotto rice	good 1½ cups
225g (8oz)	chicken livers	good 1 cup
1.2 litres (2 pints)	chicken stock (bouillon), (see page 68)	5 cups
to taste	sea salt and freshly ground black pepper	to taste
100g (3½ oz)	small button mushrooms, optional	1 cup
25g (1oz)	butter	2 tablespoons
	To garnish	
	chopped tarragon leaves	

Method

1 Heat the oil in a large saucepan, add the onion and cook gently for 5 minutes, then stir in the garlic and cook for a further 2 minutes.
2 Add the rice and turn in the oil mixture, so all the grains become coated. Remove any gristle from the livers and dice them neatly.
3 Meanwhile, heat the stock in another saucepan. Add just enough of the hot stock to moisten the rice mixture, and when this has been absorbed add a little more. Stir in salt and pepper to taste.
4 Continue adding hot stock until the rice is beginning to soften, then stir in the liver, and the mushrooms if using. Watch the pan carefully and as soon as the rice absorbs the hot liquid add more. Stop when the rice is just tender; the finished dish should still be moist.
5 Check the seasoning and stir in the butter. Top with the tarragon and serve.

Variations

* Although never included in the classic recipe you can stir in 3 (3¾) tablespoons raisins just before the rice is cooked. The sweetness of the dried fruit balances the flavour well.

* When you can include most cheeses in your diet top the dish with grated Parmesan and serve it as an accompaniment.

* Instead of fresh mushrooms soak 1 (1¼) tablespoons porcini (dried mushrooms) in a little hot water as instructed on the packet, then add to the other ingredients.

* To give a touch of luxury to the risotto add a few drops of truffle oil to the stock.

* There are many other foods you can use instead of chicken livers but during the vital first days of the diet the livers are important. Try the following:

  Chickpea (garbanzo bean) and Liver Risotto: add 175g (6oz) or 1 good cup cooked chickpeas to the risotto at step 4 after putting in the liver and mushrooms. (Chickpeas have an excellent flavour and high protein value, so should be served as often as possible.)

  Mushroom Risotto: use about 450g (1 lb) diced mixed mushrooms, including as many wild varieties as possible.

Freezing: cook to the end of step 4. Cool and freeze.

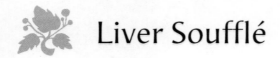

Liver Soufflé

This is an excellent way to introduce liver to anyone who is not over-fond of the flavour. It gets them accustomed to the taste.

Ingredients

METRIC (IMPERIAL)		AMERICAN
1 tablespoon	sunflower oil	1¼ tablespoons
175g (6oz)	button mushrooms, sliced	1 cup
150g (5oz)	calves' or lambs' liver, minced (ground) or very finely chopped	good ½ cup
25g (1oz)	butter or margarine	2 tablespoons
15g (½oz)	cornflour (cornstarch)	1 tablespoon
150ml (5fl oz)	milk or chicken stock (bouillon)	⅔ cup
3	large eggs	3
1	egg white	1
to taste	sea salt and freshly ground black pepper	to taste

Method

1 Lightly grease a 15–18cm (6–7 inch) soufflé dish. Heat the oil in a frying pan (skillet), add the mushrooms and cook for 3 minutes. Spoon about three-quarters into the base of the soufflé dish. Mix the remaining mushrooms with the uncooked liver.

2 Preheat the oven to 190°C/375°F/Gas Mark 5 or 180°C for a fan (convection) oven.

3 Heat the butter or margarine in a large saucepan, stir in the cornflour and cook gently for 1 minute. Gradually add the milk or stock. Bring to the boil, then lower the heat and stir until the sauce thickens.

4 Remove the saucepan from the heat and stir in the mushroom and liver mixture. Separate the eggs and put the 3 whites into a bowl with the extra egg white.

5 Beat the yolks, then stir into the ingredients in the saucepan. Add a little seasoning.

6 Whisk the whites until they stand in soft peaks. Take a few spoonfuls and beat into the liver mixture to give a softer consistency. Gently fold in the remainder. Taste and adjust the seasoning.

7 Spoon into the prepared soufflé dish and bake for 30–35 minutes or until well-risen. Serve at once with a mixed salad.

Do not freeze

Country Lambs' Kidneys

Lamb and veal kidneys are important foods in this diet. As they are tender meats they are quick to prepare and cook. I have suggested using spring onions (scallions) in this recipe as they look attractive and, like the kidneys, are quick to cook. Alternatively, you could use very small shallots, pickling (pearl) onions or thinly sliced mild onions.

Ingredients

SERVES 4

METRIC (IMPERIAL)		AMERICAN
450g (1 lb)	lambs' kidneys	1 lb
1 tablespoon	cornflour (cornstarch)	1¼ tablespoons
to taste	sea salt and freshly ground black pepper	to taste
25g (1oz)	butter	2 tablespoons
2 tablespoons	sunflower or groundnut oil	2½ tablespoons
225g (8oz)	plump spring onions (scallions) (trimmed weight)	½ lb
225g (8oz)	small button mushrooms	½ lb
300ml (10fl oz) plus extra if required	meat or chicken stock (bouillon) (see page 68)	1¼ cups plus extra if required
	To garnish	
	watercress sprigs	

Method

1 Skin the kidneys and cut each one in half; remove any gristle and excess fat. Mix the cornflour with a little salt and pepper and use to coat the kidneys.

2 Heat the butter and half the oil in a saucepan. Add the kidneys and cook steadily, turning them around several times, for 5 minutes. Remove from the pan on to a plate.

3 Check the amount of fat left in the saucepan; if little is left add the remaining oil, heat and add the onions. Cook for about 5 minutes, turning once or twice, until they are slightly golden.

4 Return the kidneys to the pan with the mushrooms and stock. Bring the liquid to the boil, check the seasoning, then cover the pan and simmer for 10–15 minutes or until all the ingredients are tender. Check during the cooking time to see there is sufficient liquid; if not add more stock.

5 Garnish and serve with cooked brown rice and mixed vegetables.

Variation

Sautéed Kidneys: skin then slice lambs' kidneys or veal kidney. Do not coat in cornflour, just season lightly. Fry steadily in hot butter and oil, or all oil, until tender.

Freezing: proceed to the end of step 4, cool and freeze.

Creamed Sweetbreads

Sweetbreads are another valuable food to include in your arthritis diet. Veal sweetbreads are not readily available but the smaller lambs' sweetbreads are very good. You may have to purchase them frozen, in which case defrost and dry well before using. Classic recipes suggest that sweetbreads are first pressed under a weight, then sliced before using, but this rather laborious step is not necessary.

Soya milk could be used in the sauce; it gives an interesting change of flavour.

Ingredients

SERVES 4

METRIC (IMPERIAL)		AMERICAN
550g (1¼ lb)	sweetbreads	1¼ lb
1–2	medium onions, sliced	1–2
2	medium carrots, sliced	2
small bunch	parsley	small bunch
to taste	sea salt and freshly ground white pepper	to taste
	For the sauce	
25g (1oz)	butter	2 tablespoons
15g (½oz)	cornflour (cornstarch)	2 tablespoons
150ml (5fl oz)	milk	⅔ cup
150ml (5fl oz)	sweetbread stock (bouillon), (see method)	⅔ cup
150ml (5fl oz)	single (light) cream or extra milk	⅔ cup
2 tablespoons	chopped parsley or other herbs	2½ tablespoons

Method

1 Wash the sweetbreads in cold water, then put into a saucepan, cover with water and bring to the boil. Strain immediately, discarding the water. This is known as blanching, a process which whitens the meat.

2 Return the sweetbreads to the pan with the onion(s), carrots, parsley and enough water to cover. Add a little seasoning. Simmer steadily for about 20 minutes for lambs' sweetbreads or up to 30 minutes for veal sweetbreads.

3 Strain and retain 150ml (5fl oz) or ⅔ cup of the stock. Remove the skin and any gristle from the sweetbreads. Larger sweetbreads should be cut into neat dice.

4 Heat the butter in a saucepan. Mix the cornflour with the milk and add to the pan with the stock. Stir as the liquid comes to the boil and thickens, then add the cream or extra milk and the diced sweetbreads. Heat well, then stir in half the parsley and any seasoning required. Top with the remaining parsley and serve with mixed vegetables.

Do not freeze

Sweet and Sour Lambs' Hearts

Hearts are a very good alternative to liver, and lambs' hearts are the most tender. The meat is very lean, so it fits perfectly into a low-fat diet.

Ingredients

METRIC (IMPERIAL)		AMERICAN
8	small lambs' hearts	8
to taste	sea salt and freshly ground black pepper	to taste
1 tablespoon	cornflour (cornstarch)	1¼ tablespoons
2 tablespoons	sunflower oil	2½ tablespoons
2	medium onions, finely chopped	2
150ml (5fl oz)	lamb stock (bouillon) (see page 68)	⅔ cup
150ml (5fl oz)	apple juice	⅔ cup
3 teaspoons	honey	3 teaspoons
1 tablespoon	balsamic or other vinegar	1¼ tablespoons
2	dessert apples, cored, peeled and cut into rings	2
2 tablespoons	raisins	2½ tablespoons
	To garnish	
	watercress	

Method

1 Preheat the oven to 160°C/325°F/Gas Mark 3 or 150°C for a fan (convection) oven.

2 Skin the hearts, remove any gristle and fat, then cut the meat into fingers about 2cm (¾ inch) wide. Mix a little seasoning with the cornflour and use to coat the meat.

3 Heat half the oil in a frying pan (skillet), add the onions and sauté for 3 minutes only; spoon into a casserole.

4 Add the remaining oil to the pan, heat again, then stir in the strips of heart. Cook gently for 5 minutes, turning over halfway through the cooking time. Spoon into the casserole.

5 Pour the stock and apple juice into the pan. Stir well to absorb all the meat juices, then stir in the honey and vinegar and bring the mixture just to boiling point. Pour over the meat. Cover and cook for 1 hour.

6 Add the apple rings and the raisins, taste the liquid and add more seasoning if required. Cover again and cook for a further 30 minutes. Garnish and serve. Sweet potatoes, baked in their skins and cooked red cabbage are good accompaniments.

Freezing: the dish is better if frozen without the apples. These become over-soft, so add them when reheating.

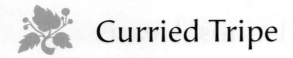

Curried Tripe

The food value of tripe has been appreciated since Roman times but it is a variety meat that has become somewhat unfashionable. This recipe gives it an up-to-the-minute taste.

Most tripe on sale today has been dressed – prepared – by the butcher so the cooking time is considerably reduced. If by chance you are sold undressed tripe simmer it slowly in water for at least 1 hour, then drain and proceed as below.

Ingredients

SERVES 4

METRIC (IMPERIAL)		AMERICAN
675g (1½ lb)	tripe, cut into 7.5cm (3 inch) squares	1½ lb
1 tablespoon	sunflower oil	1¼ tablespoons
25g (1oz)	butter	2 tablespoons
2	medium onions, thinly sliced	2
2	garlic cloves, chopped	2
1–2 teaspoons	grated root ginger	1–2 teaspoons
½ teaspoon	turmeric	½ teaspoon
¼ teaspoon, or to taste	cayenne pepper*	¼ teaspoon, or to taste
¼ teaspoon, or to taste	chilli powder*	¼ teaspoon, or to taste
1 teaspoon, or to taste	ground coriander	1 teaspoon, or to taste
¼ teaspoon	ground cumin	¼ teaspoon
300ml (10fl oz), or as required	chicken stock (bouillon) or water (see page 68)	1¼ cups, or as required
to taste	sea salt	to taste
to taste	few drops balsamic or other vinegar	to taste
	To garnish	
	sliced banana and diced pineapple	

*The combination of these two hot spices may be too strong for some people so use them sparingly until you are happy with the result

Method

1 Put the tripe into a saucepan with water to cover, bring to the boil, then strain and discard the liquid. This is known as blanching the tripe and it improves both colour and taste. Do this even if you have had to boil the tripe first.

2 Heat the oil and butter in a saucepan, add the onions and cook gently for 5 minutes. Add the garlic, ginger and all the spices. Stir over a low heat for 2–3 minutes.

3 Pour in the stock or water and bring to simmering point. Add the tripe with salt to taste and the vinegar.
4 Cover the pan and simmer gently for 15 minutes or until the tripe is tender. Check during this period and add a little more stock if required. Garnish and serve with a selection of diced, lightly cooked root vegetables and a green salad.

Freezing: cook to the end of step 4 but omit the garnish. Add this when reheating the defrosted curry.

Steak with Roquefort

This is a simple and very delicious dish using prime beef. When you feel you have gained good control over your arthritis you will want to proceed to more familiar foods, such as various meats and vegetarian dishes. At first it is wise to keep to fairly simple recipes so you can assess their effect easily.

In the case of this recipe do not serve it with an accompaniment of lots of nightshade foods, such as red and green (bell) peppers, tomatoes and potatoes, unless you have proved quite conclusively that these do not adversely affect your arthritis.

I have suggested Roquefort cheese as the topping for the steaks, as this is one of the cheeses you may well have eaten during the initial days of the diet and found it suits you well. Later on you can try other cheeses.

Ingredients   SERVES 4

METRIC (IMPERIAL)		AMERICAN
50g (2oz)	butter	¼ cup
100g (3½oz)	Roquefort cheese, crumbled	½ cup
1 tablespoon	finely chopped watercress leaves or parsley	1¼ tablespoons
4	fillet or rump steaks	4
to taste	sea salt and freshly ground black pepper	to taste
	To garnish	
	cooked mushrooms	
	watercress or parsley	

Method

1 Cream half the butter with the cheese and watercress or parsley.
2 Melt the remaining butter. Preheat the grill (broiler) and place a piece of foil over the grid of the grill pan. Brush this with a little of the melted butter.
3 Put the steaks on the foil, brush with butter and season to taste. Cook for 1–2 minutes only, then turn and brush with the rest of the butter. Cook for a further 2–6 minutes, depending upon how well done you like your steak.
4 Top the steaks with the Roquefort mixture about 2 minutes before the end of the cooking time, so the cheese just starts to melt. Garnish and serve.

Variations
Fillets of lamb (slices from the leg); or veal, chicken or turkey escalopes are excellent served the same way.

Do not freeze

Caribbean Lamb

When moving from the initial diet do try this dish, which gives lamb a great deal of flavour. The combination of chilli powder and refreshing pineapple is a very pleasant one. If you find that red and green (bell) peppers and chilli peppers do not affect your arthritis adversely then they can be included for extra taste and texture (see under Variations).

Add the chilli powder gradually as different makes vary in strength.

Ingredients

SERVES 4

METRIC (IMPERIAL)		AMERICAN
1 tablespoon	sunflower or groundnut oil	1¼ tablespoons
1	large onion, finely chopped	1
1 or 2	garlic cloves, finely chopped	1 or 2
½–1 teaspoon	chilli powder	½–1 teaspoon
8	lamb cutlets	8
150ml (5fl oz)	pineapple juice	⅔ cup
2–3	fresh pineapple slices	2–3
to taste	sea salt	to taste
	To garnish	
	diced seasonal vegetables	

Method

1 Heat the oil in a large frying pan (skillet), add the onion and cook gently for 5 minutes, then add the garlic and chilli powder. Stir over a low heat for 1 minute to bring out the flavour of the chilli.

2 Add the cutlets and turn around in the pan so they become coated with the chilli mixture, then sauté for 2 minutes on each side. Pour in the pineapple juice. Lower the heat and cook gently for 5 minutes or until the meat is almost cooked to your personal taste.

3 Meanwhile, cut away the peel from the pineapple and remove the centre hard core; dice the fruit neatly. Add to the pan and heat for 1–2 minutes. Garnish and serve.

Variations

✿ Use 4 large lamb chops instead of the cutlets. Remove any surplus fat from these before cooking.

✿ If you can eat peppers then use 1 deseeded and finely chopped chilli pepper instead of chilli powder and add 4 (5) tablespoons of diced red and green peppers just before the pineapple.

✿ Thin slices of lean, tender pork can be used instead of lamb cutlets.

Do not freeze

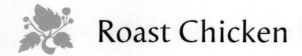

Roast Chicken

Roast chicken is allowed in the first few days of the diet, and is a good alternative to liver and fish. Ordinary meats are not recommended while you are following the first very important days of the diet. You can, however, serve turkey or game birds instead of chicken. If you can, use organically-reared poultry and game birds – these are now much more readily available.

Ingredients

SERVES 4

METRIC (IMPERIAL)		AMERICAN
1	young roasting chicken – about 2kg (4½ lb) in weight when trussed	1
2 tablespoons	butter, softened or olive oil	2½ tablespoons
to taste	sea salt and freshly ground black pepper	to taste
	flavourings – see opposite	

Method

1 Wash the chicken well in cold water, dry very thoroughly and put into a roasting tin (pan).

2 Good-quality birds can be roasted at a high temperature, so preheat the oven to 220°C/425°F/Gas Mark 7 or 210°C for a fan (convection) oven.

3 Brush the bird with the butter or olive oil, paying special attention to the breast. Season lightly.

4 Roast for about 1½ hours. You can baste the chicken with a little more butter or oil halfway through the cooking time. If cooking birds of a different weight, allow 15 minutes per 450g (1 lb) and 15 minutes extra.

5 Check carefully before serving. Pierce the bird where the leg joins the body and note the colour of the juice that flows. If it is at all pink then the bird needs a little longer cooking. When it is done the liquid will be clear.

6 Cover the bird with foil and leave to stand for 10 minutes before carving.

Variations

❋ Turkey, guinea fowl and game birds need about the same cooking time. (See Quail recipe on page 105.)

❋ With larger chickens or turkeys cook for half the time with the breast side downwards, then turn over to complete cooking. This helps to keep the breast moist.

❋ If you lay foil over the bird while roasting you need to allow another 5–10 minutes' cooking time.

❋ If you prefer slower roasting, preheat the oven to 180°C/350°F/Gas Mark 4 or 170°C for a fan (convection) oven. Allow 25 minutes per 450g (1 lb) and 25 minutes extra.

Flavourings

- ✽ Remember that you must avoid stuffings based on bread, sausages and bacon during the initial diet, and also the juice from citrus fruits.

- ✽ It is not recommended that moist mixtures, such as the Almond Relish on page 112, are put in the cavity of the bird. Put them under the skin at the neck end or between the skin and the breast meat.

- ✽ One or two peeled, whole garlic cloves or a peeled onion can be put into the body of the bird to give additional flavouring; or you could put a small bunch of mixed herbs such as parsley, chives, rosemary and thyme in the bird.

- ✽ The melted butter or oil used to brush over the bird can be flavoured with crushed garlic, grated root ginger, or chopped herbs such as thyme, tarragon or rosemary. Alternatively, mix a little sesame oil with the butter or olive oil and sprinkle sesame seeds over the bird when nearly cooked.

- ✽ If you find citrus fruit does not affect your arthritis then one of the best ways of flavouring chicken is with lemon. Put a halved lemon inside the bird and sprinkle the uncooked flesh with lemon juice before brushing with butter or oil.

Do not freeze

Turkey in Almond Sauce

This recipe uses turkey fillets (tender slices of breast meat), which are readily available. Check carefully to ensure you are buying fillets from organic turkey. The addition of a generous amount of coriander (cilantro) is important as it adds both flavour and colour. The sauce keeps the turkey flesh moist. If you dislike coriander use tarragon instead.

Ingredients

SERVES 4

METRIC (IMPERIAL)		AMERICAN
2 tablespoons	sunflower oil	2½ tablespoons
4	turkey fillets	4
2	small onions, finely chopped	2
1	garlic clove, finely chopped	1
50g (2oz)	blanched almonds, chopped	½ cup
to taste	sea salt and freshly ground black pepper	to taste
150ml (5fl oz)	crème fraîche	⅔ cup
4 tablespoons	chicken stock (bouillon) (see page 68)	5 tablespoons
1½ tablespoons	chopped coriander (cilantro)	1¾ tablespoons
	To garnish	
	paprika	
	coriander (cilantro) leaves	

Method

1 Heat the oil in a large frying pan (skillet), add the turkey fillets and cook fairly quickly until just golden brown on both sides. Remove from the pan with a perforated spoon or fish slice.

2 Add the onions to the pan and heat steadily for 4 minutes, then add the garlic and almonds and stir over a low heat until the almonds turn pale golden. The onions and garlic can be allowed to colour slightly too, but take care they do not burn.

3 Return the turkey to the pan and add seasoning. Stir in the crème fraîche and stock and simmer gently, stirring from time to time, for about 10 minutes or until the turkey is tender. Stir the coriander into the sauce just before serving. Top with a good dusting of paprika and coriander leaves. Serve with cooked brown rice and broccoli.

Variations

❉ Chicken breast portions can be cooked in the same way.

❉ Yoghurt or fromage frais could be used instead of crème fraîche.

Do not freeze

Quail with Blueberry Sauce

These small game birds are available throughout the year, and many supermarkets sell them ready boned. They are surprisingly meaty, so while I suggest allowing two per person, you may find one is enough for those with small appetites. A classic way of cooking quail is to wrap them in vine leaves. These prevent the delicate flesh from drying out, and are eaten along with the birds. Since these are not easy to obtain I often use tender leaves from a cabbage heart instead.

Ingredients

SERVES 4

METRIC (IMPERIAL)		AMERICAN
16–24	vine leaves or about 8 young cabbage leaves	16–24
to taste	sea salt and freshly ground black pepper	to taste
40g (1½oz)	butter	3 tablespoons
8	quail	8
	For the sauce	
150ml (5fl oz)	water	⅔ cup
1 tablespoon	honey	1¼ tablespoons
225g (8oz)	blueberries	1¾ cups

Method

1 Preheat the oven to 200°C/400°F/Gas Mark 6 or 190°C for a fan (convection) oven.

2 If using vine leaves wash and drain them well; if young they do not need heating but if older treat as cabbage. To heat the leaves, put a small amount of water into a saucepan, season lightly and bring to the boil. Add the leaves and boil for 1 minute only, then drain.

3 Place the leaves on a work surface. Spread the butter over the quail and season. Put each bird on enough leaves to enclose it completely when wrapped round.

4 Lift the parcels into a roasting tin (pan) or large ovenproof dish. Cover with foil or a lid and cook for 25–30 minutes.

5 To make the sauce, put the water and honey into a saucepan or bowl in the microwave. Bring to boiling point then add the blueberries and cook gently until tender.

6 Serve the quail parcels with the sauce poured around them. Roasted parsnips and/or sweet potatoes are excellent accompaniments; as is a crisp green salad.

Variation

Pheasant or guinea fowl: either of these birds can be cooked the same way. Spread the birds with Creamy Liver Pâté (see page 64) instead of butter.

Do not freeze

Salmis of Pheasant

This is a classic recipe that I have adjusted to avoid the use of flour, which contains wheat. Wheat flour is normally used to thicken the sauce, but here I have used cornflour (cornstarch), which comes from maize. Use cornflour for thickening gravies and other sauces too. Remember it has twice the thickening ability of ordinary flour, so where a standard recipe states 25g (1oz / ¼ cup) of flour use half that amount of cornflour.

This is an ideal dish to choose when entertaining as the pheasant looks pleasantly brown and there is no last-minute carving to be done.

Ingredients

SERVES 4–6

METRIC (IMPERIAL)		AMERICAN
2 large	pheasants, lightly roasted (see page 105)	2 large
900ml (1½ pints)	water	3¾ cups
to taste	sea salt and freshly ground black pepper	to taste
1 small bunch	mixed herbs – parsley, thyme, rosemary and marjoram	1 small bunch
2	fresh bay leaves	2
3	medium shallots, roughly chopped	3
3	medium carrots, roughly chopped	3
100g (3½oz)	button mushrooms	1 cup
½ teaspoon	turmeric	½ teaspoon
½ teaspoon	grated nutmeg	½ teaspoon
25g (1oz)	cornflour	¼ cup
3 tablespoons	sherry or port (not while on the strict diet) or water	3¾ tablespoons
	To garnish	
2	fresh pineapple rings	2

Method

1 Cut away the leg joints from the birds and halve them. Cut away the breast joints, making sure they are kept intact. If very large and plump these too can be halved.
2 Break the carcass into small pieces and place in a saucepan with the water and a little seasoning. Bring to the boil, then cover the pan and lower the heat.
3 Simmer for 45 minutes, then strain the liquid and return it to the pan.
4 Tie the herbs with cotton, so they can be removed easily, and put into the stock with the bay leaves, shallots, carrots, mushrooms, turmeric and nutmeg.
5 Simmer for 30 minutes; then remove the bunch of herbs and the bay leaves. Mix the cornflour

with the sherry, port or water, add to the hot liquid and stir to make a smooth, slightly thickened sauce.

6 Spoon the sauce and vegetables into a liquidizer or food processor and process to a thin, smooth purée. Taste and adjust the seasoning.

7 Preheat the oven to 170°C/325°F/Gas Mark 3 or 150°C for a fan (convection) oven.

8 Pour the sauce into a casserole and lay the pheasant joints in it. Cover and cook for 35–40 minutes. Do not overcook.

9 Cut away the skin and hard core from the pineapple rings. Dice the flesh and use to garnish the Salmis. Serve with a selection of vegetables. Mashed celeriac is a particularly good accompaniment.

Variation
Any game birds can be served in the same way.

Freezing: this particular dish is better not frozen.

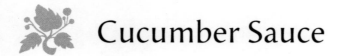

Cucumber Sauce

Do not overlook the value of cucumbers to add flavour and interest to salads and other dishes. Strips of cucumber are also excellent in stir-fries. While you are avoiding nightshade foods, such as tomatoes, sweet (bell) peppers and chilli peppers, you will find these cucumber sauces excellent alternatives with meat such as lamb or veal, or with chicken or fish.

Ingredients

SERVES 4

METRIC (IMPERIAL)		AMERICAN
115g (4oz)	small cucumber (peeled weight)	1 cup
25g (1oz)	butter	2 tablespoons
15g (½oz)	cornflour (cornstarch)	2 tablespoons
300ml (10fl oz)	milk	1¼ cups
2 teaspoons or to taste	apple, cider or rice vinegar	2 teaspoons or to taste
to taste	sea salt and freshly ground white pepper	to taste
to taste	herbs, see step 4	to taste

Method

1 Dice the cucumber, then sieve or liquidize to make a purée.
2 Heat the butter in a saucepan, stir in the cornflour and continue stirring over a low heat for 1–2 minutes. Gradually stir in the milk, then bring the sauce to the boil and whisk or stir briskly until thickened. Stir in the cucumber purée.
3 Lower the heat and simmer gently for 5 minutes, then remove from the heat and whisk in the vinegar.
4 Add a little salt and pepper, then the chopped herbs. Choose mint if serving the sauce with lamb; tarragon or rosemary with chicken; fennel or dill leaves with fish. (Parsley and basil are other herbs that blend well with cucumber.) Heat gently, without boiling, then serve.

Variations

* Instead of making the sauce simply mix the cucumber purée, or peeled and coarsely grated cucumber, with 250ml (8fl oz/1 cup) of thick yoghurt. Add the vinegar, seasoning and herbs as in the recipe. Serve cold.
* *Cucumber Coulis:* peel and coarsely grate 1 small or ½ large cucumber. Mix with 1 (1¼) tablespoons apple, cider or rice vinegar, seasoning and herbs to taste.

Freezing: neither version of the sauce freezes well, though the coulis can be frozen. It is better to add the herbs after defrosting.

Pesto Sauce

This is a classic sauce to serve with pasta. If you are avoiding wheat products while on the Eat to Beat Arthritis *Diet you can still enjoy this sauce with gluten-free pasta, or use it to add extra flavour to fish and a variety of cooked vegetables. If you find that wheat does not adversely affect your arthritis, you can enjoy this sauce with every kind of pasta. Make the sauce with a mixture of herbs or just basil leaves.*

Ingredients

SERVES 4

METRIC (IMPERIAL)		AMERICAN
about 8	flat parsley leaves, coarsely shredded	about 8
2 small sprigs	marjoram or oregano	2 small sprigs
about 20	basil leaves	about 20
2	garlic cloves	2
75g (scant 3oz)	Parmesan cheese, grated	good ½ cup
5 tablespoons	extra virgin olive oil	6 ¼ tablespoons
100g (3½oz)	pine (pignolia) nuts	1 cup
to taste	sea salt and freshly ground black pepper	to taste

Method

1 Put all the ingredients into a liquidizer or food processor and process to a thick purée. Serve cold.

Variations

* Often 1–2 tablespoons of melted butter are liquidized with the other ingredients to give greater richness to the sauce.
* You can add a second cheese. Pecorino (romano) is an Italian choice, but 2–3 tablespoons of goat's cheese could be used while on the diet.
* Use blanched almonds instead of pine nuts.

Do not freeze

Vinaigrette Dressing

This is the basic dressing for most salads though it can be varied in many ways. Virgin olive oil, which comes from the first pressing of the olives, is the classic choice for a good salad dressing but there will be occasions when you prefer to use other oils. If you are anxious to keep your fat intake low, look for light olive oil. Organic olive and other oils are also obtainable.

Wine vinegar was traditionally mixed with the oil but today there are many other types on the market, and these add individual touches to the dressing. Well-matured balsamic vinegar, though very expensive, can be added in very small quantities to give a delicious sweetness. If you find that citrus fruits do not affect your arthritis adversely you can substitute lemon or lime juice for vinegar.

Ingredients

SERVES 4

METRIC (IMPERIAL)		AMERICAN
1 teaspoon	Dijon mustard	1 teaspoon
150ml (5fl oz)	virgin olive oil	⅔ cup
4 tablespoons	red or white wine vinegar	5 tablespoons
to taste	sea salt and freshly ground black pepper	to taste
1 teaspoon	sugar or honey	1 teaspoon

Method

1 Put all the ingredients into a bowl or screw-topped jar and whisk or shake briskly. A larger quantity could be mixed together in a liquidizer (blender).

2 Use as required. Any dressing left over can be stored in a covered container for several days in a cool place.

Variations

✽ For a lighter dressing use half olive and half sunflower or other oil. To change the flavour use 2–3 teaspoons sesame seed oil and omit this amount of olive oil. Walnut or other nut oils can be used in the same way.

✽ Substitute 1 tablespoon balsamic vinegar for the same amount of wine vinegar. Do not use more than this as the flavour would be too strong for most salads. You can change the proportions of oil and vinegar according to personal taste.

✽ Add crushed garlic cloves and chopped mixed herbs; or crushed root ginger, galangal or finely chopped lemon grass to the dressing.

✽ Add spices such as chilli powder or cayenne pepper to give a hotter dressing.

✽ If you are able to eat nightshade vegetables, add finely diced sun-dried tomatoes, sweet (bell) peppers or hot chilli peppers.

Do not freeze

Mayonnaise

While you are avoiding as many prepared foods as possible it is advisable to make your own mayonnaise. This is not difficult, particularly if you use a liquidizer or food processor.

Bring the eggs out of the refrigerator about 1 hour before making the sauce as this helps to insure a smooth mayonnaise.

Ingredients

SERVES 4–6

METRIC (IMPERIAL)		AMERICAN
2	yolks, from large eggs	2
1 teaspoon	Dijon mustard	1 teaspoon
to taste	sea salt and freshly ground white pepper	to taste
up to 300ml (10fl oz)	extra virgin olive oil*	up to 1¼ cups
3 teaspoons	white wine or rice vinegar	3 teaspoons
1 tablespoon	very hot water, optional	1¼ tablespoons

*This amount of oil is the maximum most people would like, so you can reduce it to give a less oily dressing.

The choice of oils can be varied, see under Vinaigrette Dressing, opposite

Method

1 Put the egg yolks into a bowl, add the mustard and seasoning and stir well. Gradually add the oil. The best way to do this is to hold the container in one hand and trickle the oil slowly on to the yolks, while stirring or whisking briskly with the other hand. Stop immediately if there is the slightest sign of the sauce curdling (separating). If this happens, whisk very hard indeed.

2 If the sauce has already curdled, break a third egg yolk into a second bowl and gradually whisk in the curdled sauce. When sufficient oil for your taste has been absorbed and the sauce has thickened, stir in the vinegar.

3 If the mayonnaise is very thick and you would prefer a lighter sauce, whisk in the hot water.

Variations

❋ *Using a liquidizer or food processsor:* when making mayonnaise in this way you can use whole eggs, rather than just the yolks. This produces a lighter sauce. Put the whole eggs or egg yolks into the goblet or bowl, add the seasonings and, *with the motor running,* slowly pour in the oil. When the sauce has thickened add the vinegar, and hot water if using this.

❋ *Hard-boiled (Hard-cooked) Egg Mayonnaise:* if you prefer not to use uncooked eggs substitute the yolks of 2 hard-boiled eggs for the raw egg yolks.

Do not freeze

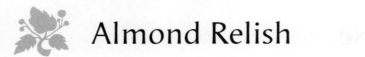# Almond Relish

This relish is included in the first week's diet as an accompaniment to chicken. It is delicious with most poultry, so suggestions for varying the flavour are given. Lemon juice would normally be used in such a recipe but in this version the wonderful herb lemon balm is used, along with lemon grass.

Ingredients

SERVES 4–6

METRIC (IMPERIAL)		AMERICAN
2 tablespoons	olive oil	2½ tablespoons
1	medium onion, finely chopped	1
50g (2oz)	raisins	⅓ cup
1 large	barely ripe dessert pear, peeled and finely diced	1 large
115g (4oz)	tenderized (ready to eat) dried apricots, finely chopped	⅔ cup
115g (4oz)	whole or blanched almonds, chopped	1 cup
50g (2oz)	ground almonds	½ cup
1	lemon grass stalk, finely chopped	1
1 tablespoon	finely chopped lemon balm or ½ tablespoon dried lemon balm	1¼ tablespoons
to taste	sea salt and freshly ground black pepper	to taste

Method

1 Heat the oil in a saucepan and cook the onion for 5 minutes; remove from the heat. Stir in the remaining ingredients and season.

2 Some of the stuffing can be inserted under the skin at the neck end of the bird and the remainder cooked in a separate dish, which should be covered.

3 Cook for 40 minutes in a preheated oven set to 190°C/375°F/Gas Mark 5 or 180°C for a fan (convection) oven.

Variations

❋ If you find that citrus fruit does not affect your arthritis substitute 1–1¼ (1¼–1½) tablespoons of lemon juice for the lemon grass and lemon balm.

❋ This stuffing is equally good with turkey or guinea fowl. You could use walnuts instead of almonds.

❋ With duck or goose: substitute a large apple for the pear. Use a cooking (baking) apple to give a sharper flavour and a dessert apple for a sweeter taste.

Do not freeze

Herbed Polenta

Polenta is made from maize flour and is very filling, so makes an ideal alternative to wheat products and potatoes. Authentic polenta needs to be cooked very slowly and stirred constantly, but this recipe is based on the quick-cooking variety. It is possible to buy ready-cooked polenta but wiser to avoid this while on the strict diet. If you wish to make the dish with authentic polenta see Variations below.

Ingredients

SERVES 4

METRIC (IMPERIAL)		AMERICAN
900ml (1½ pints)	water	3¾ cups
1 teaspoon	sea salt	1 teaspoon
225g (8oz)	instant polenta	1½ cups
good pinch	freshly ground black pepper	good pinch
2 tablespoons	finely chopped parsley	2½ tablespoons
1 tablespoon	finely snipped chives	1¼ tablespoons
1 tablespoon	olive oil	1¼ tablespoons
	For frying	
3 tablespoons	olive oil	3¾ tablespoons

Method

1 Pour the water into a saucepan and bring to the boil. Add the salt, then slowly and steadily pour in the polenta.

2 Lower the heat, add the pepper and herbs and continue stirring until thickened; this takes about 4 minutes.

3 Brush a shallow dish or tin with the oil and spoon the polenta in to it, spreading evenly to give a depth of about 2.5cm (1 inch). Leave until cool.

4 Dip a sharp knife into boiling water and cut the polenta into fingers. You could use a pastry cutter instead to give more interesting shapes.

5 Heat the olive oil in a frying pan (skillet) and fry the polenta on either side until golden brown. Serve hot with cooked fish, liver, poultry or game.

Variations

If using authentic polenta, let it run through your fingers like sand into the boiling salted water. Cook steadily, stirring all the time, for about 45 minutes. Add the pepper and herbs as described above.

Freezing: polenta freezes well. Open-freeze, then pack.

Savoury Omelettes

An omelette is a quick and easy dish for any meal of the day. I have suggested serving them as a breakfast dish. One filling – of prawns (shrimp) – may be unusual for breakfast but it insures that you have fish on that particular day.

Ingredients

METRIC (IMPERIAL)		AMERICAN
2 or 3	large eggs	2 or 3
1 tablespoon	water, optional	1¼ tablespoons
to taste	sea salt and freshly ground black pepper	to taste
25g (1oz)	butter	2 tablespoons
few drops	olive or sunflower oil, optional	few drops

Method

1. Lightly beat the eggs with a fork; do not whisk hard, as that aerates the mixture too much and makes it become slightly drier in cooking. Add the water if desired; this gives a lighter texture. Season to taste.
2. Heat the butter in a small omelette or frying pan (skillet). Ideally this should be no larger than 12–15 cm (5–6 inches) in diameter. Too large a pan means the eggs are spread too thinly. Adding the oil is not essential but helps prevent the omelette sticking to the pan.
3. When the butter, or butter and oil, is hot pour in the eggs and cook over a moderate heat. Leave undisturbed for about 30 seconds to allow the omelette to begin to set on the underside.
4. This is the time to 'work' the omelette. Loosen the eggs from around the sides of the pan, then tilt it so that the still-liquid egg runs from the top to the sides of the pan. Do this until the omelette is set to your taste.
5. Fold or roll the omelette away from the handle, tip on to a hot plate and serve at once.

Variation

To give a richer flavour and help prevent the omelette sticking to the pan, stir 1 (1¼) tablespoons of melted butter or olive oil into the eggs just before cooking.

Flavourings and Fillings

* Add a mixture of freshly chopped herbs to the eggs; this is known as *aux fine herbes*.
* *Cheese Omelette:* either add a small amount of grated cheese to the beaten eggs, or cover the top of the cooked omelette with grated cheese or spoonfuls of cheese before folding. For a main meal the omelette can be filled with a thick cheese sauce. Often this is mixed with lightly cooked vegetables.
* *Fish Omelette:* mix flaked, cooked fish with the beaten eggs and add chopped herbs to taste.
* *Mushroom Omelette:* either add finely diced, uncooked mushrooms to the beaten eggs, or fill the cooked omelette with small whole, or sliced, mushrooms of various kinds, precooked in a little oil or butter.
* *Prawn (Shrimp) Omelette:* either add a few spoonfuls of peeled and finely chopped cooked prawns (shelled shrimp) to the eggs, or heat whole prawns in a little hot butter and add to the omelette just before folding. If using frozen prawns defrost and dry well on paper towels before chopping or heating. (Avoid this omelette until you have finished the initial diet.)
* *Thai Omelette:* to give the eggs a taste of the Far East flavour them with a little finely chopped lemon grass and grated root ginger or ground ginger. Fill the cooked omelette with hot, crisp bean sprouts.
* *Tomato Omelette:* if you are satisfied that tomatoes do not adversely affect your arthritis fill the cooked omelette with thinly sliced, raw tomatoes or a thick tomato purée before folding.
* *Vegetable Omelette:* fill the cooked omelette with lightly cooked, diced root or other vegetables. (While on the diet avoid those in the nightshade family – listed page 39.)

Tortilla (Spanish Omelette)

This is a different kind of omelette, eaten cold as well as hot, and solid enough for a packed lunch. The traditional vegetables are potatoes and onions with perhaps a little chopped garlic. However, potatoes must be avoided during the initial days of the diet, so instead use rings of onion with sliced parsnips, carrots and sweet potato or yam, steamed or boiled in a very little salted water until just tender.

Strain well then heat in a little olive oil or oil and butter in the omelette or frying pan. Beat the eggs as instructed in step 1, pour over the hot vegetables and cook steadily until the eggs are set. Do not try and tilt the pan when making this omelette and do not fold. Simply slide onto a plate. Serve hot or cold cut into wedges.

Sweet Potato Rösti

Rösti is normally made with ordinary potatoes, but sweet potatoes or yams make an excellent alternative. The Swiss-inspired dish retains the full flavour of the vegetables, and is excellent served with main dishes. The chives or spring onions (scallions) are not essential, but give the sweet potatoes a more savoury flavour. Sweet potatoes and yams cook more rapidly than ordinary potatoes so do make sure they are not overcooked before grating them. The steaming time will vary slightly according to the shape of the vegetables.

Sweet potatoes and yams can also be baked in their skins, boiled, mashed, fried and roasted just like ordinary potatoes. However, they have a fairly high sugar content so they burn more easily when roasted or fried.

Ingredients

Serves 4

METRIC (IMPERIAL)		AMERICAN
450g (1 lb)	sweet potatoes or yams	1 lb
3 tablespoons	very finely chopped chives or spring onions (scallions)	3¾ tablespoons
to taste	sea salt and freshly ground black pepper	to taste
	For frying	
50g (2oz)	butter	¼ cup
2 teaspoons	sunflower or groundnut oil	2 teaspoons

Method

1　Scrub the potatoes or yams and place in a steamer. Cook for 6–8 minutes, or until the outsides begin to feel slightly softened.

2　Cool slightly, then remove the skins and rub the vegetables against a coarse grater. Let the flesh fall into a bowl as you do so. Mix in the chives or spring onions and a generous amount of seasoning.

3　Heat the butter and oil in a large frying pan (skillet). Add the potato mixture and spread out flat. Cook slowly for 7 minutes or until brown on the underside. Hold a large plate over the top of the frying pan and invert the pan so the rösti falls on to the plate with the browned side uppermost.

4　Slide the rösti back into the frying pan so the browned side is uppermost. Cook for 6–7 minutes, then tip on to a serving dish and cut into portions.

Variations

* Instead of one large potato cake make several smaller cakes, turning them over when browned on the under side, then cooking until brown on the second side.
* Use all sunflower or other oil instead of butter and a little oil.
* Parsnips and celeriac: both these vegetables make excellent rösti, either alone or mixed together. Peeled and grated raw vegetables can be used but this means a longer frying time and the need to use rather more butter and oil.

Freezing: rösti freezes well.

Minted Beans and Cabbage

This satisfying blend of vegetables and apple could make a good vegetarian main meal (see under Variations). It is also a good accompaniment to liver.

In the initial stages of the diet it is recommended that as many vegetables as possible are eaten raw. Undoubtedly there will be times when you would prefer hot vegetables; just make sure they are given the shortest possible cooking time, in the minimum of boiling water or, better still, that they are steamed. They will then retain the maximum vitamin and mineral content.

Often the thought of having several saucepans in use deters people from cooking a selection of vegetables, but if you cut them to a size that insures they need similar cooking times then they can be placed in one saucepan or steamer. Occasionally you will need to add vegetables at different times, as in the recipe below.

Ingredients

SERVES 4

METRIC (IMPERIAL)		AMERICAN
675–900g (1½–2 lb)	fresh broad (fava) beans•	1½–2 lb
1 tablespoon	olive oil	1¼ tablespoons
1	large onion, cut into rings	1
300ml (10fl oz)	water	1¼ cups
to taste	sea salt and freshly ground black pepper	to taste
1 teaspoon	grainy mustard	1 teaspoon
115g (4oz)	courgettes (zucchini), cut into thin strips about 5cm (2 inches) long	¼ lb
about ¼	red cabbage heart, finely shredded	about ¼
2	dessert apples, cored but not peeled, and thinly sliced	2
2 tablespoons	chopped mint	2½ tablespoons

•you need about 350g (12oz/2¼ cups) after shelling

Method

1 Remove the beans from the pods. Heat the oil in a saucepan, add the onion and sauté gently for 4 minutes. Pour in the water and add a little salt, pepper and the mustard. Bring to the boil.

2 Add the beans and cook steadily for 5 minutes, then put in the courgettes, cabbage and apples and continue cooking for 3–4 minutes. Stir in half the mint and strain. Keep the liquid as it makes a good vegetable stock (bouillon).

3 Spoon the mixture into a heated dish and top with the remaining mint.

Variations

- If the beans are very young they can be cooked in the pods; simply remove the ends. If you can do this allow only about 450g (1 lb).

- Dried beans: when fresh broad beans are not in season make this dish with cooked dried beans. Remember that when cooking dried beans, especially red kidney beans, they must be given 10 minutes fast boiling during the cooking process, to remove toxins. Follow step 1, then add the beans with the courgettes and other ingredients.

- Canned beans: if using canned beans, rinse and drain them well. Add in step 2 after the vegetables and apples.

- For a main dish: add 225g (8oz/½ cup) diced tofu to the pan with the beans or top the cooked dish with mint and a thick layer of blanched, flaked almonds.

Do not freeze

Garlic Mushrooms

This dish can be served as a starter or light snack. There are many kinds of mushrooms on sale but I find that medium-sized button ones hold the garlic filling best.

Ingredients

SERVES 4–6 AS A STARTER OR 2–3 AS A SNACK

METRIC (IMPERIAL)		AMERICAN
	For the filling	
3–4	garlic cloves, peeled	3–4
115g (4oz)	butter, slightly softened	½ cup
2 tablespoons	very finely chopped parsley	2½ tablespoons
to taste	sea salt and freshly ground black pepper	to taste
450g (1 lb)	medium button or small cup mushrooms	1 lb

Method

1 Finely chop or crush the garlic cloves. Mix with the butter, parsley and seasoning.
2 Remove the stalks from the mushrooms and keep them for making stock (bouillon). Wipe the caps well and place in an ovenproof dish with the stalk sides uppermost. Fill with the garlic mixture.
3 Preheat the oven to 200°C/400°F/Gas Mark 6 or 190°C for a fan (convection) oven. Bake for 10 minutes and serve hot with a green salad.

Variations
✿ Use other herbs, such as a mixture of chives, thyme and oregano instead of parsley.
✿ Cook in the microwave on High for about 6 minutes.
✿ *Cheese-topped Garlic Mushrooms:* when you can have a choice of cheese, cover the filled mushrooms with a thin layer of finely grated Cheddar or other good cooking cheese before baking.

Do not freeze

Grilled Spiced Sardines (page 85) served with Sweet Potato Rosti (page 116–17). Do not eat the lemon while on the diet.

Liver Stir-fry (page 81) and Seafood Stir-fry (page 80–81).

Peaches in Honey and Almonds (page 133).

Strawberry & Grape Sorbet (page 135) served with Macaroons (page 140).

Avocado and Pineapple Salad

This unusual salad not only makes a delicious start to a meal but can be served equally well as a dessert (see under Variations).

Ingredients

METRIC (IMPERIAL)		AMERICAN
	For the dressing	
4 tablespoons	single (light) cream	5 tablespoons
1 tablespoon	cider or apple vinegar	1¼ tablespoons
1 tablespoon	chopped coriander (cilantro)	1¼ tablespoons
	For the salad	
4	slices fresh pineapple	4
2	ripe avocados	2
to taste	sea salt and freshly ground white pepper	to taste
to taste	rocket (arugula) leaves	to taste

Method

1 Mix together the ingredients for the dressing. It is important to have this ready before cutting the avocados, to prevent the fruit discolouring.

2 Remove the skin and centre hard core from the pineapple, then cut the rings into small neat portions. Add any juice that flows from the pineapple to the dressing.

3 Halve, peel and stone the avocados. Cut the flesh into neat dice or small balls with a vegetable scoop. Add to the dressing. Taste and add a very little seasoning if desired.

4 Arrange the rocket leaves on individual plates. Top with the avocado and dressing, then with the pineapple.

Variation

To turn this into a dessert, use double (heavy) cream instead of single (light) cream. Sweeten this with a little clear honey and flavour it with a teaspoon of chopped mint. Omit the vinegar, coriander and seasoning. Stir the avocado into the cream. Spoon into individual glasses and top with diced pineapple and mint leaves.

Do not freeze

Buckwheat Salad

In spite of the name, buckwheat is not a wheat but a member of the rhubarb family. As it is filling it can take the place of potatoes while you are finding out if these have any adverse affect on your arthritis. It is an excellent ingredient in a salad. No cooking is required – just soften the grains with boiling liquid.

Ingredients

SERVES 4

METRIC (IMPERIAL)		AMERICAN
115g (4 oz)	coarse buckwheat	½ cup
300ml (10fl oz)	water	1¼ cups
¼ teaspoon	saffron strands or powder, optional	¼ teaspoon
2	pomegranates	2
	mixed salad greens	
2 tablespoons	Vinaigrette Dressing (see page 110)	2½ tablespoons
2	kiwi fruit	2

Method

1. Put the buckwheat into a bowl. Bring the water to the boil, add the saffron, if using, and pour over the buckwheat. Stir briskly, then leave until cold.
2. Strain the buckwheat, discarding the surplus moisture. Transfer to a large plate to dry out slightly.
3. Halve the pomegranates and scoop out the juicy seeds; mix with the buckwheat.
4. Arrange the salad greens on individual plates and sprinkle with the dressing. Make a neat mound of buckwheat in the middle. Peel and slice the kiwi fruits and arrange around the wheat.

Variations

* Instead of saffron use a little turmeric. This, like saffron, colours the grains and makes them look more attractive.
* If you find tomatoes have no adverse affect on your arthritis you could use freshly prepared tomato juice instead of water. Boil and use in the same way as the water. Omit the pomegranate seeds in this case and add finely diced cucumber instead.

Do not freeze

Fruit and Vegetable Salads

These simple salads can be served at any time of the day. They may well take the place of the biscuits you previously enjoyed midmorning or at tea time.

They make very good hors d'oeuvre at the start of a meal, or accompaniments to both hot and cold dishes.

Apple and Beetroot (Beet)

Mix equal quantities of peeled and diced cooked beetroot with peeled, cored and diced dessert apple. Add a few raisins and moisten with Vinaigrette Dressing (see page 110). Serve on watercress. This is particularly good with cold or hot duck. In this case, add finely chopped sage leaves.

Avocado, Celery and Cucumber

Pour 4 (5) tablespoons of Vinaigrette Dressing (see page 110) into a bowl. Halve, stone and peel 1 large or 2 small avocados. Cut the flesh into neat dice. Put into the dressing together with 6 (7½) tablespoons of finely diced celery heart and the same amount of unpeeled, thinly sliced cucumber. Serve on a bed of mixed lettuce leaves.

Green Bean, Apple and Pineapple

Cook diced green beans until tender. Strain and mix with equal amounts of unpeeled, diced dessert apple and diced fresh pineapple. Moisten with any pineapple juice that flows as you cut the fruit, and a very little extra virgin olive oil. Serve on a bed of rocket (arugula) and top with chopped walnuts. Red chillies make a colourful garnish if you find you can eat these.

Pear, Peach and Almond

Mix equal amounts of peeled, sliced dessert pears and peeled, halved and stoned ripe peaches. Make a dressing with a little apple vinegar, honey to sweeten and sea salt. Turn the fruits in this to moisten and retain their colour. Serve on a bed of shredded lettuce and top with whole blanched almonds.

Sweetcorn

Cook 2 large corn cobs, then strip away the kernels and put into 3 (3¾) tablespoons of Mayonnaise (see page 111) or yoghurt. Spoon on to a bed of lettuce and sliced cucumber and garnish with thin slices of ripe melon.

Do not freeze

Grilled Goat's Cheese Salad

Combining hot ingredients with cold gives a modern touch to this salad. It makes a good dinner-party dish as you can prepare the ingredients in advance and assemble them while grilling (broiling) the cheese at the last minute.

Ingredients

SERVES 4

METRIC (IMPERIAL)		AMERICAN
	For the dressing	
3 tablespoons	extra virgin olive oil	3¾ tablespoons
1½ tablespoons	cider vinegar	2 tablespoons
1 teaspoon	balsamic vinegar	1 teaspoon
2 teaspoons	clear honey	2 teaspoons
1	garlic clove, finely chopped	1
2 teaspoons	chopped oregano	2 teaspoons
1 teaspoon	Dijon mustard	1 teaspoon
to taste	sea salt and freshly ground black pepper	to taste
	For the salad	
2	celery sticks, chopped	2
2	dessert apples, peeled, cored and sliced	2
	mixed salad greens, shredded	
	For the cheese	
4	small individual goat's cheeses	4
1 tablespoon	butter, melted	1¼ tablespoons

Method

1 Mix together the dressing ingredients. Add the celery and apple and leave to marinate for 30 minutes. Arrange the salad greens on individual plates and top with the celery, apple and dressing.
2 Place the cheeses under the preheated grill (broiler), brush with the butter and heat for 2–3 minutes or until the cheese is just starting to melt.
3 Spoon on to the salad and serve at once.

Do not freeze

Liver and Herb Salad

The liver for this salad can be grilled (broiled) or sautéed – see pages 89 and 90. Whichever method you choose, cut the still-warm cooked liver into narrow strips and marinate it in the dressing so it absorbs the flavour and becomes beautifully moist.

Ingredients

SERVES 1

METRIC (IMPERIAL)		AMERICAN
2	slices of calves' or lambs' liver or about 4 chicken livers, cooked	2
	For the dressing	
2 tablespoons	virgin olive oil	2½ tablespoons
1 tablespoon	rice or red wine vinegar	1¼ tablespoons
½ teaspoon	grated root ginger	½ teaspoon
1 teaspoon	finely chopped lemon grass	1 teaspoon
2 teaspoons	chopped basil	2 teaspoons
1 teaspoon	chopped tarragon	1 teaspoon
1 teaspoon	honey	1 teaspoon
	For the salad	
a few	rocket (arugula) leaves	a few
a few	watercress sprigs	a few
a few	lettuce leaves	a few
1 or 2	fresh pineapple slices, diced	1 or 2

Method

1 Cut the cooked liver into narrow strips while still warm. Mix the ingredients for the dressing together and pour into a shallow casserole. Add the liver, cover and leave in the refrigerator for several hours or overnight.

2 Arrange the salad ingredients on a large plate. Scatter the strips of liver on top and sprinkle with the dressing.

Do not freeze

Mushroom and Liver Salad

The combination of hot mushrooms and a cold salad is very pleasant. Although the liver is given as cooked in the recipe you could have it uncooked if you enjoy it that way.

Ingredients

SERVES 1

METRIC (IMPERIAL)		AMERICAN
2 teaspoons	olive oil	2 teaspoons
100g (3½oz)	mushrooms, preferably chestnut, wiped and thickly sliced	1 cup
to taste	sea salt and freshly ground black pepper	to taste
100g (3½oz)	cooked liver (see page 89), neatly diced	½ cup
2 tablespoons	pine (pignolia) nuts	2½ tablespoons
to taste	green salad leaves	to taste
to taste	Vinaigrette Dressing (see page 110)	to taste

Method

1 Heat the oil in a frying pan (skillet) and cook the mushrooms for 5 minutes. Season to taste and keep warm while preparing the salad.
2 Mix the liver and nuts with the salad leaves and sprinkle with a little dressing. Pile on to a serving plate and top with the warm mushroom slices.

Variations

❧ Use cooked chicken livers and walnuts instead of mushrooms and pine nuts.
❧ Add a few tablespoons of alfalfa sprouts to the salad.
❧ Microwave: cook the mushrooms in just one teaspoon of oil in a bowl in the microwave for about 2 minutes.

Do not freeze

Sweet Potato Salad

Sweet potatoes or yams make a delicious and very satisfying salad. It is better to steam the vegetable before peeling as it will then be firmer and easier to dice neatly.

Ingredients

SERVES 4

METRIC (IMPERIAL)		AMERICAN
	For the dressing	
2 tablespoons	olive oil	2½ tablespoons
2 tablespoons	cider vinegar	2½ tablespoons
3 tablespoons	single (light) cream	3¾ tablespoons
1 teaspoon	clear honey	1 teaspoon
2 teaspoons	chopped mint	2 teaspoons
2 teaspoons	snipped chives	2 teaspoons
to taste	sea salt and freshly ground white pepper	to taste
	For the salad	
1	large sweet potato	1
2	dessert apples, unpeeled but cored and sliced	2
to taste	salad greens	to taste

Method

1 Mix all the ingredients for the dressing together in a large bowl. Scrub the sweet potato, place in a steamer with a little salt and pepper and steam for about 8–10 minutes, or until tender but not over-soft.

2 Put the prepared apples into the dressing. Make sure it covers them completely, to prevent discolouration.

3 When the sweet potato is cooked, peel it and cut the flesh into neat small dice. Carefully stir into the dressing, taking care to keep the dice unbroken. Spoon the potato, apple and dressing mixture over the salad greens and serve.

Do not freeze

Main Dish Salads

It is important to have as many of the salad ingredients uncooked as possible. If you have not tried shredded raw spinach, Brussels sprouts and other green vegetables you will find their flavour unexpectedly delicious.

Try grated, raw root vegetables too – carrots are familiar but young celeriac, parsnips, turnips and swedes (rutabaga) are also excellent. A suitable dressing for these salads is found on page 110 and hints on varying this are given below. All these salads serve four.

Duck and Apple Salad

Remove the skin from a whole cooked bird or cooked duck portions, then cut the flesh into long narrow strips.

Make the Vinaigrette Dressing on page 110 and add to this a crushed garlic clove, 1–2 teaspoons of grated root ginger and 2 teaspoons of chopped sage leaves. Put the duck strips into the dressing and leave for 30 minutes.

Halve, but do not peel, 2 red-skinned dessert apples; remove the cores and cut each apple into about 8 slices. Add to the dressing together with 50g (2oz/⅓ cup) of raisins.

Prepare a large platter of shredded raw spinach, grated carrots, grated turnip and lightly cooked chopped green beans. Spoon the duck, apple and dressing on top.

Variations

Cooked chicken, pheasant or guinea fowl could be used instead of cooked duck. Substitute finely chopped rosemary for the sage.

Roquefort and Asparagus Salad*

If the asparagus is very young you could serve it raw, but most people prefer it lightly cooked. Put the asparagus into lightly salted water and cook for just a few minutes; the stalks should still be firm and a little crunchy. Drain carefully and arrange on a bed of sliced cucumber and shredded raw spinach.

Make the Vinaigrette Dressing on page 110, then add 150g (5oz/1 cup) of finely diced Roquefort cheese and 2 (2½) tablespoons of snipped chives. Spoon over the salad.

*Do not serve this salad during the initial diet.

Lentil and Pine (Pignolia) Nut Salad

Any kind of lentils can be used but the famous Puy type have the best flavour. First peel and chop 2 onions and 2 garlic cloves. Heat 2 (2½) tablespoons of olive oil in a large saucepan, add the onions and cook gently for 2 minutes, then put in the garlic and cook for a further 2 minutes.

Pour 600ml (1 pint/2½ cups) of water into the pan. Bring to the boil, then add 115g (4oz/½ cup) lentils together with a little sea salt and freshly ground black pepper. Cover the pan and cook steadily for 15–25 minutes until tender but still firm. Puy lentils take the longer time. Do not over-cook, the lentils should retain a firm texture.

If any liquid remains, drain well. Leave until cold, then stir in 2 peeled and finely chopped dessert apples or small ripe pears, 115g (4oz/1 cup) pine nuts, 2 (2½) tablespoons chopped parsley and 2 (2½) tablespoons finely snipped chives.

Mound the lentil mixture on individual plates and surround with a border of watercress and rocket (arugula) leaves. Spoon a little Vinaigrette Dressing over just before serving.

Variations

* *Bean and Walnut Salad:* use cooked borlotti (pinto) beans, or raw or lightly cooked broad (fava) beans when in season instead of lentils; and coarsely chopped walnuts instead of pine (pignolia) nuts.

* If you find you can eat tomatoes with no ill effect add 2 large peeled, deseeded and chopped tomatoes to the onions and garlic before adding the water.

Do not freeze

Apricot Rice Pudding

Rice is one of the familiar foods you can enjoy on your initial diet. Perhaps it is years since you made a rice pudding – now classed as old-fashioned. The recipe below brings the pudding up to date by using coconut milk and dried apricots, as well as the more conventional ingredients.

If you are allergic to cows' milk choose goats' or soya milk instead. I suggest sweetening the pudding with honey but other forms of sweetening are date syrup and agave syrup (both natural products), which are sold in health food stores. If you have none of these and use sugar, make sure it is natural (untreated) and organic.

Ingredients

SERVES 4

METRIC (IMPERIAL)		AMERICAN
115g (4oz)	tenderized (ready to eat) dried apricots	¼ lb
85g (3oz)	raisins	½ cup
50g (2oz)	short grain (pudding) rice	4 tablespoons
300ml (10fl oz)	milk	1¼ cups
300ml (10fl oz)	coconut milk	1¼ cups
1 tablespoon	honey	1¼ tablespoons
150ml (5fl oz)	apple juice	⅔ cup

Method

1 Preheat the oven to 150°C/300°F/Gas Mark 2 or 140°C for a fan (convection) oven.

2 Cut the apricots into small pieces. Put half of these and half the raisins into a 900–1200 ml (1½–2 pint/3¾–5 cup) pie or soufflé dish.

3 Rinse the rice in cold water and drain well. Add to the dried fruit together with the two kinds of milk and the honey. Stir gently to mix the ingredients and bake for 1½–2 hours. Reduce the heat slightly if the top of the pudding is becoming too brown. Stirring halfway through will help give a creamy texture.

4 Meanwhile, add the remaining apricots and raisins to the apple juice. Just before the pudding is ready, heat this mixture in a saucepan, or in a bowl in the microwave, until the fruit is well softened and most of the liquid has evaporated.

5 Serve topped with the hot apricot and raisin mixture.

Variation
If more convenient bake the pudding in a slower oven, 140°C/275°F/Gas Mark 1 or 130°C for a fan (convection) oven.

Do not freeze

Mango Foule

I have used the original name for this dessert instead of the more familiar word 'fool'. It comes from the French verb fouler, *meaning to chop, and the fruit should be finely diced rather than being made into a smooth purée. You can, of course, please yourself as to how you prepare it, but I think diced fruit makes the dessert seem more satisfying.*

Ingredients

SERVES 4

METRIC (IMPERIAL)		AMERICAN
2	large ripe mangoes	2
	For the custard	
2	large eggs	2
300ml (10fl oz)	milk	1¼ cups
2 teaspoons or to taste	honey	2 teaspoons or to taste
150ml (5fl oz)	double (heavy) cream or thick yoghurt	⅔ cup
	To decorate	
	blanched almonds	

Method

1 Cut a long slice from each side of the mango stones, scoop out the pulp from the slices and from around the stones. Chop finely.
2 Beat the eggs, add the milk and honey, then place the bowl over a pan of simmering water and whisk or stir briskly until the custard thickens.
3 Add the fruit to the warm custard and allow to cool.
4 Whip the cream until it just stands in peaks, then fold into the mango and custard mixture. Yoghurt will not need whipping.
5 Spoon into individual glasses and chill well. Top with the almonds and serve.

Variations

✽ Use other ripe fruit, such as peaches, nectarines and soft berries. Sieve the latter to remove the pips.
✽ Gooseberries make an excellent Fruit Foule; unless they are very ripe, cook them first in the minimum of water.

Freezing: it is better to sieve the fruit if you intend freezing the mixture.

Ginger and Lemon Pears

In this recipe the lemon flavour is provided by the use of lemon grass or the herb lemon balm. Keep the slices of root ginger fairly thick, so they are easy to remove. If you like a strong ginger taste grate the root finely so it becomes part of the sauce.

Ingredients

SERVES 4

METRIC (IMPERIAL)		AMERICAN
150ml (5fl oz)	water	⅔ cup
3 tablespoons	clear honey	3¾ tablespoons
2.5cm (1 inch)	root ginger, peeled and sliced or grated (see above)	1 inch
1	lemon grass stalk or large sprig lemon balm	1
4	large dessert pears, halved, peeled and cored	4

Method

1 Pour the water into a large frying pan (skillet) or into a microwaveable bowl. Bring to the boil, then stir in the honey and ginger.

2 Strip and discard the outer skin from the lemon grass, then finely chop the stalk. If it seems tough then crush before chopping. Lemon balm should be washed and chopped. Add to the honey syrup.

3 *In a frying pan:* add the pear halves and simmer gently in the syrup for 10–15 minutes, depending on the ripeness of the fruit.
In the microwave: make the syrup in the bowl, then add the pear halves and give 5–8 minutes on High. Stand for 3 minutes before serving.

4 If you have used sliced ginger, remove it with a slotted spoon. Serve hot or cold.

Freezing: this dessert freezes well.

Peaches in Honey and Almonds

This is a delicious way of cooking peaches, whether they are just ripe or slightly under-ripe.

Ingredients

METRIC (IMPERIAL)		AMERICAN
4 large	peaches, halved and stoned	4 large
	For the sauce	
6 tablespoons	water	7½ tablespoons
2 tablespoons	clear honey	2½ tablespoons
	For the filling	
50g (2oz)	ground almonds	½ cup
1 tablespoon	clear honey	1¼ tablespoons
25g (1oz)	flaked blanched almonds	¼ cup

Method

1 Preheat the oven to 190°C/375°/Gas Mark 5 or 180°C for a fan (convection) oven.

2 Place the peaches in a large ovenproof dish with the cut sides uppermost.

3 Heat the water with the honey in a saucepan or in a bowl in the microwave. Pour over and around the peaches.

4 Mix the ground almonds and honey together and place a little in each peach half. Stud with the almonds.

5 Cover the dish with a lid or foil and bake for 15–25 minutes, depending on the ripeness of the peaches. For a slightly browned effect, remove the foil for the last 3 minutes of cooking. Serve hot or cold.

Variation

When fresh peaches are not in season use canned peaches in natural juice, well drained. The juice can be used instead of water to make the filling.

Do not freeze

Summer Soufflé Omelette

A light fluffy omelette filled with seasonal fruit (as shown on the cover) makes an attractive and nourishing dessert. The filling can be varied throughout the year.

You are advised to avoid sugar as much as possible, particularly during the early stages of the diet, and use honey. Unfortunately this makes the eggs too sticky and spoils the lightness of the omelette, so use sugar for this purpose. If possible, choose sugar that is both natural and organic.

Ingredients

SERVES 2

METRIC (IMPERIAL)		AMERICAN
	For the fruit filling	
150ml (5fl oz)	water	²/₃ cup
1 tablespoon	honey or sugar	1¼ tablespoons
225g (8oz)	mixed summer fruits (raspberries, red and black currants, cherries)	½ lb
	For the omelette	
4	large eggs	4
2 tablespoons	caster (superfine) sugar	2½ tablespoons
a few drops	vanilla extract	a few drops
1 tablespoon	single (light) cream or milk	1¼ tablespoons
25g (1oz)	butter	2 tablespoons
	To decorate	
a little	icing (confectioner's) sugar	a little
	large sprig of mint	

Method

1 Put the water into a saucepan with the honey or sugar. Bring to the boil and simmer for 3 minutes, then remove from the heat. Add the fruits and allow to stand. This prevents the soft fruits being overcooked but allows the syrup to flavour and slightly soften them.

2 Separate the eggs and lightly beat the yolks with the sugar, vanilla and cream or milk. Whisk the egg whites in a separate bowl until they stand in soft peaks, then fold into the yolks.

3 Preheat the grill (broiler) on a medium setting. Heat the butter in an omelette or frying pan (skillet), pour in the egg mixture and cook steadily until the bottom of the omelette is set; the top should still be runny.

4 Place the pan under the grill and cook until the egg mixture is just set. Cover half the omelette with the warm fruit, fold the other half over it and slide on to a heated dish.

5 Sift over a little icing sugar, top with the mint and serve at once.

Do not freeze

Strawberry and Grape Sorbet

Sorbets (sherbets) can be made with almost any fruit. If the fruit itself is not very juicy you can add liquid in the form of apple, grape or pineapple juice. If you find you are not allergic to citrus fruits then lemon, lime or orange juices give wonderful flavours to sorbets.

One of the primary objects of this book is to insure that people with arthritis are eating helpful foods. So many commercially made products include such a wide range of added ingredients that it is difficult to ascertain just what may, or may not, be affecting your arthritis. If you make your own sorbets and ice cream (see page 136) then you know exactly what is in them.

Ingredients   SERVES 4–6

METRIC (IMPERIAL)		AMERICAN
450g (1 lb)	strawberries	1 lb
250ml (8fl oz)	grape juice	1 cup
1 tablespoon	honey	1¼ tablespoons
or to taste		or to taste

Method

1 Put all the ingredients into a liquidizer or food processor and process until smooth. The small seeds in strawberries are generally crushed after this, but if you want an absolutely smooth liquid then pass it through a sieve.

2 *With an ice-cream maker:* pour the mixture into the container, switch on until sufficiently aerated and frosted, then spoon into a suitable container and store in the freezer.
   Without an ice-cream maker: pour the mixture into freezing trays and place in the freezer until lightly frosted. Turn into a bowl, whisk briskly to aerate the mixture, then return to the trays or a suitable container and continue freezing. This stage of whisking is not essential but it gives a better texture; see also under Variations.

3 Always bring a sorbet out of the freezer about 15 minutes before serving. Store in the refrigerator, then spoon into chilled glasses or dishes.

Variations

❀ Use any fruits or combinations of fruits. If you have a juice extractor you can also freeze vegetable juices (without sweetening) or combine them with fruit juices.

❀ It is possible to lighten the fruit mixture by incorporating egg whites at step 2. This is not necessary if you have an ice cream maker but a good idea (if you do not mind eating uncooked egg whites) when making sorbets by hand. Whisk the whites of 2 large eggs until stiff, then fold into the half-frozen mixture at step 2.

Vanilla Ice Cream

Ice cream should be omitted during the initial stages of the diet and even after that it is better to make your own, unless you can buy organic ice cream that does not contain additives that could affect your arthritis. The first recipe is based on a classic method of making the dessert but it is high in both fat and calories. It does, however, produce a wonderfully smooth result, even if frozen in an ordinary freezer or freezing compartment of the refrigerator. If you want to produce low-fat and low-calorie ice cream regularly you would be well-advised to purchase an ice cream maker. Some are now quite inexpensive.

If you are allergic to cows' milk, try using goats' milk, ewes' milk or soya milk, or use tofu (bean curd) as suggested opposite.

Ingredients
SERVES 4–6

METRIC (IMPERIAL)		AMERICAN
300ml (10fl oz)	milk	1¼ cups
2	yolks from large eggs (or 2 whole eggs)	2
1 tablespoon or to taste	honey or organic caster (superfine) sugar	1 tablespoon or to taste
1	vanilla pod (bean)	1
300ml (10fl oz)	double (heavy) cream	1¼ cups

Method

1 Warm the milk but do not allow it to boil. Whisk the egg yolks or whole eggs with the honey or sugar, then add the milk.

2 Slit the vanilla pod, remove the seeds and add them to the egg mixture. (Save the pod and place it in a jar of sugar to flavour it.)

3 Pour the custard into a bowl or the top of a double saucepan and whisk or stir over hot, but not boiling, water until the mixture coats the back of a wooden spoon.

4 Place a piece of damp greaseproof paper or baking parchment over the custard to prevent a skin forming and leave until cold.

5 Whip the cream until it stands in soft peaks (do not over-whip), then fold into the custard. Spoon into a suitable container, cover and freeze. For a lighter texture freeze lightly then whisk to aerate and continue freezing.

Variations

- Use ½–1 teaspoon of vanilla extract instead of the vanilla seeds.
- *Low-fat Vanilla Ice Cream:* use single (light) cream or fromage frais instead of the double cream. Eat the ice cream when it has been freshly frozen, otherwise icicles form in the low-fat mixture. This is excellent if frozen in an ice cream maker.
- In an ice cream maker you can follow the basic recipe but use single (light) cream instead of the whipped double (heavy) cream.
- *Tofu Ice Cream:* if you are allergic to dairy products use tofu (bean curd). Buy the silken (soft) variety and either whisk or liquidize it to give a smoother texture. To 400g (14oz/good ¾ lb) of tofu use the vanilla seeds, as suggested in step 2 opposite, or ½–1 teaspoon vanilla extract with honey or sugar to sweeten. Freeze lightly, then whisk to aerate and complete freezing. I find Tofu Ice Cream is better with a fruit flavour. Use about 200ml (7fl oz/scant 1 cup) of fruit purée to the 400g (14oz/2 cups) of tofu.
- *Fruit Ice Cream:* use the basic recipe with about 300ml (½ pint/1¼ cups) of your favourite fruit purée. Add to the custard and cream mixture.
- *Spiced Ice Cream:* flavour the ice cream with a little ground ginger or cinnamon.

Freezing: store in the freezer but remove about 10 minutes before serving.

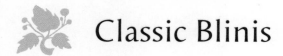

Classic Blinis

This recipe uses fine buckwheat flour. If you can obtain only coarse buckwheat and are using the American measures, use just 1 US cup and put into a food processor for a short time to make it finer.

Ingredients

MAKES 12

METRIC (IMPERIAL)		AMERICAN
225g (8oz)	fine buckwheat flour	2 cups
¼ teaspoon	sea salt	¼ teaspoon
1 teaspoon	easy-bake (instant) yeast	1 teaspoon
375ml (12½fl oz)	milk	1½ cups
1 teaspoon	clear honey	1 teaspoon
3 tablespoons	double (heavy) cream	3¾ tablespoons
1 tablespoon	butter, melted	1¼ tablespoons
2	large eggs	2
	For cooking	
a little	sunflower oil, see step 8	a little
1 tablespoon	butter, melted	1¼ tablespoons

Method

1 Mix the buckwheat flour, salt and easy-bake yeast together in a mixing bowl.

2 Warm the milk to blood heat (just comfortably warm), add to the flour and mix well.

3 Blend the honey with the cream and melted butter. Separate the eggs, add the yolks to the honey mixture, then stir into the mixing bowl.

4 Beat well for 3 minutes, then cover the bowl and put in a warm place for about 45 minutes or until almost doubled in bulk.

5 Beat the batter until smooth. Whisk the egg whites until stiff, then fold into the batter.

6 Heat 1 teaspoon of oil in a small pancake pan (skillet). Spoon in a little of the mixture to give a thickish pancake. Cook steadily for 2–3 minutes or until golden brown on the underside.

7 Turn over and brush the top of the pancake with a little of the melted butter. Cook for the same time on the second side.

8 Continue in this way. If using a non-stick pan you may not need any more extra oil but make sure the pan is well heated before cooking each pancake.

9 Serve hot with savoury or sweet ingredients.

Freezing: separate each cooked pancake with squares of waxed paper. Defrost at room temperature.

Speedy Blinis

The recipe for Classic Blinis, made with yeast, is on page 138. The recipe below uses the buckwheat in a quicker method. You will find these pancakes invaluable while you are avoiding ordinary wheat. They are delicious hot or cold. This recipe assumes you are using the coarser buckwheat. If you can obtain the finer buckwheat flour use 1 American cup and not ¾ cup, and don't liquidize the ingredients.

Ingredients   MAKES 8–10

METRIC (IMPERIAL)		AMERICAN
115g (4oz)	coarse buckwheat flour	¾ cup
½ teaspoon	sea salt	½ teaspoon
225ml (7½fl oz)	water	scant 1 cup
2	large eggs, whisked	2
1 tablespoon, or as required	oil*, optional	1¼ tablespoons, or as required
	For cooking	
1 tablespoon	oil*	1¼ tablespoons

*I like olive oil in the pancakes and groundnut or sunflower oil for cooking them

Method

1 Put the buckwheat and salt into a bowl. Bring the water to the boil, pour over the buckwheat and leave until cold.

2 Stir in the eggs and mix thoroughly. Add the oil just before cooking the pancakes. (This is not essential but helps stop the pancakes sticking and is invaluable if they are to be frozen.)

3 To give a smoother texture pour the ingredients into a liquidizer or food processor and process for about ½ minute. You will still have the nutty grains of the wheat but they will be finer.

4 Pour about 1 teaspoon of oil into a pancake pan (skillet) then add a large spoonful of the mixture. The ideal size for general purposes is about 10cm (4 inches) across. If necessary, spread out the mixture to give this size using the back of the spoon.

5 Cook over a low heat for 4–5 minutes, or until the pancake is golden brown on the underside and can be turned over easily. If you have a large pan, cook more than one at a time.

6 Continue in this way. If using a non-stick pan you may not need any more oil but make sure it is very hot before cooking each pancake.

7 Serve hot with savoury or sweet ingredients.

Freezing: separate each cooked pancake with squares of waxed paper. Defrost at room temperature.

Macaroons

As macaroons contain a high percentage of sugar they should not be eaten regularly, but I feel that a treat now and again helps one to maintain a fairly strict regime. I have tested the macaroons with the amount of sugar given below, which is slightly less than usual, and they still have a very good flavour. To insure a sticky texture in the middle put a small ovenproof bowl or tin of water into the oven under the baking sheets.

Ingredients

Makes 15

Metric (Imperial)		**American**
a few sheets	rice paper	a few sheets
2	whites from large eggs	2
a few drops	almond extract	a few drops
150g (5oz)	ground almonds	1¼ cups
115g (4oz)	caster (superfine) sugar	½ cup
	To decorate	
	15 blanched almonds	

Method

1 Place the rice paper on 2 or 3 large baking sheets. Preheat the oven to 180°C/350°F/Gas Mark 4 or 170°C for a fan (convection) oven.

2 Whisk the egg whites until just frothy, then stir in the remainder of the ingredients. Divide into 15 small portions and roll these into balls. If the mixture seems a little sticky chill for a time in the refrigerator or dampen your fingertips before rolling them. Alternatively, just use spoonfuls of the mixture.

3 Place on the rice paper, allowing at least 3.75cm (1½ inches) around each macaroon as the mixture spreads during cooking. Press an almond into the middle of each macaroon.

4 Bake for 20 minutes or until evenly golden. Cool slightly, then remove from the baking sheets and cut around the rice paper.

5 The macaroons can be stored for a day in an airtight tin but they lose their texture and tend to crumble if kept longer.

Variation
Coconut Macaroons: use 65g (2½oz/good ½ cup) ground almonds and 65g (2½oz/½ cup) desiccated (shredded) coconut.

Freezing: macaroons can be frozen for about 2 weeks; after that they tend to crumble badly when removed from the freezer.

Millet Porridge

You may be able to buy gluten-free breakfast cereals from health food shops but it is easy to prepare a hot or cold breakfast dish with millet. This is a very nutritious grain (see the comments on page 164). Porridge made with millet is familiar in many parts of the world.

The quantities below give one large or two small helpings.

Ingredients

SERVES 1 OR 2

METRIC (IMPERIAL)		AMERICAN
	For preparation	
115g (4oz)	millet	½ cup
4 tablespoons	milk or water	5 tablespoons
	For breakfast	
4 tablespoons or amount preferred	milk	5 tablespoons or amount preferred
¼ teaspoon	ground cinnamon (optional)	¼ teaspoon
amount required	honey	amount required

Method

1. Put the millet into a bowl. Bring the milk or water to boiling point and pour over the millet. If you like crisp grains allow to stand for 10 minutes; to give a softer texture cover the bowl and leave in the refrigerator overnight.
2. Tip the mixture into a saucepan or microwaveable bowl and stir in the extra milk and the cinnamon, if using.
3. Heat well, then spoon into one or two serving dishes and top with honey.

Variations

* Add 3 (3¾) tablespoons of raisins at step 3.
* *Millet Muesli:* follow step 1. At breakfast time mix 2 (2½) tablespoons raisins, 1 or 2 unpeeled grated apples and 2 (2½) tablespoons of chopped walnuts with the millet. Spoon into one or two serving dishes and top with honey and yoghurt.

Do not freeze

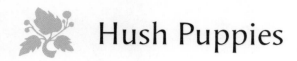

Hush Puppies

These fried corn cakes are an American speciality. They are ideal as a quick breakfast dish or as an accompaniment to savoury dishes.

All grains vary in the amount of liquid they absorb, so it is important to check the consistency at step 3.

When frying, be selective about the oil you use; discard stale oil that has been used on a number of occasions. A wok is good as you need less oil than in a frying pan (skillet) or deep fryer.

Ingredients

Makes about 12

METRIC (IMPERIAL)		AMERICAN
115g (4oz)	yellow or white maize (corn) meal	1 cup
1 teaspoon	baking powder	1 teaspoon
½–1 teaspoon	sea salt	½–1 teaspoon
1 teaspoon	honey	1 teaspoon
1 tablespoon	olive oil	1¼ tablespoons
2	large eggs	2
4 tablespoons or as required	milk	5 tablespoons or as required
2 teaspoons	chopped or grated onion or snipped chives	2 teaspoons
	For frying	
at least 250ml (8fl oz)	vegetable oil	at least 1 cup

Method

1 Sift the maize meal, baking powder and salt into a mixing bowl.

2 Beat the honey, olive oil and eggs together. Add to the maize meal.

3 Gradually beat the milk into the other ingredients. The mixture should be the consistency of a thick batter that drops easily from a tablespoon but holds its shape. Stir in the onion or chives.

4 Pour the oil into a wok or frying pan (skillet). You need a depth of about 5cm (2 inches). Heat to a temperature of 170°C (340°F). To test without a thermometer drop in a cube of day-old bread; it should turn golden in 1 minute.

5 Drop in tablespoons of the mixture and fry for about 1½ minutes, or until golden. Turn over and cook for 1½ minutes on the second side, then lower the heat and cook more slowly for 2 minutes.

6 Lift the Hush Puppies out of the oil, drain on kitchen towels and serve hot.

Do not freeze

Corn Bread

Classic recipes for corn bread loaves are made with two parts maize (corn) meal to one part wheat flour. As that is not possible while avoiding wheat, the following soft bread is the best to bake. This is better eaten hot when freshly baked but it can be cooled, then cut into squares and reheated for a few minutes in the oven. Alternatively, toast it under a preheated grill (broiler) and use as a base for poached or scrambled eggs.

Ingredients

MAKES ABOUT 9 SQUARES

METRIC (IMPERIAL)		AMERICAN
115g (4oz)	yellow or white maize (corn) meal	1 cup
1 teaspoon	baking powder	1 teaspoon
½–1 teaspoon or to taste	sea salt	½–1 teaspoon to to taste
40g (1½oz)	butter, melted	3 tablespoons
2 teaspoons	honey	2 teaspoons
250ml (8fl oz)	water, boiling	1 cup
250ml (8fl oz)	milk	1 cup
3	large eggs	3

Method

1 Preheat the oven to 190°C/375°F/Gas Mark 5 or 180°C for a fan (convection) oven. Line a 20cm (8 inch) square cake pan with baking parchment or grease thoroughly. (As the mixture is very liquid do not choose a pan with a loose base.)

2 Sift the maize meal, baking powder and salt into a mixing bowl. Mix the butter and honey with the boiling water, then add the cold milk.

3 Separate the eggs and whisk the yolks into the water and milk. Gradually beat into the maize meal.

4 Whisk the egg whites until they stand in soft peaks, then fold into the batter.

5 Pour into the prepared cake pan and bake for 35–40 minutes until golden brown and firm to a gentle pressure.

6 Cool in the pan for 5 minutes, then turn out on to a wire cooling tray.

Freezing: replace in the cake pan. When cold, cut into squares and freeze. This means you can remove any number of squares as required. When frozen place in a container and cover.

PART FIVE

Taking It Further

CHAPTER 1

Foods that heal

Many foods have healing qualities that can help arthritis sufferers. Try including the following ingredients in your cooking whenever possible.

Almonds – a rich source of calcium.

Angelica – a tall robust plant that has spread across Europe as a weed. Candied stalks are used in decorating cakes and other sweets. Toss young leaf shoots with salad greens and serve with a dressing of olive oil and concentrated apple juice.

Avocados – a good source of the omega-6 essential fatty acid, linoleic acid. Some nutritionists believe these delicious fruits also contain a substance that helps the elimination of uric acid from the body.

Bananas – a rich source of potassium, a mineral needed for the balance of fluids in the body, the transmission of nerve impulses, and muscle function. As you drink water, potassium is flushed from your body. Bananas are filling, come in a safe natural wrapper, are easy to digest and rarely cause food sensitivity.

Black pepper – improves circulation and thus helps control inflammation.

Black treacle (molasses) – rich in iron, potassium, magnesium and calcium, this sweet food should be taken daily and is an important part of the *Eat to Beat Arthritis* Diet.

Brazil nuts – an excellent source of selenium, and also S-adenosyl-methionine [SAMe], a chemical with pain-relieving properties similar to ibuprofen. Sunflower seeds also contain SAMe. As the quantities of SAMe are small, eat these foods as frequently as possible (you would need to eat about 250g (9oz) of Brazil nuts, or 500g (18oz) of sunflower seeds to receive the same benefit as from a single dose of a SAMe dietary supplement.) James A. Duke, Ph.D., author of *The Green Pharmacy*, said 'It is not feasible to eat that many nuts and seeds, but I believe that every little bit helps ...'

Brewers' yeast – taken daily as part of the *Eat to Beat Arthritis* Diet, this is an excellent source of folate and other members of the B-vitamin family, as well as the minerals iron, copper, phosphate, magnesium and zinc. It is an excellent natural supplement to promote healthy bones, joints and muscles.

Broccoli – a good source of glutathione, a powerful natural antioxidant that is thought to be beneficial in controlling symptoms of arthritis.

Camomile – used since the time of the ancient Egyptians to aid healing. Tea made with camomile calms the nerves and reduces stress. As stress promotes pain, sipping a warm cup of camomile tea in the evening helps you relax before going to bed.

Carrots – a rich source of beta-carotene, a precursor molecule the body turns into vitamin A. Beta-carotene is a powerful antioxidant. It is best consumed as a natural part of food, rather than as a manufactured dietary supplement. Other good food sources include sweet potatoes, apricots, mangoes and watercress.

Celery – contains compounds that help the body eliminate uric acid. Also contains an anti-inflammatory substance. Include raw celery in your diet at least three times a week, and use crushed celery seeds to top salads and savoury baked products.

Cherries – although there is no real scientific proof, some scientists claim that a substance in cherries helps the body eliminate uric acid.

Chilli peppers – capsaicin, a substance found in hot peppers, triggers the release of the body's own opiates, known as endorphins. Red peppers also contain salicylates, compounds that are closely related to aspirin. After you have tested your sensitivity to members of the nightshade family, try adding some peppers to your diet for healing as well as for flavour.

Fish – enjoy fresh fish rich in omega-3 fatty acids, such as mackerel, tuna, salmon and albacore. Fish eat green water plants that contain small amounts of linoleic acid. The body of the fish transforms this vital nutrient into DHA and EPA, which are then stored in the body fat of the animal. Some experts believe that eating foods rich in omega-3 fatty acids reduces the need for certain prescription medicines. Talk to your doctor about this after you have established your new diet programme.

Ginger – helps relieve the pain associated with inflammation, and stimulates the circulatory system. Combine with coriander in curries and sauces for meat. Jean Carper, author of *Food: Your Miracle Medicine*, drinks ginger tea for her osteoarthritis.

Liver – a rich source of B-vitamins and many of the minerals necessary for muscle, bone and joint health. (People with gout should avoid liver, however.) It is an excellent source of iron. Calves' liver has the best flavour.

Offal – this term refers to a number of internal organs eaten as meat, including liver, kidney, tripe and sweetbreads. High in protein, offal also contains significant amounts of key nutrients including the B-vitamins and minerals. As the liver is the most biologically (metabolically) active organ in the body, it is also the richest in those nutrients needed for normal human health and development. In terms of nutrient value, kidney and sweetbreads rank second and third. Tripe is a muscle, and has little value other than as a source of protein.

Olives – have had a reputation as a mild diuretic, a useful characteristic in the control of gout. There is some evidence from Japan that the daily consumption of about a quart (litre) of tea made from olive leaves increases the daily output of urine by 10–15 per cent, thus helping the body rid itself of uric acid.

Oregano – contains rosmarinic acid, which research has shown has powerful properties as an antioxidant, anti-viral, antibacterial and anti-inflammatory substance. Infused in combination with members of the mint family, oregano makes a satisfying and useful tea for arthritis sufferers. The pizza and pasta herbs – basil, marjoram and rosemary – all contain antioxidants that research suggests have anti-arthritic properties, so top up your food with flavours from the Mediterranean.

Parsley – used for centuries as a natural diuretic, it aids the elimination of uric acid from the body. Parsley is also a rich source of iron and vitamin C.

Pineapple – research suggests that bromelain, a substance found in fresh pineapple but not in canned, helps prevent inflammation and improve healing. This fruit also contains substances that block the formation of cancer-causing nitrosamines in the stomach.

Tea (green) – is the only caffeinated drink of potential benefit for people with bone disease. All tea contains isoflavonoids, which have a weak oestrogenic activity thought to protect bones against mineral loss, but their concentration in green tea is greater than in black tea. Recent scientific studies compared the bone-mineral density of women between the ages of 65 and 76 years who were either tea drinkers or non-tea drinkers. Statistically excluding factors such as HRT, smoking and coffee-drinking, the bone mineral density of tea drinkers was approximately 5% greater than that in women who drank no tea.

Turmeric – contains a useful substance that aids the pain of chronic arthritis. Curcumin, which gives the spice its brilliant yellow colour, is thought to block a neurotransmitter involved in carrying pain signals to various parts of the body. Curcumin also acts as an antioxidant, an antimicrobial and an anti-inflammatory.

According to Susan Clark, British Health Journalist of the Year and *Sunday Times* expert on alternative medicine, curcumin may work as well as the steroid cortisone in relieving acute inflammation. The recommended dose is 400–600mg per day. Turmeric contains between 0.3 and 5.4 per cent curcumin, so either prepare to eat large amounts of yellow food, or use a food supplement containing this substance. No toxic level has been established for curcumin, but it is always unwise to exceed recommended amounts of any supplement.

Walnuts – are good plant sources of omega-3 fatty acids. There is evidence that eating an ounce of walnuts three or four times a week can help reduce blood cholesterol levels.

Some important food tips

* Other foods supply specific nutrients that help combat arthritis. For example, avocados, peaches, watermelons, cabbage and cauliflower are all good sources of glutathione, a natural antioxidant which has been linked with arthritis. People who have low levels of this substance in their bodies are more likely to have arthritis. Asparagus and citrus fruit are also are good sources of glutathione, but do not include these in your diet until after you have tested your sensitivity to them (see pages 50-51). Asparagus is high in purines, substances which can increase the level of uric acid in the blood, and so should be avoided by those with gout. If you suffer from arthritis, try this vegetable after Week Two.
* Remember: if you are taking aspirin on a regular basis to cope with the pain of arthritis, eat plenty of vitamin C-rich foods. Aspirin destroys significant quantities of vitamin C.
* If you love the cheerful pink colour and sweet-sour taste of rhubarb, remember that it contains oxalate, a substance that interferes with the absorption of calcium needed for strong bones. Enjoy rhubarb in limited quantities.

Questions and answers about arthritis

What is arthritis?

Arthritis is a general term used to describe any disease or illness that causes inflammation of one or more joints. More than one hundred conditions are classified as arthritis by the medical profession. Some have names we recognize at once: rheumatoid arthritis, osteoarthritis and gout are examples. However, most forms of arthritis are relatively rare and receive limited public notice; these include carpal tunnel syndrome, ankylosing spondylosis, scleroderma, Lyme disease and systemic lupus.

What is a joint?

Joints are structures that occur where two bones meet. There are several types of joints: some allow movement while others do not. For example, joints linking bones in the arms and legs move, but those between the flat bones of the skull do not. Most joints contain a cartilage pad at the end of each bone, a fibrous capsule, a lining of synovial membrane, a space partially filled with fluid secreted by the membrane, and ligaments. Fibrous connective tissue links bones in immobile joints.

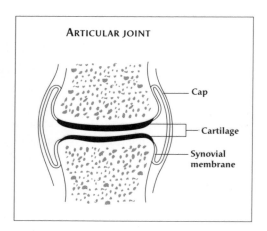

ARTICULAR JOINT

Cap

Cartilage

Synovial membrane

Mobile joints, also known as synovial joints, are found in the jaw, spine, arms, shoulders, hands, hips, legs and feet. They are characterized by a fibrous wall lined with a thin sac that secretes a lubricating substance known as synovial fluid. These joints also contain cartilage pads at the end of adjoining bones; these act as shock absorbers during physical activity.

What is osteoarthritis?

The rubbery tissue (cartilage) covering the ends of bones meeting inside synovial joints is damaged by osteoarthritis (OA), leading to pain during movement. Abnormal spurs of bone may grow inside the damaged joint and add to discomfort. Although the exact cause of OA is unclear, the following are important risk factors:

* Joint injuries – caused by sports injuries or physical labour.
* Gender – women are affected more often than men.
* Age – people over 45 are at greatest risk.
* Inherited conditions affecting the joints or cartilage.
* Excess body weight.
* Any disease, or medication, that affects the normal production and function of joint cartilage.

It is most likely that OA will affect the fingers, spine and weight-bearing joints, including those in the hips, knees and feet. Swelling may occur, especially in the knee joints.

Osteoarthritis is the most common form of arthritis. It rarely develops before the age of 40 and almost everyone over the age of 75 is affected to some degree. It can be very mild, causing only an occasional twinge, or so severe that even the simplest activities become painful and difficult.

What is rheumatoid arthritis?

Rheumatoid arthritis (RA) is a chronic inflammatory disease that most commonly affects the synovial lining of joints; it can also cause inflammation of the lining surrounding the lungs and heart, and the membranes lining blood vessels. RA is caused by the body's own immune system attacking normal tissue. If the attack continues untreated over a long period of time, the cartilage and bony parts of joints may be destroyed. Individual cases vary widely in severity, however.

About one per cent of the world's population suffer from RA: every ethnic group is affected. Two to three times more women than men develop RA, and some experts believe hormones may be a factor because the risk decreases after the menopause. Genetics also plays a role in susceptibility to this condition and close relatives of people affected by RA are at risk of developing it. Siblings of RA patients have the highest risk of developing the disease.

Unlike other forms of arthritis, RA is symmetrical, attacking the same joints on both sides of the body. An attack can be extremely painful. Membranes surrounding a joint becomes inflamed, thickened, and produce an excessive amount of fluid. The build-up of this fluid produces pressure on the soft tissues surrounding the joint and damages the soft cartilage 'cushions' within the joint. The disease progresses at different rates, and its severity usually waxes and wanes over a number of years. RA will go into remission in a few people, usually within the first two years.

RA most commonly attacks the joints of the hands and feet, causing tenderness, swelling and pain. Generalized stiffness on getting out of bed in the morning is common. Usually late in the course of the disease, one in four RA patients develop hard *rheumatoid nodules* under their skin on the elbows, heels, hips, back of the head, fingers and toes.

What is gout?

Gout is a form of arthritis that occurs when crystals of uric acid accumulate in soft tissues, such as the kidneys and the joints of the feet and hands. The big toe is most frequently affected. Uric acid is a natural by-product of metabolism that is normally excreted in the urine. Gout occurs when the kidneys do not function adequately to remove uric acid from the body, or when the diet contains excessive quantities of foods containing substance called *purines* (proteins primarily found in the nucleus of cells). In both cases, the level of uric acid in the blood reaches abnormal concentrations and crystals of sodium biurate begin to form in soft tissues and joints. The crystal deposits grow for as long as the condition remains untreated.

Diet plays an important role in controlling this form of arthritis, and certain foods, including red meat, shellfish, anchovies, sardines, liver and sweetbreads should be avoided. The risk of an attack is increased by the excessive consumption of alcohol.

Gout tends to run in families, and men are more susceptible than women. Diabetes, high blood pressure and obesity are important risk factors.

What medications and treatments are used for the various forms of arthritis?

OSTEOARTHRITIS

The two most commonly prescribed treatments for OA are corticosteroids and non-steroidal anti-inflammatory drugs (NSAIDs), such as aspirin, ibuprofen and fenbufen. These work by blocking the action of specific hormone-like substances (prostaglandins), which are responsible for producing inflammation and, therefore, pain. Medications such as Tylenol and paracetamol relieve pain but do not reduce inflammation.

Recent scientific research demonstrates that glucosamine, a naturally occurring substance in the body, can reverse the damaging processes that destroy cartilage in the joints (see page 154).

RHEUMATOID ARTHRITIS

Anti-rheumatic drugs are designed to relieve pain and stiffness, maintain mobility and prevent deformation of joints affected by rheumatic disorders. Three types of anti-rheumatic drugs are available:

* those that relieve symptoms;
* those that slow or halt the underlying condition causing the symptoms;
* corticosteroids.

Drugs used to reduce symptoms are usually prescribed as a first line of treatment, and include aspirin and non-steroidal anti-inflammatory drugs (NSAIDs) such as acemetacin, benorylate, diflunisal, fenbufen, fenoprofen, ibuprofen, mefenamic acid and tolmetin. They are called 'non-steroidal' to separate them from corticosteroid drugs, which also reduce inflammation. Although NSAIDs do nothing to stop the progress of the illness, they effectively reduce pain, swelling and stiffness that result from tissue inflammation. However, because the damage to joints remains, symptoms may recur.

If symptoms increase, drugs are prescribed which slow further damage to joints and tissues. These include:

* gold-based drugs, such as auranofin;
* immunosuppressants, such as azathioprine and chlorambucil;
* chloroqine and hydroxychloroquine;
* penicillamine (which is not an antibiotic);
* sulphasalazine.

Corticosteroids control pain by blocking the biochemical processes that trigger inflammation. These drugs are used for short periods of time because they temporarily depress the immune system. All anti-rheumatic drugs should be used under medical supervision to control side effects, some of which can be distressing.

Gout

Drugs used to prevent gout lower blood levels of uric acid. These include allopurinol, probenecid and sulphinpyrazone. Those prescribed to treat gout include NSAIDs and colchicine.

Which dietary supplements are helpful in treating arthritis?
Fish oil

For decades, arthritis sufferers have experienced less pain and debilitating illness when they supplemented their diet with fish oil. No one knew why this was, and some medical experts doubted that the improvement was real and not simply a placebo effect. At the turn of this century, scientists at Cardiff University conducted a series of experiments exposing the cells responsible for the growth and repair of joint cartilage, called chondrocytes, to various mixtures of fatty acids. Not surprisingly, they found that adding omega-3 fatty acids (those found in oily fish and fish oil supplements) produced a dose-dependent decrease in cellular activity linked with cartilage damage. While there is undoubtedly more to learn, it is now clear that stories about eating fish 'to oil your joints' are based on more than hearsay.

Fish oil is extracted from the flesh of oily fish such as herring, mackerel, salmon and trout. It is the best source of the omega-3 fatty acids needed to maintain healthy joints. These fatty acids have the added benefits of discouraging the formation of blood clots and helping to maintain normal blood pressure and cholesterol levels. They also are vital for healthy skin and hair.

Unlike cod liver oil, fish oil contains neither vitamin A nor D, and will not add to a build-up of these nutrients in the liver, which can be toxic in large amounts.

Take fish oil with food, as it may cause nausea when taken on an empty stomach. The usual recommended dose is 1000mg taken three times a day.

COD LIVER OIL

Cod liver oil has been associated with healthy bones and joint mobility since 1922, when it was discovered that a daily dose of cod liver oil prevented rickets, a crippling disease that causes bow legs in children. As the name states, this dietary supplement is derived specifically from the livers of cod fish. Scientists later found that its success in preventing rickets was specifically due to the amount of vitamin D in the oil. Cod liver oil differs from fish oil because it contains substantial amounts of both vitamins A and D, but lower levels of omega-3 fatty acids EPA and DHA (see *Fish Oil*). It is now recognized that the omega-3 fatty acids – which were unknown in 1922 – play an important role in maintaining healthy bones and joints.

A maximum of 3000mg per day is thought to be safe. Higher doses should not be used without a practitioner's supervision because cod liver oil is rich in vitamin A, which can be toxic in large amounts.

GLUCOSAMINE SULFATE

Glucosamine sulfate is used in the body to build and repair joints, and maintain healthy ligaments, muscles and tendons. It has also been shown to act as an effective non-steroidal anti-inflammatory drug in the treatment of osteoarthritis.

In normal joints a balance exists between the processes that build, or synthesize, cartilage and those that break down or degrade it. In osteoarthritis the balance is tipped in favour of the processes that degrade cartilage. Other anti-inflammatory agents do not restore this balance, and research has shown they can actually add to the negative imbalance. Glucosamine, however, supports the biological processes responsible for synthesis, and so helps restore joint mobility.

Medical treatment for osteoarthritis aims to reduce or stop the degeneration of joint cartilage and control pain and other symptoms associated with this debilitating condition. According to European studies, glucosamine has about the same effect as the NSAID ibuprofen – a common treatment for this form of arthritis – but without the same degree of gastric side effects. Using both reductions in pain and increased movement as indicators, the value of this natural compound was found to be significant.

Some anti-inflammatory drugs reduce pain but inhibit the body's ability to build new joint cartilage. Research strongly suggests that glucosamine actually supports the synthesis of cartilage, and may reduce the inhibition caused by NSAIDs.

The recommended dose is 500–1500mg per day, taken in 500mg doses up to three times a day. Take it with meals to avoid heartburn and indigestion. If you have a sensitive stomach take only one tablet per day. Usually it takes 4–6 weeks before the full effects of glucosamine are felt.

Glucosamine is generally thought to be non-toxic, and at the time this book was written there was no published scientific evidence that it interacted adversely with any medication. However, people sensitive to shellfish may experience mild stomach upset.

Evening primrose oil (EPO)

Seed oil from the evening primrose (no relation of the wild primrose) has been used as a food supplement for decades. It is an excellent source of GLA (gammalinoleic acid), an omega-6 fatty acid that some people fail to produce in adequate amounts, and one that has been shown to aid joint mobility, improve skin conditions, and reduce breast tenderness associated with PMS. Certain medications, viral infections, smoking, alcoholic beverages, ageing and excessive amounts of saturated dietary fat all slow the body's production of this vital substance.

When self-supplementing, 3000mg per day is a safe maximum dose. This should be taken separately from fish oil. Note: starflower oil, extracted from the seeds of the borage plant, is frequently taken as a source of GLA. People with certain mental disorders, or those taking tranquillizers, should check with their doctors before using supplements containing GLA.

Which vitamins and minerals are important in preventing and treating arthritis?

Calcium

Calcium makes up about 1.5% of the body's weight, and 99% of this is in bone. It is required for strong bones and teeth, and for normal biological activity in muscles, nerves and blood. Severe deficiency can produce rickets in children, and osteomalacia in adults. It is thought that the development of osteoporosis may be due to a mild deficiency of calcium over a number of years.

It is recommended that adults consume 800mg of calcium per day. The intake for adolescents, nursing mothers and pregnant women should be between 1.0 and 1.4g per day.

Good food sources of calcium include dairy products, canned fish, tofu, dried figs, dark green leafy vegetables and pulses (legumes).

Vitamin D and calcium

Vitamin D and calcium are necessary to prevent bone loss and fractures associated with osteoporosis. For many years it was believed that a balanced diet and normal exposure to sunlight provided adequate levels of this important pair of nutrients, but scientists have reconsidered the matter. In the mid-1990s, calcium's role in the prevention of osteoporosis was reviewed and the recommended daily intake for people over 65 was substantially increased from 800mg to 1500mg, or the equivalent of five 240ml/ 8fl oz glasses of milk. Most women in the United States, where the relevant studies took place, consume on average only 600mg each day.

Vitamin D helps the body absorb calcium and transport it to bones. Unfortunately, as we age our digestive systems are less able to absorb calcium; an additional boost of vitamin D helps correct this slow-down. Vitamin D is produced when a compound in the skin absorbs sunlight. As little as 15 minutes exposure per day is adequate to supply normal requirements of the nutrient. However, older people may tend to avoid the sun, and this compounds problems caused by their lowered capacity to absorb the nutrient. Reduced kidney and liver function make matters even worse.

For these reasons, supplements containing vitamin D and calcium are recommended. If you are over 65, or think your diet and sun exposure do not provided adequate levels of these nutrients, experts advise consuming 400 International Units (IU) a day. However, avoid taking excessive amounts of vitamins D. Prolonged intake of 600 micrograms or more a day may have toxic effects, including kidney damage and high blood pressure. Consult your doctor if you are taking digoxin, glycoside medication, or thiazide diuretics before using any supplement containing vitamin D.

Boron and vitamin K also work with calcium to maintain healthy bone structure. When you buy calcium supplements, check to see if these are included in the product.

VITAMIN E

There was a time when scientists did not believe that humans required vitamin E for good health. Recent research has shown, however, that this oily substance is a powerful antioxidant with anti-ageing properties. It is thought that vitamin E protects against cardiovascular disease by protecting the HDL cholesterol (sometimes called 'good' cholesterol) from damage by free radicals in the body. This reduces the build-up of atherosclerotic plaques on the walls of blood vessels.

There are other considerable benefits from vitamin E. When taken with vitamin C, vitamin E may also slow the effects of Alzheimer's disease. Damaging free radicals are thought to play a significant role in the development of this debilitating illness, and an increasing number of scientific studies suggest antioxidant vitamins may prevent or slow its progress.

Experts believe it is safe to supplement the diet with 400 IU per day. However, prolonged use of large amounts of vitamin E (more than 1000 IU per day) may cause bleeding in people taking medication to thin the blood.

VITAMIN C

People with damaged or painful joints may have an increased need for vitamin C. Heavy smokers, athletes, heavy drinkers and people who are ill or recovering from illness or injury may also wish to supplement their diet with this nutrient.

Recent scientific studies have shown a link between diets rich in vitamin C and lower rates of cardiovascular disease and certain cancers. Vitamin C is also thought to enhance the immune system's response to viral and bacterial infections, and help relieve cold symptoms by acting as a mild antihistamine.

Vitamin C is vital for the production of collagen, found in bone, tendons and skin. Also, in combination with vitamin E, vitamin C is a powerful antioxidant that helps fight any damaging build-up of oxidative free radicals in the body.

According to the National Institutes of Health (NIH), in the United States, a healthy adult should consume 200mg of vitamin C each day. Only a third of Americans achieve this, and one third consume less than 60mg per day. People eating processed foods as part of westernized diets fail to meet their body's requirements for this crucial vitamin. Happily, the *Eat to Beat Arthritis*

Diet provides plenty of fruits and vegetables rich in this vital nutrient.

Experts generally agree that, over the long term, 1500–2000mg of vitamin C a day is safe. Good food sources include red and green peppers, strawberries, kiwi fruit, and citrus fruit.

MAGNESIUM

Magnesium helps maintain healthy bone structure. In Great Britain, tea is a major source of this mineral. Other food sources include avocados, nuts, pulses (legumes) and wholegrains.

SELENIUM

Selenium is a mineral that acts as an anti-inflammatory in the body, and is therefore useful in controlling the symptoms of arthritis. Diets rich in selenium have been linked with lower rates of certain cancers and heart disease. Brazil nuts are the best food source of selenium, but it is also found in liver and other forms of offal, red meat, fish, and wheat grown in soil rich in this mineral. (Note: those suffering from gout should avoid liver and other offal.)

Selenium intake in Great Britain and most of the rest of Europe is very low – half the recommended daily allowance or less. In Finland, the general dietary intake of selenium dropped so low the government considered it a public health hazard, and fertilizers used to grow crops were supplemented with the mineral.

A safe long-term dose is 200 micrograms per day. Do not exceed 700 micrograms, as over time this and higher amounts can become toxic.

What other natural substances hold promise as treatments for arthritis?

CHONDROITIN SULPHATE

Chondroitin is a building substance in cartilage that was once thought to have as much therapeutic value as a dietary supplement as glucosamine. The two were combined in many commercial products. However, research has shown that chondroitin is poorly absorbed by the body, and its value as a supplement appears to be limited. Nutrimax, a company that makes a patented product containing both chondroitin and glucosamine, is funding research to assess its effectiveness.

MSM (METHYLSULFONYLMETHANE)

MSM is found in tiny quantities in every cell in the body. Although we know comparatively little about it, research suggests it is a necessary building block for a number of proteins, including those in muscles, connective tissue and joints.

As it appears to inhibit pain impulses and also act to control inflammation, MSM is one of the newer dietary supplements used to control arthritis. Early work suggests it may be especially useful for people suffering from osteoarthritis.

Testimonials suggest MSM reduces muscle spasms, increases blood flow, and may help repair cartilage. It has also been used to treat lupus and other auto-immune conditions, chronic back pain and to slow the growth of certain cancers.

Ronald M. Laurence, M.D., Ph.D., assistant clinical professor at UCLA School of Medicine, has written a book on this subject (*The Miracle of MSM*, Putnam, 1999). In an interview conducted by www.wholehealth.com, Dr Laurence was asked about the safety of this new supplement. He reportedly said: 'In the thousands of patients I have treated who took 2000mg and more of MSM daily for months and years, I haven't heard of any serious complaints to date.' He continued, 'In fact, I feel comfortable telling people that MSM is safer than water. Remember, though, MSM is a biologically active substance and can sometimes produce side effects, such as skin rash or minor gastrointestinal upset, in some people. If you're on anticoagulants, you should check with your doctor before taking MSM, because it can occasionally have a blood-thinning effect.'

Dr Laurence recommends taking a combination of MSM and 500mg of glucosamine three times a day, and many patients experience less pain when they use this combination of supplements.

Take with food to minimize gastric upset.

BOSWELLIA

This herb is used as a treatment for arthritis in the traditional medicine of India. It is thought that boswellic acid blocks the action of leukotrines that stimulate an inflammatory response.

CAYENNE CREAM

A topical cream containing capsaicin, the substance in hot peppers that give them their sting, has been found useful in controlling the pain of arthritis. It appears to create a temporary diversion, and inhibits the production of a chemical substance that sends pain messages to the brain.

Use only as recommended on the product.

DMSO (DIMETHYL SULFOXIDE)

An industrial solvent approved by the United States Food and Drug Administration for a bladder disorder known as interstitial cystitis, DMSO was once widely used as an alternative treatment for several forms of arthritis. However, the highly unpleasant smell it caused in users lessened its appeal. It can also have toxic effects in some people. It is now used as a solvent in some products.

NIACINAMIDE

A double-blind study has shown that this form of vitamin B3 is an effective treatment for knee pain. Do not use this supplement without being monitored by your doctor, as high doses (about 3000mg per day) may have serious side effects.

SAMe (S-ADENOSYLMETHIOINE)

It has been found that an anti-inflammatory effect similar to that of ibuprofen can be produced by SAMe (pronounced sammy), which is a form of the amino acid methionine. Compared with other non-prescription treatments, this supplement is expensive. It should not be taken by people with manic-depressive illness.

What are some of the alternative therapies used in the treatment of arthritis?

Acupressure – a massage technique in which the fingertips and thumbs apply pressure on specific points along the acupuncture meridians.

Alexander technique – a means of improving movement and posture by the effective and minimal use of muscles.

Aromatherapy – the use of aromatic essential oils to treat pain, inflammation and the underlying cause of many forms of ill-health.

Art therapy – by using art to express their feelings, patients gain relief from pain and the tensions that increase the sensation of pain.

Ayurvedic medicine – an ancient system of holistic healing originating in India. Remedies are based on diet, breathing exercises and yoga.

Bach flower remedies – the use of infusions of different plants to treat health-threatening emotional and physical imbalances.

Chiropractic – a system of manual manipulation of the spine used to relieve pain and illness throughout the body.

Colour therapy – use of colour to affect a person's mental and physical state.

Feldenkrais – the system of yoga, stretching and exercise that improves one's awareness of movement patterns and encourages the proper use of muscle groups.

Herbal medicine – holistic system of medicine based on the healing properties of plants.

Homeopathy – a healing system based on the belief that minute amounts of substances that cause a symptom in a healthy person will cure that same symptom in one who is ill.

Hydrotherapy – therapy based on the use of different temperatures of water and compresses.

Meditation – a system of spiritual healing in which a person learns to focus their attention on a neutral object and relax.

Microwave therapy – deep heat treatment in which electrodes placed on a person's skin pass electromagnetic waves to deeper parts of the body. The heat created increases blood flow to the area and relieves joint and muscle pain.

Nutritional therapy – the use of specific foods and food supplements to treat illness.

Occupational therapy – a system of care in which trained professionals devise ways for individuals to perform everyday tasks.

Osteopathy – a system of medical practice based on the theory that the loss of physical integrity, or form, causes illness. Treatment involves manipulation of the spine and joints, plus other therapeutic techniques.

Physiotherapy – a system of healing care in which a medical professional uses exercise to help restore movement and strength to the body.

Rolfing – a system of healing based on deep massage intended to realign the body's structure by strengthening the body's connective tissue, thus improving posture and balance.

Shiatsu – a system of treatment similar to acupressure, but here the therapist uses elbows, knees and feet as well as fingers and thumbs when applying pressure to the body's meridian points.

Ultrasound – the use of sound waves to stimulate blood flow to an area of pain.

Yoga – a holistic system of therapy, originating in India, that utilizes breathing, exercises, meditation and relaxation to heal.

Zen – a system of spiritual care, based on Buddhist philosophies, that aims to integrate the mind, body and spirit in achieving a state of total fulfilment.

Glossary

This section includes items not mentioned in this book, but which may be of interest to the reader.

Acute disease: A short, severe illness.

Allergens: Substances that cause allergies.

Allergy: An abnormal immune response to harmless substances causing one or more of the following symptoms: itching (especially around the mouth), hay fever (sneezing), rash and swelling. Extreme reactions may lead to bronchospasm, anaphylactic shock and death.

Amaranth: A grain discovered in ancient caves in Mexico. It is high in the amino acid lysine, and is favoured by some nutritional therapists for its healing properties. It is usually available in health food stores.

Amino acids: The basic building blocks for proteins. There are 20 amino acids in the human body, and most can be manufactured by it. However, there are eight amino acids that must be supplied by food. These are tryptophane, isoleucine, leucine, lysine, threonine, methionine, phenalanine and valine. Two other amino acids (histidine and arginine) can be made in the adult body, but not that of young children, and are therefore known as 'semi-essential' amino acids.

Dietary protein should include all the essential amino acids, because the absence of any one acid can cause protein deficiency. Including meat in your diet eliminates this possibility. Protein supplied by plant sources, such as grains and pulses (legumes), does not contain the full complement of amino acids: some are missing in grains, while others are missing in pulses. If you are a vegetarian, you should therefore mix grains and pulses in the same meal.

Two ancient grains from South America, quinoa and amaranth, are excellent plant protein sources because they both contain all the amino acids required for good health.

ANA (antinuclear antibody) test: A means of determining if the body is producing antibodies that cause auto-immune disorders by attacking the nuclei of healthy cells in connective tissue.

Analgesic: Any medication that controls pain.

Ankylosing spondylitis: A form of rheumatic arthritis affecting the spine and lower back.

Antibody: A protein produced by white blood cells in response to a specific substance, or *antigen*. The antibody binds itself to the antigen and neutralizes it.

Antigen: Any substance introduced into the body that stimulates the production of antibodies by the immune system. (See *Immune system*.)

Antioxidant: A substance that is able to block the harmful effects of excessive free radicals produced during the process of oxidation. Vitamins E and C are examples of powerful natural antioxidants. (See *Free radicals*.)

Atrophy: Wasting away of a body part or tissue. Muscles, for example, atrophy following long periods of inactivity.

Auto-antibodies: Antibodies that react to and destroy normal body cells and tissues, thus causing illness. (See *Auto-immune disease*.)

Auto-immune disease: Any abnormal condition arising when a person's immune system produces antibodies that attack normal tissues. Examples are rheumatoid arthritis, SLE (*Systemic lupus erythematosus*), auto-immune infertility, diabetes mellitus type 1, and auto-immune haemolytic anaemia.

Benign illness: A relatively mild form of a disease; non-life threatening.

Bone marrow: The spongy soft tissue found in the cavities of bones. Two forms exist: yellow bone marrow, which mostly consists of connective tissue and fat; and red bone marrow, which is the source of most blood cells including red blood cells, stem cells and platelets. In adults, red marrow is found in the collarbones, breastbone, ribs, spine, pelvis, shoulder blades and bones of the skull.

Bursa: A sac-like structure, lined with cells that secrete a lubricating fluid. It serves as a cushion between bones, muscles and tendons, and helps them glide over one another.

Bursitis: Inflammation of a *bursa*. Examples are 'frozen shoulder', 'student's elbow' and 'housemaid's knee'.

Carbohydrates: The components of food that are its primary source of energy. About 50 per cent of calories in a healthy diet come from carbohydrates. These are made up of chains of molecules of different building blocks, or 'sugars'. These can be simple in form, or complex.

Simple sugars are sweet, and add enjoyment to many of the foods we eat. When used in purified form – such as table sugar – simple sugars have little nutritional value other than as a source of fast energy; when this energy is excessive, and not burned off through exercise, it is stored in the body as fat. Simple sugars – like that used on cereal or in sweets – can cause the blood sugar level to fluctuate, sometimes causing mood swings.

By contrast, long chain sugars (polysaccharides, also known as starches) release their energy slowly into the body, and help keep blood sugar levels within healthy limits.

Some complex carbohydrates we eat are not digested by the human body, and pass unused through the digestive system. Known as 'dietary fibre', these complex carbohydrates form a vital part of nature's internal cleansing process.

Cartilage: A flexible, tough form of connective tissue. For arthritis sufferers, the most important cartilage is found at the ends of bones, where it acts as a shock absorber during motion. In osteoarthritis, cartilage is slowly destroyed through wear and tear (see *osteoarthritis*). Cartilage also forms structural parts of the body, including the ears and nose.

Cell: The smallest complete unit in the body, consisting of a membrane, nucleus, cell fluid and small structures called organelles. Cells are the metabolic engines of life.

Chronic illness: A lingering illness – the opposite of *acute*.

Chronic degenerative diseases: Illnesses associated with the processes of ageing and the slow deterioration of body structures.

Collagen: The main protein component of connective tissue. Collagen is damaged during many inflammatory illnesses, including rheumatoid arthritis.

Connective tissue: Structural tissue that holds parts of the body together and gives it form. For example, blood vessels and bone have shape because of connective tissue. Cartilage and tendons are forms of connective tissue.

Contracture: Crippling joint deformity resulting in the loss of motion and shrinking of surrounding tissues.

Elimination diet: The process of identifying foods which cause sensitive or allergic reactions. Two methods commonly used are either to introduce foods one at a time and watch for symptoms; or to eliminate individual foods until a food sensitivity or allergic reaction clears.

Endorphins: Natural substances in the brain that stop pain. Exercise, chocolate, chillies and honey all increase endorphin levels.

Enzymes: Protein catalysts produced by cells that support the biological processes of life without changing their own structure.

ESR (*erythrocyte sedimentation rate*): A clinical test that measures the rate at which red blood cells settle to the bottom of a test tube. A high ESR indicates an inflammatory disease, such as rheumatoid arthritis.

Essential fatty acids: A group of fats required by the human body for normal health. These fats cannot be manufactured by the human body, and must be obtained from food, or consumed as dietary supplements. Two forms exist, each having its own biological structure and significance; these are omega-3 and omega-6 fatty acids.

Omega-3 fatty acids help prevent heart disease and maintain healthy joints. Oily fish are excellent sources of these substances.

Linolenic acid, the basic omega-3 fatty acid, is most commonly obtained from oily fish, some nuts, and certain green foods. This molecule is metabolized by the body to form *DHA* and *EPA*. Under certain circumstances (illness, stress, using excessive amounts of alcohol, smoking and taking certain medications) the body fails to metabolize adequate amounts of linolenic acid. In these cases DHA- and EPA-rich supplements are helpful. The metabolic process responsible for the first step in the conversion of both linoleic and linolenic acid is the same and, therefore, there is competition between these nutrients.

Omega-6 fatty acids are important structural parts of normal cell membranes and small hormone substances (prostaglandins) that regulate body functions. Plant seed oils are good sources of these nutrients.

Linoleic acid, the basic omega-6 fatty acid, is most commonly consumed as part of seed and nut oils. This molecule is metabolized by the body to form gamma-linolenic acid (GLA), which are then further converted into other fatty acids vital for good health. Under certain circumstances (illness, stress, using excessive amounts of alcohol, smoking, and taking certain medications) the body fails to metabolize adequate amounts of linoleic acid. In these

cases, GLA-rich supplements are necessary.

Three important metabolites of essential fatty acids are:

GLA (*gamma-linolenic acid*): An omega-6 fatty acid found useful in treating a number of conditions, including premenstrual tension. It is produced by the body during the metabolism of linoleic acid.

DHA (*docosahexaenoic acid*): An omega-3 essential fatty acid that has been shown to have a positive effect on inflammation. It is also important for normal brain function.

EPA (*eicosapentaenoic acid*): An omega-3 essential fatty acid shown to have a positive effect on inflammation. It is important for a normal central nervous system.

When used as dietary supplements, omega-3 and omega-6 fatty acids should be taken at different times and always with food.

Evening primrose oil: An oil extracted from the seeds of an ancient healing plant found in North America, which is now used as the major source of *GLA*.

Fat: An important source of energy and building material for a healthy body, dietary fat is also the sole source of essential nutrients such as vitamins D and E, and the essential fatty acids (see *Essential fatty acids*). As part of a normal healthy diet, fat should provide about one-third of the total calories consumed. The type of fat we eat is important to our health. Saturated fat, like that found in red meat and dairy products, should make up no more that 10 per cent of our total fat intake. Many vegetarians are unaware that their diet is high in saturated fat due to their dependence on dairy products for protein.

Most of the fat in a healthy diet should be monounsaturated, like that found in olive oil and avocados.

Polyunsaturated fats are the most biologically beneficial of the fats, and should make up about 20 per cent of total intake. Vitamin E is needed to protect these fats against oxidation. Good food sources include wheatgerm oil, safflower oil, sunflower oil and almonds.

Remember: processing foods destroys the delicate structure of polyunsaturated fatty acids and removes their biological benefits.

Fish oil (marine oil): Oils extracted from the bodies of oily fish, such as mackerel, herring and salmon. Fish oil is not the same as cod liver oil, which is extracted from the livers of fish. Pure fish oil naturally contains a higher concentration of the essential fatty acids DHA and EPA, but contains less vitamins A and D than oil extracted from fish livers.

Remember: vitamin A levels in fish liver oil are high, and excessive amounts can be toxic.

Flare: A hot, red area often seen over, or around, an arthritic joint. A sign of inflammation.

Free radical: A molecule of a substance that has lost part of its electrical charge through the process of oxidation. Free radicals are part of normal chemical processes in the body; in excess, however, they are a contributing cause in many degenerative illnesses, including rheumatoid arthritis. (See *Antioxidant.*)

Gluten: A form of protein found in wheat, rye and barley that may cause food sensitivity, including coeliac disease. Oats contain a substance with properties similar to gluten.

Gluten is not used by the human body, and is therefore not a necessary part of a healthy diet. However, because its presence enhances the texture and appearance of many foods, it is frequently added to processed foods.

Gout: A type of arthritis caused by crystals of uric acid forming in joints. Symptoms are inflammation, swelling and acute pain. Gout affects more men than women, and frequently occurs in a big toe. (See *Uric acid.*)

Gram (g): A measure of weight equal to one thousandth of a kilogram.

Immune system: The combination of organs and cells in the body that work to protect the body from invasion by bacteria, fungi and viruses.

Inflammation/Inflammatory response: Localized pain, heat, redness and swelling that develop as part of an immune response. Increased blood flow, the concentration of fluid in an area, and the accumulation of white blood cells are involved. Inflammation is normally observed following an infection, although it also occurs under abnormal conditions, such as an *auto-immune* reaction.

Isoflavins: Natural plant compounds. Populations enjoying diets rich in these substances have lower risks of heart disease, certain cancers and menopausal symptoms. Good food sources are soya products, such as tofu, and linseed. The western diet is low in isoflavins.

Joint: A place where two bones meet. There are several types of joints: some are mobile, like those in the arms and legs, and others are immobile, such as those between the bones of the skull.

Joint capsule: See *Synovial sac.*

Juvenile rheumatoid arthritis: A chronic and crippling form of arthritis seen in children.

Leukotrines: Hormone-like substances, derived from omega-6 essential fatty acids, that play a role in inflammation.

Ligaments: Strap-like fibres attached to bones that help maintain their normal alignment.

Marine oils: See *Fish oil.*

Metabolism: The continuous chain of chemical reactions that take place in the living body. Food and tissues are broken down (*catabolism*), while new substances are built-up for use in the production of energy, or to replace parts of body cells and cell products (*anabolism*).

Microgram (ug): A measure of weight equal to one millionth of a gram.

Milligram (mg): A measure of weight equal to one thousandth of a gram.

Molecule: The smallest existing amount of any chemical compound that maintains the characteristic of that substance.

Nodules: Areas of confined inflammation that commonly appear under the skin of people suffering from rheumatoid arthritis.

NSAIDs: Non-steroidal anti-inflammatory drugs used to suppress pain and inflammation. Aspirin and ibuprofen are examples.

Remember: NSAIDs inhibit the production of prostaglandins in the lining of the stomach and may encourage the formation of ulcers.

Nutrition: The balance of basic substances that the body requires from food to enable it to maintain normal growth and good health. Well-balanced nutrition protects the body, whereas poor nutrition encourages disease. Poor nutrition can cause illness by itself, through dietary deficiency, or it can increase the possibility of illness by damaging the immune system and reducing the disease-resistance of body tissues.

Osteoarthritis (also known as *degenerative joint disease*): Damage to joints that affects the cartilage pads at the ends of bones. Cartilage may fray, wear, or even wear away entirely. The onset of osteoarthritis frequently follows damage or prolonged stress on a joint.

Osteoporosis: The loss of bone mass and strength that increases the risk of fractures. Believed by many to be a natural part of ageing, osteoporosis is most common in post-menopausal women, elderly men and people who do not consume adequate quantities of calcium in their diet.

Pauciarticular: Arthritis affecting four or fewer joints.

Polyarticular: Arthritis affecting five or more joints.

Prostaglandins: Substances in the body with hormone-like activity. Essential fatty acids make up a part of their molecular structure. Certain prostaglandins cause the symptoms of inflammation.

Proteins: One of the four major components of food (protein, carbohydrate, fat and water) that are needed for the normal structure and activity of all cells in the body. Proteins are complex molecules made up of basic building blocks called *amino acids*. Protein should provide 10–15 per cent of the total calories in a healthy diet.

Purines: Natural substances found in anchovies, asparagus, cauliflower, game, mushrooms, offal (liver, kidneys and heart), peas, poultry, pulses (beans, chickpeas, lentils), sardines, shellfish and spinach. These foods can increase the level of uric acid in the blood, thus making it more likely to precipitate in joints and soft tissues, such as the kidneys. (See *Uric acid*.)

People suffering from gout should avoid foods high in purines.

Range of motion (ROM): The extent to which a joint can progress through its normal movements. ROM exercises are important in arthritis because they increase or maintain movement and flexibility of muscles, joint, ligaments and tendons.

Rheumatism: A general term used to describe inflammatory conditions of the skeleton and muscles. Also used as a general term to describe aches and pains.

Acute rheumatism, also known as rheumatic fever, most frequently occurs in childhood following a streptococcal throat infection. Symptoms include polyarthritis of the larger joints, fever, and inflammation of the heart, which can result in long-term consequences. Treatment with penicillin is effective.

Rheumatoid arthritis: A chronic inflammation of joint linings (synovial linings) that causes pain, swelling and stiffness. Loss of joint function may occur.

Rheumatoid factor (RF): An antibody found in the blood of most people suffering from rheumatoid arthritis.

Quinoa: Called the mother grain by the Incas, quinoa is actually a distant relative of the beet family, and is not really a grain but a fruit. It is nutritionally valuable as it contains all eight essential amino acids, in perfect balance. It is available in health food stores.

Serous membrane: The thin layer of cells that form a lining over all the closed surfaces of the body, including the joints. They secrete a watery fluid that serves as a lubricant between moving body parts.

Serum: The clear fluid that separates from blood when it clots.

Spurs: The bony outcrops that occur within joints afflicted by osteoarthritis.

Sugars: See *Carbohydrates*.

Synovial fluid: Fluid found in synovial sacs surrounding joints.

Synovial sac: The fibrous capsule encasing the contents of a joint.

Tendons: Cords of tough fibrous tissue that connect muscles to bone.

Uric acid: A waste product from the metabolism of proteins. Under normal conditions this relatively insoluble substance is released into the blood, carried to the kidneys, and excreted in the urine. Under abnormal circumstances – such as the long-term use of certain medications – the kidneys fail to excrete adequate amounts of uric acid, which remains in the blood. As the level rises, it crystallizes out of the blood and forms deposits in various tissues around the body, including the joints. Gout can be extremely painful and although there are drugs that can help reduce the problem, dietary measures to control the amount and type of protein eaten are an important part of any treatment programme. (See *Gout*.)

Vitamins: A group of nutrients that cannot be manufactured by the human body, but are absolutely essential for specific metabolic activities in living tissue. Absence of one or more vitamins over time leads to deficiency diseases, such as scurvy (vitamin C deficiency).

There are two types of vitamins: those soluble in water (vitamin C and all the B vitamins are examples), and those vitamins that are soluble in oil (such as vitamins A, E and D).

The body's demand for individual vitamins varies with age, physical condition and lifestyle. Smoking, for example, greatly increases the need for vitamin C. Menstrual bleeding and childbirth increase the need for iron.

Helpful Resources

SELECTED READING

A Doctor's Proven New Home Cure for Arthritis, Giraud W. Campbell D.O., Thorsons, London. 1989.

8 Weeks to Optimum Health, Andrew Weil, M.D., Little, Brown and Company, London. 1997.

Clear Body Clear Mind: How to be Healthy in a Polluted World, Leon Chaitow, Gaia Books Ltd., London, 1990.

The Everyday Wheat-free and Gluten-free Cookbook, Michelle Berriedale-Johnson, Grub Street, London. 1998.

The Fats We Need to Eat, Jeannette Ewin PhD., Thorsons, London. 1995.

The Green Pharmacy, James A. Duke, Ph.D., Rodale Press, Emmaus, Pennsylvania. 1997.

Healing with Whole Food: Oriental Traditions and Modern Nutrition, Paul Pitchford, North Atlantic Books, Berkeley, California. 1993.

USEFUL ADDRESSES

All addresses were correct at the time of going to press. Do remember, however, that website addresses (usually those not attached to established organisations) tend to change.

The United States

National Institute of Arthritis and Musculoskeletal and Skin Diseases (NIAMS)
National Institutes of Health
Bethesda, Maryland
USA

United Kingdom

The Arthritic Association
1st Floor Suite
2 Hyde Gardens
Eastbourne BN21 4PN
Telephone (01323) 416550
www.arthriticassociation.org.uk

Arthritis Care (Help line)
18 Stephenson Way
London NW1 2HD
(020) 7916 1500
www.arthritiscare.org.uk

The Institute for Optimum Nutrition
Blades Court
Deodar Road
London SW15 2NU
Telephone: (020) 8877 9993
www.ion.ac.uk

National Osteoporosis Society
P.O. Box 10
Radstock
Bath
BA3 3YB
(01761) 471771
www.nos.org.uk

Arthritis Research Campaign, Medical Research Charity
Copeman House
St Mary's Court
Mary's Gate
Chesterfield
S41 7TD
(01246) 558033
www.arc.org.uk

Australia

Australian Nutrition Foundation
1-3 Derwent Street
Glebe
NSW 2037
Telephone: 02 9552 3081

OTHER USEFUL WEBSITES

Arthritis

Arthritis Information Resources –
www.pslgroup.com/arthritis.htm

The Arthritis Society of Canada –
www.arthritis.ca

Arthritis Victoria –
www.arthritisvic.org.au

National Institute of Arthritis and Musculoskeletal and Skin Diseases, National Institutes of Health –
www.nih.gov/niams

Arthritis News Break Newsletter –
www.hsc.missouri.edu/~arthritis/anbtp.html

www.arthritiswebsite.com

General medical information

American Academy of Family Physicians
www.aafp.org/healthinfo

www.bbc.co.uk/health

www.britannica.com (One of the best free websites available. Provides links to other sites.)

www.docguide.com

www.healthy.net

www.mayohealth.org

www.netdoctor.co.uk

www.webmd.com

www.wholehealth.com

Index